CAMDEN MISCELLANY
XXXII

Chris Evans
November 1994

CAMDEN
MISCELLANY
XXXII

CAMDEN FIFTH SERIES
Volume 3

LONDON
OFFICES OF THE ROYAL HISTORICAL SOCIETY
UNIVERSITY COLLEGE LONDON, GOWER STREET, WC1E 6BT
1994

British Library Cataloguing in Publication Data

Camden Miscellany XXXII—(Camden Fifth Series; v. 3).
  1. History—Periodicals
  I. Royal Historical Society   II. Series
ISBN 0–86193–300–1

Printed and bound in Great Britain by
Butler & Tanner Ltd, Frome and London

CONTENTS

I
PRIVATE INDENTURES FOR LIFE SERVICE IN PEACE AND WAR 1278-1476

Edited by Michael Jones and Simon Walker

CONTENTS

CONTENTS

ACKNOWLEDGEMENTS

The documents edited below are to be found in widely dispersed libraries and record offices. We are grateful to the many owners, librarians and archivists who have assisted us by giving permission to publish, for providing access to documents or supplying photographs or other information on the indentures in their keeping. Because of their number, individual acknowledgement of such help is in most cases made below at the relevant entry; however, particular gratitude is owed for help received from three major repositories. Crown copyright material in the Public Record Office is reproduced by permission of the Controller of Her Majesty's Stationery Office; that from the British Library by permission of the Trustees and that from the Bodleian Library by permission of the Keeper of Manuscripts.

Whilst we are certain that there are still other private life indentures to be discovered, the thoroughness of our trawl has been immensely assisted by the generosity of many friends and colleagues who have kindly drawn our attention to indentures or other relevant material of which they had knowledge. Most of these debts are also acknowledged at an appropriate point in our edition, though we would especially wish to thank Professor J. M. W. Bean, Dr Christine Carpenter, Miss Elizabeth Danbury, Professor Robin Frame, Dr Rosemary Horrox, Dr Philip Morgan, Professor Tony Pollard, Professor Michael Prestwich and Dr Alix Sinclair for particularly valuable assistance. The circumstances in which this edition has been brought to completion by the present editors are explained more fully in the Introduction that follows. Here they wish to place on record their deep appreciation of the generosity of the late Professor Norman Lewis and of Professor Michael Powicke for placing material that they had collected for a project that was originally their own in the present editors' hands.

In carrying out the requisite research, the editors are particularly grateful for financial support from the British Academy, through its Small Grants in the Humanities Fund, and to the research funds of their respective Universities of Nottingham and Sheffield.

MICHAEL JONES   SIMON WALKER
University of Nottingham   University of Sheffield

Candlemas 1994

ABBREVIATIONS

Bean	J. M. W. Bean, *From Lord to Patron. Lordship in Medieval England* (Manchester, 1989)
BIHR	*Bulletin of the Institute of Historical Research*
BL	British Library
BPR	*Black Prince's Register*, 4 vols. (HMSO, 1930–3)
CAD	*Calendar of Ancient Deeds*
CChR	*Calendar of Charter Rolls*
CCR	*Calendar of Close Rolls*
CFR	*Calendar of Fine Rolls*
CPR	*Calendar of Patent Rolls*
CIM	*Calendar of Inquisitions Miscellaneous*
CIPM	*Calendar of Inquisitions Post Mortem*
CRO	County Record Office
DKR	*Annual Reports of the Deputy Keeper of the Public Record Office*
Dunham	W. H. Dunham jr., *Lord Hastings' Indentured Retainers, 1461–1483. The Lawfulness of Livery and Retaining under the Yorkists and Tudors, Connecticut Academy of Arts and Sciences*, vol. 39 (1955), reprinted 1970
EHR	*English Historical Review*
Ellis	Roger H. Ellis, *Catalogue of Seals in the Public Record Office. Personals Seals*, 2 vols. (HMSO, 1978–81)
GEC	G. E. Cockayne, *The Complete Peerage*, revised edn. by Vicary Gibbs et al., 13 vols. (London, 1910–59)
Given-Wilson	C. Given-Wilson, *The Royal Household and the King's Affinity* (New Haven and London, 1986)
HC, 1386–1421	J. S. Roskell, Linda Clarke, Carole Rawcliffe, eds. *The House of Commons, 1386–1421*, 4 vols. (Stroud/Wolfeboro Falls, 1992)
HMC	*Historical Manuscripts Commission*
Holmes	G. A. Holmes, *The Estates of the Higher Nobility in Fourteenth-Century England* (Cambridge, 1957)
Moor	C. Moor, *Knights of Edward I*, Harleian Soc., vols. lxxx (1929), lxxxi (1929), lxxxii (1930), lxxiii (1931), lxxxiv (1932)
NLI	National Library of Ireland
NLW	National Library of Wales
PPC	*Proceedings and Ordinances of the Privy Council of England,*

	ed. Sir Nicholas Harris Nicolas, 7 vols. (London, 1834–7)
PRO	Public Record Office
RO	Record Office
Rot. Parl.	*Rotuli Parliamentorum*, ed. J. Strachey *et al.*, 6 vols. (London, 1767–83)
S&G	Sir N. H. Nicolas, *The Controversy between Sir Richard Scrope and Sir Robert Grosvenor in the Court of Chivalry*, 2 vols. (London, 1832)
TRHS	*Transactions of the Royal Historical Society*
VCH	*Victoria County History*
Wedgwood	Josiah C. Wedgwood & Anne D. Holt, *Biographies of the Members of the Commons House, 1439–1509 (HMSO, 1936)*
YAS	*Yorkshire Archaeological Society*

INTRODUCTION

The proposal for an edition of selected private life indentures for service in peace and war was first made to the Royal Historical Society by Professor Norman Lewis shortly after he had contributed 'Indentures of Retinue with John of Gaunt, duke of Lancaster, enrolled in Chancery 1367–1399' to *Camden Miscellany* xxii (1964). After the Society accepted this proposal, Lewis discovered that Professor Michael Powicke was also working on a similar project and they agreed to cooperate. Lewis agreed to be responsible for indentures before 1327 and Powicke worked on those between 1328 and 1462. Texts of thirty-seven surviving original indentures were selected and a brief introduction was written, reflecting their division of labour, but the project then hung fire. In the interim other work had revealed that many further indentures survived than had been suspected and a considerable literature developed of which at least brief notice was required; despite working to the end of his long life on a subject which he had made peculiarly his own, when Lewis died in 1986 there still remained much to be done to prepare the proposed edition for publication, whilst Professor Powicke found himself with other obligations that prevented him from bringing it to completion.

A query by one of the present editors about the fate of the edition to Dr Blair Worden, then Literary Director of the Society, following up an earlier interest which had lain dormant for almost twenty years, resulted in a correspondence with Professor Powicke. He generously indicated a willingness to hand over the material he and Lewis had gathered to a third party if that would assist in bringing the project to completion. When a year later Michael Jones became in turn Literary Director and inherited the file relating to the Lewis-Powicke edition, he suggested to the Society that the project could yet be brought to a successful conclusion, especially if he might be allowed to associate Dr Simon Walker with the edition. This was accepted. Dr Walker kindly agreed to help; he is responsible for the substantive part of this introduction while the other results of the editors' collaborative efforts may be seen in the documents that follow.

Briefly, the new editors realised that despite a long interest in the subject, much of the literature of which was surveyed in the recent monograph by J. M. W. Bean, *From Lord to Patron. Lordship in Late Medieval England* (Manchester, 1989), scholars were still hampered by a lack of information on the numbers and location of surviving original indentures; that there had been no systematic attempt to list them with the exception of those contracted by John of Gaunt, duke of Lancaster and William, lord Hastings; and that because of their dispersal, patchy or inadequate publication, many private life indentures were still difficult of access. Consequently they have included in the present edition a complete working list of such indentures for which full texts survive, excepting only those drawn up with Gaunt and Hastings which have received treatment elsewhere.

The list comprises 156 documents, the majority of them life indentures of retainer for service in peace and war, but it also includes examples of letters patent of retainer and a few agreements for a fixed period of service (not less than a year). One hundred and thirty nine documents are printed in full, of which only twenty three have previously appeared in print. These latter are republished here either because the first publication is difficult of access or seriously flawed, or because a significant new, normally an original, text has come to light. In addition a further sixteen life indentures are listed for completeness: ten of these have been published already in good modern editions of which details are provided, whilst the rest have been listed because *mutatis mutandis* they repeat verbatim the terms of a previous document for which a full text has already been provided.

These documents are intended to show a representative range of the diplomatic forms and conditions on which private life retaining was conducted. As will be seen, individual lords or families often used a preferred or standard form of indenture; we have attempted to provide the widest possible selection of these forms but where several indentures in common form survive for one of the contracting parties we have simply calendared the text briefly. We must emphasise strongly here that our efforts have been limited to tracing full texts of private life indentures: as will be evident from details given below, we are aware of many lost indentures, brief terms of which may survive in financial accounts and other records. But a systematic search to compile a comprehensive list of such retainers would be an enormous task requiring study of every leading noble family and its records. Monographs by Professor Bean and Dr Rawcliffe on the Percies and the Staffords respectively, or the Appendix of Noble and Gentry Affinities in Warwickshire in Christine Carpenter's *Locality and Polity* (Cambridge, 1992), indicate the extent of that particular problem. We hope, however, that our work will at least serve as a reference point for some of that future research.

The indenture of retainer for life in peace and war was the most distinctive of the written instruments used to regulate relations between lords and their men in later medieval England. It was the domestic version of a widespread phenomenon in western Europe, the development of a non-feudal contract designed to replace the grant of land and obligations based upon tenure as a means of securing service by the grant of a money fee. Within the French kingdom, this contract took the form of the *alliance*, which created a relationship of mutual aid and service that differed from the grant of a money fief for term of life principally in the absence of the act of homage.[1] In northern Italy, pacts of *accomandigia* between *signori* and their clients, placing the military resources of the rural nobility at the disposal of a lord in return for political guarantees and privileges, emerged in the mid-fourteenth century to supplement the continuing grants of fiefs in land.[2] In parts of Germany in the fifteenth century, particularly Bavaria and the Rhine Palatinate, the *Dienerbrief* bound the contracting party to serve his lord for life, or a fixed term of years, with a specified number of troops whenever required, and imposed an oath of loyalty similar to that required of a vassal, though moderated by the ability to refuse in advance to serve against certain named persons.[3] Closer to home, the Scottish bond of manrent developed, *c.* 1450, as the principal means by which the comital families sought to secure the loyalty and manpower of lesser lords in return for a promise of maintenance and protection.[4] Though differing in detail, each of these forms of contract were very similar in their general terms – the promise of service and loyalty in return for fee and favour; the use of the money fee rather than the fief in land; the concern to secure sometimes substantial resources of manpower in time of war; the absence of homage – while each was given a distinctive form by the particularities of the political and social structure from which it emerged.

Besides the importance the indenture of retainer possesses as the principal English evidence for a definable phase in the development of western European lordship, its language and diplomatic exercised an influence beyond the legal boundaries of English authority. In 1366 Sir Stephen de Cosington was 'retained' with a *fief-rente* by Charles II, king of Navarre, and the dukes of Brittany, counts of Foix and earls

---

[1] P. S. Lewis, 'Decayed and Non-Feudalism in Later Medieval France', *BIHR*, xxxvi (1964), 157–84; idem, 'Of Breton Alliances and Other Matters', *War, Literature and Politics in the Late Middle Ages: Essays in Honour of G. W. Coopland*, ed. C. T. Allmand (Liverpool, 1976), 122–43, both reprinted in *Essays in Later Medieval French History* (London, 1985), 41–90.

[2] G. Soranzo, 'Collegati, raccomandati, aderenti negli stati italiani dei sec. XIV e XV', *Archivio Storico Italiano*, xcix (1941), 3–35; T. Dean, 'Lords, vasals and clients in Renaissance Ferrara', *EHR*, c (1985), 106–19.

[3] H. J. Cohn, *The Government of the Rhine Palatinate in the Fifteenth Century* (Oxford, 1965), 152–61; F. Redlich, 'The German Military Enterpriser and his Work Force', *Vierteljahrschrift für Sozial- und Wirtschaftsgeschichte*, 47 (1964), 7–29.

[4] J. Wormald, *Lords and Men in Scotland: Bonds of Manrent 1442–1603* (Edinburgh, 1985).

of Douglas all made occasional use of the indenture,[5] while the characteristically precise enumeration of the benefits and conditions of service it contained seems also to have exercised an influence on the contracts of both the counts of Flanders and dukes of Bourbon in the mid-fourteenth century.[6] Conversely, the indenture was sometimes used within the British Isles as a vehicle for agreements displaying elements of the *alliance* and *accomandigia*, such as the contract concluded between Hugh Despenser the younger and John Bermingham, earl of Louth, in 1321 or the pacts by which successive earls of Kildare and Ormond sought to assure the loyalty and service of their noble Irish clients.[7]

For historians of later medieval England, the interest of surviving indentures of retainer has lain principally in the evidence for the nature and exercise of aristocratic power that they provide, and discussion of their contents has frequently been linked to the wider question of the nature and alleged failings of English society in the later Middle Ages.[8] When doing so, it is important to be aware of the limitations, as well as the value, of the evidence these indentures provide. They formed only one of a variety of bonds by which men were bound to the service of a lord; besides the tenurial relationship, which continued to exercise a residual influence on the composition of many magnate affinities, the annuity for past and future services, the grant of livery robes and appointment to posts within the household and estate administration of the lord constituted popular alternative means of rewarding good service, while in addition to such acknowledged clients and servants a magnate often enjoyed the support of a larger, and less easily definable, body of 'well-wishers'. These latter might receive the lord's livery device or be invited to serve with him on campaign but were bound by no more definite obligation than those transactions might imply.[9]

Indentures of retainer were the most formal and explicit, but by no means the most common, of these bonds of service; among the 141

---

[5] B. Leroy, *Le Royaume de Navarre à la fin du moyen âge. Gouvernement et société* (London, 1990), 94; Lewis, *Essays in Later Medieval French History*, 46, 88–9; *Registrum Honoris de Morton*, ed. T. Thomson *et al.* (Bannantyne Club, 1853), ii. 101.

[6] M. Vale, *War and Chivalry. Warfare and Aristocratic Culture in England, France and Burgundy at the End of the Middle Ages* (London, 1981), 67; Lewis, 68.

[7] Oxford, Bodleian Library, MS Dugdale 18 f. 39v; *The Red Book of the Earls of Kildare*, ed. G. MacNiocaill (Dublin, 1964), nos. 139, 165–9; *Calendar of Ormond Deeds*, ed. E. Curtis (Dublin, 1932–43), ii. nos. 22, 34–6, 38, 90, 219 and 347.

[8] K. B. McFarlane, 'Bastard Feudalism', *BIHR*, xx (1945), 161–80; N. B. Lewis, 'The Organization of Indentured Retinues in Fourteenth-Century England', *TRHS*, 4th ser. xxvii (1945), 29–39 were the pioneering modern studies of the subject.

[9] M. Cherry, 'The Courtenay Earls of Devon: Formation and Disintegration of a late Medieval Aristocratic Affinity', *Southern History*, i (1979), 71–99; C. Carpenter, 'The Beauchamp Affinity, A Study of Bastard Feudalism at Work', *EHR*, xcv (1980), 514–32; S. Walker, *The Lancastrian Affinity 1361–1399* (Oxford, 1990), 8–38.

known annuitants of Humphrey, first duke of Buckingham, for instance, only 31 had their conditions of service regulated by an indenture of retainer.[10] Nor were they always a necessary adjunct to the exercise of lordship. Though indentures concluded by many of the major noblemen of later medieval England have survived, and references to many more, now lost, are preserved in contemporary administrative and financial records, there were nevertheless other magnates who maintained an efficient local hegemony, facilitated either by the access to the resources of Crown patronage they provided for their clients, or by the concentration and predominance of their estates within a single region, without any apparent recourse to formal contracts of service.[11] The indenture of retainer was never, therefore, more than one element in the complex mechanism of later medieval lordship, the product of a social order rather than its defining feature, and one that cannot be properly understood without some wider consideration of the circumstances that produced it.

The complex question of the origins of the indenture of retainer helps to demonstrate the point. The increasing shortage of land available for redistribution as reward had already reduced the scale of new enfeoffments undertaken by tenants-in-chief by the end of Henry I's reign. The threat to the exercise of their feudal lordship posed by the gradual evolution of hereditary tenure, combined with the profits to be gained from the direct management of their estates in a period of inflation, rendered lords still more reluctant to engage in grants of land that would lead to a permanent depletion of their patrimony. As a consequence, tenants-in-chiefs began to seek to substitute a variety of rewards, in cash and kind, for the grant of a heritable fee in land. The simultaneous growth of practical literacy meant that this was increasingly effected by lords concluding with their followers written contracts, which preserved the ideals behind the acts of homage and fealty without insisting upon their performance, and spelled out in detail the conditional, and time-limited, nature of the rewards offered for service.[12] The form taken by many of these contracts, an indented chirograph divided into two identically-worded copies, had been popularized by its use to record the 'final concords' of the king's courts, while the practice of inter-changeable sealing, by which each of the contracting

[10] C. Rawcliffe, *The Staffords, Earls of Stafford and Dukes of Buckingham 1394–1521* (Cambridge, 1978), 232–40.

[11] Cherry, *op. cit.*; S. J. Payling, *Political Society in Lancastrian England. The Greater Gentry of Nottinghamshire* (Oxford, 1991), 95–8, 140–7, 195–200.

[12] P. Coss, 'Bastard Feudalism Revised', *Past & Present*, 125 (Nov. 1989), 30–9; D. Crouch, D. A. Carpenter, 'Debate: Bastard Feudalism Revised', *ibid.* 131 (May 1991), 165–89; S. L. Waugh, 'Tenure to Contract: Lordship and Clientage in Thirteenth-Century England', *EHR*, ci (1986), 811–39.

parties authenticated the copy of the agreement retained by the other, was familiar from the procedures of ecclesiastical administration.[13] The kind of service promised in these contracts was often specific and limited in nature, such as acting as the lord's pleader in the courts or in the office of estate steward, but it could also be more open-ended, involving the lord in an undertaking to maintain a man as a member of his household or 'company', in return for a promise of fealty or service.[14] A consequence of this development was that magnate 'affinities' of a type familiar in the fourteenth and fifteenth centuries, a group of client gentry drawn from the general region of their lord's principal estates but possessed of a direct tenurial connection with him in only a minority of cases, became an increasingly prominent feature of thirteenth-century society, while the corruption of central and local government through the influence of the nobility and their clients – a phenomenon usually associated with the later Middle Ages – was already widespread by the middle years of Henry III's reign.[15]

What was new in such agreements was largely their form rather than their content, for one of their major purposes was to continue to offer the benefit of association with, and sometimes residence in, a noble household to favoured followers. The Anglo-Irish magnate, John Fitz-Thomas, lord of Offaly, was, by 1290, receiving letters of obligation from his followers, promising him service 'as if my lord', in return for a grant of the status of a *familiaris* and *fidelis*.[16] The prestige and desirability of such an association was to be repeatedly attested over the following century by the popularity of maintenance agreements sometimes drawn up in chirographic form, by which the impoverished, the ambitious and the lazy surrendered quite considerable properties in return for an assurance of sustenance within a magnate household.[17]

---

[13] M. T. Clanchy, *From Memory to Written Record. England 1066–1307* (Oxford, 2nd ed. 1993), 87–8; C. R. Cheney, *English Bishops' Chanceries 1100–1250* (Manchester, 1950), 132.

[14] PRO, E40/391 (Philip, lord Basset and William de Wydendon); E40/14378 (Philip, lord Basset and William Aylwyn); DL25/1308 (Hugh de Neville and John Filliol).

[15] G. G. Simpson, 'The *familia* of Roger de Quincy, earl of Winchester and Constable of Scotland', *Essays on the Nobility of Medieval Scotland*, ed. K. J. Stringer (Edinburgh, 1985), 102–29; D. Crouch, *William Marshal* (London, 1990), 135–68; H. Ridgeway, 'William de Valence and his *Familiares*, 1247–72', *Historical Research*, lxv (1992), 239–57; D. A. Carpenter, 'Simon de Montfort: the first leader of a political movement in English history', *History*, lxxvi (1991), 10–13; idem, 'King, Magnates and Society: The Personal Rule of Henry III, 1234–1258', *Speculum*, lx (1985), 39–70.

[16] *Red Book of the Earls of Kildare*, nos. 11–15.

[17] P. A. Brand, 'Oldcotes v. Darcy', *Medieval Legal Records*, ed. R. F. Hunnisett and J. B. Post (London, 1978), 64, 69–70; PRO, CP40/134 m. 202d (Sir William Devereux and Walter Langton, bishop of Coventry and Lichfield); CP40/207, enrolled deeds m. 1 (Hervey de Stainton and John de Bradfield); N. Saul, 'A "Rising" Lord and a "Declining" Esquire: Sir Thomas de Berkeley III and Geoffrey Gascelyn of Sheldon', *Historical Research*, lxi (1988), 345–56.

Before the reign of Edward I, however, it was rare for these contracts to include any reference to military service, though systematic use of paid troops to supplement the feudal obligations of the Crown's tenants-in-chief was a long-established one: 'its essential features were already established custom, *mos familiae regis*, by the beginning of Henry I's reign'. What brought about this change were the increased demands for military service from the Crown's tenants-in-chief created by Edward I's ambitions and commitments in Wales, France and Scotland. These were of a scale that could no longer be supplied solely by the resources of the magnate household, with the result that contracts that temporarily expanded the size of a lord's household during a campaign, while preserving the traditional nature and rewards of household service, began to appear.[18] The earliest surviving contracts of this type were concluded in 1270 by the Lord Edward in preparation for his Crusade. Though the arrangements they embodied were traditional ones, it is possible that the precise form of the contracts was novel, borrowed from contemporary French practice. The efforts at recruitment by those contracted to serve Edward produced, in any case, one of the earliest agreements for life service in peace and war embodied in a chirograph, between Thomas de Clare, the younger brother of the earl of Gloucester, and Sir Nicholas Sifrewast.[19] The agreements the king's demands subsequently generated included undertakings both for service additional to the feudal quotas and, especially in the case of ecclesiastical tenants-in-chief, contracts regulating the fulfilment of existing feudal obligations. In the earliest of these, for example, Sir Henry Erdington was party to an indenture in June 1277 to perform the bishop of Lincoln's knight service in Wales for the payment of 55 marks.[20]

The influence of the Crown's military demands on the development of the indenture of retainer can be most clearly seen in the relatively large number of early contracts concluded for a limited term of service:

[18] J. O. Prestwich, 'The Military Household of the Anglo-Norman Kings', *EHR*, xcvi (1981), 2–35 (quotation p. 33); B. D. Lyon, 'The Feudal Antecedents of the Indenture System', *Speculum*, xxix (1954), 503–11; M. Prestwich, *War, Politics and Finance under Edward I* (London, 1972), 41–91.

[19] H. G. Richardson and G. O. Sayles, *The Governance of Medieval England from the Conquest to Magna Carta* (Edinburgh, 1963), 464–5; S. D. Lloyd, 'The Lord Edward's Crusade 1270–2: Its setting and significance', *War and Government in the Middle Ages: Essays in Honour of J. O. Prestwich*, ed. J. Gillingham and J. C. Holt (Woodbridge, 1984), 120–33.

[20] Shakespeare Birthplace Trust, Gregory Hood Collection, DR 10/2094. For other examples of agreements to discharge the service of ecclesiastical tenants-in-chief: *William Thorne's Chronicle of St Augustine's, Canterbury*, ed. A. H. Davis (Oxford, 1934), 286; *Registrum Ricardi de Swinfield, episcopi Herefordensis*, ed. W. W. Capes (Canterbury & York Soc., 1909), 375–6; *The Register of Roger Martival, bishop of Salisbury*, iii. ed. S. Reynolds (Canterbury & York Soc., 1965), 97–8, 193; N. B. Lewis, 'The Summons of the English Feudal Levy, 5 April 1327', *Essays in Medieval History presented to Bertie Wilkinson*, ed. T. A. Sandquist and M. R. Powicke (Toronto, 1969), 248–9.

six months;[21] nine months;[22] a year;[23] or a more open-ended agreement for 'as long as the war between the king of England and the king of France lasts'.[24] Though clearly intended to augment the military resources a lord could offer the Crown for the duration of one or more campaigns, these contracts do not confine the service required of the retainer to warfare alone but envisage him as a member of the lord's household throughout the term of the agreement. This is what distinguishes them from the sub-contracts for military service alone between a captain and his men-at-arms, which begin to appear once the system of recruitment by indenture took final form in the early years of Edward III's reign,[25] although, even in the late fourteenth century, a soldier contracting with a captain for a single campaign could still occasionally be offered the privileges of residence within his household.[26] Though these temporary contracts do not conform exactly to the definition of the indenture of retainer adopted in this edition, as an agreement for service *for life* in peace and war, it has seemed excessively teleological, as well as potentially misleading, to exclude them from consideration on that ground alone. The indenture of retainer passed through nearly half a century of experimentation in its form and content before becoming relatively standardized and, during that period, the comparative frequency of temporary contracts is significant, first, in emphasising the importance of military service in influencing the precise content and form of the indenture and, secondly, in suggesting a volatility and impermanence in the composition of some magnate affinities in these years hinted at by other sources.[27]

The text of an indenture of retainer, of the relatively uniform type

---

[21] E.g., the indented letters patent of Hugh Despenser the elder retaining Sir Robert Fitzwalter for six months, granting him robes and saddles in time of peace and a fee of 200 marks in time of war, for the service of Fitzwalter and his company of 20 men-at-arms: PRO, E42/271, 29 Oct. 1317.

[22] E.g., the indenture between Gilbert Umfraville, earl of Angus and Sir William Swynburne, retaining Swynburne and two valets for three quarters of a year at a fee of 20 marks: Northumberland RO, Swinburne of Capheaton, ZSW 1/58, 22 Sept. 1334.

[23] *Infra*, nos. 11, 16, 26, 29, 30.

[24] *Infra*, 8.

[25] A. E. Prince, 'The Indenture System under Edward III', *Historical Essays in Honour of James Tait*, ed. J. G. Edwards, V. H. Galbraith and E. F. Jacob (Manchester, 1933), 283–99; A. Goodman, 'The Military Subcontracts of Sir Hugh Hastings, 1380', *EHR*, xcv (1980), 114–20; S. Walker, 'Profit and Loss in the Hundred Years War: the subcontracts of Sir John Strother, 1374', *BIHR*, lviii (1985), 100–6.

[26] Northumbs. RO, ZSW 4/50; PRO, E101/68/9/202.

[27] Note, for instance, the very few names that occur in both the lists of the earl of Norfolk's household drawn up in 1294–5 and 1297 and the considerable turnover in the names of Henry, earl of Lancaster's annuitants, 1330–2: PRO, C47/2/10/8; *Documents Illustrating the Crisis of 1297–8 in England*, ed. M. Prestwich (Camden Soc., 4th ser. xxiv, 1980), 157–8; PRO, DL40/1/11 ff. 45v, 51v.

that began to predominate during Edward III's reign, usually consists of five separate clauses, though the order in which these clauses are combined is, except in the case of the first and final elements, very fluid. The five elements in most indentures of retainer are: i. an introduction, announcing the fact of an agreement for service between the two parties named; ii. a clause or clauses setting out the terms of the retainer's service in both peace and war; iii. a clause or clauses detailing the rewards to be granted in return for the faithful performance of this service; iv. a penalty clause, setting out the remedies available in the case of the failure of one party or the other to fulfill the foregoing conditions; v. a validating clause. The evolution and development of each of these elements is worth scrutinising with care, for changes in the wording and form of these indentures of retainer can provide valuable evidence to contribute to a consideration of the much wider question of the nature of lordship at the end of the Middle Ages.

The distinctive opening phrase of the indenture of retainer – *Ceste endenture faite parentre* ... (or in the fifteenth century, its English equivalent) – took some time to evolve; the earliest surviving instance of its use dates from 1317.[28] Prior to that, practice had varied between the use of indented letters patent, with their characteristic address *A touz ceux qi cestes lettres verront ou orrount* (or its Latin equivalent),[29] and the employment of a hybrid introductory and dating clause which made no mention of the form of the instrument in which the agreement was couched.[30] In addition, a few agreements preferred to retain the standard opening of *conventiones* of all types, *Hec est convencio facta ...*[31] During this initial phase of definition, several of the surviving examples of indented letters patent were issued by the retainer rather than by the lord. This must imply that each party to the contract issued separate letters patent, embodying their respective obligations within the relationship, in a fashion similar to the reciprocal bonds of maintenance and manrent that emerged in fifteenth-century Scotland.[32] In England, however, this form of agreement was generally superseded by the identically-worded but interchangeably sealed indenture of retainer in the course of the fourteenth century.

The characteristic opening of this type of agreement appears to have originated in the Lancastrian chancery under Earl Thomas and spread from there to other baronial households by the 1330s,[33] though it was not until the second half of the fourteenth century that it became the

[28] *Infra*, 23.
[29] 1, 2, 8, 13, 20, 22, 29, 38–9.
[30] 3, 4, 7, 10, 11, 12, 14–18, 21, 26, 28, 30, 33, 43, 45.
[31] 6, 9, 19.
[32] 2, 8, 13, 20; Wormald, *Lords and Men in Scotland*, 30–1.
[33] 23–5, 27, 32, 34–7, 40–2, and *passim*.

virtually invariable introductory phrase. The most significant alternative to it continued to be the use of indented letters patent, which still occasionally appear in the early fifteenth century.[34] Their survival serves to emphasize the more general point that, although the distinction between an indenture of retainer and letters patent granting an annuity for past and future services was clear in legal theory, it was not always observed or understood in practice. While an agreement of retainer for life could be couched in the form of letters patent, letters patent could, on occasion, go well beyond the simple grant of an annuity to detail many of the benefits and conditions associated with the indenture of retainer.[35] The situation was further complicated in the later fifteenth century by the growing practice, apparently adopted in order to circumvent the restrictions of the legislation against retaining passed in 1468, of granting annuities for past and future services which were themselves defined and specified in more detail in an indenture of retainer concluded between the two parties.[36] The 'sea of varying relationships'[37] that constituted the world of late medieval lordship had its counterpart, therefore, in the varied range of diplomatic instruments used to reduce those relationships to a contractual form. The indenture of retainer was the dominant but not invariable instrument of mutual obligation and the continuing element of indeterminacy in its form is a warning not to seek to define those obligations with an artificial precision.

This is immediately apparent in considering the range of peacetime service to which retainers were committed by their indentures. In essence, their duties consisted of attending the lord in his household when summoned to do so and accompanying him in his riding retinue as he travelled around the country. Many contracts amplify this undertaking with the retainer's promise to take his lord's part against all others, though this reservation of loyalty was generally omitted from contracts concluded between c. 1360 and 1400.[38] There was a further assumption, sometimes articulated, that peacetime service would only take place 'within the realm of England',[39] though Henry, prince of Wales, unusually required his retainers to be prepared to travel abroad on diplomatic business.[40] To these general obligations some early

---

[34] 98, 112.

[35] E.g., the letters patent of William, lord Zouche, granting John Clifford a fee of 8 marks p.a. together with bouche of court for himself and a valet, and livery for two horses: PRO, C66/398 m. 15, 24 Sept. 1414.

[36] This was the practice of Richard, duke of Gloucester: PRO, DL29/648/10485 m. 14.

[37] Holmes, 79.

[38] 1, 2, 10, 12, 13, 23–7, 31–2, 38, 43–5, 91–2, 94–6, 100, 102, 105, 116, 119 and passim.

[39] 118, 133; Dunham, forms B, C, D, F–K, N, Q, S, W.

[40] 104, 106–11.

indentures add the duty of attending the lord at Parliaments – the last instance of this provision dates from 1332[41] – and other contracts envisage the possibility of service away from the household or in the 'country' of the lord.[42] Two of Thomas, lord Despenser's indentures extended the frequent requirement that retainers bring with them a specified number of followers in war to peacetime service as well.[43] In general, however, the 'multiplicity of peacetime service'[44] performed by retainers on behalf of their lords remains largely unstated in the terms of the surviving indentures. Thomas Fairfax's undertaking to 'ride and work in peacetime with the said earl [Marshal] and others on business touching the salvation of the honour or right and inheritance of the earl' is as comprehensive a statement of the mutual expectations of lord and retainer as they provide.[45] The main exception to this widespread lack of precision lies in those hybrid contracts which combine a general agreement of retainer with appointment to a more specific office in the lord's service, whether as his steward, chamberlain or as a member of his council.[46] Still more specific in their terms are those indentures retaining a man for particular professional services, such as those provided by minstrels and trumpeters, cooks and physicians.[47] Contracts with lawyers, retaining them to be 'of counsel' with a lord for life or for a term of years, fall into a similar category, though their comparative scarcity suggests that a grant of an annuity for past and future services was generally felt to be a more appropriate means of obtaining legal counsel.[48]

One particular form of service requires more extended discussion. Professor Bean has argued that the description of a retainer as a 'bachelor' in an indenture indicates 'a person of superior knightly status, who occupied a position of special trust within the entourage of the lord', his obligations perhaps regulated by an additional contract –

[41] 11, 24–5, 27, 31–4.

[42] 85, 92.

[43] 87, 93. Despenser was clearly anxious to secure himself a substantial peacetime retinue. For his request to the prior of Llanthony-by-Gloucester to supply him with five men-at-arms and 15 archers to attend the Parliament of September 1397: PRO, C115/K2/6684 f. 193.

[44] R. Horrox, *Richard III. A Study of Service* (Cambridge, 1989), 7.

[45] *Infra*, 77.

[46] 37, 68, 75, 79, 89, 90.

[47] 112, 113; *John of Gaunt's Register, 1372–1376*, ed. S. Armitage-Smith (Camden Soc., 3rd ser., xx–xxi, 1911), nos. 792, 797; A. Compton Reeves, 'Some of Humphrey Stafford's Military Indentures', *Nottingham Mediaeval Studies*, xvi (1972), 91. Note also the indenture between Sir Philip Thornbury, his wife Margaret, and Richard Whitwick, retaining him in the offices of lardyner, 'catour' and cook in their household for the term of their lives. Whitwick was to receive a fee of 20 shillings *p.a.* and a suit of yeoman's livery and to hold a tenement at Pottern Green (Herts.) for a rose rent: PRO, E210/1172.

[48] 117, 119; T. Madox, *Formulare Anglicanum* (London, 1702), no. cclxiii.

though none of these have survived.[49] While certainty is difficult to achieve on this question, in view of the many shades of meaning attached to the word in later medieval sources, a careful study of the use of the term 'bachelor' in the indentures printed below indicates that it will not bear so precise a definition. In general, the usage of the indentures suggests that the commonest contemporary meaning of the word was the sense in which it was understood by the contracting parties; that is, that a 'bachelor' belonged to a particular rank within the order of knighthood – below a knight banneret and, according to some authorities, above a knight *sans phrase* – rather than being the possessor of any particular office or position within the noble household.[50] This is clearest in those indentures which refer to the 'estate' or 'degree' of bachelor, and to the retainer's subsequent advancement to the 'estate' of baron.[51] It was necessary to specify a knightly retainer's status so exactly because, in time of war, a banneret was expected to bring a larger company on campaign than a knight bachelor and received in return more generous wages from the Crown. Indentures retaining knights banneret do survive, though they are considerably less common than contracts with knights bachelor, while Sir Nicholas Kyriel's undertaking to Sir Stephen Segrave that, if he becomes a banneret on inheriting his estates, he will continue to serve him in the same manner as he did while a knight bachelor (*de luy servir ausi com devaunt*) suggests that the difference in the nature of a bachelor and a banneret's service was one of degree rather than kind.[52] This is not to deny that some bachelor knights *did* enjoy a position of special trust within the household of their lord – Sir John Sully, one of the 'bachelors of the chamber' of the Black Prince was also a member of the prince's 'special retinue'[53] – but the additional elements of favour and trust in this relationship arose from Sully's position as a knight of the prince's chamber, fulfilling duties very similar to those required of the royal chamber knights, rather than from his status as a knight bachelor.[54]

[49] J. M. W. Bean, ' "Bachelor" and "Retainer" ', *Medievalia et Humanistica*, n.s. iii (1972), 117–31; Bean, 22–32.

[50] E.g., *Rotuli Parliamentorum* (London, 1783), iii. 57–8; *The Babees Book*, ed. F. J. Furnivall (Early English Text Soc., o.s. xxxiii, 1868), i. 186, 284. For a general discussion of the distinction between knights banneret and knights bachelor see N. Saul, *Knights and Esquires. The Gloucestershire Gentry in the Fourteenth Century* (Oxford, 1981), 7–10; D. Crouch, *The Image of Aristocracy in Britain 1000–1300* (London, 1992), 114–19.

[51] *Infra*, 70, 122. Note also the provision that knights of the royal household were to be 'xij bachelers sufficiantz and most valent men of war of that *ordre* of every cuntrey': *The Household of Edward IV. The Black Book and the Ordinance of 1478*, ed. A. R. Myers (Manchester, 1959), 108.

[52] 13, 24, 27, 31.

[53] 41, 42.

[54] Given-Wilson, 160–74, 204–12 for the King's chamber knights and, for a similar group in John of Gaunt's household, Walker, *Lancastrian Affinity*, 11–13. Note too the

Some indentures contained provision for the variation or relaxation of the various obligations of service they set out under certain conditions, such as the concession that William Daventry secured from Thomas, lord Despenser, that he be excused from service when busy on his own legal affairs.[55] The most common clause of this type was one reserving the retainer's allegiance to the king and, in the appropriate circumstances, his eldest son.[56] In general, this did no more than state the obvious. Only in the case of Richard, duke of York's contracts in 1460 is the omission of a specific reservation of allegiance to the king, always included in the duke's contracts during the previous decade, likely to have been purposeful.[57]

Yet the uncertainties of political life in later medieval England sometimes left their mark on this clause. The insistence in John Holland, duke of Exeter's indentures, concluded in September 1399, that his retainers should serve him 'before all living [men], except his liege lord' left the object of that allegiance conveniently undefined, while Sir William Stanley's reservation of his loyalty to King Edward 'and all other that should be King of England after the death of the said King Edward' suggests some uncertainty over the permanence of the Yorkist dynasty.[58] In the fifteenth century, lords began to allow other magnates to appear in the exception clause, though such relaxations of the retainer's duty of loyalty, recognizing a pre-existing obligation on his part, were never very frequent.[59] Indeed, some lords sought to insist that their retainers were not to take fee or service with any other lord without their consent.[60] Once again, this was not a frequent stipulation, largely because it did not need to be. The kind of regular and menial service envisaged in most indentures was such that a retainer could discharge his duty adequately to only one lord at a time. Much commoner was the exception of some or all of the retainer's family and kindred from the terms of the contract, though the group thus excepted rarely extended as far as the three degrees of kindred allowed Sir James Strangeways by Richard Neville, earl of Salisbury.[61]

While the majority of indentures were relatively vague in defining the nature and extent of the peacetime services required of a retainer, they were usually much more precise in setting out his obligations in

indenture retaining Camoys Mavow as an esquire of the earl of Cambridge's chamber (69).

[55] *Infra*, 87.

[56] 12, 13, 20, 23–7, 31–2, 43–5, 100, 102, 105, 116, and *passim*. All Lord Hastings' indentures reserve the retainer's allegiance to the king.

[57] 129–31, 134–7

[58] 91–2, 141.

[59] 116, 126; Dunham, forms C, I, L, Y. For one fourteenth-century example, *infra*, 43.

[60] 5, 94–6.

[61] 8, 119, 121, 126, 132, 150.

time of war. This was principally because large sums of money, the payments made by the Crown to the lord for the wages and regard of his war retinue, as well as the ransoms and other profits of war that might accrue to both lord and retainer, were potentially at stake. The number and status of the men a retainer was required to bring with him in time of war, the wages and other benefits he would receive for doing so, the day on which his service would commence, and the theatres of operation in which he would be required to serve were all, in consequence, the subject of careful regulation in his indenture. It was generally assumed that a retainer would campaign whenever his lord did, though some indentures dispensed with this obligation, allowing the retainer to decide whether he would serve or not.[62] The geographical scope of this service was usually taken to be within the British Isles and in France, though the obligation to serve in France was omitted in some early indentures and, in the fifteenth century, service in war as well as peace began to be confined to England alone. By 1447, when the earl of Salisbury specifically exempted Ralph, lord Greystoke, from the duty of serving him in France, indentures making no specific provision for war service at all, or confining the retainer's obligations to England, were relatively common.[63]

This was a development reflected in the language of the indentures themselves, which began to replace the promise to serve 'in peace and war' with a more general undertaking by the retainer to serve his lord 'term of his life against all folks saving his allegiance'. Though this was a far from uniform development, with some of Lord Hastings' indentures preserving the 'peace and war' formula as late as 1483,[64] the gradual disappearance of a natural expectation of service in war from the indenture of retainer lends some weight to the argument that the commitment of the English upper-classes to chivalric values in general, and to the vigorous prosecution of the war in France in particular, faded in the course of the fifteenth century.[65]

Two further conditions of service, both closely related to the retainer's obligation to serve his lord in time of war, require brief discussion. Tournament service was an obligation included in many early indentures,[66] for a tournament was one of the occasions on which a lord was

---

[62] 21, 73, 87.

[63] 118, 127, 130–1, 133, 142, 151; Dunham, forms C, F, G, H, J, K, N, W.

[64] Dunham, forms D, H, Q, S, T, U, V.

[65] P. Maddern, 'Honour among the Pastons: gender and integrity in fifteenth-century English provincial society', *Journal of Medieval History*, xiv (1988), 357–72; M. Keen, 'The End of the Hundred Years War: Lancastrian France and Lancastrian England', *England and her Neighbours, 1066–1453. Essays in Honour of Pierre Chaplais*, ed. M. Jones and M. Vale (London, 1989), 297–311.

[66] 7, 11, 14, 16, 28, 33.

most anxious to secure honourable escort. Aymer de Valence's contract with John Darcy, which allowed the retainer to serve with whichever lord he wished at tournaments, with the additional condition that, if Valence wished Darcy to remain in his service at such times, he was to offer him as much as he could have gained from any other lord, indicates how stiff the competition was for suitable attendants.[67] The last separate provision for such service occurs in 1339, though tournaments themselves were to remain an important element in English chivalric life for at least another half century. Thereafter, the duty of attendance at tournaments seems to have been subsumed within the general obligations of war service.[68] Largely excepted from the routine provisions of the early indentures of retainer was the question of the Crusade. Service in the Holy Land was felt to be a special case, requiring separate provision; the contract for service *outremer* between Henry Lacy, earl of Lincoln, and Richard Tanny is the only surviving example of such an agreement.[69] Whatever the hardships, the lure of the Crusades remained strong until the end of the fourteenth century. One retainer was allowed to join the 'common voyage' to the Holy Land even if his lord remained at home, and once the focus of Crusading endeavour switched from Palestine to the *estranges marches* of Prussia – first mentioned in 1347 – the inclusion of an obligation on the retainer to crusade together with his lord became a little more common.[70]

The rewards offered a retainer by his lord for these various forms of service usually consisted of a combination of benefits in cash and kind. The benefits in kind could be considerable and, in some instances, constituted the full extent of the rewards granted the retainer.[71] Retainers might be offered the privilege of eating within the household when summoned by the lord (*bouche de court*); full stable provision – hay, oats, bedding and shoeing – while resident in the household; a livery robe of the lord's whenever a general distribution was made, together with a new saddle each year. These benefits are itemised in some detail in the earlier fourteenth-century indentures and were, in some cases,

---

[67] *Infra*, 15.

[68] *Infra*, 37; J. Vale, *Edward III and Chivalry* (Woodbridge, 1982), 57–75; J. Barker, *The Tournament in England, 1100–1400* (Woodbridge, 1986), 12–16, 120–3.

[69] 3, 5–7, 18.

[70] 14, 40, 85, 93; N. B. Lewis, 'Indentures of retinue with John of Gaunt, duke of Lancaster, enrolled in Chancery, 1367–1399', *Camden Miscellany* xxii (1964), no. 1; Walker, *Lancastrian Affinity*, 294–5.

[71] 13, 19, 21, 28. Note also the terms of the indenture, preserved in a sixteenth-century transcript, by which Maurice FitzThomas, first earl of Desmond, retained Thomas, son of Walter Mandeville, 22 Sept. 1341, granting him two suits of livery and a war-horse, with suitable saddle and bridle, each year: K. W. Nicholls, 'Abstracts of Mandeville Deeds, NLI Ms. 6136', *Analecta Hibernica*, xxxii (1985), 18–19.

considered preferable to a cash fee.[72] But, with the exception of *bouche de court*, most had ceased to be mentioned by the end of the century. Individual items of stable provision, like the separate distribution of a saddle, were increasingly commuted into a cash payment of household wages while in attendance on the lord.[73] Equally, the robe of the lord's livery – once considered so important an indication of loyalty that, in two of Thomas, earl of Lancaster's indentures, the retainer was only to receive the benefits enumerated if he was wearing Lancaster's livery[74] – began to be the subject of a separate and less regulated provision by mid-century. Although lay and ecclesiastical magnates continued to make regular distributions of their livery robes throughout this period,[75] it was only at a lower social level, in contracts between gentry and yeomen, that the granting of a livery robe continued to be comprehended within the terms of the indenture.[76]

In the majority of cases, however, the most valuable of the benefits offered was the retaining fee itself. This usually took the form of a rent charge, payable in two annual instalments, assigned on one of the lord's manors or receiverships, though it was occasionally the case, particularly in Ireland, that the retaining fee was paid as a lump sum over a term of years.[77] It was also quite common, in the case of favoured retainers, for the lord to alienate a whole manor to his servant for the term of the latter's life; the social consequence that lordship over land and men conferred could be a substantial additional benefit in itself.[78]

The size of the fee paid naturally varied in proportion to the wealth of the lord and the consequence of the retainer. What is most noticeable is the absence of standardization in the early indentures, some of which offer very large money fees – as much as £1000 for the service of Sir William Latimer and his company of 40 men to Thomas, earl of Lancaster in time of war[79] – while others offer no fee at all. This variety had been replaced, by the end of the fourteenth century, by a reasonably

---

[72] E.g., PRO, CP40/235, enrolled deeds, m. 1: letters patent of Sir John Cockfield, 16 April 1320, announcing that whereas Sir Richard Damory was obliged by his writing to pay him a fee of 100 shillings a year, he now wished Damory to substitute for the fee two robes and a saddle suitable for a knight 'of such livery as he makes for his bachelors each year'.

[73] 59, 62, 64, 66, 69–70.

[74] 27, 31.

[75] K. B. McFarlane, *The Nobility of Later Medieval England* (Oxford, 1973), 111–2. The lists of livery distributed by successive priors of Christ Church, Canterbury, between 1439 and 1466, for instance, suggest a provision for up to 80 *generosi*: Bodl., MS Tanner 165 ff. 155v–176v.

[76] 115, 150.

[77] 11, 26, 29, 43–5.

[78] 5, 31, 34, 38, 48, 52, 65, 90, 118, 126.

[79] 31.

standard set of expectations; £20 or 20 marks *p.a.* for a knight, £10 or 10 marks *p.a.* for an esquire. Even so, substantially larger fees were still not uncommon; Henry, prince of Wales offered 250 marks *p.a.* to the two earls he retained, while Humphrey, duke of Buckingham, could contemplate paying a fee of 100 marks *p.a.* in 1440.[80] In this respect, Professor Dunham's suggestion that the later Middle Ages witnessed a development in the articulation of lordship 'whereby fiefs gave way to fees, and fees to favour'[81] appears to place too much emphasis on his own analysis of the evidence furnished by Lord Hastings' indentures.

Hastings rarely granted his retainers a money fee, substituting instead (to take a representative example) an undertaking to be a 'good and tender lord' to the retainer 'in all things reasonable he hath to do, and him to aid and succour in his right as far as law and conscience requireth'.[82] Though the promise of good lordship appears in some contemporary contracts concluded by lords other than Hastings,[83] this emphasis on favour was only making explicit an assumption so central to the relationship codified in the indenture of retainer that it was rarely written down; though its intended operation – as in Hugh Despenser's promise to procure the marriage of his sister for Sir Peter Uvedale, or the earl of Northumberland's undertaking to advance the brother of his retainer to a benefice worth £40 *p.a.*[84] – is sometimes set out. Money fees continued to be offered, even in the indentures of magnates as powerful as Richard Neville, earl of Warwick and Richard, duke of Gloucester,[85] and the tie between lord and man created by the cash fee remained a substantial element in the creation and maintenance of a magnate affinity well into the early Tudor period. John de Vere, earl of Oxford, for instance, left instructions for the continued payment of annuities to twelve knights and forty six other gentlemen, at the cost of over £200 *p.a.*, in his will in 1513.[86] The exclusive emphasis on good lordship in the Hastings indentures seems, in consequence, more likely to represent the exception than the rule. It is best explained by the exceptional nature of the affinity he was seeking to construct, for Hastings' role in the north Midlands was primarily to act, in his capacity as steward of the duchy of Lancaster honour of Tutbury, as the representative of the absentee Edward IV. His indentures were consequently more

---

[80] 104, 111, 122.
[81] Dunham, 10.
[82] *ibid.* form D.
[83] 149, 155.
[84] 22, 99.
[85] 138–40, 142–5, 152–3.
[86] W. H. St John Hope, 'The Last Testament and Inventory of John de Vere, Thirteenth Earl of Oxford', *Archaeologia*, lxvi (1915), 318–20.

concerned to secure the loyalty of the county gentry to the king than to create an effective local affinity for himself.[87]

The financial benefits on offer in the indenture of retainer could be varied, at the discretion of either party, in time of war. Most indentures offer a flat fee in return for the retainer's service in both peace and war, though the custom of allowing the retainer to keep the wages of war paid by the Crown meant that, in practice, a prolonged period of campaigning would bring a significant increase in his fee income.[88] A substantial minority of indentures were more favourable in their provisions, offering an increment on the retainer's fee in time of war,[89] while a few were less generous, demanding that any wages of war received from the king be deducted *pro rata* from the peacetime fee.[90] Much depended on the custom and practice of the particular noble family concerned: the Beauchamps were consistently generous in granting increments, the Nevilles generally insisted on rebating; Edward, prince of Wales, pursued a policy of granting substantial fees but requiring his retainers and annuitants to campaign entirely at their own charge.[91]

The whole question of a retainer's rewards for his service in war was further complicated by the need to make provision for the division of any spoils of war that might be gained while on campaign, in the form of ransom of prisoners and plunder from the countryside. The conventions governing the division of such spoils were first spelled out in an indenture of retainer in 1347, when half of all the gains of war won by the retainer were claimed by the lord.[92] Prior to this, more concern had been shown for the potential losses of warfare than for the possible gains, with particular attention paid to the lord's obligation to compensate his retainers for their horses lost while on campaign; some early contracts for war service were almost entirely taken up with the precise enumeration and valuation of the horses to be comprehended

---

[87] S. M. Wright, *The Derbyshire Gentry in the Fifteenth Century* (Derbys. Rec. Soc., viii, 1983), 75–82; I. Rowney, 'The Hastings Affinity in Staffordshire and the Honour of Tutbury', *BIHR*, lvii (1984), 35–45; M. A. Hicks, *Richard III and his rivals* (London, 1991), 229–46; C. Carpenter, *Locality and Polity*, 516–46.

[88] 67, 76, 78–9, 84, 87–8, 93–6, 101, 142.

[89] 4, 5, 31, 40, 52, 54, 62, 71–2, 82; Walker, *Lancastrian Affinity*, 68–9 for John of Gaunt's practice in this respect; approximately a quarter of his indentures, most of them concluded in 1372, offer an increment for the retainer's service on campaign.

[90] 97, 102, 105, 114, 128, 132.

[91] *Infra*, 55–6; PRO, CHES 2/48 mm. 2, 2d, 49 m. 1 for the Prince's letters patent, announcing grants of £40 *p.a.* for past and future services to nine knights, all of whom were to serve him in war with two esquires '*saunz aucun autre fee prendre de nous pour lui ou pour les dictes esquiers...*'.

[92] *Infra*, 40.

within the agreement.[93] The rule that a captain was entitled to half his retainer's spoils of war but was, at the same time, obliged to restore the value of any horses lost by his men while on campaign appears to have been generally observed until *c.* 1370, when it was gradually replaced by a new understanding that the lord was no longer responsible for the restoration of horses lost but would, in return, lay claim to only a third of his company's winnings of war.[94]

This was a far from simultaneous or uniform development, however; the entitlement of the captain and the Crown was reduced to a quarter in some contracts[95] and the practice of individual magnates varied. Some were content to follow the custom of the country – 'in the way that is reasonably done in the places and voyages where they campaign' – while others drove a notably hard bargain. As late as 1400, the earl of Warwick could insist on half of all his retainer's gains of war, without any corresponding concession over the restoration of lost horses.[96] Although, by the time of Richard II's Durham Ordinance in 1385, the 'third' was generally accepted as the standard entitlement,[97] there still remained considerable scope for discussion and bargaining between lord and retainer, for there was more than one interpretation of the convention governing the 'third'. A number of late fourteenth-century indentures sought to claim a third of the winnings of the retainer *and* his company for the lord, if they were all at his wages;[98] this was a less favourable arrangement for the retainer than the convention that was eventually accepted as standard practice, which allowed the lord a third of his retainer's booty and only a third of the retainer's third of his followers' gains of war.[99] The general adoption of this convention in the fifteenth century represented a significant improvement in the inducements offered a retainer for his service

[93] 4, 5, 7, 11, 13, 18, 19, 23–5, 27, 29, 30, 32–4, 36–7, 39; N. B. Lewis, 'An early indenture of military service, 27 July 1287', *BIHR*, xiii (1935–6), 85–9.

[94] 40, 54; D. Hay, 'The Division of Spoils of War in Fourteenth-Century England', *TRHS*, 5th ser. iv (1954), 91–109; H. J. Hewitt, *The Black Prince's Expedition of 1355–7* (Manchester, 1958), 155–7; M. H. Keen, *The Laws of War in the Late Middle Ages* (London, 1965), 146–7; Bean, 238–46. Note also the contract between Richard, earl of Arundel and Sir Gerard de Lisle for service for a year with 30 men-at-arms in which Arundel offered restoration of horses lost to Lisle and his company and claims half of all their gains of war: Berkeley Castle, Select Charter 526, 5 March 1350.

[95] BL, Add. MS 37494 ff. 8v, 9; PRO, E364/8 mm. 9–10.

[96] 64, 70, 97.

[97] *The Black Book of the Admiralty*, ed. Sir T. Twiss (Rolls Series, lv, 1871), i. 456. Note also Richard II's mandate to the earl of Northumberland to regulate the ransoming of prisoners on the March, with full powers to punish those who ransomed prisoners without the consent of their masters 'to whom the third belongs, as it is determined by the law of arms and the usages of war': PRO, C81/1349/13, 5 Feb. 1386.

[98] 59, 62, 65, 66, 82, 85, 94–6, 98, 102, 105, 126, 128.

[99] 75, 80, 101, 104, 106–11, 114, 122, 124–5, 127, 132, 138–9, 144–5, 147–8, 152–3.

overseas, at a time when many captains were finding it increasingly difficult to meet the quotas of knights and men-at-arms agreed in their contracts with the Crown.[100]

What recourse was available to either lord or man if any of the conditions set out in their indentures of retainer was broken? The enforceability of annuities granted for past and future services was clearly recognized by the Common law courts but the status of a fee regulated by the terms of an indenture of retainer remained more uncertain.[101] The one known legal case directly concerned with the issue seemingly did not reach a conclusion, though the justices' initial judgement indicates that they were prepared to regard a retaining fee as a recoverable free tenement.[102] How it was to be recovered remained a matter of judgement; in 1314 Richard de Kellawe, bishop of Durham, allowed Sir Edmund Mauley to recover the £20 p.a. he had granted him either by a writ of annuity or of novel disseisin, whichever seemed best to the retainer.[103] In any case, the inequality of power and social position prevailing in the relations between many lords and their retainers ensured that the legal niceties were not always observed. Edward, prince of Wales, simply wrote to two Cornish knights in 1351, dismissing them from his service on the ground of their oppression of his tenants 'notwithstanding any letter which has heretofore reached you from us, or any speech or indenture between us and you touching your retainder with us'.[104]

All the same, a substantial number of indentures addressed themselves to the questions of default and enforceability. Some were careful to delimit the area of dispute, specifically exempting the retainer from service in the case of illness, incapacity or other 'reasonable' cause,[105] while others were prepared to accept the performance of the retainer's service by deputy.[106] Many more included a distraint clause which, typically, allowed the retainer to distrain on the manor or other source of revenue to which the payment of his fee was assigned if it remained unpaid after a stated period of time – variously defined as twelve days, a fortnight, a month, forty days or two months.[107] The lord's reciprocal right to cease payment of the fee if the service for which it was granted went unperformed was explicitly stated far less often, though it must

---

[100] M. R. Powicke, 'Lancastrian Captains', *Essays ... presented to Bertie Wilkinson*, ed. Sandquist and Powicke, 371–82.

[101] Saul, *Knights and Esquires*, 96–7, 265–6; Bean, 14–17.

[102] *Infra*, 81.

[103] *Registrum palatinum Dunelmense. The Register of Richard de Kellawe, lord palatine and bishop of Durham, 1314–16*, ed. Sir T. D. Hardy (Rolls Series, lxii, 1873–8), iii. 1256–7.

[104] *BPR*, ii. 9–10 (Kindly brought to our attention by Chris Given-Wilson).

[105] 35, 70, 81, 98.

[106] 33–4.

[107] 58, 77–80, 84, 87, 91, 93, 115, 118.

have been taken for granted within most relationships.[108] Such distraint clauses were not, in any case, universal. The most powerful magnates, such as the Black Prince and John of Gaunt, generally omitted them from their contracts.[109] The inclusion of a distraint clause in an indenture was, in this respect, an additional inducement offered to the retainer, since it allowed him to recover his fee without recourse to the expensive and uncertain process of litigation. The disappearance of such clauses from most contracts after *c.* 1430 consequently suggests a relative deterioration in the terms and conditions of service offered most retainers.

As with many other aspects of the indenture of retainer, however, the relative standardization of the distraint clause discernible by *c.* 1370 was preceded by a period of experimentation, in which a number of alternative solutions to the problem of enforceability were canvassed. One was for either or both parties to oblige themselves in all their lands, or for a punitive sum in damages, to the fulfillment of the conditions of the indenture.[110] Another was for the distraint to be executed by the stewards and marshals of the king's household – a provision that emphasises the background of insistent and increasing Crown demands for military service against which the early contracts developed.[111]

One vital element in the legal enforceability of the indenture of retainer was the final validating clause, for by *c.* 1300 the royal courts had evolved the doctrine that contracts were only cognisable if made under seal.[112] The effectiveness of any surviving indentures that appear not to have been sealed, such as those concluded by Richard, duke of York, in 1460, must consequently remain doubtful.[113] The sealing clause was at once the most distinctive and the most stable of the indenture of retainer's constituent elements. Apart from one unexplained case,

---

[108] 59, 61, 66, 70.

[109] Bean, 251–68 for a tabulation of Gaunt's practice. Only 15 of his 160 surviving indentures include a right of distraint.

[110] 7, 12, 13, 22. Note also the indenture between Sir Nicholas de Loveyne and Simon, son of Walter de Woodham in which Loveyne enters into a bond of £100 to provide Woodham with the wardship of an heiress, to the value of 20 marks *p.a.*, and to maintain him '*en aussi covenable manere come un des meillours esquiers estaunt demorant et servant en lostil*', in return for Woodham's undertaking to serve him as an esquire in all parts of England: PRO, C54/198 m. 7d, 1 Dec. 1360, a reference owing to the kindness of Simon Payling.

[111] 7, 8, 11, 18. Edward I wrote to the Council, 8 Sept. 1297, ordering them to take action against one of Roger de Mowbray's retainers, who had failed to go on campaign in Flanders as he had contracted to do; Prestwich, *Documents Illustrating the Crisis of 1297–98*, 146 no. 135.

[112] F. Pollock and F. W. Maitland, *The History of English Law before the time of Edward I* (Cambridge, 1898, repr. 1968), ii. 219–20.

[113] 134–7.

which has no sealing clause at all,[114] every indenture either describes itself as sealed 'interchangeably' or, in a more elaborate exposition of the same process, states that the lord has sealed the half of the indenture remaining in the possession of the retainer, and that the retainer has sealed the half remaining with the lord. The only exceptions to this are those contracts in the form of reciprocal bonds which, though interchangeably sealed, preserve evidence for only one half of the procedure.[115] Variations or developments in the form of the sealing clause are few. Prior to c. 1350, a list of witnesses was sometimes included for greater security;[116] the retainer might occasionally be required to take an oath on the gospels to fulfill all the conditions of the indenture;[117] some Neville indentures add, instead, that the retainer has 'pledged his faith', though no details of what this act involved are given.[118] After 1450, the spread of lay literacy is reflected in the fact that some indentures begin to be signed, as well as sealed, interchangeably.[119]

The latest of the indentures of retainer listed in this edition dates from 1476; the last of Lord Hastings' indentures was concluded in May 1483, a month before his summary execution. No later indentures of retainer for life appear to have survived, nor even any reference to the terms of one, although English armies for service abroad continued to be, in part, recruited by indentures for a fixed term of military service until 1512.[120] The practice of retaining and the presence of retainers within the noble household remained an important political phenomenon throughout the sixteenth century but there is nothing to indicate that it continued to be regulated, as it had been in the fourteenth and fifteenth centuries, by a formal written contract between lord and man.[121]

The disappearance of the indenture of retainer, the instrument by which the obligations of lordship and service had been most characteristically expressed for two centuries, is so rapid as to require,

---

[114] 40.

[115] 8, 13, 20.

[116] 6, 7, 23–4, 31–2, 35, 38–9, 43–4, 81, 97.

[117] 2, 22, 24, 32, 43–4, 91–2; Wormald, *Lords and Men in Scotland*, 70 for the same practice.

[118] 100, 105, 116.

[119] 129, 152–3; all Lord Hastings' indentures, except forms A, B and U, bear the retainer's sign manual.

[120] C. G. Cruickshank, *Army Royal. Henry VIII's Invasion of France, 1513* (Oxford, 1969), 197–8.

[121] Dunham, 90–116; L. Stone, *The Crisis of the Aristocracy 1558–1641* (Oxford, 1965), 201–17; A. Cameron, 'The Giving of Livery and Retaining in Henry VII's Reign', *Renaissance and Modern Studies*, xviii (1974), 17–35; J. P. Cooper, 'Retainers in Tudor England', *Land, Men and Beliefs* (London, 1983), 78–96.

in conclusion, some brief attention. An important part of the explanation for its disappearance clearly lies in the increasing legislative restrictions placed upon the practice of retaining by indenture. The parliamentary Commons had petitioned against retaining *de pace* as early as 1330 but the first statutory limitations on the extent and rewards of retaining did not materialise until 1399, when liveries of cloth were witheld even from indentured retainers, unless they were also members of the lord's household and council.[122] This prohibition was confirmed and elaborated by statute in 1406 and by proclamation in 1413 but it remained the only limitation on the nobility's freedom to retain by indenture and the restriction it imposed was even slightly relaxed in 1461, when Edward IV allowed the Wardens of the March to distribute livery north of the Trent and made a further exception for those acting under 'special commandment by the King to raise people for the resisting of his enemies'.[123]

In 1468, however, Edward IV radically extended the existing prohibitions by enacting that 'no person, of whatsoever condition or degree he be ... [shall] give any such livery or sign, or retain any person other than his menial servant, officer or man learned in the one law or the other by any writing, oath or promise'. All indentures for service with retainers other than household servants or officers and the lord's councillors were thereby declared illegal and all existing indentures falling into that category rendered null and void, though annuities granted for 'lawful' past and future services were specifically excepted from the terms of the statute.[124] These prohibitions were repeated and refined by Henry VII in 1504, who made formal provision for exemptions from the terms of the 1468 statute for those granted a licence to retain by the king.[125]

The genesis, purpose and effect of Edward IV's legislation against retaining have all been the subject of considerable discussion.[126] Best understood as a manoeuvre within the context of an increasingly bitter power-struggle between the king and Richard Neville, earl of Warwick, it seems likely that Edward IV's intention in promulgating the 1468 statute was to control the extent of indentured retaining by a system of licensing rather than to outlaw it entirely. This helps to explain why magnates in the king's favour, such as Lord Hastings and the duke of

---

[122] *Rot. Parl.*, ii. 63 and iii. 428; *Statutes of the Realm* (Record Comm., 1816), ii. 113–4 (1 H. IV, c. 7); Bean, 200–30 provides a helpful survey of the statutory changes.

[123] *Statutes of the Realm*, ii, 155–6 (7 H. IV, c. 14); *Rot. Parl.*, v. 487–8.

[124] *Rot. Parl.*, v. 633–4; *Statutes of the Realm*, ii. 426–9 (8 E. IV, c. 2).

[125] *Statutes of the Realm*, ii. 658–60 (19 H. VII, c. 14).

[126] Dunham, 67–89; J. G. Bellamy, 'Justice under the Yorkist Kings', *American Journal of Legal History*, ix (1965), 152–4; C. Ross, *Edward IV* (London, 1974), 412–3; M. A. Hicks, 'The 1468 Statute of Livery', *Historical Research*, lxiv (1991), 15–28.

Gloucester, were able to continue to retain on a considerable scale,[127] while other, lesser, figures were compelled to pay some attention to the terms of the statute. The Westmorland esquire, Thomas Sandforth of Askham, for example, abandoned the conventional indenture of retainer as a means of recruiting an affinity after 1469, turning instead to a variety of reciprocal bonds and undertakings which, though similar in effect, nevertheless avoided the new statutory restrictions.[128] Yet it is unlikely that Edward IV's legislation would have achieved the formal success it appears to have enjoyed if the popularity and usefulness of the indenture of retainer had not already been on the wane. The contemporary decline in the practice of retaining lawyers *de consilio* provides a close parallel, suggesting that changes in the structure of society were at least as important as statutory prohibition in hastening the indenture's disappearance.[129]

Chief among these was the increased economic consequence and social prestige of the gentry, which rendered the assurance of a magnate's 'good lordship' less vital to their security and caused them to look with less enthusiasm on the element of menial household service still contained in the terms of the indenture of retainer.[130] The increased emphasis placed upon civilian virtues rather than military ability in fifteenth-century society was, in turn, reflected by the gradual modulation of the language of lordship into a new, and less hierarchical, ethic of friendship – into which the starkly contractual terms of the indenture of retainer could only with difficulty be fitted.[131] As a result, the nobility began to shift the focus of their efforts in creating an affinity away from the greater gentry and towards the yeomanry, seeking to reinforce the customary expectation of military service from their tenantry by elaborating the conditions of their leases into agreements that amounted, in some cases, to a form of indenture of retainer; the contract between Henry, lord Fitzhugh, and one of his tenants, concluded in 1465, provides a clear and early instance of this development.[132] It was a change in the pattern of lordship perhaps

---

[127] Besides the indentures printed below (152–5), Richard of Gloucester concluded indentures for life service with at least 15 further retainers between 1471 and 1473, for example: PRO, DL29/648/10485 m. 14.

[128] *Infra*, 149, n. 372.

[129] N. Ramsay, 'Retained Legal Counsel, *c.* 1275–*c.* 1475', *TRHS*, 5th ser. xxxiv (1985), 111–12.

[130] C. Given-Wilson, *The English Nobility in the late Middle Ages* (London, 1987), 69–83; Payling, *Political Society*, 1–19; Carpenter, *Locality and Polity*, 35–97.

[131] M. James, *English Politics and the Concept of Honour* (Past & Present Supplement, 3, 1978), 20–2.

[132] *Infra*, 146; Cooper, *Land, Men and Beliefs*, 91–3; J. Goring, 'Social Change and Military Decline in Mid-Tudor England', *History*, lx (1975), 189–90. Note also the elements of a tenancy agreement in the contract between John, duke of Exeter and Thomas Proudfoot (92).

already under way during Henry VI's minority, when the returns to the Parliamentary income tax of 1436 suggest that only the higher peerage possessed the resources or inclination to retain a substantial body of gentlemen. Most of the baronage paid fees to a few knights and esquires, at most, and commanded affinities largely drawn from the ranks of their yeomen tenantry.[133]

In the end, therefore, the indenture of retainer disappeared because it had become redundant. For both lord and retainer, the indenture had always possessed one major advantage over the grant of annuity by letters patent; its flexibility of form meant it was possible to be considerably more specific about the precise nature of the service required from a retainer and the rewards offered him. By confining indentured retaining to the personnel of the household, however, the 1468 statute rendered otiose any separate enumeration of the household benefits to be granted the retainer. The cessation of large-scale hostilities in France a few years earlier had already removed the need for another of the distinctive features of the indenture, a detailed recital of the conditions under which a retainer would be required to serve abroad. When circumstances dictated, these conditions continued to be spelled out, often with considerable elaboration, in separate indentures for war service.[134] There was, in consequence, little left, in terms of precision and assurance, in the indenture of retainer that could not be provided, with equal convenience and unquestionable legitimacy, by a grant of annuity for past and future services. It was by such grants, together with a multiplication of their estate offices, a continuing expansion in the size of their households and the generous distribution of their livery that the early Tudor nobility maintained their often substantial affinities.[135]

---

[133] H. L. Gray, 'Incomes from Land in England in 1436', *EHR*, xlix (1934), 607–34; T. B. Pugh, 'The magnates, knights and gentry', *Fifteenth-Century England, 1399–1509*, ed. S. B. Chrimes, C. D. Ross and R. A. Griffiths (Manchester, 1972), 101–9.

[134] E.g., George, duke of Clarence's lengthy indenture with John Archer, esquire, retaining him for a year's service in Normandy and France: Shakespeare Birthplace Trust, ER 3/667, 28 Feb. 1475, a reference kindly provided by Christine Carpenter.

[135] M. James, *A Tudor Magnate and the Tudor State. Henry, Fifth Earl of Northumberland* (Borthwick Paper, 30, 1966), 5–9; D. Willen, *John Russell, First Earl of Bedford* (London, 1981), 35–43; G. W. Bernard, *The Power of the Early Tudor Nobility. A Study of the Fourth and Fifth Earls of Shrewsbury* (Brighton, 1985), 156–62, 180–3; B. J. Harris, *Edmund Stafford, Third Earl of Buckingham, 1478–1521* (Stanford, 1986), 136–48; K. Mertes, *The English Noble Household 1250–1600* (Oxford: Blackwell, 1988), 136, 186–91, 218; S. J. Gunn, *Charles Brandon, Duke of Suffolk, c. 1484–1545* (Oxford, 1988), 123–30, 154–60, 210–19, 224–5; idem, 'Henry Bourchier, earl of Essex', *The Tudor Nobility*, ed. G. W. Bernard (Manchester, 1992), 158–65.

EDITORIAL NOTE

In preparing the documents for publication, every effort has been made to produce clear and accurate texts; doubtful or missing words or passages have been enclosed in square brackets, with suspension points where appropriate; attention is drawn to other emendations in textual notes; paragraphs have been introduced in some longer documents for convenience; common contractions have normally been extended; j and v have been used for consonantal i and u; punctuation has been modernised and capitals restricted chiefly to proper names.

PRIVATE INDENTURES FOR LIFE SERVICE IN PEACE AND WAR, 1278–1476

1 Letters patent of William de Swynburne announcing that he has retained William de Kellawe, Haughton in Tyndale, Northumberland, 13 March 1278 (Northumberland RO, Swinburne (Capheaton) Charters ZSW/1/36, formerly sealed on tag).[1]

Omnibus hoc scriptum visuris vel audituris Willelmus de Swyneburn' salutem in domino.[2] Noveritis me concessisse dilecto et fideli meo Willelmo de Kellawe pro servicio suo mei inpenso et inpendendo viginti solidos annui redditus percipiendos per manum meam et [heredum] meorum apud manerium meum de Halwton' ad duos anni terminos, videlicet decem solidos ad Pentecost' et decem solidos ad festum Sancti Martini in yeme et sic de anno in annum et de termino in terminum in tota vita ipsius Willelmi. Et idem Willelmus erit fidelis meus et heredum meorum et stabit nobiscum et iuvabat nos consilio et auxilio ubi presens fuerit vel sine dampno accingere poterit cum per nos premunitus fuerit contra omnes exceptis dominis suis capitalibus quibus tanquam nobis tenere. In cuius rei testimonium presenti scripto cyrograffato pro me et heredibus meis sigillum meum apposui. Et predictus Willelmus de Kellawe alteri parti penes me Willelmi residenti sigillum suum apposuit. Dat' apud Halwton in Tyndal' die dominica proxima post festum Sancti Gregorii pape anno domini m cc lxx septim'

2 Letters patent of John de Lisle announcing that he has been retained by William de Swynburne, Haughton in Tyndale, Northumbs., 19 May

[1] We are grateful to Mr J. Browne-Swinburne and Northumberland Record Office for permission to publish this document and **2** below.

[2] W. Percy Hedley, *Northumberland Families* (2 vols., Society of Antiquaries of Newcastle-upon-Tyne, 1968), i. 99–100 for the career of Sir William de Swynburne (d. 1289), of West Swinburne, parish of Chollerton, treasurer of Queen Margaret of Scotland. Kellawe was still in Swynburne's service in May 1289, when he acknowledged receipt of ten shillings for his fee for Pentecost term (Northumbs. RO, ZSW 1/44).

1278 (Northumbs. RO, Swinburne (Capheaton) Charters ZSW/1/37, formerly sealed on a tag).[3]

Omnibus hoc scriptum visuris vel audituris Johannes de Insula salutem. Sciatis me teneri et hoc scripto meo obligari Willelmo de Swyneburne quod ego ero fidelis sibi et heredibus suis in tota vita mea et stabo cum eis et iuvabo eos consilio et auxilio fideliter cum toto posse meo ubi presens fuero vel accingere potero cum per ipsos premunitus fuero contra omnes in mundo exceptis dominis meis capitalibus quibus tanquam predicto Willelmo et heredibus suis teneor et ante confeccionem huius scripti fui obligatus. Et sciendum est quod non stabo cum eis nec eos adiuvabo consilio nec auxilio contra predictum Willelmum vel heredes suos nec cum prenominato Willelmo vel heredibus suis contra prefatos dominos meos. Et ad hoc fideliter et sine fraude tenendum ego sibi feci fidelitatem et tactis sacrosanctis iuravi propter quod predictus Willelmus concessit mihi pro se et heredibus suis pro servicio meo sibi inpenso et ei et heredibus suis inpendendo toto meo perpetuo viginti solidos anni redditus percipiendo de camera sua et heredum suorum ad manerium suum de Haluton' ad duos anni terminos videlicet medietatem ad Pentecost' et aliam medietatem ad festum Sancto Martini in yeme et sic de anno in annum et de termino in terminum in tota vita mea. In cuius rei testimonium presenti scripto cyrograffato penes predictum Willelmum et heredes suos residenti sigillum meum apposui. Et predictus Willemus alteri parti huius scripti penes me residenti pro se et heredibus suis sigillum suum apposuit. Dat' apud Haluton' in Tyndall' die Jov' proximo ante assencionem domini Anno gratie mᵒ dec' lxxᵒ viij.ᵒ

3 Henry Lacy, earl of Lincoln and Master Richard de Tanny, marshal, Berwick-upon-Tweed, Northumberland, 15/17 June 1292[4] (PRO, Court of Wards, Ward 2, Box 60/234/86, formerly sealed on tag).[5]

Le Dimaingne prochein apres la feste de seint Barnabe lapostle lan de grace milyme deus centime nonantime second e lan du regne le rey Edward de Engleterre vintisme, convint entre sire Henri de Lascy,

[3] Probably John de Lisle of Woodburn, who appears as an occasional witness to Swynburne charters between 1274 and 1299, though the Swynburnes' relations with the Lisles of Chipchase were also good: Northumbs. RO, ZSW, 1/38, 45, 4/10; Hedley, *Northumberland Families*, ii. 228–38 for the Lisles.

[4] In the opening clause of the agreement the date is given as Sunday after St Barnabas the Apostle, i.e. 15 June in 1292, but in the dating clause as 17 June.

[5] GEC, vii. 681–6 for Henry de Lacy, earl of Lincoln (1258–1311); Moor, lxxxiv. 9 for Sir Richard de Tanny (d. by 1 June 1296).

conte de Nichole e conestable de Cestre de une part, e Mestre Richard
de Tanny, mareschal, de autre part: Cest asaveir ke le dit Richard est
demore en le servise le dit conte de [a]ler ove luy outre mer a servir
le taunt avaunt come il savera e purra. E prendra par an du dit conte
sustenaunce honurable en lostel le conte solom coe ke il afiert a home
de son estat ove mounture covenable. E estre coe dys livres de argent
chescun an tant come il demoert outre mer en le servise le dit conte
comencaunt de recevire la moite des dys livres avauntdites avaunt ke
le dit Richard se mette sus la mer de Grece e lautre moite dedenz le
demi an prochein suyant. E [is]si de an en an chescun an dys livres
apres le prem[ier an] passe taunt come il demorront en la terre de
outre mer. E si il aveingne par cas ke le dit Richard deveingne malades
si ke il ne puisse travailler ne servir, le dit Henri ly tr[over]a re[sonable
susten]ance e despens desky taunt ke il puisse retorner en le reaume
de Engleterre. En tesmoune de que chose les devaunt diz monsire
Henri de Lascy e Richard de Tanny a [ceste] cirograffe e[ntre-
c]hangeablement ont mis lur seaus. Don' a Berwyk en Escoce le xvij
jour de Juyn lan du Rey Edward avantdit.

4 Aymer de Valence and Sir Thomas de Berkeley, London, 2 July 1297
(PRO, E101/68/1 no. 1, formerly sealed on tag).[6]

Le Dymeygne prochein apres les utaves de la Nativite sein Johan le
Baptist en le an del regne le Rey Edward fiz le Rey Henry vintequint
a Londres, aconvenu est entre Eymar de Valence, fiz e heir sire
Williame de Valence de une part, e mon sire Thomas, seignur de
Berkele de autre part, ceo est a saver: qe meme celi mon sire Thomas
est demore ove lavaunt dit Eymar, de son mennage a banere, sey
cinkyme de chivalers; e prendra de ly par an, taunt come demort ove
ly, ausi ben en pes come en guerre, en Engleterre, en Gales e en
Escoce, cinkaunte livres, e robes pur sei cinkyme de chivalers; e bouche
a court pur li e pur memes les chivalers, e pur deus esquiers a li memes
servir, e pur quatre esquiers pur ses quatre chivalers servir, e pur trois
vallez de meyster portaunz les males memes celi mon sire Thomas e
ses chivalers. E si guerre est, il prendra gages come a banret, ceo est
assaver, quatre souz le jour; e pur checun de ses chivalers, deus souz

[6] First published in H. Gough, *Scotland in 1298* (London & Paisley, 1888), 260–1 after
the original, then PRO, Exchequer, Treasury of Receipt, Miscellanea no. 42/13. See J.
R. S. Phillips, *Aymer de Valence, earl of Pembroke 1307–1324* (Oxford, 1972), 261–7 for the
earl's relations with the Berkeleys, and GEC, ii. 127–8 for Thomas, lord Berkeley (1295–
1321). For two further indentures between Valence and Berkeley, concluded in May and
August 1298, regulating the fulfilment of the terms of this agreement, see PRO,
E101/68/1/2 and 3.

le jour; e pur checun esquier arme ove chival covert, doze deniers le jour: issi qe le avauntdit mon sire Thomas avera vint e quatre chivaus coverz partut en le servise lavaunt dit Eymar.

E sil veet en guerre ove lavaunt dit Eymar, aylours qe en Engletere, Gales ou en Escoce, il prendra de li par an cent mars, e ses gages pur li e pur ses chivalers, e pur ses esquiers, sicome est avaunt dit; e bouche a court pur li e pur ses genz avaunt nomeez. E lavauntdit Eymar aquitera le passage pur li e pur ses genz, e pur ses chivalers, ceo est assaver: louwage de neef, e lur gages come en tere; e les chivaus de armes pur lavaunt dit mon sire Thomas e pur ses genz serrount prisees avaunt ceo qil les mettent en la neef. E sil les pert apres ceo, ou en mer ou en tere, en le servise lavaunt dit Aymar, ou tuz ou partie, lavauntdit Eymar li rendra le pris de ceus que serount perduz dedenz les quaraunte jors apres la perte.

Estre ceo, sil avent qe mon sire Morice fiz lavauntdit mon sire Thomas seit a banere en sa compaignie, qe de cel oure ne prenge lavauntdit mon sire Thomas dil avauntdit Eymar fors qe pur sey quart de chivalers, ove quinze chivaus coverz partut; e mon sire Morice a banere, sei terz de chivalers, ove unze chivaus covers partut. E prenge de cel oure mon sire Thomas, en tens de pes e de guerre, en Engletere, Gales e en Escoce, trente livers e robes pur sei quart; e lavauntdit mon sire Morice, vint livres e robes pur sei terz. E si les avauntditz mon sire Thomas e mon sire Moriz, ou un de eus, vount en guerre ove lavantdit Eymar aylours qe en Engletere, Gales ou Escoce, prendra lavauntdit mon sire Thomas dil avauntdit Eymar par an seissaunte mars, e lavaundit mon sire Morice quaraunte mars, e gages pur checun de eus come pur banret; e pur lur chivalers, e pur lur esquiers, gages ausi come avaunt dit est.

E donke lavaunt dit mon sire Morice avera bouche a court pur li e pur ses deus chivalers, ausi come lavaunt dit mon sire Thomas; ceo est asaver, deus esquiers pur li memes servir en son hostel, e deus esquiers pur ses deus chivalers; et sil pert ses chivaus en son servise, qil li rendra le pris, ausi come avaunt dit est de mon sire Thomas. E eyent les avaunt diz mon sire Thomas e mon sire Morice chaumbre de liveree en le houstel lavauntdit Eymar, pur eus a pur lur chivalers saunz plus, sil y eit mesons outre les genz de son houstel ke lem le puse fere, pur estre prest a son maundement, ausi ben de nuyt come de jour. E sil avent qe les avauntdiz mon sire Thomas e mon sire Morice, ou un de eus, veignent a lavauntdit Aymar par son mandement, a ses maners, ou aylors en Engletere a viles champestres, ou il ne pusent trover vitayle a vendre pur eus, e pur lur genz, e pur lur chivaus, qil seyent a touz coustages lavaunt dit Eymar la primere nuyt, e nent plus. En temoigne de queu chose les parties en cest escrit endente entrechaunjablement ount mis lur seaus. Done lan, jor e leu avaunt nomeez.

Dorse: Eymar de Valence

5 Roger Bigod, Earl Marshal and Sir John de Segrave, Chesterford, Essex, 9 June 1297 [French] (Oxford, Bodleian Library, MS Dugdale 18 fos. 83v–84r, 17th c. copy, pub. in N. Denholm-Young, *Seignorial Administration in England* (Oxford, 1937), 167–8).

6 John de Grey, lord of Rotherfield, and Robert de Tothale, Rotherfield Greys, Oxon., 15 July 1297 (Leeds District Archives, Gascoigne Deeds, GC/DZ 364, formerly sealed on tag)[7].

Hec est convencio facta die lune proxime ante festum beate Margarete virgine[8] anno regno regis Edwardi vicesimo quinto inter dominum Johannem de Gray, dominum de Rutherfeld, ex parte una, et Robertum de Tothale ex altera, videlicet quod predictus dominus Johannes dedit, concessit et hac presenti carta sua confirmavit Roberto de Tothale, pro servicio suo faciendo, videlicet ad eundem cum corpore suo in exercitu domini regis ad transfretando mare vel alio quoque loco quod dicto domino Johanne placuerit, tempore pacis et guerre quam diu predictus Robertus vixerit extra terra Ierosol', sex marcas annui redditum ad percipendo de Elya de Yapum in villa de Yapum[9] in comite Eboracum, ad duos annui terminos, videlicet ad festum Sancti Martini tres marcas, et ad festum Pentechostes tres marcas, habendo et tenendo dicto Roberto et heredibus suis vel assignatis totum predictum redditum de capitale domino feodi illis libere, quiete, bene, et in pace jure a hereditarie in perpetuum faciendum capitali domino feodi illis servicia inde debita et consueta. Et predictus dominus Johannes totum predictum redditum predicto Roberto et heredibus suis vel assignatis warantizabit, acquetabit et in perpetuum defendebit. Preterea dictus dominus Johannes concessit dicto Roberto et heredibus vel assignatis suis districcionem faciendo quare feodo quod Elyas de Yapum de se tenet in predicta villa vel in quibus manibus predicta terra devenerit quotiens predictus redditus aretro fuerit et districcionem retinendo

---

[7] We are grateful to the Trustees of the late Mrs Yvonne Studd-Trench-Gascoigne for permission to publish this document and to W. J. Connor, District Archivist, for his help in obtaining it. Sir John de Grey (d. 1311) had succeeded his father in 1295; the family's estates included scattered but quite considerable lands in Yorkshire (GEC, vi. 144–5; *CIPM*, iii. 284; v. 345; Moor, lxxxi. 150). Robert de Tothale, lord of Enesbury, Caldecote, Hardwick and Barkford, Hunts., knight of the shire for Buckingham in 1313, was blind and unfit for service in 1324 (Moor, lxxxiv. 34).

[8] 20 July.

[9] Yapham, near Pocklington, E. R. Yorks.

aliisque dicto Roberto et heredibus vel assignatis suis de arreragiis dicti redditi fuerit satisfactum. Et si contingat dictum Robertum in exercitu domini regis non admisse nec mare in servicio dicti Johannis domini sui transfretasse, excepto maemium sui corporis in servicio dicti domini Johannis, domini sui, recepisse, ex tunc bene licebit predicto domino Johanne et heredibus vel assignatis suis totum predictum redditum resumere et sine contradiccione vel impedimento dicti Roberti, here-dorum aut assignatorum suorum in perpetuum retinere et possidere, ad maiorem securitatem faciend' uterque pars alternatim sigilla sua apposuerint. Hiis testibus Ivone Roberto de Houlton, milite, Ricardo Boustard, Willelmo de la Dale, Martino Malure, Johanne Byset et aliis. Datum apud Rutherfeld mense et anno predictis.

Dorse: Dominus Johannes de Grey, Dominus de Rutherfield[10]

7 Sir John Bluet [of Raglan] and William Martel, Ellcestre, 10 August 1297 (British Library, Additional Charter 1531, ruled parchment, sealed through turn up).[11]

An du rengne le Rey Edward fiz le Rey Henr' vintime et quint issi acovint par entre sire Johan Bluet chevaler et Williame Martel,[12] cest asaver qe le dist Johan Bluet reconust pur lui et ces heyrs sey estre tenuz alvauntdit Williame Martel seon vallet a toute le vye memes celui Williame en seisaunte souz de argent de bone moneye et de leale a receviere de an en an a deus termes al hockeday et a la feste Seint Michel de seon maner de Langeston en Netherwent,[13] Cest asaver des teres et des tenemens qe Wautier le Swan, Johan le fiz Thomas, Roberd le Ioevene, Annes le Swan et Aliz Ketyng de lui tenent en la more de Langeston, issi qe le vauntdit Williame ou seon certayn atturne les avauntdis tenemens par la vauntdite rente lever a lur volunte en queus mayns qe memes ceus tenemens devenent peussent destreindre saunz contredit de nully e celes destreces en seon park fermement tener ieskes taunt qe de memes cele rente seit purpaye,[a] ensement deus robes par

---

[10] In a seventeenth-century hand.

[11] A small armorial seal, an eagle displayed; first edited in Edward Owen, *A Catalogue of Manuscripts relating to Wales in the British Museum*, iii (1908), 641–2, no. 1130, and reading the legend: IESU SEL BON E BEL. Contemporary rolls of arms give Bluet variations on the arms of a double-headed eagle displayed; he was dead by 24 March 1322 (Moor, lxxx. 100).

[12] No firm evidence has been discovered on the branch of the Martel family to which William belonged (cf. Moor, lxxxii. 82).

[13] Bluet held two knights' fees at Langstone and Wyteston, Gwent, of the late Gilbert de Clare in 1314.

an pris de quarante souz de sa chaumbre a toute la vye le devauntdit Williame, la une a Nowel et lautre a Pentecouste, et a sustenir le devauntdit Williame taunt come il vivera en manger et en bewere avenauntement come a gentil homme a peut, e ces deus garsuns. E a trover a ces deus chevaus feyn et aveine et litere et ferure a toute la vye memes celui Williame, cest asaver chescune nuth un bussel de aveine, E pur cest ben fet le devauntdit Williame Martel servira le dist Johan Bluet ben et lealment come a vallet apent en la guerre mue par entre le Rey de Engletere et le Rey de Fraunce. E ausi en Engletere si guerre nule sourde, qe Deu deffende, et en Gales, et en totes teres de sa la meer, et de la la meer la ou sien cors demeyne y est hors pris la tere seinte. E en tornemens en tens de pees od un graunt cheval de armes, le quel le dist Johan lui trovera et armure bonne et avenaunte saunz nule defaute pour seon cors. E a greynnur seurte fere par cest covenaunt en la fourme susescrite[b] ben et lealment tener le vauntdit Jean Bluet oblige lui et ces heyrs et ces exseketurs et totes ces teres et tenemens qe il aveit en Engletere et en Gales le jour de la confection de cest escrit en ky mayns qe il devenderunt en tens en avaunt. E ausi en la destresce des seneschaus et des mareschaus nostre seyngnur le Rey de Engletere. E des baillifs de la fraunchise de Kaerlyon ky qe il seyent, si il en nul poynt defaillent des covenaunz sus nomes. E si nul des chevaus le devauntdit Wylliame en tens de pees ou de guerre en le service le vaunt nome Johan Bluet seit periz, le dist Johan Bluet oblige lui et ces heirs et ces exseketurs plenement de les restorer. En tewmon' de quele chose les parties sus nomees entrechaungablement a cest escrit parti ont mis lur seaus par y ces Tewmoynes Sire Jean ApAdam, Sire Thomas de Coudray, Sire Jean de Knoyvyle, Rauf de la Grave, Jean de Howel et autres. Done a Ellcestre[14] le jour Seint Laurens an du rengne nostre seyngnur le Rey Edward vintime et quint.

Dorse: viij *in top left hand corner.*

a. Followed by *En* struck out
b. Word written around hole in MS

8 Letters patent of Philip de Hardreshull announcing that he will serve Edmund de Stafford in war and peace, Ghent, 3 October 1297 (Cheshire

---

[14] Owen prints *Cilcester*; neither placename has been securely located.

RO, DCR 26/3D/6, formerly sealed on tag through fold).[15]

A tous ceus ke ceste lettre verrount ou orrunt, Phelipe de Hardeshulle[16] saluz en nostre seygnur. Sachez mey estre tenuz a sire Edmound de Estafforde seygnur de Madeleye a servir ly tawnt come la gwere dure entre le Rey de Engletere e le Rey de Fraunce, la quele gwere fust entre eus le jowr de la confection de cest escrit. E par ceste presente lettre apres le avaunt dite gwere je le avaunt dit Phelipe me oblige a le avaunt dit sire Edmownd de mey atacher en sa compaygnye de ly servir avaunt touz autres, par quey il me face autaunt come autres me voddrunt fere, for pris le servise e la retenaunce sire William de Hardeshulle, mon frere, ke je forpreng sus touz autres. E si issi seyt, ke je le avaunt dist Phelipe sey chivaler, ke les robes ke je dei prendre de sire Edmound li seyent returnez. E si il aviengne, ke je le avaunt dit Phelipe reen de cestes choses defaylle, je me oblige a la destresce des senescaus e des mareschaus nostre seygnur le Rey de Engletere, ke donkes seyent, ausi bien de hors la verge cum de dens. En tesmoyne de quele chose a ceste presente lettre ay mys mon seel. Done a Gawnt en Flawndres le jeofdy procheyn apres la feste seyn Michel en le an de le regne le Rey Edward le vintime quint.

Dorse: Madley

9 Sir Nicholas Kingston and Sir William Mansel, 5 December 1298 [Latin] (Berks. RO, Pusey Archives, E Bp/fl; pub. by K. B. McFarlane, 'An Indenture of Agreement between Two English Knights for mutual aid and counsel in Peace and War, 5 December 1298', *BIHR*, xxxviii (1965), 209–10; reprinted in his essays *England in the Fifteenth Century*, ed. G. L. Harriss (London, 1981), 54–55.

10 John Fitz Thomas, lord of Offaly and Niall O Mórdha (O'More)

---

[15] We are grateful to Mary Duchess of Roxburghe for permission to publish this document and to Jonathan Pepler, Principal Archivist, Cheshire RO, for help in obtaining this. It was first published in G. Barraclough, 'The Earldom and County Palatine of Chester', *Trans. of the Historic Society of Lancashire and Cheshire*, ciii (1951), 54 and reprinted with a reproduction in G. Barraclough, *The Earldom and County Palatine of Chester* (Oxford: Blackwell, 1953), 36–7. Edmund, baron of Stafford, came of age in 1294 and died in 1308 (GEC, xii, pt 1. 173).

[16] Michael Jones, 'Sir John de Hardreshull, King's Lieutenant in Brittany, 1343–5', *Nottingham Medieval Studies* xxxi (1987), 76–97 places Philip de Hardreshull in his family context.

of Laois (Leix), Leix, 18 July 1303 (Trinity College, Dublin, MS 9825, The Red Book of Kildare, c. 1514–19, fo. 22v).[17]

Anno regni regis Edwardi tricesimo primo die Jovis proximo ante festum sancte Margarete virginis apud Leye ita convenit inter dominum Johannem filium Thome dominum Offalye ex una parte et Nigellum O Morth' ex altera, ita videlicet quod predictus dominus Johannes dedit [et] concessit omnia castra et tenementa de Moyrath et de Sawfyntyn[18] dicto Nigello ad totam vitam ipsius Nigelli, quasquidem terras idem dominus Johannes emit de domina Emelina Lungespee et de domino Alano de la Zousch; reddendo inde annuatim dicto domino Johanni et heredibus suis duo ostoria sorum vel quadraginta solidos argenti; ita tamen quod dictus Nigellus servicium suum auxilium et consilium ad totam vitam suam integre et fideliter contra omnes gentes sine aliqua fictione dicto domino Johanni et heredibus suis prestabit et arma militaria pro voluntate ipsius domini Johannis recipiet. Et si contingat quod absit quod dictus Nigellus servicium suum auxilium et consilium in tota vita sua integre et fideliter dicto domino Johanni et heredibus suis modo supradicto non prestaverit et arma militaria ad voluntatem ipsius domini Johannis non receperit vult et concedit quod liceat dicto domino Johanni et heredibus suis omnes terras et tenementa prenominata intrare absque aliqua contradictione et inde voluntates suas facere. In cuius rei, etc.

11 Aymer de Valence, lord of Montignac and Sir Robert FitzPayn, Dunfermline, Fife, 8 November 1303 (PRO, E101/27/11, sealed on tag).[19]

Le Vendredy prochein avaunt le Seint Martin lan du rengne nostre seignur le Rei Edward trentisme primer, acovint entre monsire Eymar de Valence, seignur de Mountignak dune part et monsire Roberd le Fuiz Paen dautre part: cest a saver qe lavauntdit monsire Roberd demorera ove lavauntdit monsire Eymar pur le turnement de le Noel

[17] Drawn to our attention by Prof. Robin Frame; published in *The Red Book of the Earls of Kildare*, ed. G. Mac Niocaill (Dublin, 1964), 70 no. 76 after a photostat copy, National Library of Ireland, MS 5769. For John FitzThomas, created earl of Kildare in 1316, see GEC, vii. 218–21.

[18] Morett, Coolbanagher parish, Laois; Saint Fintans, Clonenagh and Clonagheen parish, Laois.

[19] A good impression of an armorial seal in red wax (Valence) survives (cf. Ellis, i. no. P818 after an impression on PRO, E40/68). The indenture was later cancelled by a series of wavy cuts; see also Phillips, *Aymer de Valence*, 308. FitzPayn was dead by 30 August 1315 (Moor, lxxxi. 50–1).

prochein a venir apres la confection de ceste lettre tanke a la Pasche prochein ensuiant en un an. Et deit launtdit monsire Eymer trover au dit monsire Roberd covenable et honorable monture au tornement pur soun cors, covenable monture pur ses deus bachelers, e restor de deus chevaux pur deus bachelers aparfere sei quint. E robes et seles pur luy et pur ses deus bachelers et pur soun fuiz sil est chivaler dedenz le terme susdit. E avera lavauntdit monsire Roberd bouche a court pur luy, et pur ses iij valetz, et pur ses quatre bachelers et pur chascun chivaler deus esquiers en la ville du tornement, et sy lavantdit monsire Robert veingne ou seit mande en cheminaunt vers le tornement alavantdit monsire Eymar il avera bouche a court pur luy et pur ses deus chevalers et pur chascun chevaler deus esquiers.

E pur les covenaunces susdites bien et leaument fere et tenir lavantdit monsire Eymar dorra au dit monsire Roberd cent livres desterlinges a paier amesmes celuy monsire Robert ou a soun certein attorne ceste endenture eiaunt, cest a saver, a la Pasche prochein a venir apres la confection de ceste letre vint livres, e a la Nativite Seint Johan ensuiant vint livres, e a la Seint Michel prochein suiaunt vint livres, e a Noel prochein suiaunt vint livres, e a Careme Prinaunt prochein suiaunt vint livres. E si issi aveingne qe lavantdit monsire Eymar aille la outre de denz le dit terme pur le turnay lavantdit monsire Robert voet et grante de aler ove luy par mesmes les covenaunces susdites. Et si lavantdit monsire Roberd veingne au dit monsire Eymar par soun mandement as parlementz ou aillours pur les bosoingnes le dit monsire Eymar il avera bouche a court pur luy et un bacheler et treis esquiers et deus someters, e fein et aveingne pur dogge, chevaux e gages pur uyt garcouns pur le temps qil demorera en les bosoingnes le dit monsire Eymar. E a touz ses covenaunces bien et leaume[n]te tenir lavantdit monsire Eymar se oblige luy et ses eyrs et touz ses biens a la destrecce de queu ministre le Rey qe lavantdit monsire Roberd vodra elire. En tesmoingne de queu chose les avantditz monsire Eymar et monsire Robert a cest escrites endentes entrechaungablement ount mis lour seaux. Donne a Dounfermelyn en Escoce lan et le jour susdits.

12 John Wogan, justiciar of Ireland and Henry de la Roche, lord of the Rower, Kilkenny, Dublin, 10 February 1306 (National Archives of Ireland, RC7/11, 435–8, two nineteenth-century versions from now lost original).[20]

[20] This transcript, published by kind permission of the Director of the National Archives, was prepared by Prof. Robin Frame, to whom we are deeply indebted for help with this and other Irish indentures, from a document presenting severe textual problems. It survives in transcript only in the Irish Record Commissioners' draft calendar of rolls of the Dublin Bench. The transcript was prepared by a clerk who made some mistakes

Ces sunt les covenantes feits entir Monsire Johan Wogan adonk justice Dyrlaunde dune part e Henri De La Roche seigneur de Roure dautir part

Coe est asaver qe le dit Henri est demurre ove lavaundit Mounsire Johan de sa retenaunce a de seon mesnage aservir le a tout seon poer en Irlaunde ausi bien en les busoignes le Rey cum en ses busoignes propres de guerre e de pees encountir touz gens save la fey le Rey a totte la vye le dit Monsire Johan

Et sil avigne qe le dit Monsire Johan survyve le dit Henri donk le heyr ou lassigne le dit Henri ky de age serra e ses terres tendra [ ] mesme le service al dit Monsire Johan ou a celuy qe en leu de luy sera par tote la vie le dit Monsire Johan

Et graunte le dit Henri pur luy e ses heyris qe luy ne ces heyris ne nul qe de sa retenaunce [ ] seon acorde soit peusse de autri retenaunce demorrer ou le dit Monsire Johan ou seon leu tenant ne soient forpris issi ke lour demoere soit ove le dit Monsire Johan contre touz altres sauve la fey le Rey si com avaunt est dit

Et lavauntdit Henri taunt cum il est esquier prendra [ ] del dit Monsire Johan pur luy & pur un compaignoun a tottes les foitz qil fait sa pleine liveree a ses altres esquiers

Et graunte mesme celuy Henri qil serra chivaler ala volunte le dit [ ] Johan & prendra les armes de luy ales coustages le dit mesmes celui Sire Johan & quant il serra chivaler donk prendra robe pur luy e pur un compaignoun si cum les altres chivalers a tot les foitz qil fait sa pleine liveree a ses altres chivalers

Et le dit Monsire Johan aquitra le dit Henri [ ] mars les ques il deit au Rey an le escheker de Duvelyne

Et quant mesmes celi Henri serra maunde de venir ove gentz darmes donk eit ses gages apres le primer jour de sa montre [ ] lascoiant des gentz qil avierra par tiel maundement coe est asaver douse deners le jour pur le [ ] coverte ou bouche en court pur luy & ses gentils homes mountez a lur aferant & sis deners [ ] aveines ferrure e gage des garceons pur le chival coverte al chois le dit Monsire Johan

Et quant il serra en guerre ou en chivalchers ove le dit Monsire Johan dounk eit bouche en court [ ] e ses gentils homes e sa altre

and left a number of gaps, which he blamed on the condition of the original roll. His work was revised by a superior, who corrected some more obvious errors and succeeded in reading some missing words. However, revision did not stop there: it was also designed to save space – and possibly to gloss over difficulties – by means of deletions and crude contractions (for instance, the repeated *Monsire* is consistently deleted, and the dating clause contracted to *10 Fev' a' r' r' 34*). There are thus, within a single heavily-emended MS, two unsatisfactory versions of the text. The text presented here is not a critical edition of these nineteenth-century transcripts, but a working text based on them, correcting only the most obvious errors.

mesne viveent de lour purchas & et de lour foreer si le pais [ ] de guerre soit a coe suffisaunt

Et pur ses altres aveneuees e demorrees quant il serra maunde [ ] fein & avoyne ferrure & gages des garcons pur luy & soun compaignoun taunt cum il demeurt esquier & quant il serra chivaler dounk eit pur luy & seon compaignoun deus esquieres ou trois quaunt il les avera ensi ove luy

Et grantent les avauntditz Monsire Johan e Henri pur eux e lour heyrs qe si nul de eux viegne contre les covenauntes avauntdites qi celui qi les ensiendra seit e miz al altre partie en mille librarum dargent en pure dette e qe les covenauntes desus escrites veynt les meims ses tegnent

Et a tottes les choses avaundites tenir se obligent eux pur eux e pur lur heyrs tottes lur terres & leur tenementz en ky meims qil demoergent

En tesmoniaunce de quoi chose les parties avauntdites a cest escrit endente unt mys lur seals entrenchangablement

Escrit a Duvelyne le x. jour de Feverer an du regne le Rey Edward trentisme quart[21]

13 Sir Nicholas de Kyriel (*Cryel*) announces that he has agreed to serve Sir Stephen de Segrave, 1307 x 1325 (Berkeley Castle, Gloucs., Select Charters no. 490, sealed on a tag).[22]

---

[21] John Wogan was Justiciar of Ireland from 1295–1308 and 1309–13 (E. Curtis, *A History of Mediaeval Ireland from 1100 to 1513* (Dublin, 1923), 186–94; Moor, lxxxiv. 208–9). Henry de la Roche was probably a younger brother of Sir Thomas de la Roche of Pembroke who served in Ireland from the early 1280s (Moor, lxxxiii. 83). See also R. Frame, 'Military Service in the Lordship of Ireland 1290–1360: Institutions and Society on the Anglo-Gaelic Frontier', *Medieval Frontier Societies*, ed. Robert Bartlett and Angus MacKay (Oxford, 1989), 117 for further comment.

Wogan also retained John son of William Butler of Waterford on 1 February 1310 (*Rotulorum Patentium et Clausorum Cancellariae Hibernie Calendarium*, vol. 1, pars 1, *Hen. II – Hen. VII* (1828), 16 no. 57 after Patent Roll 3 & 4 Edward II, destroyed in 1922). Butler agreed to serve for life in any place in Ireland to which he was summoned and against all men, saving his liegeance to the king, and with as many armed men and horses as he could raise, in return for maintenance, robes and wages as Wogan's other household valets, namely 12d a day for each mounted man, *bouche en court* for himself and his men-at-arms, 6d per day each for hay, oats etc. 'nisi fuerit in loco guerre et tempora annis quo homines pabulari poterint', and pledging to pay £200 if the contract was broken.

[22] Fine impression of armorial seal (Two chevronels, a canton = Pecche), diameter 24 mm., in white wax. Stephen de Segrave witnessed documents from 1305, was knighted by 1307, succeeded his father in October 1325 but was dead by Christmas (GEC, xi. 608–9; Moor, lxxxiii. 238–9). We are obliged to David Smith, Archivist, Gloucestershire RO, for help in arranging for us to see this document and others from Berkeley Castle and for permission to publish.

A touz ceaux qe ceste lettre orrount ou verrount Nycholaz de Cryel[23] saluz en Dieu. Sachez mey estre demorre ove monsire Estevene de Segrave a tote ma vie com son Bachiller pur luy servir de pees et de gere countre totez gentz sauve le fey le Roi; issint qe le dit monsire Estevene me trouvera robes et seales com afiert a Bachiller et restor de Bachiller pur ma mounture pur luy servir a tournement. Et gages pur ix garcons et feyn et aveyne pur ix chivaux tauncom il demeurt en ville. Et si aveyngne qe quant mez teres me serrount escheeues qe jeo voil estre a banere, jeo me oblige adoncs au dit monsire Estevene de luy servir ausi com devaunt, sauve qe jeo prendray robes et seales pur mey tiers de Bachiller, et gages pur xij chivaux et pur xij garcons, et bouche a court pur mey et pur mez bachillers, et la mounture pur mon cors prisee. Et en tens de gere prendray du dit monsire Estevene tauncom jeo suy bachiller, gages pur vij garcons et feyn et aveyne pur vij chivaux en tens quant hom deit livere fere, et restor de ma monture si jeo le perde en son servise, et bouche a court pur mey et pur mes esquiers. Mes quant jeo seray a banere adoncs auray ma mounture prisee, et bouche a court pur mey et pur mes ij bachilers et pur vj esquiers, et gages pur xij garcons, et fein et aveyne pur xij chivaux.

Estre ceo, com sovent qe jeo veyngne au dit monsire Estevene par mi son maundement a demorer ove luy en tens de pees come a parlementz ou a ses maners, jeo aurai gages pur v garcons, feyn et aveyne pur v chivaux, et bouche a court pur mey et mes ij vallets. Et si aveyngne qe jeo defaille en ces covenaunz tenir issi qe jeo ne serve le dit monsire Estevene de pees et de gere en la fourme susdite, tauncom luy plest ma demeure en sa compaynie, jeo oblige fermement par cest escrit mey et mes heirs et mes asseketours a payer mil marcs a la croyserye vers la tere seinte; a la destresce dez queux deners, si il seyent encorewes, jeo oblige mon maner de Walmere[24] en le conte de Kent enqi mains qil deveyngne et touz mes biens meubles et non-meubles a la destresce chescun ministre nostre seingnur le Rei et de chescun ministre de seynt eglise tauntqe la dite dette de mil marcz seit pleinement paye. En temoyngne de queu chose a ceste escrit ay mis mon seal.

Dorse: De Nicolas Criel
　　　　Leyc' – Croxt' Kyriel[25]

[23] Nicholas de Kyriel (Crioll), succeeded in 1303 and was knighted with Prince Edward on 22 May 1306; his mother was Margaret Pecche (Moor, lxxx. 253).

[24] Walmer, Kent.

[25] Croxton Keerial, Leics.

14 Humphrey de Bohun, earl of Hereford and Essex and Sir Bartholomew de Enfield, knight bachelor, Lochmaben, Dumfries, 15 February 1307 (PRO, DL 25/92, sealed on tag).[26]

Le meskredi proschein apres la feste seint Valentin lan du regne nostre seignur le Roi Edward trentisme quint, convynt entre mounsire Hunfrai de Bohun, counte de Hereford et Dessex, seignur du Val de Anand de une part, et mounsire Berthelmeu Denefeud dautre part: cest a savoir qe le dit sire Berthelmeu demorra tote sa vye por pees et por guerre ove le dit counte en totes terres de sca la mer et de la, et por la Terre Seinte si le dit counte il y aille. Et prendra le dit sire Berthelmeu robes et seles come ses autres bachelers. En temps de pees fein et aveigne por quatre chevaux, gages por treis garscouns et son chaumberlein mangaunt en sale; en temps de guerre et por le turnoi fein et aveigne por owyt chevaux, gages por sept garscons et son chaumberlein mangaunt en sale, et soffissaunte mounture por guerre et por le turnoi.

Et por ceo service bien et leaumente faire, le dit counte ad donne au dit mounsire Berthelmeu, por touz autres coustages, quaraunte marcheez de terre[a] en la Val de Anand a terme de la vye le dit sire Berthelmeu, cest a savoir Hoton' et Lokardeby,[27] ove totes maners de aportenaunces. Et si issi soit qe riens faille en les dites villes de quaraunte de marchez de terre, le dit counte fournira le plein aillours en le Val de Anand en tieu manere qe le dit sire Berthelmeu se tendra a paye. Et si aventure avigne qe le dit sire Berthelmeu se feint ou retret de le service le dit counte par qui il ne soit servi de guerre ne de pees auxi come il est sus dit, qe a donqes lise au dit counte a prendre les terres et a reseisir a la volentie le dit counte saunt countredit de nuly, si le dit sire Berthelmeu ne soit destorbe par mahayn ou par maladie, qe Dieu luy defend, par qui il ne poet le dit service faire.

Et si avigne qe commun veiage soit vers la Terre Seinte, et le dit counte demoerge en pays par certaines enchesouns, qe donqes lit bien au dit sire Bethelmeu aler cel veiage en autri compaignie et quil peuse les espleitz de sa terre prendre auxi come avaunt est grauntie, nient countre esteaunt la demoere le dit counte. En tesmoignaunce de queu chose les avauntditz counte et sire Berthelmeu a cest escrit endentee ount my lour seaux. Donne a Loughmaban le jour et lan avauntditz.

[26] A fine impression of Enfield's seal in green wax: an antique gem with head in deep relief. For a contemporary example of Bohun's seal from PRO, DL 25 no. 42 see Ellis, ii. no. P1063. Humphrey de Bohun succeeded his father as earl of Hereford in 1298 and was killed at Boroughbridge in 1322 (GEC, vi. 467–70). For Enfield cf. Moor, lxxx. 305.

[27] Hutton and Lockerbie in Annandale, Dumfries; Bohun was granted Annandale and Lochmaben castle on 11 April 1306 (CChR, iii. 66).

Dorse: la retenaunce mons. Barthelm' Denefeld

vacat

a. MS *terra*

15 Aymer de Valence, earl of Pembroke and John Darcy (the nephew), valet, Exning, Suffolk, 29 November 1309 (PRO, E40/A11547, formerly sealed on tag).[28]

La veille de Seint Andreu Apostre lan du regne le Roy Edward fuiz le Roi Edward tierz aconvient entre noble home monsire Aymer de Valence, counte de Pembrok', seigneur de Weseford et de Mountiniak dune part et Johan Darcy dautre: Ceo est assaver qe le dit Johan ad graunte et est demorre de cy en avaunt a tote sa vye ove le dit counte auxi en temps de pees et de guere, prenaunt du dit counte en temps de pees sustenaunce et robes covenables com un des autres valletz et en temps de guere autre sustenaunce, mounture et armure sicom apent au vallet covenablement et serra entendaunt au dit counte en tour soen corps. Et le dit counte ad graunte qe le dit Johan, en temps de pees quaunt tourneymentz sey prendront, peusse demorer au quiel seignur qil vodra, sauve ceo qe sil plest au dit counte qil demeurge entour luy, il demorra et adounk le dit counte luy durra, ceo qe le dit Johan purra prendre dautre seignur, et pur ceste demeure feire en la manere desus dite le dit counte ad done au dit Johan et a ses heirs de soen corps loiaument engendrez cente soude de rente a tenir en la ville de Geynesburgh,[29] sicom il est contenu en la chartre qe le dit counte lui ad de ceo feite.

Et sur ceo, le dit counte luy deit profeire les responses renables qil mettra en la bat passager sil ne seit qe la farme de la passage encrest pluis qe ore nest. Et a quiel houre qe la vaundit Johan sey fez feire chivalier, le vaundit counte est tenu a feire et a feffer le vaundit Johan pur luy et pur ses heirs de soen corps loiaument engendrez de tresze marchez et demye de terre ou de rente a tenir en la fourme sicom il est contenu en la chartre de les cent soude de rente qe le counte lui ad done en la ville de Geynesburgh. Et a dounk le vaundit Johan est tenu a servir[a] le vaundit counte entour soen corps auxi bien en temps de pees com en temps de guere de cea la miere et de la et pour le veiage de la Terre Seinte. Et le dit Johan deit prendre du counte sustenaunce et mounture, robes, gages et totes autres choses com un des autres bachelers. Et a ceo covenaunt endente profeire bien et

---

[28] GEC, iv. 54–8 and Moor, lxxx. 264–5 for John Darcy *le neveu* (d. 1347).

[29] Gainsborough, Lincs.

loiaument tenir le dit counte et Johan ount mys lour seaix. Escrites a
Ixening le jour et lan avaundites.[30]

a. MS appears to read *sertiir*

16 Humphrey de Bohun, earl of Hereford and Essex retains Sir
Thomas de Mandeville, knight bachelor, for a year in peace and war,
Writtle, Essex, 2 February 1310 (PRO, DL 25/L1981, formerly sealed
on tag).[31]

Le Lundy en la feste de la Purification Nostre Dame et lan du regne
nostre seignur le Roi Edward fuiz le Roi Edward tierz convynt entre
monsire Hunfrai de Bohun, counte de Hereford et Dessex dune part
et monsire Thomas de Maundevill', chevaler, dautre part: cest assaver[a]
qe le dit monsire Thomas est demore por pees et por guerre ove le dit
counte du jour de la Purification Nostre Dame avauntdit tauntque a
m[ei]s[me] le jour pour un an aco[mp]l[i]e. Et prendra le dit monsire
Thomas robes et seles comme ses autres bachelers; et en temps de pees
feyn et aveig[ne] p[or] quatre chev[au]x g[ag]es por trois garscons et
son chaumberlein mangaunt en sale; en temps de guerre et por le
turnoy fein et aveigne por owy[t ch]evaux, gages por sept garscons et
son chaumberlein mangaunt en sale, et soffisaunte mounture por guerre
et por le turnoy. Et por ce service bien et loiaument fair tauntque au
jour avauntdit le dit counte dorra[b] au dit monsire Thomas vynt mars
desterlings por touz coustages; apaier as deus termes, cest assaver, la
une moitie a la Pentecouste proschein avenir apres la date de cest
escrit, et lautre moytie a la seint Michel proschein suyaunt sau[nz] plus
lung delai. Au queu paiement bien et loiaument faire nous obligioms
nous et noz heirs. En tesmoignaunce de queu chose les avantditz counte
et monsire Thomas a cest escrit ount mys lour seals. Donne a Writele
le jour et lan avauntditz.

a. *ass* inserted
b. *sic* for *donra*

17 Aymer de Valence, earl of Pembroke and John Darcy the nephew,

[30] cf. Phillips, *Aymer de Valence*, 309 for Valence and Darcy; F. J. Tanquerey, 'Actes
privés en Anglo-Normand', *Mélanges ... M. Alfred Jeanroy* (Paris, 1928), 202–3 for an earlier
edition.
[31] The indenture, rubbed in places, has been mounted for conservation; Moor, lxxxii.
105 for Mandeville.

Hertford, 10 April 1310 (PRO, E 40/A6404, formerly sealed on a tag, amplifying terms of **15** above).[32]

Decimo die mensis Aprilis regni Regis Edwardi tercio convenit inter dominum Adomarum de Valencia comitem Pembrochie ex parte una et Johannem Darcy ex altera, videlicet quod predictus comes feoffabit dictum Johannem et heredes suos de corpore suo legitime procreatos de passagiis aput Trentam ad maneria euisdem comitis de Geynesburgh et de Doneham[33] spectantibus in com' Lincoln' et Notingham' quousque idem comes vel heredes sui dictum Johannem et heredes suos de corpore suo legitime procreatos de viginti marcatis de terre sive redditus aliunde feoffamentis pro qua quidam donacione dictus Johannes infra quindenam Pasche proximo venturus post confectionem presencionem[34] debet ordinem militis suscipes et circa corpus dicti comitis tam tempore pacis quam guerre in partibus cismarinis et transmarinis atque pro viatico ad terram Sanctam cum temptis evenerit ad totam vitam euisdem Johannis sollicite esse intende[n]s viriliter que ministrans capiendo de dicto comite equitaturam pro suo corpore[a] tempore pacis et guerre et vesturam et huiusmodi necessaria prout unus de militibus euisdem comitis. Et si contingat quod prefatus Johannes deficiat in aliquo ei hiis convencionibus suprascriptis et de servicio dicti comitis sponte se alienat nisi morbo gravi sive alia causa resonabili impediatur ex tunc licebit dicto comiti passagia predicta vel viginti marcatis terre sive redditus tanquam libera tenementa sua quiete que seisinus et omnino revocare. In cuius rei testimonium huic indenture partes predicto sigillo sua alternatim apposuerunt. Dat' aput Hertford die et anno supradictis.

a. *corpore* interlined

18 Robert, lord Mohaut and Sir John de Bracebridge, Walton on Trent, Derbys., 30 August 1310 (University of Nottingham, Middleton Deeds, Mi D 1909, sealed on a tag).[35]

[32] cf. Phillips, *Aymer de Valence*, 309; Bean, 25.
[33] Gainsborough, Lincs. and Dunham, Notts.
[34] 3 May 1310.
[35] A small natural wax armorial seal, a lion rampant (Mohaut); cf. *HMC*, Middleton, i. 87 with incorrect date, 5 September 1311; pub. in Michael Jones, 'An Indenture between Robert, lord Mohaut and Sir John de Bracebridge for life service in peace and war, 1310', *Journal of the Society of Archivists* iv (1971–2), 391. For recent comment and a photograph see Peter Coss, *The Knight in Medieval England 1000–1400* (Stroud, 1993), 114–6. We are grateful to the Hon. Michael Willoughby, owner of this indenture and **46** below, and to the University of Nottingham as custodian, for permission to publish, and to Dr Dorothy Johnston and her staff at the Department of Manuscripts, The Hallward Library, University of Nottingham, for their help and advice.

Le Dymenche prochein apres la Decollacion Seint Johan lan du regne le Roi Edward fuiz le Roi Edward quart, acovint entre Mons. Robert de Mohaut, seneschal de Cestre, dune part et Sire Johan de Bracebrugge, chivaler, dautre part. Cest assaver qe lavauntdit mons. Robert de Mohaut a done et graunte a lavauntdit mons. Johan de Bracebrugge dys livrees de annuele rente en la ville de Walton' sur Trente en le counte de Derby a recevire des tenauntz lavauntdit mons. Robert, aussi bien des francs come des neifs a terme de la vie lavauntdit mons. Johan de Bracebrugge. Cest assaver de Will' Dunstan, vynt et deus soutz vuyt deniers, de Robert de Charteleye, trente et un soutz, de William de Meisham, quatre soutz, de Roger Adam, trois soutz maille, de Thomas Symenel, sys soutz quatre deniers, de Richard fuiz Johan deus soutz, de Will' Griffin, deus soutz un denier, de Will' le Pestour, doze soutz maille, de Robert Jacob, doze deniers, de Rauf de Fenton', doze deniers, de Roger Jacob, deus soutz, de Robert fuiz Andreu, doze deniers, de Robert de Knytele, deus soutz, de Roger fuiz Renaud, doze deniers, de Robert fuiz Richard le Pastour, doze deniers, de Will' le Noble, neof soutz, de William le Fevre, sept soutz, de Richard le Charrett' le fuiz, sept soutz sys deniers, de Rauf Lengynour, quatre deniers, de Richard Broun, treze soutz, de Robert fuiz Robert ate Cros, quinze soutz, De Margeri de Wortburton, quatorze soutz, de Robert ate Cros, quatorze soutz, de Richard le Charett' le pere, doze soutz, de Richard fuiz Roger de Borgh', treze soutz, et de Richard Matheu, trois soutz, as termes de la dite ville de Walton' usueles. Et a la rente avantdite bien et loiaument faire alavaunt dit mons. Johan a terme de sa vie, voil et graunte qe lavauntdit sire Johan ait plein poeir a destreindre dedens ville et dehors et les destresses retenir tant qe il soit de la rente avauntdite pleinement parpaie, sanz contredit de moi, ou de mes hoirs ou de mes assignes enqoi meyn qe la terre demegne. Cest assaver qe lavantdit Sir Johan a done et graunte affaire son leal servise de chivalerie a lavantdit sire Robert a toute sa vie pour la rente avantdite aussi bien en temps de pees come de guerre, et en touz lieus ou ili bosoignera de son serviz par la ou la presence lavauntdit Sire Robert serra et en toutes terres et en touz regions hors pris la Terre Seynte quant des foiz et quel houre qe il serra de lui covenablement garni et maunde a la mounture et a les robes et a les propres custages lavantdit Sire Robert resonablement sicome il affiert a chivalier estre trove de son seignur et restor des chivaus, de palefroi, de somer et de rouncyn, son vadlet son hakeney et son somer en temps de guerre solum resonable pris par lavantdit Sire Robert prisie. Et sil aviegne qe lavantdit Sire Johan de son servise avant nome defaille sanz encheson resonable encontre la volente le dit Sire Robert, lavantdit Sire Johan graunte et par cest escrit cirographe se oblige de rendre et de releser a lavantdit Sire Robert les dys livrees de rente avant nomez, les queus ili a graunte et feoffe a recevire en la dite ville de Walton' des tenantz susescritz sanz nul contredit. Et a ceste chose loiaument faire lavantdit Sire Johan se oblige ala destresse de seneschaus et de mareschaus nostre seignur le Roy sur peine de Cent livrees a paier a lavantdit Sir Robert si des avantditz dys livrees de rente soit destourbe. Et lavantdit Sire Robert par la tenure de cest escrit se oblige aparfaire au dit Sire Johan les covenances susescrites a terme de sa vie sur la peine avauntdite. En tesmoinaunce de quele chose les parties avantdites a cest escrit cyrographe ount mys leur seaus. Donne a Walton' sur Trente le jour et lan susescrites.

19 Sir Ralph FitzWilliam and Sir Nicholas de Hastings, Hinderskelfe, Yorks., 21 August 1311 (San Marino, California, Henry E. Huntington Library, Hastings Manuscripts, Personal Papers Box 1 no. 5, sealed on tag)[36].

Ceo covenaunt fu fet le samady procheyn apres la feste del assumpcioun de nostre dame lan du regne le Rey Edward fiz le Rey Edward quint, enter Sire Rauf le Fiz William de une parte e Sire Nichol de Hastyngges de auter part, cest a saver qe levaundit Sire Nichol demorera ove levaundit Sire Rauf en pees e en guerre a terme de lure deux vyes, issint qe levaundit Sire Nichol irra ove levaundit Sire Rauf en guerre la hou sun corps demyn irra e qe levaundit Sire Nichol vendra a la dit Sire Rauf a cheskune foyz qe renablement serra garny en temps de guerre ove deux vallets e lure munture e dis garcuns. En temps de pees ove deux vallets e quater garcuns. E qe levaundit Sire Rauf trovera a levaundit Sire Nichol covenable munture pur sun corps demeyn e deux robes par an e une sele solum ceo qe apent a chivaler, e sil aveygne qe le dit Sire Nichol perde nul graunt chival de armes en le servis de dit Sire Rauf qe le dit Sire Rauf seyt tenuz a fere a dit Sire Nichol allouuaunce solum ceo qe le dit chival par deux homes serra prisee. E de quel lyu en le cunte de Everwyke qe le dit Sire Nichol seyt movaunt vers le dit Sire Rauf a sun maundement qe le dit Sire Rauf trovera a le dit Sire Nichol ses resonables mises e despenses, e qe les gents le dit Sire Nichol avaunt nomez eyent lure guages en temps de guerre e de pees de le dit Sire Rauf solum ceo qe apent. En temeygnaunce de quel

---

[36] cf. *HMC*, Hastings, i (1928), 197–8 for précis of document and description of the fine armorial seal: Six barrulets, over all three chaplets (FitzWilliam); first published in Dunham, 134. A further agreement augmenting these terms appears to have been drawn up on 25 March 1312 (BL, Harl. MS 4774 f. 18v; ibid., 3881 f. 4, and cf. W. Dugdale, *The Baronage of England* (London, 1676), i. 579). GEC, vi. 190 and Moor, lxxxi. 69–70 for Sir Ralph FitzWilliam of Hinderskelfe (d. 1317), who also granted Nicholas de Hastings and his heirs a rent of £8 on Thorpe Basset, Yorks. (Moor, lxxxi. 197). We are grateful to William A. Moffett, Librarian, Henry E. Huntington Library, for permission to publish this indenture and **47**.

covenaunt cheskun de eux a auter endenture ad mis sun seal. Done a Hildirskelf le jour e lan avaundits.[37]

20 Philip Sammelsbury announces that he has been retained by Hamo de Massy, Dunham [–Massey], Cheshire, 3 May 1312 (Lancs. RO, de Trafford deeds, DDTr/bundle 5/3, Massy chs., sealed on tag through a fold).[38]

Sachent touz qe ceste lectre verrunt ou orrount qe joe Fylippe de Samlisbury sui par ceste escrite fermement lye a mons. Hamon de Masscy chivaler, et ovek ly demorre contre tute gent mortel, sauve la fey le Rey, a ly leuement server del jour qe ceste lectre fu fete, en pes et en gwerre solom mon saver a tute ma vie pur un annuele rente qe le avandist mons. Hamon ad a moi et a ma compaygne, la file sa soere, graunte par sa lectre avant fete. E od mes aveygne, qe Deu defend, qe joe defaile a luy server solom mon poer bonement et leusment, l'ust a ly avandist mons. Hamon a moi destreindre par tus mes beins mobles et non mobles en qi poer qe il seint tenuez et la destresse tener jekes pleynez amendes a ly seint fetes solom sa leute demeygne. En tesmoygnance de ceste choese a ceste escrite joe ad mis mon seel. Done a Donham le mekerdy procheyn avant le Assencion le an de regne de Rey Edward le fiz le Rey Edward quinte.

21 John de Grey, lord of Dyffryn Clwyd and Thomas Fillol, Hemingford [Grey], Hunts., 24 June 1313 (Longleat House, Wilts., Muniments of the Marquess of Bath, MS 2832, sealed on tag through fold).[39]

A la feste de la Nativite de Seyn Johan de Baptist en lan du Regne le Rey Edward syme a Hemmyngford en la counte de Huntyngdone,

---

[37] The tag contains writing and was probably a former indenture: Rauf en pees . . . ; sun corps demeyn . . . e lur; en alaunt . . .

[38] We are grateful to Sir Dermot de Trafford Bt for permission to publish and to B. Jackson, County Archivist, for help in obtaining this; fragments only of a seal survive. P. Morgan, *War and Society in Medieval Cheshire, 1277–1403* (Manchester, 1987), 34 outlines (after Moor, lxxxii. 82) the career of Sir Hamo Massy, sixth baron of Dunham-Massey, who took livery of his lands in 1277 and died in 1325; for this indenture see *ibid.* 50.

[39] We are grateful to the Marquess of Bath for permission to publish this and other documents from Longleat, and to Kate Harris, Librarian, for her advice and help. A small armorial seal in blackened wax survives: 3 trefoils between 2 chevrons, a label of 3 points (Fillol). In Edward I's reign Sir Thomas Fillol is recorded as bearing 'de or a une fesse et ii chevrons de goules, en la fesse iii tryfoyls dargent' (BL, MS Stowe 440 f. 94v). Aged 12 in 1281, he held lands in Essex and still fl. 1324 (Moor, lxxxi. 26). For a modern copy of this indenture see Oxford, Magdalen College, McFarlane Papers III, 126–7.

acovynt entre le honurable bier moun sire Johan de Grey seignour de
Deffrencloyt dune part,[40] et moun sire Thomas Fillol dautrepart, cest
a savoir, qe le dit moun sire Johan ad graunte pur li et pur ses heyrs
au dit moun sire Thomas retenaunce a tote la vie le dit moun sire
Thomas pur li meymes et deus esquiers, cynk garzouns et cynk chivaus.
E prendra le dit moun sire Thomas a tote sa vie de le dit moun sire
Johan et de ses heyrs chekun an treys robes en une sele si cume apert
a chivaler, et si cume les autres chivalers le dit moun sire Johan pernent
et bouche a court pur li et deus esquiers en ses venues kaunt li plerra.
E de se cynk garzouns, le un eyt a table et les quatre a gages ou a
table si cume les garzouns de le houtel le dit moun sire Johan serount
et sustenaunce pur ses cynk chivaus. E le dit moun sire Thomas servira
le dit moun sire Johan a touz faitz de pes et de gere en Engleterre
sauve le Turney a les custages le dit moun sire Johan en mounture et
en totes autres choses si le dit moun sire Johan li voille maunder. E ne
covient mye qe le dit moun sire Thomas aille ove le dit moun sire
Johan ne ove ses heyrs en Escoce ne en Gales pur gere si noun a sa
volente demeyne. E a cest covenaunt de retenaunce en la fourme
avauntdite leaument a tenir le dit moun sire Johan oblige soun maner
de Purle en la counte de Essex' en ky meyns qil devigne a la destresce
le dit moun sire Thomas qil puisse destreyndre deynz le dit maner et
la destresce retenir quel houre qe les avauntdites covenaunts li seyent
freynts en nul poynt taunkil iseit pleynementes servi solum les
covenaunts avaunt tailles. En temoignaunce de queu chose les avauntdites parties a cest escrit endente ount mys lour seaux entrechaungeablement. Escrites a Hemyngford le jour et lan avauntdits.

22 Hugh le Despenser, the son and Sir Peter de Uvedale, knight,
London, 30 August 1316 (PRO, E40/A8019, ruled parchment, sealed
on tag through turn-up).[41]

Sachent touz ceux qe cest escrit parti verront ou orront qe cest le
covenant fait entre mons. Pierre de Ovedale, chevalier, dune part et
mons. Hue le Despencer le fuiz dautre part. Cest asaver qe le dit mons.
Pierre doit servir lavantdit mons. Hue le Despencier le fuiz soi et disime
homes darmes a terme de sa vie en temps de pees et de gere en les
parties Dengleterre, Descoce et de Gales, totes loures qe le dit mons.

[40] John de Grey of Ruthin and Wilton (d. 1323) succeeded his father in 1308 and in
1311 had a licence to entail the castle of Ruthin, the cantred of Dyffryn Clwyd and the
manor of Rushton, Cheshire, on his son Roger (cf. GEC, vi. 173–4).
[41] cf. *CAD*, iv. no. 8019. For a later example of Uvedale's small armorial seal see
below **28**; Tanquerey, *Mélanges ... Jeanroy*, 205–7 for an earlier edition.

Hue lui garnira ou lui f[er]ra garnir suffisaument un mois devant la
mayn. E qe le dit mons. Pierre prendra pur toutes choses dudit mons.
Hue bouche a court pur lui et pur ses gentz darmes avantnomez. Et si
lavenoit qe le dit mons. Pierre defailist du service et des gentz darmes
avantdiz, ou soit james en ascun temps encontre ledit mons. Hue, en
nul point parla qe il porra resonablement monstrer q'il estoit encontre
lui, save le foi le Roi et de mons. Johan de Dovedale, son pere, adonqes
voit et grant le dit mons. Pierre de doner et paier au dit mons. Hue,
ou a son attorne, quatre cent livres desterlings en les queux il est tenu
au dit mons. Hue par une lettre obligatorie sealle de son seal. E si le
dit mons. Pierre ne soit james en nul point encontre lui ne defaile dudit
service ne des gentz darmes en la manere susdit, lavantdit mons. Hue
voit et grante pur lui, pur ses heirs et pur ses assignez, qe la dite lettre
obligatorie de quatre centz livres desterlings avantditz soit adonqes
cassee et anyentie et tenue pur nule atouz jours.

E si ensi soit qe le dit mons. Pierre eit espose ou esposera la dame
de Hastinges, soer dudit mons. Hue, adonqes voit et grant ledit mons.
Pierre de doner et paier audit mons. Hue, ou a son attorne, quatre
centz marz desterlings a la Purification de Nostre Dame prochein
avenir apres la date de ceste endenture saunz plus delai, en les queux
il est tenu audit mons. Hue par une lettre obligatorie sealle de son seal.
E as toutes les choses avantdites bien et leaument tenir et acomplier
en la forme avantnome le dit mons. Pierre adjure sur les seintz
Evangelies Dieu corporament touchez de sa mayn destre toute neuve.
E si nule manere de contrarie soit fait au dit mons. Pierre par encheison
dudit mariage, voit et grante le dit mons. Hue de lui eider et conseiler
en quanqe il siet et poet solom son poer en ceo cas, horspris lestat
nostre seignur le Roi et mons. Hue le Dispensier, son pere. E a ces
covenaunces bien et leaument tenir et acomplier les parties avantnomez
ount oblige eux, lun a lautre, lour heirs et lour essecutours et touz lour
biens moebles et nonmoebles presenz et avenirs, ou qil soient trovez.
En tesmoignaunce de verite a cest escrit endente les parties avantnomez
entrechaungablement ount mys lour seaux. Done a Loundres le Lundi
prochein apres la feste de la Decollacion de Seint Johan le Baptistre
en lan du regne le Roi Edward fuiz le Roi Edward disime.[42]

Dorse: Endenture Pieres de Ovedale chevaler de retenaunz

23 Thomas, earl of Lancaster and Sir Thomas Lovel, Leicester, 14

[42] The proposed marrage between Peter de Uvedale (1290–1336) and Isabel Despenser
did not take place (cf. GEC, xii, pt 2. 197; Moor, lxxx. 288–9).

June 1317 (Leeds, Yorkshire Archaelogical Society, Grantley MS 492 (DD53/III/492), formerly sealed on tag).[43]

Ceste endenture tesmoigne qe a covenu [en]tre le nobles homme monsire Thomas counte de Lancastre et de Leicestre, seneschal Dengleterre, dune part et monsire Thomas Lovel dautre part,[44] cest assavoir qe le dit monsire Thomas est demorre [ove] le dit counte a toute sa vie, a servir ly de pes et de guerre en Engleterre, Escoce, Irlande et Gales contre toutes gentes, sauve le corps le Roy, lui meismes a deux homes darmes, et prendra monture du dit counte covenable pour son corps et restor pur ses chevaux darmes perdutz en les dites guerres au fait dy celes solonc coe qils seront preises par les gentz le dit counte alentre des dites guerres. Et avera bouche a court pur luy et ses deux vadletz et prendra robes et seles du dit counte au foer de ses autres Bachelers et livere de fein et daveine pur ses chevaux quant le dit conte[a] donne livere a ses autres Bachelors et gages pur autant des garcons. Et vendra le dit monsire Thomas a touz les mandementz le dit counte de pes et de guerre quant il serra renablement garny par lectre le dit counte solonc coe qe le dit counte avera a fere de ly. Et le dit counte ad graunte au dit monsire Thomas pur le service avantdist a fere a ly vint marche de rente a toute sa vie a recevire des terres le dit counte en le parties de Wilteshire. Et graunte le dit monsire Thomas qe sil defaillie ou refuse a faire le service audit counte comme est susdit, qe adonqes le dit counte puisse seiser le dit rente en sa mein et retenir sanz contredit le dit monsire Thomas ou de nul autre de par luy. En tesmoignance de queu chose auxibien le dit counte come le dit monsire Thomas a cest escript endente entrechangablement ont mis [lour se]alx. Par y ces tesmoignes monsire Robert de Holand, monsire Nicholas de Segrave, monsire William Tochet, [monsire Adam] de Hudleston, monsire Hugh de Cuilly[45] et autres. Donne a nostre ville de Leicestre le xiiij jour de Juign en lan du regne le roy Edward fiz au tres noble Roy Edward disme.

---

[43] We are grateful to Mrs Sylvia Thomas, Archivist-in-charge, for obtaining permission from the YAS for publication of this document and for other assistance.

[44] Thomas Lovel of Titchwell, Norfolk, was a younger brother of John, first lord Lovel of Titchmarsh (*CIPM*, vii. 304; P. S. Lewis, 'Sir John Fastolf's Lawsuit over Titchwell, 1448–55', *Historical Journal* i (1958), 5–6). In the list of Lancaster's servants compiled after Boroughbridge, Lovel's fee is said to be assigned on the town of Hungerford, Wilts., and previously on the manor of Aldbourne, Wilts. Pardoned for his adherence to Lancaster in 1322, Lovel was pardoned again in February 1327 for defending the Despenser castle of Caerphilly against Isabella and Mortimer: Holmes, 71 n. 5, 140; *Parliamentary Writs* (London, 1827–34), II, ii. 200, 204; *CPR, 1327–30*, 13, 37; see also below nos. **24**, **25**, **27** and **31**.

[45] For the witnesses, all retainers of Earl Thomas see J. R. L. Maddicott, *Thomas of Lancaster* (Oxford, 1970), passim.

Dorse: Dominus Thomas Lovel

a. dit conte interlined

24 Thomas, earl of Lancaster and Leicester and Sir Adam de Swillington, Tutbury, 21 June 1317 (Oxford, Bodleian Library, MS Dodsworth 94 fos. 122v–123r, 17th c. transcript).[46]

Ceste endenture tesmoigne qil est acovenu entre les nobles home Monsire Thomas counte de Lancastre et de Leicestre, Seneschall Dengleterre, dune part et Mons. Adam de Swilyngton dautre part, cestascavoir qe le dit Mons. Adam est demoire ove le dit counte de luy servir de pes et de guerre en Engleterre, Escoce, Irlande et Gales a toute sa vie contre toutes gentz sauve le corps le Roy. Et luy servira a dis hommes darmes covenables bien armes et apparelles, suffissaument montes, des queux il serra sey tiers [de] chevaler as robes et seles le dit Counte, et en temps de guerre prendra suffissaunte mounture du dit Counte pur son corps et restor pur ses chevaux darmes perdites en le service le dit Counte en les dites guerres solonc comme qil serront prises par les gents le dit Counte a soun oeps a lentre des dites guerres. Et avera bouche a court pur luy a ses gents darmes ou temps de guerre. Et avera foyn et aveine, fers a clous de la livere le dit Counte quant autres banerets prenent livere en les dites guerres pur vint et sis chevaux et gages pur atantz de garcons. Et en temps de pees quant le dit Monseur Adam vendra audit Counte par son mandement, par lettre as parlements ou as autres assembles ove ses chevalers, robes, le dit Counte portantz, et ove son plein des gentz adonqes mangera au sale luy et ses chevalers et ses gentils gentz avantditz. Et prendra fein et aveyne, fers et clous pour douze chevaux et gages pur atantz des garcons et avera livere de vin et de chandelle com apend pour sa chambre.

Et quant il vendra a un chevalx par mandement le dit Counte pur conseiller ou pur servir[a] adonqes avera bouche a court, feyn et aveyn pur noef chevaux et gages pur a tantz des garcons et come qapend pur sa chambre de vin, et de chandelle come por baneret doit estre done. Et si ove pluis des chevalers vent preigne pur lafferant come affert solont la forme et la force du mandement le dit Counte, et sil vigne soul santz chevaler par lettre le dit Counte preigne livere pur sis chevaux et gages come apend. Et pour touz les services affaire en la susdite manere tout la vie au dit counte avera le dit Mons. Adam

---

[46] For another seventeenth-century transcript after the Dodsworth MS see YAS, MS 283 fos. 153–154r.

quarante livres de rente a retenir des franks et des bondes le dit Counte en la menere^b de Ledys de lonour de Pontfroit[47] as termes de la dite ville usuels. Et veult et grant le dit Monsier Adam qe sil defaille ou refuse de faire au dit Counte le service qest susdit adonqe le dit Counte pusse entrer et reseiser les dites rentes a queu temps que son service ly soit arere et retenir sanz contredit le dit Monsier Adam ou de nul autre de par luy. Et a service le dit Counte bien et loialment a toute sa vie et a fere a luy les services susdites ad le dit Monsier Adam juree sur Saintes Ewangelies en la presence le dit Counte et des banerets et des autres bachelors de sout' nomes. En tesmoigne de queu chose auxibien le dit Counte come le dit Monsier Adam a ceste endenture entre-changeablement ont mis lour seals, presentes tesmoignes Monsier Robert de Holand, Monsier Nicholas de Segrave, Monsier Estevenne de Segrave, Monsier Adam de Hodeleston, Monsier William Trussell et autres. Don' au chastell de Tutteburie le xxj jour de Joign en lan ou regne le Roy Edward fiz a tresnoble Roy Edward disme.[48]

a. *inueri* underlined in text; *inveri* in margin
b. followed by *toute sa vie au dit conte* struck out, and *de lonor Leedes* in margin

25 Thomas, earl of Lancaster and Leicester, and Sir Hugh de Meynill, knight bachelor, Ashbourne, Derbys., 24 July 1317 (Oxford, Bodleian Library, MS Dugdale 18 f. 39v).[49]

Cest endenture tesmoigne qe a convenu est entre le nobles homme monsire Thomas, counte de Lancastre et de Leycestre, seneschal d'Engleterre, d'une part, et monsire Hugh de Meignel d'autre part: cestasavoir qe le dit monsire Hugh est demore ove le dit conte, et lui servira de pees et de guerre a tout sa vie, en les guerres d'Engleterre, Escoce, Irlaunde et Gales, contre toutes gentz, sauve le corps le roi lui mesmes, ove trois hommes d'armes bien armez et apparailez, et covenablement montez. Et avera monture du dit counte pur son corps, restor por ses chevaux d'armes perduz en les dites guerres en le service le dit count, selonc ceo q'il serront prisez al entre des dites guerres al oeps^a le dit counte, per les gentz le dit counte. Et prendra les robes et seles le dit counte, si come il donne a ses autres bachelers, livere de

[47] Leeds and Pontefract, Yorks. W. R.; cf. Holmes, 142 where the rent on the manor of Leeds is said to be owing to 'monsieur Aleyn de Swylingtone'.

[48] Swillington (d. 1328) received a pardon for his adherence to Lancaster in October 1318 (*CPR, 1317–21*, 231; see also Moor, lxxxiii. 320).

[49] 'Ex diversis autographis mihi accomodatis per ... Dom. Bruse primogenitum Comitis de Elgin mense Nov. A° 1659'. Moor, lxxxii. 153 for Sir Hugh de Meynill of Hilton, Yorks. (d. 1333).

fein et d'aveyn por dis chevaux, et gages por a tantz dez garsons, quant
le dit counte donne livere a ses autres bachelers. Et en temps de pees,
quant le dit monsire Hugh vendra as parlements ou aillors par
mandement le dit counte, et par sa lettre, adonque prendra livere de
fein et d'aveyne por quatre chevaux, et gages por a tantz des garsons
(etc.) Et pour toutz les services (etc.) ad le dit conte done (etc.) au dit
monsire Hugh, a terme sa vie diz marcz d'annuele rent (etc.). Done a
Assheborne en le Peke le xxiiii jour de Juyl, en l'an du regne le roi
Edward filz au tresnoble roi Edward unzime.

a. MS *corps* but cf. **27** below.

26 Aymer de Valence, earl of Pembroke, and Sir John [...], knight
bachelor, Hertfordingbury, Herts., 25 November 1317 (PRO,
E101/68/2/41, badly damaged, formerly sealed on tongue).

[Connu chose soit qe le] xxv jour de Novembre lan du regne le Roi
Edward filz au Roi Edward unzisme con[venue est parent]re le noble
homme monsire Aymar de Valance, counte de Pembroke dune parte
e monsire [Johan de ... d]autrepart: cest a savoir qe le dit monsire
Johan est demore ove le counte soi [... por lui servir de] pees et de
guerre countre totes gentz sauve [le corps] nostre seignur [le roi du
feste de ... tanque a meismes le] jour en une an pleinement acompli.
Et prendra du dit counte robes [et seles ... comme ses aut]res bachelers.
Et avera garscons as gages et mangeantz en sale sicome les autres
[bachelers ...]. E prendra du dit counte pur sa demoere susdite vint
livres, cest a savoir [dis livres ... pro]schein avenir e dis livres [a] la
Seint Michel proschein suant. Et avera suffisante m[ounture ...] p[ur]
son [...] et res[tor] des ses ch[ev]als dar[mes ...] prises pur ses [gents]
et serront prises par les gents le dit counte e perduz en le service le dit
counte. En temoigne de queu choses cest escripte [...] les ditz conte
et monsire Johan entrechangeablement ount mis lor seals. Donne a
Hertfordingebir' le jour et lan susdit.

27 Thomas, earl of Lancaster and Leicester and Sir John de Eure,
Pontefract, Yorks., 29 December 1317 (Oxford, Bodleian Library,
Dugdale MS 18 f. 39v).[50]

Ceste endenture tesmoigne qe Monsire Thomas Counte de Lancastre

[50] Transcript from same source as **25**. Eure (b. 1277) was executed after Boroughbridge
(Moor, lxxx. 316).

(etc.) ad done et graunte a Monsire Johan de Eure quarant mars de annuele Rent, a rescevire d'an en an de ses frank tenantz et bondes en son manoir de Emeldon en Northumbreland,[51] por le service qe le dit Monsire Johan ferra au dit Counte, a toute sa vie, de pees et de guerre, en les guerres d'Engleterre, Escoce, Irlaunde et Gales, contre toutes gentz sauve le corps le Roi, a dis hommes d'armes suffisantz, bien armez et apparailez, et covenablement montes, tout a sa monture demeine, des queux il serra soit tiers de chevaler as Robes et Seles le dit Counte. Et avera bouche a court por lui et ses gentz d'armes; et restor por ses chevaux d'armes perduz en le service le dit Counte en les dites guerres, selonc ce q'il serront prisez par les gentz le dit Counte a son oeps al entre des dites guerres, et avera livere de fein et d'aveine, fers et cloes, quant autres Banerets prenent livere en les dites guerres por vint huit chevaux, et gages por a tanz des garcons. Et en temps de pees, quant le dit Monsire Johan vendra au dit Conte, per son mandement et per lettre as parlementz, ou as autres assemblees ove toutz ses chevalers, robes le dit Counte portants, et son plein des gentz, adonqe mangera en sale, lui et ses chevalers, et ses gentils gentz, et prendra livere de fein et de avein, fers et cloes, por vint huit chevaux, et gages por a tantz des garzons, et avera livere du vin, et de chaundaille, come apend, por sa chaumbre. Et quant il vendra a un chevaler au dit Counte, per son mandement, por conseiller, ou por iner [sic][a] adonque prendra a bouche a court, fein et avein por sept chevaux, et gages por a tantz des garzons, livere du vin et de chaundaille, come apend por sa chaumbre (etc.). Done au chastel de Pountefret le xxix jour de Decembre, l'an de Roy Edward filz a Roy Edward unzime.

  a. For *servir* (cf. above **24**)?

28 Humphrey de Bohun, earl of Hereford and Essex, and Sir Peter de Uvedale, knight bachelor, London, 19 March 1318 (Oxford, Bodleian Library, MS Dugdale 18 f. 39v).[52]

Le dymenge prochein apres la feste de Seint Gregorie l'an du regne nostre seignur le Roi Edward filz au Roy Edward unzime, convenaunt entre le noble home monsire Humfrai de Bohun, conte de Hereford et d'Essex, d'une parte, et monsire Peres de Ouvedale, chevaler d'autre part: Cestasaver, qe le dit monsire Peres demorra ove le dit counte a terme de la vie le dit monsire Peres; pernaunt robes et seles, come ses

---

[51] Embleton, Northumbs., lying just over a mile to the west of the earl's castle of Dunstanburgh.
[52] Transcript from same source as **25**.

autres Bachelers, et bouche en court, fein, et aveyne pour quatre
chevaux, et gages pour quatre garsons, en temps de pees, quant il
vendra a court par maundement du dit counte; Et en temps de guerre
et pour le Tourney, fein et aveyn pur viij chevaux, et gages pour viij
garsons; Et restor de chevaux d'armes perdus en guerre en le service
le dit counte, dont le dit monsire Peres se montera meismes, en le
primier an de sa demoere (etc.). Done a Loundres le jour et l'an
susditz.[53]

29 Hugh le Despenser, the son and Sir Hugh de Neville of Essex,
knight bachelor, York, 22 August 1318 (PRO, DL 27/186, sealed on a
tongue).[54]

Conue chose soit as toutz qe cestes escritz endenteez verrount ou
orrount qe le Mardy proscheyn devant la feste de Seynt Augustyn
levesque[55] lan du regne le Roy Edward fuiz au Roi Edward duzisme
ensi acovynt entre monsire Hugh le Despenser le fuiz dune part, et
monsire Hugh de Nevill' del counte de Essex dautre part: cest asavoir
qe le dit monsire Hugh de Nevill' demorra soi disme homes darmes,
cest asavoir soi tierce bachillier ove sept vadletz par un an entier
proscheyn ensiwant apres la confection de cestes, de pees et de guerre,
prenant du dit monsire Hugh le Despenser en totes choses quatre vint
marcs; cest asavoir le primer quarter del an avant la meyn vint marcs
quant il va de guerre, e ensi de quartier en quartier vint marcs selonc
ceo qe lem veet de guerre[a] e robes et seles pour lui et ses deux
bac[h]illiers. E le dit monsire Hugh le Despenser outre ceo trovera au
dit monsire Hugh de Nevill' en temps de guerre manger et boire pour
lui et ses bachilliers et esquiers avantditz, et pour les deux chaumberleyns
le dit monsire Hugh de Nevill et pour les deux sometiers ses bachilliers
avantditz. E covenable mounture pur son corps et pur un de ses
bachiliers. E lui fray restor de ses chivaux darmes renablement prises
en la garderobe le dit monsire Hugh le Despenser et perduz en son
service. Estre ceo le dit monsire Hugh le Despenser trovera au dit
monsire Hugh de Nevill en temps de pees manger et boyre pour lui et
ses homes desusditz en temps de parlement quant il y vendra au renable
mandement par lettres le dit monsire Hugh le Despenser; et feyns et
aveynes pour vint chivaux, si tauntz y amene ovesque lui, et robes et

---

[53] In margin, a drawing of Uvedale's seal: a shield of arms, [Argent], A cross moline
voided [Gules], a bordure engrailed. Son of John de Uvedale and Margaret de Campania,
Peter was aged three in 1296 (Moor, lxxx. 288–9).

[54] A very fine impression of Despenser's armorial seal survives: Ellis, ii. no. P1291;
Moor, lxxxii. 251–2 for Hugh Neville (before 1283–1335).

[55] 28 August.

seles en la forme desusdite. En tesmoignance de quele chose les parties desusdites a cestes escritz endenteez entrechaungeablement ount mis leurs seals. Donne a Everwyk le jour et lan avantditz.

a. de guerre interlined

30 Ralph, lord Basset of Drayton retains Philip de Chetwynd for a year's service, Drayton, 4 March 1319 (Stafford, William Salt Library, H. M. Chetwynd, Box A, File 1, sealed on a tongue).[56]

Le dymeyn procheyn apres la feste seynt Chadde en laan de regne le Roy Edward fiz le Roy Edward duszisme acovient entre mounsire Rauf Basset segneur de Drayton' de une part et Phelip de Chetwynde[57] de altre part, ceste asaver qe le dist Phelip se tenust e se oblige a lavaundit mounsire Rauf de ly server en pies e en guere por laan ensuvaunt apres le confectioun de ceste escript countre tote gentz sour bone mounture de soen demeygne salve por le turney. Et por ceo covenauns le dist mounsire Rauf graunt a dist Phelip ces costages quaunt yl serra travayle por guere por treys chivals e treys garsouns solom ceo qe yl fet a ces altres esquiers. En tens de pies deuz chivals e deuz garsouns e cinz mars deysterlyngns a payer solom ceo qe yl est travayle par laan entier. Et restor de soun graunt chival sy perde par fet de guere. Et sy le dit Phelip prengne le ordre de chivalryre den laan, dounqe graunte le dist Phelip qe yl servera al dyst Rauf devaunt touz altres solom ceo qyl pussent acovenir de covenauns. Et a grendre suerte de ces covenauns tener le un a lautre a ceste endenture ount mys lour seals. Donez a Drayton[58] le jour e laan avaundit.

31 Thomas, earl of Lancaster and Sir William Latimer, York, 15 May 1319 [French] (PRO, DL 36/2 p. 33, pub. in Holmes, 122–3).

32 Henry, earl of Lancaster and Sir Philip Darcy, Higham Ferrers,

---

[56] An impression of Basset's seal survives. We are grateful to D. V. Fowkes, Librarian, The William Salt Library, for permission to publish this indenture; it was first published by M. Prestwich, 'An Indenture between Ralph, lord Basset of Drayton, and Philip de Chetwynd, 4 March 1319', *Stafford Historical and Civic Society, Transactions* (1971–3), 18–21 at p. 20. GEC, ii. 2–3 for Ralph, second lord Basset of Drayton (1299–1343).

[57] Philip Chetwynd came of age in 1316 and was knighted in 1339 (Prestwich, after H. E. Chetwynd-Stapylton, *The Chetwynds of Ingestre* (London, 1892). For a later namesake, **125** below.

[58] Drayton, Staffs.

Northants., 1 October 1327 (PRO, DL25/L3254, sealed on tag).[59]

Ceste endenture tesmoigne qe acovenu est entre le nobles homme
monsire Henri counte de Lancastre et de Leicestre seneschal Dengleterre dune parte et monsire Phelip' Darci dautre part: Cest asavoir
qe le dit counte ad done et graunte au dit monsire Phelip' qaraunte
marche de rente issaunt de la ferme de son manoir de Burreth' en le
counte de Nicole et de son manoir de Donington' en mesme le counte.[60]
Cest asavoir du manoir de Burreth' vynt livres et de son manoir de
Donington' dys mars a resceviere dan en an par les mayns de ses
tenaunz et de ses baillifs illoeqes issauntz de lour fermes en les ditz
manoirs as termes illoeqes usueles a avoir et tenir au dit monsire Phelip'
a tote sa vie les ditz qaraunte marche de rente pur les services quil
f[e]ra au dit counte de pees et de gerre.

Cest asavoir en les gerres Dengleterre, Escoce, Irlaunde et Gales
countre totes gentz, sauve le corps le Roi, a sept hommes darmes des
queux il sera soi tierz des chivalers as robes et seles le dit counte. Et
sera soun corps demeigne a la mounture le dit counte et il mountera
mesmes ses bachilers et ses esquiers et serount ses chevalers darmes
prisez al entre des dites gerres par les gentz le dit counte, et avera
restor de ses chivaux qe serount perduz au fait de gere en le service le
dit counte soulunc le dit pris. Et mangerount en sale, ly et ses gentz
darmes avantdites, et avera feyn et avayne, fers et cloues de la livere
le dit counte quant autres prendrount livre en les dites gerres pur vynt
et qatres chivaux et gages pur ataunz des garsouns, et en temps de
pees quant le dit monsire Phelip' vendra au dit counte par soun
mandement par lettre as parlementz, ou as autres assembles, ove son
pleyn des gentz. Adonques mangerount en sale ly et ses chivalers et ses
gentz avantdites et prendra feyn, avayne, fers et cloues pur noef chivaux
et gages pur ataunz des garsouns et avera livere du vyn et du chaundoille
come apent pur sa chaumbre. Et quant il vendra ove un chevaler par
mandement le dit counte pur counseiler, il vendra as coustages le dit
counte, et adonques avera bouche a court, feyn, avayne pur sept
chivaux et gages pur ataunz des garsouns et ceo qe apent pur sa
chambre du vyn et du chaundoille, et si ove plus des chivaux viengne
ou meyns, preigne pur lafferaunt come affiert soulunc la forme del
mandement le dit counte. Et vendra le dit monsire Phelip' a touz les

[59] Fragment of the seal of Philip Darcy (c. 1259–1333); for a near contemporary
enrolment see also DL42/2 f. 490r–v; GEC, iv. 51–2 and Moor, lxxx. 266 for his career.
He drew his annuity of 40 marks in 1330–1 (DL40/1/11 f. 45v; cf. R. Somerville, *The
History of the Duchy of Lancaster*, i (London, 1953), 81–2).

[60] Burreth, a lost placename in Tupholme wapentake, and Donington on Bain, Parts
of Lindsey, Lincs., identifications owing to the kindness of Prof. Kenneth Cameron.

mandementz le dit counte de pees et de gerre soulunc la forme del mandement le dit counte.

Et voet et graunte le dit monsire Phelip' qe sil defaille, ou refuse affaire au dit counte les services suzditz en nul poynt, qe adonques lirra bien au dit counte de seyser la dite rente en sa mayn et retenir a touz jours saunz contredit du dit monsire Phelip' ou de nul autre depar ly. Et voet et graunte le dit counte qe si la dite rente soit arere au dit monsire Phelip' a nul terme qe bien ly lirra a destreindre en le dit manoir de Burreth' pur les dites vynt livres et en le dit manoir de Donington' pur les dites dys mars et la destresse detenir tanques soun assetz ly soit fait de ceo qe arere ly serra de la dite rente. Et a servir le dit counte a tote sa vie bien et loialment.

E affaire a ly les services avant dites de pees de gerre en la forme avant dite ad le dit monsire Phelip' jure sur saintz ewangelies en la presence des bones gentz desouthnommez. En tesmoigne de queu chose a la partie de ceste endenture demoraunt devers le dit monsire Phelip' le dit counte ad mis soun seal et a lautre partie demoraunt devers le dit counte le dit monsire Phelip' ad mis soun seal par yces tesmoignes monsire Thomas le Blount, monsire Henri de Ferers, monsire William le Blount, monsire Johan de Sapy, monsire Johan le Blount et autres. Done en la ville de Hegham Ferers le primer jour Doctobre lan du regne nostre seignur le roi Edward primer.

Dorse: lxv
$\qquad$ S^{a}

33 Henry, lord Percy and Sir Ralph Neville, Clifton near York, 5 August 1328 (Oxford, Bodleian Library, MS Dugdale 18 fos. 39v–40r).[61]

Fait a remembrer, qe le primier jour de Aust lan du regne nostre seignur le roy Edward tierce apres la conquest secound, monsire Rauf de Neville est demorres ou monsire Henri de Percy pur pees et pur gerre, a totes lour vies, ove vint hommes d'armes, des queux soi quinte de chivaler. Et prendra pour cele demoere par aan, cent livers d'esterlings, a deux termes de l'an a la quinzeyme de S. Martin cinquant livers, et as octaves de la Trinite autres cinquant liveres. Cest asavoir sesaunte liveres issaunts du manoir de Topclive, et quarante liveres issaunts du manoir de Pokelingtone as termes avantditz (Etc.).[62] Et

---

[61] Transcript from same source as **25**. GEC, x. 459–62 for Henry, second lord Percy (1314–52). Ralph Neville, second son of Ralph, first lord Neville of Raby, succeeded his father in 1331 (see below **34**).

[62] Topcliffe, Yorks. N. R., and Pocklington, Yorks. E. R..

prendra le dit monsire Rauf robes et seles pur lui et ses chivaliers come ses autres compaignons. Et quant il vendra de gerre il avera mangeaunt en sale, lui et ses gentiz gentz, et sys vallez de mester, feyn et avene, fers et cloves pur cinquant et noef chivaux, et gages pour cinquant et tros garzons. Et avera le dit monsire Rauf de le dit monsire Henri, suffisant mounture pur son corps demeigne. Et servera le dit monsire Rauf le dit monsire Henri ove les vynt hommes darmes bien et apertement apparaillez de mounture et d'armoures que part qe le corps le dit monsire Henri irra countre totes gentz sauve la ligeaunce nostre seignur le Roi et ses heirs, et avera restor des chivaux darmes preises et perdutz en gerre. Et quant le dit monsire Rauf vendra par mandement le seignur pur le turnoi, soi quarte de chivaler ou les gentiz gentz qe afferent, il mangerount en sale, et cynk valletz de mester et avera feyn et aveynes, fers et clous pur trente et seet chivaux et gages pur trente et deux garzons, et avera suffisaunte monture pur son corps demyne du dit seignur et restor des chivaux de ses compaignions preises.

Et quant il vendra en temps de Parlement ou en autre temps, par le mandement le seignur il vendra soi autre ou ses gentiz gents qe afferent ou neef chivaux, trois homes de mester mangeaunt en sale, feyn et aveyn, fer et clous pur les chivaux avantditz et gages pur sys garzouns. Et si il soit maunde de venir plus affortement per le dit seignur preignye solounc lafferaunt suisdit. Et le dit monsire Rauf graunte qe il soit maunde par le dit seignur de Percy, avenir de gerre ou de pees, en le manere susdite et soit destourbez par maladie graundez qil troeffe cheveteyn suffisant amenir les gentz darmes avant nomes, en la manere avantdit. Et quant le dit monsire Rauf vendra par mandement le seignur adunques preignye se custages venant et retournant per resonables journez acomptez. As queux covenantz bien et leaument tenir, le dit monsire Henri se oblige par cest endenture a tenir les covenaunts susditz qe lui apartient. Et le dit monsire Rauf se oblige par mesme l'endenture a faire les services susdits, en le forme susdite. En tesmoignaunce (etc.) Donez a Clifton pres Everwik le quint jour daust l'an avantditz.

34 Henry, lord Percy and Ralph, lord Neville, Westminster, 22 January 1332 (Alnwick Castle, Northumbs., Syon, D I, 1a fos. 110v–111r, copy of c. 1377 in the Percy cartulary).[63]

---

[63] cf. *The Percy Cartulary*, ed. M. T. Martin, *Surtees Society* cvii (1911), 273–4 no. DCCXXXVIII for an earlier abbreviated edition. G.E.C., x. 459–62 for Henry, second lord Percy (1314–52) and *ibid.*, ix. 499–501 for Ralph, second lord Neville of Raby (1331–67). We are grateful to the Duke of Northumberland for permission to consult his manuscripts and to Colin Shrimpton, Archivist at Alnwick, for his help.

Ceste endenture tesmoigne qe monsire Rauf de Nevyll est demorez od monsire Henri de Percy pur peas e pur gere, pur totes lour deus vies od xx hommes darmes, des queux soi quint de chivaler. E le dit^a monsire Rauf avera pur cele demure le manoir de Neuburn^{64} od totes le apurtenances en le counte de Northumbr' a terme de sa vie, e le dit monsire Rauf prendra robes e seles pur luy quint de chivaler, auxsi come ses autres compaignons. E quant il vendra de guere il avera mangauntz en sale, luy e ses gentiz gentz come affiert, e vj valletz de mestier, feyn et aveynes, feres e clowes pur lix chivaux, e gages pur liij garcons, e le dit monsire Rauf avera du dit monsire Henri suffisaunt mounture pur son corps demeyn, e le dit monsire Rauf servyra le dit monsire Henri od les xx hommes darmes bien e covenablementz apparrillez de mounture e darmes, queu part qe le corps le dit monsire Henri irrad, countre totes gentz, save la ligaunce nostre seignur le roi e ses heirs a totes les foiz qil sera covenablementz garny come affiert. Et le dit monsire Rauf avera restor de chivals darmes preisez et perduz en guere. E quant le dit monsire Rauf vendra par covenable maundement du dit seignur pur le turnoy, il vendra soy quart de chivaler od les gentiz gentz come affierent, e mangerount luy e ses gentiz gentz en sale e v valletz de mestier, e averad fein e aveynes, feres et clowes, pur xxxvij chivals, et gages pur xxxij garcons, e averad suffisaunt mounture pur son corps demen du dit seignur, e restor des chivaux de ses compaignons priseez. E quant il vendra en temps de parlement, ou en autre temps, par maundement le seignur, il vendra soy autre od ses gentiz gentz come affiert od ix chivals et iij hommes de mestier mangauntz en sale, fein et aveynes, feres e clowes, pur les ditz chivaux, e gages pur vi garcons, e sil soit maunde par covenable garnissement de venir plus efforecementz par le dit seignur, preigne solom lafferaunt, e le dit monsire Rauf graunt qe sil soit maunde par covenable garnisement par le dit seignur a venir de guere ou pur le turnoy en la manere susdit, e soit desturbe par maladie, qil troef cheventeyn suffissaunt amener les gentz darmes avaunditz queu part qe le dit seignur irra, en manere avaundit. Et quant le dit monsire Rauf vendra par maundement le dit seignur e auge par garnissement, preigne ses coustages venant e returnaunt par resonables jornees accomptez. E sil aveigne qil ne pleise au dit monsire Rauf fere le dit servys ou qil ne le face point come il soit covenablementz garny en la manere come avaunt est dit, qe bien lise au dit monsire Henri le dit manoir entrer e tenir santz contredit ou desturbaunce du dit monsire

---

^{64} Newburn, Northumbs. Neville quitclaimed and released to Percy his previous retaining fee of £100 p.a. from the manors of Topcliffe and Pocklington on 5 Feb. 1332 and surrendered to Percy the manor of Newburn, which he held by lease of Sir John Clavering for the term of Clavering's life, on the same day. Percy issued letters patent, announcing the re-grant of Newburn to Neville, on 10 Feb.: Alnwick Castle, Syon D I la fos. 110–110v, printed in abbreviated form in *The Percy Cartulary*, nos. DCCXXXV–VII.

Rauf. E a les ditz covenauntz bien e loiaumentz tenir e faire le dit monsire Henri e monsire Rauf se obligent par cestes endentures entrechaungablementz enseales de lour sealz. Escritz a Westmoustier, le xxij jour de Janeuaire, lan du regne le Roi Edward tierz puis le conquest qynt.

Marginated: la demeure mons' Rauf de Nevill od mon seignur

   a. dit interlined

35 Henry, earl of Lancaster and Philip of Castle Martin, esquire, Leicester, 27 August 1333 (PRO, DL25/3397, sealed on tag).[65]

Ceste endenteure tesmoigne qe le nobles homme Mons. Henri counte de Lancastre et de Leicestre, seneschal Dengleterre, ad done et graunte et par cest escrit confirme a Philip de Chastelmartin dis et sept mars et demie de annuele rente a prendre en le manoir de Munstreworth[66] en le countee de Glouc' as termes usueles. Cest assavoir a la fest de Seint Michel, Seint Thomas la Postle, Pasques et de Seint Johan le Baptistre par oweles porciouns a avoir et tenir au dit Philip a toute sa vie fraunchement quitement bien et en pees pur le bon service qil ad fait et fera au dit counte a toute sa vie aussibien en temps de guerre come de pees partout en touz lieux ou le dit counte meismes irra. Et en temps de guerre avera du dit counte covenable mounture pur soun corps. Et prendra en temps de pees et de guerre[a] robes, feyn, aveyne, fers et clowes et gages pur ses garsouns aussicom un autre des esquiers le dit counte.

   Et veult et graunte le dit counte pur ly et pur ses heirs qe si la dite rente ly soit arere en partie ou en tout ainsi terme qe bien li lise adestreindre partout en le dit manoir en qi mains qil devigne et la destresse detenir tauntqe soun assez soit fait de ceo qe arere lui serra de la dite rente. Et graunte le dit Philip qe sil defaille ou refuse affaire les ditz services de pees et de guerre ou de venir as maundementez le dit counte de pees et de guerre quant il serra resonablement garni, sil ne soit destorbe part maladie ou par autre resonable enchesoun, qe le dit counte puisse retenir la dite rente en sa mayn saunz contredit de nuli. Et le dit counte graunte pur lui et pur ses heirs par cest escrit de garaunt au dit Philip a toute sa vie la suzdite rente pur soun service avandite. Et pur ceo doun et graunt le dit Philip ad graunte et renduz suiz au dit counte dis mars de rente qil avoit en soun manoir de

---

   [65] Castle Martin's small damaged red armorial seal (A fesse between three castles) survives; cf. Ellis, ii. P1171 for another complete example from DL27/302 (1341). Bean, 62 gives an incorrect reference.

   [66] Minsterworth, Gloucs.

Noefchastel souz Lyme[67] et cent soutz en ses molins de Monemouth[68] a terme de sa vie de soun graunt.

En tesmoigne de quieu chose aussibien le dit counte come le dit Philip a cestes endentures entrechangeablement ount mis lour seals par[m]y ces tesmoignes Mons. Williame le Blount, Mons. Williame de Walkynton', Mons. Johan de Seymor, Edmund Waldehef', Geffrey de Walcote et autres. Done a la ville de Leicestre le xxvij jour daust lan du regne le Roy Edward tiercz puis le conquest septisme.

Dorse: Anual' Phi Castelmartyn

    a. MS. *gurre*

36 Sir Henry Percy and William, son of John de Roddam, Alnwick, Northumbs., 1 September 1337 (Oxford, Bodleian Library, MS Dugdale 18 f. 40r).[69]

Ceste endenture faite a Alnewik le primer jour de Septembre l'an du regne le roy Edward tierze puis le conquest undszime, entre luy nobles home, monsire Henri de Percy d'une parte et William le fuitz John de Rodhum d'autre, tesmoigne qe le dit William est demoure od le dit monsire Henri, pur pees et pur gerre, od un compaignon suffisant, tanque au plein age John fitz et heir John de Rudhum. Et irra le dit William, od son dit compaignon queu part qe le corps le dit monsire Henri va de guerre, et prendra pur lui, et son dit compaignon, robes comes autres valletz, feyn, aveyn, fers et clowes pour sys chivaux, et gages pur sys garceons et ses chivaux d'armes prisez quant ils irront de guerre, et restor de ses chivaux perdutz en guerre. Et pur sa dite demoure le dit monsire Henri veult et graunt au dit William, la garde des terres mesme cesti Johan fuilz et heir le dit Johan de Rodhum en Houghtone,[70] tanq'il soit de plein age. Et serra le dit William preste de venir au dit monsire Henri, quele houre q'il soit resonablement garny, devant. Et si mesme cesti William soi alloigne nul part hors du service le dit monsire Henri, par qecunque cause qe ce soit, saunz la bone volunte le dit monsire Henri, qe adonques bien list a mesme celui monsire Henri, de raseissir mesme la garde en sa meyn, saunz chalenge du dit William. En tesmoignance (etc.)

---

[67] Newcastle under Lyme, Staffs.
[68] Monmouth, Gwent.
[69] Transcript from same source as **25**.
[70] Little Houghton, Long Houghton parish, Northumbs., which was held by John son of John de Roddam in the 1330s (*A History of Northumberland*, 15 vols., 1893–1940, ii. 407).

37 Thomas Beauchamp, earl of Warwick and Sir Robert Herle, Wanborough, Wilts., 20 April 1339 (BL, Add. MS 28042, f. 174r, late 14th cent. copy in the Beauchamp cartulary).[71]

Ceste endenture faite entre les nobles hommes sire Thomas de Beauchamp, count de Warr' dune part et mons. Robert Herle dautrepart tesmoigne, cestassavoir que le dit mons. Robert est demoure devers le dit count a terme de sa vie, soy quatre hommes darmes pour guerre daler par tout la ou le corps le count irra auxint bien par dela la mer come par desa, et pour pees come un autre bacheler de son hostel quant le seigneur avera de lui affaire pour certeins terres que le dit count lui ad done. Et quel heure que le dit count lui ad maunde le dit mons. Robert prendra ses costages resonables en alaunt et en retournaunt pour sa demoure, bouche de court pour lui et pour ses esquiers, gages pour ses garsouns, feres et clous et livere pour ses chivaux. Et le dit count trovera covenable mounture pour le corps le dit mons. Robert pour guerre et pour turnemantz. Et le dit mons. Robert trovera mounture pour ses esquiers et le ditz chivaux serount prisez et le dit count fera lui restorer. Et le dit mons. Robert avera la garde du Chastel Bernard[72] od ses appartenauntz a terme de sa vie et se charge bien et loialement garder terres et tenementz, forest et chaces et totes choses au dit chastel appendantz a ses costages demesne et se oblige de loial accompte rendre des issues et proffitz des ditz terres sourdantz et au dit chastel appendanz au dit count et ses heirs et ses executours. Et mettra toutz ministres et tielx pour queux il vaudra respondre et les trovera a ses costages demesne. Et le dit count trovera a ses costages touz mures, de reparailementz de murs, mesons, molyns, enclostures de parke, gard' de foire et custages pour la peise de venison a toutes les foitz que le dit count le vaudra avoir et mettra custages de plee si nuly soit ensemblement od toutz maners des custages pour la suisdite gard et chastel ove ses appartenaunz meyntendre forspris les custages des ministres come suisest dist. Et le dit count trovera en temps de guerre vitailles pour le dit chastel vitailler et covenable garnizaun des gentz darmes et autres defensables solom ceo que la place demande a ses custages forspris les custages le avauntdit mons. Robert et ses autres ministres come desuis est dist.

Et le dit mons. Robert prendra pour lui et pour touz ses ministres feyn pour deys chivaux et buche covenablement pour ses despenses deins le chastel et si damage au trespas soient faitz en les terres,

[71] GEC, xii, pt. 2. 372–5 for Thomas Beauchamp, earl of Warwick (1315–60); there is no good brief account of the important military career of Sir Robert Herle (d. 1364), who fought at Crécy under Beauchamp, and was captain of Calais (1350–2), lieutenant in Brittany (1358–60) and Admiral to the North and West (1361–4).

[72] Barnard Castle, Durham.

tenementz, forestes et chaces ou en autres choses au dit chastel
appendantz par le dit mons. Robert ou par ses ministres le dit mons.
Robert fera les amendes par vewe du seneschal le dit count et par
serement des bones gens del homage. En tesmoignance de quele chose
les ditz count et mons. Robert a ses endentures entrechangeablement
ont mys lours sealx. Escrit a Wanbergh'[73] le marsdy proschein devaunt
la feste de seint George lan du regne [nostre] seignur le Roy Edward
tierz puis le conquest xiij^e.

38 William Bohun, earl of Northampton and Sir William Tollemache,
Ipswich, 20 June 1340 (PRO, DL25/32, sealed on tag).[74]

Sachent touz ceaux qe sount et serrount qe nous William de Bohun,
counte de Northampton et conestable Dengleterre avoms done et
graunte et par ceste presente chartre endente conferme a Mons. William
Thalemache, chyvaler, le manoyr de Lachelye[75] en la counte Dessex
en touz les apartenaunces et avoir et tenir le dit manoir en touz les
apartenaunces a terme de la vie le dit Mons. William Thalemache et
des chiefs seigneurs du fee fesaunt a eux pour nous et pour nos heirs
les services et custumes qe au dit manoir apartenount a terme de la
vie le dit Mons. William. Et nous avauntdit William de Bohun et
nos heirs garanteroms et defendroms lavantdit manoir en touz les
apartenaunces au dit Mons. William Thalemache a terme de sa vye
com avaunt est dit countre totes gentz. Issi qe lavauntdit manoir en
touz les apartenaunces apres le disses du dit William Thalemache a
nous et nos heirs rettourne et remeigne a touz jours pur quel doun a
confermement avauntdit le dit Mons. William Thalemache est demere
au nous pour [pees] et pour guerre par tote sa vie. En tesmoignaunce
de quele chose a ceste partie de chartre endente qe envers le dit Mons.
William Thalemache remeynt nous avauntdit William de Bohun avoms
mys nostre seal et al partie de ceste chartre endente qe envers nous
remeynt le dit Mons. William Thalemache ad mys soun seal par cestes
tesmoignes Mons. John Enganye, Mons. Symoun de Drayton, chyvalers,
Robert de Teye, Johan Sampson, Robert de la Lee et Richard Ayscrop',
Johan atte Grene et austres. Don' a Gippwiz le samady procheyn

---

[73] For Wanborough see 'Abstracts of Feet of Fines relating to Wiltshire for the reigns
of Edward I and Edward II', ed. R. B. Pugh, *Wilts. Rec. Soc.*, i (1939), 126 and 'The
Wiltshire Tax List of 1332', ed. D. A. Crowley, *ibid.* xlv (1989), 26.

[74] Tollemache's small (fragmentary) armorial seal survives. He was going abroad with
William Bohun, earl of Northampton (1337–60) in 1337 (*CPR, 1334–8*, 530; GEC, ix.
664–7) and may be identical with the man pardoned for murder in 1339 (*CPR, 1338–40*,
386; ibid. *1340–3*, 188).

[75] Latchley's Farm, Steeple Bumpstead, Hinchford Hundred, Essex.

devaunt la feste de Nativite Seint Johan Baptist lan du regne le Roy Edward tierce apres la conqueste quatorsyme.[76]

Dorse: Latcheley

39 Henry, earl of Lancaster and Sir Edmund de Ufford, London, 1 March 1347 [French] (PRO, DL27/155, pub. in K. A. Fowler, *The King's Lieutenant. Henry of Grosmont, first duke of Lancaster, 1310–1361* (London, 1969), 234; see also Somerville, *Duchy of Lancaster*, 362).

40 William Montague, earl of Salisbury and Geoffrey Walsh, London, 12 July 1347 (PRO, E101/68/3 no. 68, no trace of sealing. MS damaged).[77]

Ceste endenture faite a Loundres le xiime jour de Juyl lan du regne nostre seignur le roy Edward tierz puis le conquest vintisme primer parentre luy nobles homes mounsire William de Montagu counte de Salesburs dune part et Geffrei Walsh dautre part tesmoigne qe le dit Geffrei est demorre devers le dit counte auxi bien pur pees come pur la guerre, cest assavoir pour la guerre luy mesmes, un chamberleyn maungeauntz en sale ou a livree solunc ceo qe autres de sa condicioun y serount et iij chevaux a livere ou come chevaux des autres de la retenaunce le dit counte y serount, et pour chescun cheval le jour que pour ferure ou comme chevalx de la retenaunce le dit counte y serount, et ii garsouns a table ou a gages come autres garsouns y serount. Et le dit Geffrei sera a mounture propre et son chival darmes sera preise et encas qil sera perdutz en le service le dit counte le dit Geffrei avera restitutioun. Et si le dit Geffrei ou nul des soeuns preigne nul prisoner par fortune de guerre le dit counte avera la moite de sa raunsoun et le dit Geffrei avera lautre moite et ainsi de toutes autres gaynes quecunqes qe serount gaynes sur les guerres mettaunt le dit prisoner au tiel raunson come les ditz counte Geffrei et prisoner pount aconvenir, sur quoi le dit Geffrei prendra du dit counte pur sa demoere en la manere susdite sur les guerres pur lan entier dys livres, cest assavoir la moite au comencement de lan come il sera garniz de venir devers le dit counte pur la guerre et apres de quartier en quartier come il demorra

---

[76] This indenture was drawn up just before Bohun sailed with Edward III's fleet which won the battle of Sluys a week later on St John's day. J. Sumption, *The Hundred Years War. Trial by battle* (London, 1990), 314, claims that in May 1340 he was helping to defend Valenciennes.

[77] GEC, xi. 388–90, for William Montague, earl of Salisbury (1344–97), who served in the Crécy campaign; see also below **48**.

ove le dit counte sur les guerres [. . .] ie le dit Geffrei sera garniz depar le dit counte de venir devers luy pour la guerre le dit counte lui ferra paier le [. . .] gages Dengleterre a comptant resonablement ses journes de son propre pays et en venant et retornant.

Et en cas qe le dit Geffrei passera la mer sur les guerres ove le dit counte, le dit count luy ferra aucun resonable eskipesoun pour luy ses gentz et chevaux susditz passaunt et retornaunt par le bon et agreable counge le dit counte. Et le dit Geffrei prendra du dit counte par an pur sa demoere devers le dit counte pur la pees seisaunte souz et sept deniers as quatre termes de lan principalx luy meismes mangeaunt en sale, un chamberleyn et un garsoun maungeaunt en sale ou a gages solunc ceo qe autres de lour condiciouns y serount et ij chivaux a liveree et a fers et clowes ou come autres chevaux des autres de sa condicioun y serount. Et en cas qe le dit counte se taille de passer devers estranges marches de guerrir sur les enemys Dieu le dit Geffrei ne prendra plus du dit counte sinoun come il ad pris pur la pees.

Dorse: Ceste end. sa tee.
      Endenture des covenances G. Walsh

41 Edward, prince of Wales and Sir John de Sully, London, 27 January 1353 (PRO, E36/278 f. 48v, contemporary enrolment).[78]

Ceste endenture faite parentre lui nobles homme mons. Edward eisnez filz etc. dune part et mons. Johan de Sully chivaler dautrepart tesmoigne que le dit mons. Johan est a terme de sa vie demoree ove le dit prince tant pour le pees comme pour la guerre ove un esquier, et seront en temps de pees le dit mons. Johan et son esquier mangeantz en sale ou as gages de deux deniers le jour, cynk chivals a liveree et quatre garceons as gages, et prendra des autres liverees com[me] un autre des bachelers de la chambre le dit prince. Et en temps de guerre a bouche a court ou a liveree ou as gages come les autres bachelers de la dite chaumbre et avera pour cel temps des chivaux as gages ou a liveree a noefs garceons as gages et sera son corps a la mounture le seigneur pour la guerre. Et prendra le dit mons. Johan annuelement du dit prince quarrante livres pour son fee par les meyns le recevour general le dit prince a Londres que pour le temps sera a les festes de Pentecoste et de Touz Seintz par oweles porcions tanque le dit prince lui est pourveu dautre part ou estre plus en certein del paiement de mesme

---

[78] cf. *BPR*, iv. 91. Sir John Sully K.G., of Iddesleigh, Devon, claiming to be 105 years old, gave evidence in the Scrope-Grosvenor dispute (S&G, i. 74 and ii. 240–3). His first major battle was Halidon Hill (1332).

le fee. En tesmoignance de queu choses les parties devantdites ount a
ceste endenture entrechaungeablement mys lour seals. Don' a Londres
le xxvij jour de janever lan du regne le Roi Edward tierz apres la
conquest Dengleterre vintisme septisme et de France quatorszime.[79]

42 Edward, prince of Wales and Sir John Sully, London, 10 March
1353 (PRO, E36/280 f. 31v, contemporary enrolment).[80]

Ceste endenture faite parentre lui nobles homme mons. Edward eisnez
filz etc. dune part et mons. Johan de Sully dautre part tesmoigne que
le dit mons. Johan est a terme de sa vie de la especiale retenue le dit
Prince demore ove lui tant pour la pees come pour la guerre ove un
esquier. Et seront en temps de pees le dit mons. Johan et son esquier
mangeantz en sale et son chamberlein mangeant en sale ou as gages
de deux deniers le jour, cynk chivalx a liveree de fein et aveines et
ferrure come autres prenont liveree selonc son afferant et quatre
garceons as gages a ses demoers devers la court sil ove tantz des chivals
viegne ou meyns sil viegne ove meyns et prendra des autres liverees
com un autre des Bachelers de la chambre le dit Prince. Et en temps
de guerre a bouche a court ou a liveree ou as gages come les autres
Bachelers de la dite chambre et avera pour cel temps neof chivals as
gages ou a liveree et oet garceons as gages et sera son corps a la
mounture le seigneur pur la guerre. Et quant il vendra devers le
seigneur a ses mandementz et par ses lettres il avera ses custages en
venant par resonables journees que seont acompter et allowez el hostiel
le dit Prince. Et prendra le dit mons. Johan annuelement du dit Prince
quarrant livres pour son fee des issues de son manoir de Bradenynche
el countee de Devenes'[81] a les festes de la Pentecoste et de Touz
Seintz par oweles porcions. En tesmoignance de que chose les parties
devantdites ount a ceste endenture entrechangeablement mis lours
seals. Don' a Londres le x jour de Marcz lan du regne le Roi etc.
Dengleterre xxxvij et de France xiiij.[82]

[79] Noted in margin that payment of the fee was later assigned to receipts from Devon;
see below **42**.
[80] cf. *BPR*, ii. 45.
[81] Bradninch, Devon.
[82] This indenture is followed in the register by letters of the prince (12 March 1353)
announcing that Sully's fee was to be taken from the manor of Bradninch at the Feast
of St John the Baptist and All Saints and ordering his receiver there to make payment
(another copy of which appears on PRO, C66/301 m. 12); by further letters (14 March
1353) to the auditors of the prince's accounts to allow this expense in the accounts of the
receiver and further letters (14 March 1353) to John Dabernoun and John de Kendale,
steward and receiver of the duchy of Cornwall, informing them of the retaining of Sully,
whose fee was to be paid from the issues of Bradninch previously used to pay the fee of
100 marks which the late Henry Eam received on that manor.

43 James Butler, earl of Ormond and Oliver Howell, Clonmel, Tipperary, 9 May 1356 (NLI, Ormond Deeds D 1008, formerly sealed on tag).[83]

Nono die Maii anno Regis Edwardi tercii post conquestum regni sui Anglie tricesimo apud Clomell. Ita convenit inter nobilem virum dominum Jacobum le Botiller, comitem Ermonie ex parte una et Oliverum Howell' ex parte altera videlicet quod dictus Oliverus moram suam cum dicto domino comite fecit ad serviendum ei tota vita ipsius Oliveri cum toto posse suo infra comitatum Kilkenn'[84] et marchias suas ubique adiacentes tam de pace quam de guerra et alibi per totam terram Hibernie cum quatuor hominibus ad arma equis coopertis, duodecim hobellariis et quadraginta sufficientibus peditibus de Kethern[85] per racionabilem premunicionem contra quoscumque domino Rege et heredibus comitis Dessemon[86] exceptis sumptibus dicti comitis Ermonie nisi ad domum suam reddire valeat percipiendo de dicto domino comite Ermonie pro mora sua predicta centum marcas argenti inde incontinentis solvendis decem marcas et ad festum Sancti Michaelis proxime futuro sex marcas et ad festum Pasche tunc proxime sequens sex marcas et sic de anno in annum proxime sequenciis ad terminos consimiles sex marcas quousque de predictis centum marcarum plenarie fuerit persolutis. Ita videlicet quod si dictus dominus comes Ermonie in solucione dictarum centum marcarum predicto Olivero ad terminos predictos in forma predicta solvend' defecerit quod bene liceat predicto Olivero de servicio suo in forma predicta faciend' cessare quousque ei satisfact' fuerit et predictus Oliverus concedit pro se heredibus et executoriis suis quod si ipse de servicio suo eidem domino comite Ermonie ut predictum est faciend' defecerit quod extunc teneatur restituere predicto domino comite Ermonie dampna sua que sibi contigerit habere pro defectu servicii dicti Oliveri in hac parte. Insuper dictus Oliverus concedit quo ipse arma militaria a predicto domino comite Ermonie preceteris aliis dominis recipiet cum ad illa fuerit paratus ita quod dictus dominus comes Ermonie taliter facere et deserviet erga dictum Oliverum qualiter aliquis alius dominus faceret sibi pro armis militariis ab eo recipiend' et ad maiorem huius rei

[83] This document and nos. **44, 45, 68, 90** and **129** are published by kind permission of the Council of the Trustees of the National Library of Ireland, to whom we are deeply grateful. See also *Cal. of Ormond Deeds*, ed. E. Curtis, ii. *1350–1413 A.D.* (Dublin, 1934), no. 33. GEC, x. 119–21 for James Butler, second earl of Ormond (1338–82); Robin Frame, *English Lordship in Ireland 1318–1361* (Oxford, 1982), 299 for Howell, fragments of whose seal survive.

[84] Kilkenny.

[85] *Kethern*, kerns, light-armed soldiers.

[86] Morice Fitz Thomas, first earl of Desmond died on 25 January 1356 and was succeeded by his son Morice, a minor (GEC, iv. 237–41).

securitatem convenciones predicta fideliter tenend' dictus Oliverus
tactis sacrosanctis Ewangeliis sacramentum prestitit corporale apud
Waterford[87] in presencia abbatis de Jeryponte,[88] magistri Walteri Reve,
Decani Waterford, Thome le Botiller, Petri le Botiller, Nicholai le
Lumbard, Willelmi de Fallesleye, Willelmi Ilger et aliis. In cuius rei
testimonium huic indenture parti penes dictum dominus comes Ermonie
residenti dictus Oliverus sigillum suum apposuit.

44 James Butler, earl of Ormond and Sir Richard de Burgh, Cashel,
Ireland, 16 July 1356 (NLI, Ormond Deeds D 1012, formerly sealed on
tag).[89]

Hec indentura facta apud Cassell' sextodecimo die Julii anno Regis
Edwardi tercii post conquestum regni sui Anglie tricesimo inter nobilem
virum dominum Jacobum le Botiller comitem Ermonie ex parte una
et dominum Ricardum filium Edmundi de Burgo ex altera testatur
quod dictus dominus Ricardus moram suam fecit cum dicto domino
comite ad deserviendum sibi cum toto posse suo tota vita ipsius domini
Ricardi in omnibus ipsius dicti domini comitis agendis tam in guerra
quam in pace contra quoscumque, domino Rege et suis liberis filiis
dumtaxat exceptis, sumptibus ipsius domini Ricardi in partibus ubi
eadem nocte ad propria declinare poterit, et alibi sumptibus ipsius
domini comitis. Pro quaquidem mora dictus dominus comes concessit
dicto domino Ricardo centum libras argenti solvendas inde dicto
domino Ricardo vel suo certo atornato infra istam mensem proximam
futuram decem libras et ad festum Pasche proxime sequitur decem
libras, et exinde viginti libras per annum ad festa Michaelis et Pascha
per equales porciones quousque predicte centum libre plenarie fuerint
persolute. Preterea dictus dominus comes concessit et manucepit dictum
dominum Ricardum juvare, fovere et manutenere in omnibus iustis
querelis suis sicut dominus suum militem aut suum vassalum fovere,
juvare et manutenere tenetur. Quomodo idem dictus Ricardus ad
pacem et fidelitatem dicti domini comitis se gesserit. Et eciam si
contingat dictum dominum Ricardum in comitiva dicti comitis aliquos
suos equos interfectos habere quod dictus dominus comes tenetur dicto
domino Ricardo pro eisdem respicere. Et ad istam concordiam fideliter
observandam partes predicte tactis sacrosanctis evangeliis sacramentum

---

[87] Co. Waterford.

[88] Jerpoint, Kilkenny.

[89] cf. *Cal. of Ormond Deeds*, ed. Curtis, ii. no. 37, for an earlier edition; Frame, *English Lordship*, 45 for commentary. Richard de Burgh was a grandson of Richard de Burgh, earl of Ulster (1271–1326): GEC, xii, pt. 2. 173–7.

prestiterunt corporale in presencia venerabilium patrem Radulphi dei gracia Cassellensis Archiepiscopi et domini Thome Laonensis[90] episcopi, fratris Stephani prioris de Athessell', domini Johannis Lerchedekne militis, Johannis Laffan, magistri Thome Reve clerici, Ricardi filii Galfridi de Burgo, Nicholai le Lumbard et aliorum. In cuius rei testimonium huic indenture sigilla sua alternatim apposuerunt. Data die et anno ut supra.

45 James Butler, earl of Ormond and Geoffrey son of John le Poer, Carrickmagriffin, 25 August 1356 (NLI, Ormond Deeds D 1014, formerly sealed on tag).[91]

Die Jovis proxime post festum Sancti Bartholomei apostoli anno Regis Edwardi tercii post conquestum regni sui Anglie tricesimo apud Cargemagriffyn, ita convenit inter nobilem virum dominum Jacobum Le Botiller comitem Ermonie ex parte una et Galfridum filium Johannis le Poer ex altera, videlicet quod predictus Galfridus moram suam fecit cum dicto domino comite ad serviendum sibi contra quoscumque, domino Rege excepto, ad totam vitam ipsius Galfridus cum toto posse suo, sumptibus suis propriis in marchiis suis ubi eadem die ad propria redire valeat et alibi in Hibernie sumptibus ipsius dominus comes. Pro quaquidem mora dictus dominus comes concessit sibi viginti libras argenti solvendas inde decem marcas per annum ad festum Michaelis et Pasche per equales porciones termino inapiente ad festum Sancti Michaelis proximo futuro. Et dictus dominus comes concessit dictum Galfridum juvare et manutenere sicut et dominus tenetur facere. Et ulterius concessit quod si contingat dominum Galfridum aliquos equos in servicio ipsius dominus comes habere interfectos vel arma perdere, quod dictus dominus comes teneatur pro valore eorumdem sibi satisfacere. Et ad ista fideliter observandum dictus Galfridus tactis sacrosanctis Evangeliis juramentum prestitit corporale. In cuius rei testimonium partes predicte huic indentura sigilli sua alternatim apposuerunt. Datum die et anno supradictis.

46 Edward, prince of Wales and Sir Baldwin de Freville, London, 8 August 1358 (University of Nottingham, Middleton Deeds, Mi F 10/8, formerly sealed on tongue, with a tying thong).[92]

---

[90] Killaloe, Clare.

[91] cf. *Cal. of Ormond Deeds*, ed. Curtis, ii. no. 39, with date 1 Sept. 1356.

[92] We are grateful to the Hon. Michael Willoughby as owner and to the University of Nottingham as custodian for permission to publish (cf. above **18** and *HMC, Middleton*, 98); for a near contemporary copy see PRO, E36/278 f. 148v (*BPR*, iv. 80, 259).

Ceste endenture faite parentre lui nobles homme monsieur Edward
eisnez filz au noble Roi Dengleterre et de Fraunce, prince de Gales,
ducs de Cornewaille, et counte de Cestre, dune part, et Monsieur
Baudewyn de Frevill',[93] dautre part, tesmoigne que le dit Monsieur
Baudewyn est pour terme de sa vie demoree ove le dit prince prenant
pour son service qil ferra au dit prince annuelement quarrante livres a
terme de la vie de le dit Monsieur Baudewyn des issues et profitz
sourdantz du manoir de Cheillesmore de la ville de Coventree et de la
feeferme de la Priorie de Coventree, par les meyns du receivour ou
autre gardein le dit prince illeoques, qi pour le temps serra, a les termes
de Seint Michiel et de Pasques par oweles porcions.[94] Et que a quele
heure que le dit prince irra pur la guerre, le dit monsieur Baudewyn
prendra pour tauntz des gentz come il amenera ove le dit prince ataunt
come autres de son estate prendront pour l'afferant des gentz q'il
amenera. En tesmoignance de quele chose auxibien le dit prince come
le dit monsieur Baudewyn ount a ceste endenture entrechaungeablement mis lour seals. Donne a Londres le viij jour d'Augst, lan du
regne le Roi Edward tierz apres le conquest Dengleterre trentism
secound et de Fraunce disneofism.

47 Sir Ralph de Hastings and John de Kirkeby of Wigginthorpe, York,
14 July 1362 (San Marino, California, Henry E. Huntington Library,
Hastings MSS, HAP Box 1 no. 18, sealed on tongue).[95]

Ceste endenture fait parentre monsire Rauf de Hastinges chivalier dune
part et Johan de Kyrkeby de Wyginthorpe[96] daultre part tesmoigne qe
le dit monsire Rauf et le dit Johan sount acordez en manere qe ensuyt.
Cest asavoir qe le dit Johan demurra devers le dit monsire Rauf a ses
robes au terme de sa vie saunz estre remowe se il ne soit par resonable

---

[93] Sir Baldwin de Freville (c. 1315–75) of Tamworth, Staffs., had his fee increased to
100 marks p.a. for good services past and future in 1362 (*ibid.*, 427).

[94] Temporary arrangements for payment were made in April 1359 when Edward III
assigned these revenues to the executors of Queen Isabella but the original terms came
into force at Michaelmas 1359; in the interim Freville was appointed keeper of the park
of Cheillesmore (*BPR*, iv. 271, 288, 311).

[95] Seal: A lion rampant (Hastings); born about 1339, Ralph succeeded his uncle,
Robert Herle, in his Leicestershire estates and testified in the Scrope-Grosvenor case (S&
G, i. 103–4, ii. 283–5).

[96] Hastings and Kirkeby had been in disagreement for some time, their dispute
apparently arising from Kirkeby's former position as steward and receiver to Hasting's
father; in Feb. 1353 Kirkeby had sought a commission of *oyer et terminer* to investigate
assaults allegedly committed on him at Wigginthorpe by Sir Ralph Hastings and others:
W. Dugdale, *The Baronage of England* (London, 1676), i. 195; *CPR, 1350–4*, 447. For another
grant of a livery robe to an esquire by Hastings: Huntington Library, HAD 3329.

cause trove par bones gentz, cest assavoir monsire Brian de Stapleton, Richard de Aske, Johan de Fencotes, Johan de Aymunderly, Johan de Pykerynge et aultres. Et si encas qe riens soit parle de asqune manere de grevance chargeant de part le dit Johan touchant le dit monsire Rauf le dit Johan vendra en presence le dit monsire Rauf et si il ne purroit estre escuse des grevances en tiele manere faitz le dit Johan fera les amendes au dit monsire Rauf par descretion des bones gentz avantditz. Et si ensy soit qe le dit monsire Rauf face riens si bien noun devers le dit Johan bien lise au gentz susditz de redresser les trespasses myewez entre eux a manere susdit. En tesmoinance du quele chose a icestes endentures les avantditz monsire Rauf et Johan de Kirkeby entrechaungeablement ount mys lour seals. Escrit a Everwyk le quatorszime jour de July lan du regne le roy Edward tierce apres le conqueste trent[e]sisme.

48 William de Montague, earl of Salisbury and Sir Edmund Donmere, Christchurch, Hants., 29 March 1364 (PRO, E326/B4915, sealed on tag).[97]

Ceste endenture feate parentre monsire William de Montagu counte de Sarum dun part et monsire Edmund Donmere[98] daultre part tesmoigne que od le dit monsire Edmund eit le manoir de Swire[99] a terme de sa vie de doun le dit counte pur son bon et greable service feate et a faire le dit monsire Edmund grante par le dit doun par cest endenture que il demorra pardever le dit counte si bien en temps de pees come en gerre par la ou en queux parties le dit counte seo prendra une viage a gerre, issint que le dit counte face a dit monsire Edmund paiement et[a] allowance pur son eskier et ces aultres gentez les queux il est assigne par le dit counte[b] et pur ces chivalx come il feat a aultres de sa retenue de soun estat. En tesmoignance de quele chose al une partie de ceste endenture demorant devers le dit monsire Edmund le dit counte ad mys son seal et al autre partie de la dite endenture demorant dever le dit counte le dit monsire Edmund as mys son seal. Don' a Cristchurch le vynt et noefysme jour de marz lan du regne le roi Edward tierce puis le conqueste trentisme utisme.

Dorse: Edward. Endenture de la demeure monsire Esmond de

---

[97] A fair impression of Donmere's armorial seal survives.
[98] From a Dorsetshire family, Sir Edmund witnessed two deeds of Montague dated at London on 31 July 1360 and at Canford, Dorset, on 24 June 1364 (*CCR, 1364–8*, 205, 489).
[99] Swyre, Dorset.

Dunmere devers lui conte de Sarum.

xxiij[100]

a. paiement et interlined
b. counte interlined

49 Edward, prince of Aquitaine and Wales and Sir Geoffrey de
Warburton, Chester, 6 June 1365 (Manchester, John Rylands University
Library, Arley Charters, Box 14 no. 5, sealed on tongue).[101]

Ceste endenture tesmoigne que monsire Geffrey de Werberton'[102] est
demore devers lui nobles et puissant seignur le Prince Daquitaine et de
Gales pur paix et pur guerre ove deux esquiers comenceant le jour qil
remuera par mandement le dit Prince de sa maison vers la mier a
passer as parties Daquitaine. Et prendra le dit monsire Geffrey quarrant
livres par an pur son fee dount il serra paie de la moitie devaunt la
meyn et gages pur lui, ses gentz et chivalx come autres de son estat
prendront ses journees acomptees tanqa sa venue au dit Prince a queu
temps il serra a bouche au court et prendra gages pur ses ditz gentz et
chivalx come autres ses compaignons ensemble eskipson sufficeant pur
lui, ses gentz et chivalx en passant la mier et retournant en service du
dit Prince. En tesmoignance de quele chose les parties avauntditz a
ceste endenture entrechangeablement ount mis lours sealx. Donne a
Cestre le sism[e] jour de Juyn lan du regne le Roi Edward tierce puis
le conquest trent neofism[e].

50 Edward, prince of Aquitaine and Wales and Sir Aubrey de Vere,
London, 1 October 1367 (PRO, C66/300 m. 6, *inspeximus* of 22 March
1378).[103]

Ceste endenture tesmoigne que mons. Aubry de Veer est demorez pour
terme de sa vie avec li nobles et puissant seignour le Prince Daquitaine

---

[100] No further indentures of William Montague, earl of Salisbury (1344–97) have been
discovered though by letters patent of 15 August 1381 he announced that he had retained
Sir William Faringdon for life with a fee of £40 p.a. (*Monumenta de Insula Manniae*, ed. J.
R. Oliver [The Manx Society, vii, Douglas 1861], ii. 205–7).

[101] Damaged impression of the prince's seal in white wax: England, a label of three
points, 41mm. diameter; this indenture is reproduced by courtesy of the Director and
University Librarian, the John Rylands University Library of Manchester.

[102] G. Ormerod, *The History of the County Palatine and City of Chester*, ed. T. Helsby, 3
vols. (Chester, 1882), i. 570 for Sir Geoffrey de Warburton (b. before 1338 – d. after 1381),
citing this indenture; see also below **141**.

[103] cf. *CPR, 1377–81*, 161.

et de Gales pour paix et pour guerre et prendra le dit mons. Aubry de dit Prince pour le bon service que li a fait einz ces heures et ferra pour le temps avenir centz marz desterlinges par an pour soun fee, en partie de quele somme le dit Prince a grantez et donez au dit mons. Aubry durante sa vie son manoir de Newport en Essex[104] ove les appartenances en value de cinquante marz par an forspris toufoiz feodez de chivalers, avoesons des esglise, gardes, mariages, forfaites et eschetes. Et sera le dit mons. Aubry servez de cinquante marz que demoerent en leschequer de dit Prince a Cestre. En tesmoignance de quele choses les parties avantdites ont a ceste endenture entrechangeablement mys lours seelx. Donne a Londres le primier jour Doctobre lan de regne le Roy Edward tiers apres le conquest quarantisme primier.[105]

51 Edward, prince of Aquitaine and Wales, and Sir Baldwin de Bereford, London, 1 October 1367 (PRO, C66/302 m. 36, *inspeximus* of 22 March 1378).[106]

Ceste endenture tesmoigne que mons. Baudewyn de Bereford est demoree pour terme de sa vie devers le noble et puissant seignour le prince Daquitaine et de Gales pour paix et pour guerre. Et prendra le dit mons. Baudewyn du dit prince pour le bon service qil li ad fait et fera quarrante livres par an pour son fee dont il sera serviz de issues sourdanz de la seignourie de Coventre par les mayns du seneschal, fermier, recevour ou autre ministre illeoques que pour le temps sera as termes de Seint Michel et de Pasques par owelles porcions. Et trouvera au dit prince en temps de guerre deux esquiers sufficeantz saunz autre fee prendra pour li ou pour les ditz esquiers. En tesmoingnance de quele chose les parties avandictes ont a ceste endenture entre-chaungeablement mys lour sealx. Donne a Londres le primier jour doctobre lan du regne le Roy Edward tiers apres le conquest qua-rantisme primier.

[104] Newport, Essex.
[105] Three further letters of the prince re-assigning Aubrey de Vere's fee of 50 marks p.a. on the Exchequer of Chester to £100 p.a. on the Stannaries of Cornwall (31 August 1369), naming him constable of Wallingford Castle at £40 p.a. (22 July 1375) and adding £10 p.a. to that fee (23 July 1375), were also confirmed by Richard as prince of Wales (15 February 1377) and subsequently as king (cf. also *DKR* 36 (1875), 494).
[106] cf. *CPR, 1377–81*, 209–10; Bean, 61 inadvertently cites C66/301 m. 36. A marginal note mentions that on 12 March 1395 Richard II gave Bereford the manor of 'Fertyngton' [Fortyngton, Dorset] for life, cancelling the annuity granted in this indenture (cf. *CCR, 1391–6*, 582–3); for his career as a chamber knight, see C. Given-Wilson, *The Royal Household and the King's Affinity* (New Haven & London, 1986), 31, 62, 161–2, 219, 232.

52 Roger, lord Clifford and Sir Robert Mowbray agree on terms augmenting a previous indenture, Skelton, Cumbria, 28 October 1368 (Oxford, Bodleian Library, MS Dodsworth 70 f. 41v, 17th c. transcript).

Ceste endenture fait parentre mons. Roger de Clifford, seigneur de Weymorland, dun part et mons. Robert Moubray[107] daltrepart tesmoigne que come le dit mons. Robert est demore od le dit mons. Roger pour peas et pour guerre a tout la vie le dit mons. Roger, pernant pour sa demore en temps de peas dys livres par an et de guerre quarrant marcez comme en une endenture ont entre eux fait plus pleynement appiert, le dit mons. Roger pour greignour surete faire al dit mons. Robert de les dys livres avantditz ad lesse et par ceste endenture confirme al dit mons. Robert son manoire de Skelton ov les appurtenauntes en la counte de Cumbirland a avoir a tout la vie le dit mons. Robert, salva[n]t la revercion al dit mons. Roger et ses heirs, le quel manoire est extendu a dyssoeit livres rendant[a] par an al dit mons. Roger et ses heirs seit livres as festes de Pasque et de Seynt Michiell par oweles porcions, et sil le dit rent de oeit[108] livres soit a dere du partie ou du tout par un mois apres nule des termes avantditz, adonqes bien lise al dit mons. Roger et ses heires en le dit manoire destreindre et les destresces retenir tanque gree lour soit fait del rent susdit, ou du tiel qe le dit rent de seit livres soit a derer par quarant jours apres nuls des termes susditz bien lise al dit mons. Roger et ses heires dentrer le dit manoire et saunz contredit du dit mons. Robert en son primir estate tenir sur tiell condicion que si le dit manoir soit destraint[b] par les enemys en temps avenir ou degaste[c] ou empayre par cause de pestilence ou ascune alters sodeygne chaunce dont home ne pint[d] a ore avoire conisaunce et ne mys en difaute, le dit mons. Robert, adonqes en le paiement ad les oeit livres avantditz tant sera receps dedanz en an solonc le ferrant del gaste et destitucion, par discretion de meultz norrys du pais, et le dit mons. Roger et ses heirs le dit manoir ou les appurtenaunts al dit mons. Robert pour toute sa vie en le fourme avant dite garont, tenront et defendront contre toutz gentz, pour quel lese, conferment et garantie suisditz le dit mons. Robert ad relesse al dit mons. Roger la dit rent de dize livres pour temps de peas a prendre. En tesmoignaunce de[e] quele chose les parties avantditz a les parties de

---

[107] Robert Mowbray of Bolton in Allerdale, Cumbs., a manor he held for life by grant of Edward III. In the years following this indenture Mowbray occupied a prominent position in county affairs, representing Cumberland in the Parliaments of June 1369, Nov. 1372, Oct. 1377 and Jan. 1380 and acting as sheriff of the county Dec. 1372 – Nov. 1375 (*CCR, 1369–74*, 101, 476; ibid., *1377–81*, 105, 355; *CFR, 1369–77*, 190). The arrangements outlined in this indenture had already been confirmed by the king in July 1367 (*CPR, 1364–7*, 424–5).

[108] The figures given do not add up; our edition prints those provided in the MS.

cestes endentures entrechaungeablement ont[f] mys lours sealx. Escrit a Skelton le jour des Appostoiles Seyntz Symond et Jude lan du regne le Roi Edward tierce puis le conquest quarantisme secounde.[109]

a. Followed by *ent* in MS
b. *Sic* for *?destruict*
c. Followed by *le dit mons. Robert* struck out
d. After *puit* struck out
e. Followed by *chele* struck out
f. Followed by *my* struck out

53 Letters patent of Humphrey Bohun, earl of Hereford announcing that he has retained William de Stapleton, esquire in peace and war for life for an annual fee of £20, Camelot, 10 May 1370 (PRO, C66/288 m. 23, *inspeximus* of 18 March 1373).[110]

Sachent tout gent nous Humfrey de Bohun, conte de Hereford, Dessex et de Norhampton et Conestable Dengleterre avons done et grauntee a nostre bien ame esquier William de Stapleton une annuele rente de vint livres a terme de sa vie pur son bon et greable service qil nous ad fait et ferra si bien en pees come en guerre ou qi nous sumes durant sa vie a prendre dan en an la dite annuele rente de nostre manoir de Longbenyngton[111] et de touz noz terres en le countee de Huntyngdon as termes de Seint Mich' et de Pasque par oweles porcions. Et nous volons qe si la dite annuele rente de vint livres soit aderiere en partie ou en tout oet jours apres aucunes des termes avantditz durant sa vie qe bien lise a dit William et a son attourne en nostre dit manoir de Longebenyngton ou ses appurtenances en touz les terres en le countee de Huntyngdon susdite destreindre et les destresces enchacer et retenir tanqe gree lui soit fait de la dite annuele rente ensemblement ove les arrerages si aucuns y soient, et a greindre sieurte faire au dit William de mesme celle annuele rente nous lui avons done pour lui mettre en possession sys souldz oet deniers de noz coffres. Et nous Humfrey de Bohun et noz heirs la dite annuele rente de vint livres au dite William garantrons a terme de sa vie. En tesm' de queu chose a ceste nostre fait endente avons fait mettre nostre seal. Done a Camelot[112] le dysme

---

[109] T. D. Whitaker, *The History and Antiquities of the Deanery of Craven in the County of York*, 3rd edn., ed. A. W. Morant (Leeds & London, 1878), 315 notes this indenture and prints two indentures of war (1369, 1379) contracted by Roger, fifth lord Clifford (1345–89), for whom see also S&G, i. 197–8, ii. 469–72, GEC, iii. 292 and below **67** and **74**.

[110] cf. *CPR, 1370–4*, 261; GEC, vi. 473–4 for Humphrey, earl of Hereford (1361–73).

[111] Long Bennington, Parts of Kesteven, Lincs.

[112] Camelot, county unidentified.

jour de May lan du regne le Roy Edward tiercz puis le conquest quarant quart.

54 Thomas Beauchamp, earl of Warwick and John Durant, London, 24 October 1370 (Burghley House, Stamford, Exeter MS 76/88, sealed on tag).[113]

Ceste endenture faite parentre mons. Thomas de Beauchamp, conte de Warr' et seignour de Gower dune part et Johan Duraunt[114] dautre part tesmoigne que come le dit conte eit graunte au dit Johan a terme de sa vie dys livres dannuele rente a prendre de son manoir de Bernghdon' come piert par un escrit du dit conte ent fait as termes contenuz en le dit escrit, le dit Johan veut et graunte a demorer ove le dit conte de peas et de guerre pour terme de sa vie en manere que senseut, cest assavoir pour la peas lui mesmes, deux chivaux et un garzon as quelle houre qil serra mande de venir au dit conte par tiele manere. Et quant il serra mande de venir au dit conte pour la guerre, il vendra mesmes a sa mounture propre ou un chaumberlain, trois chivaux et deux garzons prenant gages acustumez par le chemin et en loistiel du dit conte bouche a court pour lui mesmes et son chamberlein, fein et aveigne et ferrure pour ses trois chivaux avantditz, gages acustumes pour ses deux garzons, sil les eit, et eskipison ove le dit conte en alant et retournant, et serra la mounture le dit Johan prise et a lui restore solent le pris alloue par le Roi sil perisse de guerre. Et a quelle houre que le dit Johan travaille de guerre ovesque son dit seignour, il prendra par an dys marcz dencres outre les dys livres avantdites par les meins du gardein del hostiel le dit conte. Et avera le dit conte la moite des ranceons des prisoners et dautres quecumques profitz que pourront happer de guerre au dit Johan ou a ses gentz. Et si le dit Johan preigne prisoner, qil ne soit mys a ranceon sanz assent le dit conte ou autre son depute a ce par lui assigne. En tesmoign' de quelle chose a cestes endentures les avantditz conte et Johan entre-changeablement ont mys lours sealx. Donne a Loundres le vintisme quart jour Doctobre lan du regne le Roi Edward tierz puis le conquest quarant quart.

[113] Published by permission of the Marquess of Exeter. Sealed in red wax, with an armorial seal, four crosses on a large cross imposed on an escutcheon (Beauchamp); cf. GEC, xii, pt. 2. 375–8 for Thomas, earl of Warwick (1369–1401). We are grateful to Dr Alix Sinclair for bringing this document to our attention and to Nicholas Humphrey, Assistant House Manager at Burghley for providing a copy and other information.

[114] Durant may be connected with the Durants of Barston, Warwicks., rather than those of Alsthorpe, Rutland (cf. *HC, 1386–1421*, ii. 810–11).

Dorse: Johannes Duraunt retent' p[r]o ad[ ]ediat'

55 Edward, prince of Aquitaine and Wales and Sir Thomas Guysing, Caernarvon, 5 October 1371 (PRO, C66/304 m. 13, *inspeximus* of 5 May 1379).[115]

Presens indentura facta inter illustrissimum dominum nostrum dominum Edwardum, illustris Regis Anglie et Francie primogenitum, Principum Aquitanie et Wallie, Ducem Cornub', comitem Cestri et dominum Biscaye et Castri de Ordialibus, ex parte una, et Thomas Guyssyng chivaler,[116] ex altera parte, testatur quod idem dominus nostri Princeps pro bono et laudabili servicio eidem domino nostro principi per prefatum Thomam hactenus impenso et impendendo in futuri, idem dominus princeps dedit et concessit eidem Thome, durante vita sua, quadraginta libras percipiendas quolibet anno in scaccario eiusdem domini nostri principis apud Caern' per manus camerarii dicti nostri principis ibidem, qui pro tempore fuerit, ad terminos Pasche et Sancti Michaelis per equales porciones, pro qua quidem annuitate idem dominus nostri princeps vult quod idem Thomas teneatur eidem domino nostro principi cum uno armigero sufficienti tempore guerre de servire absque eo quod idem Thomas aliquid aliud feodum de dicto domino nostro principe per se aut armigero suo percipiat antedicto. In cuius rei testimonium huic parti presentis indenture penes dictum Thomas remanenti idem dominus nostri principis sigillum suum cancellarii sue quo utitur in North Wall' apponi demandavit, alteri vero parti presentis indenture pene dictus dominum nostrum principum remanenti idem Thomas sigillum suum apposuit. Dat' apud Caern' quinto die Octobri anno regni illustrissimi domini nostri Regis Anglie quadragesimo quinto et Francie tricesimo secundo.

[115] cf. *CPR, 1377–81*, 345; cf. Bean, 61 n. 76 with incomplete reference.

[116] Sir Thomas Guysing (Gissing, Norfolk) complained on 10 March 1371 that while he had recently been in the Prince's service in Aquitaine and his properties were in the king's protection, Robert Harsent and others, including several clerics, had ravished his wife, Agnes, taken her and his goods away and still detained them (*CPR, 1370–4*, 104–5). As late as 1376 he was pardoned for £60 demanded from him for the goods of Harsent, put in exigent for felony, which were forfeit to the king (*ibid.*, 288). He had been a prominent member of the Bench in Cambridgeshire from 1361 (*CPR, 1361–4*, 21, 285, 371, 529; *ibid., 1367–70*, 195), sat as shire knight for Norfolk in the Good Parliament (*CCR, 1374–7*, 429) and was a member of the commission of *oyer et terminer* which inquired into the assault on Henry Despenser, bishop of Norwich by the inhabitants of Bishop's Lynn in 1377 (*CPR, 1374–7*, 502). Reunited with Agnes, in 1373 he delivered seisin of his manor of Kingston, Cambridgeshire, to Sir Robert Swillington the uncle in a complicated transaction (*CCR, 1369–74*, 552–4).

56 Edward, prince of Aquitaine and Wales and Sir William Wasteneys, Caernarvon, 5 October 1371 [Latin] (PRO, C66/302 m. 1, *inspeximus* and confirmation of letters of confirmation of Richard as Prince of Wales, Caernarvon, 28 Feb. 1377).[117]

57 Edward Le Despenser, lord of Glamorgan and Morgannwg and Sir Thomas Arthur, London, 16 November 1372 (PRO, C66/359 m. 18, *inspeximus* of 23 Feb. 1400).[118]

Hec indentura facta inter illustrem et magnificum dominum dominum Edwardum le Despenser Glamorg' et Morg' dominum generalem ex parte una et dilectum suum militem Thomam Arthur ex parte altera testatur quod idem dominus Edwardus libere concessit et confirmavit predicto Thome Arthur militi pro bono et laudabili servicio suo[a] et impenso et ad totam vitam suam imposterum impendendo quandam annuam pensionem viginti librarum sterlingorum recipiendo annuatim de scaccario suo in castro de Kerdife[119] ad duos terminos Pasche videlicet et Sancti Michaelis Archangeli per equales porciones omnes annos ad totam vitam Thome Arthur militis supradictus prefatus, tamen Thomas Arthur miles sponte promittit de sua fidelitate stare et venire per totum tempus antedictum serviens et mandatis quibuscumque dicti domini Edwardi licitis et honestis tam in tempore pacis quam guerre pro predicta annua pensione viginti librarum quocienscumque per ipsum seu aliquem alium sui parte debite fuerit premunitus et hoc ad omnes expensas licitas et usuales in curie dicti domini Edwardi et eciam ad eius expensas licitas eundo et redeundo omni vice que pro suis negociis per ipsum aliunde transmittatur. In cuius rei testimonium presentibus indenturis sigilla parcium alternatim sunt appensa, hiis testibus Johanne Daundesey, Johanne de Thorp, Edwardo Dalyngrigg, militibus, Thoma Mortymer, Thoma Lyouns, Johanne Fallesley et aliis militis. Dat' Londonie die decimo sexto mensis novembris anno domini millesimo CCC[mo] septuagesimo secundo anno vero regni Regis Anglie Edwardi tercii post conquestum quadragesimo sexto.

a. suo interlined

[117] This indenture repeats the terms of **55** verbatim; cf. *CPR, 1377–81*, 249 and Bean, 61 n. 76 with incorrect reference. The domestic career of Wasteneys is traced in *Trans. Worcs. Arch. Soc.*, 3rd ser. 5 (1976), 20; he received a protection for service as a knight with the prince on 12 Feb. 1369 (PRO, C61/82 m. 12).

[118] cf. *CPR, 1399–1401*, 244. GEC, iv. 274–8 for Edward, fourth lord Despenser (1357–75), and *HC, 1386–1421*, ii. 57–8 for Sir Thomas Arthur (d. 1404) of Clapton in Gordano, Somerset.

[119] Cardiff.

58 Edward, Le Despenser, lord of Glamorgan and Morgannwg and Nicholas Bernak, esquire, London 25 November 1372 (PRO, C66/313 m. 12, *inspeximus* of 4 Nov. 1382).[120]

Hec indentura facta inter illustrem et magnificum dominum dominum Edwardum Le Despenser Glamorg' et Morg' domini generalem ex parte una et suum dilectum scutiferum Nicholaum Bernak ex parte altera testatur quod idem dominus Edwardus libere concessit et confirmavit predicto Nicholao quandam annualem pensionem viginti marcarum sterlingorum pro bono et laudabili servicio suo sibi impenso et ad totam vitam suam imposterum impendendo recipiendo annuatim de manerio predicti domini Edwardi de Bokland in com. Bokyng'[121] ad duos anni terminos Pasche videlicet et Sancti Michaelis Archangeli per equales porciones. Et si contingat predictam annuam pensionem viginti marcarum aretro esse ad aliquam termini in parte vel in toto per duodecim dies quod extunc bene liceat prefato Nicholao Bernak in predicto manerio de Boklond cum omnibus suis partem distringere districionesque si quas invenerit abducere et eas penes se retinere quousque de predicta annua pensione viginti marcarum cum omnibus dampnis et expensis super huiusmodi detencione factis plenarie et integre sibi fuerit satisfactum, prefatus tamen Nicholaus Bernak sponte promittit de sua fidelitate stare et venire serviciis et mandatis quibuscumque dicti domini Edwardi licitis et honestis per totum tempus antedictum tam in tempore pacis quam guerre quocienscumque per ipsum vel aliquem aliam sui nomine debite fuerit pronunnciis per predicta pensione viginti marcarum et hoc ad omnes expensas licitis et usuales in curie dicti domini Edwardi et eciam ad eius expensas licitas eundo et redeundo omni vice que pro suis negociis per ipsum aliunde transmittitur. In cuius rei testimonio presentibus indenturis sigilla predicti alternatim sunt appensa hiis testibus Johane Daudeseye, Johane de Thorp, Edwardo Dalyngrigg, militibus, Thoma Mortymer, Thoma Lyons, Henr' Zakesley et aliis multis. Dat' London' die vicesima quinta mensis Novembri anno domini millesimo CCC^mo septuagesimo secundo regni vero Regis Anglie Edwardi tertii post conquestum quadragesimo sexto.

59 Edmund Mortimer, earl of March and Walter Bromwich, Hereford, 4 April 1373 (PRO, C66/312 m. 15, *inspeximus* of 3 May 1382).[122]

[120] cf. *CPR, 1381–85*, 181.

[121] Buckland, Aylesbury Hundred, Bucks.

[122] cf. *CPR 1381–5*, 116; GEC, viii. 445–8 for Edmund Mortimer, third earl of March (1360–81).

Ceste endenture faite parentre lui nobles homme mons. Esmond' de Mortemer counte de la Marche dune parte et Wautier Bromwych[123] dautre parte tesmoigne que le dit Wautier est demoriez devers le dit counte pour luy servir a tote sa vie sibien pour pees come pour guerre queu par que le dit counte lui vodra avoir en sa compaignie, cestassavoir pour la guerre bien mountez et adrestez a sa mounture propre, et quant il vendra au dit counte par soun commandement de pees, il avera bouche au court pur lui mesmes, un chamberleyn, un garceon, feyn, aveynes, litere, fers et clowes pur trois chivalx sil les eit, ou gages resonables, et pour la guerre il avera bouche a court, livere ou gages pur lui mesmes, un chamberleyn, troys garceons sil les eit, feyn, aveynes, litere, fers et clowes pur cynk chivalx sil ceo est et eskipeson convenable pur lui, ses gentz et chivalx avauntditz ove le dit counte en alant et retournant. Et si prisoner prenre ou autre profit de guerre soit par le dit Wautier ou ses gentz pris en gaigne, le dit counte eut avera la tierce partie forspris de chevetyn ou de chevalier(?) de guerre si nulle y soit pris lui quele demoura entierement devers le dit counte, faisant au dit Waltier regard covenable en maniere comme les autres seigneurs ferront a lours en la voiage en tieu cas, issint totesfoitz que nul prisoner par le dit Wautier ou ses gentz pris le raunceon le quel passeroit la valu de cent souldes desterlinges soit delivrez ne mys a raunceon sanz accord ledit counte ou autre de par lui a ce assignez.

Et prendra le dit Wautier gages accustumez en venant et retournant par maundement le dit counte pour quel demoure et service fait au dit counte mesme le counte ad done et grauntez au dit Wautier un annuele rent de vint marcz a prendre a tote la vie le dit Wautier des issues de manoir de Malmeshull' Lacy[124] el counte de Hereford a les termes de Pasques et Seint Michel par oweles porcions le primer terme comenceant a le fest de Paske proschein avenir, et si le dit annuite soit a derere en partie ou en tout que adonques bien lise au dit Wautier a destreindre en le dit manoir et les destres retenir tanques gre lui soit fait des arrerages et si le dit Wautier refuse ou de faile a servir le dit counte comme desus est dit en sa defaute sanz cause resonable, adonques bien lise au dit counte la dit annuite sustrere et retenir a lui et ses heirs a touz jours sanz contredit le dit Wautier ou de nul autre depar lui, ceste endenture

---

[123] Walter Bromwich had a licence to impark 20 acres of woodland and 200 acres of meadow and pasture at his manor of Sarnesfield Coffyn, Herefords. in 1377 (*CPR, 1377–81*, 69), and at the supplication of the earl of March, was exempted for life from serving on a wide range of commissions or from holding any county office against his will, though in fact he was named commissioner of array in Herefordshire in 1380 (*ibid.*, 345, 474). Previously in 1377 he had shared that task with, among others, his relative John Bromwich (*ibid., 1374–7*, 499), for whom see **66**.

[124] Mansell Lacy, Herefords.

nient contresteant. En tesmoignance de quel chose si bien le dit counte come le dit Wautier a cest endenture entrechangeablement ont mys lours sealx. Donne a Hereford lundy en le fest de Seint Ambrose lan du regne le Roy Edward tierce puis le conquest Dengleterre quarrant septisme.

60 Thomas Beauchamp, earl of Warwick and Robert Massy and Margery, his wife, Warwick, 2 September 1376 (Oxford, Bodleian Library, MS Dugdale 15, pp. 296–7, after an original in the possession of Robert, lord Bruce in 1659).[125]

Ceste endenture faite a Warrewyk la seconde jour de Septembre lan du regne le roy Edward tierce puis le conquest cynkauntisme parentre luy nobles hommes monseigneur Thomas de Beauchampe counte de Warrewyk, seigneur de Gower, dune parte, et Robert de Massy esquier et Margerie sa femme, une des coheirs sire Piers de Mountfort, qe Dieux assoile, dautrepart, tesmoigne qe sur le clayme qe les avantditz Robert et Margerie fesoiont vers le dit counte pur la purpartie la dite Margerie del heritage de Mountfort susdit,[126] les parties susdits sount accorde en la forme qe ensuit: cestassavoir qe les avantditz Robert et Margerie sei tendront pur agrees et contentes del manoir de Gunthorp et Loudham el counte de Notyngham, ove les appurteignances, pur tote la purpartie la dyte Margerye del entier heritage susdite: sur quei Johan Danyel et autres, per le dit counte enfeffez du dit manoir de Gunthorp et Loudham en fee symple ount enfeffez Johan Bacon, viker de Coton, Rauf de Waltone et Roger Daryel, chapellayns, de mesme le manoir, a avoir et tener a terme de deux ans proscheyns ensuants apres la date de cestes: rendant ent per an un flur de rose a la feste de S. Johan le Baptiste; et fesaunt as chiefs seignurages des fees services ent dues et accustumes. Deyns queux deux ans les avantditz Robert et Margerie serrount prestes, quant ils serrount garnys per le dit counte, de faire au dit counte et a ces heirs tiel estate de la reversion du dit manoir de Gunthorp et Loudham apres la deces les avantditz Robert et Margerye, et Johan de Sudleye fitz au dite Margerie, ensemblement ove tiel seurtee de tote la remanant de la dite heritage, come le counseil

---

[125] Robert Massy may be the man who served in Guyenne with the Black Prince in the 1360s and, as Sir Robert, at Calais in 1382 (Morgan, *War and Society in Medieval Cheshire, 1277–1403*, 127; M. J. Bennett, *Community, Class and Careerism. Cheshire and Lancashire Society in the Age of Sir Gawain and the Green Knight* (Cambridge, 1983), 167).

[126] For the fine levied in 1350 regulating the descent of the Montfort inheritance, including the manor of Gunthorpe in Lowdham, Notts., see *Warwickshire Feet of Fines, 1345–1509* (Dugdale Soc., xviii, 1943), no. 2028; *Abstracts of inquisitions post mortem relating to Nottinghamshire 1350–1436*, ed. K. S. S. Train (Thoroton Soc., Record series, xii, 1952), 63.

le dit counte voudra devise per la ley, per fyn de court ent a lever, relees, ou autre voie de leye quecomques.

Et est accordez qe le dit Robert demorra devers le dit counte de pees et de guerre de terme de sa vie a ytiels conditions come autres esquiers de son estat sount retenuz, en pernant de fee pur sa demoere de pees et de guerre les issues du dit manoyr de Gunthorp et Loudham, en quy meigns qil devigne, par leese ou feffement des enfeffes susdits. Et sil avigne qe le dit Robert devie vivant la dite Margerie, adonques la dite Margerie tendra la dite manoir a terme de sa vie, per service du rose susdit, et fesant as chiefs seigneurs des fees services ent dues et accustumes. Et apres la decese la dite Margerie, le dit Johan tendra le manoir susdit a terme de sa vie, rendant ent per an es ditz enfeffez et a lours heirs et assignes dys marcs desterlings as termes del Annunciacioun nostre Dame et seint Michel, et fesant as chief seigneurs des fees services dues et accustomez: Et apres le deces de dit Johan le dit manoir ove les appurtenances entirement retournera et remeyndra au dit conte, ses heirs et assignez a touts jours. En tesmoigne (etc.). Done jour, lieu et an susditz (etc.).

61 Edmund Mortimer, earl of March and Ulster and Sir Hugh Cheyne, London, 2 November 1376 (PRO, C66/369 m. 24, *inspeximus* of 22 May 1403).[127]

Ceste endenture faite parentre lui tresnoble seigneur mons. Esmon de Mortemer counte de la Marche et Dulvestier dun part et mons. Hugh Cheyne chivaler dautre part tesmoigne que le dit mons. Hugh est demourez ovesque le dit conte pour lui servir a toute sa vie sibien pour pees come pour guerre, cestasssavoir pour la pees a toutes les foiez que le dit mons. Hugh vendra devers le dit conte par soun maundement il aura bouche a court pour lui mesmes, un chamberlayn, deux garceons et un page, fein, aveigne et ferrurs pour cynk chivaux si les eit ou gages resonables. Et pour la guerre sera le dit mons. Hugh montez et adrescez a ses costages propres et aura bouche a court, livere ou gages pour lui mesmes, un chamberlayn, trois garceons et un page, fein, aveigne et ferrurs pour cet chivaux si les eit. Et si le dit mons. Hugh sera prest a faire le service qil pourra come a soun estate atteint a comandement du dit conte. Et prendra le dit mons. Hugh gages accustumez en venant et retornant par mandement au dit counte ensemblement ove eskipesoun covenable pour lui ses gentz et chivaux suisditz pour quele

---

[127] cf. *CPR, 1401–5*, 229; Sir Hugh Cheyne (d. 1404) of Cheyney Longville, Salop, had been a King's yeoman since 1358 (cf. *HC, 1386–1421*, ii. 545–7). For his indenture with Roger Mortimer, earl of March in 1397 see below **89**.

demore et service faire au dit counte en la maniere susdite mesme le counte ad graunte a dit mons. Hugh un annuel rente du quarante marcz a prendre a toute la vie du dit mons. Hugh des issues du manoir et ville de Lodelowe[128] ove les appartenances el counte de Salop as termes de Pasqe et de seint Michel par oweles porcions. Et si la dite rente soit aderere en partie ou en tout as ascuns des termes suiditz durante la vie du dit mons. Hugh, qadonques bien lise a dit mons. Hugh a destreindre en les avantditz manoir et ville ove les appartenantz et les destresse[s] retenir tanques plenere gre lui soit fait des arrerages.

Et si le dit mons. Hugh refuse ou defaille a suivre le dit counte en la maniere susdite sanz cause resonable, qadonques bien lise a dit counte la dit annuel rente souztrere et retenir et que delors mesme la rente et poair a destreindre pour icelle cesse pour touz jours, cest graunt nientcontresteant. Et si le dit conte et ses heirs la dit annuel rente de xl marcz a dit mons. Hugh a toute sa vie en la forme et condicioun suisditz garanteront. En tesmoignance du quele chose a ceste endentures sibien le dit conte come le dit mons. Hugh entrechangeablement ont mys lour sealx. Donee a Londres le secunde jour de Novembre lan du regne le Roy Edward puis le conquest cynquantisme.

62 Thomas Beauchamp, earl of Warwick and John Russell, esquire, Warwick, 2 January 1377 (Oxford, Bodleian Library, MS Dugdale 15 p. 297, transcript of 1659).[129]

Ceste endenture faite parentre lui noble home Mons. Thomas Beauchamp conte de Warwick, d'une parte, et Johan Russell, escuier d'autre part, tesmoigne qe le dit Johan est demourez ove le dit Conte de peas et de guerre, a terme de sa vie. Et, si aura le dit Johan pour son fee de peas cent solds d'esterlings par an, bouche en court pur ly mesmes, livere ou gages pur un guarsoun et deux chivaux quant il serra maundes per le dit conte tielx, et pour le temps comme autre de soun estate del hostel le dit conte pernaunt. Et prendre le dit Johan pur soun fee de guerre pur an quarant livers d'esterlings pur toutes maneres des custages, ove bouche en court pur lui mesmes come autres Escuiers de sa condicion ount, des queux quarant livers suisditz, le dit Johan sera

---

[128] Ludlow, Salop.

[129] After the original then in the possession of Robert, lord Bruce, eldest son of the earl of Elgin; for a later indenture between Beauchamp and (Sir) John Russell (d. 1405) of Strensham, Worcs., see below **71**. In the end he deserted the earl for Richard II during the 'tyranny' (cf. C. Carpenter, *Locality and Polity. A Study of Warwickshire Landed Society, 1401–1499* (Cambridge, 1992), 362; *HC, 1386–1421*, iv. 248–51). A brass commemorating him survives in Strensham church.

paies de vint et cinq livers devant q'il depart de soun hostell, l'an de
guerre commenceant le jour q'il departira de soun hostell arraiez de
guerre per mandement le dit count. Et si le dit conte ne demoerge sur
la mere pur le temps qe le dit Johan seit ainsi devant la main paiez,
q'adonq le dit Johan fera restituccion a dit conte de ses fees de peas
pour la rate de temps qe soit ainsi devant la main paiez et nient pas
deserviz. Et graunte le dit Johan qe serra armez et mountez covenablement pur soun estate. Et si aura le dit Johan eskypesoun covenable
pour son passage et repassage outre meer as custages le dit conte. Et
aura le dit counte le tiers de gain de guerre quecunqs per lui ou null
des soens pris ou happez de ceux qe prendront guages du dit Conte.
Et si prisoner soit pris il ne serra mys a finance saunz assent du dit
conte ou autre pur lui et ceo assignez. En tesmoigne (etc). Done a
Warwyk le second jour de Janvyvere l'an de Roi Edw[ard] tierce puis
le conquest cinquantisme.

63 James, lord Audley of Red Castle and Heighley and Sir John de
Massy of Tatton, 23 September 1377 (Cheshire RO, Egerton of Tatton
Deeds, DET/303/14(42), sealed on tag through fold).[130]

Ceste endenture fait entre mons. James Daudelegh seigneur de Rouge
Chastel et de Helegh dune part et Johan de Massy chivaler[131] dautrepart
tesmoigne que le dit mons. James sour les condiciones qenseuont[a] ad
graunte et relesse et quitclame au dit Johan, ses heirs et a ses assignes,
tout soun droit et cleim quele il ad en sesaunte soldes de rente issaunz
del manoir de Tatton[132] de quele manoir de Tatton le dit Johan est seisi
et en possessioun a temps de la confection dycestes, issint que le dit
mons. James ne ses heirs, ne nulle autre de par ly, droit ne cleim en le
rente de sesaunte soldes susdit devers le dit Johan, ses heirs ne ses
assignetz de ceo jour en avaunt puissent clamer eins par ceste fait soient
forclos a toux jours, salvant toute foithe les condicions queu seront,
come desus est dit,[b] pur quele graunt, relesse et quitclamanz en la
maner avantdite fait le dit Johan de Massy ad done, graunte et en

---

[130] Published by permission of Cheshire County Council Archives and Local Studies
Service; we are grateful to Jonathan Pepler, Principal Archivist, for his help in obtaining
this. Fragments of an armorial seal (Fretty = Audley) survive. For James, lord Audley
(1313–86) of Red Castle, Salop, and Heighley, Staffs., see GEC, i. 339–40.

[131] Sir John Massy of Tatton succeeded his father c. 1371 and was retained for life by
Edward, prince of Wales on 28 March 1373 for 50 marks p.a. (Ormerod, *Hist. of the
County Palatine and City of Chester*, ed. Helsby, i. 440–1). He died in 1427 (S&G, i. 79–80, ii.
262–4). The family descended from a cadet line of the Massys of Dunham-Massey (cf.
above **20**)

[132] Tatton, Cheshire.

eschaunge conferme au dit mons. James, ses heirs et a ses assignez, deux mees et trent et sys acres de terre ove les apurtenances en warenne buryfrith deins la ville de Wrennebury,[133] les queux mees et terre susditz Henri Hugynessone et Johan le Flecher tiegnent a terme daunz de dit Johan de Massy[c] le jour de la confeccion dycestes, si largement et si entierement et par mesme les boundes come les ditz Henri et Johan le Flecher le dites terres et tenemenz tiegnent le jour defesaunte dycestes, a avoir et tener au dit mons. James, ses heirs et a ses assignez ove touz maneres, comunes, fraunchises et aisements a les avantditz terres et tenemenz regardanz sur les condicions enseuanz des chiefs seigneurs des fees par les services dues et acustumes, salvant toute foithe que si le dit mons. James ou ses heirs en temps avenir cleiment le dite rente de sesaunte soldes vers le dit Johan de Massy,[c] ses heirs ou ses assignez ou ascun parcel dycelle et celle eient par recovrer ou par ascun autre maner que bien lise a dit Johan de Massy[c] et a ses heirs les mees et terres avantditz dentrer et les tener a toux jours sanz countredit de dit mons. James et ses heirs et de toux autres en que meins que les dites mees et terres devingnent.

Et en cas que le dit mons. Johan de Massy[c] ou ses heirs ou ascun autre les mees et terres et tenemenz avauntditz ou ascun parcel dycelles de ceo jour enavant cleymant vers le dit mons. James, ses heirs ou ses assignetz et les eient par voi de recouvrer ou par ascun autre maner que bien lise au dit mons. James et a ses heirs le rente de sesaunte soldes avantdit clamer et reaver saunz countredit de dit Johan de Massy ou de ses heirs et cestes reles soit aneinty et de tout perde sa force en que meins que le dit manoir de Tatton devient. Et auxint le dit Johan de Massy pour terme de sa vie est demoure ovesque le dit mons. James, salvant soun retenu et service a son seignour liege, issint toute foithe que a quele heure qil travaillera par maundement de dit mons. James, il avera ses gages de ly resonablement. En tesmoignance de quele chose a cestes endentures les parties avauntditz entrechaungeablement ount mys lours seals. Donne le mesgerdy proschein devaunt la feste de seint Michel larchaungle lan de regne le Roi Richard primer.

Dorse: Carta domini de Audeley [d]
      Tatton

    a. *sour les condiciones qenseuont* interlined
    b. *come desus est dit* interlined
    c. *de Massy* interlined
    d. Written twice, once now very faint

64 Thomas Beauchamp, earl of Warwick and Piers de la Holte,

[133] Wrenbury, Cheshire.

esquire, *Gudereste* near Warwick, 23 March 1378 (Lancs. RO, DD Pt 23/9, sealed on tongue).[134]

Ceste endenture fait parentre lui nobles home mons. Thomas de Beauchamp, conte de Warrewyk, dune part et Piers de la Holte, e[s]quier, dautre part tesmoigne que le dit Piers est demourez ove le dit conte a terme de sa vie de pees et de guerre, cestassavoir pur la pees lui meismes a bouche en court ove dieux chivals et un garcion a fein, ferrure et provendre, liveree ou gages come as autres esquiers le dit conte est liverez, et quant il sera mande per le dit conte de venir a la court.[a] Et avera le dit Piers pur ses fees du pees unne annuete de dys livres aprendres del manoir de Beoleye[135] come plus pleynement piert per autres endentures ent faites. Et pour la guerre lui meismes bien armez et mountez ove un archier, quatre chivals et six garceons sil les eit, lui meismes a bouche en court, liveree ou gages pour lui, ses gents et chivaux, a y tiels et pour le temps come autres esquiers de sa condicion prendront. Et prendra le dit Piers outre son fee du pees susdite pour lan entier de guerre dys livers del garderobe du dit conte dont il serra paiez de la moite al comencement del an de guerre et del remenant apres les quarters del an come y est defeniz. Et si le conte ne demoerge sur la guerre pour le temps que le dit Piers soit ensi devant la mein paiez de la moitie de les dys livers susditz qadoncqs le dit Piers ferra restitucion a dit conte pour la rate du temps qil est ensi devant la mein paiez et nient pas deserviz[b] par resonable acompte de fere parentre le garderope le dit conte et le dit Piers. Et avera le dit Piers eskippeson convenable sur la mier de passage et repassage pour lui, ses gents et chivaux. Et avera le dit conte de dit Piers la moite de qiconque gayn de guerre par lui et ses gents qeconques pris ou happes et si prisoner soit pris par le dit Piers ou ascun des soens il serra mye mitz a finance sanz expresse assent de dit conte ou dautre par lui a ceo assignez. En tesmoignance de quelle chose a cestes endentures les parties susditz entrechangeablement ont mys lours seals. Donez a Gudereste[136] iouste Warr' le vynt et tierce[c] jour de marcz lan de regne le Roi Richard secund puis le conqueste Dengleterre premier.[137]

Dorse: 'Holte'

---

[134] We are grateful to the Agents of Capt. R. C. Petre for permission to publish.

[135] Beoley, Worcs.

[136] *Gudereste* has not been identifed; it appears as *Godereste* in a document of 1375 (Holmes, *Estates*, 77 n. 5).

[137] Holt remained in possession of his annuity until at least 1404. He was the first man to bring news of the birth of his eldest son to Earl Thomas, receiving a gift of £10 as a result (*CIM, 1392–99*, no. 302; Birmingham Reference Library, 168234 m. 2d; *CIPM*, xviii. 855). Fragments of Beauchamp's seal survive.

a. et quant il sera mande per le dit conte de venir a la court interlined
b. deserviz written around hole in MS
c. et tierce interlined

65 Richard, earl of Arundel and William Rees, London, 1 October 1379 (PRO, C66/348 m. 29, *inspeximus* of 17 Nov. 1397).[138]

Ceste endenture faite parentre Richard counte Darundell et de Surr' dune part et William Rees[139] dautre part tesmoigne que le dit counte ad retenuz devers luy le dit William a terme de sa vie pour pees et pour guerre. Et que le dit counte ad donez et grauntez et par cestes endenture confermez a dit William pour le bon et greable service qil luy ad fait et ferra tut son manoir de Ovesham[140] ove les appartenauntz en la countee Dessex a avoir et tener tut le dit manoir ove toutz les appartenauntz a dit William pour son fee a terme de sa vie fesaunt as chiefs seignours des fees les services ent duez et acustumez. Et le dit William durant tut le temps qil soit hable et de tiel poair qil pourra travailler sera prest sur resonable garnissement et mandement de venir al dit counte et a demourer ove le dit counte solonc ceo qil ad ove luy a faire. Et a quele heure que le dit William soit venuz a dit counte a son mandement en temps de pees adonques le dit William aura un vadlet et dieux chevalx as costages de dit counte, cestassavoir le dit William et son vadlet a bouche de court et pour sez deux chivalx prenaunt provendre et fein et ferrures come les autres esquiers du dit counte. Et quele heure que le dit William veigne a dit counte pour la guerre adonqes le dit William aura un vadlet, un garcion et trois chivalx as costages du dit counte, cestassavoir le vadlet a bouche de court, le garcion a gages come les garcions des autres esquiers, et les trois chivalx a fein, provendre et ferrure come les chivalx dautres esquiers du dit counte.

Et si ascune viage soi taillera sur la mer ou ailours la ou bosoigne ne sera pas des chivalx qadonqes en le mesmes temps le dit counte soit descharge des costages des chivalx suisditz. Et le dit William sera tenuz de rendre la tierce de queconques gayne de guerre qil prendra ou gaynera par luy ou par son vadlet avantdit en temps de guerre. Et outre ceo si ascun viage se ferra en quele le dit counte ne soy taille daler adonqes si le dit William se vodra travailler et eit congie de dit counte daler en ycelle, qadonqes le dit William sera tenuz de rendre la tierce de queconque gaine par luy mesmes gayne de guerre en mesme la viage en temps de guerre. Et apres ceo que le dit William eit ensy

[138] cf. *CPR 1396–1399*, 255; GEC, i. 244–5 for Richard, earl of Arundel (1376–97).
[139] *HC, 1386–1421*, iv. 187–9 for the career of William Rees (d. 1410) of Tharston, Norf.
[140] Ovesham, Essex.

cungie de travailler en ascun viage en absence du dit counte et le dit
counte soi taille de travailler en mesme le viage ou aillours, qadonqes
le dit William apres ce que son quartier et demi an soit finiz sera
tenuz de venir a dit counte par son maundement et par resonable
garnissement. Et le dit counte et sez heirs tut la dit manoir ove les
appartenauntz a dit William pour terme de sa vie en la forme come
desuys est dit encontre toutz gentz garanteront et defenderont. En
tesmoignance de quele chose a lune partie de ceste endenture demourant devers le dit William le dit counte ad mis son seal et a lautre
partie demourante devers le dit counte le dit William ad mis son seal.
Donez a Loundres le primier jour Doctobre lan du regne le Roy
Richard puis le conqueste tierz.

66 Edmund Mortimer, earl of March and Ulster and Sir John Bromwich, Hereford, 18 October 1379 (PRO, C66/312 m. 28, *inspeximus* of
24 February 1382).[141]

Ceste endenture faite parentre le tresnoble seigneur mons. Esmon de
Mortemer counte de la Marche et Dulvester dune part et mons. Johan
de Bromwych[142] chivaler dautrepart tesmoigne que le dit mons. Johan
est demourez devers le dit counte pur lui servir a toute sa vie sibien
pur pees come pur la guerre quieu part que le dit counte lui voudra
avoir en sa compaignie, cestassavoir pur la guerre lui mesmes ove un[a]
esquier bien montez et adresciez a lours coustages propres, et quant il
vendra au dit counte par son mandement de pees il aura bouche a
court pur lui mesmes, un esquier, un chamberleyn, trois garceons, feyn,
aviegnes, litere, fers et clous pur sys chivaux si les eit ou gages resonables
et pur la guerre il aura bouche a court, livere ou gages pur lui mesmes,
un esquier, un chamberleyn, sys garceons, fein, aveigne, litere, fers et
clous pur noef chivaux si les eit, et eskipeson covenable pur lui et ses
gentz et pour mesmes les chivaux et plusours si les eit ove le dit counte
en alant et retournant. Et pour a tant des chivalers, esquiers et archiers
come le dit mons. Johan amenera en la compaignie le dit counte par

---

[141] cf. *CPR, 1381–5*, 99; Bean, 85 calls these 'letters patent of indenture'.
[142] Sir John Bromwich of Tregate, Herefords., claimed to be 55 years old when he
gave testimony in the Scrope-Grosvenor case (S&G, i. 205–6). He was in Mortimer
service by 1371 and acted as justiciar in Ireland during the earl of March's lieutenancy
there, receiving a protection for a year on 16 November 1379 (*CPR, 1377–81*, 403). He
had previously been in the service of Lionel, duke of Clarence and was subsequently
retained by John, duke of Lancaster, acting as surveyor and governor of his son's lands
between 1385 and his death in 1388: *CIPM*, xii. 408; *CPR, 1370–4*, 87; *ibid., 1377–81*,
380; Holmes, *Estates*, 60–1; Simon Walker, *The Lancastrian Affinity, 1361–1399* (Oxford,
1990), 265; Somerville, *Duchy of Lancaster*, 386.

son acord, il prendra de mesme le counte a taunt come autres de lour estat prendront de lui pur le temps qils demoureront en son service. Et si prison[er] preis ou autre profit de guerre soit par dit mons. Johan ou nul de ses gentz prez ou gaines le dit counte eut aura la tierce partie, issint toutez foitz que nul prisoner par le dit mons. Johan ou ses gentz pris soit delivrez ne mys a raunceon saunz acord du dit conte ou dautre depar luy a ceo assignez. Et prendra le dit mons. Johan gages acustumez en venant et retournant par mandement le dit conte pur la guerre pur lui et ses gentz pur quele demoere et service faire au dit conte en la manere susdite mesme le conte ad grauntez a dit mons. Johan une annuele rente de cent marcz a prendre a toute la vie le dit mons. Johan des manoirs et seignouries le dit counte de Clifford et Glassebury[143] ove les appartenantz en la marche de Gales joignant al counte de Hereford as les termes de Pasques et de Seint Michel par owels porcions. Et si la dite rente soit aderiere ou partie ou en tout a ascun des termes susditz durant la vie du[b] dit mons. Johan, voet et graunte le dit counte qadonques bien lise au dit mons. Johan a destreindre en les ditz manoirs et seignouries ou les appartenances et les destresses retenir tanques pleine gree lui soit fait des arrerages.

Et si le dit mons Johan refuse ou defaille a servir le dit counte en la manere suisdite sanz cause resonable qadonques bien lise au dit counte la dite annuele rente cesse pur toutz jours cest grant nient contresteant. Et a quiele heure que le dit conte ne soit ordenez de travailler de guerre ou neyt affaire du service le dit mons. Johan pur la guerre en la manere susdite, adonques le dit conte de sa bone seignourie soeffra le dit mons. Johan travailler ou lui plerra pur un temps tanques mesme le conte se verra ordener pur la guerre come est dit. Et le dit conte et ses heirs la dite annuele rente de cent marcz par an al dit mons. Johan et toute sa vie en la fourme et condicion susdites garanteront. En tesmoignance de quelle chose sibien le dit conte come le dit mons. Johan as cestes endentures entrechangeablement ont mys lour seals. Donez a Hereford en la feste de Seint Luk' lan du nostre seignour le Roy Richard le secunde puis le conquest tierce.

a. MS *une*
b. *du dit* interlined

67 Roger, lord Clifford retains John Lowther for a year, reserving the right to renew the agreement annually, Skipton, 26 October 1379

[143] Clifford and Glasbury, Herefords. The keeping of these lordships, then in the king's hand, was committed to Bromwich in May 1382: *CFR, 1377–83*, 295; *CCR, 1392–6*, 391.

(Cumbria RO, Carlisle, D Lons/L/MD/Lo 104, sealed on tongue).[144]

Ceste endenture fait parentre monsire Roger de Clifford, seigneur de
Westmorland, dunpart et Johan de Lowthir[145] dautrepart, tesmoigne
que le dit Johan est demore ove le dit monsire Roger pur un an entier
comensaunt a la fest de Seint Hillar' proschein venaunt destre du
conseill le dit monsire Roger et pur server a Thomas de Clifford, filtz
et heir le dit monsire Roger, et deprendre garde a les gentz, chivaux
et hernoys le dit Thomas come a le dit Johan appent. Preignant de le
dit monsire Roger par le dit an pur la pees dys livres as deux termes
del an, cest asavoir Pentecost et Seint Martyn par owels porcions, et
issint de an en an sils purront acorder. Et le dit Johan prendra de le
dit Thomas pour la guerre sil aveigne les gages du Roy et regarde[a] et
le dit Johan acounttera loyalment a la dit monsire Roger de tout qil
ressayvera par endenture sibien en argent come en autre araye. Et le
dit Johan sera a bouche du court, son vadlet et deux[b] chivaux a bouche
de court ou a gages come autres ount destre demourant devers lui
devant cest forch.[c] En tesmoignance de quelle chose les parties suisdites
a cestes endentures entrechaungablement ount mys lour seals a Skipton
en Craven[146] le xxvj jour doctobre lan du regne le Roy Richard puis
le conquest tirce.

  a. *et regarde* interlined
  b. *deux* interlined
  c. MS *sic* for ?*foith/foitz*

68 James Butler, earl of Ormond retains Sir Robert de la Freigne as
his steward for life, Carrick [-on-Suir], Tipperary, 10 July 1380 (NLI,
Ormond Deeds D 1272, sealed on tongue).[147]

Ceste endenture fait parentre le noble seignour James le Botiller conte
Dormond dune part et Robert de la Freigne chevalier dautrepart

---

[144] This indenture and **149–51** and **153** are published by kind permission of the
Trustees of the Lowther Family Trusts and we are especially grateful to the Earl of
Lonsdale and David Bowcock, Assistant County Archivist, for their help. A good
impression of Clifford's seal survives.

[145] Of Lowther, Westm., and Newton Reigny, Cumbs. The eldest son of Sir Hugh
Lowther and Matilda, daughter of Sir Peter Tilliol, he was returned as MP for
Westmorland to the Parliaments of Jan. 1377, Oct. 1378, April 1379 and Jan. 1380: C. M.
Lowther Bouch, 'The Origins and Early Pedigree of the Lowther Family', *Trans. Cumbs.
and Westmorland Antiqs. Soc*, n.s. xlviii (1948), 120–1.

[146] Skipton, Yorks. W. R.

[147] An impression of De la Freigne's seal survives; cf. *Cal. of Ormond Deeds*, ed. Curtis,
ii. no. 247.

tesmoigne que le dit conte ad depute, fait et ordine le dit Robert son chief seneschal, estiward et surveour des totes ses terres et seignouries en Irland, as ses terres asseer et au ferme doner en encresce et avantages du dit conte, ses officiers corriger et lour defautes amender et tesmoigner, et si ne vuillent eaux amender, autres covenables en lours lieu mettre et ordiner par assent de mondit seignour si bien deinz lostell comme de hors, et prenant pour son fee par an diz livres des rentes du dit conte de Courduf,[148] la moyte a receyvre a la fest seynt Michell' et lautre moyte a la Pask', et ensi de an en an et terme en terme come plerra as dites conte et Robert, et avera le dit Robert poair pour destreyndre pour les deniers suditz en cas qils ne soient paiez as termes susescriptz en totes les terres de Courduf, et auxint avera ils de mon dit seignour gages resonables et[a] quant il travalera en le service du dit conte si bien en temps de guerre come de pees solonc la descrescion de mon dit seignour et son conseill, et le dit Robert soit en lostell du dit conte il, ses gentz et chivaux serront as coustages mon dit seignour. En tesmoygnantz de quele chose les avantditz conte et Robert as cestes endentures entrechangeablement ount mys leur seals. Don' a Carryk le x jour de Juyll' lan du regne nostre seigneur le Roi Richard le second apres le conquest quart.

a. *et* interlined

69 Edmund, earl of Cambridge and Camoys Mavow, Hatfield, Herts., 1 January 1381 (PRO, C66/373 m. 23, *inspeximus* of 14 May 1405).[149]

Ceste endenture fait a Haytefeld parentre Esmon fitz au noble Roi Dengleterre et de France le counte de Cantebrigg' dune part et Camoys Mavow de altre part le primer jour de Janvier lan du regne le Roy Richard secunde puis le conquest quart, tesmoigne que le dit Esmon ad retenu devers lui sibien pur la pees come pour la guerre a demourer en sa compaignie le dit Camoys par terme de sa vie et destre un des esquiers de sa chaumbre. Et le dit Esmon ad grantee que le dit Camoys prendra annuelment vynt marcz pour terme de toute sa vie pour son fee des profites sourdantz de son manoir de Fasterne en la countee de Wildshire,[150] cest assavoir a les festes de Pasques et Seint Michell' par owels porcions et il aura bouche a court en temps du pees pour luy

---

[148] Courduff, County Dublin; cf. *The Red Book of Ormond*, ed. N. B. White (Dublin, 1932), 25–7 and Robert Bartlett, *The Making of Europe. Conquest Colonization and Cultural Change, 950–1350* (London, 1993), 147.

[149] cf. *CPR, 1405–8*, 16; GEC, ii. 494 and xii, pt 2. 895–9 for Edmund, earl of Cambridge (1362–1402).

[150] Fasterne, Wilts.

mesmes, un vadlet et un garsoun ou autrement gages pour les dites
vadlet et garsoun et il aura feyn, provendre, litere et ferrure pour trois
chevalxs en maniere come altres esquiers de sa condicioun averont a
toute la temps qil demoura dedenz lostell du dit Esmon ou autrement
gages pour la liveree des ditz chevalxs. Et en cas que le dit Camoys
travaillera en la compaignie du dit Esmon en temps de guerre il aura
a tant de gages come ascune altre de sa condicioun. Et le dit Esmon
voet et graunt que si les avantditz vynt marcz soient aderer en partie
ou en toute a ascun terme qadonques bien lise au dit Camoys et a ses
attournez en toute le manoir suisdit et en chescune partie dycelles
manoir en qi mains qil deviendra destrindre et mesme la distresse
enchacer et retenir par la ou lui plest tanques gree a luy soit faite de
les dites xx marcz suisditz et de les arrerages si nules seront. En
tesmoignance de quele chose a cestes endentures les partiez suisditz
entrechaungeablement on[t] mys lours sealxs. Donne le jour, lieu et an
suisditez.[151]

70 Edmund Mortimer, earl of March and Ulster and Sir Henry
Conway, 1 August 1381 (PRO, C66/312 m. 12, *inspeximus* of 12 May
1382).[152]

Ceste endenture faite parentre le treshonure seigneur mons. Esmon de
Mortemer counte de la Marche et Duluestier dune part et mons. Henry
Coneway chivaler dautre part tesmoigne qe come le dit mons. Henry
autrefoiz par noun de Henry de Coneway esquier par autres endentures[153] sur ceo entre eux faites estoit retenuz et demourez devers le dit
counte de lui servir a toute sa vie sibien pur pees come pur la guerre
souz certaine forme en les dites autres endentures plus pleinement
expresses pur quele terme ensy a faire au dit counte, mesme le counte
avoit grauntez au dit Henry un annuel rente de cinkante marcz a
prendre annuelment des issues des manoirs, chastell et seignourie de
Clifford et Glasebury[154] ove les appartenances en Gales et en la marche
de Gales a toute la vie le dit Henry sicome en les dites autres endentures

---

[151] Also confirmed by Henry IV at the same time were letters patent of Edmund as
duke of York, given at Bury St Edmunds, 2 November 1398, granting Piers Mavow
esquire an annuity of 10 marks a year on his lordship of Wakefield. For Mavow's petition,
asking for confirmation 'because the said suppliant has nothing to live on apart from the
abovesaid annuities alone', see PRO, E28/21/40. He was still in receipt of the annuity
from Fasterne at Michaelmas 1412 (BL, Egerton Roll 8780 m. 1).

[152] cf. *CPR, 1381–1385*, 119.

[153] This earlier indenture has not been traced; for Conway's relations with Mortimer
see Holmes, 61.

[154] Clifford and Glasbury, Herefords. (cf. above **66**).

pluis pleinement est contenuz puis, apres le dit mons. Henry ay prist du dit counte lordre de chivaler, est demorrez devers mesmes le counte de lui servir en estat du bacheler sibien pur la pees come pur la guerre a toute le vie du dite counte en la forme qensuit, cestassavoir a toutes les foiz qe le dit mons. Henry vendra devers le dit counte par son mandement de pees il aura bouche en court pur luy mesmes, un esquier, un chamberleyn, quatre garcons, feine, aveine, fers et clous pur sys chivaux sil les eit ou gages resonables pour ses ditz garcons et chivaux, et a toutes les foiz qil vendra devers le dit counte par son mandement pur la guerre il aura bouche en court, livere ou gages resonables pur lui mesmes, son dit esquier, son chamberleyn et cink garcons, feine, aveine, fers et clous ou gages resonables pour oet chivaux si les eit, et pour toute les hommes darmes et archiers qil amenera ovesque le dit counte pur la guerre del ordenance du dit counte outre les persones suisdites il prendra du dit counte^a au tieux feods et gages come il dorra as autres de lour estat et degree en mesme le voiage, endroit de prisoners prises et autres profitz de guerre qe par le dit mons. Henry ou ascun de ses gentz serront pris ou gaignes le counte ferra devers le dit mons. Henry et le dit mons. Henry devers le counte en maniere come serra resonablement fait et usez en les lieux et voiages ou ils travailleront du guerre, pur quel service ensy affaire au dit counte par le dit mons. Henry et aussint pur ceo que le dit mons. Henry ad susrenduz et relessez et sustrent et relest par ycestes au dite counte la dite annuele rente de cynkante marcz a lui grauntez come desus mesme le counte ad donez et grauntez et par icestes au dit mons. Henry une annuele rente de quarante livres a prendre a tout la vie le dit mons. Henry des issues et profitz de la terre et seignourie de Kedewyng en Gales¹⁵⁵ a les termes de Seint Michel et Pasques par oweles porcions. Et si la dite rente de quarant livres par an soit aderere a auscun des termes susditz duraunt la vie du dit mons. Henry qe bien lise a lui et ses assignez pur la dite rente destreindre en les ditz terre et seignourie et les destresses retenier tanques gree ent lui soit fait. Et si le dit mons. Henry refuse a servir le dit counte en maniere susdite sanz cause resonable qe alors cesse le paiement de la dite annuele rente de quarante livers et le poair a destreindre pour ycelle. Et le dit counte et ses heirs lavauntdite annuele rent de quarante livres au dit mons. Henry a toute sa vie en la forme et condicion susditz garanteront. En tesmoignance de quele chose al une partie du ceste endenture demurrant devers le dit mons. Henry le dit counte ad fait mettre son seal et al autre partie dycelle demourrant devers le dit counte le dit mons. Henry ad mys soun seal. Donez le primer jour Daugst lan du regne le Roy Richard secounde puis la conquest quinte.

---

¹⁵⁵ Cydewain, Powys.

a. dit counte interlined

71 Thomas Beauchamp, earl of Warwick and Sir John Russell, Warwick, 29 March 1383 (PRO, C66/314 m. 6, *inspeximus* of 25 April 1383).[156]

Ceste endenture faite par entre lui nobles hommes Thomas Beauchamp count de Warrewyk dune part et monsire Johan Russel de Strengesham[157] chivaler dautre part tesmoigne que le dit monsire Johan est demore ove le dit counte par terme de sa vie pur la peas et pur guerre, et prendra pur la peas du dit counte annuelment vynt lyvres pur terme de la vie du dit monsire Johan del manoir le dit counte de Chedworth en le counte de Gloucestre,[158] et pur la guerre quarrant livres, et sera paie annuelement as termes de la nativite seint Johan le Baptistre et de Nowel par oveles porciones des issues de dit manoir de Chedworth par les mayns de gardein de mesme le manoir, et avera le dit monsire Johan pur la pees qant il sera maunde de venir au dit counte bouche au court pur lui mesme, un chamberleyn et un garson, feyn, provendre et ferure pur trois chivalx pur le temps de sa demoere. Et pur la guerre le dit monsire Johan[a] mountera lui mesmes covenablement et avera bouche au court ove liveree pour lui mesmes, un chamberleyn et trois garzons ou gages al afferant et feyn, provendre et ferure pour cynk chivalx, en manere come autres de son estate ove le dit counte prendront. Et sil preigne prisoner soit entre le dit counte et le dit monsire Johan sicome il fait parentre lui et autres bachilers de sa retenue pour terme de vie. Et voet et graunte le dit conte par cestes presentes lettres que sil dit rent annuel de vynt livres pur la peas ou de xl li. pur la guerre soit aderere et nient paie par un moys apres ascuns des termes avantdites, que bien lise au dit monsire Johan, ou a son attorne en celle partie, en le dit manoir de Chedworth destreindre pur les arrerages de le dit rente et la destresse retenir tanque plein paiement lui soit faite des ditz arrerages. Et si le dit Johan ne soit mye paie de la dit rent de xx li. et xl li. aprendre en la forme susdite de dit manoir de Chedworth, le dit conte voet et grante que le dit Johan puisse destreindre pur terme de sa vie pur les arrerages des dites xx li. et xl li. aprendre en la forme susdite en toutes ses terres et tenementz les

---

[156] cf. *CPR, 1381–1385*, 283. There is a truncated copy of this indenture transcribed in November 1659 after the original then in the possession of Robert, lord Bruce in Oxford, Bodleian Library, MS Dugdale 15 pp. 297–8. See also above **62** for an earlier indenture between Beauchamp and Russell, for whose later career as a chamber knight of Richard II, see Given-Wilson, *passim*.

[157] Strensham, Worcs.

[158] Chedworth, Gloucs.

queux le dit conte ad en le dit counte de Gloucestre. Et voet auxint et graunte le dit conte que le dit monsire Johan ne soit mye astrynt ne arce par my ses covenances de travailler de guerre si noun ovesque le dit conte et en sa presence et comensera son an de guerre le jour de son remuement de son hostiel propre vers les parties ou le dit count lui maundera par ses lettres. En tesmoignance de quele chose as cestes presentes endentures les avantditz conte et monsire Johan entre-changeablement ont mys lour sealx. Done a nostre chastel de Warrewyk le xxix jour del mois de Marcz lan de regne[b] le roy Richard second puis le conquest sisme.

    a. Johan omitted in enrolment
    b. regne interlined

72 Thomas Beauchamp, earl of Warwick and Walter Power, Warwick, 31 March 1383 (PRO, C66/315 m. 6, *inspeximus* of 8 June 1383).[159]

Ceste endenture faite parentre lui nobles hommes monsire Thomas de Beauchamp counte de Warrewyk dune part et Wauter Powere esquier[160] dautre part tesmoigne que le dit Wauter est demouree ove le dit counte pur terme de sa vie pur la pees et pur la guerre et prendra du dit counte pur la pees annuelement cent soldz pur terme de la vie du dit Wauter del manoir du dit counte de Chedworth en la countee de Gloucestre[161] et pur la guerre vynt livres et serra paie annuelement as termes de la nativitee seint Johan le[a] Baptistre et de Nowel par ovels porcions del issues del dit manoir par les mayns del gardein de mesme le manoir. Et avera le dit Wauter pur la pees quant il sera mande de venir au dit counte bouche en courte pur lui mesmes et pur la guerre auxint par manere come autres esquiers de son estat pernont. Et sil preigne prisoner soit entre le dit counte et lui sicome il fait parentre lui et autres esquiers de sa retenue pur terme de vie. Et voet et graunte le dit counte par cestes presentes lettres que si la dite rente annuele de cent soldz pur la pees ou de vynt livres pur la guerre soit aderiere et nient paie par un moys apres ascun des termes avandites que bien lise au dit Wauter ou a son attorne en celle partie en le dit manoir de Chedworth pur les arrerages de la dit rent destrendre et la destresse retenir tanque plein paiement lui soit faite des ditz arrerages. Et si le

---

[159] cf. *CPR, 1381–1385*, 277–8.
[160] For another indenture between the same parties see below **82.** Power was steward of Earl Thomas's household by 1393 and remained in Beauchamp service until at least 1401/2. For his career, A. F. J. Sinclair, 'The Beauchamp earls of Warwick in the later Middle Ages', Unpublished Ph.D thesis, London 1987, 354.
[161] Chedworth, Gloucs.

dit Wauter ne soit mye paie de la dite rent de cent soldz et vynt livres
apprendre en la forme suisdite, du dit manoir de Chedworth le dit
counte voet et graunte que le dit Wauter puisse destrendre pur terme
de sa vie pur les arrerages des ditz cent soldz et vynt livres apprendre
en la forme suisdite en touz les terres et tenementz les queux le dit
counte ad en le dit countee de Gloucestre. Et voet auxint et graunte le
dit counte que le dit Wauter ne soit mye astrint ne arce parmy ses
covenances de travailler de guerre sinon ovesque le dit counte et en sa
presence et comencera son an de guerre le jour de son^a remuement de
son hostel propre vers les parties ou le dit counte lui mandra par ses
lettres. En tesmoignance de quele chose a cestes presentes endentures
les avantditz counte et Wauter entrechangeablement ont mys lour sealx.
Don a nostre chastel de Warrewyk le xxxi jour de mois de Marcz lan
du regne nostre seigneur le Roi Richard puis le conqueste sisme.

a. interlined

73 Walter, lord Fitzwalter and Sir Alexander Walden, 22 June 1385
(PRO, C66/323, m. 6, *inspeximus* of 28 May 1387).[162]

Sachent toutz gentz moy Waltier sir ffitz Waltier et de Wodeham avoir
done graunte et par ceste fait endente conferme a Alisandre de Walden
chivaler[163] un annuel rente de dys livres desterlinges pur terme de vie
le dit Alisandre apprendre annuelment de mon manoir de Asshedon[164]
en le counte de Essex as deux termes del an, cest assavoir al feste de
seynt Michel larchangel et de Pasch par ovels porcions. Et sil aveigne
que la suisdite rente soit aderere en partie ou en tout a ascun terme
suisdit, qadonque bien lise a dit Alisandre et a sez assignes en lavandit
manoir ove les appurtenantz entrer et distrendre et les distresses
prendre, enchacer et emporter et devers eux retenir tanque gree soit
fait sibien des damages come des arrerages dicell. Et le dit Alisandre
de sa part ad graunte a moy Waltier sire ffitz Waltier avantdit que a
quele hore aveigne moy a travailler en les guerres nostreseigneur le
Roy et le dit Alisandre soit en volunte et voet travailler adonqes qil
serra prest a travailler ovesque moy en la dicte guerre devant toutz
autres, pregnant de moy Waltier sire ffitz Waltier suisdit pur ycelle a
tant des gages pur chescun viage de guerre et reward semblable come

---

[162] cf. *CPR, 1385–1389*, 307. For Walter, third lord Fitzwalter (1361–86), who in a long
and active military career served in Richard II's Scottish expedition of 1385 and died at
Orense in Galicia in Gaunt's company in October 1386, see GEC, v. 477–80.

[163] Sir Alexander Walden of Matching and Rickling, Essex (d. 1401): see *HC, 1386–
1421*, iv. 739–40, where his military service with Fitzwalter from 1378 is traced.

[164] Ashdon, Essex.

jeo avantdit Waltier sire ffitz Waltier prendra pur mes autres chivalers de ma retenue, et ovesque ceo destre a bouche de ma court ove son chamberlayn et un page, de quel annuel rente avantdit pur greindre surte affaire au dit Alisandre je avantdit Waltier sire ffitz Waltier ay mys lavantdit Alisandre en seisine et possession par le paiement de dusze deners. Et je avantdit Waltier sire ffitz Waltier, mes heirs et mes assignes le dit annuel rente de dys livres au dit Alisandre pur terme de sa vie en forme avantdit encontre toutz gentz garantarouns. En tesmoignance de quele chose a lune partie de ceste endenture demurant devers le dit Alisandre jeo Waltier sire ffitz Waltier avantdit ad mys mon seal, al autre partie de mesme lendenture demurrant devers moy Waltier sire ffitz Waltier le dit Alisandre ad mys son seal. Done le jeody proschein devant le feste de seint Johan le Baptiste lan du regne le Roi Richard secunde puis le conquest neoffisme.

74 Roger, lord Clifford and Roger Hornby, Brough under Stainmoor, 13 January 1387 (PRO, C66/323 m. 3, *inspeximus* of 7 June 1387).[165]

Hec indentura testatur quod nos Rogerus de Clifford dominus West-merland dedimus, concessimus et hac presenti carta nostra indentata confirmavimus Rogero de Horneby unum mesuagium, sexaginta et decem acras terre, sex acras prati et quatuor acras vasti cum pertinentiis in Whinffell et ballivam de Whinffell[166] cum pertinentiis habendum et tenendum predicto Rogero filii Willelmi de Horneby ad terminum vite sue post terminum vite[a] Willelmi patris predicti Rogeri filii predicti Willelmi de Horneby, reddendo nobis et heredibus nostris annuatim ad terminos Pentecost' et Sancti Martini per equales porciones triginta septem solidos bone monete Angliae. Et predictus Rogerus nobis serviret tam in guerra quam in pace capiendo de nobis tantum sicut ceteri homines de statu suo capient pro guerra. Et nos vero predictus Rogerus de Clifford et heredes nostri predicto Rogero filii Willelmi de Horneby omnia terras et tenementas predictas simul cum balliva foreste de Whinffell contra omnes gentes warantizabimus et defendemus modo et forma quibus dictus Willelmus pater predicti Rogeri de Horneby de nobis habet dictam ballivam. In cuius rei testimonium tam nos prefatus Rogerus de Clifford quam predictus Rogerus filii Willelmi de Horneby hunc indenture sigilla nostra alternatim apposuimus. Dat' apud

[165] cf. *CPR, 1385–1389*, 311; for Roger, fifth lord Clifford, see above **52.**
[166] Whinfell in Brougham, Westmorland.

Burgham[167] terciodecimo die mensis Januarii anno regni Regis Ricardi secundi post conquestum decimo.[168]

    a. *vite* omitted in enrolled text

75 Edmund, duke of York and Sir Thomas Gerberge, London, 9 May 1388 (PRO, C66/373 m. 25, *inspeximus* of 6 April 1405).[169]

Ceste endenture fait parentre le treshonoure et trespuissant seignour Esmon Duc Deverwyk Counte de Cantebrigg et seignour de Tyndale dune part et sire Thomas Gerberge chivaler[170] de la counte de Norf' dautre part tesmoigne que le dit sire Thomas est retenuz et demorez devers mon dit seignour le Duc a terme de sa vie et pour le bone service qil ferra le dit Duc luy ad ordeigne et assigne pur estre seneschall de son hostell durant le temps qil plerra au dit mon seignour le Duc et dez toutez les terres et tenementz que mon dit seignour le Duc ad en Engleterre il ad ensi ordeigne et assigne le dit sire Thomas pour estre chief seneschal en la manere que monsire Rouger de Welesham estoit le temps qil fuist en vie[171] durant le temps qil plerra au dit monseignour le duc. Et prendra le dit Thomas du dit monseignour le duc pour son feez quarante marcz desterlinges chescon an a terme de vie avantdite dont serra paiez de an en an des issues et profitez issantez annuelment de son manoir de Somerforth Keynes[172] par les mainz de le fermour qi ore est illoeques ou qi pour le temps serra, cestassavoir as deux termes de Paskez et de Seint Michell par oweles porcions comenseant son primer paiement al fest de seint Michel proschein ensuant la date dicestes. Et veult le dit monsire le duc que si le dit Thomas trovera aucouns officers en lostell mon dit seignour ou dehors en defaute quils ne fuissent a le profit mon dit seignour qil ad plein poair de les remouer par ladvys et ordenaunce de mon dit seignour et de son conseil et y mettre autres plus suffisante et profitables en lour lieu et de toutes autres choses faire qappartienent au autres offices en

---

[167] Brough under Stainmoor, Westmorland.

[168] In August 1389 William Hornby, chief forester of Whinfell, was said by an inquisition jury to hold 40 acres within the forest, 5 messuages and a rent of 30 s. p.a. by virtue of his office: *CIPM*, xvi. 836. For Roger Hornby occupying the same office in 1392, *ibid.*, xvii. 13.

[169] cf. *CPR, 1405–1408*, 12; for Edmund of Langley, duke of York (1385–1402) see GEC, xii pt. 2. 895–9.

[170] *HC, 1386–1421*, iii. 178–81 for the career of Sir Thomas Gerberge (c. 1342–c.1413) of Marlingford, Norfolk. He was already acting as York's steward of lands by Nov. 1386 (PRO, E403/515 m. 19).

[171] Welesham was dead before 1 Dec. 1386 (*CPR, 1385–9*, 272).

[172] Somerford Keynes, Wilts.

mesme la manere que monsire Roger de Welsham avoit de mon dit seignour. Et quant le dit sire Thomas sera travaillant sur les bussoignez monditseignour il avera quatre souldz desterlinges pour son gagez chescon jour qil travaillera dount serra paiez par les mains de son Tresorer et avera bouche a court pour luy et un esquier et ij vadlettes et quatre chivaux a la livere de feyn et provandre et ferrure ou autrement gagez pour les ditz chivaux quant il serra al hostell et si le dit monseignour le duc travaillera en la mier ou aillours le dit sire Thomas travaillera ovesque luy et avera tieux gagez et regard pour son corps come le dit monseignour le duc prendra pour luy de notreseignour le Roy. Et pour sa retenue de quele il pourra accorder ovesque monseignour avantdit il avera tieux gagez come mon dit seignour le duc prendra pour eux de nostre seignour le Roy et avera monseignour le tierce part de toute la gayn de guerre que le dit monsire Thomas ferra de sa main propre et la tierce des tierces de sa retenue et si aveigne que le dit Thomas ou ascun de sa retenue preigne ascun cheveinteigne ou piere de reyme, ville, chastell ou forteresse de noz ennemys le dit monseignour le Duc le avera devers soy fesant resonable gree aceluy que lavera pris come entre eux purront bonement accorder, et pour toutz cestes choses tenir fermez et stablez dun part et dautre les ditz partiez ount mys lour sealx entrechaungeablement a ycestes endentures. Donee a Loundres le ix jour de May lan du regne le Roy Richard seconde puis le conquest unsisme.

76 Thomas Mowbray, Earl Marshal and earl of Nottingham and Sir Thomas Clinton, London, 6 February 1389 (PRO, C66/354 m. 15, *inspeximus* of 15 October 1400).[173]

Ceste endenture faite parentre nous Thomas conte Mareschall et de Notyngham seignur de Moubray et de Segrave dun part et nostre trescher et bien ame bacheler monsire Thomas de Clynton[174] dautre part tesmoigne que nous avons graunte par ycestes au dit monsire Thomas un annuel rent de vynt livres aprendre de an en an de nostre manoir de Caludon[175] a toute sa vie as festes de Pasque et de Seint Michel par oveles porcions, pur la quel annuite le dit monsire Thomas de Clynton est demore et retenu pur toute sa vie ovesque nous sibien pur la pees come pur la guerre en la forme qensuyt. Cestassavoir que

[173] cf. *CPR, 1399–1401*, 28. The same *inspeximus* confirmed a further grant to Clinton and Alice, his wife, dated 24 Feb. 1394, of 20 marks p.a. from the manor of Chacombe, Northants., with effect from the death of the Countess Marshal. GEC, ix. 601–4 and 781 for Thomas Mowbray, earl of Nottingham (1386–99).

[174] *HC, 1386–1421*, ii. 595–6 for Sir Thomas Clinton (d. 1415).

[175] Caludon in Wyken, Warwicks.

le dit monsire Thomas Clynton travaillera et chivachera ovesque nous quel part que nous irrons deins le roialme Dengleterre et demorera ovesque nous a nostre volunte deins nostre houstel ove deux vadletz pur nous faire honure et service come appent, et avera de nous pur la pees bouche a court pur luy et ses ditz vadletz tant seulement pur toutes choses. Et prendra pur la guerre pur luy et ses servantz gages et regard tieux come nous le dit Conte prendrons pur luy et ses ditz servantz de nostre seigneur le Roy pur la viage ou journe quel nous ferrons et sera a bouche de courte ovesque nous ove deux valletz pur mesme le viage. Et si le dit annuel rent soit aderere et nient paie au dit monsire Thomas Clynton apres ascuns des termes susditz qadonque bien lise au dit monsire Thomas en nostre dit manoir destrendre et la destresse retener tanque gree luy soit fait, parensy qil nous face et perfourne son service avantdicte bien et covenablement. En tesmoignance de quele chose sibien nous come le dit monsire Thomas a cestes endentures entrechangeablement si avons mys noz sealx. Done a Londres le sisme jour de Feverer lan du regne le Roy Richard second puis le conquest douzisme.

77 Thomas Mowbray, Earl Marshal and earl of Nottingham and Thomas Fairfax, esquire, York, 27 March 1389 (Berkeley Castle, General Charter 3829, sealed on tongue).[176]

Ceste endenture faite parentre Thomas conte mareschall et de Notyngham, seigneur de Moubray et de Segrave dune parte et Thomas Farefax[177] esquier dautre part tesmoigne que le dit Thomas est retenuz pour terme de sa vie a demourer ovesque le dit conte sibien pour la pees come pour la guerre. Et sera le dit Thomas tenuz par ycestes de chivacher et travailler de pees ove le dit conte ou aillours es choses que touchent la salvacion de lonour ou droit et enheritance du dit conte par resonable garnissement au faire au dit Thomas de par le dit conte. Et prendra du dit conte chescun jour qil sera ensi chivachant vers le dit conte ou travaillant ovesque luy de pees a son mandement autielx gages pour luy et ses chivalx come un autre esquier mesneal de mesme le conte y prendra ove bouche du court pour luy et un vadlet et quant le dit Thomas chivache ou travaille en absence du dit conte as choses que touchent lonur et droitures de mesme le conte si prendra le dit

---

[176] Mowbray's small (15 mm.) signet seal in red wax, displaying a crown above a letter n, flanked by two ears of wheat.

[177] Thomas Fairfax of Walton, near Wetherby, was retained to stay with the king in July 1382 and granted the stewardship of the forest of Galtres, Yorks. N. R., an office he held until his death in Jan. 1395 (*CPR, 1381–5*, 165; York, Borthwick Institute of Historical Research, Bishops' Register 14 f. 48).

Thomas en tiell travaille greignour gages par advis du dit conte ou de soun conseil. Et prendra le dit Thomas du dit conte pour la guerre autielx gages et regard come le dit conte prent du Roy pour homme de soen estat et sera a bouche du court ove un vadlet ovesque luy, pur quel retenu et service faire au dit conte come desuis est dit mesme le conte ad graunte au dit Thomas pour terme de sa vie un annuel rent de dis marcz a prendre de an en an en soun manoir de Hovyngham deinz le countee Deverwyk[178] par my les mayns de soun receyvour illeoques que sera pour le temps as festes de Seint Michel et de Pasques par ovelles porcions.

Et si par cas aveigne que le dit annuel rent soit aderer en partie ou en tout a nient paie au dit Thomas deinz un moys apres ascuns des termes suisditz qadonqes bien lise au dit Thomas a destreigner en le manoir suisdit et la destresse tenir tanques gree a luy soit fait pleinement du dit annuel rent par ensi toutz voies que le dit Thomas perfourme et face les services et devoirs suisditz. Et si aveigne que heritage descende en apres au dit conte a la value de toutz ses terres et services quelx il ad au present entre mayns, qadonqes le dit conte soit tenuz par ycestes de graunter annuelment au dit Thomas pour terme de sa vie autres dys marcz pour ses services et autres devoirs suisditz par luy affaires en la fourme suisdite au dit conte. En tesmoignance de quele chose a la partie de ceste endenture demourant devers le dit conte le dit Thomas ad fait mettre soun seal. Don' a Everwyk le xxvij jour de Marcz lan du regne le Roy Richard second puis le conquest duszisme.[179]

Dorse: Fairfax

78 Thomas Mowbray, Earl Marshal and earl of Nottingham and Sir Robert Legh, London, 7 May 1389 (PRO, C66/373 m. 15, *inspeximus* of 11 June 1405).[180]

Ceste endenture faite parentre nous Thomas conte Mareschall et de Notyngham seignour de Moubray et de Segrave dune parte et nostre

---

[178] Hovingham, Yorks. N. R.

[179] On the tongue is the signature of the clerk *Brunham* which in the form *Burnham* appears on other Mowbray documents (e.g. Berkeley Castle, General Charter 3819, quittance of Thomas Etton for part of his annuity from the Earl Marshal, York, 19 March 1389). Thomas Burnham of Axholme was one of the most active of Mowbray's councillors (R. E. Archer, 'The Mowbrays, Earls of Nottingham and Dukes of Norfolk to 1432', Unpublished D. Phil thesis, Oxford 1984, 347).

[180] cf. *CPR, 1405–1408*, 29.

trescher et biename bachiler monsire Robert de Legh[181] dautre part tesmoigne que le dit monsire Robert est demorez et retenuz devers nous pour terme de sa vie sibien pour la guerre come pour la pees. Et prendra le dit monsire Robert pour la pees une annuite de vint marcz par an pour terme de sa vie as termes de Seint Michell et de Pasque par oveles porcions des issues de nostre manoir de Melton Moubray[182] deinz le countee de Laycestre par les mayns de noz fermers, baillifs ou provostes quy pur le temps serront, pour quelle annuite le dit monsire Robert serra tenuz daler et chivacher ovesque nous quel partie que nous travaillerons deins le roialme Dengleterre a quel heure qil soit comandez depar nous. Et a quelle heure que nous serrons encresce par descent deritage de noz terres adonque le dit monsire Robert serra encresce de son annuitee par dys marcz. Et auxi sovent que le dit monsire Robert serra commandez depar nous pour venir devers nous le dit monsire Robert serra allouez de ses costages pour le temps qil demorera entour nous en manere come autres bachilers de son estat serront alouez. Et avera a bouche de court luy mesmes un esquier et un vadlet en temps de pees. Et sil aveigne que le dit annuitee de vynt marcz soit aderer en partie ou en tout par un moys apres ascun des ditz termes adonque bien lise au dit monsire Robert en le dit manoir de Melton Moubray destreindre et les destresses ent retenir tanque gree luy soit fait de ferme susdicte. Et prendra le dit monsire Robert pour la guerre pour luy et ses gentz darmes et archers qil amesnera tielx gages et regard come nous prenderons de nostre seignour le Roy pour le dit viage. Et averons du dit monsire Robert la tierce partie de toutz maneres de profitz ou gaignez par voie de guerre. En tesmoignance de quel chose a les parties de cestes endentures sibien nous come le dit monsire Robert entrechangeablement avons mys noz sealx. Donnee a Loundres le vij jour de May lan du regne le Roy Richard seconde puis le conquest duszime.

79 Thomas Mowbray, Earl Marshal and earl of Nottingham and

[181] Of Adlington, Cheshire, Legh was one of the most prominent of the Cheshire gentry; sheriff of the county, Oct. 1393–Aug. 1394 and Feb. 1397–Sept. 1400, he was retained for life by Richard II at a fee of £40 p.a. in Aug. 1397 and appointed constable of Oswestry castle in the following Oct. Though his fee was confirmed by Henry IV, he was involved in the Percy rebellion of 1403. Subsequently pardoned, he entered the service of Prince Henry, fought with him in Wales in 1406 and acted as his deputy in the office of justiciar of South Wales in 1407. The origin of his connection with Mowbray may lie in the earl's need to raise a retinue for service in the East March in 1389; the links between the two men remained strong until at least 1396 (*DKR*, 36 (1875), App. II, 290–1, 293; *CPR, 1391–6*, 177, 204, 573; *ibid., 1401–5*, 259; *ibid., 1405–8*, 145; *CFR, 1391–9*, 122, 195; R. A. Griffiths, *The Principality of Wales in the Later Middle Ages* (Cardiff, 1972), 128.

[182] Melton Mowbray, Leics.

Richard Burgh, London, 22 February 1390 (PRO, C66/359 m. 28, *inspeximus* of 24 February 1400).[183]

Ceste endenture faite parentre nous Thomas Count Mareschall et de Notyngham seignour de Moubray et de Segrave dune part et nostre trescher et bien ame esquier Richard de Burgh dautre part tesmoigne que nous confiaunce en les loialtee, sen et bon discrecion du dit Richard luy avons ordenez et constitut nostre chief chamberlein a avoir le dit office pur terme de sa vie ovesque toutz les fees et profitz a ycell regardantz, a demorer continuelment entour nostre person ou aillours par nostre assignement. Et serra le dit Richard tenuz de nous faire honur, profit et service en le dit office come appent au chaumberlein de faire a son seignour. Et volons que le dit Richard preigne toutz les biens et hernoys qappartienent au dit office par endenture et les livera par endenture quant et solonc ceo qe busoignera et come il vorra respoundre sur son acompt. Et pour le bon et greable service que le dit Richard nous ad fait et ferra en temps avenir luy avons donez et grantez par ycestez un annuel rent de vint livres a prendre dan en an de nostre manoir de Burton en Lonesdal[184] a toute sa vie as festes de Pasche et de Seint Michell par oveles porcions par quel annuitee le dit Richard est retenuz et demorez devers nous pour toute sa vie sibien pour la pees come pour la guerre en la forme qensuit. Cest assavoir que le dit Richard travaillera et chivauchera ovesque nous quele partie que nous irrons deinz le roialme Dengleterre et demorara ovesque nous a nostre volunte deinz nostre hostell ove un vadlet pour nous fair[e] honour et service come appent, et avera de nous pour la pees bouche de court pour luy et un vadlet et pour ses chivaux gages de nostre hostell acustumez, et prendra pour la guerre pour luy et ses servantz gagez et regardez tielx come nous le dit conte prenderons pour luy et ses servantz de nostre seignour le Roy pour la viage ou journee quele nous ferrons, et serra a bouche de court ovesque nous ove un vadlet pour mesme la viage. Et si le dit annuel rent soit aderer en partie ove (*sic*) en tout et nient paie au dit Richard par un moys appres ascuns des termes suisditz qeadonqe bien lise au dit Richard en nostre dit manoir destrendre et la destresse retenir tanque gree luy soit fait parensi qil nous face et parfourne bien et co[ve]nablement son service avantdit. En tesmoignance de quel chose si bien nous le dit conte come le dit Richard as parties de cestes endentures entrechangeablement avons mys noz sealx. Donnee a Loundres le xxii jour de Feverer lan du regne le Roy Richard second puis le conquest treszisme.[185]

---

[183] cf. *CPR, 1399–1401*, 234.

[184] Burton in Lonsdale, Yorks. W. R.

[185] Burgh held the manors of Colthorp, Bykerton and Couesby, Yorks. For his service to the Mowbrays between 1389 and 1404, see Archer, 'The Mowbrays', 347. He also

80 Thomas Mowbray, Earl Marshal, earl of Nottingham and Sir Richard Basset, Epworth, Parts of Lindsey, Lincs., 26 May 1391 (PRO, C66/358 m. 10, *inspeximus* of 16 February 1400).[186]

Ceste endenture faite parentre nous Thomas conte mareschall et de Notyngham, seignur de Moubray et de Segrave dun part et nostre trescher et bien ame bacheler monsire Richard Basset[187] dautre part tesmoigne que le dit monsire Richard est demourez et retenuz devers nous pour terme de sa vie si bien pour la pees come pour la guerre. Et prendra le dit monsire Richard de nous pour la pees une annuite de dys marcz des issues provenantz de nostre manoir de Eppeworthe en lisle Daxholm de an en an a terme de toute sa vie as festes de seint Michel et de Pasques par ovelles porcions. Et serra le dit monsire Richard tenuz de chivaucher ovesque nous quele part qil nous chivacherons deinz le roialme Dengleterre, et avera le dit monsire Richard en temps de pees bouche de courte en nostre houstelle pour luy mesmes, un vadlet et un servant au temps que nous envoierons pour le dit monsire Richard et avera gages pur ses chivaux comes autres bachelers de son estate prendront de nous. Et avera le dit monsire Richard en temps de guerre tielx gages et regardes pour luy et pour les gentz qil amenera come nous le dit conte prendrons de nostreseignur le roy pour luy et ses ditz gentz et avera le dit conte la tiers de la tierz de ses gentz et la tiers de soy mesmes des gaignes de guerre par luy et ses ditz servantz, et avera en temps de guerre bouche de courte pour luy mesmes un vadlet et un servant. Et si le dit annuite de dys marcz soit aderer en partie ou en toute par deux moys apres ascuns des termes suisditz qadonque bien lise a dit monsire Richard en nostre dit manoir destreindre tanque gree luy soit fait de ceo que luy est aderere de son annuite suisdit issint toutz foitz qil face et perforne son service bien et convenablement. En tesmoignance de quele chose as parties de cestes endentures les parties susditz entrechangeablement ont mys lour sealx. Donne a nostre manoir de Eppeworth le xxvi jour de May lan du regne le roy Richard second puis le conquest quatorzisme.

81 Sir Ivo FitzWarin and Ralph Brit, Caundle Haddon, Dorset, 27 January 1392 (PRO, JUST 1/1519 m. 30).[188]

---

held the manors of Kirkby Malzeard, Yorks., and Weston by Chiriton, Warwicks., by grant of the Earl Marshal: *CIM, 1392–9*, nos. 388–9.

[186] cf. *CPR, 1399–1401*, 196.

[187] Basset was apparently a professional soldier in the Calais garrison; his indenture with Mowbray follows soon after the earl's appointment as captain of Calais on 1 Feb. 1391: *CPR, 1396–9*, 42; *ibid., 1399–1401*, 438; *CCR, 1396–9*, 364; *ibid., 1399–1401*, 314.

[188] This indenture was recited in a plea of novel disseisin brought by Brit against FitzWarin before the justices of assize at Dorchester, 23 Feb. 1411. A truncated version is preserved on the dorse of a contemporary copy of the assize proceedings (BL, Add. Roll

A touz yceux qi cestes lettres verront ou orront Ioun fitz Wareyn chivaler saluz en Dieux. Sachez moi avoir done et graunte et par icest escript endente conferme a Rauf Bryt fitz Rauf Bryzt del Merssh toutz mes terres et tenementz, rentes, services et reversions en Antiokes al countee de Dors' qux Richard Charleton nadgairs tenoit a tout sa vie. Et auxi jai done et graunte a dit Rauf fitz Rauf Bryt del Merssh toutz les rentes et servicez William Hoke qux il a moy rent annuelement pur touz lez terres et tenementz ove lour appurtenauncez appellez le Wythye qil de moi tient a terme de sa vie en Caundell Merssh en mesme le countee ensemblement ove la reversion de mesme lez terres et tenementz ove lour appurtenauncez come eschut apres la mort le dit William a avoir et tenir a dit Rauf fitz Rauf pour terme de sa vie rendant ent par an au dit Ioun, ses heires ou assignes un rose al fest de Seint Johan le Baptistre et a labbe de Shirbourne annuelment tresze soultz quatre deniers durant la vie le dit Rauf fitz Rauf sur tiel condicion que le dit Rauf fitz Rauf serra retenuz ove le dit Ioun fitz Wareyn come son esquier si bien pour guerre come pour la pees pour tut sa vie. Et le dit Rauf fitz Rauf prendra annuelment tiel vesture come autres gentils preignont de dit monsire Ioun et bouche de court pour luy et un valet, feyn et provendre pour deux chivalx as coustages le dit monsire Ioun pour la pees. Et si le dit Rauf fitz Rauf irra ove dit monsire Ioun as guerres le Roy, prendra lez gages et regard du roy pour luy et son archer du dit monsire Ioun et auxint skippeson pour eux et lours chivalx come affiert a lour estat. Et le dit Ioun voet et graunte par ycestes que si aveigne que le dit Rauf fitz Rauf veigne a tiel age ou qil soit malades ou autrement pris par ascun infirmite issint

74138). FitzWarin justified the dissesin on the grounds that, on 4 Oct. 1403 at Elkstone, Gloucs., he had asked Brit to do his service as an esquire in time of peace and ride with him to his manor of Blunsdon, Wilts., but that Brit, though in good health and in possession of the disputed tenements, had refused. Brit justified his refusal on the grounds that FitzWarin had previously refused to give him the clothing of an esquire or to provide any of the other benefits specified in the indenture and had expelled him from his household at Caundle Haddon, Dorset. Both parties put themselves on the assize and were given a day to appear before the justices of the Common Bench at Westminster on Monday next after the month of Easter 1411. The case was postponed until Hilary 1412, when both sides rehearsed their previous pleadings, and the justices found that Brit should recover the disputed tenements. Fitzwarin immediately sued out a writ of error and the case was called into King's Bench, where it was subsequently non-suited by the death of Henry IV. Fitzwarin obtained a second writ of error and pleading resumed in Trinity 1413, when he again repeated the substance of his original defence, adding only the secondary point that Brit's title to the tenements formerly held by William Oke was insufficient. A day was given for Easter 1414 but no further record of the case appears on the roll for that, or the three subsequent terms. Fitzwarin's death in September 1414 effectively brought the case to a close (PRO, CP40/601 m. 319; KB27/604, Attornies, m. 1; 605 m. 31). For Brit in FitzWarin's service in 1401 see *PPC*, ii. 109 and for FitzWarin (1347–1414), *HC, 1386–1421*, iii. 84–7.

qil soit en nonpoar de travailler en manere come desuis est dit ou que
le dit monsire Ioun defaille envers le dit Rauf fitz Rauf en null des
covenantz avantditz que le dit Rauf fitz Rauf ayt et emoise touz lez
terrez et tenementz, rentes, services et reversions avantditz ove lez
appurtenantz en manere come desuis est dit, et outre ceo que le dit
Rauf fitz Rauf soit descharge devers le dit monsire Ioun a luy servir
come est avantdit, porveu toutzfoitz qa quelle temps que le dit Rauf
soit sayn et en poair de travailler et que le dit monsire Ioun tiegne et
perfourne toutz les covenantz avantditz de sa part a tenir qadonque le
dit Rauf fitz Rauf soit tenuz deservir le dit monsire Ioun en manere et
forme avantdit. Et le dit monsire Ioun et [ses]ᵃ heirs garaunteront,
acquiteront et defenderount touz les ditz terrez et tenementz, rentes,
servicez et reversions ove lour appurtenauntz a dit Rauf fitz Rauf pour
terme de sa vie sur la condicion et en la forme et manere avantdit. En
tesmoignance de quelle chose sibien le dit monsire Ioun come le dit
Rauf fitz Rauf a ycestes endentures entrechaungeablement ount mys
lour sealx par yceux tesmoignes Johan Tower, Johan Glaunnvill,
Thomas Peytevyn, Johan ffauntlerey, Johan Plumber et altres. Don' a
Caundell le dymenge proschein apres la Chaundelhure lan du regne
nostre seignur le Roy Richard quinzisme.

a. Omitted in text.

82 Thomas Beauchamp, earl of Warwick and Walter Power, Warwick,
12 September 1392 (PRO, C66/340 m. 28, *inspeximus* of 4 July 1394).[189]

Ceste endenture fait parentre luy nobles hommes monsire Thomas de
Beauchamp conte de Warr' dune part et Wauter Power esquier[190]
dautre part tesmoigne que le dit Wauter est demore ove le dit conte
pur terme de sa vie sibien pur la pees come pur la guerre preignant
annuelment du dit conte pur le pees dis livrez et pur la guerre vint
livrez des manoirs de Buddebrok la Grove et Haseley en le contee de
Warr'[191] a les festes de la Nativite seint Johan le Baptistre et de Nowell
par oveles porcions des issues de mesmes les manoirs par les mayns des
baillis ou provostes illoesqes qui pur le temps serront. Et serra le dit
Wauter meynal ove le dit conte sibien en temps de pees come en temps
de guerre et avera bouche en court pur luy mesmes et un vadlet et
feyn, provendre et ferrure pour deux chivalx come autres esquiers de

[189] cf. *CPR, 1391–6*, 238.
[190] For an earlier indenture between these two parties, see above **72**.
[191] Budbroke, Grove Park by Warwick, and Haseley, Warwicks.; *CIM, 1392–9*, nos.
305–6.

son estat preignont du dit conte. Et avera le dit conte la tierce de qanque le dit Wauter et ses servantz preignont par voie de guerre issint que null prisoner soit mys al finance sanz lassent du dit conte. Et voet et grante le dit conte que si le dit annuel rent de dis livrez par an pour la pees ou de vint livrez pur la guerre soit aderere par un moys apres ascuns des termes avantditz, que bien lise au dit Wauter ou a son attourne celle partie en les manoirs avantditz destreindre et les destresses retinir tanque plein paiement luy ent soit fait. Et comencera le dit Wauter son an de guerre le jour de son remuement de son hostiel propre vers les parties ou le dit conte luy mandra par ses lettres. En tesmoignance de quel chose a cestes presentes endentures les avantditz conte et Wauter entrechangeablement ont mys lour sealx. Don' a nostre chastel de Warrewyk le duszisme jour de Septembre lan du reigne nostre seigneur le Roy Richard second puis le conquest seszisme.

83 Thomas Mowbray, Earl Marshal and earl of Nottingham and William Sutton, piper, Epworth, 26 July 1393 (Berkeley Castle, General Charter 3876, formerly sealed on a tag).

Ceste endenture faite parentre nous Thomas conte Mareschall et de Notyngham, seigneur de Moubray et de Segrave dune part et William Sutton piper dautre part tesmoigne que le dit William est demorez et retenuz devers nous pur nous servir de son mestier pur toute sa vie sibien pour la pees come pur la guerre. Et prendra de nous en temps de pees un annuite de quatre marcs a prendre annuelment pour toute sa vie des issues de nostre manoir de Thresk[192] en le contee Deverwyk as termes de Seint Michel et de Pasques par oveles porcions et sera tenuz le dit William de venir a nous a nostre commandement pur nous faire service come appent. Et avera bouche de court pur luy et[a] liveree pur son cheval en manere come ses compaignons noz autres ministralx prendront de nous a chescun temps que le dit William viendra a nostre houstel a nostre commandement.[b] Et prendra de nous en temps de guerre autieux gages et regardes come ses compaignons noz ministralx prendront. En tesmoignance de quele chose as parties de cestes endentures sibien le dit conte come le dit William ont mys lour sealx. Don' a Eppeworth'[193] le xxvj jour de Juyl lan du regne le Roy Richard second puis le conqueste dys et septisme.

Dorse: William Sutton sa rendre au service par indenture

[192] Thirsk, Yorks. N.R.
[193] Epworth, Parts of Lindsey, Lincs.

a. *et* interlined
b. *a nostre commandement* interlined

84 Thomas, lord Despenser and John Willicotes (Wilcotes), Cardiff, 29 September 1395 (PRO, C66/358 m. 17, *inspeximus* of 15 February 1400).[194]

Ceste endenture tesmoigne que Johan Willicotes esquier[195] del counte Doxenford est detenuz et demourez ovesque son treshonure seigneur Thomas sire le Despenser pour pais et guerre pur terme de vie de dit Johan preignant annuelment de son dit seigneur pur son fee x li. en le Brodeton[196] en le counte de Wilts' a les festes de Paske[a] et de seint Michel par oweles porcions a terme de vie de dit Johan sur les condicions qensuent. Cestassav[oir] que en cas que son dit seigneur travaille a fere de guerre hors de roialme Dengleterre ovesque nostre seigneur le Roy ou en son service ou ove ascun autre pur queles viages, son dit seigneur prendra fees et gages et le dit Johan soit requis et charge pur aler et travailler ovesque son dit seigneur en les ditz viages, le dit Johan sera tenuz daler et travailler ovesque son dit seigneur luy mesmez, et ses gentz bien et covenablement arme et montez chescun solonc lour estat et degree pernant de son dit seigneur pur les ditz viages outre son dit fee de x li. fees et gages pur luy mesmes et ses gentz qil soit charge et comande de mesner ovesque luy a tant come autres gentz de son estate et degree prendront de son dit seigneur pur les ditz viage. Et outre ceo si le dit Johan soit charge par message ou par lettre de venir a son dit seigneur vers ascuns parties deinz le roialme Dengleterre ou de Galys ove ascun nombre des gentz que soit greindre ou meindre, le dit Johan est tenuz sur resonable garnisement de venir et lez amesner si ensy soit qil ne poet luy excuser par cause resonable, et pur tantz des gentz qil amesne avera et prendra gages solonc lour estat et degree pur le temps qills serront en le servise de lour dit seigneur. Et en cas que le dit Johan soit charge ou mande par lettre ou par ascun autre mandement de venir a son dit seigneur vers ascuns parties deinz le roialme Dengleterre ou de Galis, le dit Johan est tenuz de venir a son dit seigneur ove un[b] vadlet, un garson et trois chivaux preignant gages pur luy et ses deux gentz et trois chivaux come autres de son estate et degree ent preignont de lour dit seigneur. Et si les x li. pur le fee de dit Johan soient aderere en partie ou en tut par qarant jours apres ascuns des termes suisditz et pur terme du vie du dit Johan

[194] cf. *CPR, 1399–1401*, 189. For Thomas, fifth lord Despenser (1375–1400), see GEC, iv. 278–81.
[195] *HC, 1386–1421*, iv. 860–3 for John Wilcotes of Great Tew, Oxon. (d. 1422).
[196] Broadtown, Wilts.

qadonqs bien lise au dit Johan en tout le dit Brodeton distrendre pur le dit rent si soit aderer et la distresse amesner et recever tanque pleine gree luy soit fait de la dit rent ove les arrerages saunz contredit de nully. En tesmoignance de quele chose sibien le dit Thomas come le dit Johan aycestis endentures entrechageablement ont mys lour sealx. Done a Kerdef le jour de seint Michel larchang[el] lan du reigne le Roy Ric[hard] seconde puys le conquest ditzneofisme.

   a. de Paske interlined
   b. MS *une*

85 Thomas, duke of Gloucester and William Cheyne, Pleshey, 30 September 1395 (PRO, C66/356 m. 8, *inspeximus* of 13 November 1399).[197]

Ceste endenture faite parentre Thomas Duc de Gloucestre dune parte et William Cheyne esquier[198] dautre parte tesmoigne que le dit William est demoerez et retenuz devers le dit Duc pur paix et guerre a terme de sa vie et le dit William est tenuz de servir le dit Duc sibien en temps de paix come de guerre es quelx parties que plerra au dicte Duc bien et covenablement montez et arraiez solenc son degree, et prendra le dit William du dicte Duc pour son fee sibien en temps de paix come de guerre sesze livres par an de la seignurie de Holdirnesse[199] par les meynes del Recevour de la dicte seignurie qui pour le temps serra as termes de Pasqes et de Seint Michell par egales porceons, et avera le dit William pour lui et un valet, son chamberleyn, bouche de court as toutz les foitz quil serra en la courte du dicte Duc de mandement et voluntee le dicte Duc et le dit William avera trois chivalx a livere de feyn, aveynes et ferrure pour la guerre, et en temps du paix qant il serra en la contre du dit Duc il avera livere ou gages pour ses chivaux tieles et en manere come autres de sa condicion averont. En droit des prisoners et autres profitz de guerre de tout ce que serra gaigne par le dit William ou par nul de soens le dite Duc avera la tierce partie entiere et si persone roiale, chivetayn ou lieutenant de guerre soit pris par le dit William ou par nuls des soens le dicte Duc sil voet avera les prisoners par devers lui, resonable gree fesant a lui qui les ad pris, et ferra le dit William moustre de lui et de touz ceux quil avera en sa compaignie en la guerre quant et atant des foitz quil enserra requys par le dit Duc ou par son lieutenant qui pour le temps serra de les

[197] cf. *CPR, 1399–1401*, 117. For Thomas, duke of Gloucester (1385–97) see GEC, v. 719–28.

[198] Of Stainton-by-Irford and Searby, Lincs. (*CFR, 1391–9*, 127; *CPR, 1399–1401*, 152).

[199] Holderness, Yorks. E. R.

guerres, et le dit William ove touz les soens serra entendant et obeisant au dit lieutenant selonc les ordenances et volentees du dite Duc, et si le dit Duc travaillera sur les enemys Dieux et plese avoir le dit William en sa compaignie le dit William serra au bouche de courte et son dicte chamberlein pernant son dicte fee sanz autres fees ou gages pur celle viage prendre. En tesmoignance de quelle chose les dictes Duc et William as cestes endentures entrechaungeablement ont mys lour sealx. Donne a Plecy[200] le darrein jour de Septembre lan du regne nostre seignur le Roy Richard second puis le conquest Dengleterre dys et neofisme.

86 Thomas Mowbray, Earl Marshal and earl of Nottingham and Sir John Inglethorpe (Ingoldisthorpe), London, 26 April 1396 (PRO, C66/358 m. 13, *inspeximus* of 17 November 1399).[201]

Ceste endenture faite parentre nous Thomas counte de Notyngham et mareschall Dengleterre, seignur de Moubray et de Segrave dune parte et monsire Johan Ingelthorpe dautre parte tesmoigne qe le dit monsire Johan est demorrez et retenuz devers nous pour toute sa vie si bien pour la pees comme pour la guerre. Et prendra le dit monsire Johan pour la pees annuelment durant sa vie vynt livres des issues de nostre manoir de Wylingtone en la countee de Bed[ford]e[202] par les mayns des ffermers ou resceyvours illeoqes quy pour le temps seront as festes de Paske et seynt Michelle par owelles porcions. Et prendra le dit monsire Johan en temps de guerre pour luy et sa gent quil amesnera al tielx gages come nous le dit conte prendrons de nostre seignur le Roy pour le dit monsire Johan et ses ditz gentz pour le viage ou journe affaire. Et volons outre que apres ceo que nous sumes encresce par descent de heritage par la morte de nostre treshonoure dame et miere qadonque la dicte annuyte de vynt livre sera chaungez a quel lieu que nous et le dit monsire Johan purrons accorder que soit pluis pres leritage de dit monsire Johan. Et a quel heure que nous enveions pour le dit monsire Johan par noz lettres il prendra de nous autielx gages come nous durrons a autry bacheler de son estat. En tesmoignance de quele chose sibien le dit counte come le dit monsire Johan a ycestes endentures entrechangeablement ont mys lours sealx. Donne a Loundres le vynt et sisme jour daprill lan du regne le roy Richard le secound puis le conquest dys et noefisme.

[200] Pleshey, Essex.
[201] cf. *CPR, 1399–1401*, 193; *HC, 1386–1421*, iii. 475–7 for Sir John Ingoldisthorpe (*c.* 1361–1420) of Ingoldisthorpe and Raynham, Norf.
[202] Willington, Beds.

87 Thomas, lord Despenser and William Daventry, Sherston, 1 October 1396 (PRO, C66/358 m. 4, *inspeximus* of 14 November 1399).[203]

Ceste endenture tesmoigne que William Daventre esquier[204] del counte de Northampton est retenuz ademurrer ovesque mon treshonoure seigneur Thomas sire le Despenser, seigneur de Glamm' et Morg' pur pees et pur guerre pur terme du vie de son dit seigneur sur certeinez condicions qensuont. Cestassavoir que qant le dit William soit requis ou charge par son dit seigneur ou par mandement de sa lettre de venir a luy quel part qil soit deinz la roialme Dengleterre ou de Gales par sa lettre, le dit William viendra a son dit seigneur sur resonable garnisment ove trois chivaux et deux servauntes, preignant gages en manere come autre de son estat preignont enalant et retornant, et a sa venue tanque come il soit demurant en la compaignie de son dit seigneur il, sez servantez et ses chivaux serront a bouche de court. Outre ceo en cas que le dit William soit charge par son dit seigneur ou comande par sa lettre damesner ascunz gentz de quelle estat qills soient par la comandement susdit, que par tantez qil amesne il prendra gages pur eux accordantz a lour estatez pur aler demurer et retorner a lour hostiell. Et auxi en cas que son dit seigneur veulle travailler ou prendre ascun viage hors de roialme Dengleterre pur le quell il prendra gages de Roy ou dascun autre seigniour qeconque, si le dit William soit requis daler ovesque luy, il est tenuz daler ovesque luy et ove null autre en cas que le dit William veulle travailler, pernant de son dit seigneur tiellx gages come autrez de son estat et degree preignont, purveu toutfoiz qil ne travaillera ovesque null autre hors de roialme santz conge de son dit seigneur. Et outre ce si le dit seigneur veulle travailler en ascunz partiez hors de roialme Deingleterre sur les enemys nostreseigneur Jhesu Crist, a ses costages propres, et le dit William soit requis par son dicte seigneur daler ovesque luy, il serra tenuz de le faire, en cas que le dit William veulle travailler hors de roialme come desuiz est dicte prendra bouche de court pur luy et deux servantez et trois chivaux come desuiz est dit saunz autres gages. Et si le dit William plede ou soit emplede par ascun issint qil soit necessarie et busoignable dattendre, il serra excuse devers son dit seigneur dattendre entour sez busoignes avantditz pur le temps qil serra necessairement occupie entour ycell. Et si le dit William veulle aler hors de roialme en ascune pilgremage nient armez, il est tenuz pur demander conge de son dit seigneur de ceo faire le quell luy serra graunte. Et pur ycestez demure, service et retenue le dit Thomas son seigneur grante au dit William pur terme de vie une annuelte de vynt

[203] cf. *CPR, 1399–1401*, 182–3.

[204] Of Potcote in Cold Higham, Northants. (*CIPM*, xvii. 737). Daventry was already in possession of an annuity of £20 from Sherston, granted him by Edward, fourth lord Despenser, in April 1373. He was also constable of the Despenser castle of Llantrisant, Glamorgan (*CPR, 1388–92*, 397).

marcz de bone monee Dengleterre apprendre de son manoir de Scherston en le counte de Wilts'[205] a lez festes de Pasch et de seint Michel par owells porcons. Et si le dit annuelte soit aderere en parcell ou en tout par quinsze jours ascunz des termes susditz durant toute la vie du dit William bien lise au dit William ou son attorne en le dit manoir ove toux les appurtenances distreindre et la distresse amesner ou que luy plest tanque il soit pleignement paiez de la dite annuelte et de les arrirages si ascunz isseront et sez costages. Et le dit Thomas, son seigneur, et sez heires la dite annuelte de prendre de la dit manoir ove lez appurtenancez en la forme susdite au dit William pur terme de sa vie encontre toux gentz garrenteront. En tesmoignance de quele chose a la partie de ceste endenture entrechangeablement avons mys nostre seal. Don' a Scherston le primer jour doctobre lan du regne le Roy Ric[hard] seconde puis le conquest vintisme.

88 Thomas Mowbray, Earl Marshal and earl of Nottingham and Richard FitzNichol, London, 18 April 1397 (PRO, C66/359 m. 36, *inspeximus* of 16 November 1399).[206]

Ceste endenture fait parentre Thomas conte de Notyngham, mareschall Dengleterre, seigneur de Moubray, de Segrave et de Gower dune part, et nostre cher et biename esquier Richard Fitznycholl,[207] dautrepart, tesmoigne que le dit Richard est retenuz et demurez devers nous pur terme de sa vie sibien pur la pees come pur la guerre. Et prendra le dit Richard de nous pur la pees une annuittee de dys marcs par an dont il sera paiez annuelment des issues et profitz provenantz de nostre manoir de Hynton en la countee de Cantebrigg[208] a les festes de seint Michel et de Pasch par owelles porcions parmy les mayns de noz fermers ou receyvours qui sont ou seront pur le temps. Et prendra le dit Richard de nous pur la guerre autielx gages pur luy come nous prendrons de nostre seigneur le Roy pur ascun autre de son degree pur le voiage ou journe afaire. En tesmoignance de quele chose as ycestes endentures sibien nous le dit counte come le dit Richard entrechaungeablement avons mys noz sealx. Don' a Londres le xviii jour daveryll lan du regne le Roy Richard secund vintisme.

---

[205] Sherston, Wilts.

[206] cf. *CPR, 1399–1401*, 224.

[207] Of Halstead, Essex. In 1386 he was an esquire in the service of Sir John Stanley, but was already associated with several established Mowbray servants by 1390 (*CCR, 1409–13*, 206; *ibid., 1413–19*, 80, 508; *CPR, 1388–92*, 231). For his subsequent career in Mowbray service, Archer 'The Mowbrays', 352. By 1408 he is described as a king's esquire (*CPR, 1408–13*, 3; *CCR, 1405–9*, 451).

[208] Cherry Hinton, Cambs.

89 Roger Mortimer, earl of March and Ulster and Sir Hugh Cheyne, Connaught, 20 October 1397 [French] (PRO, C66/369 m. 24, pub. in Holmes, 129–30).[209]

90 Roger Mortimer, earl of March and James Butler, earl of Ormond and William, son of Piers Butler, Trim Castle, Co. Meath, 23 November 1397 (NLI, Ormond Deeds D 1365, sealed on tag).[210]

Ceste endenture faite parentre Roger de Mortemer conte de la March et Dulvestier, seignur de Wiggemore, Clare, Trym et Connaght dune parte et James le Boteller, conte Dormond et William filz Piers Boteller dautre parte tesmoigne que les ditz conte Dormond et William et chescun de eux pour le bone cousinage et entiere naturesce que le dit conte de la March lour ad fait et monstre, donant et grantant par sa chartre parentre eux endente au dit William, ses manoirs de Dunboigne et Moiemet[211] ove les appartenances en la contee de Mid' a avoir et tenir au dit William et a les heirs masles de son corps engendrez, issint que si le dit William devye saunz heir masle de son corps engendre qadonques, apres la mort du dit William, les ditz manoirs ove les appartenances remeignent au dit conte Dormond et as heirs masles de son corps engendrez, la reversion des ditz manoirs ove les appartenances apres la morte des ditz William et conte Dormond, sils et chescun de eulx devyent saunz heir masle de lour corps engendre, au dit conte de la March et ses heirs reserve, sont demurrez envers le dit conte de la March pour paix et guerre a terme de loures vies, destre du conseil le dit conte de la March et luy foialment conseiller a tout lour seen[a] et poair et de travailler en la companye le dit Conte de la March et ses deputes en sabsence[b] en ses guerres Dirlande ove tauntz des gentz come ils purront bonement amesner selonc ceo qils ou lautre de eaux seront ou serra resonablement garniz depar le dit conte de la March a ses coustages resonables. En tesmoignance de quele chose les parties avantditz a cestes endentures entrechangeablement ont mys lours sealx. Don' al Chastel de Trym le vyngtisme tierce jour de Novembre lan du regne le Roy Richard second vyngtisme primer.

[209] cf. *CPR 1401–5*, 229; GEC, viii. 448–50 for Roger Mortimer, earl of March (1381–98), and *HC, 1386–1421*, ii. 545–7 and above **61** for Cheyne.
[210] An impression of March's seal survives; cf. *Cal. of Ormond Deeds*, ed. Curtis, ii. no 323 (2); GEC, x. 121–3 for James Butler, third earl of Ormond (1381–1405). D. B. Johnston, 'The Interim Years: Richard II and Ireland, 1395–1399', *England and Ireland in the Late Middle Ages*, ed. J. Lydon (Blackrock, 1981), 189–90 for the circumstances in which this indenture was concluded.
[211] Dunboyne and Moiemet, Co. Meath.

a. Possibly *seeu*

b. *et ses deputez en sabsence* interlined

91 John Holland, duke of Exeter and Thomas Trevarake, London, 22 September 1399 (PRO, C66/359 m. 9, *inspeximus* of 6 April 1400).[212]

Cest endenture fait parentre Johan Duc Dexcestre, Counte de Huntyngdon et Chamberlein Dengleterre dune parte et Thomas Trevarake esquier[213] dautre parte tesmoigne que lavantdit Thomas est retenuz et demurrez devers le dit Duc pour estre ovec luy devant toutz vivantz forpris soun seignur lige sibien pur la pees come pur la guerre suffisantment arraies come appartient a soun estat del jour de la fesance dicestes a terme de sa vie. Et prendra le dit Thomas du dit Duc annuelment durant sa dicte vie dys livres des issuez et proffitz prevanantz du seignurie du dit Duc de Comartyn en la countie de Devenshire[214] as termes de Pasques et de Seint Michel par ovelles porcions par les mayns de son resceivour illoeques pur le temps esteant. Et pour la guerre tielx gages et regard pur luy mesmes come null autre de son estat ou condicion avera ou prendra du dit Duc. Et si aveigne que le dit Thomas soit envoiez en message du dit Duc le dit Thomas prendra tielx gages et regard come null autre de son estat ou condicion avera du dit Duc. Et pour le temps que le dit Thomas sera a lostel du dit Duc par son commandement il avera et prendra les gages de lostiel come les autres de son estat. Et en cas que le dit anuelte de dys livres soit aderere en partie ou en tout as ascuns des termes desuisditz que bien lise au dit Thomas et a ses assignes en le dit seignurie distreindre et enprendre distresse tanque le dit Thomas soit pleinement de toutz les arrerages paiez de tout le temps ency encorruz. Et cestes covenantz bien et loialment tenir garder et acomplir le dit Thomas ad fait seurement au dit Duc sur les Saintz Ewangilx. En tesmoignance de la quele chose les parties desuis ditz entrechangeablement ont mys lour sealx. Done a Londres le xxij jour de Septembre lan du regne le Roy Richard second vint et tierce.

92 John Holland, duke of Exeter and Thomas Proudfoot, London, 24

[212] cf. *CPR, 1399–1401,* 255. For John Holland, duke of Exeter (1397–9), see GEC, v. 195–200.

[213] In Feb. 1401 Trevarake was granted the keeping of the manor of Winkleigh Tracy, Devon, which Thomas Proudfoot (below **92**) formerly had of the grant of John Holland (*CFR, 1399–1405,* 104).

[214] Coombe Martin, Devon.

September 1399 (PRO, C66/359 m. 18, *inspeximus* of 18 March 1400).[215]

Ceste endenture fait parentre Johan Duc Dexcestre Counte de Hunt-yngdon et Chamberlein Dengleterre dune parte et Thomas Prodefote esquier[216] dautre parte tesmoigne que lavantidt Thomas est retenuz et demores devers le dit Duc pur estre ovesque luy devant toutz vivantz forpris son seignour lige sibien pour la paes come pour la guerre suffisantment araies come appartient a soun estat del jour de la faisance dicestes a terme de sa vie. Et prendra le dit Thomas du dit Duc annuelment durant sa dite vie dys livres, pour les quelles dys livres le dit Duc done et graunte au dit Thomas toutz les terres et tenementz, rentes et services de Wynkelegh Tracy ove les appurtenantz en la countee de Devenshire[217] a terme de la vie du dit Thomas. Et le dit Thomas maintiegnera et susteindra bien et covenablement durant sa dicte vie toutz les ditz terres et tenementz, rentes et services ove toutz les appurtenantz en auxi bon estat et degre ou meillour quilx ne furent le jour quil les resceupt. Et pour la guerre le dit Thomas avera tielx gages et regard pour luy mesmes come nul autre de son estat ou condicion prendra du dit Duc. Et si aveigne que le dit Thomas soit envoyes en message du dit Duc il avera tielx gages et regard come nul aultre de soun estat ou condicioun prendra du dit Duc. Et pour le temps quil soit en lostiell du dit Duc par soun comandement il avera les gages de soun hostiell come aultres esquiers ount. Et cestes covenantz bien et loyalment tenir, garder et accomplir le dit Thomas ad fait seurement au dit Duc sur les Seintz Ewangilx. En tesmoignance de la quelle chose les parties dessuis ditz entrechangeablement ont mys lour sealx. Don' a Loundres le xxiiij jour de Septembre lan de regne le Roy Richard second vingt et tierce.

93 Thomas Despenser, earl of Gloucester and William Hamme, London, 27 October 1399 (PRO, C66/359 m. 4, *inspeximus* of 17 April 1400).[218]

Ceste endenture tesmoigne que William Hamme esquier del countee de Hereford est detenuz a demurer ovec mon treshonure seigneur

---

[215] cf. *CPR, 1399–1401*, 244.

[216] Proudfoot, of Dunmow, Essex, was reported beheaded in the rebellion of John Holland but subsequently appeared before the Council to testify that he had taken no part in the earl's rising. All his goods were forfeit to the king by Aug. 1401, however, on account of a felony (*CIM, 1399–1422*, no. 17; *CCR, 1399–1402*, 137–8; *CPR, 1399–1401*, 536).

[217] Winkleigh Tracy, Devon.

[218] cf. *CPR, 1399–1401*, 263. Despenser was promoted to the earldom of Gloucester at Michaelmas 1397 and beheaded on 13 Jan. 1400 (GEC, v. 729).

Thomas le Despenser conte de Gloucestre pour pees pour terme de
vie du dit William preignant annuelment de mon dit seigneur pour son
fee dys marcz en le manoir de Burford[219] en le counte Doxenford a les
festes de Pasqz et seint Michel par oveles porciouns a terme de vie du
dit William sur les condicions qensuent. Cestassavoir qen cas que mon
dit seigneur travaille affaire de guerre hors du royaume Dengleterre
ovesqz nostre seigneur le Roy ou en son service ou ove aucun autre
pur quelles viages mon dit seigneur prendra fees et gages et le dit
William soit requis et charge pour aler et travailler ovesqe mon dit
seigneur en les ditz viages le dit William sera tenuz daler et travailler
ovesqe mon dit seigneur luy mesmes et ses gentz, bien et covenablement
armez et mountez chescun selonc lour estate et degree, pernant de
mon dit seigneur pur les ditz viages fees et gages pour luy mesmes et
ses gentz qil soit charge et comaunde de mesner ovesqe luy a tant
come autres gentz de son estat et degree prendront de son dit seigneur
pur les ditz viages saunz rien prendre du dite annuitee de dis marcz
durante le temps du dit viage. Et outre ceo sil aveigne que mon dit
seigneur veut travailler vers les parties de Sprws,[220] Rodes ou vers
aucuns autres parties quelconques hors du roiaume Dengleterre ou de
Galis en queles parties qil plest a mon dit seigneur sur ses coustages
demesnes et le dit William soit requis de travailler ovec mon dit
seigneur[a] vers les parties suisditz le dit William est tenuz daler et
chivacher ovec mon dit seigneur luy mesmes covenablement arraie
preignant pur luy come autres de son estat et degree preignont. Et en
cas que le dit William soit charge ou mande par lettre ou aucun autre
mandement de venir a mon dit seigneur vers aucuns parties deinz la
roiaume Dengleterre ou de Galys le dit William est tenuz de venir a
mon dit seigneur ove un vallet, un garson, troys chivaux pernant gages
pour luy et ses deux gentz et trois chivaux come autres de son estat et
degree ent prendront de mon dit seigneur. Et outreceo si le dit William
soit charge par message ou par lettre de venir a mon dit seigneur vers
aucuns parties deins la roiaume Dengleterre ou de Galys ove aucun
nombre de gentz que soit greindre ou meindre le dit William est tenuz de
venir et les amesner si ensy soit qil ne puet luy excuser par cause resonable
et pur tantz de gentz qil amesne avera et prendra gages selonk lour estat
et degree pur le temps qils serront en le service mon dit seigneur. Et si les
ditz dis marcs pur le fee du dit William soit aderere en partie ou en tout
par carante jours apres ascuns des termes desuisditz et pour terme de vie
de dit William qadonques bien lise au dit William en tout le dit manoir
distreindre pur le dit rent qi soit aderere[b] et la distresse amesner et retener
tanque plein gree luy soit faite de le dit rent ove les arrerages sanz contredit

---

[219] Burford, Oxon.
[220] i.e. Prussia.

de nully. En tesmoignance de quelle chose sibien le dit Thomas come dit William a ycestes endentures entrechangeablement ont mys lours seales. Don a Londres le xxviiime jour doctobr' lan du regne le Roy Henry quart puis le conquest primer.[221]

a. *seigneur* interlined
b. *qi soit aderere* interlined

94 Ralph Neville, earl of Westmorland and John Pirian, London, 15 February 1400 (PRO, C54/245 m. 16d, contemporary enrolment).[222]

Cest endenture faicte parentre Rauf cont de Westm[orland] seignur de Nevill et mareschall Dengl[eterre] dune part et Johan Pyrian esquier dautre part tesmoigne que acorde est que le dit Johan demora ove le dit cont pur terme de sa vie quant il serra hors du service du Roi par licence ou par congie du Roi quell temps qil serra resonablement garniz par le dit cont sibien pur le peax come pur la guere, pernant du dit count pur la peax par an cynkaunt livres desterl[inges] de la manoir et vil de Boston en la countee de Nicol.[223] Et prendra le dit Johan du dit cont pur la guerre come il fait as autres de son degree et condicione. Et avera le dit cont les tierces du gaignie du guere againiers par le dit Johan et par ses gentz queux il avera as gages ou coust du dit count. Et le dit Johan serra mounte, arme et araie et prest pur traveiller ovesqe le dit cont et ove son depute quell temps qil serra garnie, come affiert a son degree, sil ne soit en la service nostre seigneur le Roy. Et le dit Johan ne traveillera hors du service du dit count ovesqe nully forsqe en la service nostre seigneur le Roy saunce especiale congie du dit cont. En tesmoignance de quell chose a ycestes endentures entrechaungeablement les partiez avauntditz ount mys lour sealx. Don' a Loundres le quinszyme jour de Feverer lan du regne le Roi Henri le quart puis le conquest primer.[245]

---

[221] There is no evidence that Hamme joined Despenser in rebellion against Henry IV in Jan. 1400. In March 1402 he was granted a fee of £12 p.a. from the hundred of Dudstone, Gloucs., 'for his probity and good service to the king' (*CPR, 1401–5*, 37; *CCR, 1399–1401*, 465).

[222] cf. *CCR, 1399–1401*, 116. For Ralph Neville, first earl of Westmorland (1397–1425), see GEC, xii, pt. 2, 544–9.

[223] Boston, Lincs.

[224] The enrolled indenture is followed by a note that both the parties to it came into the Chancery at Westminster on 20 Feb. 1400, and acknowledged its contents. On the previous day a further indenture was concluded between the two, witnessing a covenant that if the manor and town of Boston was taken into the king's hand, the earl should be discharged of paying Pirian's fee (*CCR, 1399–1401*, 117). Pirian was a Breton servant of Henry IV's second wife, Joan of Navarre, who took out letters of denization in 1411. He settled for a period at Lockley in Welwyn, Herts. (*CPR, 1408–13*, 368; *ibid.*, *1413–16*, 335). He is to be distinguished from his near homonym Jean Périou, treasurer and wardrober (1407–20) of Joan of Navarre as duchess of Brittany (cf. Jean Kerhervé, 'Les gens de

95 Ralph Neville, earl of Westmorland and Anthony Ricz, London, 15 February 1400 (PRO, C54/245 m. 23d, contemporary enrolment).[225]

Ceste endenture faicte par entre Rauf cont de Westm[orland][a] seignur de Nevill [et mareschall] Dengle[terre] dune part et Antoyne Rycz dautre part tesmoigne [que le dit Antoyne] demora ove le dit cont pur terme de sa vie quant il serra hors du service du Roy par licence ou per congie du Roi quell temps qil serra resonablement garniz par le dit cont sibien pur la peax come pur la guerre, pernant du dit cont pur la peax par an cent livres de nostre manoir de Crowhirst[226] et de noz autres manoirs, terres et tenementz en le counte de Sussex pertenant al seigneurie de Richm[ond]. Et prendra le dit Antoyne du dit conte pur la[b] guere come il fait as autres de son degree et condicione. Et avera le dit cont le tierces du gaignie du guerre agaigniers par le dit Antoyne et par ses gentz queux il avera as gages ou coust du dit cont et le dit Antoyne serra monte, arme et arraie pur travailler ove le dit cont et ove son deputee quell temps qil serra garnie come affiert a son degree sil ne soit en la service nostre seigneur le Roy. Et le dit Antoyne ne travaillera hors du service du dit cont ovesque nully forsqe en la service nostre seigneur le Roy saunce especiale congie du dit cont. En tesmoignance de quel chose a ycestes endentures [les parties avantditz] entrechangeablement ont mys lour sealx. Don a Loundr[e]s le quinzisime jour de Feverer lan du regne le Roy Henry le quart puis le conquest Dengl[eterre] primer.[227]

---

finances des ducs de Bretagne 1365–1491', Thèse de Doctorat d'Etat, Paris 1986, Catalogue Prosopographique, i. 22–3).

[225] cf. *CCR, 1399–1402*, 104–5.   [226] Crowhurst, Sussex.

[227] For an indenture subsidiary to the indenture of retainer, regulating the terms under which Ricz (Ricze, Rize, Rys) might sue out a writ of annuity against Neville, concluded on 19 Feb. 1400 see *CCR, 1399–1402*, 112–3. Like **94** and **96**, this agreement arose from the confused tenurial position of the honour of Richmond between 1398 and 1400. Ricz was a trusted councillor and servant of John IV, duke of Brittany, and it was presumably as an agent of the duke that he had a grant, together with Joan, lady Basset (the duke's sister) and Nicholas Aldrewich of the honour of Richmond in April 1398. Whether this grant was superseded by the subsequent restoration of the earldom of Richmond to John IV remains unclear, with the result that Ricz and Aldrewich could plausibly contest Henry IV's grant of the honour to Neville in October 1399. It is in the context of their residual claims on the Richmond lands that the generosity of Neville's retaining fees should be seen.

Ricz remained in England, acting as attorney for Joan of Navarre, John IV's widow. He was proctor for her second marriage to Henry IV, but suffered from the rise of anti-alien sentiment and had sold out all his interest in Crowhurst for a lump sum of £300 by 1406: *Recueil des actes de Jean IV, duc de Bretagne*, ed. Michael Jones (Paris, 1980–3), ii. nos. 655, 726, 791, 816, 930, 995, 1050, 1119; Michael Jones, *Ducal Brittany, 1364–1399* (Oxford, 1970), 195–6; *CPR, 1396–9*, 350; *ibid., 1399–1401*, 24; *CCR, 1402–5*, 212; *CPR, 1405–8*, 178, 185. Possibly of English but more probably of Welsh origins, he was in John IV's service as early as 1374 (Rymer's *Foedera*, Record Comm. edn., iii, 1010), was banished

a. Letters and words in brackets omitted in the enrolled text
b. MS *le*

96 Ralph Neville, earl of Westmorland and Nicholas Aldrewich, London, 15 February 1400 (PRO, C54/245 m. 16d, contemporary enrolment).[228]

Cest endenture faicte parentre Rauf cont de Wesm[orland] seigneur de Nevill et mareschall Dengle[terre] dune part et Nicholas Aldirwyche esquier dautre part tesmoigne que le dit Nicholas demora ovesque le dit cont pur terme de sa vie quant il serra hors du service du Roy par licence ou par congie du Roy quell temps qil serra resonablement garniz par le dit cont sibien pur la peax come pur la guerre, pernant du dit cont pur la peax par an cent et dys marcz de la manoir de Qwassyngburgh[229] et des terres et tenementz de mesme la ville en le countee de Nicol pertenaunt al seigneurie de Richm[ond]. Et prendra le dit Nicholas du dit conte pur la guere come il fait as autres de son degree et condicion. Et avera le dit cont les tierces du gaignie du guere agaigniers par le dit Nicholas et par ses gentz queux il avera as gages ou coust du dit cont. Et le dit Nicholas serra mounte, arme et araie et prest pur traveiller ovesqe le dit cont et ove son depute quell temps qil serra garnie come affiert a son degree, sil ne soit en la service nostreseignur le Roy. Et le dit Nicholas ne travellera hors du service du dit cont ovesque nully forsque en la service nostreseigneur le Roy sanz especial congie du dit cont. En tesmoignance de quell chose a ycestes endentures les parties avantditz entrechaungeablement ount mys lour sealx. Don a Loundres le quinzsime jour de Feverer lan du regne le Roy Henry le quart puis le conquest Dengl[eterre] primer.[230]

97 Thomas Beauchamp, earl of Warwick and John Longville, esquire,

with his wife, Peronelle Aldrewich, by Parliament in 1406 (*Rot. Parl.*, iii. 572) but still flourished in Brittany as Master of the duke's household as late as 1418 (Kerhervé, Catalogue Prosopographique, i. 11–12).

[228] cf. *CCR, 1399–1402*, 116.

[229] Washingborough, Lincs.

[230] Acknowledged by both parties in Chancery at Westminster, 20 Feb. 1400, and with a subsidiary indenture regulating payment of the fee and Aldrewich's right to distrain as in **94** and **95** (*CCR, 1399–1401*, 115). Like Ricz, Aldrewich was a servant of John IV granted the honour of Richmond in 1398. An Englishman from a family with a long tradition of service to the Montfort duke, he continued in the employ of Joan of Navarre until at least 1413. In addition he was granted a fee of £40 p.a. by Henry IV in Feb. 1401 and served as sheriff of Lincolnshire Nov. 1412–Nov. 1413: *CPR, 1396–9*, 350; *ibid., 1399–1401*, 546; P. S. Lewis, 'Of Breton Alliances and other matters', *Essays in Later Medieval French History* (London, 1985), 88–9; *CPR, 1413–16*, 130, 272; *List of Sheriffs for England and Wales* (PRO, Lists and Indexes, 9, 1898), 79.

Warwick, 8 June 1400 (Oxford, Bodleian Library, D. D. Radcliffe a.2 (218), formerly sealed on a tag through a turn up).[231]

Ceste endenture fait parentre Thomas Beauchamp, conte de Warr' dune parte et Johan Longevylle esquier[232] au dit conte dautre parte tesmoigne que le dit Johan est demoerre pur terme de sa vie ove le dit conte de peas et de guerre pernant annuelment pur soun fee pour la peas dys marcz a toute la vie le dit Johan del manoir de Multon en la conte de Northamton[233] quel fee le dit conte ad done al dit Johan par ses lettres patentes, a avoir a toute la vie le dit Johan come par ses lettres patentes au dit Johan ent faits piert pluis au pleyn. Et viendra le dit Johan au counte quant il serra mande depar le dit conte ove un valet et deux chivaux et avera bouche de c[our]te pur luy mesmes et liveree ou gages pur soun vadlet et ses chivaux pur le temps de sa demoerre. Et pour la guerre al temps que le dit conte trava[ill]era mesmes en propre persone viendra le dit Johan par resonable garnissement du dit conte bien et sufficealment armez et monte come affiert a soun estat ove ses hommes arraiez covenablement. Et avera pur le temps de guerre pur luy et ses hommes gages atantz et tielx come le Roy donne as autres esquiers de soun estat ove bouche de courte pur luy mesmes et liveree ou gages pur ses gentz et chivaux pur le temps esteantz issint toutefoitz que pur le temps de guerre la dite fee de dys marcz pur la peas cessera. Et avera le dit conte la moyte de quanque le dit Johan ou ses gentz gaynera ou gayneront par voie de guerre et sils un ascun de eaux preigne ou preignont ascun prisoner il ne serra mys au fynance ou a reanceon sanz lassent du dit conte et soun counsaill. Et avera le dit Johan pur luy, ses gentz et chivaux esqipesoun a la maer en alant et retornant a les custs le dit conte. En tesmoignance de quelle chose les parties avanditz entrechangeablement ont mys lour sealx a y ces tesmoigns Mons. Nich' Lillyng, Mons. Johan Trussell, Mons. Averey Trussell, Mons. Gilles Mallory, Rauf Par[ker] et autres.[234] Don' a Warr' le viij^e jour de Juyn lan du regne le Roy Henry quart puis le conquest primer.

98 Michael de la Pole, earl of Suffolk and Sir William Berdewell

[231] Published by kind permission of the Trustees of Dr John Radcliffe. GEC, xii, pt. 2. 375–8 for Thomas Beauchamp, earl of Warwick (1369–1401).

[232] John Longville of Wolverton, Bucks., was escheator of Bedfordshire and Buckinghamshire, 24 Oct. 1392–24 Nov. 1394 and 8 Nov. 1401–29 Nov. 1402: VCH, Bucks., iv. 507; List of Escheators for England and Wales (PRO, Lists and Indexes, 72, 1971), 4; CCR, 1402–5, 36.

[233] Moulton, Northants.

[234] All the witnesses except Parker are known to be Beauchamp servants: Sinclair, 'The Beauchamp earls', 320, 322–3.

(Bardwell), London, 8 February 1401 (Suffolk RO, Borough of Eye Records, EE 2/T/1, sealed on tag through turn up).[235]

Sachent toutz gentz, Nous Michel de la Pole Count de Suff' avoir done et graunte par cest fait endente a nostre chier et bien ame Mons. William Berdewell[236] un annuel rente de vynt livres a prendre annuelement del fest de Seynt Michel proschein avenir as festes de Pask et Seynt Michel par ovelles porcions a terme de vie naturell du dit Mons. William des issues et profites del Chastell, ville et manoir de Eye[237] pur le bon et greable service que le dit Mons. William ad fait a nous[a] en temps passe et ferra en temps avenir sibien en temps de guerre come en temps de peas, a avoir et tener a dit Mons. William et a sez assignes le dit annuel rente come devant est dit pur terme de vie le dit Mons. William. Et voillons et grauntons par ycestes pur nous et pur noz heirs et pur noz assignes qe a quele heure qe le dit annuel rent soit aderrere en partie ou en tout al ascun terme susdit, qe bien lise a dit Mons. William ou sez assignes distreindre en les ditz Chastell, ville et manoir ove les a[rrerages et ...][b] les distresses ove luy chacer tanqe gree luy soit faite de ceo qe soit aderrere ove les costages et damages. Et le dit Mons. William serra tenuz de servier le dit Count, sibien en temps de guerre come en temps [de peas ...]serr[...] et garny de part le dit Count bien et covenablement montez et arraiez come a son estat appartient.

Cest assavoir luy mesmes ove un Esquier, deux Vadlettes et un Garcion et cynk chivaux. Et [...] qe [...] Mons. William soit a bouche de nostre Courte ove sez ditz servantz et chivaux en temps de peas ou[...]ment qe un vadlet et un Garcion et Chivaux soient a gages come autres seront del meigne du dit [count], et aura pur sez chivaux [...]gnable.[c] Et si le dit Mons. William soit travaillant en Engleterre del comandement du dit Count hors de son hostell il serra allowe resonablement pur sez costages et dispenses. Et avera vesture un foitz par an appurtenant a son estat quant le dit Count donera vesture as autres gentils.[d] Et auxint si le dit Mons. William soit

[235] Drawn to our attention by Elizabeth Danbury after *HMC, 13th Report*, 516–7, which describes the seal as 'a singularly fine example of the engraver's art'. It displays, Quarterly, 1 and 4, a fesse between three Catherine wheels, 2 and 3, on a bend three pairs of angels' wings. Legend in Gothic script: SIGILLU[M]:MICHAELIS: DE:LA:POLE:COMITIS: SUFFOLCHIE. We are grateful to David Jones, Branch Archivist, for obtaining permission to publish this document from Eye Town Council and for supplying a photograph of the seal. Michael de la Pole was restored to his father's earldom of Suffolk in 1398, forfeited it in 1399 and was subsequently restored by Henry IV; he died at the siege of Harfleur in 1415, cf. GEC, xii, pt. 1. 441–2.

[236] Sir William Bardwell (*c.*1361–1434) of Bardwell, Suffolk and West Harling and Gasthorpe, Norf. (*HC, 1386–1421*, ii. 125–7).

[237] Eye, Suffolk.

maheimez ou maladez ou de tiel age qil ne poet travailler pur servier le dit Count, nient contresteant le dit Count voet et graunte par yceste qe le dit Mons. William eit et enjoise le dit annuel rente de vynt livres come est susdit a toute sa vie. Et le dit Mons. William sera tenuz de servier et travailler luy mesmes ove un vadlet a bouche courte[c] ove le dit Count en temps de guerre bien arraiez come a luy affiert et ovesqe a tantz des[f] gentes darmes et Archiers al chival ou a la meere sanz chivaux solonc ceo qe le viage demande, come serra accorde parentre eux preignant tielx fees et gages et paiement de guerre et regarde pur luy mesmes et sez gentz come le dit Count prent du Roy pur autres de lour estat et condicion. Et endroit de prisoners et autres profites de guerre prisez ou gaignez par le dit Mons. William ou par ascun de sez gentz en le service du dit Count, le dit Mons. William et ses gentz auront les deux parties et le dit Count aura la tierce partie. Et en cas qe le dit Mons. William ou ascun de sez gentz preigne Seignour ou Capitaigne des gentz darmes qils ne purront mettre a finance ne eaux delivrer sanz licence du dit Count. Et del comensement de son an, demi an, ou quart del an, ou autre temps de guerre ensemblement de leskippeson et reskippeson de luy, sez gentz, chivaux et harnoys, le dit Count ferra a luy en maniere come nostre dit Seignour le Roy ferra a dit Count pur autres de son estat en celle viage. En tesmoignance de quele chose a cestes endentures sibien le dit Count, come le dit Mons. William entrechangeablement ount mys leur sealx. Donez a Loundres le viii[e] jour de Fevrier lan du regne nostre Seignour le Roy Henry quart puis le conquest seconde.

    a. *a nous* interlined
    b. Three small holes in MS affecting text indicated here and elsewhere by square brackets
    c. *et aura pur sez chivaux [. . .]gnable* interlined
    d. This whole sentence interlined
    e. *luy mesmes ove un vadlet a bouche courte* interlined
    f. *des* interlined

99 Henry Percy, earl of Northumberland and Sir William Curwen, Warkworth, 8 May 1401 (Cumbria RO, Carlisle, D Lons/L/MD/WO 5, sealed on tag through fold).[238]

Ceste endenture faite a Werkeworthe le viij jour de May lan du regne nostre seigneur le roy Henry quart second tesmoigne qe accorde est

[238] Fragments survive of a seal showing a man in armour resting a shield of the Percy arms on the ground; first published in F. W. Ragg, 'De Culwen', *Trans. Cumberland and Westmorland Antiquarian Soc.* n.s. xiv (1914), 402–5. GEC, ix. 708–14 for Henry Percy, earl of Northumberland (1377–1408) and his son Henry Hotspur (d. 1403).

parentre le treshonore et puissant seigneur le Conte de Northumbr'
Conestable Dengleterre dune part et Mons. William de Curwen[239]
dautre part, qe le dit Mons. William ferra feoffement et seure estat
estre fait en fee simple a Johan de Curwen frere au dit Mons. William
et certeines persones a nomer par assent sibien du dit Conte come
par le dit Mons. William en les manoirs de Wirkyngton, Seton et
Thornethwayt en Derwentffelles[240] en le contee de Cumbr' ove les
appurtenances, sur tiele condicion qe les ditz enfeffez refefferont le dit
Mons. William en les manoirs susditz ove les appurtenances a avoir au
dit Mons. William et ses heirs de son corps engendrez, issint qe
par defaute de issue de dit Mons. William les ditz manoirs ove les
appurtenances remayndrent au dit Conte et ses heirs de son corps
engendrez. Et si le dit Conte devie sanz heir de son corps engendrez
que touz les ditz manoirs ove touz lour appurtenances remayndrent a
Mons. Gilbert de Curwen piere au dit Mons. William pour toute sa
vie; le remeyndre apres le decees du dit Mons. Gilbert a ses droitz
heirs. Pur quel feffement et [   ] faire come desus est dit, les susditz
Conte et Mons. Henry de Percy son filz ferront seure estate au dit
Mons. William de une annuitee de vyngt marcs par an a prendre a
terme de sa vie as termes de Seint Martyn et Pentecost par oveles
porcions; pur quele annuitee le dit Mons. William est demorez par
toute sa vie en chief as ditz Conte et son filz en temps de pees, savant
sa legeance. Et le dit Conte ferra seure estat au dit Johan de Curwen
de une annuitee de vyngt lyveres par an a prendre a mesmes les termes
tanque il soit avancez a un benfice de Seinte Esglise a la value de
quarant livres par an ou plus par le dit Conte ou ses heirs ou lour eide.
Et en cas qe le dit Conte ou ses heirs soient prestz pour luy avancer a
tiel benfice come devant est dit et le dit Johan ne le voet acceptier,
qadonques la dite annuitee de vyngt livres a luy grantee par le dit
Conte cesse et soit quasse a touz jours. Et outre ce le dit Conte ou son
dit filz ferra seure estat a Christofre de Curwen filz au dit Mons.
William dune annuitee de cent souldz pour terme de sa vie a prendre
as termes susditz. Pur quele annuitee le dit Christofre sera ove le dit
Conte et son dit fils en chief a terme de sa vie en temps de pees. Et en
cas qe le dit Christofre change son estat et preigne lordre de chivaler
il serra adonqes en chief ove le dit Conte et son dit fils a toute et
prendra annuelement apres le dit ordre pris as termes susditz pur la
pees dys marcs par an et cessera la fee de cent souldz susdit. Et plus
outre est accorde parentre les parties avantdites qe les ditz Conte et
Mons. Henry son filz relesseront au dit Mons. William toutes accions

---

[239] *HC, 1386–1421*, ii. 723–6 for Sir William Curwen of Workington (d. 1403) and his
son Christopher, with an account of the circumstances leading to this indenture.

[240] Workington, Seaton and Thornthwaite, Cumbs.

de obligacions de reconissances et toutes autres accions personeles,[241] et le dit Mons. William relessera as ditz Conte et son ditz filz et a tous leurs servantz et autres par eux a nomer touz maners de trespas avant ces heures faitz a luy ou a sez tenantz et servantz dedeinz les contees de Westmerland et Cumbr'. Et si ascune chose soit amender en les matires susdites qil soit amende par avys et conseil de ambedeux parties a ce eslieuz, toutes voies les substances des matires susdites esteantz en lour force et effect. En tesmoignance de quele chose a y cestes endentures les parties susdites entrechangeablement ont mys lour sealx. Escrit les jour et lieu susditz.

Dorse: le cont de Northumland et Sir W. Curwen

100 Ralph Neville, earl of Westmorland and Sir Thomas Grey of Heaton, 6 August 1404 (PRO, E326/3515, sealed on tag through a fold).[242]

Ceste endenture faite par entre Rauf conte de Westmerland, sire de Nevill et mareschal Dengleterre, dune part, et monsire Thomas Grey, sire de Heton,[243] dautre part, tesmoigne que le dit monsire Thomas est demore avec le dit conte a terme de sa vie si bien pour la pees come pour la guerre contre toutz gentz hors pris nostre tressouverain seignur le Roy et ses filz, Roys Dengleterre. Et pour ce que le dit conte a achate et purchase par ses deniers loffice de la conestablerie du chastel de Banbourgh,[244] quel office il vouche saf sur le dit monsire Thomas et lui ent a fait avoir graunt a terme de sa vie par lettres patentes de nostre dit seignur le Roy,[245] tant mesmes monsire Thomas relesse par icestes au dit conte toutes manieres accons et demandes dascun fie aprendre du dit conte par an pour toute sa vie pour sa demouree susdite. Et toutes heures que le dit monsire Thomas travaillera de guerre avec le dit conte ou par son assignement le dit counte paiera a lui et a ses gentz comme il faira a autres de leur degree sanz aucun rebat afaire en leur gages par cause du dit office. Et le dit monsire Thomas et ses gentz feront arrere au dit conte tielles devoirs des gaignes de guerre et dautres services comme autres gentz de leur degre feront a le conte susdit. Et pour les covenances avantditz tenir fermement al dit conte par le dit monsire Thomas en maniere avant dite, le dit

[241] Cumbria RO, Carlisle, D Cu/4/3.
[242] cf. *CAD*, ii. 412.
[243] Heaton, Northumbs.
[244] Bamburgh, Northumbs.
[245] Grey was granted the office of constable of Bamburgh for life, with the accustomed fees and wages, by royal letters patent issued at Lichfield, 29 Aug. 1404 (*CPR, 1401–5*, 412).

monsire Thomas a plevy sa foy a mesme le conte. En tesmoignance de quelle chose les parties avant ditz as parties dicestes endentures entrechangeablement ont mis leurs sealx. Le vi^e jour de August lan du regne du Roy Henry le quart puis le conqueste quint.[246]

Dorse: Gray

101 Henry, prince of Wales and John Legh of Booths, Chester, 18 October 1404 (PRO, CHES 2/78 m. 3, contemporary enrolment).[247]

Ceste endenture fait parentre le treshault et puissant prince Henry eisne filz au noble roi Engleterre et Ffraunce, prince de Gales, duc de Guyenne, Lancastre et de Cornewaill et counte de Cestre dune part et Johan de Legh de Bothis[248] esquier dautre part tesmoigne que le dit Johan est retenuz et demourez vers le dit prince pour luy servir tant en temps de pees come de guerre a terme de sa vie et pur travailler ovec luy as queles parties qil plerra au dit prince bien et covenablement mountez, armez et araiez come a son estat appartient. Et sera le dit Johan en temps de pees as gages et bouche de court du dit prince a ses diverses venues illoeques quant pur luy sera envoiee par lettres de mesme le prince ou de son mandement en manere come seront ses autres escuiers de son estat et condicion, pur quele demoure mesme celluy prince de lavys de son conseil ad graunte au dit Johan pur son fee la ville de Sutton[249] ove les appurtenantz deinz la forest de Macclesfeld a avoir pur terme da sa vie tanque a value de vynt marcz par an, rendant au dit prince annuelment a son Eschequer de Cestre le surplusage provenant des issues et revenues de mesme la ville outre les vynt marcz annueles avantditz a la fest de seint Michell pur tout lan, et sil aveigne que le dit Johan faille en paiement du dit surplusage en partie ou en tout par quarant jours apres ascun fest suisdit durant sa vie qadonqes bien lise au dit prince et a ses heirs de rentrer en mesme la ville et ycelle tenir en son primere droit, ceste endenture non obstant. Et outre ce prendra le suisdit Johan de lavantdit prince en

---

[246] Grey was married to Alice Neville, one of Westmorland's daughters. For an account of his career, T. B. Pugh, *Henry V and the Southampton Plot of 1415* (Southampton Rec. Soc., xxx, 1988), 102–5.

[247] For details of Legh's career and rewards as one of Richard II's seven 'esquires masters of the watch of Cheshire' see J. L. Gillespie, 'Richard II's Cheshire Archers', *Trans. of the Historic Soc. of Lancs. and Cheshire*, cxxv (1974), 3, 13–22. He had previously enjoyed a grant of £20 p.a. from Sutton, in addition to a retaining fee of 100 s., by grant of Richard II; he surrendered these to the prince in July 1401 and received in return 20 marks from Sutton (*CPR, 1396–9*, 461; PRO CHES 2/71 m. 12 and 75 m. 3).

[248] Boothes in Knutsford, Cheshire.

[249] Sutton Downs, Cheshire.

temps de guerre autielx gages de guerre ou autrement autielx gages et bouche de court du dit prince come prendront ses autres esquiers de son degree pur le viage, des queles gages il sera paiee par les mains del Tresorer du dit Prince pur la guerre qi pur le temps sera. Et le dit Prince avera sibien la tierce des prisoners et profitz de guerre par le suisdit Johan prises ou gaignez come le tierce del tier[c]e prises ou gaignez par ascunz de ses gentz en le service du dit Prince, et sil aveigne que ascun chieftain, ville, chastell ou forteresse soit pris ou gaignez par le suisdit Johan ou par ascun de ses gentz en le service du dit Prince mesme celluy Johan ferra deliverance au dit Prince de tiel chieftein, ville, chastell ou forteresse ensi par luy ou par ascun de ses gentz prises ou gaignez preignant du dit Prince suffisant regard en ce partie, et endroit del commencement de son an de guerre ensemblement et de leskippeson de luy, ses gentz, chivalx et hernois mesme celluy prince ferra a luy en manere come il ferra a ses autres esquiers de son estat et condicion. En tesmoignance de quele chose a la partie de ceste endenture remaignant vers lavantdit Johan le dit Prince ad mys son seal. Don' a Cestre le disoitisme jour Doctobr' lan du regne nostre tresredouteseignour[a] le Roi Henri quart puis le conquest sisme.[250]

a. *Tresredouteseignour* interlined

102 Ralph Neville, Earl Marshal, earl of Westmorland and John de

[250] Two mandates relating to this indenture are enrolled with it on the same membrane: i. Letters of the prince, dated at Coventry, 18 Oct. 1404, informing the Chamberlain of Chester that he had retained Legh, reciting the terms of the indenture, and ordering him to cancel the existing letters patent by which Legh had possession of the town of Sutton by the prince's gift and to issue to him instead 'noz lettres patentes endentees solonc la forme del copie dune endenture quele nous vous envoions encloos deinz cestes'; ii. Letters of the prince to the Chamberlain of Chester, dated at Hereford, 20 April 1406, informing him that Legh had certified that the tenants of Sutton were anciently accustomed to pay their annual dues and rents at Michaelmas only, with the result that Legh is committed by the terms of his indenture to paying half the surplus of the vill a term before he has received it. By advice of his council, the prince had therefore granted Legh's petition that he be required to render the surplus revenues at Michaelmas only: 'volons de lavys de nostre conseill et vous mandons que sur nostre dit primere graunte et de mesme la date desouz nostre seal de vostre office illoeques en vostre garde esteant vous facez avoir au dit Johan noz lettres patentes endentes en due forme rendant a nous annuelment a nostre Eschequer de Cestre le surplusage provenant des issues et revenues de mesme la ville outre les vynt marcz annueles suisditz a les festes de Seint Michel tant soulement'. This is the form in which the indenture appears on the roll, which thus differs in two significant respects from the original agreement concluded between Legh and the prince.

Thorp, esquire, Raby, Co. Durham, 24 April 1406 (PRO, E327/BX 176, sealed through fold on tag).[251]

Ceste endenture faicte parentre Rauf conte de Westmerland, Sire de Nevill et mareschal Dengleterre dune part et Johan de Thorp esquier dautre parte tesmoigne que le dit Johan est demore et retenu ovec le dit conte pur terme de sa vie encontre toutes gentz sauvant nostre tressoverein seignur le roy et ses heirs rois Dengleterre pernant par an du dit conte en temps de pees quarrant souldz par an pur son fee as termes de seint Martyn en yver et Pentecost par ovelles porcions par les maynes de nostre resceivour de Richmond qui pur le temps y serra, et prendra en temps de guerre autielx gages come le dit conte donera as autres de son degree, rebatuz toutesfoiz lafferant de son dit fee pur le temps de guerre. Et serra le dit Johan bien et covenablement montez, armez et arraiez et prest toutdiz a chivaucher ovec le dit conte ou son depute a toutes les foiz quil serra garny a ce faire. Et le dit conte avera les tierces de guerre gaignez par le dit Johan ou par sez gentz quelx il avera as gages ou coust du dit conte. Et saucune capitayn ou homme destat soit pris par le dit Johan ou par ses dictes gentz le dit conte lavera faisant al pernour resonable regarde pur lui. En tesmoignance de quelle chose a ycestes les parties susditz entrechangeablement ont mys lour sealx. Don' a Raby le xxiiij jour daverill lan du regne le roy Henry quart puis le conquest septisme.

Dorse: Thorp

103 Sir John de Lumley and Robert de Lumley, esquire, 20 September 1407 (Sandbeck Park, Maltby, Rotherham, Yorks., Muniments of the Earl of Scarbrough, MTD/A2/12).[252]

Ceste endenture faite parentre Johan de Lumley chivaler dune part et Robert de Lumley son frere esquyer dautre part,[253] tesmoigne que le dit Robert est demurre et retenuz en chief ovesque le dit Johan sibien

---

[251] Remnants of a seal (a fleur-de-lys with a decorated border); first printed in Thomas Madox, *Formulare Anglicanum*, 97 no. clxxvi.

[252] Originally drawn to our attention by Elizabeth Danbury; we are grateful to Lord Scarbrough for allowing us to see this and other documents, and to the Trustees of the Earl of Scarbrough's Childrens Settlement for permission to publish it. Measuring 245 x 105 mm., it is sealed in red wax on a tag through a turn up with an irregular octagonal signet displaying the Lumley popinjay. GEC, viii. 270–1 for Sir John Lumley (1382–1421). In 1413 he drew up an indenture, granting residence in his household, with John Neville, lord Latimer (Oxford, Bodleian Library MS Dugdale 18 f. 40v).

[253] Robert Lumley was retained for life by the king and granted £20 p.a. from the manor of Nunwick, Yorks., in March 1406 (*CPR, 1405–8*, 163).

pour la guerre come pour la pees pour terme de sa vie, et serra le dit
Robert covenablement mountez et arraiez pour travailler ovesque le
dit Johan en sa compaignie quant il serra a ceo resonablement requise
et avera le dit Robert bouche de court pour luy, une vadlet et un
garsoun pour lour chivalx pour la temps qil serra travaillant ou meyniell
en la compaignie le dit Johan, pur quele demourer le dit Johan ad fait
mons. Rauf de Eure chivaler, Robert de Wyclyff clerc et William
Mayhu doner et graunter a dit Robert et ses heirs males un annuell
rente de vingt livres issant de lour manoirs de Morton' et Hesilden'[254]
les queux manoirs ils ount du doun et graunt le dit Johan, de quele
graunt du dit annuite certeynes endentures sount faitz parentre les ditz
mons. Rauf, Robert de Wyclyff et William et le dit Robert de Lumley
de annullere le dit graunt sur condicions comprisez en les endentures
susditz en cas qils soient enfreyntz par le dit Robert de Lumley ou ses
heirs malez come en les endentures ent faitz pleynement est contenuz.[255]
En tesmoignance de quele chose les parties avauntditz a y cestes
endentures entrechangeablement ount mys lour seals. Don' le vintisme
jour de Septembre lan du regne le Roy Henr' quarte puis le conqueste
oeptisme.[256]

---

[254] Murton and [Cold] Hesledon manors in the parish of Dalton-le-Dale, Co. Durham.

[255] The agreement between Robert de Lumley and the feoffees of Murton and
Hesledon manors is dated 18 May 1407 (MTD/A2/11).

[256] On 11 April 1410 Sir John de Lumley released his brother from the penalty clauses
of the indenture for the next six years in this form:

A toutz iceux qi cestes lettres verront ou orront Johan de Lumley chivaler salutz en
Dieu. Comant que mon tresamee frere Robert de Lumley esquier soit demouree ovesque
moi en chief pour la guerre et pees pour terme de sa vie issent que sil face sa demoere
pour terme de vie ou dans ou voluntee ove ascune autre persone que moy saunz mon
assent, voluntee et congie, qadonques un annuell rent de vint livres graunte a dit Robe[rt
mon fre]re, et sez heirs madles de soun corps engendrez, par mons. Rauf de Eure, Sire
Robert de Wyclyff clerc et William Mayhu issantz de lour manoirs de Morton et Hesilden
deinz leveschie de Duresme les q[uels je] voille, et [i]ls ount de mes doun et feffement,
cesse a toutz jours et le fait endentee eut fait soit de nulle value. Saches moi avoir done
et graunte pleyn assent, voluntee et congie par icestes au d[it frer]e cesse en ascune [ ]
demourer ovesque qique seigneur que luy plerra et meulx semblera pour soun profit et
a sa voluntee demesne pour le terme de sys ans proscheins aveniers apres la date dicestes,
et ceo non obstant jeo [ ] le R[ ]este que par cause del demoere suisdite ovesque
qique seigneur que plerra et meulx semblera au dit Robert, mon frere, pour le dit terme
de sys ans come desuis est dit, le dit annuelle rent [ ]niere eyns estoise en sa pleyn
force et vertue. En tesmoignaunce de quele chose a ycestes jay mys mon seall. Don' le
unzisme jour del mois daprill lan du regne [le roi Henri q]uart puis le conquest
Dengleterre unzisme.

MTD/A2/13, MS holed, sealed through turn up on tag with similar but slightly smaller
seal to MTD/A2/12 and inscribed with the letters I and L (for John de Lumley) on
either side of the popinjay. William Mayhu was still in Lumley's service in 1419
(MTD/A1/8).

Dorse: Haseldine
      Morton

104 Henry, prince of Wales and Thomas, earl of Arundel, Westminster, 20 February 1408 (PRO, CHES 2/80 m. 3, contemporary enrolment).[257]

Ceste endenture faite parentre le hault et puissant prince Henry prince[a] de Gales, duc de Guyen, de Lancastre et de Cornewaille et cont de Cestre dun part et son trescher et tresame cousyn Thomas cont Darondell et de Surr' dautre part tesmoigne que mesme le count est retenuz et demurrez devers mon dit seigneur le prince pur lui servir sibien en temps de pees come de guerre, a pees et a guerre sibien depar decea come de la ou sur la miere, pur terme de sa vie, et pour estre ovesque monditseigneur le prince a pees et a guerre encountre touz gentz du monde except nostre tresredoubteseigneur le Roy Henry piere a mesme monseigneur le prince, pur le quel service prendra le dit cont de mon ditseigneur le prince deux centz et cynquant marcs par an a son Eschequer de Cestre as termes de Pasque et de Seint Michell par oveles porcions. Et avera le dit cont quant il sera deinz lostiel de mon ditseigneur le prince ovec luy quatre de ses escuiers et sys vadlettes a bouche de courte de monseigneur le prince avantdit. Et avera mon ditseigneur le prince de lavantdit cont par tout la vie du dit cont quant il sera as gages de mon ditseigneur le prince la tierce partie de lui et la tierce partie de les tierces de touz ses gentz de lour gaignes de guerre. Et si le suisdit count ou ascun de ses gentz prendra ou prendront aucun chieftayn, chastell ou forteresse en aucun voiage quant il sera as gages de mon suisditseigneur le prince il sera tenuz pur les ditz chieftayn, chastell ou forteresse[b] livrer a mon avantditseigneur le prince, faisant a luy resonable gree pur le chieftayn, chastel ou forteresse avantditz. Et outre ce si mon ditseigneur le prince envoie au dit cont pur venir devers lui soit il deinz le roiaume ou dehors ou sur la meere ovec aucun nombre de gens outre les ditz quatre escuiers et sys vadletz pur lui servier en sa presense ou aillours par son comandement le dit cont serra tenuz pur venir a mon ditseigneur le prince et pur les gentz queux il ainsi amesnera outre le dit nombre de quatre escuiers et sys vadletz il avera gages tielx come autres gens prendront de lours estatz et come le bosoigne de lour venue requiert. Et si mon ditseigneur le prince ferra aucune armee ou voiage en aucune partie dedeinz Engleterre ou dehors ou sur la meere sibien en le droit le Roy nostreseigneur avantdit come en la droit le suisditseigneur le prince, pur le quel il

[257] cf. *DKR* 36 (1875), App. II, 9.

ferra aucune retenue de gens le dit cont sera tenuz pur servir mon ditseigneur le prince ovec un tiel nombre come autres averont de son estat, selon lafferant de la noumbre de gens queux mon ditseigneur le prince avera. Et sil plest a mon ditseigneur le prince pur envoier lavantdit cont outre la meer en son message, le suisdit count sera tenuz pur aler et luy servier a son comandement, et pur le noumbre des gens quelle serra appointz pur le dit cont davoir ovec lui il prendra de mon ditseigneur le prince gages ou regarde solonc les estates de les gentz queux il avera en sa compaignie. En tesmoignance de quele chose a la partie de ceste endenture demurant devers le dit cont mon ditseigneur le prince ad fait mettre son seal. Donne a Westm[inster] le vingt jour de Feverer lan du regne du Roy nostre tresredouteseigneur Henr' quart puis le conquest noefisme.[258]

    a. Henry prince interlined
    b. en aucun voiage ... forteresse interlined

105 Ralph Neville, Earl Marshal and earl of Westmorland and Richard Otway, esquire, 21 June 1408 (Formerly Muncaster MSS Bundle 47 no. 13).[259]

Ceste endenture faite parentre Rauf conte de Westmerlande sire de Nevill' et mareschal Dengleterre dune parte et Richard Otway escuier[260] dautre part tesmoigne qe le dit Richard est demore et retenu ovec le dit conte pur terme de sa vie encontre touz gentz savant nostre tressoverein seignur le roy et ses heirs roys Dengleterre sibien en temps de pees come de la guerre, preignant du dit conte pur son fee en temps de pees quatre marcz issantz annuelment hors du seignurie de Cokermouth[261] par les mayns del receivour illeoques qui pur le temps

[258] For Thomas, earl of Arundel (1400–15) see GEC, i. 245–6, and for his relations with Prince Henry, *Henry V. The Practice of Kingship*, ed. G. L. Harriss (Oxford, 1985), 32–3, 69–70; C. Allmand, *Henry V* (London, 1992), *passim*.

[259] cf. *HMC. 10th Report*, pt. 4, 226 and W. Denton, *England in the Fifteenth Century* (London, 1888), 289–90. The present location of this document is unknown: a search at the Cumbria RO in the Penington papers revealed a note referring to it being sent to the John Rylands Library on 10 January 1930. It appears to have been seen there by Prof. Lewis, whose transcript is followed here. But despite a thorough search, Dr P. McNiven, Head of Special Collections, John Rylands University Library, has been unable to locate it. Some Muncaster MSS from the library have been transfered more recently with a deposit of Crawford MSS to the National Library of Scotland, but a search there has also failed to reveal the original indenture. We are particularly grateful for Dr McNiven's help in this matter.

[260] Otway, of Seaton in Coupland, Cumbs., was dead by 1429: Cumbria RO, Carlisle, D Pen/14/10, 29/17.

[261] Cockermouth, Cumbs.

serra as termes de seint Martyn proschein commenceant et Pentecost par ovelles porcions. Et prendra en temps de guerre autielx gages come le dit conte donera as autres de son degree, rebatant toutfoiz lafferant de son dit fee en temps de pees pur lafferant de ses gages en temps de guerre. Et sera le dit Richard bien et covenablement montez armez et arraiez, prest toutdiz a chivaler ovec ledit conte quant il sera garny depar lui. Et avera le dit conte lez tierces de guerre agaigners par le dit Richard ou par ses genz queux il avera as gages ou cost du dit conte. Et si aucune capitayne ou homme destat soit pris par le dit Richard ou par ses ditz gentz le dit conte lavera faisant al pernour resonable regarde pur lui. As queles covenancz bien et loialment tenir et perfournir depar le dit Richard ad plevy sa foit a dit conte par icestes. En tesmoigne de ce a ycestes les parties suisditz entrechaungeablement ont mys lour sealx. Donne le xxi jour de Juyn lan du regne le roy Henry quart puis le conqueste noefisme.[262]

106 Henry, prince of Wales and Walter Dalehay, esquire, Westminster, 15 November 1408 (PRO, E101/69/2 no. 327).[263]

Ceste endenture faite parentre le hault et puissant prince Henry prince de Gales, duc de Guyen, Lancastre et de Cornewaille et cont de Cestre dune part et son trescher et biename escuier Waulter Dalehay[264] dautre part, tesmoigne que le dit Waulter est retenuz et demurrez devers mon dit seignur le prince pur lui servir sibien en temps de pees come de guerre a pees et a guerre sibien depar decea come dela ou sur la meer pur terme de sa vie, et pur estre ovec mon dit seignur le prince a pees et a guerre encontre tous gens de monde excepte nostre tres redoubte seignur le Roy pere a mesme monseignur le prince pur le quel service

---

[262] Seal of Otway on a double panel tag: bird (?stork) passant, wings folded behind, with trumpet in mouth, within a plaited rush border.

[263] Formerly sealed on tongue now missing.

[264] Dalehay was one of eleven Herefordshire esquires retained on the same day by Prince Henry. Besides the five for whom indentures survive (nos. **106–110**) the others were: John Baskerville, John Boddenham, Thomas de la Hay, Philip Dumbleton, Richard Wiseham and Thomas Borghope. They form a coherent group, all drawn from established local families and connected, in some cases by inter-marriage. The prominence of these Herefordshire gentry in the prince's affinity faithfully reflects the importance of the county in his affairs up until this point. With the virtual cessation of the Welsh campaigns by 1408, Henry was now seeking to consolidate a regional standing created by shared military experience: W. R. M. Griffiths, 'The Military Career and Affinity of Henry, prince of Wales, 1399–1413', Unpublished M. Litt. thesis, Oxford, 1980, 198–201. Dalehay's own indenture may have been ineffective, however; he was the only one of the eleven esquires not to be paid the first instalment of his fee the following Feb. (PRO, SC6/1222/10 m. 3).

prendra le dit Waulter de mon dit seignur le prince dys mars par an pour terme de sa vie par les mayns de le chamberlein de Suthgales pur le temps y esteant as termes de Pasque et de seint Michel par oueles porcions. Et avera mon dit seignur le prince de lavantdit Waulter pur toute la vie du dit Waulter quant il sera as gages de mon dit seignur le prince la tierce partie de lui et la tierce partie de les tierces de tous ses gens de lour gaignes de guerre. Et si le dit Waulter ou aucun de ses ditz gens prendra ou prendront aucun chieftayn, chastel ou forteresse en aucune voiage quant il sera as gages de mon dit seignur le prince il sera tenuz pur les ditz chieftayn, chastel ou forteresse liverer a mon dit seignur le prince faisant a lui resonable gree pur le chieftayn, chastel ou forteresse avantditz.

Et outre ce si mon dit seigneur le prince envoie au dit Waulter pur venir devers lui soit il deinz le roiaume ou dehors ou sur la meer ovec aucun nombre de gens pur lui servir en sa presence ou aillours a son commandement, le dit Waulter serra tenuz pur venir a mon dit seigneur le prince et pur les gens queux il ainsi amesnera il avera gages tielx come autres gens prendront de leures estates et come le bosoigne de lour venue requert.

Et si mon dit seignur le prince ferra aucune armee ou voiage en aucune partie dedenz Engleterre ou dehors ou sur la meer sibien en le droit le Roy nostre seignur avantdit come de le roiaume pur le quel il ferra aucune retenue de gens le dit Waulter sera tenuz pur servir mon dit seignur le prince ovec un tiel nombre come autres escuiers averont de son estat. Et sil plest a mon dit seignur le prince pur envoier lavantdit Waulter outre la meer ou aillours en son message pur quelconque cause que ce soit le dit Waulter sera tenuz pur aler et lui servir a son commandement et pur le nombre de gens quel sera appointez pur le dit Waulter davoir ovec lui, il prendra de mon avantdit seigneur le prince gages ou regarde selon lestates de les gens queux il avera en sa compaignie. En tesmoignance de quel chose a la partie de ceste endenture demurrant devers mon dit seignur le prince lavantdit Waulter ad mys son seal. Donne a Westm' le xv jour de Novembre lan de regne du Roy nostre tresredoubte seignur Henry quart puis le conquest disme.

107 Henry, prince of Wales and Thomas Bromwych, Westminster, 15 November 1408 (PRO, E101/69/2 no. 328).[265]

---

[265] Formerly sealed on a tongue now missing; the name of the retainer has been filled in by a separate hand. Thomas Bromwych of Fownhope, Herefords., was the son of Sir John Bromwych (cf. **66**) and had acted as a collector of the income tax in Herefordshire in 1404 (*CFR, 1399–1405*, 258; *CCR 1416–22*, 326).

In identical terms to **106**.

108 Henry, prince of Wales and Thomas Holcot (Holgot), Westminster, 15 November 1408 (PRO, E101/69/2 no. 329).[266]

In identical terms to **106** except that the third sentence of the indenture begins: 'Et avera mon dit seigneur le prince de le dit Thomas quant il sera en son service de guerre en sa presence ou de son commandement la tierce partie de lui et la tierce partie des tierces ... '; this is written over an erasure.

109 Henry, prince of Wales and Geoffrey Ardern, Westminster, 15 November 1408 (PRO, E101/69/2 no. 330).[267]

In identical terms to **108**.

110 Henry, prince of Wales and Walter Devereux, Westminster, 15 November 1408 (PRO, E101/69/2 no. 331).[268]

In identical terms to **108**.

111 Henry, prince of Wales and Richard Beauchamp, earl of Warwick, Lambeth, 2 October 1410 (PRO, E101/69/2 no. 338, formerly sealed on tongue).[269]

Ceste endenture faite parentre le hault et puissant prince Henry aisne filz au noble Roy Dengleterre et de France prince de Gales duc de Guyen et de Lancastre et de Cornwaille et conte de Cestre dune part et son treschier et tresame cousin Richard counte de Warrewyk dautre

---

[266] Formerly sealed on a tongue now missing. *HC, 1386–1421*, iii. 397 for the career of Holgot (d. *c.* 1420); see also below **134**.

[267] Formerly sealed on a tongue now missing. There is a 17th century transcript of this indenture in Oxford, Bodleian Library, MS Dugdale 2, p. 264.

[268] Formerly sealed on a tongue now missing and previously printed from the transcript in Oxford, Bodleian Library, MS Dugdale 2, p. 261 by Dunham, 138–9. Walter Devereux of Weobley, Herefords., succeeded his father in 1403 and married into the Bromwych family. He was aged about 22 at the time of this indenture: J. Duncumb, *Collections towards the history and antiquities of the county of Hereford* (Hereford, 1804–11), ii. 37–8; *CIPM, 1399–1405*, no. 701.

[269] Carpenter, *Locality and Polity*, *passim* for the fullest treatment of the career of Richard Beauchamp, earl of Warwick (1401–39).

part tesmoigne que le dit count est retenuz et demorrez devers mon dit seigneur le prince pur lui servir sibien en temps de pees come de guerre a pees et a guerre sibien depardecea come dela ou sur la meer pur terme de sa vie et pour estre ovec mon dit seignur le prince a pees et a guerre encontre tous gens du monde excepte nostre tresredoubte seignur le Roy Henry pere a mesme monseignur le prince. Pur le quel service prendra le dit count de mon dit seignur le prince deux centz et cynquant marcz par an a son eschequer de Kermerdyn as termes de Pasqe et de seint Michell par ovelles porcions. Et avera le dit cont quant il sera deinz lostiel de mon dit seigneur le prince ovec lui quatre de ses escuiers et sys vadletz a bouche de courte de monsire le prince avantdit. Et avera mon dit seigneur le prince de lavantdit conte pur tout la vie du dit cont quant il sera as gages de mon dit seignur le prince la tierce partie de lui et la tierce partie de les tierces de toutz ses gens de leur gaignes de guerre. Et si le suisdit conte ou auscun des ses gents prendra ou prendront ascun chieftain, chastell ou forteresse en auscune voiage quant il sera as gages de mon dit seignur[a] le prince il sera tenus pur les dites chieftain, chastell ou forteresse liverer a mon avant dit seignur le prince faisant a luy resonable gree pur le chieftain, chastell et forteresse avantditz.

Et outre ce si mon dit seignur le prince envoie au dit cont pur venir a luy soit il deinz le royaulme ou dehors ou sur la meer ovec auscun nombre de gens outre les ditz quatre escuiers et sis valletz pur lui servir en sa presence ou aillours a son commandement le dit conte sera tenuz pur venir a mon dit seignur le prince. Et pur les gens queux il ainsi amesnera outre le dit nombre de quatre escuiers et sis valletz il avera gages tielx come autres gens prendront de leurs estatz et come le bosoigne de lour venue requiert. Et si mon dit seignur le prince ferra ascun armee ou voiage en ascun partie dedenz Engleterre ou dehors ou sur la meer sibien en la droit le Roy nostre seignur avantdit come en la droit le susdit seignur le Prince pur le quel service il fera auscun retenue des gens le dit conte sera tenuz pur servir mon dit seignur le prince ovec un tiel nombre de gens come autres averont de son estat selon lafferant de le nombre de gens queux mon dit seignur le prince avera.

Et sil plest a mon dit seignur le prince pur envoier lavantdit conte outre la meer ou auilours en son message le suisdit conte sera tenuz pur aler et luy servir a son commandement et pur le nombre de gens quel le sera appointez pur le dit conte davoir ovec lui, il prendra de mon dit seignur le prince gages ou regarde selon lestatz de les gens queux il avera en sa compaignie. En tesmoignance de quelle chose a la partie de ceste endenture demourant devers mon dit seignur le prince lavantdit conte ad mys son seal. Donne en le manoir de Lambehith le seconde jour doctober lan de regne de nostre soverein seignur le roy Henry le quart puis le conquest douszisme.

Dorse: Warr'

a. MS here and elsewhere *ditseignur*

112 Henry, lord Beaumont and Hugh Cok, trumpeter, Folkingham, 5 April 1412 (PRO, C66/392 m. 15, *inspeximus* of 12 November 1413).[270]

A toutz yceaux que cestez presentes lettres verront ou orront Henry sir de Bealmont salutz. Sachiez moy pur le bone et greable service que Hugh Cok trumpet moy ad fait, et a moy et mes heires ferra, avoir luy graunte deux mees ensemblement gisauntz en la ville de Folkyngham[271] ove deux boefes de terre en mesme la ville, les queux deux mees et deux boefes William Champer ore tarde tient, et un annuele rent de xl s. aprendre annuelment par les mayns de coillour ou resceivour de ma dite ville de Folkyngham as termes de Seint Michel et Pasche par oveles porcions, a avoir et tenir a dit Hugh en le maner avantdit pur terme de sa vie, rendant a moy et a mez heirs annuelment un rose al fest de Seint Johan Baptist. Et sil aveigne que le dit rent de xl s. soit aderer en partie ou en tout as ascuns des termes avantditz nient paiez que bien lise a dit Hugh en la dit ville distrendre et destresces reteigner tanque pleine gree a luy soit fait del rent avantdit ensemblement ovesque les arrerages si aucuns ysoient. Purveu toutfoitz que lavantdit Hugh serroit tenuz a servire en son office a moy et a mes heirs pur terme de sa vie avantdit. En tesmoignance de quele chose a lune partie de ceste endenture demourant devers le dit Hugh jay mys mon seal et a lautre partie de ceste endenture demourant devers moys le dit Hugh ad mys son seal. Don a mon chastell de Folkyngham le maresdy proschein apres le fest de Pasche lan du regne nostre seigneur le Roy Henry quart puis le conquest treszisme.

113 Henry, lord Beaumont and Nicholas Duke, minstrel, Grimsthorpe, 14 December 1412 (PRO, C66/392 m. 22, *inspeximus* of 14 November 1413).[272]

Cest endenture fait le xiiij jour de December lan de regne nostre seignour le Roy Henry quarte puis le conquest quatorzisme tesmoigne que Nicholas Duke mynstrall est retenuz pur demourer ovec Henry Sir

---

[270] cf. *CPR, 1413–16*, 137; *CCR, 1413–19*, 207–8. Cok was still in receipt of the annuity granted him by this indenture in 1435 (PRO, E163/7/31/2 m. 27), though Henry, fifth lord Beaumont (1396–1413) was long dead (GEC, ii. 61).

[271] Folkingham, Lincs.

[272] cf. *CPR, 1413–16*, 132; *CCR, 1413–19*, 129.

de Bealmont seignour de Folkyngham[273] pour luy servier a terme de sa vie sibien de peas come de guerre. Et prendra le dit Nicholas del dit Sir de Bealmont quarant souldz par an des issues et revenuz del seigneurie de Barton sur Humbre[274] par les mayns del Baylif pour le temps esteant as termes de Pasque et de seint Michell par oveles porcions. Et sil aveigne que lavantdit rente soit aderer en partie ou en tout as ascuns des termes avantditz nient paiez qadonques bien lise a dit Nicholas en toutz les terres et tenementz de Barton distrendre et les destressez retenir tanque a luy plain paiement soit fait del rent avantdit ensy aderer esteant, ensemblement ovec les arrerages dicels si ascuns ysoient. En tesmoignance de quel chose as icestez presentz endentures les parties avantditz enterchanchablement ount mise lour seals. Doune a Grymesthorp[275] lan et jour susditz.

114 John, duke of Bedford and Sir Robert Plumpton, Bishopthorpe, Yorks. W.R., 15 October 1415 (Leeds, City Archives, Plumpton Coucher Book, Acc. 1731/3, no. 373).[276]

Ceste endenture fait dentre le haut et puissant prince Johan fitz et frere des Roys, duc de Bedford, count de Richmond et Kendale, et connestable d'Engleterre, dun part, et Robert de Plompton, chevaler, dautre part, tesmoigne que le dit Robert est retenuez et demorrez pardevers le dit tres noble et puissant prince a terme de sa vie pour lui servir, sibien en temps de pees come de guerre, au mielz qui resonablement il pourra estre en son pouoir, preignant annuelement du dit haut et puissant prince pour son fe a cause de sa dite demoere vingt marcs en temps de pees de les cofres de mesme le haut et puissant prince. Et sera le dit Robert montez, armes et arraies come a son degre et estat appartient, et prest de chivalcher ovec le susdit tres noble et puissant prince en sa compaignie, a quel temps que a ce fair il sera deper mesme le puissant prince garniz ou requiz, preignant en temps de guerre du dit tres noble et puissant prince, quant traveillera ovec luy, pour luy mesmez et ses gentz, lesquex il amesnera ovec luy par comaundement de le dit haut et puissant prince, tieulx gagez come autres gentilx de lour degree prendront pour le temps, rebatant toutesvoies lafferant de son fe en temps de pees pour lafferant de ses gagez en temps de guerre, en cas qil travaille ove le dit tresnoble et puissant prince a aucuns journes que se tiendra pur un quarter del an ou plus, et

[273] Folkingham, Lincs.
[274] Barton on Humber, Lincs.
[275] Grimsthorpe, Lincs.
[276] Published first in *The Plumpton Correspondence*, ed. Thomas Stapleton (1839), xlii note g. We are grateful to W. J. Connor, District Archivist, Leeds District Archives, for permission to publish.

nemye pour nulle autre petit journes que se namontera al quarter dan.

Et aura le dit Robert quant il traveillera ovec le dit tresnoble prince en sa compaigne en temps de pees, ou veigne a son houstell per son comaundement, bouche du courte pour luy mesmes, un escuier, et deux ses valetts, en tiel regarde come au dit tres noble prince il plerra. Et de toutez maners de prisoners et autres profittz et gaignes de guerre quelconques en aucune manere per le dit Robert prisez ou gaignes, le dit tres noble et puissant prince aura la tierce; et de tous autres ses ditz gentz lesqueulx il aura as gages, de mesme le tres noble prince la tierce de la tierce. Et si aucun chevitaigne ou autre grand sera soit pris per le dit Robert ou aucun de ses ditz gentz, le dit tres noble et puissant prince aura le chevitaigne ou seigneur avant dit, fesant a celly que luy prist resonable regarde. En tesmoignance du quele chose sibien le dit prince come le dit Robert a cestes endentures entrechangeablement ount mys lour sealx. Donne a la manor de Bisshopthorp le xv jour d'octobre, l'an du reigne notre soverain sire le Roy Henri quint puis le conquest tierce.[277]

115 William de Burgh, esquire, and William de Hesilton and Katherine, his wife, Brough, Yorks. N. R., 19 July 1419 (North Yorks. RO, ZRL 1/22, sealed through turn-up on two tags).[278]

Hec indentura facta inter Willelmum de Burgh armigerum ex parte una et Willelmum de Hesillton de Tunstall[279] et Katerina uxorem eius ex parte altera testatur quod prefatus Willelmus de Burgh concessit et confirmavit pro se et heredibus suis predictis Willelmo de Hesillton et Katerine uxori eius quod ipsi habebunt et precipient de prefato Willelmo de Burgh et heredibus suis apud Burgh singulis tribus septimanis post festum Sancti Martini[280] in yeme proxime futuro post datum presencium venturis duos bussellos frumenti grani tanabilis durantibus vitis pre-

[277] *Ibid.*, xxi–xlix and *HC, 1386–1421*, iv. 90–2 for the career of Sir Robert Plumpton (1383–1421) of Steeton, Yorks., and Kinoulton, Notts. We are grateful to Mrs Joan Kirby, who is preparing a new edition of the Plumpton correspondence, for help with this indenture.

[278] William Burgh (d. 1442) of Brough Hall in Catterick, Yorks. N.R., also held land in Leeming, Walborn and Richmond (NYCRO, ZRL 1/19). For the family see A. J. Pollard, 'The Burghs of Brough Hall, c. 1270–1574', *North Yorkshire County Record Office Journal* 6 (1978), 5–33 and below **152**. We are grateful to the representatives of the late Sir Ralph Lawson for permission to publish this document and to M. Y. Ashcroft, County Archivist, for help in obtaining this and for other assistance. The first tag bears the impression in red wax of a small seal inscribed with an initial W; the second seal is missing.

[279] Tunstall in Catterick, Yorks. N. R.

[280] 11 November.

dictorum Willelmi de Hesillton et Katerine ac utriusque eorum diutius viventis. Et ulterius idem Willelmus de Burgh concedit pro se et heredibus suis prefato Willelmo de Hesillton unam robam de liberata et secta valettorum suorum habendam et percipiendam robam predictam annuatim ad terminum vite sue[a] pro qua quidem roba predictus Willelmus Hesillton super debita pronnuncionem ei faciendum paratus erit ad eundum vel equitandum cum prefato Willelmo de Burgh quocumque ei placuerit ad custus et expensas ipius Willelmi de Burgh. Et si contingat predictum frumentum aretro fore per duos menses non solutum quod tunc bene liceat prefatis Willelmo de Hesillton et Katerine uxori eius pro predicto frumento et qualibet parcella eiusdem sic aretro existente in omnibus terris et tenementis ipsius Willelmis de Burgh in Tunstall distringere et districciones sic captas abducere et imprecare quousque de predicto frumento et arreragiis eiusdem plenarie eis fuerit satisfactum et solutum. In cuius rei testimonium partes harum indenturarum presenciorum[b] sigilla suo alternatim apposuerunt. Datum apud Burgh duodecimo die mensis Julii anno regni regis Henrici quinti post conquestum Anglie septimo.

Dorse: Carta Willelmi de Burgh de terra in Tunstall

a. *sue* interlined
b. *presenciorum* interlined

116 Sir Richard Neville, Warden of the West March, and Thomas Womewill, esquire, Pontefract, Yorks., 6 October 1426 (PRO, E210/D4972, damaged original, formerly sealed on tag).[281]

This endenture made betwix sir Richard Nevill knyght wardein of the Westmerche of England ayenst Scotland of that on part and Thomas Womewill squier[282] of that othir part bereth witness that the sayde Thomas Womewill is belest and wytholden with the said Sir Richard for terme of lyve agaynes all folke savyng his ligeaunce and the duke of Yhork. Takyng for his fee forty shyllyngs of monye to be payed of the fee of the said sir Richard at Pountfreit by the handys of the resceyveour ther beyng for tyme at the termes of Martinmaes and Whyssonday by even porcions draying othir ... the said fee ... of the

[281] Neville was Warden of the West March, 8 June 1420–12 Sept. 1435: R. L. Storey, 'The Wardens of the Marches of England towards Scotland, 1377–1489', *EHR*, lxxii (1957), 613.
[282] Of Wombwell, Yorks., W. R. He was Neville's deputy as Steward of Pontefract from Feb. 1425 until his death in 1453: *Testamenta Eboracensia*, ii. 163–4; Somerville, *Duchy of Lancaster*, 513.

said sir Richard att Pountfreit ... And yf so be that the said sir Richard be discharged of his office(?) forsaid then he will and graunts to the said Thomas that the foresaid [forty] shyllyngs of monye to be taken at his maner of Coryngham[283] att the termes forsaid by the handes of his resceyveour ther beying for tyme. And the said Thomas sall be allway redy to ryde with the said sir Richard or his depute att his commaunde [well arraied at] all tymes that he be resonably warned on his behalf ... Takyng the said Thomas for hym and ... travaill with the said sir Richard siche wages als he gifes to othir of hys degree. For the whiche covenauntz whele and trewly to be holden and performed on the behalf of the said Thomas as(?) he has plight his troth to the said sir Richard. In witnenes herof the parties be forsaid to the parties of this endentures entrechaungeably have set ther seals. Written at Pountfreit sext day of Octobre, The yhere of kyng Henry the sext after conquest the fifte.

117 Richard, earl of Salisbury and John Hotoft, Warwick, 9 May 1429 (PRO, E315/40/154, mounted in a book; no trace of seal surviving).[284]

Hec indentura facta inter Ricardum comitem Sar' ex parte una et Johannem Hotoft armigerum[285] ex parte altera testatur quod predictus comes per presentes retinuit predictum Johannem essend' de concilio ipsius Comitis tota vita ipsius Comitis, pro quo quidem concilio prefato comiti per prefatum Johannem imposterum inpendendo idem Comes concessit prefato Johanni quandam annualam pensionem quatuorum marcarum percipiendo annuatim ad totam vitam suam in manibus suis propriis, videlicet de certis redditis quos prefatus Johannes annuatim solvere consuevit prefato comiti ad manerium suum de Ware in com' Hertford[286] de diversis terris et tenementis ipsius Johannis in eadem villa ad festa sancti Michaelis et Pasche per equales porciones. Ita quod bene licebit prefato Johanni et assignatis suis dictas quatuor marcas annualis quas prefato comiti pro dictis terris et tenementis suis in villa predicta solvere tenebatur ad proprium usum suum durante vita sua penes se detinere absque calumpnia sue inpedimento prefato Comiti aliquali. In cuius rei testimonium presentibus indenturis partes predicte sigilla sua alternatim apposuerunt. Datum apud War[wick] nono die Maii anno regno Regis Henrici Sexti post conquestum septimo.

[283] Corringham, Lincs.

[284] GEC, xi. 395–8 for Richard Neville, *iure uxoris* earl of Salisbury (1428–60).

[285] *HC, 1386–1421*, iii. 427–9 for John Hotoft (d. 1443) of Knebworth, Herts., and E. Acheson, *A Gentry Community. Leicestershire in the Fifteenth Century, c.1422–c.1485* (Cambridge, 1992), 236–7 for his family.

[286] Ware, Herts.

118 Thomas, lord Roos and Sir John Cressy, Belvoir, Leics. 12 November 1429 (PRO, C66/435 m. 18, *inspeximus* of 5 December 1433).[287]

Ceste endenture fait parentre Thomas seignour de Roos et de Troussebous[288] dune parte et Johan Cressy de Dodford en le countee de Norhamton chivaler[289] dautre parte tesmoigne que le dit Johan est retenuz et demorez ovesque le dit seignour pur luy faire service a terme de vie du dit Johan en Engleterre, et pur le dit service ensi fait et affaire par le dit Johan a dit seignour mesme le seignour ad graunte et demyse par ycestez au dit Johan soun manoir de Braunston en le countee de Norhamton[290] suisdit ov lez appurtenunces, forpris lavoeson del esglise de Braunston avauntdit et lez heriottes des tenants au dit manoir appurtenauntez, a avoier et tener au dit Johan le dit manoire ove les appurtenunces forprisez les forsprisez (*sic*) suisditz pur terme du vie de mesme le Johan saunz ascun gaste faire de mesme le manoire ove les appurtenunces. Et outreceo le dit Thomas seignour de Roos ad grauntee par icestes a dit Johan Cressy chivaler pur soun dit service ensi fait et affaire a dit seignour en le forme et manere suisdit une annuell rent de vingt marcez par an apprendre de soun manoire de Eykeryng[291] ove lez appurtenunces en le countee de Notyngham pur terme de la vie du dit Johan a avoir, tenir et levier a dit Johan lez ditz vint marcz par an du dit manoire de Eykeryng ove lez appurtenunces a lez termes de Pasqes et Seint Michell par owellis porcions par lez mayns de lez baillifs et collectours dez rents et fermes illouques qi sount ou qe pur le temps serount durant la vie du mesme le Johan avantdit. Et surceo le dit seignour voiet et commaunde par icestes a sez ditz baillifs et collectours de dit manoir qe a dit Johan facent deue paiement de lez ditz vint marcz par an a lez termes et en le forme suisdit. Et a ses auditours de sez accoumptez que a lez ditz[a] baillifs et collectours de paiement et paiement par acquitance et acquitancez de dit Johan

[287] cf. *CPR, 1429–36*, 330. GEC, xi. 104–5 for Thomas, eighth lord Roos (1421–30) who died in Normandy in the king's service.

[288] *Troussebous*, i.e. Trussebut: Thomas's ancestors had inherited lands from the Trussebut family in the thirteenth century (cf. GEC, xii, pt. 2, 49 and I. J. Sanders, *English Baronies* (Oxford, 1960), 56).

[289] J. C. Wedgwood, *History of Parliament: Biographies of the Members of the Commons House, 1439–1509* (London, 1936), 235 for an account of the career of Sir John Cressy (1407–45) of Wheathamstead, Herts. and Dodford, Northants., which can be much augmented. He divided his time in the 1430s and 1440s between England and France, dying as captain of Pont l'Evêque, though he is buried at Dodford. His widow, Constance, daughter of Reginald, lord Grey of Ruthin died in 1486 (information kindly provided by Dr Anne Curry). Roos' inquisition *post mortem* recites the substance of this grant as far as it refers to Eakring (*Abstracts of the Inquisitiones post mortem relating to Nottinghamshire, 1350–1436*, ed. Train (Thoroton Soc., Record ser., xii, 1952), 189–90).

[290] Braunston, Northants.

[291] Eakring, Notts.

facent deue alloance de an en an et de terme en terme par icestes. Et outreceo le dit seignour graunte par icestes qe si le dit annuite de vint marce soit aderere en partie ou en tout as ascuns dez termes avantditz que bien lise au dit Johan et a sez assignez a distreigner et distresses prendre durant sa dit vie en le manoir de Eykeryng ove lez appur-tenances et distresses par luy prisez emporter et amesner et ovesque luy deteinger tanque a luy soit pleinement agreez et content de la dite annuitee et de lez arrerages dicell ovesque lez damages et costages par luy eus et sustenuz a cause de detenue du paiement avantdite. Et pluis outre le dit seignour ad graunte par icestes a dit Johan pour soun dit service en le forme suisdite bouche de courte pour luy, j esquier, j vadlect, j garceon et quatre chivalx a tout temps qil sera en sa presence et service du dit seignour en Engliterre duraunt la vie du dit Johan avantdit. En tesmoignaunce de quell chose sibien le dit Sire come le dit Johan a ycestez endentures entrechaungeablement ount mys loure sealx. Donnez a Beauvier[292] le dousze joure de Novembre lan du regne de Roy Henry sisme puis le conquest Dengleter oytysime.

a. ditz interlined

119 William, lord FitzHugh and John Wencelagh (Wensley), Rav-ensworth, 24 December 1433 (Leeds, Yorks. Arch. Soc., DD 42/175, sealed on tag with signet).[293]

This endenture made betwix William[a] lorde ffitzhugh on Þe to party and John Wencelagh Þe yongar[294] on the tother party wyttenes Þat Þe sayde John is belesst and fully withaldyn for terme of his lyffe to be of counsaill with Þe sayde lorde and with his heires in Þe faculte of lawe agayns all man[ere] of men except Þas persones Þat ar or shall be of kyn or alye to Þe same John and such services shall do after his conyng in Þe sayde faculte as resonabilly Þe sayde lorde wyll comaunde hym, takyng yerly of Þe sayde lorde atte feste of Seynt Martyn in Wynter for his fee xiij s. iiij d. duryng all Þe lyffe of his fadir and after[b] Þe decesse of his sayde fadir to have and to halde in Þe name of his fee a mese, a croft and foure oxgang of lande in Þe toune and felde of

[292] Belvoir, Leics.
[293] A helm topped by a dragon's head. GEC, v. 426–7 for William, fourth lord Fitzhugh (1425–52).
[294] The connection betwen the Fitzhughs and the Wensley family was a long lasting one: John Wensley the elder was acting as collector of rents and farms on the Fitzhugh estates in 1410/11 and his son was still doing business for Lord Fitzhugh in 1451: North Yorks. CRO, ZJX 3/2/47 m. 1; YAS, MD 116/4, 5.

Brandesburton in Holdernes[295] for terme of his lyffe afftir the fourme and Þe effect of a dede endentid made to his sayde ffadir and to hym. In wyttenes wherof to this present endentures aither of Þe partys afforesayde enterchaungeabilly has put Þaire seles. Gyffen at Ravenswath[296] Þe xxiiij^{te} day of Decembre Þe yere of Kyng Henry sext after Þe conquest xij^e.

    a. William interlined
    b. after interlined

120 Richard Neville, earl of Salisbury and Sir Thomas Dacre, 22 April 1435 (Northants. RO, Fitzwilliam (Milton) Muniments, MS 2049, sealed on tongue, with tying thong).[297]

This indenture made bitwix Richard Erle of Salisbury on the one parte and Thomas Dacre knyght son and heire of the lorde Dacre on the other parte bereth witnesse that the said Thomas is belast and witholden with the said Erl for terme of lyve of the said Thomas ayenst al folke, saving his ligeance, aswele in tyme of paix as of werre, wele and covenably horsid, armed and arraied and alwey redy to ride with or for the said Erle, at al tymes that he be reasonably warned on his bihalve, takyng the said Thomas of the said Erle, yereli for his fee, living Johanne contesse of Westmorl', twenty marke of moneie and after hir decesse or in cas the said lord Dacre dye twenty pound, at termes of Michaelmesse and Pasque bi even porcions, and the said Erle shal have the thirdes of wynnyng of werre geten bi the said Thomas or bi his men, which he shal have at wages or cost of the said Erle. And if eny capitaigne or man of state be taken bi the said Thomas or bi eny of his said men the said Erl shal have him, doyng to the said taker reasonable rewarde for him. In witnesse of which thing the said Erle and Thomas to the parties of this indenture entrechangeably have set their sealx, yifen the xxij dai of Avrill the yere of the Regne of King Henry sext syn the conquest thirtened.

Dorse: Indentura Thomas Dacre chivaler[298]
      Of no valu'[299]

---

[295] Brandsburton, Yorks. E.R.

[296] Ravensworth, Yorks. N.R.

[297] We are grateful to the Trustees of the Estate of the late Earl Fitzwilliam for permission to publish this indenture and **126** and **127**, and to Miss R. Watson, County Archivist, for help in obtaining this. A small round red signet (10 mm) survives: I. H. Jeayes, in a typescript catalogue of these deeds (1930), suggests '?a dragon's head'; it may be a dolphin. Thomas Dacre, eldest son of Thomas, sixth lord Dacre (1399–1458), predeceased his father (GEC, iv. 7–8).

[298] Contemporary endorsement.

[299] In late seventeenth/early eighteenth-century hand.

121 Joan, countess of Westmorland with Richard, earl of Salisbury, and Robert Eure, esquire, 1 May 1435 (BL, Lansdowne Charter 629).[300]

This endenture made bitwix Johane contesse of Westmerl[and] and Richard Erl of Salisbury on yat one parte and Robert Eure squier[301] on yat other parte bereth witnesse yat wher ye said Robert by an other endenture bering date ye first day of Marce ye yere of ye regne of King Henry sext syn the Conquest thirtened is bilast and witholden with ye said Contesse and Erle ayenst al folke saving onely his ligeance as in ye same endenture it appereth. Neverthelesse ye saide Contesse and Erle wil and grauntes by thies yat it shal be leful to ye said Robert to be of consail and helping with Sir William Eure[302] his brother and with his children ayen ye said Contesse and Erle if eny materes of difference in lawe happen to fal bitwix theym, which God defende,[a] ye first[b] endentures of bilevying of ye said Robert with ye said Contesse and Erle notwithstanding. In witnesse of which thing ye said parties to the parties of this endenture entrechangeably have set theyr seals. Gifen ye first day of May ye yere of ye regne of King Henry sext syn ye conquest thirtened.

Dorse: Indent' of belefing for ye brother Sir Will' Eure.

a. A clause deleted at this point: *and if it happen also yat God so wil yat eny mattere of difference or vareance fal bitwix ye said Contesse or Erle and Thomas of Lumley yat ye said Robert shal not be constreyned to be with ye said Contesse and Erl of conseil ayenst ye said Thomas*

b. *ye first* interlined

122 Humphrey, earl of Buckingham and Sir Edward Gray (Grey), London, 20 April 1440 (National Library of Wales, MS Peniarth 280

[300] Cut for a tongue but then sealed on a tag, the seal now missing; for Joan Beaufort, dowager countess of Westmorland (1425–40) and her son Richard Neville, earl of Salisbury (1428–60), cf. GEC, xii, pt. 2. 547 and xi. 395–8.

[301] Son of Sir Ralph Eure (*HC, 1386–1421*, iii. 38–43), Robert Eure of Bradley, Durham, acted as sheriff and escheator of Durham and Sadberge under Bishop Langley between 1420 and 1436 and was appointed steward of the palatinate by Bishop Robert Neville in 1438 (R. L. Storey, *Thomas Langley and the bishopric of Durham, 1406–1437* (London, 1961), 61; *DKR* 34 (1873), 167). Joan, countess of Westmorland's association in this agreement was the result of her tenure of the Neville lordships of Penrith, Middleham and Sheriff Hutton as dower.

[302] Wedgwood, 306 for Sir William Eure.

fols. 6–7, transcript between 1620–48 by Robert Vaughan from the now lost *Redd Book of Caures Castle*).[303]

This endenture made betwene the right worshipfull lord Humfrey Erle of Bukingham etc. on the one partye and Sir Edward Gray knight[304] on the other partye, Wittnesseth that the said earle hathe yeven and graunted by these present endentures to the sayd Sir Edward an annuel fee of an C. mark to take yearly during the life of the said Sir Edward. Wherof the paiement of xl mark shall sese unto the tyme that God provide the said Sir Edward to the estat of Baron so that he shall take of the said erle during the time he standeth at the degre of bachelor xl l. yerely and when he is at the stat of Baron an C. mark yerly to have and take of the lordshippys of Okeham[305] in the counte of Rutland and Tyso[306] in the counte of Warwyck bi the hands of the recevour, farmours, baylife, provostes and other ministres and occupiers therefor the tyme being at the terms of St Michel and Estren be even porcions, for the whiche the seid erle hath witholde toward him the said Sir Edward to do him servise terme of lyf in the maner and forme as followeth. That ys to wite in pece and werre and that for the tyme of pease the said Sir Edward schall be redy at all dayes when he schall be send for or commaunded to come to the seyd Erle upon resonable warning to do him service and with him to ride in all parties on this side of the sea with j escuier, iij yemen, j grome, j page and vij hors or as many persons and horse as the said erle liste to assigne or commaunde for the tyme he standeth at the degre of bachelor, and whanne the seid Sir Edward be at the stat of baron he schall have with hym two escuiers, iiij yemen, j grome, ij pages and x horses, or as many persons and horses as the said Erle in tyme of pees list to commaunde or assigne, for the which he schall have suche bouche of court and livere during the tyme of his demure as is covenable to his degre or estat with resonable costes in comyng to the said Erle and retournyng ayen as ofte tymes as he is send for bi the said Erle. And in cas that the seid Erle be ordeyned in any voiage of warre be it on this side of the see, or beyond, in the service of the king our sovereyn lord or of any other, the said Sir Edward schall be redy upon resonable warning with suche numbre of men of armes and archers as the said Erle shall assigne or

[303] Published by courtesy of the National Library of Wales. Cf. C. Rawcliffe, *The Staffords, Earls of Stafford and Dukes of Buckingham 1394–1521* (Cambridge, 1978), 3 for the Red Book and for Buckingham's career; we are grateful to Dr Christine Carpenter for loan of a microfilm of this MS. This indenture was first published by A. Reeves, 'Some of Humphrey Stafford's Military Indentures', *Nottingham Mediaeval Studies* 16 (1972), 88–9.

[304] GEC, v. 358–9 for Sir Edward Grey, later lord Ferrers of Groby (1446–57).

[305] Oakham, Rutland.

[306] Tysoe, Warwicks.

appoint according to his degre or estat to be accompagnied with him
well and suffisantly armed, horsed and arayed after the maner and feet
of warre, for the which armes and viage the said Sir Edward schall
take of the said Erle such wages and reward for him and his seid men
so accompaigned with him as the said Erle schall take of the king or
any other his capitains, with shippyng and reshippyng resonable for
him, his seid men and horse as other of his degre or estat schall have
in the compaignye of the said Erle, the which viage during the said
Erle schall have of the said Sir Edward the thryddes of all maner
prisoners and of all other prises and wynnyngs bi him taken and the
thriddes of the thriddes of his souldiours of the prisoners, prises and
wynnynges bi hem taken or geten bi way of fortune or aventure of
werre, and the said Sir Edward nor non of his men so accompaignied
with him schall putte ne prisoner bi hem or any of hem taken at any
time duryng the said viage to finance nor ransoum but as law of armes
woll. In witnesse wherof the said Erle to on parte of these present
endentures toward the said Sir Edward remaygnyng hath putte to his
seal and to the other part of the same endentures toward the said Erle
remaignyng the said Sir Edward hath putte to his seal. Yeven at London
the xx^{ti} day of Averyll the yere of the regne of King Henry the sixte
after the conquest the xviij^{the}.

123 Humphrey, earl of Buckingham and Sir Richard Vernon, London,
31 October 1440 [English] (NLW, Peniarth MS 280 fos. 11–12, pub. in
Nottingham Mediaeval Studies 16 (1972), 89).[307]

124 Humphrey, earl of Buckingham and Sir John Mainwaring, Stafford
castle, 5 September 1441 (Manchester, John Rylands University Library,
Supplementary Mainwaring Deeds 9, sealed on tag through turn up).[308]

This endenture made betwene the righte worshipfull lorde Humfrey
Erle of Bukyngham, Hereford, Stafford, Northampton and Perche on

---

[307] *HC, 1386–1421*, iv. 712–7 for the career of Sir Richard Vernon (1390–1451) of
Harlaston, Staffs., and Haddon, Derbys. His younger son and heir, Sir William Vernon
was also retained by Buckingham for service in peace and war, at a fee of £10 p.a. by
an indenture dated 1 August 1454 (PRO, SC6/1040/15 m. 3).

[308] Reproduced by courtesy of the Director and University Librarian, the John Rylands
University Library of Manchester. We are grateful for help from Dr Peter McNiven,
Head of Special Collections, in tracing the original; it is counter-sealed with a small
armorial seal (a chevron) on a double tag through the turn up. It was first pub. after
NLW, Peniarth MS 280 fos. 17–18 in *Nottingham Mediaeval Studies* 16 (1972), 89–90.

the on partie and Sir John Maynwarynge knyght[309] on the other partie
witnesseth that the seyde Erle hathe yeven and graunted by these
presentes endentures to the seyde Sir John an annuell fee of x li. to
take yerely durynge the lyf of the seyde Sir John of the issues, proffites
and revenues comyng of the lordship of Rothewell[310] in the counte of
Northampton by the handes of the resceivour, baillyf, fermour, provost
or other minyster or occupiour there for the tyme beynge at the termes
of Estern and of Seynt Michell be even porciouns, for the whiche
annuell fee the seyde Erle hath withholde toward hym the seyde Sir
John for terme of lyf to do hym service before alle other in pees and
werre in manere and fourme as foloweth: That is to witte that in tyme
of pees the seyde Sir John uppon resonable warnynge shall be redy at
alle tymes when it shall like the seyde Erle to comaunde hym to come
to his presesence to and in alle parties and places on this syde of the
See to do hym service and with hym to sojourne and ride with as
many men and horses moo or fewer as the seyde Erle lyste to comaunde
or assigne reasonably after the degree and power of the seyde Sir John,
for the whiche the same Sir John shall have suche bouche of courte
and lyvere for hym, his seyde men and horses durynge the tyme of his
demure in the presence of the seyde Erle as other of his degree shall
have and take in the houshold of the seyde Erle with resonable
allowance of his costes for his comynge and retournynge hom ayeyn
as often tymes as he is sende fore or comaunded to come by the seyde
Erle. And in cas that the seyde Erle be ordeyned in any vyage of werre
be it on this syde the See or beyonde, the seyde Sir John shall be redy
uppon resonable warnynge to go with the seyde Erle in the seyde vyage
with such noumbre of men of armes and of archers well and suffisantly
armed, horses and arayde after the feet of werre as the seyde Erle shall
liste to assigne or appointe acordynge to his degree for the whiche the
seyde Sir John shall have for him, his seyde men of armes and archiers
acompaignyed with hym, suche wages and rewarde as the seyde Erle
shall take of the Kynge oure soverayn lorde or any other his capitaigne
durynge the seyde viage with skypesoun and reskypesoun resonable for
him, his seyde men and horses such as other of his degree shall have
in the compaigne of the seyde Erle. And the seyde Erle shall have of
the seyde Sir John the thriddes of alle maner prisoners, prises and
wynnynges by hym taken or geton by way of fortune or aventure of
werre, and the thriddes of the thriddes of alle maner prisoners, prises
and wynnynges by any of his men accompanied with hym taken or
geton by way of fortune or aventure of werre durynge the seyde vyage.
And the seyde Sir John nor none of his men so accompaignied with

---

[309] Rawcliffe, *The Staffords*, 224, 233 for Buckingham and Sir John Mainwaring.
[310] Rothwell, Northants.

hym shall put no prisoner by hym or any of his seyde men taken or geton to finaunce nor raunsoun but as lawe of armes wole. In witnesse wher of the parties beforeseyde to these presentz endentures enterchaungeably have put her seelles. Yeven at the Castell of Stafford the v^the day of Septembre the yere of the regne of Kynge Henry the sixte after the conquest the xx^ti.

125 Humphrey, earl of Buckingham, Hereford, Stafford, Northampton and Perche and Sir Philip Chetwynd, London, 13 February 1444 (Staffs. RO, D 4597, pp. 32–3).[311]

This endenture made betwene the right worshipfull lord Humfrey, Erle of Bukyngham, Hereford, Stafford, Northampton and Perche on the oon parte, and Sir Philip Chetewynd knyght[312] on the other partie witnesseth that the said Erle hath yove and graunted be these presente endentures to the said Sir Philip an annuell fee of xx li. to take yerely, during the lyf of the seid Sir Philip, of the issues, proffits and revenus comyng of the lordship of Holdernesse bi the hands of the Resceivor of the seid Erle there for the tyme being, at the termes of Estier and Seint Michell, be even portions, for the which annuell fee the seid Erle hath witholde toward him the seid Sir Philip for terme of his life, to do him service tofore all other in pees and were, in such maner and forme as followeth, That is to wite that in tyme of pees, the seid Sir Philip upon reasonable warnyng shall be redi at all tymes whanne it shall like the seid Erle to comaunde him to come to his presence, to and in all parties and places on this side of the see to do him service, and with him to sojorne and ride with as many men and horses, mow or fewer as the seid Erle liste to comaunde or assigne resonably, after the degree and power of the seid Sir Philip, for the which the same Sir Philip shall have suche bouche of court and liveree of the seid Erle, for him, his seid men and horses, during the time of his demure in the presence of the seid Erle, as other of his degree shall have and take in the houshold of the seid Erle, with reasonable allowance of his costis,

[311] 'Chetwyndorum Stemma ... Ex ipsis Autographis penes Walterum Chetwynd Arm. deducta' (1690), printed as 'The Chetwynd Chartulary', ed. G. Wrottesley, *Collections for a History of Staffordshire*, xii (1891), 318–9.

[312] P. J. C. Field, *The Life and Times of Sir Thomas Malory* (Cambridge: D. S. Brewer, 1993), 66–7, 83–4, 86–8 for a recent account of Chetwynd's career; see also H. E. Chetwynd-Stapylton, *The Chetwynds of Ingestre* (London, 1892), 95–106. He was with Humphrey, earl of Stafford in Paris at Henry VI's coronation and his annuity of 10 marks was doubled in 1431 (Staffs. RO, D 4597, pp. 26–7; ed. Wrottesley, 312–13). On the same day as this indenture, he contracted to serve as Buckingham's lieutenant at the castle of Calais (D 4597 pp. 33–5; ed. Wrottesley, 319–20) where he died on 10 May 1444. We are grateful to Dudley Fowkes, County Archivist for help in locating this document.

for his comyng and returning hom ayen, as often tymes as he is sende for, or comaunded to come bi the seid Erle.

And in case that the seid Erle be ordeined in any viage of werre, be it on this side of the see or beyonde, the seid Sir Philip shall be redi upon resonable warnyng to go with the seid Erle in the seid viage with such nombre of men of armes and archers, well and sufficiently harmed, horsed and araid, after the feet of werre, as the seid Erle shall liste to assigne or appointe according to his degree, for the which the seid Sir Philip shall have for him his seid men of armes and archers accompaignied with him such wages and reward as the seid Erle shall take of the Kyng oure soverain lord, or of any other his capitaine duryng the seid viage, with skyppeson and reskyppeson resonable for him, his seid men and horses, such as other of his degree shall have in the compaigne of the seid Erle, and the seid Erle shall have of the seid Sir Philip, the thrides of all maner Prisoners, Prises, and wynnynges be him taken or getyn by wey of Fortune and aventure of werre, and the thrides of the thrides of all maner Prisoners, Prises and wynynges, bi any of his seid men then accompaigned with him, taken or geten by way of Fortune or aventure of werre, duryng the seid viage. And the seid Sir Philip nor non of his men so accompaigned with hym, shall putte no prisoner bi him or any of his men, taken or geten, to fynaunce nor ransom but as lawe of armes woll. In witnesse whereof ye parties aforesaid to these present endentures enterchaungeably have putte to here sealles. Writen at London the xiiith day of Fevrier the yer of the reigne of Kyng Henry the sixte after the Conquest the twenty second.

126 Richard Neville, earl of Salisbury and Sir James Strangeways, 1 October 1446 (Northants. RO, Fitzwilliam (Milton) Muniments, MS 2051, sealed on tongue; tying thong lost).[313]

This endenture made bitwix Richard Erl of Salisbury on that oon partie and James Strangways knyght on that othre partie beres witnesse that the same James is bilast and witholden with the said Erl for term of lyfe ayenst al folkes, savyng his ligeance and the high and myghty princesse Katerin duchesse of Norff', the reverent fadre in God Robert Bisshop of Duresme[314] and the kynne and alies of the said James at and

---

[313] A small round signet measuring 9 mm in diameter, it displays a sexfoil. J. S. Roskell, 'Sir James Strangeways of West Harsley and Whorlton', *Yorks. Arch. Journal*, xxxix (1958), 455–82 [reprinted in *Parliament and Politics in Late Medieval England* (London, 1981), ii. 279–306] calls Strangeways' connection with Richard Neville 'the most important single *motif*' in his political career (he was Speaker in 1461) but does not mention this indenture.

[314] Katherine Neville, widow of John, duke of Norfolk (d. 1432), who survived until 1483; Robert Neville, bishop of Durham 1438–57.

within the thride degree of mariage, takying the said James yerely terme of his lyfe for his fee of the said Erl, thissues and profettes of the manoir of Hundburton[315] within the countie of York with al thappurtenaunces accordyng to a deede of gyfte thereof made by the said Erl to the said James, and the said James shal be wele and convenably horsed, armede and arrayede and alway redy to ryde, come and goo with, too and for the said Erl aswele in tyme of paix as of werre at al tymes and into al places, except the parties of Fraunce, that he shal be resounably warnede on his bihalve at the wages and costes resounables of the said Erl as othre take of his degree, takyng the said James of the said Erl in tyme of werre such wages as he yeveth to othre of his degree, rebatyng alwayes in tyme of werre his fee of tyme of paix aftre thafferant of his wages in tyme of werre, and the said Erl shal have the thriddes of al wynnyng of werre to be wonne or geton by the said James or eny of his men that he shal have at the wages or costes of the said Erl, and if eny capitaigne or man of estate bee taken by the said James or eny of his said men the said Erl shal have him dooyng to the taker resounable rewarde for him. In witnesse of which thing the parties afore said to the parties of this endenture entrechaungeably have set their sealx, yeven the first day of Octobre the yere of the Reign of Kyng Henry sext sith the conquest twenty and fyve.

Dorse: Sir James Strangways

127 Richard Neville, earl of Salisbury and Sir Ralph Greystoke, Sheriff Hutton, Yorks. N.R., 10 July 1447 (Northants. R O, Fitzwilliam (Milton) Muniments, MS 2052, sealed on tongue, with tying thong).[316]

This endenture made bitwen Richard Erl of Salisbury on that oon partie and Raufe Graystoke knyght[317] on the othre bereth witnesse that the said Raufe is bilast and bilaste[a] towarde and with the saide Erl terme of his lyve ayenst al personnes savyng his liegeance wele and convenably horsed, armed and arraied and[b] alway redy to ride and goo too, with and for the same Erl aswele in tyme of paix and of werre into al places and coostes except the parties of Fraunce[c] at the costez resounablez of the saide Erl at al tymes that he bee by him or eny on

---

[315] Humburton, Yorks. N.R.
[316] Within an octagonal surround (10 mm diameter), a small signet displaying ?a flower or leaf, red wax.
[317] Ralph succeeded his father, John, lord Greystoke in 1436, when he was already aged 22, and lived until 1501 (GEC, vi. 196–8).

his bihalve warnede or required and the saide Erle shalle doo his devoire that[d] the said Raufe in the name of his fee shal have the fee graunted him by Richard late Erl of Warwic' of the lordship of Bernard Castell[318] accordyng to his dede to the saide Rauf thereof made and the said Raufe shal take of the saide Erl in tyme of werre suche wages as dothe othre of his degree and yif eny capitaigne or man of estate bee taken by the saide Raufe or by eny of his men that he shal have at the costes or wages of the saide Erl the same Erl shal have him dooyng to the taker resounable rewarde for him, and the said Erl shal have the thirdes of al wynnyng of werre to bee wonne or geton by the said Raufe and the thirdes of thirdes of al wynnyng of werre to bee wonne or geten by eny of his saide men. In witnesse of which thing the parties aforesaide have set their sealx. Writen at Shirriſhoton the tent day of Juyl the yere of the Reyn of King Henry sext sith the conquest twenty and five. And in cas the said Raufe be unpaied of his said fee that then this endenture bee voide and of no value, writen as above.

Dorse: Rad[ulfu]s Graistok' mil'

    a. *and bilaste* interlined
    b. *and* interlined
    c. *except the parties of Fraunce* interlined
    d. *the saide Erle shalle doo his devoire that* interlined

128 Richard Neville, earl of Salisbury and Walter Strickland, 1 September 1448 (Sizergh Castle, Kendal, Strickland Deeds, sealed on tag).[319]

This endenture made bitwen Richard Erl of Salysbury on Þat one partie and Waultier Strykland son and heir of Sir Thomas Strykland knyght[320] on Þat othre bereth witnesse Þat the same Waultier is bilaste and witholden with the said Erl for terme of his lyfe ayenst al folkes

[318] Barnard Castle, Durham; for relations between Richard Beauchamp, earl of Warwick (d. 1439) and the Greystokes, cf. Carpenter, *Locality and Polity*, 392 n. 187.

[319] We are grateful to Mr Thomas Hornyold-Strickland for permission to publish. This is the unique case where both parts of the indenture have survived: one is sealed with York's Griffin signet within a plaited rush wreath; the counter indenture has been badly holed, lacks its seal and has shrunk considerably. First pub. in Joseph Nicolson and Richard Burn, *The History and Antiquities of the Counties of Westmorland and Cumberland* (London, 1777), i. 97–8, cf. *HMC, Fifth Report*, 330; Denton, *England in the Fifteenth Century*, 290; Daniel Scott, *The Stricklands of Sizergh Castle* (Kendal, 1908), 67–8, with the date 1 September 1449.

[320] Strickland was born c. 1411 and died in 1467 (Wedgwood, 823–4).

savying his ligeance. And the said Waultier shal bee wele and convenably horsede, armede and arrayede and alway redy to ryde come and goe with to and for the said Erl at al tymes and into al places on this side and beyonde the see aswele in tyme of paix as of werre Þat he bee warnede by the said Erl on his bihalve at the wages and costes resonnables of the same Erl. Takyng the said Waultier yerely for his fee of the said Erl ten marcs of money of thissues and profitts of the lordship of Penreth[321] with thappurtenances comyng by the handes of the receivor Þere beeyng for the tyme at the festes of Martynmesse and Whitsonday by even porcions. And the said Waultier shal take of the said Erl in tyme of werre suche wages as Þen he yeveth to othre of his degree rebatyng of such wages of were thafferant of his wages in tyme of paix. And the said Erl shal have the thrid of al wynnynges of werre to be wonne or geten by the said Waultier or eny of his men Þat he shal have at the costes and wages of the same Erl. And if eny Capitaigne or man of estate bee taken by the said Waultier or eny of his said men, the said Erl shal have him dooyng to the taker resonnable rewarde for him. In witnesse of which thing the parties aforesaid to the parties of this endenture have entrechangeably set their sealx. Yeven the furst day of Septembre the xxvij yere of the reign of king Henry sext sith the Conquest.

129 Richard, duke of York and James Butler, earl of Ormond, Dublin, 28 July 1450 (NLI, Ormond Deeds D 1735, sealed on tongue).[322]

This endenture made at Divelin the xxviij. day of Juille the xxviij. yere of the Regne of oure souverain Lord Kyng Henry the sext, betwix the right high and mighty prince Richard Duc of York, lieutenant of Irland on the toon part, and James Erle of Ormond[323] on the other part, bereth witnesse that the saide Erle of Ormond is witholden and belast with my saide lord the duc for terme of his lyf, forto doo hym service aswel in werre as in pees, aswel in England whan hit shal hapen hym there forto bee as in this land of Irland. And with hym forto bee ayenst al other creatures of what estat, preeminence or condicion soo evere thay bee next the Kyng oure souverain lord and his heirs Kyngs of England and of France. For the which beleving and witholding the

---

[321] Penrith, Cumbs.

[322] An impression of Ormond's seal survives; cf. *Cal. of Ormond Deeds*, ed. Curtis, iii. 167–8 no. 177; a 17th c. copy after an original then in the possession of William Pierpont may be found in Oxford, Bodleian Library, MS Dugdale 18 fos. 77v–78r.

[323] GEC, x. 123–6 for James Butler, 'the White Earl', fourth earl of Ormond (1405–52), and for his relations with York, K. Simms, 'The King's Friend: O'Neill', *England and Ireland in the Later Middle Ages*, ed. Lydon, 219–24.

saide Erle shal take and perceyve yerely during the terme of his lyf of
my saide lord the Duc C marcs sterling, to bee taken after the teneur
and effecte of certain lettres patentes made unto the saide Erle undre
the seel of my saide lord the Duc in that behalve. And yif the saide
Erle of Ormond doo not service unto my saide lord the duc aswel in
England whan hit shal fortune hym forto bee Þere, as in Irland,
according unto the witholding aforesaide, that than the lettres patentes
which the saide Erle hath of the graunte of the saide duc stande in
noo force ner vertu. In witnesse of which thing to the toon part of Þees
endentures remaynyng toward my saide lord the Duc the saide Erle
hath doo set his seel the day, yere and place aforesaide.[324]

J[ames] B[utler] ORMOND[325]

130 Richard, duke of York and George Darell, esquire, Fotheringhay,
Northants., 30 January 1453 (PRO, C146/6400, sealed on tongue).[326]

This endenture made at Fodringey the xxx[ti] day of Janvier the xxxj[ti]
yere of the Regne of oure souverain lord Kyng Henry the Sext, betwix
the right high and mighty prince my lord Richard duc of York on the
toon part and George Darell' squier[327] on the other part, bereth witnesse
that the saide George is belaste and witholden with my saide lord the
duc for terme of his lyf. Prometting by the feith of his body and binding
him by thees endentures forto doo true and feithful service unto my
saide lord the duc. And with him forto be[a] ayenst all erthly creatures
of what estate, preeminence or condicion soo evere they bee next the
kyng oure soverain lord and hys yssu kynges of England and of France.
For the which witholding the saide George shal take of my said lord
the duc yerely the somme of x. li. sterling' to bee taken of the issues,
proufits and revenues of his manoir and lordeship of Fasterne in

---

[324] In another indenture concluded at Dublin, 22 August 1450, York appointed Ormond
his lieutenant and governor throughout the land of Ireland at a fee of 500 marks p.a.
while York remained in Ireland and £1000 p.a. after his departure for England. These
terms were further modified in a third indenture, concluded the following day: Oxford,
Bodleian Library Ms. Eng. hist. c. 34, part I, f. 1.

[325] Autograph.

[326] A fragmentary impression of York's signet survives; cf. *CAD*, vi, no. C 6400, and
pub. by P. Johnson, *Duke Richard of York, 1411–1460* (Oxford, 1988), 225 with incorrect
date 30 Jan. 1458.

[327] Of Littlecote and Fittleton, Wilts. Darell was sheriff of Wiltshire, Nov. 1454–5, but
was obliged to purchase a pardon for all treasons and other offences in March 1460.
Following Edward IV's accession, he was appointed Keeper of the Great Wardrobe and
became one of the mainstays of Yorkist government in the West Country, acting as sheriff
of Wiltshire, Nov. 1460–1, 1464–5, 1468–9, and of Somerset and Dorset, Nov. 1466–7:
CPR, 1452–61, 576; *ibid., 1461–7*, 17, 90; *ibid., 1467–77*, 419; *List of Sheriffs*, 124, 153.

Wiltshire[328] by the handes of ye receveurs, fermers and other occupiers of the same for the tyme being atte festes of the Annunciacion of Oure Lady and Mighelmasse by even porcions, unto the tyme yat ye saide George bee provided by my saide lord the duc unto an office or an other resounable rewarde of the valeu of xx. mark by yere as by lettres patentes and lettres of warrant made theruppon unto the saide George, undre the seel of my saide lord the duc hit may more clerely appere. In witnesse wherof to the toon part of thees endentures remaynyng toward ye saide George my saide lord the duc hath doo set his signet the day, place and yere aforesaide.[329]

a. *be* interlined

131 Richard, duke of York and John Alington, esquire, London, 16 January 1456 (Cambridge University Library, MS Mm I. 42 (Baker MS 31), p. 260, late 17th-century/early 18th-century transcript).[330]

This Endenture made at London the xvi. day of Janvier the xxxiiii[ti] yere of the Reyne of oure soverain lord Kyng Henry the Sext betwen the Right High and Mighti Prince Richard Duc of York on that oon partie, and John Alyngton Sqyer[331] on that other partie bereth witnesse that the same John is belast and withholden [for] terme of his lyf, with and towardes the seide Duc, promitting be y[e] feith of his body, and binding him by this endenture with the same Duc for to be, holde and abide ayenst all erthly creators, his ligeance except, taking the same John yerely during his said lif for his fee of the said Duc the summe of x. marks sterling of the yssues and proufits of the castle and Honour of Clare[332] with thappurtenance comyng by the handes of the Recevour of the same for the tyme being, at the Festes of Thannunciation of oure Lady and St Michel Tharchangel by even porcions. And the said John shal be wele and conveneably horsed, armed and arrayed and alweys redy to ride, come and go to, with and for the said Duc at al tymes and into al places in England and in Wales, upon warnyng resounable therunto by the said Duc, or on his behalve to be yeven

[328] Fasterne, Wilts.

[329] Autograph signature *R. York* in left margin.

[330] Kindly drawn to our attention by Dr M. J. Bennett. We are grateful to the Syndics of the University Library, Cambridge, for permission to publish.

[331] Alington, of Horseheath, Cambs., was active in county government, serving as escheator for Cambridgeshire and Huntingdonshire, Nov. 1447–8; sheriff of Cambridgeshire, Mar.–Nov. 1461, and as a justice of the peace, Feb. 1466–Dec. 1470, and from Dec. 1473 until his death in August 1480: *List of Escheators*, 17; *CFR, 1461–71*, 9; *ibid., 1471–85*, 196; *CPR, 1461–7*, 560; *ibid., 1467–77*, 609; *ibid., 1476–85*, 555.

[332] Clare, Suffolk.

him. In witnesse wherof to the parties of this endenture the Partie aforesaide entrechaungeably have set theire sealles. Yeven the day, place and yere abovesaide.[333]

132 Richard Neville, earl of Salisbury and Richard Musgrave, 22 November 1456 (Cumbria RO, D/Mus/H 123, formerly sealed on a tongue).

This endenture made bitwen Richard Erl of Salisbury on Þat oon partie and Richard Musgrave yong[er][334] on Þat othre partie bereth witnesse Þat ye said Ric' Musgrave is bylast and witholden toward and with the said Erl terme of his lyf ayenst al persounes savying his ligeance, John, lord Clifford and Thomas, lord Dacre in Þeir owne propre materes,[335] wherin if eny hapne, Þat God defende, Þe said Richard shal not assist Þe said lordez ne neiÞer of theim in his person, his men, with counseil ne oÞerwise ayenst Þe said Erl. And if in suche cas it shal lust Þe said Ric' to labour as a tretour for Þe wele of eny suche matere, the said Erl aggreeth him not to take in Þat bihalve Þe same Ric' to eny straungenesse or displeasour. And Þe said Ric' wele and covenably horsed, armede and arraied and alway redy to ride and goo too, with and for Þe said Erl aswel in tyme of paix as of werre into al places and coostez at costez resonablez of Þe said Erl at al tymes Þat he be by him or on his bihalve resounably warnede or requirede, shal take of Þe said Erl for his yerely fee during the life of his grauntsire Sir Richard Musgrave knyght and William Stapleton squier ten markez of money of the revenues of Þe lordship of Penreth[336] comyng by the handes of the receivore Þere for the tyme beyng at termes of Pasche and Michelmesse by even porcons. And Þe same Ric' if it hapne him to overlif Þat oon of his said grauntsires shal immediatly

---

[333] When transcribed the original still had a seal attached; this agreement is cited by Catherine E. Parsons, 'Horseheath Hall and its Owners', *Proc. Cambridge Antiquarian Soc.*, xli (1948), 3 with the date 1455, but there is no mention of Alington's service or annuity in Johnson, *Duke Richard of York*.

[334] Eldest son of Thomas Musgrave of Hartley, Westmorland, the son of Sir Richard Musgrave of Musgrave, Westmorland. His mother was Joanna, daughter and co-heir of Sir William Stapleton (*CCR, 1476–85*, 205–6; Nicolson & Burn, *Hist. of Westmorland and Cumberland*, i. 595). Musgrave's connection with the Nevilles paid off handsomely after the accession of Edward IV. In Feb. 1462 he was appointed constable of the castles of Brougham, Pendragon and Brough and bailiff and chief forester of Brough and Kirby Stephen, Westmorland (*CPR, 1461–7*, 74, 143); he was dead by 1491 (Wedgwood, 619).

[335] Musgrave was married to one of John, ninth lord Clifford's sisters. For the hostility between Clifford and the Neville supporters of the duke of York, GEC, iii. 293–4; Nicolson & Burn, i. 284–5.

[336] Penrith, Cumbs.

aft[er] Þe decesse of him soe dissessede take yerly of Þe said Erl for his fee ten poundez commyng by Þe handes and at Þe [termes] abovesaide. And Þe said Ric' shal take of the saide Erl for his fee immediatly aftre Þe decesse of both his said grauntsires, him lyvyng, twenty markez of money yerely during his life at Þe said termes of Þe said revenuez by the said handes. And Þe same Ric' shal take of Þe saide Erl in tyme of werr suche wagez as doo othre of his degree, rebating alway in tyme of werr his wagez after Þafferant in tyme of paix. And if eny capitaign or man of estate bee taken by the saide Ric' or by eny of his men Þat he shal have at wagez or costez of Þe said Erl the same Erl shal have him, doyng to the taker resounable rewarde for him. And Þe said Erl shal have Þe thirdes of all wynnynges of werr to bee won or goten by the said Richard and the thirdes of thirdes of all wynnynges of werr to be won or goten by eny of his said men. In witnesse wheroff the parties aforesaide to Þe parties of Þis endenture entrechaungeably have set Þeir sealx. Yeven Þe xxij day of Novembre Þe xxxv^{to} yere of Þe reign of King Henry sext sith Þe conquest.

133 James Butler, earl of Wiltshire and Ormond and John Audley, esquire, Hook, Wilts., 18 March 1457 (PRO, E 159/257, Adhuc Communia, Adhuc Recorda, Easter, m. 20 b).[337]

This indenture made at Hook[338] the xviij^{th} day of Marche the xxxv yere of the reigne of oure soveraigne lord Kyng Henry the sexte, wytnesseth that John Audeley squier, son and heire of James the lord Audeley, is witholde and beleffte for the terme of his lyff toward James Erle of Wilteshire and of Ormond,[339] promittyng and byndyng hym by the feith of his body and by this endenture that nexte oure said soverayne lord before all the lordes of England, he shall do the said Erle as good, true and feithfull service as he best can or may duryng his lyff wythin the Realme of Englond as hoften as it shall lyke the said Erle hym to commaunde or desire in all thynges apperteignyng to the same Erle, for the which foresaid wytholdyng and belevyng in manere and fourme abovesaid, and for the good service that the said John hath doon and shall doo to the saide Erle, the same Erle hath yeve and

---

[337] Recited in a plea before the Barons of the Exchequer at Easter 1480 as warrant for the sum of £26 13s 4d in demand against Audley. Though Edward IV had confirmed the fee in May 1478 the process was not terminated until Easter 1488, when Audley appeared by his attorney and exhibited a pardon for the disputed sum (CPR 1476–85, 68; PRO, E 159/264, Adhuc Communia, Adhuc Recorda, m. 21).

[338] Hook, Wilts.

[339] For James Butler, earl of Wiltshire and Ormond (1449–61) see GEC, x. 126–9, and for John, later sixth lord Audley (1459–90), ibid. i. 341–2.

graunted by this present endenture to the foresaid John an annuitee of xx^{ti} marcs sterling yerely, to have take and receyve to the foresaid John duryng his lyff in and of the manor of Hasilbere in the shire of Dorset[340] wyth thappurtenaunces by the hands of the said Erlys Receyvour, Baillyff, Fermour or other occupiour there for the tyme beyng at the festes of seynt Michell the archangell and of Estre by even porceons. And yf the said annuitee of xx^{ti} marcs be behynde in parte or in all at eny terme of payment above lymited ayenst the fourme abovesaid, be it than lawfull to the said John or to his assignes in the foresaid manor wyth the appurtenaunces to entre and to distrene, and the distresse so taken lawfully to lede and carye away and thaym wytholde untyll tyme that the said annuite and arrerages therof to hym be fully payed and satisfied. And the said Erle woll and graunteth by this said endenture that whan and as often as the foresaid John is wyth the foresaid Erle in his houshold in England he shall have budge of courte for hym self and for as meny of his men, horses and hakeneys as the said Erle shall assigne hym to come wyth. And also he shall have his resonable costs and expenses in doyng and observyng elles where the foresaid Erlys commaundements at all tymes whan it shall lyke the same Erle to assygne the said John to doo hym service wythin this said realme of Englond. In wytnesse whereof as well the seall of the said Erle as the seall of the said John to these endentures enterchaungeably ben put. Wreten at the place, day and yere abovesaid.

134 Richard, duke of York and Thomas Holcot, Gloucester, 2 October 1460 (Longleat House, Wilts., Muniments of the Marquess of Bath, MS 10491, ?formerly sealed on tongue).[341]

This endenture made at Gloucestur the secunde dai of Octobre the yere of oure lord M^l cccc lx betwix the Right heghe and myghty prince Richard duc of York on that on partie and Thomas Holcot[342] on that othur partie berith witnesse that the said Thomas is belast and witholdyn for time of his lyf with and toward the said Duc and his sonne Edward

---

[340] Haselbury, Dorset.

[341] This indenture and nos. **135-6** were first discussed by K. B. McFarlane, 'The Wars of the Roses', *Proc. Brit. Acad.* L (1964), 87–119 at p. 93 [reprinted in McFarlane, *England in the Fifteenth Century*, ed. G. L. Harriss (London, 1981), 231–61 at pp. 236–7]. They are all written by the same clerk and all confer annuities to be drawn on York's lands in Herefordshire. No trace of wax remains and it is doubtful whether a seal was ever attached. We are grateful to the Marquess of Bath for permission to publish and to Kate Harris, Librarian at Longleat, for help when consulting these documents.

[342] cf. Johnson, *Duke Richard of York*, 233; presumably a son or grandson of an earlier Herefordshire Thomas Holcot (above **108**).

erl of Marche, promitting and byndyng hym by the faithe of his body
and by this present endentures to do trew, diligent and faithfull service
un to the said Duc and Erle, and with thaym for to be ayenst all erthly
criatures of what estate, condicion or preeminence so ever thay be, for
the whiche witholding and service of the said Thomas the saide Duc
hathe grauntyd un to hym ane annuite of x marcs sterling during the
lyff of the saide Thomas, to be by hym yerely persayvid of thissues,
profettes and revenues of the saide Duc of his lordeships within the
counte of Herford by the hondes of his ressayvour of the same for the
tyme being at the fest of Estur and Michelmas by evyn porciones as in
the lettres patentes of the saide Duc therupon made un to the saide
Thomas more playnly it apperithe. In witnesse where of to the part of
this endendure remaynyng toward the said Duc the said Thomas has
set his seall the day, yere and place abovesaid.

Dorse: Hereford[343]

135 Richard, duke of York and Henry Hakleton, Gloucester, 2 October
1460 [English] (Longleat House, Wilts., MS 10492).[344]

136 Richard, duke of York and Simon Milburne, Gloucester, 2 October
1460 [English] (Longleat House, Wilts., MS 10494).[345]

137 Richard, duke of York and Simon [   ], Gloucester, 2 October
1460 [English] (Longleat House, Wilts., MS 10493).[346]

138 Richard Neville, earl of Warwick and Salisbury, and John Vaux of
Caterlen, Middleham, Yorks. N. R., 20 April 1461 (PRO, E315/49/157,

---

[343] In a ?17th-century hand.

[344] In exactly the same terms as **134**. A tying thong remains but there is no trace of
wax on the tongue, suggesting that it was never sealed.

[345] In the same form as **134** and **135**; the tying thong is missing and once again there
is no trace of a seal. Wedgwood, 593 for Simon, son of Richard Milburne (1395–1451),
of Laverstock, Wilts., aged 24 at the time of his father's death.

[346] In the same form as **134–6** but MS shrunken and partly damaged; only the first
two letters of the name of the second party survives (*Sy* ...) but sealed with York's signet
seal (18–19 mm., England, a label of three points). It is probable, as McFarlane states,
that this is York's counterpart of **136** but some doubt must remain since the space for
the name (*Symond Milburne*) appears inadequate. In any event York's letters patent in
Latin and sealed with his large seal (55 mm., England, a label of three points) announcing
the grant of 10 marks p.a. to Milburne survives (Longleat MS 10495).

formerly sealed on tag, no indenture and currently mounted in a book).[347]

This endenture made betwene Richard Neville erle of Warrewyk and Salisbury, lieutenant to Þe king oure souverain lord, great chamberlain of England, capitaine of Calays, and wardeyn of Thest and West Marches of England forgeinst Scotland on Þat one partie and John Vaux of Caterlen[348] on Þat oÞir bereth witnesse that Þe said John is belest and witholden with and toward the saide Erle ayenst all persones his liegeance except. And the same John wel and convenably horsed, armed and arrayed shalbe redy to ride, come and goe with to and for the said Erle at all tymes and in to all places upon resonable warnyng to be yeven him on the bihalve of the said Erle at his costs or resonable reward. The said John takyng for his fee yerely terme of his lyf foure marcs sterling of thissues and profits of oure lordship of Penreth[349] commyng by the hands of Þe recyvor, fermor or occupior of ye same for Þe tyme beyng at Þe termes of Michelmesse and Estre by even porcions. And the said erle shal have ye IIIdes of all wynnynges of werre wonne or gotten by the said John and the IIIde of IIIdes of all his servants Þat he shal have at ye wages or costes of the same erle. And yf any capitaine or man of estate be taken by Þe said John or eny of his said men Þe said erle shal have him doyng to Þe taker resonable reward for him. In witnesse wherof Þe parties aforesaid to Þe parties of thies endentures entrechangeably sette their sealx. Yeven at our castel of Midilham ye XX[to] day of Aprill Þe ffirst yere of Þe regne of Þe king our soverain lord Edward Þe IIIIth.

139 Richard Neville, earl of Warwick and Sir John Trafford, 26 May 1461 (Lancs. RO, Trafford MSS, DD Tr B3/156, formerly sealed on a tag through a fold).[350]

This endenture made Þe xxvj day of May the fyrst yere of Þe regne of the King our souverain lord Edward Þe iiij[the] betwen Richard Neville erle of Warrewyk and Capitain of Caleys of Þe one partie and Sir John

---

[347] Space has been left for an initial ornamented letter T which has not been executed. GEC, xii, pt. 2. 385–93 for Warwick.

[348] Nicolson & Burn, ii. 394 for the Vaux family of Caterlen, Cumbs.

[349] Penrith, Cumbs.

[350] We are grateful to Sir Dermot de Trafford Bt for permission to publish. '*sire John Trafford*' is written on the face of the fold in a contemporary hand. *English Historical Documents 1327–1485*, ed. A. R. Myers (London, 1969), 1127 no. 663 provides a modern version of this indenture.

Trafford knyght³⁵¹ of the oþer partie bereth wittenesse þat þe said Sir John Trafford of hys fre and mere mocion ys beleft and reteynned to ward and with þe said Erle duryng þe terme of hys lyffe to be with hym and do hym service and attendance ayenst all manere persones except hys alligeance. And þat þe said Sir John Trafford shal be redy at þe desir or commandemant of þe said Erle to come unto h[ym at all] such tymes and in such places as þe said Erle shal call upon him or yeve him warnyng sufficiant, horsed, harnessed, arrayed and accompanyed as þe cas shall require and according to þat that þe said Erle shall call hym to at þe costes of þe said Erle resonable. And þe said Erle for þe same have graunted unto þe said Sir John Trafford to have by patent undre þe seal of his armes an anuyte duryng hys lyf of þe summe of xx marc st[erling] to be leveyed, taken and reteyned of thissues and revenues of his lordship of Midelham³⁵² by þe hands of his receyvor þere at þe termes of Mikelmasse and Passch. And over this þe said Erle hath graunted unto þe said Sir John Trafford þat in tyme of werre he shal have such wages rewarde and profits as oþir persones of hys degre shal have, yeldyng unto þe said Erle his iij des and þe iij de of iij des in like wise and forme as it ys accustumed in þe werre. In witnesse wherof þe yere and day aboven said þe said parties entrechaungeably to þes presentes have pute to their seall.

140 Richard Neville, earl of Warwick and John Faucon, gunner, Carlisle, 24 June 1461 (PRO, E326/6402, formerly sealed on tag).

This endenture made between Richard Nevill Erle of Warrewyk, Great Chamberlain of Englande, Capitaine of Caleys and Wardeyn of Thest and West Marches of England forgeinst Scotland on þat one partie and John Faucon gonner on that oþer, witnesseth þat the said John is belest and witholden with and toward the said Erle ayeinst all persounes his ligeance except, and the same wel and convenably horsed, armed and arrayed according to his occupacion. And the said John shall be redy to ride come and goo with to and for þe said Erle at all tymes and in to all places upon resonable warnyng to be yeven him on the bihalve of saide Erle at his costes or resonable rewarde. The saide John takyng yerely terme of his lyf fyve marcs sterling of thissues and proffitts of þe lordship of Penreth³⁵³ comyng by the hands of the Receyvor of the same for the tyme beyng at the termes of Martynmasse and

---

³⁵¹ Of Trafford and Stretford, Lancs. (*VCH, Lancs.*, iv. 332).
³⁵² Middleham, Yorks. N. R. There is no record of this fee on the incomplete list of fees in the Middleham receiver's account for 1464–5 (PRO, SC6/1085/20 m. 13).
³⁵³ Penrith, Cumbria

Witsonday by even porcions, and the said John shal have his table for him and his man in the castell of Karlile at Þe costes of the saide Erle. And the saide Erle shal have the threddes of all wynnynges of werre wonne or gotten by the saide John and yf any capitaine or man of estate be taken by the said John the said Erle shal have him doyng to the taker resonable reward for him. In witnesse whereof Þe parties aforesaid to Þe parties of this endenture have entrechangeably sette their sealx. Yven under our signet at Carlile the XXIIII day of Juyn the first yere of the regne of the king oure souverain lord Edward the IIIIth.

141 Sir William Stanley and Piers Warburton, esquire, Chester, 27 October 1461 (Manchester, John Rylands University Library, Arley Charters, Box 9 no. 7, defaced red wax seal on a centrally cut detached tongue).[354]

This endenture made betwene William Stanley knyght on that on partie and Piers Werberton squyer[355] on that othir partie witnessethe that the saide Piers is reteigned and witholden for terme of his life with the saide William and grauntes to do hym service duryng the same tyme in pease and werre before all othir persones excepte oure soveraigne lorde kynge Edwarde the iiij^te and all othir that shall be kynges of Englond after the dethe of the saide kynge Edward, takyng therfore yerely duryng the life of the saide Willyam v marcs of money of the ffe that the saide William has of the graunte of the lordes of Bromfeld and Yale for terme of his life be the hands of the receyvour of the Holt[356] for the tyme beyng at the feestes of Estur and Michelmas be even porceouns. In witnes wherof to these presentz endentures the parties afforesaid entrechaungeable have set to thaire sealx, yeven at Chestre the xxvij day of Octobre the yere of the regne of the saide kynge Edward the iiij^te the furste.

142 Richard Neville, earl of Warwick and Robert Peret, London, 7

---

[354] Pub. first in Ormerod, *Hist. of the County Palatine and City of Chester*, ed. Helsby, i. 572n.

[355] Piers Warburton succeeded his father, Sir Geoffrey, in 1448 and died 1494/5; a namesake was retained for life at 10 marks p.a. by Henry, prince of Wales in 1407 (ibid., 571n, cf. *DKR* 36 (1875), App. II, 506), whilst Sir Geoffrey had been retained by Humphrey, duke of Buckingham (Rawcliffe, *The Staffords*, 233); all descended from Sir Geoffrey de Warburton, retained by the Black Prince in 1365 (above **49**). For Stanley and his affinity, see M. K. Jones, 'Sir William Stanley of Holt and Family Allegiance in the late Fifteenth Century', *Welsh History Review* 14 (1988), 1–22.

[356] Receiver of Holt castle in the lordship of Bromfield and Yale, Clwyd.

March 1462 (BL, Cotton Charter V. 39, formerly sealed on tag through turn up).

This endenture made bitwen Richard Neville Erle of Warrewyk, Great Chambrelain of England and Capitaine of Calais on that one partie and Robert Peret on that othre, bereth witnesse that the saide Robert is belest and withholden with and toward the saide Erle ayenst all personnes, his ligeaunce except, and the same wel and convenably horsed and arayed, according to his occupacion, shalbe ready to come to the saide Erle foure tymes in the yere withoute warnyng to be yeven unto him, that is to say at the festes of Cristmasse, Estre, Witsontid and All Halowes, in what place that the saide Erle shalbe withine this Reawme of England, the saide Robert takyng for his fee five marcs sterlinges yerly of thessuez and profitz of the lordshyp of Olney[357] comyng by the handes of recevour, fermour or occupiour of the same for the tyme beinge, at the termes of Eastre and Mighelmasse by even porcions, and overemore the saide Robert shalbe redy to ride, come and goo with, to and for the saide Erle at all tymes and in to all places upon resonable warnyng to be yeven unto him on the behalve of the saide Erle at his costes, wages of werre longing to men of his occupacion or resonable rewarde beside the saide fee, and if any capitaine or man of Estate be taken by the saide Robert, the saide Erle shal have him doing to him resonable rewarde for him. In witnesse wherof the parties aforsaide to the parties of this endenture have entrechaungeably sette their sealx. Yeven undre oure signet at London the vij day of Marche the secounde yere of the Reigne of the King our soverain lorde Edwarde the iiij[th].

143 Richard Neville, earl of Warwick and Christopher Lancaster, Middleham, 27 April 1462 [English] (PRO, E101/71/5/945, pub. in C. L. Scofield, 'An engagement of service to Warwick the Kingmaker, 1462', *EHR* xxix (1914), 720).

144 Richard Neville, earl of Warwick and Robert Warcop, Middleham, 27 April 1462 (PRO, E327/185, formerly sealed on double tag through fold).[358]

This endenture made between Richard Neville, Erle of Warrewyk,

---

[357] Olney, Bucks.
[358] First pub. by Madox, *Formulare Anglicanum*, 104–5 no. clxxxv.

Great Chamberlain[359] of England, Capitaine of Calais and Warden of Thest and Westmarchez of Englond forgeinst Scotland, on that one partie, and Robert Warkop the yonger, squier, sone and heir of Robert Warcop thelder,[360] on that othre, bereth witenesse that the said Robert is belest and witholden with and towarde the said Erle ayenst all parsounes, his ligeaunce except. And the same Robert well and convenably horsed, armed and araied shalbe redye to ride, come and goo with, to and for the said Erle at all tymes and into all places upon resonable warnyng to be yeven him on the behalve of the said Erle at his costes or resonable reward, the said Robert takyng for his fee yerely terme of his lyf [a] sterlings of thissues and profites of oure lordeshipes within the countee of Westmerland comyng by the handes of the receyvour of oure said lordshipes for the tyme beyng at the termes of Michelmasse and Eastre by even porcons. And the said Erle shal have the iij[dez] of all wynnynge of werre won or gotton by the said Robert and the iij[de] of iij[dez] of all his servauntes yat he shal have at the wages or costes of the same Erle. And if any Capitaine or man of estate be taken by the said Robert or any of his said men the said Erle shal have him, doyng to the taker resonable reward for him. In witnesse wherof the parties of thies endentures have entrechaungeably sette their sealx. Yeven at oure Castell of Midelham the xxvij day of Aprill, the seconde yere of the reigne of the Kyng oure souverain lord Edwarde the iiij[th].

Dorse: retenuz

a. blank in MS

145 Richard Neville, earl of Warwick and Thomas Blenkinsop, esquire, Middleham, 27 April 1462 (PRO, E326/6415, sealed on tag).[361]

This endenture made betwen Richard Neville erle of Warrewyk, Great Chamberlain of England, Capitein of Caleis and Wardeyne of Thest and Westmerches of Englond forgeinst Scotland on that oon partie and Thomas Blencansop squier[362] on that othre bereth witnesse that the said Thomas is belest and witholden with and toward the said Erle ayeinst all personnes his liegeance except and the same Thomas welle

[359] The whole of the first line of the indenture is written in upper-case letters, with some decoration.
[360] Of Langholme and Gamblesby, Cumbs. He married Agnes, youngest daughter of Sir Richard Musgrave of Musgrave and succeeded his father, a justice of the peace in Cumberland and Westmorland, in 1467 (*CPR, 1461–7*, 562, 575; *ibid., 1467–77*, 13; Nicolson & Burn, i. 594).
[361] The first line is double the height of the following lines, and has ornamental capitals.
[362] Of Helbeck, Westmorland (Nicolson & Burn, i. 583).

and convenably horsed, armed and arraied shalbe redye to ride come
and goo with to and for the said erle at all tymes and into al places
upon resonable warnyng to be yeven him on the bihalve of the said
Erl at his costs or resonable reward. The said Thomas taking for the
fee yerely terme of his life thre pounds sex shillings and eight pennes
sterlinges of thissues and proffits of oure lordshipes beyng within the
countie of Westmerland comyng by the handes of the receyvour of
oure said lordeshipes for the tyme beyng at the termes of Michelmasse
and Eastre by even porcones. And the said erle shal have the IIIdes
of al wynnyngs of werre woon or gotton by the said Thomas and the
IIIde of IIIdes of all his sirvaunts that he shal have at the wages or
costs of the same erle, and if any capiteine or man of estate be taken
by the said Thomas or any of his said men the said erle shal have him
doyng to the taker resonable reward for him. In witnesse wherof the
parties aforesaid to the parties of thies endentures have entrechaungeably sette their sealx. Yeven at oure castel of Midelham the
XXVII day of Aprill the seconde yere of the reigne of the king oure
souverain lord Edwarde the IIIIth.

Dorse: Thomas Blencansop [?yevyn]

146 Henry, lord Fitzhugh and Abraham Metcalf, Ravensworth, 5 May
1465 (Leeds, Yorks. Arch. Soc., DD 53/III/119, formerly sealed on a
tongue).[363]

This bill indented made at Ravenswath fift day of May fift yere of the
reigne of King Edward iiij[te] by twex Henry lord Fitzhugh on that one
party and Abraham Metcalfe of Askerige, yoman, on that other party,[364]
witnesseth the seid lorde Fitzhugh hath grantid to the seid Abraham
that he shall have upon his good beringe ye demayne lande of Askerige
to ferme next after Thomas Person. And also yis yere bedone the seid
Abraham shall have to ferme upon his good beringe all the tenaments
of the seid lorde with ye appurtanans which he and Henry Smyth
occupies at yis day, duringe the term of vij yere next followinge, yeldyng
for them both yerely to the seid lorde like as thei paye[a] at this daye.
And the for said Abraham graunts by this indenture to be left with the
seid lorde and to be his sworne man and to do hym service next the
kings highness a fore al other person or persones and to be redy upon
lawful warnynge to ride or goo with ye seid lorde or his assignes at
tymes resonabill, and finde to the seid lorde sufficiaunt soudrtry to pay

---

[363] GEC, v. 428–9 for Henry, fifth lord Fitzhugh (1452–72).
[364] Askrigg, Yorks. N.R.

his fermes at tymes usuall, and to be good tenant and agreable and of good reuill and demenynge to all the seid lords tenants. In witnes wherof ayther part to thies billes indentid interchaungeable hath set to yeir sealles. Yevyn day and yere aboveseid.

    a. paye interlined

147 Richard Neville, earl of Warwick and Salisbury and Robert Cuny, esquire, 25 September 1467 (Oxford, Bodleian Library, MS Dugdale 15 p. 8, after the original at Stafford castle in 1638).

This Indenture made bitwene Richard Earle of Warwyk and Salisbury on ye one parte, and Robert Cuny Squier[365] on ye other bereth wittenesse y^t that said Robert is w^{t}holden and belest w^t and toward ye said Erle ayenst all persons his ligeance except, and the same Robert well and covenably horsed, armed and arrayed shallbe redy to ride, come and goo w^t, toward and for the said Eerle at al tymes and into al places upon resonable warninge to be yeven unto him on ye behalfe of ye said Erle at his costs or resonable reward, the said Robert taking for his fee yeerly to terme of his life an hundreth shillings sterling to be perceived and had of the issues[a] of Yardeley[366] within ye countie of Warr. etc.

And the said Erle shall have ye thirds of all wynings of werre won or gotten by the same Robert and ye iij^d of iij^{ds} of all his servants y^t he shall have at the wages and coste of the said Erle. And if any captayn or man of astate be by the said Robert or eny of his servants taken the said Erle shall have him doing to the taker resonable reward for him.

Yeven at Warwyk xxv^o Sept[ember] vij^o E[dwardi] iiij^{ti}.

    a. MS appears to read *wosps*

148 Ralph, lord Greystoke and John Fleming, esquire, 9 December 1467 (Cumbria RO, Kendal, WD/Ry, Medieval Deeds, 127, formerly sealed on tag through fold).[367]

This indenture made the ix day of Decembre in the vij yere of the regne of King Edward the fourt be twix Rauff lorde of Graystok and Wemme, on ye ton party, and John Flemyng esquier[368] on ye todir

---

[365] Of Western Coyney, Staffs. Appointed escheator of Staffordshire in Nov. 1460, and re-appointed in March 1461: *CFR, 1452–61*, 292; *ibid., 1461–71*, 10, 223.

[366] Yardley, Worcs.

[367] Drawn to our attention by Dr Simon Payling and published by permission of the Cumbria RO, Kendal; first published in Nicolson & Burn, *Hist. of Westmorland and Cumberland*, i. 158 with no indication of source. GEC, vi. 197–99 for Ralph, lord Greystoke (1436–1501) and above **127**.

[368] John Fleming of Rydal, Westm., was a justice of the peace in Westmorland, Jan. 1471–July 1474 and was dead by 1483 (Nicolson & Burn, i. 158–9; *CPR, 1467–77*, 635; *CFR, 1471–85*, 259).

party, witness Þat the said John is retenyd and beleft wᵗ the said lorde
for terme of his lyffe als welle in were as in peasse, agayns all maner
of men, except his legeance, the said John takyng yerly of ye said lorde
iiij li. of lawfull monie of Yngland and in the tyme of werre suche
wages as ye King gyffes to suche men of suche degre, and he go wᵗ the
saide lorde. And ye said John to take his said fee by ye handez of the
receviour of Graystok,[369] Þat is or shalbe, Þat is to say at Whitsonday
and Martynmes. And if the said John go wᵗ the said lorde over the se
or in to Scotland, Þat yen it happyns the said John Flemyng or any of
his servants to take any prisoners, Þat Þan the saide lorde to have the
thirde and ye thirde of thirdes. And if it happyn Þat the saide lorde
sende for the said John to com to hym and to ride wᵗ hym to London
or for any other matt[er], Þat yan the said lorde to pay for his costez
and to gyffe hym bowchecurte for hym and his ffeliship. In witnes
herof ayther party to ye partyes of this indenture entirchaungeable
hayth set to ther seales. Wretyn the day and ye yere aforsaid.

149 Thomas Sandforth of Askham, esquire, and William Bradley of
Knipe, yeoman, 17 January 1468 (Cumbria RO, Carlisle, D
Lons/L/MD/AS 63, formerly sealed on a tag through a fold).

This indentore made at Ascom Þe xvij day of Januar Þe yer of Þe
regne of Kynge Edward Þe fourt after Þe conquest of Ingland Þe vij
betwexe Thomas of Sandforth of Ascom[370] esquier on Þe ton partie
and William Bradle of Gnyp[371] in Þe counte of Westmerlond yoman
on Þe toder partie bers witnes Þat Þe said William Bradle is withaldyn,
belevyt and becomyn Þe said Thomas man for terme of lyve and Þe
said William, his frends and all Þat he may caus and streyn, sall take
trew and faytfull part with Þe said Thomas as oft as he make Þe said
William sufficient warnynge aȝanest all maner of men except Þe soveran
lord Þe Kynge, for Þe whilke withold, beleve and service Þe said
Thomas salbe to ye said William gud and tender maister and Þe said
Thomas sall pay or make to be payd to Þe said William duryng ye said
termᵃ yerly atᵇ Witsonday and Martynmes by even porcons xiij s. iiij
d. Þe whilke salbe ressavyt of Þe said Thomas Graves with in Þe
parochynge of Bampton, ho so ever happyns to be for Þe tyme. And
at (*sic*) all thyes premisses and condicions abowen said salbe trewly
kepyt and fullfyllyt ayder partie of thes indentore to oder ar assuryt. In
witnes wher of to Þe toÞir partie of this indentore Þat is remanynge

---

[369] Greystoke, Cumbs.
[370] Askham, Westmorland.
[371] Knipe, Westmorland.

with Þe sayd William Bradly the said Thomas Sandforth hath sett to his seall. Yeven Þe place, day and ȝer abowen said.[372]

a. *duryng ye said term* interlined
b. *ye fest of* struck out

150 Thomas Sandforth of Askham and John Clibburn of Bampton, gentleman, 24 April 1469 (Cumbria RO, Carlisle, D Lons/L/MD/BM 119, sealed on a tag through a fold).[373]

This indenture mayd at Ascom ye xxiiij day of April ye ix ȝer of ye reygne of Kynge Edward ye iiij be twyx Thomas of Sandforth of Ascom on ye one partty and John Clebburn of Banton gentill man[374] on ye oÞer partte specyffyce, wettnesyse and recordys yat John Clybburn [. . .]ᵃ beleste man to ye sayd Thomas Sandforth with hym to be and trew partte take for ye terme of hys lyffe in pesse and wer as oft and when he schall be suffycyenly requryed aȝnes all oder men excepe ye Kynge and Rowland Clybburn his awne fadir with all hys awne bredir and Sir Thomas Curwen his fadir in law with all hys chylldyr in syche matteris as is yeir owne parte, yat is ye sayd John is agred be this indentur him to fullfyll in all hys powyr as well with all hys men and tenandis now beyng or yat may be in tyme comyng to be wyth and

[372] Thomas Sandforth succeeded his father in the family estate at Askham in 1460; he married Margaret, daughter of Thomas Musgrave of Hayton (Nicolson & Burn, i. 425, 594). He was retained by Richard Neville, earl of Warwick in April 1462 and was appointed a deputy to the escheator of Cumberland and Westmorland between the waters of Eamont and Lowther in 1464 (Cumbria RO, D Lons/L/MD/AS 59, 60). He appears to have remained loyal to Warwick, since he was appointed a justice of the peace in Westmorland during Henry VI's brief readeption and an order for his arrest and forfeiture was issued in July 1471 (*CPR, 1467–77*, 634). Sandforth's connection with the Nevilles, and his good relations with the influential Yorkist knight Sir William Parr, allowed him to establish a position of considerable local influence during the 1460s (Cumbria RO, D Lons/L/MD/AS 61, 62A, 64). The two indentures of retainer printed here (**149–50**) represent only the most formal of a variety of agreements by which he built up an affinity of 'friends, tenants and servants' among the local yeomanry. In Oct. 1470 Henry Walker and his sons entered into a bond of £40 'to be true and faithful to Thomas Sandforth and with him and his take part in peace and war during their lives before all other except the King'; and in the following year William Yate granted Sandforth and his son William the rule, governance and *manrydyn* of his place of Leadgate for the term of both their lives, in return for a promise from the Sandforths to maintain and fortify him and the other tenants there as they would any of their own; and in 1477 the Noble family of Butterwick obliged themselves under a bond of £40 to 'abide . . . and fulfil the rule and governance' of Thomas Sandforth (*ibid.*, AS 65, 66, 67).

[373] Fragments of a seal remain.

[374] John Clibburn of Bampton Cundale and Knipe; he married Elizabeth, a younger daughter of Sir Thomas Curwen (Nicolson & Burn, i. 466–7).

assyste ye sayd Thomas as by hys awne person. Wherfor ye sayd Thomas Sandforth is agreyd and by this indentur bownd for ye terme of hys lyffe in all hys powyr to assyst and manten ye sayd John[b] of Clebburn as hys man in yat as ryght or conscience may reqyre and over yat to gyff to ye sayd John[b] a ȝerly fee of xl s. duryng ye terme of ye two lyffys of lawfully mony of Ingland to be payd to ye sayd John or hys asignes by ye sayd Thomas or hys assignes at ij termes of ye ȝer, yat is to say in ye feste of ye Nativite of our Lord and of Sante Peter commonly callyd Lamesseday by ewyn porcions with a gown ȝerly of hys clothyng acordyng to ye sayd John, and ye forsayd Thomas to ber ye costys of ye forsayd John when he is in hys servyce. In wettenes herof both ye parttes aboffsayd enterchaunlybly hath sett to yeir seales, ye place, day and ȝer afor sayd.

a. Four words illegible
b. *John* interlined

151 Henry Percy, earl of Northumberland and Christopher Curwen, esquire, Cockermouth, 16 December 1469 (Cumbria RO, Carlisle, D Lons/L/MD/WO 8, seal missing).[375]

This indenture maid betwix Henry Percy Erle of Northumbr' and lord of the honor of Cokermouth on the one part [and Christofer] Curwen squier[376] on the other parte witnessith that the said Christofer is beleft and retenyd with the said Erle [ ][a] hym service afor all other persone, his aliegeince except, in pease and in werre within the Reame of England [ ][a] he gudly may make and stur accordyng to his degres, takyng therfor yerely of the said Erle [ ] vi li. of the rents and ferme of Bretby and Allerdale[377] and xxvi s. viij d. of the ferme of Co[kermouth …] be the hands of the Colliyers, fermours, tenants and occupiors of the same fro the tyme beyng at terms [of Whitsunday] and Martynmas be even porcions. In witnes where of the foresaid Erle and the said Christofer Curwen hase put there sealis at Cokermouth[378] aforesaid the xvj th day of December the yere of our Lord [ ]LXIX.

Dorse: Cristofer

[375] First pub. in F. W. Ragg, 'De Culwen', *Trans. Cumbs. & Westmorland Antiquarian & Arch. Soc.*, n. s. xiv (1914), 422. GEC, ix. 717–9 for Percy; technically the family had forfeited the earldom of Northumberland in 1461 and it was held between 1464–70 by John Neville, lord Montagu.

[376] Of Workington, Cumbs., the son of Sir Thomas Curwen (d. 1464), who was also in receipt of a fee from the Percies (Nicolson & Burn, ii. 54; J. M. W. Bean, *The Estates of the Percy Family 1416–1537* (Oxford, 1958), 96).

[377] Allerdale, Cumbs.

[378] Cockermouth, Cumbs.

a. Damaged; one or two words illegible

152 Richard, duke of Gloucester and William Burgh, esquire [Middleham], 4 October 1471 (North Yorks. CRO, ZRL 1/35, formerly sealed on a tag).[379]

This[a] endenture made bitwene the right high and myghty prince Richard, duc of Gloucestre, Gret Chamberlain, Constable, Admiral and Wardin of the Westmarches of England forgainst Scotland oon Þe oon partie and William Burgh, squyer,[380] on Þe other partie, witnessyth that the same William is witholden and belest for terme of his lief with and toward the said duc ayeinst alle persons, his ligeaunce except, and the same William wele and covenably horsed and harnesed shalbe redie to ride, come and goo, with, toward and for the said duc aswel in tyme of peas as of werre at alle tymes and into alle places uppon resonable warnyng to be yeven unto hym on the behalf of the said duc at his costes or resonable rewarde, the said William taking yerely for his fee ten marcs sterling of thissues, prouffits and revenues comyng and groweing aswel of the ferme of the vaccarie of Sleighholme[381] as of the fermes and revenues of the lordship of Midelham by the handes of the receivours, fermours, baillyfs or other occipiours therof for the tyme beyng at the termes of Martynmas and Whitsontyde by even porcions, and the said duc shal have the iij[des] of alle wynnynges of werre wonne or goton' by the said William, and the iij[de] of iij[des] of alle his servauntes that he shal have at the wages or costes of the said duc, and if any capitain or man of estate by the same William or any his servauntes be taken, the said duc shal have hym, yevyng to the taker resonable reward for hym. In witnesse wherof aswel Þe said duc as the said William to thies endentures entrechaungeably set thair sealx, yeven the iiij[th] day of October the xj[th] yere of the reigne of the king our souverayn lord Edward the iiij[th].

a. Autograph signature *R. Gloucester* in margin

[379] First pub. by C. P. Perceval, 'Notes on a selection of ancient charters, letters and other documents from the muniment room of Sir John Lawson of Brough Hall, near Catterick in Richmondshire, Baronet', *Archaeologia* xlvii (1882), 195; reproduced in *Richard III and the North of England*, ed. Barbara English (University of Hull, Primary Sources for Regional and Local History, no. 1, 1985) for a copy of which we are grateful to Prof. David Palliser. For Gloucester's letters patent announcing the grant of this fee, and his order to the farmer of the vaccary of Sleightholme to pay it, both dated at Middleham, 4 Oct. 1471, see NYCRO, ZRL 1/37 and 36.

[380] For William Burgh (who succeeded his father in 1465 and d. 1492) and his family, cf. above **115**.

[381] Sleightholme in Stainmore Forest, Yorks. N. R.

153 Richard, duke of Gloucester and Henry Denton, 3 September 1473 (Cumbria RO, Carlisle, D/Lons/L/MD/D 65, sealed on tag through a fold).[382]

This endenture made the first day of Octobre the xiij[th] yere of the reigne of Kyng Edward the iiij[th] betwene the right high and myghty prince Richard duc of Gloucestre on the on part and Herry Denton son and heir of John Denton squier[383] of Þat other part witnesseth Þat the said Herry is beleste, witholde and reteyned wyth the said duc for terme of his lyff, his aliegeaunce to the kynges highnes only except. So Þat he shalbe redy at all tymes when he shalbe requyred to awayte and attende upon hym aswel in tyme of pease as of werre without any delaye, sufficiently horsed, harnessed and accompanyed to [...] Þat he may make in al feldes as other journeys and places, takeyng of Þe said duc resonable costes and expensez for the same, provided ever Þat in tyme of werre if it fortune any man of worship or capteyn to be taken by the seid Herry or any of his accompanye, the seid duc to have hym, yeldyng a resonable reward to the taker of Þe same, and also the seid duc shall have all the third of thirdes. For the whiche reteynder the seid Herry shall have yerely duryng the lyff of his fader c.s, and after his decease x marc' of fee to be taken of the revenuez of two closes called Coltclose and Blaberythwayt withyn the forest of Inglewode[384] comyng by the handes of the fermor ther for the tyme beyng, as in the lettres patentes therupon made more pleynely it shall appere.[385] In wytnesse wherof the parties abovesaid to these present indentures entrechaungeably have sette Þeir seales the day and yere abovesaid.

154 Richard, duke of Gloucester and Henry, earl of Northumberland, 28 July 1474 (Alnwick Castle, Northumberland, MS Y.II.28, formerly sealed on tongue, now missing).[386]

---

[382] A good impression of Gloucester's seal survives. Autograph signature *R. Gloucestre* in top left-hand margin.

[383] Of Cardew, Cumbs. (Nicolson & Burn, ii. 318).

[384] Inglewood, Cumbs.

[385] For an example of the letters patent issued by Gloucester consequent upon an indenture of retainer, see C. H. Hunter Blair, 'Two Letters Patent from Hutton John near Penrith, Cumberland', *Archaeologia Aeliana* 4th ser., xxix (1961), 367–70, plate xxxv.

[386] We are grateful to the Duke of Northumberland for permission to publish this document and to Colin Shrimpton, archivist to the Northumberland Estates, for facilitating this and for other help. It was first pub. in E. B. de Fonblanque, *Annals of the House of Percy* (London, 1887, 2 vols.), i. 549, and in a modernised English version in Dunham, 140; cf. also *HMC, 6th Report*, part i. 223b. GEC, ix. 717–9 for Henry Percy, earl of Northumberland (1470–89). For the circumstances in which this indenture was concluded see Bean, *The Estates of the Percy Family*, 128–35; R. Horrox, *Richard III. A Study of Service* (Cambridge, 1989), 61–4.

This endenture made the xxviij[th] daie of July in the xiiij[th] yere of
the reigne of oure soveraine lorde King Edward [the][a] fourthe bitwix
the right high and mighty prince Richard, duc of Gloucestre, on
the oone partye, and [the][a] right worshipfull lorde Henry, Erle of
Northumberland, on the other party, witnesseth that the said Erle
by thies presentes promitts and grauntz unto the said duc to be his
faithfull servaunt, the said duc being his good and faithful lorde,
and the said Erle to do service unto the said duc at all tymes
lawfull and convenient whan he therunto by the said duc shal be
lawfully required, the duetie of the alegiaunce of the said Erle to
the kinges highnes, the Quene, his service and promise to Prince
Edward, thair first begoten son, and all the kinges issue begoten
and to be begoten, first at all tymes reserved and hadd.

For the which service the said duc promitts and grauntz unto the
said Erle to be his good and faithfull lorde at all tymes, And to sustene
hym in his rights a fore all other personnes, except to fore except. Also
the said duc promittes and grauntes to the said Erle that he shal nat
aske, chalenge nor clayme any office or offices or fee that the said Erle
hath of the kinges graunt, or of any other personne or personnes, at
the making of thies presents, nor interrupt the said Erle nor any of his
servauntz in executing or doing of any the said office or offices by hym
or any of his servauntz in tyme to come. And also the said duc shal
nat accept nor reteigne into his service any servaunt or servauntz that
was or any tyme seth hath been, with the said Erle reteigned of fee,
clothing or promise according to thappoyntment taken bitwix the said
duc and Erle by the kinges highness and the lordes of his counseil at
Nottyngham the xii[th] daie of May in the xiiij[th] yere of the reigne of
oure said souveraingn lorde, except John Wodryngton.[387] In witnes
wherof the said duc and the said Erle to thies endentures entre-
chaungably have set thair sealis the daye and yere above said.

J. Newton'[388]

a. damaged

155 Richard, duke of Gloucester and Elizabeth, lady Scrope of Masham
for Thomas, lord Scrope, 14 January 1476 [English] (New York,
Collection of Mr and Mrs Harry Spiro, seals missing). Pub. in Lorraine
C. Attreed, 'An Indenture between Richard Duke of Gloucester and
the Scrope Family of Masham and Upsall', *Speculum* 58 (1983), 1025.

[387] Of Chipchase, Northumbs., he was the earl's master-forester at Alnwick: M. A.
Hicks, 'Dynastic Change and Northern Society: the Fourth Earl of Northumberland,
1470–89', *Northern History* xiv (1978), 83, 107.

[388] The seals are missing and there is no contemporary endorsement but a list of
household objects (blankets, coverlets, towels, quilts, feather beds, etc.) was jotted down
on the dorse before the end of the fifteenth century.

Addendum*

156 Humphrey, earl of Buckingham and Sir John Hanford (Handeforthe), London, 26 October 1441 (Manchester, Chetham's Library, Adlington MS f. 153v).[389]

Whilst the orthography of this indenture differs considerably, largely because of the conventions used by its early seventeenth-century copyist, it otherwise follows **124** verbatim, except that Hanford's pension of £10 p.a. is assigned on the manor of Thornbury, Gloucs. and the dating clauses differ.

[389] An early seventeenth-century transcript first published in J. P. Earwaker, *East Cheshire*, 2 vols. London, 1877–80, i. 241–2. We are grateful to Michael Powell, Librarian, for help in locating this document. A monumental effigy presumed to represent Sir John Hanford (1391–*c.*1461) in Cheadle parish church displays a version of the SS collar (Plate facing Earwaker, i. 212), who also provides a genealogy and other details on his career). Rawcliffe, *The Staffords*, 233 notes Buckingham's award to Hanford of an annuity for life service in peace and war at home and abroad of £10 p.a. on the revenues of Rothwell, Northants., by indenture in Sept. 1441, after NLW, Peniarth MS 280 f. 24. The present indenture presumably replaces this earlier agreement, unless there has been some confusion in compiling the Peniarth MS where the indenture (dated 5 Sept. 1441) with Sir John Mainwaring (**124**), also assigned his annuity on Rothwell.

* As predicted in the Introduction, a further indenture has come to light even while our MS was with the printer. And, as midnight struck, Philip Morgan drew our attention to a remarkable indenture between Hondekyn Mainwaring the elder and Sir John Mainwaring [cf. above **124**] and Thomas Alkemontelowe, 5 March 1443, for his life 'service to oure ouen persones in such occupacion as he most useth, Þhat is to say wᵗ Penne and Inke and Counsell be fore all oÞer men oute take the Kyng and his Mynystres' in return for their 'gode Maystreshippe', an annual livery gown and 'during his lyve covenable mete and drynke and beddyng to hym and hys servaunt' (William Dugdale's MS *Chartularium Mainwaringianum*, 12.i, currently in private hands).

INDEX

Figures in Italic refer to page numbers of the Introduction; those in Roman to Indentures. Bishop, duke and earl have been abbreviated to b., d. and e; n signifies note. References to regnal years of individual kings have been omitted.

II
WILLIAM ATKINS,
A RELATION OF THE
JOURNEY FROM ST OMERS
TO SEVILLE, 1622

Edited by Martin Murphy

CONTENTS

CONTENTS

PREFACE

An abridged version of this *Relation*, edited by Joseph Stevenson S.J., was published serially in *The Month* in 1879–80.[1] The editor modernised the spelling and cut the text, notably omitting the section describing social, political and religious life in the Moroccan enclave of Salé. He was chiefly interested in the *Relation* as a document of recusant history, illustrating the risks and dangers undergone by English Catholic students abroad, and since *The Month* was largely limited to a Roman Catholic readership, its version of the *Relation* escaped the wider attention of historians. Although it contains the first extensive account of the pirate state of Salé written by a European, it is not included in Sir Robert Playfair's bibliography of Morocco published in 1893, nor is it mentioned in any studies of the Barbary pirates published since.[2] The *Relation* contains much of interest also to social and maritime historians. The purpose of the present edition is to make the document accessible to a wider readership, to restore the full text along with the original spelling which gives the language its savour, and to provide an introduction and commentary which attempt to set the story in its context.

The manuscript of the *Relation* is reproduced by kind permission of the Rector of Stonyhurst College. I am particularly indebted to Father F. S. Turner, the Librarian of Stonyhurst, for allowing the manuscript to be deposited in the Bodleian Library for transcription. Professor T. A. Birrell carefully checked the text and contributed a number of valuable suggestions and emendations based on his expert knowledge of recusant literature. Dr María Rodríguez-Salgado gave me the benefit of her knowledge of piracy and suggested improvements. Mrs Joy Rowe took the trouble to investigate the Cambridgeshire origins of William Atkins, and Mrs Bohija Dottridge indicated some features of seventeenth-century Salé which survive in twentieth-century Rabat. Finally I am deeply indebted to Dr Colin Heywood, of the School of Oriental and African Studies, who shared with me his knowledge of Ottoman history and the Turkish language.

---

[1] *The Month* xviii (December 1879), 534–49; xix (January 1880), 44–58, 392–410; xx (July 1880), 395–412.

[2] Robert L. Playfair, *A Bibliography of Morocco*, Royal Geographical Supplementary Papers, vol. 3, Part 3 (1893), 203–476. For recent work on Salé, see p.204, n.16.

ABBREVIATIONS

ARSI	Archivum Romanum Societatis Jesu, Rome
CRS 73	Catholic Record Society Publications, Records Series volume 73, *St Gregory's College, Seville, 1592–1767*, ed. Martin Murphy (1992)
CSP (Dom)	*Calendar of State Papers (Domestic)*
Dan	Pierre Dan, *Histoire de Barbarie et des Corsaires* (Paris, 1637)
Dunton	John Dunton, *A True Journall of the Sally Fleet* (London, 1637; facsimile edition, Amsterdam, 1970)
Foley	H. Foley, *Records of the English Province, S.J.*, 8 vols in 7 (London, 1877–83)
Friedman	Ellen Friedman, *Spanish Captives in North Africa in the Early Modern Age* (Madison, Wisconsin, 1983)
García Figueras	Tomás García Figueras and Carlos Rodríguez Joulia Saint-Cyr, *Larache: datos para su historia en el siglo XVII* (Madrid, 1973)
Hambye	Étienne Hambye, *L'aumônerie de la flotte de Flandres au XVIIe siècle* (Namur, 1967)
HMC	Historical Manuscripts Commission
Israel	Jonathan Israel, *The Dutch Republic and the Hispanic World 1606-1661* (Oxford, 1982)
Lithgow	William Lithgow, *The Totall Discourse of the Rare Adventures and Painefull Peregrinations* (London, 1632; Glasgow, 1906)
Redhouse	J. W. Redhouse, *A Turkish and English Lexicon* (Constantinople, 1921).
SIHM	*Sources inédites de l'histoire de Maroc*, ed. H. de Castries, 1e série, Dynastie Saadienne: *Archives et Bibliothèques de France*, vol. 2 (Paris, 1909) *Archives et Bibliothèques de France*, vol. 3 (Paris, 1911) *Archives et Bibliothèques de l'Espagne* (Paris, 1921) *Archives et Bibliothèques de l'Angleterre* (Paris, 1925)
Stradling	R.A. Stradling, *The Armada of Flanders* (Cambridge, 1992)
VCH	*Victoria County Histories*
Wadsworth	James Wadsworth, *The English Spanish Pilgrime* (London, 1629. Facsimile edition, Amsterdam, 1979)
Wright	Joseph Wright, *The English Dialect Dictionary*, 6 vols. (Oxford, 1981)

INTRODUCTION

I THE *RELATION* AND ITS AUTHOR

The Manuscript

The manuscript, preserved at Stonyhurst College, Lancashire, consists of 56 sewn leaves (31 x 20 mm), the two exterior leaves forming the covers. The pages, *recto* and *verso*, have been numbered 1–83 by a recent hand in pencil. The opening opposite page 1 bears the inscription 'Francis Whitgreave, Burton Manor, near Stafford. This M.S. I found among some old books which had been packed in an oak chest and so removed from our ancient family seat of Moseley Hall near Wolverhampton. F.W.'.

The lacunae in the manuscript and evident examples of misreading, dittography and omission make it clear that this is a copy of an earlier text, now lost. The copper-plate hand is that of a practised scrivener, who is faithful to the frequently archaic spelling and syntax. The fact that he appears unfamiliar with relatively well-known classical allusions and theological terms[1] suggests that he was not a priest. The only visible watermark is a crowned shield enclosing a fleur-de-lis, a motif which was commonly used between c.1627 and c.1679 and later from c.1717. The first editor of the text, Joseph Stevenson, thought that the orthography could 'probably be referred to the reign of our Charles the Second'. Since Stevenson was a palaeographer who worked for the Historical Manuscripts Commission before joining the Society of Jesus, his opinion carries some weight, but other experts have assigned the hand to the eighteenth century. There are no signs of the manuscript having been prepared for publication.

Authorship

Some clues as to authorship may be obtained from a comparison between the names of the twelve students given in this narrative and those listed by James Wadsworth in *The English Spanish Pilgrime* (1629).[2] Wadsworth claims to give the students' 'true' names, as opposed to their aliases. Most students attending English Catholic colleges on the continent at this time went under one or more aliases, and this was

---

[1] See the lacunae on p.231 n.37 and p.267 n.107.
[2] Wadsworth, p.32.

particularly necessary in Flanders and Seville, where they were liable
to surveillance by government spies.

'A Relation'	*Wadsworth*
James Wadsworth	'myself'
Thomas Coniers	Conniers
William Appleby	Appleby
Peter Middleton	Middleton
John Robinson	Robinson
Robert Neale	Naile
Peter Edwards	Evely
Thomas Kensington	Gerard
William Fairfax	Clifford
George Champian	Farmer (? = Fermor)
John Woodas	Hausby (? = Hansby)
'myself' (p. 277)	Atkins

The first six names and the last in the two lists correspond, and Peter
Edwards is known to have been the alias of the student Amesius
Eveleigh.[3] Thomas Kensington, who may be identical with Wadsworth's
'Gerard', is said by the author of the *Relation* (p.237) to have died.
Nothing is known of William Fairfax, George Champian and John
Woodas, nor of how they correspond with Clifford, Farmer and Hausby.
Atkins, however, may be identified as William Atkins, a native of
Cambridgeshire who was ordained priest at St Gregory's College,
Seville, in 1628, joined the Society of Jesus in Flanders in 1629, returned
to England by 1631, and spent the remaining fifty years of his life (1631–
81) in the Staffordshire district.[4] The fact that the MS copy of the
Relation was discovered at Moseley Old Hall in Staffordshire may be
taken as further evidence that Atkins was the author.

Though Cambridgeshire, which is given in the Jesuit catalogues as
Atkins' county of origin, was not Catholic territory, a number of
recusant families are recorded in the fenland region bordering north-
west Norfolk. A Richard Atkyns of Outwell, a parish divided between
Cambridgeshire and Norfolk, was regularly listed as a recusant at
Norwich between 1593 and 1615. He was described as a yeoman 'of
good worth and quality', and in 1596 his lands were valued as being
worth 20 marks per annum. He is probably the Richard Atkyns who
wrote reports on fenland drainage schemes in 1602–4 and 1618. He
was married at Outwell to Catherine Bateman in 1584 and died in
1627. The terms of his will show that he was survived by his wife, his
sons William and Richard, and two daughters, one of whom was

---

[3] CRS 73 (1992), 65.
[4] CRS 73 (1992), 50.

married to a Thomas Blyth.[5] The elder son William, christened in 1585, is known to have been a student at Douay College between 1601 and 1603, having been sent there on the recommendation of the priest Edward Hughes. The Douay Diaries record that he was recalled to England by his father in 1603.[6] In his will, Richard Atkins left this son all his 'bookes, printed and written, mappes, chartes, writings and papers', which suggest that he was a travelled as well as an educated man.

The author of the *Relation* cannot be the William Atkins just mentioned, for that would make him 37 years old in 1622, but he may have been the son of Richard Atkins' daughter and her husband Thomas Blyth. It was common practice for students abroad to take their mother's maiden name as an alias. The younger William Atkins' career after his arrival at Seville in November 1622 can be traced in outline. In July 1624 the Jesuit General in Rome wrote to the Rector of the English College, Seville, about the young man's wish to join the Society, instructing that 'before he does so, his father wants to meet him in Flanders to discuss arrangements for his patrimony'.[7] In the event Atkins did not become a Jesuit until four or five years later, after his ordination at Seville in 1628. He was at the novitiate at Watten (Flanders) in 1629–30, and thereafter was listed in the catalogues of the English Province as resident in the 'College', or district, of St Aloysius, then covering the counties of Lancashire, Derbyshire, Cheshire and Staffordshire. In the supplement to the catalogue of 1629 he is described under the conventional headings as being 28 years of age, of one year's standing in the Society and a native of Cambridgeshire. His report goes on to assess him with a series of double negatives as not unintelligent, somewhat lacking in judgment and sense, not inexperienced, rather backward in his studies, choleric in temperament and in other respects as yet unproven. (*'Ingenio non caret, iudicium non satisfacit, prudentia similis, experientia non caret, in litteris non multum profecit, complexio cholerica, caetera nondum constant'*). The 1631 supplement notes his robust health.[8] The comments on temperament were based on the Hippocratic-Galenic doctrine of the mixture (*complexio*) of the humours. In those of choleric temperament the yellow or red bile was thought to predominate. If Atkins was true to form he would have been impetuous, red-haired and overly fond of female company. Doubtless the third of these characteristics did not apply, but he tells us that he was judged by some

[5] Norfolk Record Office, DIS 9/1a: lists of presentments at Archdeaconry Courts and indictments at Quarter Sessions, 1593–1616; ibid., Probate Register, Traver 19: Richard Atkins' will of 7 April 1627.

[6] CRS 10 (1911), 37, 52.

[7] ARSI Baet. 5 II, f.18r.

[8] ARSI Anglia 10, ff.97–8.

people at Salé by his 'person, complexion and favours much to resemble the natives of Ireland' (p.244) – which might be taken to mean that he had reddish hair or a reddish complexion.

Atkins was based throughout his working life in Staffordshire, an area which was originally within the Jesuit 'College' (sub-province) of St Aloysius but was given the title of the Residence of St Chad in 1661 and became a College in its own right in 1670. In 1652 he is recorded as a witness to the inspection of the relics of St Chad. In 1653 he was appointed Rector of the College of St Aloysius, and in 1656 he is said to have carried out an exorcism at Halfcote in Kinver Forest – performing a role in which Catholic priests were thought to have the advantage over their reformed brethren. But most of his apostolate was exercised in and around Wolverhampton, which in 1654 was described as swarming with Papists and 'by many styled little Rome'.[9] He was still living at Wolverhampton in his late seventies when he fell victim to the persecution provoked by Titus Oates. On 13 August 1679 he and Andrew Bromwich appeared at Stafford Assizes before Lord Chief Justice Scroggs on a charge of being 'Romish priests'. Witnesses testified that they had seen him exercise his priestly functions 'at Mrs Stanford's' at Wolverhampton, and at Well Head, Ham. Atkins had suffered a stroke six years earlier and had to answer through a spokesman since he was deaf, virtually speechless and unable to lift his hand. The sentence of death had to be shouted in his ear. The judge could not prevent one of the prosecution witnesses from acknowledging the old man's charity: 'He is a man that hath relieved me and my children oftentimes when I was in want'.[10] Both priests were subsequently reprieved, Bromwich because he agreed to take the oaths and Atkins because of his age. He died in Stafford Gaol on 17 March 1681.

History of the Manuscript and Date of the Original Text

The copy reproduced here was discovered by Francis Whitgreave (1819–96) soon after his removal from his family's ancestral seat at Moseley Old Hall, Bushbury, four miles north of Wolverhampton, to the new house he built in 1855 on the site of Burton Manor, near Stafford. Moseley Old Hall is only six miles from Boscobel House, which is known to have been one of the centres of the Staffordshire Jesuits, and it may be assumed that Atkins was closely acquainted with

[9] Foley iii.795, ii.22–3; *VCH Staffs* iii (1970), 104–7.

[10] *The Trial, Conviction and Condemnation of Andrew Bromwich and William Atkins for being Romish priests, before the Right Honourable Lord Chief Justice Scroggs at Summer Assizes last at Stafford* (London, for Robert Pawlett, 1679); Michael Tanner, *Brevis Relatio Felicis Agonis quem pro Religione Catholica subierunt aliquot e Societate Jesu Sacerdotes* (Prague, 1683), 86; Foley v.450–4.

Thomas Whitgreave (1625–1702), the squire of Moseley. Whitgreave achieved celebrity as one of those who sheltered the future King Charles II when he was a fugitive in the area in September 1651. It was at Moseley that the King first met the priest John Huddlestone who was to receive him into the Catholic Church on his deathbed thirty four years later.[11] After the Restoration Huddlestone was appointed chaplain to the Queen Dowager at Somerset House, and possibly Atkins succeeded him in that capacity at Moseley.

Internal evidence suggests that the original *Relation* was composed at some time between 1637 and *c*.1655, probably earlier rather than later. The Dunkirk admiral Jean Colaert is said by the author to have died, so the date of his death, 1637, may be taken as a *terminus a quo*.[12] On the other hand he refers to his fellow-traveller James Wadsworth as being still alive, persevering 'to this day in his apostacie'. Wadsworth is last heard of in 1655, when according to Sir William Sanderson he was living in Westminster, 'a common hackney to the basest catchpole baylifs'.[13] It is perhaps more likely that the *Relation* was written in the reign of Charles I when Catholics had more freedom of association and expression, when the author's powers of recall were still fresh, and when Wadsworth's account of the same journey (published in 1624) had not yet faded from memory. Wadsworth is said by Atkins to have been the cause of the 'utter undoing of manie vertuous Catholicks'. Though he was chiefly notorious for giving evidence at the trials of the Jesuits Thomas Holland and Henry Morse in 1642 and 1645 (evidence which led to their conviction and execution) Wadsworth is known to have been an informer against Catholics from as early as 1626. The House of Lords Calendar recorded in August 1642 the names of priests 'indicted and attainted' by Wadsworth and two other 'messengers' during the previous three years. On a lighter note, the 'unseemelie fashion of naked dressings' which Atkins denounces as prevalent 'amongst our vaine gentlewoemen of England' (p.233) is hardly applicable to the style of the Commonwealth – though animadversions upon female immodesty were a commonplace of pious rhetoric throughout the seventeenth century (and beyond).

Purpose of the work

There is no evidence that the *Relation* was intended for printed pub-

---

[11] A.H. Chatwin, 'The Whitgreaves of Moseley', *Staffordshire Catholic History* xix (1980), 1–11; Stebbing Shaw, *The History and Antiquities of Staffordshire* (1801), i.74–80.

[12] Colaert became Admiral of the Dunkirk fleet in 1635 and died in August 1637 (Stradling, 86–8, 101).

[13] William Sanderson, *A Compleat History of the Lives and Reigns of Mary Queen of Scotland and of her Son and Successor James the Sixth* (1656), 491.

lication, and it does not fall into any of the genres adopted by Jesuit writers for the press. The legible scrivener's hand suggests that this is a reading copy intended for circulation, perhaps among Atkins' brethren and the circle of Staffordshire Catholic gentry in which he moved. The references to feast days and quotations from the Vulgate are only some of the many touches which assume a Catholic readership. Possibly, like John Gerard and Henry Morse before him, Atkins was asked to compose the *Relation* by his superiors.

In his concluding paragraphs the author goes out of his way to rebut some of the allegations made in Wadsworth's book *The English Spanishe Pilgrime*, but this passage is incidental rather than central to his work. Similarly, though the narrative is interspersed with passages explicitly praising the workings of divine Providence, this pious and didactic note is not allowed to dominate. The author is careful to vary the pace and tone of the narrative which ranges from the high to the low style, from fanciful poetry to earthy realism, from tragedy to comedy. The section relating the students' overland journey from Gibraltar to Cadiz, blending realism with fantasy, has some of the elements of a picaresque novel. The common feature underlying all this variety is the evident desire to entertain. The writer aims to hold the reader's attention, and he seems to have in mind a readership of like-minded persons who will enjoy a good story with a moral attached. Though he can be smug (for instance in telling us on several occasions what an edifying impression he and his companions made on all who met them) he does not beat the Jesuit drum, and though he indulges in some sarcasm at the expense of Puritans, Anabaptists and Huguenots, his account of the Muslim inhabitants of Salé is by contemporary standards relatively dispassionate.

Style

The *Relation* is a highly mannered composition in which the author is at pains to display his literary talent. Sentence structure is often carefully balanced (e.g. 'he ... wee', p.216; 'some ... others', p.215). At moments of high drama the historic present tense is brought into play, as in the account of the storm at Mamora (p.262). The third person narrative is varied by apostrophe. Set speeches, such as those of the stage Dutchman (p.221) and the French merchant (p.256) are introduced for dramatic effect. There is an abundance of high-flown literary vocabulary, such as 'prognosticate' (p.215), 'parthenian' (p.236), 'cornucopia', 'amphitheatrum' (p.240). Other terminology is perhaps deliberately archaic (e.g. 'derne', 'faintie', 'rascaldrie'). The narrative is rich in allusions to classical literature, in particular to the *Aeneid*, and in one passage describing the journey from Gibraltar to Medina Sidonia the author fancifully imagines himself and his companions as actually crossing the

Elysian Fields and wading the river Lethe. The influence of Virgil is also evident in epic formulae such as 'we furrowed the liquid soyle' (p.272) and in allusions to Charon, Palinurus, etc. The most interesting feature, however, is the use of verse to paint a scene (such as the appearance of Cape St Vincent, p.230) or to dramatise an episode (such as the sea battle on pp.215–9). The former passage is introduced in the high literary manner: 'And I at the gratefull remembrance of these swete solaces wee tooke ... have more minde now to sit a while and sing them then goe forward in my tragicall narration'.

Though the narrative has some features of epic and comedy, this 'tragic' note is struck on two other occasions. The capture of the Dunkirk ship by Jacob May (p.220) is described as a 'tragick scene', and the homosexual abuse of one of the students by the pirate 'Arch' is referred to as a 'tragicall passage' (p.238). According to James Wadsworth, after the students reached Seville the Jesuits there made a 'tragicall comedy' of their voyage, 'whereby they got much money and honour, whereupon all people admired Gods providence and our delivery out of such manifest dangers, which the Jesuits ascribed only to their protector S. Ignatius, we being their schollers, and thereupon they collected no small summes of money'.[14] It is possible that Atkins' narration may contain some elements of this 'tragicall comedy', even though this would originally have been performed in Latin or Spanish for the benefit of the Seville audience. Though the theme of divine providence and protection is present in the *Relation*, St Ignatius is not mentioned. While the author's style is derivative – the verse passages being reminiscent of Sidney's *Arcadia* – his handling of the story is confident and vivid. For one whose proficiency in literature is described in his early reports as 'unsatisfactory' it is an impressive achievement.

James Wadsworth's account

James Wadsworth's account of the same journey in *The English Spanish Pilgrime* (1629; second edition, 1630) is much shorter than that of Atkins. The chapter devoted to the voyage amounts to only fifteen pages out of a total of ninety-five. Wadsworth's avowed purpose was to 'discover diverse subtilties and policies of the English Jesuits, Fryers, Monkes and other Seminary Priests beyond the seas', so that those inclined to Rome might 'see the vaile unmaskt wherwith they were hoodwinkt'.[15] Wadsworth made a living by selling 'revelations' and by exploiting his inside knowledge of the Catholic world through which he had passed. The chapter on the journey from St Omer to Seville (where Wadsworth

[14] Wadsworth, 47.
[15] Wadsworth, A3.

was supposed to enter the English college) is relatively neutral in tone (unlike his description of the college at St Omer) and does not differ in its main outlines from Atkins' account. Wadsworth gives himself the credit of having secured the students' eventual release from captivity at Salé by persuading the French merchant Jehan de la Goretta, somewhat against his will, to negotiate their ransom. Atkins ingenuously describes this merchant as a 'verie charitable man' who had ransomed many captives, whereas Wadsworth says more bluntly that he was a trafficker in slaves. It is perhaps characteristic of Wadsworth that he does not bother to justify his action in jumping ship at Larache and abandoning his companions.

The main discrepancy occurs at the end of the story. According to Wadsworth the Jesuits at Seville reneged on the ransom promised by the deceased merchant to the pirates, thus leaving the merchant's daughter penniless since she lost the value of the goods left at Salé by her father on deposit. Atkins makes no mention of this daughter and states that the merchant secretly took 'most' of the deposit away with him. Wadsworth also takes the opportunity to accuse the Jesuits of exploiting the students' adventures for gain and of dishonesty in appealing for contributions to a ransom that was never paid. The two versions are irreconcileable. Atkins was closer to events, since he remained in Seville and was able to follow developments in the case, whereas Wadsworth knew of them only by hearsay. The latter's claim to motives of altruism (on behalf of the merchant's daughter) is not wholly convincing in the light of what is otherwise known of his character.

II THE JOURNEY AND ITS HISTORICAL CONTEXT

The Salé Pirates

As already indicated, this *Relation* is the first substantial account in any language of life among the 'Salley pirates', as they were known in seventeenth-century England.[16] 'New' Salé (modern Rabat), on the south bank of the Bou-Regreg river on the Atlantic coast of Morocco, was settled c.1609 by Arabic-speaking Muslim emigrants from Hornachos in Extremadura who were allowed by the Sherif of Morocco to rebuild the old and abandoned Casbah. Between 1609 and 1614 they were reinforced by large numbers of Spanish-speaking Moriscos (known

---

[16] For what follows, see *SIHM, France*, iii (1911), 187–98; R. Coindreau, *Les corsaires de Salé* (Paris, 1948); K. Brown, 'An urban view of Moroccan history: Salé, 1000–1800', *Hesperis-Tamuda* xii (Rabat, 1971), 5–106; Friedman, 25–8.

at Salé as Andalos) expelled by Philip III from southern Spain. These two groups, divided from each other in language and mentality, were then joined by some of the English and Dutch pirates who lost their base of operations at Mamora, eighteen miles to the north, when it was captured by the Spanish in 1614. The *Relation* provides valuable evidence also of the presence at Salé of Anatolian Turks: not only does the writer on several occasions make the distinction between 'Turks' and 'Moors' but he uses the Turkish rather than the Arabic form of the Muslim hours of prayer — which suggests that he heard them from a Turkish speaker. Elsewhere in the North African dominions of the Ottoman Empire — at Algiers and Tunis, for example — Anatolian Turks were the ruling ascendancy: at Salé they seem rather to have been freelance soldiers or corsairs of fortune. It is possible that Turkish served as a *lingua franca* among the corsairs. This heterogeneous community (if it can be called such) was nominally subject to the Sherif of Morocco and his resident representative, the Caïd, but in practice it was virtually independent. After the death of Ahmad al-Mansur (1578–1603), who had expanded his Empire as far as the Sudan, Morocco had split into two rival kingdoms, with capitals at Marrakech and Fez, and both were preoccupied with the problem of insurgency among the Arabic or Berber-speaking tribes of the interior, led by inspirational marabouts, or holy men.

Salé's position on the Atlantic coast, only 100km south of Tangier, made it an ideal base for attacks on shipping passing through the Straits of Gibraltar, and it was also in striking distance of the Canaries and the Spanish sea-lanes. Piracy now became not merely a Mediterranean but an Atlantic phenomenon. Moreover there was an added edge to the activities of the Salé pirates. The majority of them had been expelled from Spain and therefore had reason to bear a grudge against those who had driven them from their homeland. They used their knowledge of Spain well, and proved more dangerous without than they had been within the kingdom. Their organisation was strengthened by the English and Dutch pirates who joined them after 1614 and contributed their technical skills of seamanship. In 1624 a Dutchman, Jan Jansz of Haarlem, was Captain of the 'Sallee fleet' which amounted to some thirty or forty ships. It was he who led the spectacular raids on Reykjavik in 1627 and Baltimore, Co. Cork, in 1631. Between 1618 and 1626 the 'Salleymen' were at the height of their power and are estimated to have taken over six thousand captives. The Dutch found the pirates a useful weapon in their war against Spain, but the British and French also made alliances with Salé at different times in order to protect their shipping, to obtain favourable trade agreements, to recover captives and to gain the advantage over their rivals. In 1627 the envoy John Harrison signed a treaty with Salé, assuring it of British support, but Charles I withheld ratification.[17] In 1637 the government sent a naval expedition under William Rainsborough which imposed terms on the pirates by force. One of Rainsborough's captains, John Dunton, had himself been a prisoner at Salé before being sent on a raiding expedition to the south coast of England by his Morisco master, leaving his young son behind as a pledge. He was captured off the Isle of Wight, brought to trial in Winchester, acquitted, and then enlisted for the expedition against his former captors. His diary of the expedition, *A True Journall of the Sally Fleet* (London, 1637) is the first published work in English specifically about Salé, though it confines itself to the events of Rainsborough's mission.

The Trinitarian friar Pierre Dan visited Salé in the 1630s and devoted some pages to it in his *Histoire de Barbarie et des Corsaires* (Paris, 1637) in which he deals with all the Barbary states.[18] However he describes Salé at a later stage of its development, after its declaration of independence from the Sherif of Morocco in 1627. Atkins' *Relation* is unique as an eyewitness account of Salé in its formative stage, affording evidence about its everyday life and customs, government, the conditions in which slaves were held and relations between the Governor and his subjects as well as between the immigrant population of the town and the indigenous tribesmen of the interior. The *Relation* is also valuable in giving a first-hand account of the Spanish *presidio* at Mamora, established in 1614, where the twelve students lent a hand with the artillery as the garrison defended itself against one of the frequent attacks by local tribesmen. These assaults on Mamora and the other *presidio* at Larache further north were, as Wadsworth testifies, led by the charismatic *marabout* Sidi (*seyyid*) Muhammad Zayani, known as al-Ayyashi, the 'Saint of Salley', who regarded the Spanish, the Sherif of Morocco and the Moriscos of Salé with equal contempt. He established his base at old Salé, and in 1637 Captain Rainsborough found him a useful if unpredictable ally against the pirate republic of new Salé on the opposite bank. The terms of the treaty Rainsborough signed with 'the right excellent Saint', later approved by the government in London, are included in John Dunton's account of the expedition.[19]

St Omers and Seville

The College of St Omers in Artois, the point of departure for the twelve students, was founded in 1593 by the Jesuit Robert Persons for

[17] *SIHM, Angleterre*, ii (1925), 445–6.
[18] Dan, 173–90, 285, 407, 421–2.
[19] Dunton, E2–3.

the education of sons of English recusants.[20] The town lay within the territory of the Spanish Netherlands and the college was founded with the aid of a Spanish benefaction. Students followed the normal Jesuit curriculum in the humanities, and on completing the course those who wished to study for the priesthood normally proceeded to those seminaries on the continent which were under Jesuit direction, rather than to the nearby seminary at Douai, which was administered by the secular clergy. The English College at Rome had been established under Jesuit direction in 1579, but shortage of funds and a dramatic rise in the number of applicants soon made it necessary to find alternatives. The resourceful Persons took advantage of a visit to Spain in 1589 to found a new college under the patronage of Philip II at Valladolid, and three years later made a similar foundation at Seville, where the English College of St Gregory was formally inaugurated on 25 November 1592. The Rector was a Spanish Jesuit and the students followed their course of philosophy and theology at the nearby college of St Hermenegild, where the professors were Jesuits from the Andalusian Province, but there were several English Jesuits at St Gregory's who were concerned with discipline, spiritual direction and training in the skills of controversy and pastoral theology needed for the mission. Many of the students joined the Society after ordination, and it is significant that of the twelve mentioned in this Relation no fewer than six did so.

From its foundation in 1593 the college at St Omers regularly sent batches of candidates to the seminaries at Rome, Valladolid and Seville. The dissensions at Rome and Valladolid in the 1590s made Seville an attractive alternative. The dangers of the journey and the problems of heat and disease endemic in that city were offset by the high standard of the studies at St Hermenegild's and by the spirit of harmony which prevailed at St Gregory's under its sympathetic Rector, Francisco de Peralta (1592–1607). The Jesuit Annual Letters record the admission of 22 students in 1597, 20 in 1601, 22 in 1603, 15 in 1605, 9 in 1609 and 14 in 1616. As these figures suggest, there was a consistent decline in numbers. 70 students are recorded there in 1597, at the height of the Catholic resistance to Elizabeth and Cecil, but by 1624, in the changed circumstances of Stuart rule, numbers had fallen to 31.[21]

The ages of the twelve students sent from St Omers to Seville in 1622 are surprisingly wide-ranging. Of those whose dates of birth are known, Wadsworth was 18 (the normal school-leaving age), Atkins and Middleton 21, Neale 22, Appleby 31 and Robinson 34. It can only be

[20] On St Omers see T.E. Muir, *Stonyhurst College, 1593–1993* (London, 1992); Hubert Chadwick, *From St Omers to Stonyhurst* (1962).

[21] CRS 73 (1992), 123–5.

presumed that the other six were the 'tender youthes' for whom their
seniors showed such concern. The presence of students in their thirties
suggests that while most of them (including Atkins himself) proceeded
from College, others (such as Appleby and Robinson) had simply
undergone a time of trial at St Omers after being sent there with letters
of recommendation from Jesuit missionaries in England.

It was normal for the St Omers contingent, or 'mission', to proceed
to Spain by sea, and the close relationship between the Jesuits of
Flanders and the captains of the Dunkirk fleet, which served the Spanish
crown, was useful in affording the travellers passage on friendly and
reliable ships. The destinations varied. The destination of the twelve
students was Sanlúcar de Barrameda, at the mouth of the Guadalquivir,
where Persons had established a staging-post in 1591, but on other
occasions students landed at ports on the northern coast of Spain, or
at Lisbon, whence they travelled to Seville overland. In view of the
dangers of capture by English or Dutch ships it is remarkable how few
of these voyages came to grief. However the danger from pirates
became an increasing problem. In 1607 a priest on his way from Seville
to England after completing his studies at St Gregory's was captured
by an English pirate who took him to Larache on the Moroccan coast
before setting him free.[22] Larache was captured by the Spanish in 1610,
and Mamora – another pirate nest – four years later, but the growing
power of the Salé corsairs in the years following posed a constant threat
to those travelling by sea between northern Europe and southern Spain.

[22] CRS 73 (1992), 124 and note.

EDITORIAL PRINCIPLES

In general this edition follows the conventions established in *The Bulletin of Historical Research*, i (1925), 6–25.

The page numbers of the manuscript are indicated within square brackets in the text.

The original spelling has been retained except that u and initial i have been rendered where appropriate as v and j.

Modern punctuation, including quotation marks and the use of capital letters at the beginning of sentences, has been adopted for the sake of readability.

Words or phrases in foreign languages have been italicised.

Abbreviations have normally been extended, and modern pound signs are used.

Where the text is illegible or defective, conjectural readings have been given wherever possible in italics within square brackets. Words which have evidently been omitted by the copyist appear within square brackets in Roman type.

In the interest of the reader all notes have been combined at the foot of the page. A date accompanying a glossarial note indicates the first use of a given word recorded by the *OED* in the sense specified.

ITINERARY

7 August	St Omer to Calais.
12 August	Departure from Calais.
20 August	Off Cape Finisterre.
21 August	Capture by the Dutch. Transfer to Hamburg ship.
23 August	A day's sail from Cape St Vincent, the Hamburghers turn north.
26 August	A day's sail from Plymouth, they turn south.
3 September	At Cape St Vincent. Capture by pirates.
3–10 September	At the mouth of the Straits of Gibraltar.
11 September	Arrival at Salé.
13 October	Departure from Salé.
14–18 October	At Mamora.
22–26 October	Off Larache.
28 October –	
3 November	At Tangier.
4 November	Arrival at Gibraltar.
4–14 November	Gibraltar – Medina Sidonia – Puerto Real – Cadiz – Sanlúcar – Seville.
14 November	Arrival at Seville.

Location of main sites named in text

A RELATION OF THE JOURNEY OF 12 STUDENTS FROM THE ENGLISH COLLEDGE AT ST OMERS IN ARTOIS, TO THE ENGLISH COLLEDGE OF SEVILL IN SPAINE ANO DNI 1622, STYLO NOVO.

Upon the 7th day of August in the yeare of our Lord 1622 wee departed from St Omers towards Callies in France[1], full of content & jollitie as well as for haveing happilie ended our lower studies of humanitie as also & especiallie for that wee were thought worthy to be preferr'd to those studies which must make us fit instruments to labour in the harvest of our English Mission, with hopes one day [*there either*][2] gloriouslie to shed our bloud for our sweete Saviours sake or at leastwise so to imploy our labours there that by meanes of us manie wandering soules mighte be brought back to the flock and fould of the true sheepheard, Jesus Christe.

With this uniforme intension wee happilie arrived the same day at Callies, where wee remain'd the three dayes following in dayly feasting and merriments, now with our Captaine and shipmen, now amongst our selves, by these externall offices of love the faster to linck our affection to each other, for avoyding the inconvenience of future dissention, which is sometimes wont to fall out amongst travellers of divers cuntries and dispositions.

Heere wee furnished our selves with varietie of provision to be sent on shipboard for the preventing of all future wants, for besides the ordinarie provision of dyet which our Captain by agreement was to provide us, wee layd in mutton pies, turkey pies, live turkeys, capons, pullets, &c, with manchets, wines, strong waters, preserves, conserves, candies, and many comfortable spices for makeing brothes & sawces.[3]

Being thus furnished of all necessaries for a three weeks journey by

---

[1] Calais became the main sea outlet for the Spanish Netherlands in April 1621, when Dunkirk and the other Flemish ports were blockaded by the Dutch. Hostilities between Spain and the United Provinces resumed that year. See Israel, 86.

[2] Two words are illegible in the MS where the leaf has split.

[3] Manchets = fine wheaten loaves. Preserves, conserves and candies are distinguishable as crystallised fruits, jams and crystallised sugar.

water, uppon the eleventh day in the morneing wee went all aboard,[4] where because some parte of our fraighte was wanting, wee remain'd in that port all that day and the next, untill towards evening [p.2] when wee weighed [anchor] and with a prosperous gale set to sea, being six ships in companie, all French but our owne, which was the vice Admirall of the association, a Dunkerker, under the King of France his culloures, conducted and commanded by Captaine John Collatt[5] of Dunkerk who was also owner of the same, a strong built ship of 200 tunn, haveing in her 22 peece of ordinance, six murderers,[6] muskets, pistoles, pikes, swordes, according to the number of our men, also 2 trumpeters, being balased with butter, cheese and wheate, greate comodities in Spaine.[7]

In this good fellowship and appointment of all necessaries for peace or war wee sayled eight daies continuallie, nothing occurring in this time save onlie wee received two more ships into our companie, where of one was a French mans, a little ship of lighte sayle without any greate Ordinance for defence, the other an Almaine[8] Hamburgher subject to the Emperour, of whome I shall have occasion to speake more largelie hereafter. All these eight daies weë had a prosperous navigation, the winde & weather attending so favourablie upon us as if wee could have chosen our season we could not have had it more seasonablie.

Whilst our ship furrowed on thus prosperouslie, wee passed our time in all sports, pastimes & ule games[9] which the wits of our shipmen imagine and the compass of a shipp would permit, sometimes againe feedeing our curious eyes with the variety of novelties which those vast

---

[4] 'Inbarked in a shippe belonging to Dunkerke which was then newly loaded for St Lucas in Spaine, having taken a false certification from the Governor of Callis that the ship and goods belonged thereunto' (Wadsworth, 33). The Dutch had imposed punitive tariffs on Flemish goods.

[5] sc. Jean Colaert. For his later career, culminating in his appointment as Admiral of Spain's Armada of Flanders in 1635, see Hambye, 3–11; Stradling, 86–8; Israel, 264. Wadsworth calls him Jaques Banburge, which was in fact the name of the French admiral of the convoy (see below, p.219). The Jesuit Province of Flanders, to which St Omers belonged, had a close connection with Dunkirk and in 1624 set up a 'naval mission' there to provide chaplains for its fleet. Seven Jesuits from this mission accompanied Colaert's victorious expedition against the Dutch in October 1624, and the English Jesuit Peter Stanihurst served as chaplain on Colaert's flagship in 1626–7. Colaert was later to declare: 'Je préfère partir en mer au plus fort de danger mais accompagné d'un jésuite, que sortir du port sans lui bien qu'avec la certitude d'une navigation heureuse' (Hambye, 3–11, 121–2).

[6] = small cannon of brass or iron.

[7] According to Wadsworth (p.33) the ship was of 100 tons, with a crew of forty sailors, a surgeon and two trumpeters.

[8] = German.

[9] = Yule, or Christmas, games.

waters did object unto us, amongst which it was no small content to
see the whale fish like a little iland play above the water, spouting a
shower out of the top of his heade into the ayre eight or ten fadom
highe. Amidst all this jollitie and content being now over against the
promentorie called Finis terrae, upon the [p.3] coaste of Galicia, on
the twentieth day about sunset wee could from the topp of our mast
discover a single lone shipp a far of, whereof some began to prognosticate it was a Hollander, others prayd God this greate mirth did
not presage some greate alteration. Thus, the sun being set and day
shut upp, wee haveing all well supp'd betooke us to our rest.

[A battle off Finisterre]

The next morning before wee could see the sunn, wee espied the
ship againe, which wee had seen over nighte, now not farr of us,
whence wee could manefestlie discover that it was a Holland man of
warr. Here needed no spurrs to hasten everie man to his charge, some
to setting out the ordinance, others to scower up the muskets and
calivers,[10] some to loade the murderers with broken yron, crooked
nailes, small flints and all other unmercifull stuffe that the wit of an
enemie could imagin, others to lay traines & boxes of powder and
stones to blow up the enemie with all if neede required, some to
naileing downe the decks, others to crossing the hatches with cabells,
8 or 10 inches platted in forme of a net to hinder him from boarding
us, others in fine building tents and cabbins for the musketeeres to
stand in above the hatches. We 12 only unexpert in that kinde of
warfare betooke ourselves to our prayers, not out of any feare wee yet
conceived, but that wee mighte have good successe to take this proude
encounterer that durst venture upon 8 ships.[11]

Scarse was halfe an houre passed when all things being in good
order on ship boarde our 8 ships had set themselves into the forme of
a half moone to receive their enemie in the midst, intending to give
him there a warme entertainement, whereof our ship and the Admirall
as being sharpest set for battaile made the 2 hornes.

It was now about seaven of the clock in the morning when this
Hollander[12] undantedlie sayl'd up to us and, as wee desired, enter'd
into our half moone where, our Admirall haveing first saluted him with
a single bullet, wee lost no time but takeing our warn word [p.4] from
this discharge laid on thick and threefould with yrone balles, meaning

---

[10] = light muskets.

[11] 'The Vice-Admiral, seeing how the case stood, said unto us 12 that wee were now
to die with honour or survive with infamy; and because we were young and unexpert in
sea fight, to encourage us the better made us to drinke each one of us a good draught
of *Aqua vitae* with gunpowder' (Wadsworth, 35).

[12] According to Wadsworth this vessel was of some 200 tons, with a crew of 150.

to make *concavum lunae* too hot an abideing place for him, which he perceiveing, and findeing that all the heat of the combate came from the left horne, which wee sharpened, he buckled up to us close and (O misfortune!) at his third charge at us he clincht our sterne so fast on the one side with a chained bullet that from that time forward wee could never more turn our ship, so that here the enemie got a maine advantage against us that he had his whole ship at command, now turning the one side, then the other, discharging his broad side at his pleasure. Wee could onlie flie from him with our sterne towards him as he persecuted us, whence wee had the use but of 2 peeces of ordinance which lay in the pupp of the shipp. Yet this disadvantage tooke not away our currage but rather (findeing our selves by so much weakened) struck a deep impression into us of our future danger which hitherto wee had not apprehended, and thence also followed a more eager resolution of our owne defence, and what wee wanted in the number of our ordinance was supplied with the dilligent and heedfull use of those 2 wee could make use of, so that wee gave blowe for blowe with him. He batter'd and tore our shipp, wee rewarded him in as faire a stamp; he cut our tacklings, rent our sayles, and wee restored againe as bountifullie what wee had received. He slew our barber surgeon,[13] wee his lieuetenant, and in fine wee put him so to it that he had spent almost all his shott & powder (for when he tooke us he swore he had but one more shott remaineing), and wee able to hold out fighte yet 3 times so long had not other disadvantages (as now I said) cut us short.

Amidst all this smoake, fire, noyse of gunns, shouting & calling to & fro, clattering of ships sides and the like, it being now about one of the clock in the afternoone, our [p.5] master gunner with a hastened voice came runing up to our Captaine, who was neither careles nor idle all this while. 'Yield, Master,' quoth he, 'for the passion of God, yield! The gun roome is beaten all open to the ayre; they levill their ordinance at the sighte of our bodies, moreover our 2 peeces of ordinance are so fyerie hot with the often discharging that there is danger least they flie to peeces in our faces or set fier on your ship.' The undaunted courage of our valiant Captaine waxing not pale at these words of his chief gunner, in whose skill and valloure he had reposed his chiefest confidence, returned him an answer in this disdaineing manner:

'And thou in whome my greatest hopes did stand,
Thou with thy often sworne fidelitie!
Thou which hast allwaies brag'd in my comand

---

[13] 'The chirurgion, saying these words, *Si Deus nobiscum, quis contra nos?* was slaine on a sudden with a common bullet, and having one hand on my shoulder pulled mee downe along with him, his blood streaming out upon me' (Wadsworth, 36).

> To spend thy life, thy goods, thy libertie!
> Go hollow harted coward yield thyselfe,
> Go periured friend call in the enemie,
> Betray thy Masters life, his ship, his wealthe;
> When thou art gone Ile win the day or die.'

Scarce had our Captain ended but our stout hearted gunner, bristleing like a lion or strucken or exasperated by his keeper, or like some noble or generous hart that had received the greatest wrong from his dearest friend or where least expected, made him this replie full of noble but desperate courage:

> 'No coward I, no faithless perjur'd friend:
> Love, linck'd with oathes, hath sway'd to wish your good.
> If you but speake, my life, and limbs Ile spend
> And bathe your decks in never daunted bloud.
> Ile go, I scorne the name of coward, I,
> Ile burn i'th' shipp, and sink i'th' brinie maine,
> Ile lay my naked breast to th' enemie,
> Ile rather die than beare a tainted name.'

With that he rann desperatelie back to the gunnroome with a resolution to winn the day or make himself within few houres a prey for the [p.6] fishes. Here began a second peale of 2 peece of ordinance against 10 of the enemie; of 20 marriners against 30 ould train'd soldiers upon a heavie laden marchants ship, and that craz'd[14] with blowes, against a lighte shipp for warr, which continued above two howres.

  In which meane while our Captaine according to his generall care came into the cabbin which was at the hinde deck directlie over the lower gunn roome, whereat the enemie had all this while discharged and where wee 12 were at our prayers for our safetie with more than ordinarie devotion: and in this our prayers were heard that wee had all of us hitherto (I may say) miraculouslie escaped death and all manner of hurt, all the end of the cabbin being beaten open to the ayre and wee discovered to the levell of the enemie. Yea, the yron balles and musket bulletts then verie often passe through the midst of us, breaking and taking away evrie nerest thing, yea some of our hats from our heades, yet not tuching any part of our bodies, and for my parte I had one fell in my lapp where I sate which burnt my hand when I tooke it up, but for further hurt I found none. The Captain (as I was saying) came into the cabbin to see how his English youthes fared all this while, where when he sawe us all alive and sound, in admiration he blessed himselfe and praised Gods providence over us,

---

[14] = broken.

deemeing it a thing morrallie impossible that wee should all of us, all this while, have escaped death and woundes in that most dangerous place of all the ship. Then he advised us by all meanes to remove our selves into the bodie of the ship, where there was lesse danger: which that it might be donne, not being perceived by the enemie, he with his hand held up a broaken dore betwixt us & them which had given entrance into the little gallerie without the hinde deck but now was beaten downe, which the enemie perceiveing discharged at him a single bullet of 4 pound weighte of yron, which glaunceing from a post about a foote from him hit such a thump upon the small ribbs of his left side that it tooke away with it all that side of his wastcoate and turned him over and over upon the floore. Wee that were present with all speede catched him up in [p.7] our armes, searched his side, but found neither wound nor bone broaken nor life in his bodie, wherefore wee hasted to our aqua vitae bottels and powred a prettie quantitie into his mouth wherewith he by & by came to himselfe againe. Wee asked him how he felt himselfe, he answered, 'No hurt, no hurt' (though wee afterward understood he was sorelie bruised). Thus he went forth of the cabbin, and the most part of us along with him. Peter Middleton,[15] James Wadsworth and myself remaineing behinde, whereas Wadworth crept under a good fetherbed, we two cast our selves flat on the ground. And of this I remained an eye witnes that no sooner was our captaine with our companie gone forth but a chain'd bullet came sweepeing over the forme whereon six of them had sitten. Thence it penetrated to the midst of the ship, where it cut downe the staires whereby wee ascended to the hatches, neither was there anything could stop it till it entered 5 or 6 inches deepe into our maine mast.

The deliverance of those six from this bullet was a manefest and speciall favoure from Almightie God, for if they [had] sitten still there, but whilst one mighte have counted fortie they had been all cut of by the midst, which bredd in us greate cherefulnes and confidence in the most Blessed Virgins favoure towards us, to whome wee had all this while with our best devotions been commending ourselves, saying her office, beades, littanies, but above all wee often repeated with more tender feeling her proper hymne *Ave maris stella*.

Our Captaine, findeing his ship sorelie batter'd and his master gunner with some of his most faithful servants allmost spent with laboures, went above hatches to see what the Admirall and the rest of the association did all this while, for indeed playing both Captaines and soldiers parte he had hitherto been so intent in his owne charge that he had taken no heed how his companie behaved themselves, but when he came above and found they were all fled from him and gonne

[15] See CRS 73 (1992), 84.

almost all out of sighte, he [p.8] broake forth into most passionate words against the perfidious dealings of the French and especially of Jaquez Bamberge his Admirall, as also in indignation against inforced submission to the base & treacherous Hollander, which now he is constrained toe, vowing if after this combate life and limbes were spar'd him, he would turne the remainder of his state into a ship of war and righte his disgrace & wrongs, which he afterwards performed, and became himselfe a Captaine of the same, and before his deathe was for his valloure made Admirall of the Dunkirk navie;[16] but our pilote who was an ancient grave well tempered man and who by long experience had learn'd to governe himselfe by reason, without passion as well in adversitie as in prosperitie, gave advice in this distresse to lay passion aside and, in expectation of better fortunes hereafter, for the present save his owne and his friends lives by submitting himselfe and his to the enemie rather than prolong delayes till wee were surprized by constraint or swallowed up in the merciles waters. Who at length giveing place to necessitie, went above hatches and with hatt in hand craved quarter, for our topsaile which is wont to be striken was allreadie strucken downe before wee intended it. It appear'd Gods speciall motion that we yielded at this instant, for (as after wee understood) the enemies next shott had beene wilde fire to have burned us in despaire of takeing us.

[The Dutch Captain]

This signe being therefore given with a hatt, the Hollander sends his cockboate with halfe a dozen hongrie weatherbeaten ragamuffins to fetch our Captaine prisoner abord theire ship, then he sends a trumpetter with halfe a score of his prime men to take possession, lastlie the Captaine came himselfe aboard us. Here it was worth observing how everie man now free from danger of bullets were attentive to what concern'd his own perticuler, everie man in a trice being in cuerpo,[17] or at leastwise [p.9] in his shirt, for it was our Captaines advice that he which had on his worst should now put on his best apparrell, and he that hitherto had but one shirt should now put on two, and some failed not to put on three or foure, for whatsoever was not found about us would infalliblie be taken from us. Those that [had] money or such like portable commodities in theire chests now put them in theire pockets, and those that had none had the lesse to care for.

By that time everie man had dress'd him againe, our new masters were come aborde us, where the first possession they tooke was the hatches, but the first plunder they made was in our ambrie;[18] which

---

[16] In 1635 (Stradling, pp.86–8).
[17] = in undress (*OED* 1625).
[18] = pantry.

they set upon with such violence, not of cannon or musket shott but of sharpe teethe and stomaks, like some hongrie hounds that haveing all day had in pursute the sillie hare, at length takeing her would spare neither head nor scut[19] nor stand to examine what was the best parte, but everie one catching where he first may devour both flesh and bones, intralls & skin & all; so these tame cormerants spare neither bacon, beef, mutton, puddings, souce,[20] pies, hens, capons, turkies, butter, nor cheese: all goes down with a little ocean of our fatt Duch beares,[21] whence wee came to understand that they had desperatelie ventured upon us, and fought it out thus resolutelie more for meate and drink then for enmitie or covetousnes of greater bootie, haveing beene sustain'd six weekes with a verie small daylie allowance of bread & water, and had they mised of us at this time they had all likelie perrished by famine.

This Holland Captaine was called Jacob May, a proper portlie man of person but of a sterne countenance and of a swarthie complexion of about fiftie yeares of age, his gilt sword hanging in a taffatie scarf sutable to his coloures streamed with blew and orange tawnie, the rest of his apparrell such as might befit a gentle Dutch skipper; who haveing likewise revived his spirits and warm'd his blood from the comfort of our Cornucopia began his revells, or rather his baccanalia, first with most violent rayleing words against those that had thus insolentlie withstood an officer of the high & mightie states, that they had battered his ship, cutt his tacklings, torne his sails, that they were all unworthie of mercie, deserving no better than to be cast into the sea, then draweing his sworde and brandishing it [p.10] a while about his head he let flie with such furie upon our master-guner with the back of it, for haveing beene a cheef agent in all this mischeef but especiallie for haveing killed his lieuetenant, who was most deare unto him, and his cosen german, that wee verilie thought he would have kill'd him with dry blowes,[22] & surelie he so bruised him about the back and shoulders that he made him go double or creepe on all-foure.

Will you now heare how wee twelve English youthes fared all this tragick sceane? Marrie for our fare this day it was temperate, for as well wee as our fellow-Dunkerkers dined with Duke Humphrie,[23] for the rest wee were like a housefull of young children, where when the angrie mother falls to whipping one or two, all the rest though guiltlesse stand trembling with teares in their eyes, each one expecting his turne

---

[19] = tail.
[20] = pickle.
[21] = full-bodied Dutch ales.
[22] = blows that do not draw blood.
[23] = went without a meal.

to come next; thus wee. But Almightie God [who] brought his [*chosen*][24] people out of the captivitie of Egipt through manie troubles by a fortie yeares journey which mighte have beene dispatcht in a month without anie difficulty or resistances, it seemes neither intended our deathes nor our returne as prisoners towards England, which wee then much feared, nor to hinder our intended course, but to teache us, as them, *qui clamaverunt ad Dominum cum tribularentur*, 'who cryed to our Lord when they were afflicted,'[25] in our more tender yeares to know him better, more confidentlie to trust in him, more zealous to call upon him, and to learne to suffer something for his sake before wee should be admitted to our ayme & desired happines. He moved the hearte of this Hollander in the heighth of his furie to shew favoure and curtesie towards us.

Wherefore calling us together he demaunded of us who wee were and whence wee came and whither wee intended. Wee, as fearfull as doubtfull of his intentions, answered (though he knew well before by private information of some of our shipmen) that wee were Englishmen, and wee had landed in the Lowe Cuntries with intention to travaile into Spaine for our better education. Then he in the [p.11] best English he was able, 'English men, be not afraid. By Godt, I wat well enough who yee been and dat yea come from Sint Omers, and dat yea go to Sevill, dare to studie, and dough yea gae to Spaine yea shall ha none hurt vrome me, vor I love Englishmen well, but I hate de Spaniard, and ben altimes a profest enemie to them, vor de Inquisite in Spaine brant my grote vader for one heretick, my vader was hangt dare, and I myself ha ben dare eleven times in de prison. But vor dat yea ben English men I shall put u in the virst shipp that I shall vinde bond for Spaine, and dare vore I ha geaven order dat my tacklings and sayles be in hast repaired to overtake another shipp of uwer companie, dat ben vled, yea sall also have all uwer good way with [you], and if my souldiers ha taken any ding vrom you, let me wat it and day sall it all restore againe.'

This speech, though homelie and scarce well understood by us all, revived us, and wee all most submissivelie gave him heartie thanks. And Champian, who spake the Dutch language well, made an acknowledgment in the name of us all, how much wee were obliged unto him, and that if ever it should ly in our powers to do him any kinde office wee would not prove ungratefull, and for a remembrance of the same wee made him a present of English knives, gloves, and toothpicks, such small commodities as for our own use wee had brought aboard, which were kindelie accepted of by him. In those and such like passages the afternoone was spent: and it was about eighte of the

[24] Lacuna of one word in MS.
[25] Psalm 106.6.

clock at nighte when by the twylighte wee could discern our Holland
conqueror returning from the pursuite of our flying companions, with
on of them brought back in his companie, which was an Hamburgher,
a ship of an hundred tunne, of verie slow sayle and of no defence at
all, haveing neither ordinance nor muskets nor any other weapon for
offence or defence; against this ship the Hollander had no quarrell,
because a newtrall to the Holland state, because she had not offended
by violent resistance, and because she transported to Spaine such as
was [p.12] thought onlie lawful wares, viz. a comoditie of deale boards.
This ship as they made shew was brought back for no other end then
to set us forward in our journey, although if they could have laid hould
on any other against whome they could have taken any advantage,
wee doubted not but wee should have beene sooner carried back to
Holland then furthered in our journey to Spaine, but in fine wee had
warneing to provide ourselves and to go aboard this Hamburgher;
when least wee mighte seem troublesome or give offence by acceptance
of theire kinde offer in taking away with us our bagg and baggage,
which was to be transported by them and in theire boate, of whose
true love to us wee had no greate reason to be verie confident, wee
resolved (notwithstanding the Captaines faire offer) to leave our trunks
behinde us and all but what wee could well carrie about us, takeing it
(for our present condition) for a sufficient favour that with our onlie
persons wee mighte be set forward, and accordinglie takeing our leave &
giveing manie thanks to the Captaine for the favour donne us, wee
were disimbarqued and in the cockboate conveyed by half a dozen of
his men to our new master Hamburgher who lay about a mile distant
from us.

[*The Hamburg Anabaptists*]

It being now about nine of the clocke at nighte and dark, when
neither eyes could see nor eares could heare our outcryes for iustice,
and wee in the midway betwixt the two shipps, those merciles ferrimen,
more cruell and inhumane than ever old Charon was, laying aside
theire owers, tooke everie one hould of his next neighboure, bidding
us deliver our purses or presentlie to be turn'd over into the sea, where
it should never be knowne what was come of us. Wee at first made
some small resistance, where by our striveing one of the robbers was
against our wills turn'd out of the boat; but wee more charie of their
lives than of our owne purses catcht him by the heeles and pulled him
up againe, but his thirst after our moneys never a whit [p.13] quenched
with the salt waters he went on with his companions to rifle us. Though
wee were twelve to six of them, yet a distrust in our own dexteritie in
so narrow a compasse and in a tottering boate amidst the mercilesse
waters, with the observation of theire desperate resolution, perswaded

us rather to make no greate resistance then to hazard any one of our lives.

Amongst these knaves was an English man, who formerlie for cuntrie sake had profered us great curtesies and amongst others had at our departure stolen us a faire Holland cheese out of our former shipp into this boate. To this friend wee appeale for iustice and his assistance, but wee found his love more to our money then to us; who alleaged that he was but one against so manie, and what good could he do us? But he sufficientlie discovered his false hearte to us in that he guided the boate whilst his companions rifled us, like another Saule, who houlding the garments of those that stoned St Stephen was judged to have stoned them with the hands of all those cruell murtherers: so this our kinde cuntrieman robb'd us with all these false caytifs hands and no question shared also with them in the bootie. Beside private moneys in no small summe they layd hold on our comen purse kept by Thomas Coniers, the properest man of our companie, with a round summe of gold in it. Thus haveing lightened our carriage not onlie of money but of all other things that they found in our pockets, they set us on shipp board upon our new master Hamburgher.

Those Hamburghers were as unfit men to governe a ship as ever set to sea, being mere animals in their education, downe righte dunces in their capacitie and nastie clowns to the eye, wanting both forecast to prevent inconveniences and wit to make the best use of adversitie. Their religion (if any they had) was Anabaptisticall, houlding manie strainge extravagant opinions. Amongst others this was one, that no Christian ought ever to fighte in his owne defence, though against Turks, and this was the cause why they were [p.14] unprovided of all kinde of weapons or defence for their ship or themselves.[26]

Now with these doults begins our tragedie, for no sooner were wee come aboarde them but they, flocking all about us, whineing and ringing theire hands, made mournfull complaints of want of provision for themselves, but now that wee were there also put upon them they were all likelie to perish for want of foode: that the Hollander had drunk up all theire beere and plundered them of a barrell of herrings, which was the principall of theire foode. Wee shewed to take greate compassion of theire wants, yet since it was our lott to be put upon them wee intreated theire patience, promiseing they should finde us verie reasonable & faire conditioned sojourners, intreating no more then an abideing place and so much of their coursest provision as would preserve life in our bodies till wee might be set on Spanish land,

---

[26] In view of their pacifism and place of origin, these are likely to have been Mennonites. The founder of the sect, Menno Simons (1496–1561), settled at Oldesloe, near Hamburg.

beside that they should be most liberallie paide for all when wee should
come to our journeys end. This our modestie somewhat alay'd theire
distemper and a little woone theire affections to us, wherefore observeing
that wee had a cheese of our owne given us, as I said before, they gave
us to it a little course bread and a canne of water. With this wee sat
us downe to supper, giveing God as heartie thanks for this as ever wee
had done for our aboundance aboard the Dunkirker. Our lodgeing this
nighte was in the open ayre above hatches, though afterwards wee had
the cabbin under the hind deck assigned us for our quarter where,
having given Almightie God with his Blessed Mother our holie saints
and angels thanks for the manie & singuler benefits received that day,
wee betooke our selves to our rest upon the naked hard bordes. Our
covering was Gods holie protection.

All that nighte and the next day wee furrowed on verie prosperouslie,
when about noone, being now a daies sayle from the Cape of St
Vincent, which was the first point of Spaine that wee were to steere
upon, wee discovered a ship steereing her course [p.15] from the coaste
of Spaine directlie upon us and by reason of her contrarie course
presentlie encounterd us. This was also an Hollander, as at first sighte
we discovered by her coloures, a lighte ship of a hunderd tunn, with
six peeces of ordinance standing forth at theire loopeholes,[27] one of
which he discharged over us as a warneing to strike sayle, which being
instantlie done he came in with some of his men aboard us, but finding
naught but passengers & lawfull wares, and that wee had beene all
readie rifled by a Statesman,[28] used no violence but seemed rather to
have great compassion upon us for the eminent danger wee were in,
affirming that that verie morneing he had beene verie hard persecuted
by seaven Turkish pirates, and had verie narrowlie escaped them, who
were not farr out of sighte, towards the Cape of St Vincent. If therefore
wee would follow him, he would safelie conduct us out of danger. Wee
beleeved him, and like geese went along with the fox for shelter, or as
sillie sheepe followed the butcher to the slaughter, for this Hollander
was not a Statesman but a pyrate roveing about for his owne private
lucre, whose intentions (as afterwards wee understood) were either to
carrie us all to Turkey, or at his best oppertunity to cast us all over
board into the sea and make his prey of our ship and marchandise.

But Allmightie God, whose singuler Providence was manifestlie seene
over us in all wee suffered, would not that wee should perrish by the
hand of this pirate, for wee had not followed him back towards the
Irish sease past three or four houres when by the riseing of a most
horrible storme, or rather by the fatherlie providence of Allmightie

[27] = portholes (*OED* 1627).
[28] = a ship of the United Dutch Provinces.

God over us, wee were parted from him and quite lost him, as wee also tooke our selves for lost. For all this long, dark, fierce and horrid nighte the waves did swell and insult upon us with such a continuall batterie of windes and rayne that our Palinurus pilote, unable to deale anie longer with such boysterous encounters, bound his sterne with ropes to the peace, the marriners let fall the sayles, the Master nail'd down his decks to keepe forth the overflowing waves which [p.16] eftsoones dashed over us with such furie that wee seemed quite overwhelm'd. Yet the strength of the ship not any way crazed, and the close covering brought it up againe, and manie times that little sayle that was left us in ouer head to some though an uneven course who by the wilde and vehement rage of some shorkes drawne under the waters and oftentimes little wanted of turning our keele[29] upside downe. Wee in the cabbin were tossed like balls from side to side with reciprocall and perpetuall knocks and rebounds, rowleing with tables, stooles, pots and all that was nere us in a confused manner from side to side, sometimes sorelie bruising our heads and bodies, and constantlie expecting no other then certein death, takeing everie wave that rushed upon us for the fatal stroke. Our best prayers and *Comendatio animae* were by jaculatories,[30] no place nor rest being afforded for one *Pater Noster*, and which afflicted us worse was that now at our departure to an other world our vitall spiritts were dull'd, partlie by want of sleepe, which had now fail'd us allmost two whole nights, and partlie by the faintnes of our bodies by defect of necessarie foode, haveing fedd but verie sparinglie the two last daies past, and partlie also because our bodies were wearied and toyled out with the unquiet nighte and continuall frights of water dashing in at the windowes of our lodgeing, which were beaten downe with a constant assault of the battering surges. Thus passing over this tedious and comfortlesse nighte, the long-desired morning gave a little refreshment to our languishing sences but no releasement to our dangers. Here by day lighte you mighte have seene us droopeing like so manie drowned mice, most of us wet to the skinn from top to toe without ever a rag to shift withall, so ill at ease in our heades, others in theire stomaks, others all over, everie one beareing a burthen of his owne not without some sence and feeleing also of his neighboures, and therefore they would be ever and anon casting forth such sentences as might any waies alleviate theire sufferings or encourage on another to the best use of them as, *Dabit Deus his quoque finem, Olim haec meminisse iuvabit, Quae nocent, docent, Non sunt condignae*

---

[29] MS: 'koole'. The text of this sentence is evidently corrupt, and difficult to reconstruct. 'Shorkes' may be a misreading of 'strokes'.

[30] = short prayers 'darted' up to God (*OED* 1624).

passiones hujus temporis ad [p.17] *futuram gloriam*[31] and such like others, according to everie ones present disposition and inward feeling.

Now our fare grew everie meale worse then other, for haveing set up our cheese (which was the onlie food wee had of our owne) in our mariners custodie, wee saw no more of it, but made our dinner this day with some few fragments of gnawne beef bones, never examineing what slovins teeth had had that happines to rake them first, nor whether his hands had been washed since the new yeare that had had the handleing them – so farr is squemishnes bannished from true honger – and of this good chere, alas, wee had but verie short commens. Our water also in the midst of the oceans was given us by stint. If wee would refresh ourselves with the consideration of Gods wonders, as sometimes wee had done, nothing was now to be heard but a confused roareing of windes and waves, nothing to be seene above us but racking clouds, nothing about us but mountaines & precipices of threatning waters, nothing under us but a tottering heavie vessell without either sayle or guide, and oftentimes this under the waves too; insomuch that when anie thing was to be visitted, repaired or fetched in, no man durst venture himself upon the hatches that did not first ty a rope about his middle made fast to the shipp, for otherwise he would be infallibly turn'd overboard with the furie of the windes or violence of some sturdie billowes. In this woefull plighte, time that devoures all things had consumd this nighte & day, to which a second nighte succeeded in no respect more favourable to us then this, and to this a third day. All this while that little way wee made was towards Ireland or England, we know not well whether, in pursute of our pyrate guide whome by Gods singuler providence, as after appear'd, wee had lost.

[*Encounter with an English ship*]

This morning about nine or tenn of the clock wee discover'd a ship comeing from the coaste of Spaine, now rideing up the highe mounteins of waters, or rather, as it seemed to our watery eyes, upon the cloudes, then againe falling into abbisses of vallies, whome shee was not [p.18] seen by us againe of almost a quarter of an houre, thus cutting forward her uneven course by ascents and descents till at length she overtook us. This sight a little cheered us up, when we observed there were yet some people floating above the waves besides ourselves, conceiveing hence that there were some hopes remaineing of escapeing death at this time as well for us as our neighboures. This was an English ship, as his red crosse upon his sprete[32] made shewe, but better able to beare of & encounter the billowes than wee were by reason of his lighter

---

[31] Vergil, *Aeneid*, 1.199, 1.203; Anon; *Romans* 8.18.
[32] = sprit.

burthen as especiallie by the industrie, skill and courage of her pilote
and marriners. To this English man wee made signes with hats in
handes to drawe nere us, for now all voyces were drowned betwixt
winde and water, who verie curteouslie ventured himself within our
ships length of us, for nerer it was not safe, least by force of some wave
the ships mighte on rush against the other.

Here some of our companie, lesse confident in the providence of
Allmighty God over us, or too fearfull of apprehending death by famine
if not by water, sollicitted this our cuntriman with more importunitie
than I am able to expresse to receive them into his shipp and set them
in a parte of England, and he should be rewarded according to his
desire, for here wee wanted necessarie foode and our ship being of
verie slowe saile and without any defence was subject to the pillageing
of everie enemie. His answer was that he should be glad to doe his
cuntrimen any good office lay in his power, but for the present he
could not do what they requested, for it was impossible to set his
cockboate upon the roughe waves without iminent danger both of
men & boate, and to come so nere us that wee might leape from ship
to ship was neither safe for himself nor us, least he mighte venture the
splitting of both ships, desired us therefore to pardon him, and so bade
us adieu.

Our mariners, amonst other things, had demanded of these English
men what danger of pyrates there was towards the Cape of [p.19] St
Vincent, and whether they had not heard of seaven Turkish pyrates
that rode thereabouts. He answered that the coast was clere, and if
wee had two daies since come that waies wee mighte have had a most
safe convoye to St Lucar, because seaven of the King of Spaines
galloons had been that way to scowre the coaste. Whence wee began
to understand the fraude of our Holland guide, perceiveing he had
brought us from the safeguard of the Spaniards to wee know not what
danger. This newes put divers doubts into our marriners heades,
whether it were better now againe to turne back againe for Spaine, or
to hould on theire course for England. Theire certificate and letters of
ingrosment from the city of Hamburgh were for Spaine, as also the
hopes of greater gaines by theire marchandise. On the other side, the
safetie of the way towards England, with the more speedie returne to
theire cuntrie and the indifferencie of theire commodities they carried,
invited them to steere forwards. It is not unlikelie they also consulted
whether anie benefit mighte be made by presenting us twelve to the
Counsell in England, but of this wee could not be certeine. Yet wee
well perceived they neither loved our companie nor our religion.

Whilest these things and manie others which wee were not privie to
were in agitation, the windes began to blowe more mildelie and cloudes
dispersed, the comfortable sunn appeared warme, and wee came

creeping forth of our holes to receive the comfort of Gods blessings. All our mouthes were so seasoned, or rather sweetened, with jaculatories that everie ones wordes sounded nothing but Gods praises & the magnifying & excelling his goodnes towards us. Our marriners, like weathercocks, not able to guide theire course by reason but following the motion of the windes, held on theire course towards England all this day and the next, when being within a daies sail of Plimouth it came into theire shallowe braines that the exchange of bay salt[33] which they were to returne to theire masters, a greate comoditie in Almainie, was not to be had in England. This objection convinced [p.20] them quite, wherefore without more discanting the matter they returne the prou round and once againe for Spaine, after foure daies back for England. Which their inconstancie was a direct cour[s]e to clem[34] us to death, haveing so small store of provision in theire shipp, such was the weaknes and want of discretion in our Master and his mariners.

From this time forward our constant diet was bread (if it mighte deserve so good a name) made of beanes and barlie, which as wee could prudentlie conjecture could not be lesse then three or foure yeares ould, and had twice so manie times beene mouldie and rotten in mustie ould hoales, and as often baked or dried againe. It had in it more coloures than the raynebow: white, black, blew, yellow, greene, red, and some other medlies, yet by the often rebakeing made as hard as brick batts, that before wee could proportion or accommodate it to our mouthes it must be knockt in peeces with mallets and hatches, dulling, turning or nicking the edges of our best knives to cutt it. Yet would it have been tollerable mighte but water have been allowed to soake it in. Thus wee fed, our marriners haveing for the most parte better for themselves. This we were wont to lay to ayre halfe a day in the sunn and winde before wee eate it, such an unsavorie stench came from it.

Our drink was water, such as even now [I] abhor to describe, for besides that it was in a verie small alowance, viz. a quarte cann at a meale amongst twelve of us, a proportion fitter for so manie sparrowes then so manie parched emptie stomaks, it was so corrupted with keeping in uncleane vessels and stunck soe abhominablie that when wee supped of our pittance in a little wooden dish, which wee kept for that division, wee stopt our noses least by the offence of that sence wee might be at losse & turne it up againe. Yet this water was of such price with us that it was held no small stratagem to cheate the slovin Hans, our draw water, of a kann of it, and if wee [p.21] missed in such a project, manie times to our paine wee would be makeing tryall of salt

---

[33] = salt of Bayonne or Bourgneuf.
[34] = starve (northern dialect).

water, which both scortched our intralls & augmented our thirst. Otherwhiles we were wont to hang our handkerchiefs upon the tacklings to gather the dew of the nighte, which wee sucked to refresh our mouthes, or if anie drops of rayne had falne wee would lick them from the ropes. This was our constant fare for tenn dayes at least.

[Admiral Quast]

Upon the first of September, being now againe about a daies sayle from the Cape of St Vincent, wee were overtaken by a very statelie built ship of about 800 tunn, setting forth 50 brasse peeces of ordinance and haveing in her 80 men of service. This was the Admirall of the Holland navie, comanded by Captaine Quest,[35] a man in person and apparrell more like some rich nosed brewer in his red capp and wa[s]tecoate then an Admirall of the high & mightie States, as they terme themselves. This was a true Statesman, and therefore, findeing us friends and that wee conveyed lawfull wares, had nothing to say either to our men or ship. Yet some few questions he demaunded about our Dunkirker that was taken to Holland by Jacob May; how he was taken & what merchandize he carried, expecting it may be his share out of the prize. He had also notice given him of the other Hollander whome wee had lost in the storme, but he presentlie tould us that was no Statesman, but a pyrate, & therefore God had blessed us well from him, for doubtlesse if time & season would have permitted him, he had either sould us to the Turks or throwne us over board. Then he asked our Master what companie he had in his ship; to whome the steeresman in a jeering manner made answer that besides ten of themselves they had also twelve Apostles, travaileing to Spaine, there to studdie to convert England. Amongst others that attended upon this Hollander two were Englishmen, Londoners, which heareing of English men going to studie in Spaine thought they mighte do their King & cuntrie a greate [p.22] peece of service if they should make some strainge discoverie upon us. Wherefore in their red caps and blew wastcoates they sate downe & like Justices of the Peace they examined us about our native cuntries, our names, our parents, our intentions in going to Spaine, our education at St Omers and the like, & wee considering their commission were nothing short (for all our miserie) in returning them unhappie answers, and nothing being proved against us wee were quit, and with a prosperous gale upon the third day of the month,

[35] *sc.* Hillebrant Quast. At this time the Dutch fleet was concentrating on its blockade of the Flemish ports and rarely took the offensive against the Spanish, but in November 1622 (two months after this encounter) a squadron under Quast's command scoured the Portuguese coast for three weeks, captured two Brazil ships and then reconnoitred the Canaries (Israel, 115). In 1635 Quast suffered a heavy defeat in the North Sea at the hands of Jean Colaert (*ibid.*, 264). Wadsworth does not name him.

betimes in the morning, wee discovered the Spannish coaste and within 2 houres after came under the forte of the long desired Cape of St Vincent, where being now in safetie from enemies and stormes a sweete calme arrested us, as willing to refresh our wearied bodies and benumed spiritts. And I at the gratefull remembrance of these sweete solaces we tooke and delicious objects wee enjoyed, have more minde now to sit a while and sing them then goe forward in my tragicall narration.

The heavens this day were of a silver hiew
Not shadowed with the vayle of any cloude,
Brighte Phebus walk'd in fields of azure blew,
No duskie vapoure did his glorie shroude,
    No blemish did eclipse the glorious skie
    From setting forth heaven's all reviveing eye.

Noe murmuring winde did wave our loftie mast,
Our sayles and tacklings loos'd the wearied raigne,
The storme presageing Porpus took's repast
I'th' quiet bottome of a milkie maine
    And everie prettie fish did take delighte
    To see the quiet heavens shine so brighte.

The windie gods lay slumbering in theire caves,
The ayre was silent in his concave sphere
And Neptune with his trident curb'd his waves
For putting wearied wights to further feare.
    The churlish planets, seldom at accorde,
    Theire milde aspects this morning did afforde. [p.23]

Faire Ladie Flora, clad in robes of greene,
Like to her self the coast did richlie suite,
Within the lande beyonde the coaste were seene
Hesperian gardens hang'd with goulden fruite.
    The nerer rocks great heards of goates did shew,
    The richer plaines with wine and oyle did flowe.

As gaudie pedlers shew theire painted store,
First lookes to winn, from lookes to purchase gaine,
The cuntrie gods[36] did also deck this shore
With natures wealth, strong objects to detaine
    Our gazeing eyes at first, from eyes to dart
    Charmeing attractives to possesse our hearte.

Victorious Mars, delighted with this seate

[36] MS: 'goodes'.

Uppon a cliffe leaneing o'r Tethis[37] lapp,
Hath raised a fort, a fort of safe retreate
For friends, and this is call'd St Vincents Cape,
    St Vincents Cape long sought, at length attain'd,
    Terrour to foes, safe harboure to thy friend.

Being now no lesse wearie of the sea then wee were taken with the
safetie of the harboure & bewtie of the pleasant cuntrie, wee earnestlie
besought our Master skipper to set us on shore, laying open to him the
facilitie of doing it, our weariness of the sea, the want of provision and
the danger wee were in of Turks if wee but stirred from the safetie of
that forte. But his answer was that if the winde favoured wee should
to morrow altogether be at our journey's end, that [if] wee were in
want of foode and in danger of Turks & pirates, his wants were no
lesse and he and his servants danger was as greate, who were more
deare to him than wee, therefore wee should expect & share like
fortunes together. But wee, conceaveing his maine difficultie to be least
wee should slipp away without paying for our waftage,[38] consulted
together what course mighte be taken, and findeing that amongst us
all there was yet remaineing (after the Hollanders [p.24] pillageing) the
summ of £10 of conceal'd money, we agreed together those which had
it should be content to disburs it for the commen good and receive it
againe when wee should come to our journeys end. Wherefore, to winn
the Masters and stere mans good will to set us on shore, we offerd
them in hand £5, and £5 more when it should be demaunded by
either of them at our English colledge at Sevill, a farr greater proportion
then was due to them, all of us offering our oathes for the performance
thereof. This goulden allurement wonne theire good will: yet because
theire owne cockboate was little, they said they were not willing to
venture us in it but promisd to set us shortlie into a fishers boate which
roam'd there not far of them and would doubtlesse ere long come
towardes them. Wee long looked for the draweing near of this fisher
boate but at length, observeing that it rather declined further from us,
we (with that little ayre which now towards the evening began to rise)
removed from under the fort, partlie to gather winde to sayle away
that nighte but especiallie to speake with this fisherman.

[Capture by pirates]

And no sooner were wee out of the reache of the ordinance of the
forte but our fisher boate turnes with all speede upon us, and scarce
had wee begunn to rejoyce in his approach but wee discovered the half
moone on the top of his little mast and by and by heard such a frightfull

---

[37] MS: 'Tet his'. The sea goddess Tethys was the wife of Oceanus.
[38] = sea passage.

celeusma[39] & shouting to us in the Turkish language that it struck our hearts into our heeles. And now it was manefest our fishermen were Turks.[40]

At this newes the Master and mariners runne all into hoales, now againe woefullie whineing and wringing theire handes, yet no one able to advise or comfort another. And wee twelve, more daunted with theire outcries then with conceived danger from so small a vessell, shut ourselves up into the cabbin where, in the best manner our feares and the confused noyse of the Turks and our owne lamentations would permit, wee settled to our prayers. Meane while the Turks rounded us about divers times, often dischargeing their muskets at our sayles and tacklings, viewing a loofe of our strength and defence [p.25] and with perpetuall clamors frighteing and disanimateing us, yet daunted with the vastnes of the prize and with they knew not what concealed ambushments they durst not venture to abborde us.

William Appleby[41] and some others, observeing the smallnes of the enemys vessell[42] and conceiving that if wee but had courage it would be impossible for them to take us, demaunded of the Master what gunns or other weapons of defence he had in his ship. His answer, as also that of all the rest of them, was that if it were the Lords will they should be taken, what would weapons boote them? And if the Lord knew they should not be taken, then were they safe enough without weapons, for the Lord would be theire protector. But wee, never a whit satisfied with this answer, urged them whether they had any weapons or not, and wee according to our religion would undertake the defence of our ship. Whereupon they brought us up from the keele of the ship a little barrell of gunn powder and 2 new muskets that never had been used nor kept for use but for sale when they should come to their journeys end, which were so cankered with long lying in the moist keele that it was impossible to drawe forth theire rammers to charge them, wherefore, demaunding the masters help and he findeing them both in the same temper, without more words but in desperate passion threw both of them and the barrell of powder into the sea. Thus giveing our selves for lost we betooke us to our prayers in the best manner wee were able for the time, to prepare our selves for death. And the Turks, after an houres deliberation, discovering no armes neither for offence nor defence, ventured to come aborde us.

---

[39] = uproar. The *OED* cites a usage in 1680 to mean 'battle-cry', but Ducange (*Thesaurus Linguae Latinae*) quotes texts where it denotes a *clamor nauticus*.

[40] Both Atkins and Wadsworth often use this as a generic term to mean Muslims of whatever origin. (But cf. p.249, n.77).

[41] See CRS 73 (1992), 50. Appleby, at 31, was older than most of his companions.

[42] 'A gally of 18 oares on each side, having in him besides about 100 Moores, Moriscoes and other runnagates' (Wadsworth, 37).

You will partlie conceive the horroure and frighte wee were in at theire entrance to us if I make a short description of the persons and demeanour of these our new masters, who for the m[*ost parte*] were of strong and big limbes, swarthie of complexion, [*with heads and*] beardes close shaven except one little tuft on the [*top of the crown*]. Theire dublets were much after the shape of [...][43] [p.26] whence it was that theire neck, shoulders and breast were shamefullie naked, theire armes covered almost downe to theire elbows with a loose & wide sleeve of the finest white holland, the rest was naked to the hand. Since which time it hath often runne in my minde whether the unseemelie fashion of naked dressings amongst our vaine gentlewoemen of England came from the Turks to us, or from us to the Turks. But surelie, whencesoever it came, the devill was both the inventor of the fashion and the messenger that brought it to us. Theire breeches were as fine as theire sleeves and, as far as I could discern, were but the skirt of theire shirt shutt at the sides and sowed together betwixt their leggs, hanging loose and open at theire knees. Theire leggs were naked, yet they had for the most parte on their feete fine red Spanish lether pumps.

At theire boarding us, findeing no resistance and overjoyed with the vastnes of the prize, they skipt and daunced and clipt and hugg'd and kissed one another, as if they would have expressed some mimicall antick shewe. Some of us they first met withall they bound with cordes, but seeing no danger of resistance they spared that laboure in the rest & conveyed us twelve with foure of our Hamburghers into theire owne boate to be sent to Argeres.[44] The rest of our ship men were left in the ship with one halfe of the Turks, spedily to be convey'd to Salle. The reason of this devision was because at that time the kingdome of England had a truce with the Castle of Salle and consequentlie no subject of the King of England was saleable there, whereas at Argeres they were verie good chaffer.[45]

This towne of Argeres is famous for pyrates, lyeth on the Numidian coaste of the Mediterranean sea southward, whence it was of necessitie first to passe the straits of Cales [*opposite*] Gibraltar before wee could be brought theither. [...][46] castle of Salle belongeth to the pettie kingdom [p.27] of Morocco, and looketh westward towards the greate Ocean.

---

[43] The corner of the leaf has been torn. I have attempted a reconstruction of the text where possible.

[44] Algiers.

[45] On Salé, see p.204. In his *Discourse on Pirates* the ex-pirate Henry Mainwaring claimed to have made 'peace with Sallee' c.1612–14 (*Navy Records Society*, lv.10), but there is no other record of any such agreement. In December 1621 John Duppa concluded a treaty with the Mokaddem of Tetuan whereby the buying and selling of English slaves was forbidden there (*SIHM, Angleterre*, ii.521).

[46] The corner of the leaf has been torn.

But he that commands the power of the seas and sendeth forth windes from his treasurie guided our course according to his infinit goodnes, not according to the intentions of men, and sent us a southerne winde so contrarie to our Turks designes that it was impossible for them to pass the gulph of the strayts with us. Wee also pray'd for a spedie passage, but our prayers were not hear'd because wee knewe not what wee asked.

Heere in dailie expectation of a favourable gale wee lay at the straites mouth from the third of September, which was the day whereon wee were taken, until the tenthe of the same, dureing which time our lodgeing was but meetelie in the keele of the boate upon stones wherewith it was ballased, in so strait a compas by reason of the narrownes thereof that when wee slept it was necessarie to rest our heades and shoulders upon each others leggs, to the great unease both of one & other. Yet this inconvenience wee thought was well recompenced with the comfort of a fuller and more savorie diet, and with our fille of [...]⁴⁷ & water. Our table was the floore, but our tabell cloth was a beares raw hide with the hair on and the fleshie side upward, whereon wee laid out butter, our cheese, our boyled rise or wheate, and fish and bread in aboundance, where when wee had eaten sufficientlie, all the fragments of breade or whatsoever of our superfluitie was cast over into the sea, it being held amongst them a grevous contamination to eate what is left or handled by Christians. Thus so full, though course, was our diet that now it seemed wee were reallie not onlie in the servitude but even in the fleshpots of Egipt, where all the specious titles wee hear'd were 'Arriva, cane! Abaxo, cane!': 'Up, dog! Downe, doggs!' and for the greater contempt theire ordinarie tearme in speaking to us was 'Christian doggs', which in theire language sounds as contemptible as Mahomet or Turk with us. And it pleas'd God to give us that speciall grace to receive at [p.28] all times a singuler content & held it for a great happines to heare our selves thus reviled by the name of our master Christe, remembering his encouragement, 'Blessed are yee when men shall revile you and say all that naughte is against you for my sake'.⁴⁸ And tould somewhat of our miseries, our Hamburgher cooke was by name Court, turn'd informer against us, gave notice to the Turkes that wee had some of us monie about us, whereupon wee were rifled and not onlie lost the most of that little stock wee had but were discovered some of us to have more shirts on then one, which were also taken from us with all comodities whatsoever which were not necessarie for the covering our nakednes, as bands, handkercheivs, knives, bookes, beades, &c. And one unhappie roguish

---

⁴⁷ Lacuna of two words in the MS.
⁴⁸ *Matthew*, v.ii.

boy, a swabber amongst them called Mucho, whome wee were wont to call Cavalero Mucho to humour & please him, spared not to take away some of our hats, and others shoes, that now wee thought wee mighte begin to say of ourselves, *Nudi nudum Christum sequimur.*

[A 'Tragicall Passage']

Hitherto you have in these imperfect lines beheld the conspiracie of heavens, fire and waters against twelve poor youthes; the earth, when time shall serve, will not faile to play its parte against us also. You have also been spectators to the assaults of atheists, heretics & Turks. It onlie remaines that hell make up the reare of this band. Behold then the powers of Hell broake loose upon us, but feare not, for wee can do all things in him that makes us strong, as St Paul hath taught us, and be our spectators to a more glorious triumph then that of chaste Lucretia, and allied with that of Nicetas[49] over incontinencie.

It was that feast day of the Nativitie of the ever most undefiled Virgin Mary,[50] joyfull to angells and men, and onlie abhorr'd by the devills and theire consorts. At the time when sunn being set and al honest mindes betaken themselves to rest, one of our master Turks whose infamous name was Arche, inflam'd with rageing lust upon the bodies of some of our more tender companie, came [p.29] downe amongst us, and after many amorous lookes & gestures to prepare his way, he first blowes forth the lighte. Wee had constantlie a lamp burning amongst us in the nighte time, for light and lust are deadlie enemies. Shame foulded up in blind concealeing nighte, when most unseene then most doth tyranize.

Then suddenlie wee heard russeling & strieving amonst us but understood not what it meant because the one desired to cloake his lewdnes in the darke and the other ashamed to name so fowle intents, though from Turks, and thinking himselfe strong enough to escape the conquerrour; but wee at length, suspecting what mighte be the matter,

---

[49] MS: 'Nuetas'. I owe the emendation to T. A. Birrell. Nicetas was the eponymous hero of *Nicetas, seu triumphata incontinentia*, by Jeremias Drexel, S. J. Originally published for Jesuit sodalities at Munich in 1624, it went through fourteen editions in Latin by 1633 and was translated into several modern languages. An English translation by 'R.S.', *Nicetas, or the Triumph over Incontinence*, was published in 1633 (facsimile edition by the Scolar Press, 1973). A. F. Allison and D. M. Rogers in their *Catalogue of Catholic Books in English* attribute the translation on the basis of the initials to Robert Stanford, a Staffordshire Jesuit who was one of Atkins' superiors at the Jesuit novitiate in Watten in 1629–30 (Foley vii(ii).731). Nicetas was a fictional Egyptian youth who, bound with silken cords to a bed of swansdown, resisted the advances of a temptress by biting off his tongue and spitting it out with the words [*sic*] 'I had rather be dumb than unchaste'.

The whole of the episode that follows was omitted in the version of the *Relation* published in *The Month*.

[50] 8 September.

urged him to tell. 'O help! O help!', quoth he, but said no more, ashamed to name the rest. But wee, conceiving this villainie to be a conspiracie of all our Turks against us, durst not venture to lay hands upon this soule murdering rogue, for fear of an uproare that might cost us all our lives, but encouraged the youthe to constancie in resistance and fell to our prayers for him, to that mother of puritie whose birth day it was and whome wee had all waies hitherto found most propitious to us. The rogue, findeing strong resistance and small bootie after much toyle, betooke him to another, and after him another, who he hoped might be more easilie conquered. But by the goodness of God and the assistance of his Blessed Mother over her parthenian[51] children all behaved themselves most valliantlie, and for that nighte wearied the traytor out. Thus passed this dismall nighte till at length, a noyse being hear'd by the watch above, they asked what doings there was amongst the Christian doggs. Arche, more cruell to us then ever proud Tarquin was to chaste Lucretia (for he but to one woeman, this threatened death & ruin to twelve of his owne sex), answered that the Christian doggs were about an insurrection and to hide theire treasure had put out theire lighte, and no question but if he, casuallie suspecting some mischieve, had not come downe before wee were all in readines, wee had infalliblie cutt all theire throates. This his false accusation [p.30] was believed by the rest, and therefore they lighted our lamp againe and set a guard over us the rest of that nighte till morneing, but never did there a more comfortable lighte shine unto us then now this lamp, nor ever could a guard be more welcome to a distressed fort then this was to our afflictions.

When day was come, a judgment was sitten upon us, what punishment wee deserved for the intended conspiracie, where Arche, our adversarie, contrarie to all law and equitie was admitted for both our accuser and judge, and according to his arbitriment wee were sentenced all to be manicled with yron boults for the present, and the remainder of our punishment to be remitted till wee come to land. Here Sodomes childe triumphs as haveing wone the field, and now surelie the prey in his owne hands when hands & arms are taken from us. Thus as condemned men wee are convey'd back to our dungeon, where the [...][52] day wee lament the miserie wee are falen into above all our former miseries, but now againe, too soone, returns the hatefull nighte

> When everie one themselves to rest betake,
> Save devills, theeves, and trembling hearts that wake.

Downe comes the devills messenger againe, now trimd, wash'd &

---

[51] = virginal.
[52] Lacuna of two words in the MS.

smugg'd,[53] his linens about his neck, breast, armes & thighes as white as snowe, with smiling cocatrices infecting lookes, but wee alas so farr from being taken with his charmes that had the devill himselfe come in his owne shape, he had beene no lesse welcome to us. He seates himself by Thomas Kensington (to thy glorie here I speake it, as being translated out of a religious state to immortalitie, to receive the rewarde of thy constancie),[54] here I say this incarnate devill places himselfe. His gestures and actions discover his poysoned hearte, for his wordes, which were barbarous, were not understood, but Thomas, to divert the venime [p.31] of this infecting basilisk, spits, sighs & prayes, and pleads in his mother-tongue

> To this fierce beaste that knows neither laws nor righte
> Nor ought obeyes then his foule appetite,
> With which repulse his uncontrouled tyde
> Turn'd not, but swell'd the higher by this lett.
> Small lightes are soone blowne out, huge fires abide
> And with the windes in greater furie frett.

Arche, perceiveing his woeings and flatteries to avayle nothing, drew forthe a knife & setting to the breaste of the innocent youth threatened present deathe if he gave not speedie consent to his desires, but the pure soule so little daunted with that fierce spectacle that reacheing forthe his chin & throate he say'd, 'Here, here is my throate! Quench here thy filthie lust, I will hazard the last dropp of my bloud rather than offend my God'.

The wicked Sodomite, findeing his threats to prevaile as little as his flatteries had donne, in a rage blew forth our lighte and by maine force thought to conquer where arte had missed, and for a while strove with the youth till both he and wee schreeking out and makeing frightefull noyses, the watche came downe to see what the matter was, where they found us all drowned in teares as over nighte they left us, fast manacled but our lighte put out and Arche sweateing in the midst of us. This bred jealousies in them concerneing Arches proceedings towards us, wherefore calling him in question and findeing him in an unreadie tale, they deferr'd the matter to a *melius inquirendum*. The next morning, observeing our countenances more heavie then ordinarie, and haveing alreadie some suspition of Arches proceedings towards us, they appointed two of theire souldiers that could speake the Spannish tongue to examine whether anyone had wronged us, & in particular what Arche had the nighte passed donne amongst us [p.32] when they found us moaneing without our lighte. Wee at first were fearefull to

[53] = smartened.
[54] See CRS 73 (1992), 77.

complaine, least being captives it mighte be il taken from us and wee some other waies speede the worse afterwards for it. But being againe urged by those two good natured young men (whose names were Amburge and Hache) to speake plainelie, for if anything were amisse it should surelie be amended, wee be righted, and the delinquent punnished, then wee appointed Jeames Wadsworth, who also amongst us spoake well the Spannish tongue,[55] to lay open plainlie to them the abuses wee had the two nightes pass'd suffered, as also the falsitie of the accusation lay'd against us and the intents of Arche therein, whereuppon the two commissioners in greate indignation against the malefactor vowed justice should be executed and incontinent went up to theire cheef commanders and in a most efficacious manner lay'd open to them the wrong that was done us. Then were we call'd above hatches and seriouslie charged to answer whether these our accusations were true or not. We all answered affirmativelie. They told us that though by the worlde they were counted & called barbarians and knowne enemies to all Christians, yet they were not so inhuman nor barbarous as to let passe such crimes unpunished, especiallie those against nature, and if they were at land (as they were at sea) the delinquent by the lawes of the greate Mahomett was to be burned alive (though they afterwards observed that this wholesome lawe is not executed amongst them), but for the present they wished us to name what satisfaction wee required and it should without delay be inflicted uppon him. But wee, weighing all things rather according to our present condition then by the rule of justice, agreed amongst ourselves and made our answer that wee did not require any, onlie wee earnestlie beseeched them that no such abuse mighte be offered us thereafter, and this should be a [p.33] sufficient satisfaction for us. For if wee (being theire prisoners) should cause punishment to be lay'd upon anyone, it might thereafter breede a sore in him or his friends against us and cost some of us our lives or some other greate mischief. [We] desired them therefore according to theire discretion they would punnish him or quitt him. They layd the delinquent upon his back and gave him some few blows on the bellie with a ropes-end.

This tragicall passage being ended, our boults were taken of from our handes and wee were quit of the suspected conspiracie against them. Thus our good God that is never wanting to those that call upon him, and our ever mercifull patronesse his deare Mother relieved us in our greatest distresse and sent us comforte when and where least lookd for, moveing those hard & savage heartes not onlie to free us from the

[55] Wadsworth's father converted to Roman Catholicism at Madrid in 1604. James (b.1604) joined him in Spain in 1610 and was educated in Madrid and Seville before proceeding to the college at St Omer in 1618.

danger of this shameless villaine but also from the suspition conceived
against us by meanes of this false accusation, as also from the paine of
the pinching yrons which had been so sharp that there was scarce one
amongst us that could shew a sound skinn on his wrists, and some that
had lesser boults and bigger joynts could discover the naked bones.

Now the 11th day of September was come, when with theire provision
faileing them they were constrained to make to land with all speede,
and since Salle (whither theire companions were gonne before with our
ship) was the neerest port of their own, theither they directed theire
course. But behould, all unexpected they discover a ship in theire chase
upon full saile, and feareing it might be some Christian [pursuing]
them, they fled with sayles and oares, and the more to hasten theire
flighte, they call'd us and our fellow Hamburghers up to help them to
rowe. But William Appleby, a man mature both in age and judgment,
and whose opinion swayed much amongst us at all times, advised us
rather to hazard a little beating than discover any skill or abilitie in
this imployment. 'For', said he, 'if our pursuers prove Christians, it
were indiscretion in us to flie from them. Let them take us, and
welcome, in God's name! If they prove otherwise, let us not inure our
handes in this kinde of service, which is the proper imployment of the
Turks slaves, for if once they perceive us able for it, wee shall be kept
to it all our lifetimes, without hope of releasement'. This advice
reallished well with us, and accordinglie, being at each oare two of us
put to assist one Hamburgher or one Turk, wee so crossed his stroake,
pulling towards when he put from, that they complaineing of us that
wee were indocill and did more hurt than they could do good, as
unprofittable servants wee were first a little [p.34] swaddled with the
ropes end & then all sent under hatches as unfitt for service.

In the meanewhile Abdolah, theire Cadie or pettie prieste, with two
or three assistants, according to theire accustomed cour[s]e in like
accidents, was conjureing with his crosse daggers, straws and knives
and I know not what other trash to finde out who theire pursuer mighte
be. And by this meanes, which is familiar to all Turks and Mores, they
have a greate advantage against honest Christians, being able not onlie
to discover afarr of what they are, but also what they carrie and of
what defence they are, and most likelie this arte had given them
incouragement to venture upon our Hamburgh ship with this theire
small vessel.[56] Yet some of our companie, either to make themselves

---

[56] 'Machaeromancy', using knives or swords, is one of the forms of magical divination
listed by John Gaule in his Πυσ-μαντία: *The Mag-Astro-Mancer* (London, 1652, 165). P.
Dan describes the use of arrows before battle to divine the likely result (Dan, 297).
According to Wadsworth the priest put his powers to other good use. 'The day before
our arrivall there [at Salé], being destitute of victuals, the priest, called their *Alfaqui*,
conjured the fish of the sea to draw neere to the gally so that they tooke them up with

merrie, or to discover of how little power the devills intentions are
against the virtue and power of Gods church, would sometimes be
repeating St Johns Ghospell whilst they were invocating theire Mammet
gods, which so put them out of their lesson that it caused them greate
vexation & sometimes jealousie over us. But at length by this arte they
found out that it was a Turke & friend that followed them: who being
come up to us, in a bravado our masters discharged a peale of musketts
and commanded theire Christian doggs to come above board to be
seene, which wee did verie submissivelie and were made a spectacle
and laughter to the enemies of our faith. Then were wee againe shutt
up under hatches where wee remained quiet untill wee arrived at the
castle of Salle, which was within three houres after.

[Arrival at Salé]

At our approach to the key of that harbour, for the greater ostentation
and triumph our men discharged divers peales with theire 15 musketts,
echoing them againe with theire 2 murderers[57], which redoubling theire
reporte from the bordering rocks of that greate Ocean made a verie
harmonious noyse even to us twelve, as being now wearie of the endles
turmoyle of the sea and desirous to set foote on land, though barbarian.
This triumphant sound, seconded with the report made before our
comeing (at the arrivall of the bringers of our ship), viz. that in theire
boate they had a multitude of brave English youthes, greate merchants
sonns, whose ransome would be worth a masse of money, drew forth
Turks & Mores of both sexes and all ages to the watersides to see and
give the welcome home to that victorous [p.35] boate which had sent
before her so statelie a prize, herself being fraught with so lovelie a
bootie. They were all of the vulgar sort of people, and the best of them
but souldiers and sharkers.[58] Through this amphitheatrum[59] or lane of
people they brought us into the castle.

This castle, which for the bignes mighte rather be calld a towne or
cittie (were it not thus tearmed by the inhabitants) containeth in
compasse about 30 acres of ground, being devided as other townes into
severall streets & dwelling houses, is thus call'd in respect of the greate
towne of Salle which lieth on the easte side a mile distant beyond the
river in the King of Fess his dominions but lying low is overlook'd and
sometimes over reached by the greate ordinance from the walls of this

---

their hands as many as sustained us till wee arrived at Sally' (p.39). It is notable that
neither Atkins nor Wadsworth questions the authenticity and efficacy of such divination.
  [57] = small cannon of brass or iron.
  [58] = rogues. On the distinction between 'Turks' and 'Moores' see p.249, n.77.
  [59] = crowd of onlookers (OED c.1630).

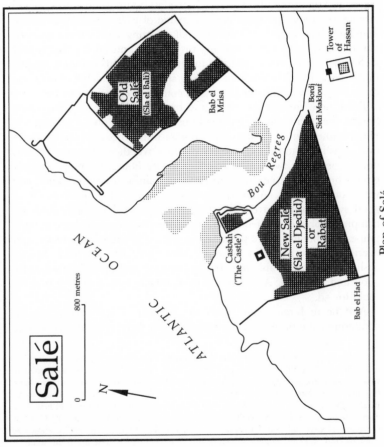

Plan of Salé

castle which is situated upon a cliff of the sea and belongeth to the kingdome of Morocko.[60]

Whilst our masters (or, as there they called them, patrons) ledd us from the waters side towards this castle, our hearts did even melt in our bodies with tendernes, considering into what mens hands wee were fallen, and that not unlikelie this was the last houre wherein wee should ever more enjoy the sighte and companie of each other. With teares, therefore, wee tooke our last farewell, begging each others prayers, pardon of offences committed in our journey, and finallie that if ever it should be any ones good happ to returne into Christendome againe, that he who should enjoy that blessing should be mindefull to acquaint the others friends with the place and condition of their distresse.

Being now entered the castle and brought into one of our patrons houses, they made theire devision of us, one takeing one of us with one Hamburgher, an other two of us, another otherwise, as everie one lik'd best or as it fell to his lott, I know not now whether.[61] But our lott was not to goe above two [of] us together to one house, the more was our grief, where when wee came our first entertainment was very faire, and with some respect. After theire manner they gave us our fill of good sweete water to drink, which was no small happines and not comprehensible of full fedd stomacks. Fruits, as pomegranates, hanged grapes and the like, were plentifull, [p.36] our bread white wheate, and everie day new baked in forme of cakes about an inch thick. Swines flesh they abhorr as abhominable, but mutton and goats flesh was verie good and plentifull. A weather with us mighte cost a mark was there sould for 5d.

And heere I may [not] omitt the manner of our eating, as well common to the masters and mistresses as to the slaves. Trenchers wee

[60] After the death of Mawlay Ahmad al Mansur ('the Golden') in 1603 his kingdom was split in two, with Marrakech and Fez as rival capitals. 'New' Salé was nominally subject to the King of Morocco at Marrakech, while 'old' Salé on the northern bank belonged to the kingdom of Fez. See *Cambridge History of Africa*, ed. Richard Gray (1975), iv.148. Whereas in this passage Atkins applies the term 'castle' to the whole of new Salé, elsewhere he uses it more correctly to denote the citadel, or Casbah, which the Caïd, or Governor, shared with the dominant Hornacheros. The Moriscos, otherwise known as Andalos, and other newcomers settled in the new town which grew up to the south of the Casbah (see map, p.241).

[61] Wadsworth's account is slightly different: 'We were carried to the Castle and there crammed like capons that we might grow fatter and better for sale, and being brought to the market were shared amongst them and sold' (pp.39–40). 'I fell', he adds, 'to the Captaine of the shippe, whose name was Alligalan, a Morisco'. This is the man referred to by Atkins (p.252) as Gallante. All the slaves, about 800 hundred in number, including Spanish, French, English, Portuguese, Italians and Flemish, were lodged at night in a 'dungeon' in the market place, manacled with irons (Wadsworth, p.41). At Salé these dungeons were ironically called *matamoros* (Dan, 407), a Hispanicisation of the local term *matmoura* – a grain silo which served as a lock-up (*SIHM, France*, iii (1911), 234, n.4).

saw none, knives and spoons all most out of use, whence theire manner
is, before they put theire meate into the pott, to chop it into taxadoes[62]
(as wee may call them, steaks) and with it good store of worts or
cabbage and pimienta (a red cod[63] of the same vertue as our blak
pepper) and some garlick, but no thickening, boiling the flesh so long
till it fall from the bones. This they serve up in greate wooden bowles,
broth, meate and cabbige altogether. The bowle is sett upon the
ground, where all that are for that mess set them downe round about
it, the gentrie upon a matt, the rest upon the bare earthe. Into this
bowle everie man falls to breaking his bread by morsels, so much as
may suffice to drink up all the broath; then with theire fingers they
eate it out againe, supplying the use of knives and spoones. Thus
haveing dispatched their broth they come to the meate and worts at
the bottome, which with theire fingers they pull in peeces, being
tenderlie boyled, and proportion it to theire mouthes as they see good.
This, and theire rediculous manner of apparell, was the cause why that
formidable and inhumane runagate pyrate Captaine Warde, who from
a Christian turn'd Turk and lived many yeares by robberies, murders
and conjureing upon the seas, and by land by rapes, adulterie, buggerie
and drunkennes at Argiers, about this time lying on his death bed, and
readie to yield forth his soule to the devill, delivered in a dispaireing
humour this limping and barbarous epitaph to be set over his beastlie
corps:

> I liv'd like a beast, like an ape was I cladd,
> I fed like a swine, like an ass was I shodd,
> And this have I deserv'd for leaveing my Lord God.[64]

Our lodgeings was upon the bare earthe, unless by a speciall favour
some matt or old sackcloth were lent us, which were also the best beds
our patrons had for themselves, wives and children, unlesse it were a
pillow or cushion under theire heades, which was not allow'd us. This
manner of lodgeing was in the begining more tedious in regard of the
moystnes more then of the hardnes of the earth, being for the most
parte in some wet kitchen or wash-house or like out roome, for upper
roomes they have [p.37] none, theire houses being all platform'd on
the top with morter and built with mudd, as well for coolenes in the
sommer time as to save timber, which is there verie scarce.

---

[62] Not in *OED*. The Spanish verb *tajar*, or *taxar* = 'to chop', so *tajados* would be diced
steak
[63] = red pepper.
[64] On John Ward, see *DNB* and Julian Corbett, *England in the Mediterranean* (London
1904), i.10–20. He was established at Tunis by about 1605 and entertained the traveller
William Lithgow there in 1615 (Lithgow, 1906, 315). He died in 1622. I have been unable
to trace Atkins' source for the 'epitaph'.

In this manner wee were at first curteouslie entreated according to the custome of the cuntrie, not haveing any imployment of difficultie impos'd upon us. The most was to dandle a childe, to fetch in a jarre of water from the well, or at the most to grinde an houre sometimes at a handmill. With this easie imployment, and encouraged by the favourable aspects of our patrons and patronesses, wee made bould now and then to walk abroad into the streets, where meeteing now with one of our companie, then heareing of anothers lodgeing, within 3 or 4 dayes wee made shift all to meete and conferr our busines together, what meanes mighte be found to procure our ransome & returne into our cuntrie, which our patrons suspecting (as being a thing they desired) winked at our private meetings.

And herein wee first made use of the counsaile of some English & Irish slaves, as also of some renegados that wish'd us well for cuntrie sake, who gave us information that no Englishman mighte at that time be bought or sold at Salle, Jeames, then King of England, whose subjects wee were, haveing truce for some yeares with that castle. Others wee found of our nation who out of malice to our religion inform'd against us that wee were no subjects to the King of England but Romish papists, and consequentlie enemies to our King and cuntrie. Others went about to prove us Irishmen, which might notwithstanding this truce be bought and sould, wherein some of us were sorelie press'd to prove our cuntrey, amongst [whom] I escaped narrowlie, being judged by my person, complexion and favoure much to resemble the natives of Ireland.

[Appeal to the Governor]

In these difficulties from our own cuntriemen (more cruell to us than Turks) wee procured meanes to make our cause known to a counsailer at lawe that spoake the Spannish tongue, whome according to his office amongst them they called Scrivanno,[65] who in his youth had beene brought up amongst Christians and at such time as the Moores were last banished out of Spaine was with manie others brought to Salle, a Captain of sweete nature and of a curteous, Christian like behaviour towards strangers. This Scrivanno proffered to make it appeare before the Santan,[66] or Governour of the Castle, that wee were [p.38] English men, true subjects to the King of England, and that if wee were bought or sould, wee had greate wrong done us, besides the breache of truce

[65] According to Father Dan the *scrivanos* (a Morisco term, from Spanish *escribano* = scribe) were receivers of the levy paid by the corsairs on their booty. For his account of the government of Salé in the decade following, see Dan, 173-7.

[66] *Santon* was the European term for a Muslim holy man, or wandering dervish. Its misapplication here may be due to a confusion with *sanjak*, the Ottoman word for a provincial governor (cf. Lithgow, 1906, 323).

which would follow betwixt them and England. The day therefore
being appointed for the heareing our cause, our patrons had warneing
given them and our witnesses were provided.

This day heareing was held in an outward corte before the Santons
house where after wee had stood a while expecting came forth the
Santon with about 4 or 5 of his grave assistants clad in theire robes of
state. One theire heades they wore shasses,[67] which is a long red cap
wreathed about theire temples with bands, or rather scarves, of differint
collours. Theire heades were shaven to the scull, one onlie tuft left in
the midst of theire crowne whereby Mahomet may pull them up to
heaven to him. Theire beards are likewise shaven to the skinn, the
upper lip onlie preserved of a greate length. Next theire bodies they
weare pure fine linen, over it a scarlet jump[68] reaching almost downe
to theire knees, garnished before most commonlie with froggs[69] and
loopes and girt about theire middle with a partie culloured scarf or
towell. Theire armes from the elbowes were partelie covered with the
loose wide sleeves of theire shirt, as also theire knees and theire hammes
with theire purest white drawers. Theire necks and legs were naked;
on their feete they wore red lether pumps. Over the one shoulder they
cast a peece of white flannell of 4 or 5 ells long, which they either
wound twice or thrice about their middle or carelesselie threwe it over
both shoulders le[as]t it traile on the ground behinde them. In this
aray (which is also used by all the better sorte) they sate them downe
to heare our cause, not in chaires or upon the bench, as with us, but
cowreing upon theire heeles and resting theire shoulders upon the
walle. Hereby, by the testimony of those that heard us speake English
and understood us, and by what our Hamburghers could say for us,
and no lesse by wit and understanding of our Scrivanno, wee were all
quit and passed not onlie for English men but for true subjects of the
King of England, and in conclusion were found not slaves but at the
most captives or prisoners, might not therefore be bought nor sould
but well compell'd to ransome our selves if we were able.

Our patrons were not well pleas'd with this order, but not knowing
how to remedie it tooke this most devillish devise of some ill willer, to
send and give us as a free gift and present to theire [p.39] King at
Morocco. This newes troubled us not a little, but when wee came
truelie to understand the nature and intent of this our preferment, to
wit that the greater parte of us being youthes and faire skinned above
the natives of the cuntrie we were to be made eunuches to wayt upon
the Kings concubins in theire chamber, according to the custome of

[67] = turbans.
[68] = a short coat (*OED* 1654).
[69] = ornamental braiding (*OED* 1746).

that cuntrey, where besides the eminent danger of our soules healthe wee understood that no money would be then taken for our ransome, it is incredible to believe how wee were frighted.[70] No sleepe would close our eyes, nor ground conteine our feete. Wee often conferr together, wee past from one counsailer to another, who all advised us that the surest way to prevent this danger was spedilie to ransome our selves and not to refuse any rates that should be exacted of us. In this almost desperate case wee thought no time to be neglected nor charges to be spared in the preventing this infernall plott against us. Wherefore, appointing a meeteing, wee conferrd together with our patrons about our ransome and returne into Europe, and in the end made this agreement with them, to give them the summe of a thousand Barberie duccats, or in English account £300, which was after a rate of £25 a man. For the procureing this money eighte of our companie are to departe for Spain with the first oppertunitie, and the other foure to remaine as pledges untill the money should come for all together.

This agreement being assented to by all parties, wee set ourselves in a second consultation (of no small weighte), to witt, who should returne for the money, and who remaine pledges, wherein everie one strove at first to bee of the number of those that should go. Yet in fine, after much debate, our conclusion was as charitable as just, that the four eldest should remaine, and younger sorte departe for the money. The reason of this our determination was, as before I noted, the Mores and Turks being most abhominablie given to the sin of sodomie had alreadie conspired against some of our tenderest youthes, either to steale them away by nighte or at any other rates to purchase theire bodies of our patrons. And for this reason also wee had made our bargaine for all together at this highe rate, for if wee had not stood true to one another, some that were elder and of a hardier complexion mighte have shifted for themselves and gonn away at a farr easier rate, but our [p.40] brotherlie resolution was steadfast, either to ransome altogether or to remaine alltogether.

It was our chance within a day or two after this agreement to meete with one Captaine Clarke,[71] an English man renegado, who haveing demanded of us upon what tearmes wee had gott our libertie & we related to him the perticulers, he tould us wee had given the knaves

[70] The students' fears were not unfounded. In 1618 Roger Hurt, the 10 year-old son of a Bristol merchant, was captured by a Salé ship while on his way to Seville to learn Spanish. By 1638 he was 'chief of the English eunuchs' at the Moroccan court, falconer to Prince Abdalah Meleh, and 'a devout Moor' (*SIHM, Angleterre*, ii.48).

[71] Possibly Captaine William Clark, one of the pirates formerly based at Mamora, who in 1614 raided the Westmann Islands, off Iceland. He later moved to Algiers. See Clive Senior, *A Nation of Pirates* (1976), 63–4, 77; Bernard Lewis, 'Corsairs in Iceland', *Revue de l'Occident Musulman et de la Méditerranée*, xv-xvi (Aix, 1973), 139–44.

too much by more than halfe. Wee then made him acquainted upon what motives, or rather constraint, wee had donne it and desired his advice if he knew any better course to be taken then what we were all readie resolved upon. He tould us that what was alreadie concluded upon amongst us would not easilie be undonne againe, yet for cuntrie sake he counsailed us by all meanes to gett away alltogether, for questionlesse the false rogues our patrons would shew us some false trick either in the receipt of our money or in letting our pledges depart. He made no question but, if we would, we might procure this by meanes of a French marchant which lived in that castle called John Agoretta, a verie charitable man and one of our owne religion, who as he had ransomed divers others of different cuntries and professions likelie would not be unwilling to lay downe money for us alltogether and take us away with him in his owne ships.[72]

Upon this advice we repair to this marchants lodgeing, by whome we were at first acquaintance kindelie entertained, as well he had before heard who wee were and the intentions of our travailes to Sevill Colledge, which was a place he well knew, as also because he had understood of our honest conversation with our neighboures and brotherlie love and fidelitie to one another since our comeing into that castle, but was sorrie wee had alreadie concluded a bargaine with our patrons at so highe and unreasonable rates, yet tould us if it lay in his power he would procure some abatement, or if that could not be donne at leaste wise to get us all away together, for he thought it dangerous for anyone of us to stay behinde as pledges. From this time forward we had free and frequent recourse to his lodgeing and large conferrences with him. And amongst others it was here not the least providence of Almightie God over us that wee never wanted language in these forraigne and barbarous cuntreys, for as before I said George Champian spake Dutch, whereby wee had the comfort of understanding, dealeing [p.41] and complying with Hamburghers, Hollanders and Flemings; Peter Middleton spake French, [*and James Wadsworth,*] who was now our interpreter with the merchants, [*spake Spanish,*] which is ordinarilie understood and spoken by the Mores of Barbarie[73], where the most of the better sorte were brought up in Spaine and are of those Moriscoes which in the yeare 1610 were by Philip the Third bannisht out of Andalusia and Granado in Spaine to the number of ninetie thousand.

[*Salé Described*]

Though manie of the Mores of this place were brought up in Spaine

---

[72] Wadsworth names him as Jehan de la Goretta, a French merchant who traded from Salé 'to Sivill and Cales, and used to traffique for slaves and other commodities' (42). Wadsworth claims that he took the initiative in seeking the Frenchman's help.

[73] The text does not make sense unless amended along the lines suggested.

and are therefore of a well-tempered naturall disposition and of Christianlike behaviour, yet the great infection which this place receives from the Alarabes or wilde Arabians[74] that much infest this barbarous cuntrie hath brought a generall corruption into their manners and an utter disorder into all theire civill government. Of the Alarabes they have learned to sell theire Christian slave in faires and markets as you would do a beast, or at other times drive him up and down the streets crying 'Who buys a slave?' And if the slave be a big lustie fellowe, the cuntrie people will not faile to buy him for the yoake, for there theire plowes are drawne by slaves yoaked by cupples, and [if] they bestir themselves not roundlie the driver beates them with a bulls peezel[75] or a ropes end. When they unyoake they are againe loaded with chaines, and if at anie time any poore fellow, wearied out with miserie, chance to get of his chaines and slip away, the patrons either kill him outrighte, for there is no more punishment due by theire lawes for a man that kills his owne slave then for him that kills his owne dogg, or else they use him as one day wee sawe a poore French man catched in the creekes of the river with hopes to have escaped over in the nighte time, and so away, but being found by his patron he first cutt of his eares, then slitt his nose, after that beate him with ropes ends till all his bodie that was not covered with gore blood was black with stripes, and lastlie they drove him naked, thus disfigured, through the streetes for an example and terrour to other slaves. In the end they threw him into a dungeon with a little strawe under him, loaden with yrons, there to refresh and comfort his bruised and torne bodie.[76]

Neither have they learned to be lesse barbarous to their own neighboures and natives of the cuntrie, since justice and equitie amongst them extends it self no further then the circuit of theire owne walls, as by this one president appeares. It fell out one day that one [p.42] of our patrons going forth of the castle to the waterside with his asse to fetch up boards from our Hamburgh ship, which had bin splitt entering into the haven, had his asse taken from him by one that was both more youthfull and better arm'd than himselfe. This put the old fellow into a greate chafe, wherefore comeing home he told us how he was served, but swore by Mahomet he would either have his owne againe or another as good, and so buckling his scemiter to his side and takeing his musket upon his shoulder, within two houres after he made his worde good and brought home another asse as good as his owne. In like manner if it chance, as often it does, that any of this castle be

[74] The tribes of the Moroccan hinterland.

[75] = a pizzel, or bull's penis, used for flogging.

[76] P. Dan relates the similar misfortune of a Breton captive caught while trying to escape to Mamora. He not only had his ears cut off but was made to eat them (Dan, 421–2).

slaine by anie one of the neighbouring townes, they require bloud for blood and haveing slaine any one, though innocent, of that towne whence the murder was committed, the faulte is remitted and reconciliation made.

As for theire religion, it is according to their Patriark Mahomets Alcoran, which they believe and followe as their true and infallible scripture, yet they are divided into two sects, if not more, of Turks and Mores. The Mores are farr more precise in their superstitions then the Turks are, and differ in their zeale, much after the manner of our Protestants and Puritans in England.[77] The Mores will not drink wine upon anie tearmes, when the Turks, though professing the observance of the same lawe, will both drink it and be drunk with it toe, especiallie when he is at sea and where he is not seene. The Turk cares not much for matters of devotion nor prayer, when the Mores are very dilligent in frequenting their Mosque, or Sinagogue, at least once everie day, and upon Frydays, which is theire sabboth day, they repaire theither seaven times a day, it may be according to the holie custome of the Prophet David, for Turcisme is a mere medley of the Catholick & Jewish religions as the Lutherans is of all ancient and modern heresies compiled together. First, two howers before day they go to *Timgilnamas*, then to *Sabahnamas* at breake of day, to *Giumanamas* at ten in the morning, to *Vilenamas* at noone, to *Kindinamas* at 3 of the clock, to *Akshanamas* at the sunset, to *Ghogunamas* two houres within nighte.[78]

---

[77] The distinction appears to be between, on the one hand, the Anatolian Turks who were present at Salé as soldiers of fortune and, on the other, Hornacheros, Moriscos, and indigenous Arabs or Berbers. The same distinction is made by William Lithgow, who was in Morocco, though not at Salé, some seven years before Atkins (Lithgow, 319–26 and *passim*). For evidence of Turkish-speakers at Salé, see note 78. The comparison of Puritanism with Islamic fundamentalism was a commonplace of recusant polemic. See William Reynolds, *Calvino-Turcismus* (Antwerp, 1597) and the works cited in Peter Milward, *Religious Controversies of the Elizabethan Age* (London, 1977), pp.145–7.

[78] Though distorted, the names of the hours of prayer are, as Dr Colin Heywood has pointed out to me, recognizably Turkish rather than Arabic in form (- *namas* being a version of the Perso-Turkish *namāz*, meaning 'canonical prayer'). Doubtless Atkins heard the terms spoken colloquially, which may account for the deformation.

Atkins	Turkish
'Timgilnamas'	*Temcid namazı*, 'a voluntary service of worship between midnight and dawn' (Redhouse)
'Sabahnamas'	*Sabah namazı*, prayers between first light and dawn
'Vilenamas'	*Öğle* (= noon) *namazı*
'Kindinamas'	*Ikindi* (= time of the afternoon prayer) *namazı*
'Akshanamas'	*Akşam* (= sunset) *namazı*
'Ghogunamas'	Possibly a corruption of *Yatsi* (from *yatmak* = to go to bed) *namazı*, rendered by Paul Rycaut, *Present State of the Turkish Empire* (London, 1670), 158, as 'Yachinamasee'
'Giumanamas'	*Cuma* (< Arabic *Jum'a* = Friday) *namazı*, the general congregational prayers on Friday morning

They have no bells in their steepels to call them together at these differint times of prayer, but choose for a signe to theire meeting at these severall houres the [p.43] strongest and loudest voice they can get, who first soundeing a horne, putteth forth a blew flagg towards the foure quarters of the neighbourhood from four windowes in the steeple, then calls them much after this manner: *Ela, Ela, Mahomet reculaca,* &c, 'God is greate, God is greate and so is his squire Mahomet. Those that will come, let them come, and those that will not, let them stay away.'[79] But among these devotes are none but men & old women, for they teache that young woemen and maydes have no soules til they growe towards three score, by this doctrine acquitting them of all scruple in immodestie and other like sinns.

Theire zeale in matters of religion is in one thing more moderate and civill than our Protestants, that they will not compell any man to their Mosque contrarie to his conscience; nay, it is paine and deathe for anie Christian to enter theire Mosque while they are at theire devotions. It chanced upon one of these Frydaies that one of our companie (knowing nothing of this lawe amongst them) out of a curiositie of seeing entered the porch of their Mosque, where he found all theire shooes standing at the doore and they within singing psalmes or songs confusedlie, much after the manner of our Geneva jiggs,[80] but as chanced he was warned by a friend to retire before he was perceived by the singers, whence it appeares that they enter theire Mosque bare foote, in reverence of the holie ground (as they conceive) they stand on. At other times wee sawe them pray in theire chambers and at the river bancks with verie strainge ceremonies, especiallie after anie uncleane sinne of the flesh committed; first they stripped themselves to the skinn, then kneeleing downe they blessed themselves, stroaking their faces with both theire hands at once from their fore head to theire chinns, then pattering some unknowne prayers they ducked downe in the ground three times, then praying againe they afterwards powred a bason or two of water upon theire heads, rubbing and washing their bodies with it runneing down; lastlie, ducking downe againe three times [p.44] as before, they gave themselves the blessing more compleatlie then before, for when their hands comeing with a gentle wipe from their fore heads reached theire mouthes, with a strong blast they blew them asunder so farr till the backs turn'd towards theire faces, with which last and violent blaste they conceited they blewe away their sinnes and so gave over theire prayers for that time. I have also

---

[79] The translation of the call to prayer (*adan*) is incorrect. *La ilaha il Allah, Muhammad al-Rasul Allah* may be rendered as 'There is no God but God, and Mahomet is God's apostle'.

[80] A term applied in mockery to metrical versions of the psalms (*OED* 1673).

seene the use of beades very familiar amongst them, but never could understand to whose honoure nor what prayers they said on them, neither was there any distinction of setts but about 60 beads all of one suite but the last beade.

They keep their month *Biran* about August or (as wee may call it) a Lent with great store of fasting and prayer[81] from which they are released when they can discover the first new moone riseing in September, when about the houre of that change you shall see thousands of people, men, woemen & children, gazeing upon hills and more eminent places to discover the riseing of the newe moone, for they hould him a greate sainte and singularlie blessed for all that yeare by Mahomet that has the happines to have the first sighte of that new moone.

This their fast is not according to the Catholick Church, nor agreeable to the Scriptures nor reason, for it is verie strict, from all manner of food till sunn set, and then they think it lawfull to eate as much as they will and what they will, commenlie stuffing themselves with greate varietie of fleshmeate, whence it is not improbable that our singuler Puritans tooke theire like manner of fast, since it is manefest they will rather runne headlong into wilfull erroure then receive anie thing from the Catholick Church, rather sociate with a Turk than a Roman Catholick, rather suffer the image of the devill then the picture of Christe in theire houses.

Theire custome is to marrie as manie wives as they are able to mainteine, with whom they have no more portion then a bride waine[82] (as wee call it), such goods and furniture as it pleases her parents to bestowe upon her, but after a man likes well of anie young woeman he bargaines with the parents about what they will take for her, and the bargaine being agreed upon & settled by writeing betweene the parents on both sides, the bridegroome, accompanied with his owne and his spouses friends, with [p.45] the bride waine and a set of winde musick solemnlie brings her away to his owne home. The saddle the bride sitts in is much like to a chaire with a highe back and sides and a canopie over head, drawne round about with silk or other rich curteines, and no man may have the least sighte of her person or bewtie, for though they be not so bad as our Puritans to say that a man hath not free will but must needs, if his foule lust or the spirit

---

[81] Atkins is not alone in confusing the fast of Ramadan with the feast of Biran. According to Lithgow 'the Lent of the Turkes is called Byrham ... Some name it also Ramadan', and the author of *A True Historical Account of Muley Hamets Rising* (1609) names among principal feasts 'the Easter which is called Rumedan'. In 1622 (A.H. 1031) Ramadan would have ended on 8 August, followed by Biran on 9 August, before Atkins' arrival in Salé.

[82] = a waggon carrying the bride's gifts to the groom's house (*OED* 1807).

move him, consent to his inordinate desire, yet they are jealous in
extreame & if at anie time they chance to take a man talking, visitting
or peepeing at theire wives, if they do not presentlie conspire his deathe
they owe him a perpetuall grudge, and for this reason they permit her
not to go abroad but upon urgent occasions, and then well attended
with Argus eyes. These woemen go verie well apparrelled, and in my
conceite farr exceed our English modestie. They are neither naked on
theire necks, breasts nor armes, though the cuntrie is verie hot, but
besides verie decent apparrell within doores, when they go abroad they
put on a long white veyle or mantle, much imitateing the Spanish
fashion, which reacheth round and decentlie to theire feete. They wear
neither black twists,[83] jewells nor braceletts about their necks nor armes,
but about the smalle of theire leggs or ankles they wear both braceletts &
plates of silver or gold, of 2 or 3 inches broade. These are onlie seene
by theire husbands or familie within doores, where they lay of theire
long mantles, and that this bewtie of theire leggs may the more appeare,
they both weare theire petticots short & go without stockings, haveing
onlie on theire feete fine, neate red lether pumps. Shee amongst manie
wives that pleases the husband best is his housekeeper and mistresse
over the familie, the rest keepe theire severall chambers and must be
contented with what is allowed them, and in all controversies which
must needs be betwixt a multiplicitie of wives they must stand to the
arbiterment of theire husband. Theire children they circumsise after
the Jewish manner, yet they hate the Jews farr more than they do
Christians and for theire greater ignominie compell them in all theire
dominions to weare black caps and black mantles, a collour generallie
abhord by all Turks and Mores. [p.46]

[Escape from Slavery]

But to returne to our owne affaires again, whilst wee were now often
at our French marchants lodgeing our patrons either began to grow
jealous of us, that these our meeteings were at length to steale away in
his ships or, which wee thought was more likelie, they had now
conspired to convey away and privatelie sell some of our handsomest
youthes to some Turks who wee well knewe had offerd verie large
summes of money for theire bodies, and this was crossed by our often
meeteing together at the marchants chamber. Therefore when one day
wee were together conferring our busines with the marchant, 5 or 6 of
our patrons (amongst which Gallante and Morena, allwaies more harsh
and cruell then the rest, were the chief) came in greate haste and furie
to the marchants house which was upon the walls nere to the southe
gate, and with manie passionate and violent words lay'd to his charge

83 = plaited cords.

that he had plotted to steale us 12 away, forbade him therefore enterteineing theire slaves any more in his chamber unlesse he desired to have his house pulled downe over his head downe to the walles and his braines beaten out.[84] Then turning to us with furie sparkeleing in theire eyes they asked us how wee durst be so bould without theire leave and good likeing to have these private meeteings. This was because wee wanted imployment at home and had too much libertie, but they would tame us in our loades of yron chaines like slaves, as wee were, and hould us to worke, and hereafter wee should never three of us meete together againe to plott our liberties. If wee did, they would make it a deare meeteing to us. The marchant, heareing these terrible thunderclaps against himselfe & us, tould us in the French tongue that it was neither safe for him nor us to gainsay or crosse these men, because they were barbarous and without either feare of God or man and would likelie do as bad as they had threatened, for if they kill'd either him or us there was no lawe against them, because we were strangers. Therefore he advised us to submit our selves to them and quietlie returne with them [p.47] and come no more to his chamber till he sent for us. He in the meane while would not be unmindefull of us, but if it lay in his power to doe us anie good we should [be sure][85] of a friend in a corner. This chainge of weather so daunted and apaled us that you mighte have seene us driven before our patrons downe the marchants staires and up to the market streete with teares in our eyes, hanging our heades like so manie malefactors attended by the publick office downe from the jayle to the gallowes. But as hitherto wee never found ourselves in any extremitie but wee presentlie found the spedie remedie from almightie God, so now whilst wee were thus conducted up the streetes (according to all probabillitie) to the uttermost of our miseries, wee espyed afar of in the farthest end of the streete our deare and constant friend the Scrivanno (before mentioned), which gave us a little comefort and hopes of our relief. Wherefore deemeing a desparet disease to be cured with a desperate remedie, wee counsailed our linguist Jeames Wadsworth to go meete him and make our distressed case knowne to him; who as he was more apprehensive of dangers and lesse patient of miseries than the rest, needed noe spurrs to set him forward, but as if it had beene a race for a wager of greate vallue he gave the start and runne upon full speede till he came to the Captaine.[86]

---

[84] MS: 'and his braines beaten out downe to the walles'.

[85] Lacuna of one or two words in the MS.

[86] The Caïd of Salé, described by Atkins as the 'Captain', and by Wadsworth as the 'Governor', was at this time Abd el-Aziz ez-Zarouri (*SIHM, France*, iii (1911), 191). He was the representative at Salé of the King of Morocco but as this episode illustrates he had difficulty in imposing his authority and was removed in 1625. Salé declared its independence in 1627 (*ibid.*, 192).

Our patrons wondered what the lad meant to doe, but knowing the castle gates were shutt, that he could not over runne them, they let him runne and with a jeereing thereat said they should find time enough to tame him shortlie. But Wadsworth layd open our dangers and our patrons threats so to the life, and tould his tale so well, that the Captaine, breaking of his discourse with his familiar friends and coming along with Wadsworth towards us, tould him hee would take an order with the rogues.

So soone as he came nere us wee showed our respects to him and begged his favour by signes, for language wee had none. Then he demaunded of our patrons what they meante by driveing us in that [p.48] disgracefull manner before them up the streetes. They answer'd we were theire slaves, and like slaves they would use us; that it nothing concern'd him how they dealt with us. With that he drewe his sworde and swore by greate Mahomat that if any of them offerd any the least violence or wrong, he would hack him in peeces, for wee were not to be counted as theire slaves but free gentlemen and friends, to whom libertie and respect was due by lawes of nations, as had alreadie been proved before the Santan.

Then they all drew their rustie blades and wished him to desist, for if any man offer'd to take theire slaves from them they would endanger the takeing of his life from him. These speeches enraged the Captaine, wherefore calling out for help against rogues and traytors he set upon, at first himself alone, but was presentlie assisted by shopp keepers and other honest minded people that came forth to him with bills, staves and swordes. Others there came forth of the rascaldrie,[87] as boatemen, souldiers and the like, to the ayde of our patrons against him and his, so that within a quarter of an houre the streetes were fill'd with all sorts of weapons. The women in the meane while in the doores and windowes out of theire good nature cryed out to the English youthes to look to themselves, for they would surelie in the midd'st of the fray be all killed, and when [we] understood not theire voyces nor screeks to us, they ventured into the streetes among the men, and catching us by the armes they drewe us into theire shopps and houses, where wee lay close till the Scrivanno with his partie had beaten our patrons and theire adherents backwards downe the streete and out of the gates. This was such a civill commotion as by the testimoney of all there had never beene seene in that castle before, especiallie between commanders and souldiers, and in the behalfe of strangers that were in little better condition then slaves, against theire owne neighboures. Haveing thus shutt the beggarlie rogues our patrons and their partners out of the castle gates and returned victors, they enquired what was come of

[87] = rabble (archaic by the 17th century).

theire English youthes for [p.49] whome they had both ventured themselves and given many a slaysh and dry blowe to theire neighboures. Where when wee were come forth of our holes and had submissivelie given thanks for the favour received, wee signified to the Scrivanno that now there was no more going home for us without eminent danger of our lives, for doubtlesse our patrons at theire first returne into the castle would revenge this theire affront upon us as the sole authors of it, and since there was no more punishment due by theire lawes for the murder of a Christian then for the death of a dogg, what could wee expect other from desperat & exasperated rogues then certeine deathe or the extremitie of miseries?

[Asylum in the Casbah]

The Scrivanno then inspired and moved by Allmightie God bade us follow him, for he would provide us a lodgeing alltogether and quit us of the slaverie of these our inhumane patrons. He brought us therefore to a chamber furnisht with mats necessarie to lodge upon, and least any violence mighte be offerd us from our patrons by way of revenge, or by any Turks to steale any one of us away, he appointed us two musketters with lighted matches for guard at our chamber dore the three first dayes and nightes. And after, as long as wee stayed in the castle wee had continuallie one to keepe centinill over us, with charge to shoote whomesoever should attempt to do us wrong.

From this day forward wee began to be housekeepers of ourselves, our good marchant daylie furnishing [us] liberallie with money to fetch in our provision, where such is the fertilitie of the cuntrie that wee 12 could fare verie well with 3 meales in the day for 18d or five groates amongst us all. For example, we eate to our breakfast (according to the custome of the cuntrie) from the cookshop 2 pounds of bonuels[88] for 2d, a food much like our fritters but fryed in oyle. These wee could rowle and bleache in good Barbarie sugar for a half pence. To our dinner wee would have a good large joynte of mutton for 5 or 6d; after that, 3 or 4 great pomegranetts or a pound of hanged grapes amongst us for a pennie; to our supper a dozen of wilde fowle as bigg as woodcock for a groate, or when time requir'd wee [p.50] could have a good dish of fish for 3d, or a groate, and out of these more than sufficient commons wee could afforde our centinell his meale. Our fowle wee commonlie pluck'd and intralled our selves, but had all roasted, boyled or baked for thanks at our neighboures pot, spit or oven as they dressed theire owne. Wheate is theire onlie graine and, I

---

[88] Possibly a misreading of a variant of *beignets* (fritters), though the earliest use of *beignets* recorded by the OED is of 1835. The fritters described by Atkins correspond with the *sfenj* still eaten in Morocco today.

believe, the best and fairest in the world. Of this wee could have everie
day fresh and newe bread to serve us all for one aspre a day, a peece
of money equivalent to 3d and is the onlie silver coyne they have of
theire owne.[89] Our drink wee fetch'd from the christaline founteine in
a greate earthen pott and could, for a pennie sugar it for the whole
day as sweet as the Turkish skerpet[90] or our meth.[91]

Now we could as often as wee thought good, some of us steale over
to our marchant. Now wee could at our leasure conferr our businesses
amongst our selves without lett or hinderance. Now wee could at our
pleasure talke with our poore Christian cuntreymen, slaves or renegados,
that made us visits or wee them. And now wee could to our fill *cantare
Domino in terra aliena*, attend to our prayers or sing to our Lord in a
strainge cuntrie. This was our course of life from the 23 of September,
when wee entered this new lodgeing, till the 8 of October, when wee
tooke shipping for Spaine.

Yet it was not wholelie quit of fights and troubles, for wee could still
heare the often threats of our patrons of sending us away to the King
of Morocco, and were in no lesse danger in looseing of some of our
yongest companions to the Turks, for which cause wee durst not at
anie time trust them out of dores, even upon necessarie occasions,
without a guard upon them. Notwithstanding, so did our friends the
Scrivanno and the marchant negociate our busines, but above all did
Allmightie God provide for us, that wee all of us escaped all dangers
from wicked men.

After that about a fortnighte was expired in this course of life, our
marchant one day sent for us alltogether to his lodgeing, which wee
speedilie perform'd. Where when we came he made us this I knowe
not whether more comfortable, by the newes of our speedie departure,
or discomfortable speeche, by reason of his distressed state, but certeinlie
most [p.51] tender and most moveing, for it caused both those effects
in us.

'My dearest English men, I am much comforted in your acquaintance
and conversation, in whome as the livelie members of the Catholick
Church I behould the sparks of true religion, devotion and brotherlie
love in this forraigne and barbarous cuntrie. Here amongst these savage
people have I lived three yeares factor to a marchant of Cales by name
John Bravo de Laguna,[92] but never since my comeing hither have

---

[89] The aspre, or asper (from Greek *aspron*) was the standard coin in the Ottoman
Empire from the earliest period until the late 17th century. Ottoman coins were regularly
struck at Algiers. Their use at Salé is further evidence of Turkish influence there.
[90] = sherbet.
[91] = mead.
[92] Perhaps related to the military engineer Luis Bravo de Laguna who in 1577 was
commissioned by Philip II to report on the coastal defences of Andalusia against the
corsairs (Friedman, 40).

received that comfort in any that I have in you. And now the course of my naturall life is a pace drawing towards its period by the violence of a burneing feaver, nor do I know where to finde a phisitian for my help, and if I did, yet durst not trust myselfe into his hands, since here the custome is that if any stranger die amongst them he forfeits all his goods to the place. Justlie therefore may I feare to put my life into his hands, least either covetousnes of what I have or their innate crueltie to strangers might hasten mine ende, or at least wise, understanding the extremitie of my disease, they should purposelie detaine me here till the violence of my sicknes make an end of me. I have therefore let my friends and your patrons understand that my intention is to depart towards Spaine with all my ships very speedilie, and that the distemper which I feele is onlie the gout, least they, understanding the danger of my disease, should detaine me here by force. Therefore in this my extremitie of dangers I entreate you all by the merrits of our deare Saviour's Passion, that if it lie in your powers you will help me to a phisitian for my poore soule, which hath wanted that comfort now these 3 yeares, and if any of you be priests, which by your vertuous conversation I have oft had reason to suspect, that you will now let me knowe, who though hitherto you mighte have just reasons to conceale your selves, yet now the obligation of charitie ties you to consider my necessities and to discover your function to me. Your rewarde for so charitable a worke shal be Allmightie God, and for my parte I have done more for you then I think for to make yet knowne to you. This onlie I tell you, that I have taken order for your ransome and tomorrow, God willing, wee will all together go on ship-board for Spaine. I onlie ask you will requite me with this last favoure.' Whilst this speech was delivered us by our interpreter, our eyes were drown'd in teares through com[p.51]passion & sorrow, though much to see the danger of his sicknes, yet much more for the spirituall want he was in which wee were not able to supplie. We return'd him therefore this short and modest answere, that our obligations to him were not to be numbered, for which wee would be his beadsmen to pray for him the longest day of our lives; that the course of our journey, as he alreadie knew, was from Flanders towards Sevill in Spaine, there to studie and, if it should please Allmightie God to make us worthie, to receive that degree which yet wee were not worthie of; let him therefore knowe that wee were none of us priests. Here he gave a sighe, and desir'd us to attend him that day with our prayers for him, which we did.

[Departure from Salé]

The next day being the eighth of October, and the most of his goods and marchandize conveyed on shipboard, wee were guarded out of the castle downe to the waterside by our good friend the Scrivanno and some of his servants, where submissivelie takeing our leave of him with thanks for the manie and great favoures received from him, and bidding farewell to all our other well wishers, both men and woemen, wee entered into one of the pinaces[93] with our marchant. You mighte have now observed manie of the cuntrie people (for the key was thronged full), especiallie of the female kinde, shedding teares at our departure, protesting they had never before seen 12 such constant friends and with all so modest and orderlie and of so sweete behaviour.

So imperfect (as I said before) are the lawes of this barbarous cuntrie that they extend no farther than the walles[94] of their owne castle, so that if they can take any straingers ship out of the command of the greate ordinance of the castle it is theire owne, and they may bring & sell it in any other haven of this kingdome of Morocco or any other, though the owner of the ship thus taken had his licence from them for free accesse and regresse in tradeing with them. This was the reason wee lay 4 or 5 daies under the command of this castle before wee durst venture to sea, seeing divers pirates (for such are all theire seamen) set out before us to watch our comeing out to sea. Yet after 4 daies, in the deade time of the nighte, the winde favouring, wee weighed anker, hoysed[95] sayles and lanced forthe into the Ocean with one ship of 2 hundred and fiftie [p.53] tunne, into which at our weighing anker wee 12 and our marchant removed, and 2 small pinaces haveing in them a hundred and fiftie men, all such as this marchant had redeem'd out of captivitie and slaverie, of verie differint sects and nations, as Englishmen, Irishmen, Dutch, Spaniards, Portugeses and others, amongst which was our Master Hamburgher who had gotten away under cullour of our first bargaine with our patrons to send money for himselfe and for the ransome of his nine companions or servants. But, as wee afterwards understood, after that he had safelie gotten home he let his servants lye by itt, and neither sent money for their ransome nor harkened any more after them. This was according to his Anabaptisticall charitie: if the Lord would redeeme them, he knewe well how to do it; if he would not, 'twas in vaine to labour about it.

[Mamora]

But whilste wee thus prolong delaies in our journey, our marchant is everie day more weake then other and hastens towards his end.[96] He spends his time in prayer, often calls upon us 12 to pray heartilie for him, for we knew not yet what he had done for us (and often he

[93] = small two-masted ships.
[94] MS: 'lawes'.
[95] = hoisted.
[96] According to Wadsworth one of the merchant's enemies had given him a 'poisoned tart', which took delayed effect.

repeates these words: wee knewe not yet what he had donne for us),
therefore earnestlie desires us to pray for him in this his last extremitie.
Upon the 14th day of the month and 6th since our comeing on
shipboard, wee observeing all signes of approaching deathe in him and
desirous if it might be possible to procure him the comfort of a ghostlie
father and Christian buriall, asked him whether he did not desire to
be carried to land, which wee understood was within halfe a daies sayle
of us; and he shewing a willingnes thereto, wee urged it with the
Captain of the ship who was as the rest a ransom'd slave and by
profession a Hugonott but being an understanding and active man was
for cuntreys sake appointed Captaine of this ship. This Captaine at
first made shew of manie difficulties & greate unwillingnes, either out
of a desire to deprive the marchant of a priest & his last rites, or
because he had rather hasten his deathe at sea, but wee layd before
him such temporall reasons for the comfort of the sick mans body and
hope of his recoverie that he could not [in] civillitie nor his loyaltie to
his friend & master deny it us. [p.54] He tould us therefore that it
should be as wee desir'd, and so steerd his course againe toward the
coast of Barbarie upon a little towne held by the Spaniards called
Mamora. Where when towards evening we came within a mile of the
towne (for nerer our ship could not ly at quiet anker by reason of the
breakeing of the violent waves upon the rocks) wee wraped our
marchant close up in his warm bedclothes and laide him into the
cockboate and carried him thus wrap'd up amongst us into the towne,
where after wee had found a convenient lodgeing wee enquire for a
prieste, and being inform'd there were three in towne whereof one was
a Frenchman, wee made choise of him to assist our marchant. But at
the comeing of the priest wee found him quite deprived of all sence
and like one that were giveing up the ghoste, it seemes strucken in his
hot fitt with the coole of the evening ayre. Some therefore falling to
theire prayers for him, and others that were more dexterous rubing
and chafeing and applying to him such things as mighte revive him,
within half an houre wee brought him to his perfect sence, speech and
understanding againe, and letting him know what a friend wee had
brought him and putting him in minde of his former desires, he shew'd
greate joy of hearte and gave God thanks for the favour, us for our
care over him, & the priest for his paines. So wee left them two together
settleing the state of his soule, and retired to our prayers for him in
another roome, where after they had beene an houre together he
againe lost the use of his sences, the priest gave him the absolution of
his sinnes and before morning he departed this mortall life, wee hope
to receive the rewarde of his good deedes in another. The same day
towards evening wee 12 attended his corps to buriall with our lighted
tapers and all other ceremonies in the Catholick Church, which was

decentlie lay'd in the chapple or oratorie of this little towne at the righte hand, nere to the comunion rayle. Where I knowe not whether our present heavines for the loss of our deare friend this French marchant were greater, or the joye we tooke in being after a long banishment gotten amongst Catholicks againe and to a place where wee might freelie and publicklie professe and practise our religion, but certeinlie we all of us felt such singuler devotion in [p.55] ourselves as wee never had found the like before. Now wee went all to the holie sacraments of confession and communion, wee were daylie present at all three masses, wee watched before the altar whensoever the chapple dore was open & scarce could the sackristan get us forth to shutt the chapple dores after evensong, whence the good Spaniards were so taken with us and edified by us, professing they had never seen so much devotion in that towne before; and nothing inferiour was our edification wee received from the Spaniards charitie in that poore and remote place towards poore Christian travellors or slaves of what nation soever that by any meanes can get out of the Turkish slaverie & fly to them for relief, whereof there are great store by reason it lies but 15 miles from the castle of Salle, devided from it by a greate river[97] which manie, to purchase theire libertie, venture to swimme over in the nighte time and sheltering themselves under the walls of this towne are in the morning received in by the Spaniards and friendlie entertain'd with good meate, drink and lodgeings of free cost till they can [find] shiping for Spaine or theire owne cuntrie, which is comenlie within 3 weekes or a month. This theire rare charitie did wee 12 abundantlie taste, with good & wholesome diet and now and then a good cupp of sack at free charges all the foure daies wee stayed with them, and mighte at the same rates have been welcome to them for 2 or 3 months if wee had not aymed at greater matters.

This little towne of Mamora lyeth within the kingdom of Fesse, situated upon a highe & steepe rock at the mouth of a verie faire river and enriched with a verie statelie and secure harboure for shipping of greate burden, guarded with 2 strong blockhouses belowe the rocks at the mouth of the harboure on either side. This, in the dayes of our late Queene Elizabeth, a professed enemie to the Spaniards and who, as the Turks yet report, stored them first with greate ordinance and taught them the use of them merely to curb & crosse the Spaniard, whereby now they curb not onlie the Spaniard but English and all Christendome (so perrillous is pollicie grounded upon passion), this, I say, in her dayes was [p.56] onlie a harboure for shiping, where our English & the Flemish pirats were wont to meete to divide theire prey

[97] Mamora (now Mehdia), occupied by the Spanish from 1614 to 1681, lies on the River Sebu, eighteen miles north of Rabat.

when they had taken any Spani[ard] or rob'd theire coasts, or otherwise to ly there at theire ease and safetie whilst they mighte heare of some bootie towards, till at length the Spaniards impatient with long abuses and daylie robberies committed upon theire coasts resolved to destroy the nest of rogues. Therefore watching a convenient time when the most of the pyrates were gone to sea, they chopped in some few ships and gallies and there at unawares surprized Captaine Nutt, Captaine Penn, Captaine Catesby and others that were left in the harboure.[98] Since which time the Spaniardes have kept this harboure, and for the better secureing they have plac'd a garrison and built this little towne consisting of small & lowe platforme buildings of earthe and fenced about with deepe trenches and highe & thick rampires of earthe, well guarded with good store of good brass ordinance and mann'd with a thousand souldiers and one troope of horse, which are the onlie and sole inhabitants of the place, unlesse it be some 10 or 12 woemen, wives to some of the souldiers. These receive their paye and daylie sustenance from Spaine. So frequent are the alarums, disquiets and sometimes assaults that the Turks and Moores give them that they can neither sowe any corne nor keepe any stock of cattle without the walls for their maintenance. It was our chance at this verie time to bee spectators to one of these alarums with a lighte skirmish betwixt the Spaniards and the Moores, when these to the number of 15 hunderd foote and horse shewing themselves in a bodie within lesse than a mile of the towne, the Spaniards within halfe a quarter of an houre after the signe by alarum bell were all in theire armes upon the walles, whence the Governour, drawing out 400 foote with his troope of horse, divided them into 4 squadrons which he leade up within musket shott of the enemie. Whence wee all out of danger upon the wals had the pleasure of the sighte, especiallie when wee beheld the Moores at the verie first encounter to begin to retyre. But the Spaniards, not knowing what ambushments there mighte [p.57] ly under the side of the hill neare to them, sounded a retreate and with all speede possible made shew to flie back to the towne, which being dexterouslie and advisedlie donne, instantlie the great ordinance from the town began to play so fast over the Spaniards heades at the Moores upon the plaine heathes that they were not able to stay in the field & so fled in a confused manner; and so dexterous were the Spaniards here at these good ordinance that they permitted not any ten Moores together within a mile and halfe of the

---

[98] On John Nutt, the Torbay pirate, see John Forster, *Sir John Eliot, 1590–1632* (1865), i.26–49. Captain Catesby may be the man who accompanied Sir Thomas Sherley on his raiding expedition to Portugal in 1602. See Kenneth Andrews, *Elizabethan Privateering* (Cambridge, 1964), 56. For the names of other English pirates operating from Mamora, cf. G. N. Clark, 'Barbary Corsairs in the 17th century', *Cambridge Historical Journal*, viii (1945–6), 22–35.

towne but sent a ball in the midst of them. In this skirmish the Spaniards received no further hurt then the losse of one horse. What damage the Moores received wee could not learne, by reason they carried theire losses away with them. And in this service wee 12 were able upon the walls to help to draw up the ordinance in theire recoyleing, to fetch or carrie when anything was wanting.[99]

Whilst these things passe with us at hand, our two pinaces have hoysed sayle and are with all speede gonne for Cales to bring the heavie newes of our marchants deathe to his executors, and our Hugonot Captaine thinks everie houre a weeke till he gett us to ship againe. Therefore to satisfie his longing, but much more because wee desired as speedilie as mighte be to be at our journeys end, we harkening for a boate, and upon St Lukes day,[100] after wee had despatch'd our devotions, understanding that two marchants had hired a boate to go a mile & halfe to sea to see our ship & the commodities shee caried, wee desir'd the favoure to go along with them. It chanced at that time that, being a spring tyde and the windes blowing strong from the western pointe directlie upon that coaste, the sea was very roughe, especiallie at the breakeing of the waves against the rocks at the river mouthe. Which our 2 Spanish marchants perceiveing, after they were gonne almost halfe the way, and apprehending greate danger in the passage, endeavoured to persuade the boatemen to returne back for the present and to take them at another time when the water should be calmer. These boatemen were six, and theire boate much after the make and biggnes of a Temmes barge, but they, covetous for money and more venterous for gaine than the marchant venturers themselves, answer'd that unlesse they might be paid for that parte of the journey they [p.58] had alreadie rowed, they would not returne. The marchants entreated them fairlie in the begining, then chidd and chafed and pleaded danger of being cast all away. The boatemen on the other side pleaded 'Pay, pay!' but row'd on, hopeing thus to squeese some money out of the marchants, till they penriouslie houlding of, at length it was too late to returne. And now the boatemen cry out 'We are all lost!', the marchants blame the boatemen of covetise, the boatemen blame the marchants of nigardise, and wee blame them all of rashnes. If wee

---

[99] According to Wadsworth (45) the attack on Mamora was led by 'the Moore whom they call the Saint of Salley, with 30,000 other Alarabes'. This was the *marabout* Sidi Muhammad ben Ahmad Zayani (1573–1641), known as al-Ayyashi (Dan, 176, calls him 'Layasse') who rebelled against Sultan Mawlay Zidan and took refuge in old Salé, using it as a base for a *jihad* against the Spanish *presidios* (*SIHM, France*, iii (1911), 189). He had earlier attacked Mamora in May 1621 and May 1622, aided in the second attempt by the Dutch. Cf. García Figueras, 145 *et seqq*. John Dunton, describes him in 1637 as 'pettie King of the old towne', at war both with new Salé and with the Sherif of Morocco (Dunton, 6–7).

[100] 18 October.

return'd back, the encroaching waves, takeing our boate at an advantage with the side towards them, would certeinelie turne it over; if we went forwards, everie stroake of the oare seemed to carrie us towards our ruine, for now the green & foameing waves, not much unlike to steepe, highe and craggie Perenian[101] or Welch mounteines, seem'd rather to overwhelme us then greete us. The marchants now begin to blesse themselves, the boatemen call to God for mercie. There are no more wordes of money, all theire thoughts are bent to save themselves. They charge us all to be still, no man to stirr upon hazard of casting all away: let evrie man looke to himselfe, least if he be cast out, no bodie dare venture to pull him up againe. The marchants close imbraced the traverse they sate upon, wee 12 cast ourselves flat on our faces to the bottome of the boate and lay'd fast hould on the ribbs or such other steedfast things as were next unto us. The boatemen have the hardest task to keepe theire seats, and also by strength of oare to hould the nose of the boate up to the waves. Now they rowe for theire lives, they strain, they sweate, and with much adoe they mount up to the topp of this first wave, and now that they are there the difficultie is no lesse to know how safelie and softlie to come down againe the other side it. Least therefore the boate should pitch endwaies into the precipice of waters, as one mighte imagin a paire of wheeles downe some steepe rock, they now againe rowe back with all mighte and maine, thus with toyle and skill makeing a gentle fall downe this liquid mounteine; and scarce were we able to lift up our heades and recover breath but behold a second wave nothing lesse formidable then the first encounters us, which wee make haste to meete least being surpriz'd betwixt the two wee mighte come [p.59] to be overwhelm'd, and as before so now our boate by the uttermost of the boatemens industrie and toyle ascends this mounteine endwaies, as steep as a ladder reared against a house side, that scarce were wee in the boate able to hold ourselves from falling forthe, & when at length wee came to the ridge, which was sharp and frothie, wee feared nothing more than the breaking and opening of the wave, which is often wont to fall out most dangerouslie, and so without mercie be all swallowed up. Yet over wee came and downe on the other side of the ridge with the same industrie of our boatemen as before. The rest of the waves betwixt us and our ship, though as greate and greater in heighthe & breadthe than these, yet were they not so steepe nor craggie and consequentlie not dangerous. For this deliverie wee gave God & St Luke the thanks, whose blessings wee had that morning received at the aultar, for questionless it was beyond all humane expectation as our skilfull boatemen did acknowledge. After wee had thus fortunatelie escaped over both Scilla and

[101] *sc.* Pyrenaean.

Caribdis, and that wee had leasure to talk one to another, wee asked each other what they did or what they thought upon all that while they lay so still without ever a worde amongst them. Whereto everie mans answer fell out alike, that he was endeavouring to make an act of contrition, supposeing, as reallie we thought that was the last houre of life, wee could not spend the remainder of our time better nor make a more secure end then by an act of contrition.

[Larache and Beyond]

Haveing thus with much toyle and danger gotten into our ship againe, wee presentlie found there an alteration in all things from what had beene in our marchants life time. Our companie were falen into factions and schisms, cheeflie by reason of the differince in religion amongst them. Our Captaine favoured his fellowes, French Hugonots, whereof there were 5 or 6. The English Protestants, 10 in number, like birds of a feather lay'd their heads together and would have no charitable commerce with any but themselves. Wee 12, as underlings, were contemn'd by our cuntriemen & sleighted by our Captaine and his faction. The Catholicks, French, Spanish, Irish &c., being more in number & formerlie in favoure with the deceased marchant, thought scorne to be awed & curbed by men of meaner capacitie and qualitie and number than themselves. When the Catholicks went to prayer, the hereticks would sing, hoote & scoffe; and when the hereticks began theire [p.60] Geneva jiggs or common prayer, the French Catholicks beate the drumme and drown'd theire musical discord. When some gott flesh meate to theire dinner others were glad of poore John,[102] other of dry bread, & others fasted. Yet as all had tasted the bitternes of the Turkish slaverie they all agreed to defend themselves & ship to the uttermost of their power from theire enemies. Therefore by day and nighte they were all verie vigillant & carefullie attended to theire severall charges. Sometimes wee sailed towards Spaine, & sometimes back againe towards Mamorra when wee were frighted, as often wee were, by enemies; and upon the 22th day of the month, being sorelie terrified by the discovery of 14 ships under sayle, doubting they might be Turks wee made towards land with all speede to a towne on the coast of Barbarie held by the Spaniards called Alarache,[103] not much above 60 miles distant from Mamorra, where we lay at anker 3 or 4 dayes, when 2 of our companie, viz. James Wadsworth and Peter Edwards, impatient of our long delayes, daylie dangers both of sea and enemies, and hard usage, finding a boate upon its journey thence for

---

[102] = salt hake.

[103] Larache (now al-Araish), 45 miles S.W. of Tangier, was captured by the Spanish in 1610 and remained a *presidio* until 1689.

Spaine, stept into it and contrarie to all faith & former constancie to one another without ever a farewell ungratefullie left us and went along with this lighte and speedie boate for Spaine.[104]

Here I am not able sufficientlie to [*relate the*] extremitie of miserie which wee ten schollars endured in tenn dayes wee lay at sea under the charge and command of this Hugonott Captain. George Champian was sick of a feaver, William Appleby of the cloudie flux,[105] I was lame in my leggs and thighes of such a swelling & sorenes that for divers daies I crawled upon my hands and knees, and allmost al the rest of us, worn out with long sufferings and want of cleane shift, were lesse able to endure inconveniences than hitherto wee had been, for it was now the latter end of October when the weather grows could, especiallie at sea. Yet our lodgeing was uppon the bare boards, with onlie one ould saylecloth amongst us to defend us from the could. Our clothes were thinne and threedbare, haveing never a cloake or coate amonst us and scarce halfe so manie shirts as bodies, and those foule & nastie of allmost a quarters weareing without shift, some moreover wanting stockings, others shooes, others hatts; and such superfluous things as bands, handkerchers [p.61] and capps were counted no want. I do even abhorre to relate how woefullie wee were besprinckled with six footed vermine, yet because I have undertaken to make an exact relation, and that you may also have some ghesse of our state in this kinde, I will tell you of a daylie practise of my owne. Because there was no end of killing these vermine I kept for the purpose in my pockett a peece of a hollowe cane which I was wont to thrust under my skirts up into my back, and rubbing my dublet a while with the open end thereof I could afterwards knock out of itt into my hand or uppon the floore 20 or 30 of those creepers. What here I write of my owne experience I knowe I mighte also bouldlie affirme of my neighbours, who were in no better a predicament than my selfe. Our victualls were course: for the most part dry ship bisket, and sometimes a little oyl'd poor Johne whereof there was good store in our shipp, but neither butter, oyle nor vinegar with itt, and this kept from us but at our meales. True it is wee had a little bottle of vinegar bestowed upon us by our marchant, but because George Champian was sick of feaver & could not eate poore John, haveing no better dainties to comfort him in his extremitie wee reserved this vinegar for him to steepe his dry bisket in, and this was his onlie foode for divers daies. If wee mighte but have had our fills of sweete water this daily want of foode would have beene more tollerable, which

---

[104] 'I and another of my companions got on shoare, unwilling to venture any further in the ship, but finding there a lighter boate of the Governors ready for Cales wee embarkt our selves therein' (Wadsworth, 45). For Peter Edwards, *alias* Amesius Eveleigh, see CRS 73 (1992), 65.

[105] = dysentery.

was at our meales given us in a verie small stint, but at other times not
a supp allowed upon any tearmes, with which want wee were now as
tormented as ever wee had been in our Hamburghers ship. One of
these nightes, I lying awake and not able to take any rest by reason of
the scortching heate that burnt mine entralls for want of some coole
moysture, at length after manie solicitous and projecting thoughts
resolved to have water before morning though it should cost me deare.
Knowing therefore where the barrells stood, I made towards them (as
lame as I was), handsomelie steping over the leggs and bodies of those
Hugonots that slept nere them as guard. Where when after many
adventures in the dark I had found them out, alas my hearte grew
could even amongst my scortching entralls, findeing a plate of yron
fast [p.62] lockt over the spigott. Then, feeleing out the bunghole, I
perceived a peece of strong lether nayled fast over that. This was also
a great disheartening, but as want ventures upon stone walls so I with
my fingars began to boare at the lether betwixt the nayles till at length
I made a passage for my fingar. Then I began to think of a quill,
strawe, keeks,[106] or any such like hollowe instrument wherewith to suck
the water out. At length it accured to my minde that I had sometimes
seene one of our English Protestants lay a long tobacco pipe nere his
heade when he layd him downe to sleepe. To him therefore I crawle
back in the dark, for all must be done by stealth, least being discovered
I mighte either hazzard a buffetting or at leaste wise be cross'd of mine
enterprize. This pipe as soone as I came nere I sooner discovered with
my nose then felt it with my hands, so furr'd and nastie it was. Yet
welcome it was when I had it, and with it I return'd back as it were
through lions, todes and serpents, so chollerick, envious & mallicious
were those against us over whose limbes I ventured now the third time
and must now venture back a fourth. This I thought to be no lesse an
adventure then if a single souldier should adventure to plunder an
enemies camp. Now therefore that I had gotten the small end of the
pipe into the bung hole, and the bigger to my mouth, methinks I still
heare how the water clinkt downe into my sides much like to a hartie
horse fed with dry provender that gulpes down his water till the skinn
stretch about his sides. In fine it did me no hurt, but I felt myself the
cooler & fresher for three dayes after, and after this comfortable draught
I stole a cupple of poore Johns along with me and arriveing back safe
to mine owne quarter I sate me downe and savorelie in the dark eate
one of them, rawe as it was, without any bread. The other I bestowed
upon some of my companions that wanted the like refreshment, who
eate it also verie savorelie but not with so cool a stomak as I had

---

[106] *sc.* kex, a hollow stalk, or straw.

donne, so good a seasoning doth hunger bring with it to whatsoever homelie food.

Upon the 28 day of this month of October wee discover'd from the coaste of Spayne three ships under sayle upon theire course directlie opposit to us. Therefore suspecting that which was probable by theire course [p.63] towards Barbarie, that they might be Turks, our Captaine, souldiers and mariners layd theire heades together with all speede to deliberate and agree what was most fitt to be done in that exigence of danger. Wee were so farr alreadie drawne from Alarache that there was no returning theither as in like occasions wee had formerlie often done, least we being of heavie burthen and slowe sayle mighte be over taken before wee could reach it. To meete and fighte it out was desperate, the enemie haveing three lighte shipps fitt for warr and wee a dull one of heavie carriage with onlie 7 peeces of small yron ordinance. The constant resolution therefore of all was to hazzard both their lives and shipp rather then fall againe under the Turks slaverie, since sad experience had taught them what it was to bee theire slaves. Wherefore upon a generall resolution they presentlie steere an oblique course on the righte hand towards the Barbarian coaste yet so as they sayled also forwards in theire journey, that in case the enemies assayled us, and wee not findeing ourselves able to deale with them, wee would not want the comfort of the mercilesse rocks, according to the comfortlesse comfort of the poet Virgil: *'Una salus victis, nullam sperare salutem'*, 'One comfort left for the [vanquished],[107] to hope for no reliefe'.

For this was all those wretched mens resolution, to have the rocks at hand whereat to dash our shipp and selves, in case wee could not otherwise escape the enemies. Yet in the meane while wee omitted no industrie that mighte availe us to escape the enemies, both Turks & shipwrack. Wee charged and set forth at their loopeholes our ordinance; we putt in order our musketts, set open our magazin for warr; those that wanted gunns, bills, pikes or swords made themselves great wooden swords of pipestaves, strong & bigg enough to knock downe an oxe withall, and all this because they would not come alive into the Turks hands, which they more feared then sinking to the bottome; and wee 10 offering our service in what wee were able, our Captaine tould us there was no neede of us, they were men enough for so small a compasse. Wee joyfullie accepted of this answere and fell to our prayers as heartilie to Almightie God & the Blessed Virgin and the 2 glorious Apostles St Simon & Jude whose feast it was,[108] beggin our safetie, as ever I think wee asked [p.64] anything; and behold, when the enemies were even now at hand and wee yet farr from land, it being highe

---

[107] Lacuna of one word in the MS.
[108] 28 October.

noone and a faire sunshine day, on a sudden descended so thick a mist uppon us that wee could scarce discerne a man from the prowe to the poope. We bouldlie therefore eschewed the rocks & sayled forwards in the encounter of our enemies yet in great silence, knowing ourselves not to be farr from them & it might be within theire heareing, and scarce was an hour passed in this obscuritie but the white cloude, sweetlie ascending againe from whence it came, left us as it found us in a glorious sunshine and plac'd us out of any greate danger of our enemies; for they, not able to discover us with eyes nor eares as they passed by, were carried above two leagues past us. Yet to let us understand theire good meaning towards us, so soone as in the cleare sunn shine they perceived us now behinde them, they turne rounde and back againe after us as fast as winde and sayles will carrie them; and therefore, haveing the start of them by at least 2 leagues, [we] spread all our cloth, hoise all our sayles, extend our goose wings[109] to gather winde, throwe out barrells and much of our coarsest loading, and fly for life & libertie towards a towne about 6 or 7 leagues distant called Tangiers. And so did God and his glorious saints prosper our flighte that the enemie could by no meanes overtake us before wee reached the towne.

Lett such as want confidence in the goodnes of God in all worldlie afflictions & distresses be here confounded, and learne to expect relief where and when itt shall seeme fitting to his fatherlie providence who was bountifull in times past in guiding the 12 tribes of Israell out of the Egiptian slaverie with a cloude in the day and with a piller of fire in the nighte, and to whome it was no harder, when neede and his glorie required, to send us 12 youthes a cloude to shelter us in the day then to give a north starre to guide by nighte, and who hath made all creatures upon earthe for the use and benefit of man, as he hath made Man for himself, will when our neede & his owne greater glorie require, supplie the want and defect of his creatures by a more particuler concourse of his owne infinit goodnes, as experience taught us in this our [p.65] present distresse or danger. *Benedictus Deus qui non dedit nos in captionem dentibus eorum,* Ps.123; *Quia timor et tremor venerunt super nos et contexerunt nos tenebrae,* Ps.54.

[*Tangier*]

This faire towne, or rather cittie, of Tangieres is a bishope seate, adorned with all varietie of learning taught there, in the possession & under the government of the Portugheses and solelie inhabitted by them, seated on the coast of Barbarie at the mouth or entrance to the strayts to the Medeterranean sea, and in diameter opposit to Cales on

---

[109] = fore and aft sails set on opposite sides of the ship to catch the wind.

the Spannish coaste & in so narrow a passage that from the one cittie
to the other may easilie be discern'd, being no more then 16 miles
distant. This nighte wee safelie sheltred ourselves under the command &
safeguard of this cittie. The next day divers officers & some marchants
came aboard us, as well to see our shipp as the wares she carried,
whome by meanes of an Irish interpreter wee entreated to obtain of
our Captaine that George Champian, who was farr spent in a burning
feaver, might be taken to land, there to gett a little fresh meate for
Gods sake to save his life, for of 10 dayes he had eaten nothing but
bread and vinegar. Which suit they verie charitablie requested and as
fortunatelie obtained, and moreover that 2 others of the most strong &
healthfull of us, viz. John Robinson and Robert Neale,[110] might be
allow'd to attend on him, for he was not able to go by himself alone.
Who as they went up the streets from the waterside, findeing him verie
feeble and too heavie a burthen to be carried betwixt them about the
towne till they should finde relief, not haveing any certaine place to
take him to, they sett him downe upon a block against a wall, meaneing
there to leave him whilst they could seeke out some prieste or other
charitable man that could understand them and answere in the Lattin
tongue, for they had not a word of the Portugese language amongst
them. But they were not parted a stones cast from him when, lookeing
back, they saw him lye groveling on his face in the dust, not able [p.66]
anie whitt to help himself. Speedilie therefore turning back they take
[him] up allmost stifled and conduct him up the streetes as well as they
may, in hopes God would move some pious hearte to commiserate and
afforde him some reliefe, when no sooner look'd for but a gentleman
souldier, takeing notice of some distressed strangers and especiallie of
the sick man in the middst, asked them in the Lattin tongue what they
were and whence they came. This was no small lightening to their
heavie hearts, wherefore haveing brieflie hear'd their distressed condition & present wants he conducted them to the Governours house,
who againe heareing a repetition of theire miseries and wants gave
order the sick man should with all speede be taken to the hospitall,
where all convenient charitie and care should be administred.[111] Where
comeing, he was imediatelie taken to a chamber, lay'd in a comfortable
bed, put into a faire shirte, attended by a servant, sweete and holesome
dyet brought him, a physitian for his soule, another for his bodie, who
observeing his extremitie commanded he should be speedilie let bloud
and other things expedient for a man in his case administered.

---

[110] John Robinson, at 34, was the eldest of the party. Both he and Neale later became
Jesuits. See CRS 73 (1992), 86, 92.
[111] The Governor of Tangier, appointed in April 1622, was Jorge Mascarenhas (García
Figueras, 153).

Wee in the meane while that were still on shipboard, emulating the good fortune of our companions at land, made suite the next day to some gentlemen that came to visit our ship, that they would aske the same favoure for us to go to land so long as our ship should lie at anker before that towne, which was likewise granted us. Wee went therefore altogether to the Governours house with an humble petition to have the libertie for some few dayes to beg the charitie of the towne. To whome he returned this no lesse charitable then curteous answer, that such of us as were not well in health mighte repaire to the hospitall to our other three companions for what wee should stand in neede of; the rest that were in health mighte also take up theire lodgeing there, but must seeke theire foode where they could get it in the towne, because it mighte not be afforded there to any but sick or lame, according to the foundation of the hospitall. Thus with no small comfort wee mett all tenn together againe and according to the order given us, those that were in health went abroad for theire victualls.

Upon All Saints Day those seaven that were well in healthe went to [p.67] the Cathedrall church to Highe Masse, and after sermon was made by the Bishopp of that place they delivered an humble petition to be reade for begging the charitie of such as were dispos'd towards relieveing theire present wants, the success whereof came to about 7s, and after service they were all severallie invited home by divers of the best of the towne and, as homelie as they were in aparrell and mute in theire language, were placed with them at theire tables to dinner. After evensong againe manie, moved with the like charitie towards them for what was now reported in the towne of our qualitie, educa-tion and miseries, tooke some two some three home with them to supper. At bedtime wee mett altogether againe at the hospitall, where [we] could with content sit and recount our dayes fortunes and shamelesse begging and the charitie of those good Portugheses. And wee again that were lame and sick had enough to say of our private chapple, and of the charitie and all kindes of comoditie wee found in the hospitall.

The next day being the Commemoration of All Soules eight of our companie repaire againe to the church service, as well to distribute theire owne spirituall almes to the faithfull departed as with hopes to finde the same charitie from the good cittizens which they had tasted the day before. In which meanewhile our Captains mate with theire Hugonote & English Protestants at shipboard, haveing a faire shipp in their possession well fraught with good marchandise not sought after by any one nor so much as knowne to any one that could then or afterwards challenge it from them, had plotted to gett her to passe the Mediterranean sea and at Argiers to sell to the Turks there not onlie the shipp and marchandise but also all the Catholicks of divers nations which were with them and were little or nothing suspicious of this conspiracie; neither should they be able to prevent it, though they mighte chance to get the knowledge of it, because all the offices and armes must be put into those hereticks hands. For this reasone our Captaine was verie sollicitous how to gett us tenn youthes from the towne into his shipp againe, that he might hoyse up sayle and be gonne. For this end he made greate complaints of us in the towne, that wee had been [p.68] ransom'd from Salle at greate rates, that he was to be accountable for us; that he justlie suspected our comeing into that towne to be for no other end then to give him the slip and defraud the deceased marchants executors of the price of our ransome; it was therefore just wee should be compeld to shipboard againe. Thus haveing handsomelie forged this complaint against us he procured a warrant for the arresting us and at the time as divine service was ended, when everie one was hastening home to his dinner, our companie, little surmising any mischief towards, were mett at the Churchdore by the Alguaziells,[112] or baylifs, which apprehending them deliverd them to the Captaine at the shipp. Yet it was the good fortune that two which were invited by a gentleman home to dinner with him went forth by a back dore and so escaped the baylifs; which two about 3 houres after brought the sad newes to George Champian and me in the hospitall, and that our ship had presentlie hoysed sayle and was gone they knew not whether. This was heavie tydings to us all, nor onlie for that wee were now separated from one another that had so much desired and endeavour'd to returne home together or suffer abroad together, but much more for that wee understood the ship was gone a wrong course up the strayts toward the Mediteeranean sea, whereas by order left by our deceased marchant they were to present both ships and marchandise & passengers to John Bravo de Laguna, the executor living att Cales, which lay on the other side the strayts directlie over against this Tangeres.

But see the singuler care & providence of Almightie God over us, for beyond all humane expectation wee had not beene 3 howers in this affliction for the losse of our six companions but a boate with 2 gentlemen, it seemes factors also to the sayd John Bravo, arrives at Tangers in quest of our ship. Who haveing received information by the two pinaces which had safelie arrived at Cales of the deathe of John Agoretta our marchant, and that a ship was left at Mamora under the charge and command of a French Hugonet, they [p.69] feared that which came to pass, least the Hugonet Captaine mighte prove false and runne away with the ship. Wherefore they undertook this dangerous journey over the maine sea towards an enemies cuntrie in a boate, first

---

[112] Spanish *alguaciles*.

to Mamora, & not findeing him there they went to Alarache, and there
also missing of him but have[ing] intelligence that [we had been][113]
there some dayes since, they made for Tangeres, where when they
understood he was also departed thence not above six howers before
their arrivall and that he was gonne upp the straights beyond his
appointed course it was manifest to them that our Captaine was a
knave and gonne for Turkey with the prize. Though this departure of
the Captaine not a little troubled them, yet they hoped well he might
be stopt at Gibraltar or elsewhere before he should passe the coast of
Spaine. For this cause they resolved not to give him over but still to
pursue him. One onlie difficultie they found remayning, that in case
they should overtake him they neither knewe the ship by sighte nor
any other person within it; they should therefore not dare to challenge
it, thoughe they should meete with it. But when they understood there
were yet in towne foure young men and came forth and belonged to
that ship who could assist them in this difficultie, they came to the
hospitall to us and earnestlie requested us to accompanie them that
nighte in pursuite of our shipp. We found great difficultie at first in
regard of our sick man, George Champian, but they makeing us large
and fayre promises to bring us againe to the rest of our companions
and to set us on Spannish land with sufficient moneys in our purses to
bring us to our journeys end, wee remitted the answer to George
Champian, who was now somewhat hartier, and though in a weak case
for such a journey yet desirous to be partaker of so comfortable and
desired promises he shewed a willingnes to go with them which was an
answere for the rest. Wee were therefore warned to be in readines
against midnighte, the appointed houre for theire setting forth to sea.
And so at the determinate houre, takeing [p.70] leave of our good
friends in the hospitall, wee walked downe to the waterside, I limping
upon my staff and George Champian susteined by our other two
companions. And because the boate could not be brought to the dry
sands, there being neither key nor banks nere whence to ship in, John
Robinson verie charitablie supply[ing] the office of a pennie porter,
there ordinarilie used, striped himself above the knees and carried the
other three upon his shoulders to the boate, whence imediatelie after
lanceing forth with sayles and oares wee furrowed the liquid soyle with
such celeritie and violence that the rebounding waves, cutt by our
encountering prowe, dashed over our heads all the nighte long like a
constant shower of raine, and by sunne riseing the next morning
brought us into the harbour of Gibraltar amongst a woode of shipps,
marchants and others.

[113] MS: 'before'.

[*Gibraltar*]

This Gibraltar is a faire haven and much frequented by the wine marchants, lying on the coaste of Spaine, and as Cales begins the straights towards the maine ocean so this towne ends them towards the Mediterranean sea. Here our Captaine, feareing lest he might be stayd and questiond by the Spaniards whether hee was bound, as commenlie they question all as they pass by, resolved of his owne accord to make his passage fair by resting himself there a nighte. When betimes in the morning wee arrived at this haven towne, our two factors rouse us up to viewe about whether wee could discover our shipp amongst the multitude, when instantlie in the greatest exultation wee threwe up our caps and hands with a '*Los compañeros, los compañeros!*', 'Our companions, our companions!', whome [we] discovered walking above the hatches, for this was all the language wee had to expresse that most joyfull spectacle the world could have afforded us at that time. To this ship therefore our factors make, and demaund to speake with the Captaine, to whome it was answered he lodged all nighte at land. Then they ask for the Captaines mate, to whome haveing related who they were and the cause of their journey they [p.71] requested him to come into theire boate and to go to the towne with them. Whether when he came, they there committed him to safe custodie, and finde[ing] the Captaines lodgeing they in like manner set a guard over him. Then takeing officers a long with them, they tooke possesion of the ship and of all that was in itt in behalfe of theire master, John Bravo de Laguna.

After this most important busines was settled, our goulden age drawes nighe and wee tenn students are set on Spanish ground. Our long expected joy returnes more full by how much longer deteyned from us, and now wee see & tread our wished coaste, so deare and welcome to us that holding it too holie to be trodden on by feete, wee stoope to imbrace it and even kisse it with our mouthes. From the waterside wee were by [the] 2 factors brought to an inne in the towne where wee remain'd two dayes to refresh ourselves, in which meane while our Captaine and his mate were discharged for knaves from all command in our ship, and for a more and sufficient rewarde of theire former charge were permitted to depart free from all punishment due for theire treacherie. The greater part of our marriners gave the slip, some into marchant ships of theire owne nation, of which were divers there in that harboure, others by land. Those that honestlie remain'd had order to weigh anker and return back with our ship for Cales, the 2 factors offering us tenne our choise to returne either by land or with them by sea. Wee answered them we had found such bad intreatie and varietie of misfortunes at sea that wee were resolved never more to trust ourselves to the salt waters when wee could go by land, wherefore desired them to lend us money to beare our charges, and within 3 or 4 daies we would by land meete them at Cales, which wee did, and upon the sixth of this month of November they set forward by sea and wee by land, in companie of 4 honest Irish men, our fellow captives, which spake a little Spannish and therefore stood us in great steed in this foote voyage.

[Overland to Cadiz]

But the cuntrie being verie scarce of townes or houses of refreshment, after [p.72] wee had traveayled 3 leagues, and nighte overtakeing us, we were faine to take up with a poor *venta* or drinking house in the highe way, where wee found neither beds nor meate for our money. Wee made a drinking therefore of bread & wine & lodged upon the floore, but before midnighte, findeing our bones wearie and could with this hard and bare lodgeing, and understanding of some cuntrie people were in their journey some part of our way, wee paid our skott[114] & the remainder of the nighte wee travailed a long with them through woodes, hills and derne[115] places amongst the howleing of wolves and the noyses of other wilde beasts, sometimes again over pleasaunt fields and meadowes. This day wee crossed the earthlie paradise commonlie known amongst the poetts by the name of the Elizean fields; now also wee waded through the memorable & famous river Lethes that deprives all of memorie of former miseries that drink of it; and after 8 leagues overcome, towards evening wee reache Medina [Sidonia],[116] the titular towne of the greate Duke of Medina, famous on our English coasts for his memorable voyage of Eightie-eighte, a verie perspicuous towne situated upon a highe hill and therefore made our wearied bodies believe wee were at it when wee had yet many heavie and heartles step[s] to measure.[117] For though wee had this day found verie good refreshment by the way in an inne for our monie, yet were all of us so spent that when wee came within a mile of the towne we could scarce crawle up the hill to it. Some were faintie, others sick, Thomas Coniers was taken with a violent feaver,[118] all of us wearie and sorelie fretted on our feete, and some so grievouslie that you mighte have discovered

[114] = reckoning.
[115] = wild, solitary (archaic by 1630).
[116] Lacuna of one word.
[117] The distance from Gibraltar to Medina Sidonia is about 74 km. For the students to have covered it in two days, as Atkins suggests, was good going. By the river 'Lethe' he means the Guadalete. For this fanciful identification, cf. Mercator's *Atlas* (Amsterdam, 1611), 120: 'Ad ostium Lethes fluminis, quod hodie *Guadalete* ... '. In fact, on the way to Medina Sidonia, the students would have crossed not the Guadalete (which flows into the Bay of Cadiz further north) but the Barbate.
[118] According to Wadsworth (47, *in marg.*) Coniers 'dyed upon his arrivall at Sivill thorow the misery he endured'.

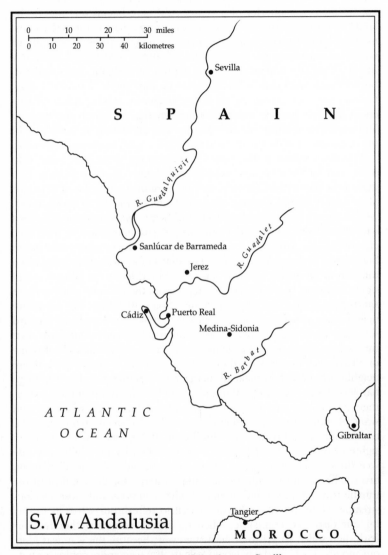

The route from Gibraltar to Seville

the naked bones, & this by want of comodious shooes and stockings
and by the rottennes of our flesh, haveing not been shifted and scarce
goone upon of a quarter of a yeare. And here begins our miserie by
land, as formerlie the heavens, fire and water had conspired against
us. One looks heavilie upon another, but none knowes how to afford
relief, yet was there no spare of charges out of small stock of money
[p.73] either to comfort the hearte within or ease the sores without,
but let everie man call for what mighte do him good. Notwithstanding,
because wee were homelie or rather beggarlie in our apparrell wee
could not obtaine any beds for money wherein to refresh our wearied
limbes but were enforced, and that by speciall favoure & authoritie of
the constables, to take up all our rest al nighte upon matts on the ground.

The next morning, the better to encourage those that were sick,
soare and faintie to a new journey both longer & more tedious than
that of the day passed, for our scarcitie of money and want of language
(if our Irish should overgoe us) would not permit us to linger there,
wee procure a large warme breakfast of beasts livers, minced & butterd
with good sallet oyle, and being arm'd with this good stuffing wee
cheerfullie set forwards for Cales. But our Irish men with theire
buckhorne heeles leade us on so fast that before wee were gotten two
miles from the towne some of our rawe bon'd feet were allmost out of
sighte behinde, pressing everie step upon theire ould soares, more
sharp then thornes or glowing coales. Some therefore stay for theire
neighboures, others complaine that if wee make no more haste forward
wee shal be benighted before wee can reache Cales. Our Irish men
threaten to leave us, those behind even cry for greef as well of paine
of theire feet as for that they are not able to complie with theire
neighboures desires in makeing better haste. Sometimes they trie to go
barefoote, and then both sand and stones frett more upon their soares,
then againe put on theire shooes, which being hard with age and
want of moysture scortch them more. Thus betweene paine & greef,
complaints and threats, wee shuffle on, though not together yet in
sighte of one another, till towards noone when by the highe way side
wee finde a pleasant spring falling from the side of a small descent,
artificiallie bewtified with a comodious cesterne for the comfort of the
thirstie traveler and stored by nature with a copious and most delicious
streame. Here wee al sit downe as well to refresh our selves as to stay
for our dispersed companie, when no sooner come together but our
Irish men solicit [p.74] to be hasteing away, because the way was long,
our money shorte, and day would faile us. But wee, more compassionate
of our neighboures sores and meanes then sollicittous of theire desired
companie, resolved to spend one howre or two there together, not onlie
by this meanes to entice them sweetelie along with us but especiallie
to comforte those that were comfortles and scarce able to set one foote

before an other in that desolate place. And blame us not if both hearte and heeles failed us allmost all, since there were scarce three amongst us perfect in health after many miseries undergone, and since our setting forthe betimes in the morning not received any refreshing till we came to this christall founteine. By which our stay wee lost the comfortable companie of our linguists the Irish men, that went forwards towards Cales with all speede.

After an houres rest, those that were more heartie began to call upon the rest to be travayleing forward, for time went on and our journey was short. Some rise with difficultie, but Peter Middleton and William Fairfax[119] resolutelie answered they were not able to go any further that nighte, therefore intreated the rest not to urge them beyond theire abilitie: they would take up their rest that day at that founteine since they could not meete with any more convenient and comfortable lodgeing. And when the rest offered to stay with them and keepe them companie they againe wished them not to do themselves that wrong, since theire stay could do them two no good and mighte do the rest much hurt, for the next day they would, God willing, meete them againe at Cales. Wherefore wee, observeing they were hearte whole though lame on theire feete and leggs, resolved that it was nothing against charitie, and more discretion, to leave them two for a nighte then to hazzard the lives or welfare of others that were sick or faintie by our staying. So leaveing them two 2 shillings of 5 wee had remayneing we bad them farewell till to morrow when we would expect them at Cales, if God prospered us in our journey.

Though wee were quit of these two lame companions, yet some [p.75] also of the rest hasting forwards with but slowe and faintie paces were the cause that John Robinson, impatient of so extreame loytering (as he tearm'd it) and finding himselfe able to reach Cales in few houres, over went[120] us after the Irishmen; to whome, for the provideing his supper that nighte, wee gave one shilling of the three that were yet remayning in our purse.

Wee were now no more in company than seaven, all of one hearte though unequall & imperfect in health and strength, viz. William Appleby, Thomas Coniers, Robert Neale, George Champian, Thomas Kensington, John Woodas[121] and myselfe, who towards three in the afternoone, wandering about the fields as well to finde some relief to our bodies, for wee were both hongrie and dry and faintie, as to get directions for the way we knew not, after a while about a mile out of the way on the left hand we discryed something like a house, but upon

[119] Not otherwise known.
[120] = outstripped (archaic by 1630).
[121] Not otherwise known.

better observation wee plainelie perceived they were but ruinns of an ould house, or square walls without roof or covering of some decayd vineyard, and so not worth our going to. Therefore wee held on our former course, when on the sudden wee discovered three souldiers upon theire full careere as it were from thence towards us, proper men, well apparrelled and singularlie mounted, the one haveing in his hand a dimilance, another his musket, the third his truncheon, and everie one his sworde at his side. These three cavaliers daunted us very sorelie, for we made noe question but they were some publick officers that went abroad to pick up rougues and vagabonds, such as by our apparrell wee mighte seeme to be: we should therefore, for a conclusion of our miseries, be lead away to the gallies, not able to speake a word for ourselves. Who when they came up to us demaunded whence wee came, whether wee went, what countrymen wee were and the like questions, to whome everie man laying to all the Spanish he had amongst us, wee made up this course answer: '*Ingleses, captivos de Berbaria, studiantes para Sevillia*', that is, 'Englishmen, captives from Barbarie, schollers for Sevill'. Haveing heard this rude answer [they] bad us follow them. Then it was manefest to us what wee had suspected, that they would [p.76] take us away for rogues. But what remedie? Wee had no language to pleade for our selves, neither durst wee refuse to follow them. But before wee had followed much above a stones cast, they made signes and bad us looke towards those ruinous houses and go meete those two men wee sawe comeing thence, which haveing saide they set spurres to their horses & rid a quite differint way with such speede that in a trice they were out of our sighte and wee left doubtfull whether we mighte not endanger our selves by going as wee were commanded, but observeing they were but two, and foote as wee, wee resolved to go meete them. When wee came nere wee beheld the former of them a compleate gentleman in all respects, both in persone, apparrell, & behaviour, of a middle age & stature: the other, following at his heeles, a venerable and comelie old man in a suite of freeze, without a hat, beareing in his righte arme 7 loaves of breade and in left a greate pitcher of wine. After a curteous salutation the former tould us he did heartilie compassionate our sufferings, and doubted not but wee were both faintie and hongrie, haveing eaten nothing since our commeing forth in the morning. He wished us therefore to refresh ourselves with that charitie he brought us. Then he gave us each one a pure white manchet and drought of sack out of his pitcher, the best, wee thought, that ever passed downe our throats, and tould us wee had travailed a long journey that day, were faintie and weake, and Cales, whether wee intended, was yet eighte miles distant. Wee would not therefore be able to reache theither that evening, but if wee turn'd on the righte hand over an hill about halfe a mile of, wee should within one

houre come to a towne called Puerto Reall where wee should find good
meate and lodgeing for our money and next morning betimes reache
Cales by water; bade us therefore be travayling on [in] Gods name.

Who these so charitable people were, wee are none of us to this day
able to say, not that there was any dwelling house whence they came,
but by all conjectures they were of the number of those [p.77] blessed
soules whose octave day this 8th of November was, as wee mighte
probably ghesse by theire charitie in seekeing to relieve us that sought
not after them, in that they understood our wants before wee made
our complaints, in that they gave us directions for our journey when
we wanted language to make it known whether wee would goe, in that
the three souldiers vanished speedilie out of sighte, in the excellencie
of theire breade and wine, in that they foretould us the successe of our
journey at Puerto Reall. Makeing therefore signes of thankfullnes for
their charitie, wee tooke our leave of them, and by the way as wee
went wee savorelie fedd upon our manna from heaven and cherefullie
repeated Gods wonderous favours towards us, *narrantes laudes Domini et
virtutes eius et mirabilia eius quae fecit*,[122] and within an houre came with
ease to the foresaid towne of Puerta Reall.

But takeing up our inne there as wee had bin advised, wee remem-
bered our selves wee had no more then 2s amongst us. Therefore
because some were sick, some lame, and all wearie, wee agreed to have
2 beds amongst us for one shilling (for beds are at six pence a peece
throughout Spaine), and with the other shilling to content our selves
with a lighte supper since wee had alreadie had a good refreshment
that afternoone, never takeing care nor forecasting how to pay for our
boate the next morneing to Cales, which was to be hired at the rate of
6d, or a royall a passenger, whence the town hath its name.[123]

After wee had sitten a while in that inne discanting over the divers
passages of that daies journey, and it being some houres yet to nighte,
William Applebie made a motion that if any one had but so much
courage lefte as to beare him companie, they would together seek out
the priest of the parrish to whome they would in Lattin make knowne
theire state and beg his assistance for some small relief for that
evening. Which motion [was] no sooner made then accepted by George
Champian, now quit of his feaver, and my self, now rid of my swollen
leggs. Thus wee three, not haveing so [p.78] much Spanish amongst
us as to ask for the parrish priests lodgeing, sauntered about the streets
from place to place nere an houre before wee could make anie one
understand what we sought for. At length, in our returne towards our

---

[122] An adaptation of Psalm 77.4.
[123] Puerto Real, the 'royal port', owes its name to Isabel the Catholic, who rebuilt it
in 1483.

lodgeing, wee observed a man in blacke walking before us, whome by his apparrell wee conjectured to be a scholler. George Champian therefore made haste after him and bouldlie salutes him with '*Loquitur Dominatio vestra Latine?*', 'Does your worship speake Lattin?', to whome he againe, '*Ita loquor. Quid vultis?*', 'I do. What would you have?' This was comfort enoughe. Then wee related to him our intentions in travaileing and the divers misfortunes wee had fallen into, and lastlie that our present desire was to make our case knowne to theire parrish priest who, we doubted not, would in his charitie afforde us some reliefe. This honest man we talked [with] with all proved to be an apothecarie of that towne and saviour like bad us '*Venite post me*', 'Come along with mee', but not findeing the parrish priest at home hee leade us downe to the waterside where he bespake a boate for us and our companions against the next morneing because hee saw wee wanted language to do it. Whome a cupple of gentlemen sitting at the river side to take the coole aire of the evening merrilie asked, 'Mr Apothecarie, what attendance have you gotte there to waite upon you?' To whome he related all wee had tould him of our state and misfortunes. The two gentlemen moved with compassion, opening theire purses, gave him 6d a peece for us. He findeing so good successe from them, tooke the same course also at everie likelie house as he returned back up the streets towards our inne, where when he came, saluteing curteouslie the rest of our companions, he layd us down 8s which he had gathered from dore to dore for us, with parte whereof he bought[124] us a verie good supper and for the next dayes brakefast at a cooks shopp, and at his owne cost gave us 2 quarts of wine. This was quite a differint conclusion from what the begining of the day had promised us, yet it was [p.79] according to the prediction of our benefactours from the ruinous house and nothing differint from the wonted goodnes of Almightie God *qui dat iumentis escam illorum et pullis corvorum invocantibus eum.*[125] Haveing therefore in gratefull manner complyed with this good apothecarie and bidden him good nighte, before wee betook us to our rest wee kneeled down upon our wearied knees, gave the glorie to Allmightie God, the author of all good, and praise to All Saints, whose octave day it was.

[*From Cadiz to Seville*]

The next morning, being Sonday, wee arrived betimes at Cales, where before all other places we repayr'd to the church of the Fathers of the Societie of Jesus and there attended to prayer, heareing of masses and thanks-giving for our safe arrivall at length at that long desir'd

---

[124] MS: 'brought'.
[125] Psalm 146.9.

place, when no sooner knowne by the good religious Fathers of that house but kindelie enterteyned and after dinner directed by them to an English Catholick marchant in the towne called John Skone,[126] consul at that time for the English marchants there resideing, who as these priests understood had order from the English Colledge at Sevill to relieve us in all wee wanted if it should be his chance to heare of 12 such youthes as wee. And here the care and charitie of the religious priests of the two Colledges of St Omers, whence we came, & of Sevill whether we were going, cannot sufficientlie be comended, in that as soone as they understood by John Collert, our first Captaine, broughte prisoner into the Lowe Cuntries, and by Jaques Bamberie and his false brethren that arrived safe at San Lucar, that wee were lost & could not learne whether wee were carried, these 2 Colledges haveing forelaid[127] most of the greatest haven townes as well in Spain and France as in the Lowe Cuntries with order for such marchants or friends as had the best intelligence to inquire us out and lay out either money or what else wee should stand in neede of, to be repaide them againe by the saide Colledges. And furthermore the Colledge of Sevill had alreadie before our arrivall dealt with the Cruciati Trinitarians, or Cruched Friars, whose proper institute it is to redeeme captives, to send into all parts of Turkey to enquire [p.80] us out & ransome us at any rates if they should chance to heare of us.[128]

Here by the care and curtesie of John Skone wee had a [...][129] who not only furnished us with good and wholesome fare & lodgeing but with shirts, hatts, bands, shooes, stockings and other such furniture as wee stood in present neede of. And now againe wee meet with John Robinson, to whome relateing the particular blessings of God upon us after his & the Irish mens departure he likewise tould us he had no lesse reason to praise Gods speciall goodnes to him then we to us, since much about the same houre as wee were refreshed with bread and wine he was mett in the way by a man rideing upon an asse, with a paire of panniers under him, who without further intercourse of wordes friendlie asked him if he were not hongrie, to whome he answered, 'Sy, senior'. Then he pulled out a large manchet and a greate pomegranett & gave it him and bade him adieu, wherewith being well refreshed he came in good time to his journeys end.

Whil'st wee were seriouslie relateing these & such like passages,

---

[126] A Juan Skerone (*Hispanice* Esquero) signed an affidavit at Marrakech in July 1609. Anthony Sherley described him in 1622 as chief of the English merchants in Morocco (*SIHM, Angleterre*, ii.545).

[127] = forewarned.

[128] On the Trinitarian order, founded by St John of Matha in 1198 for the ransoming of captives, see Dan (himself a Trinitarian), 464–514.

[129] Lacuna of ? four words.

haveing a little before taken order with Mr Skone for the sending mules to looke after Peter Middleton and William Fairfax, left the day before at the founteine, all unexpected enter the two amongst us and make upp our joys. Whome haveing cherefullie saluted wee set them to the table, and as they revived themselves with a good dinner they merrilie recounted to us theire successe since our departure from them: how towards sunset, after wee were gon from them, limping over the hills on the righte hand, within halfe a mile of the founteine they discovered a farme house, whether they went and were by the good wife of the house sufficientlie relieved with victualls, though neither could they understand her language nor shee theirs. But theire lodgeing was in the strawe in an out house attended by a sowe and piggs.

The next day Mr Skone accompanied [us] to John Bravo de Laguna his house, to whome we made our acknowledgement that we were 10 of the 12 English students ransom'd from Salle by his factor John Agoretta. Who demaunding of our names turn'd over his booke of accounts left him by his sayd factoure, but readeing the names of a hundred and fiftie, as well English as others, and the rates [p.81] of eache mans ransome, he could neither finde theire names nor any rate of our ransome, wherefore he againe asked us what wee knewe concerning any money paid for us. Wee answered him plainelie and sincerelie what had passed concerning our first bargaine with our patrons, but after wee had begun to deale with John Agoretta his factor wee remitted our whole busines to his discretion & charitie [and] could not therefore certeinlie tell what he had done for us, as he himself had often tould us & lying on his bed also said, *we knewe not yet what he had done for us*. Yet this wee certified him, his factour had lent us 40s for our maintenance whilst wee were housekeepers in Salle, which wee desired John Skone there in hand presentlie to discharge for us with that other money wee had borrowed at Gibraltar for our foote journey. Then he tould us he had no more to say to us unlesse we were able to say anything of ourselves, for according to the accounts delivered in to him either John Agoretta had paid nothing for our ransome or he had disbursed it free out of his owne purse. Thus wee were dismissed.

But before a twelvemonth came about this question was clearlie solved, for there came letters from Salle to our English Collidge at Sevill directed from the Mores our patrons, demaunding the summe of £300 from us, certifying that John Agoretta [...][130] had left them in a chamber, whereof he deliver'd them a key at his departure, £300 worth of Spanish cloth as a pawne till he should send them the £300, but hovering 3 or 4 daies in theire harboure before he sett to sea he had in the nighte time by meanes of some private friends in the castle

---

[130] Lacuna of ? three words.

defrauded them and stolen the cloth all away into his ships; threatened
us severelie, if we failed in the payment of this money due for our
ransome, they would not onlie ever after use all Englishmen the worse,
but if ever they tooke any one of us twelve again, before wee should
be ransomed it should cost us that £300 or our lives.[131] But the threats
of theeves and such as use theire extremitie of crueltie, covetousnes,
and barbarousnes towards all sorts of people little moved us, beginning
then to understand by our books that if the defect of our non payment
concern'd onlie them that had [p.82] unjustlie exacted it from us,
neither justice nor charitie did oblige us to satisfaction, and so it
remaines to this day.

Thus wee came trulie to understand the misticall words of our friend
John Agoretta, 'You know not yet what I have done for you', whose
sense he would not declare to us so long as we were at sea because
there were divers as well of our cuntrimen as other hereticks so
malicious against us that if they had come to understand wee had
cheated the Turks of our ransome would have endeavoured to have
made it knowne before wee were out of danger of being overtaken
againe, or at least wise would have borne us a grudge for it and repin'd
at the marchant for not doing them the like favoure.

Whence Wadsworths slaunder in this legend of lyes and impostures
intituled by him *The English Spanish Pilgrim* is easilie confuted, who there
gives the world to understand that wee cheated our marchant and his
executors of £300 for our ransome.[132] But the reason of Wadsworths
erroure in this pointe mighte be his owne guiltie conscience, who
neither presented himselfe to the executor, John Bravo de Laguna, to
make his acknowledgement of his being ransomed by his factour, nor
was at the English Colledge when the letters came to us from Barberie

---

[131] Eight hundred English captives were held at Salé in 1625, and over fifteen hundred
in 1626 (*CSP Dom. 1625–6*, 414, 516). In a pathetic letter sent from there to his father in
November 1625, Robert Adams of Ratcliff explained that those considered to be of
wealthy family were treated worse than the rest (*SIHM, Angleterre*, ii.591). Cf. *HMC 23,
Cowper* i (1888), 231.

[132] 'The Jesuites of Sivill, having been informed that the merchant disbursed not ready
money for their ransome but was to pay it at his returne, now (he not returning) they
affirmed that they thought in conscience they were out of debt for the matter, never
considering that the merchant had left his warehouse fraught with the value of 10,000
crowns behind, which their deceit his daughter now seeing sued them in the law, but the
Jesuites so possessed the judges that they overthrew her in the cause, so that now she
was left destitute of father and goods, the foresaid Moores and Jesuites being trebly paid.
Now the Jesuites wrote to England to their friends for their ransomes, which being
speedily sent they enjoyed themselves. Moreover they made a Tragicall-comedy of our
voyage, whereby they got much money and honour, whereupon all people admired Gods
providence and our delivery out of such manifest dangers, which the Jesuites ascribed
only to their protector S. Ignatius, we being their schollers, and thereupon they collected
no small summes of money which they pretended was to pay for our ransoming' (46–7).

and so flying the payment and understanding nothing of the truth of the case mighte out of his owne bad and apostating conscience measure and censure us all according to his owne dealeing. For it is to be noted that this our fellow travailer Wadsworth, whose father was an honest converted minister and lived divers yeares in the Courte of Madrid, never entered the Colledge at Sevill to stay as a scholler, but after his landing at San Lucar went first to see his friends at Madrid,[133] thence travelled into Flanders where he lived some time a deboish[134] Captaine, and after awhile selling his place there he came for England, where he not onlie fell from his faithe but became a notorious pursuivant, hatefull to God & man.

And here I cannot omitt to relate one passage in our journey at sea worth the observeing concerning Wadsworth, and it [p.83] was that not long after the pilote of our Hamburgh ship had in scornefull manner tould Captaine Quest that he had the 12 Apostles in his shipp, going to studie to convert England, John Robinson, a man of mature age, not endureing to be often abused by Wadsworths proude and insolent language, tould him one day to his face, 'They say wee are Apostles, but if wee be, thou art Judas, so insolent is they tongue and bad thy carriage'. Which afterwards fell out more true then John Robinson did then at that time conceive, the rest of his fellow travellers after this tedious journey to Spain takeing laudable and orderlie courses. Wadsworth alone proveing treacherous to Gods Church, abjureing his faithe, hath since beene the cause of the spilling many religious priests bloude and of the imprisonment of more, and utter undoing of manie vertuous Catholicks, and as I understand persevers to this day in his apostacie. I leave him therefore with his obdurate hearte to Gods future judgements, wishing all honest soules to beware of him and his slaunderous, scandalous writeings.

Haveing despatched with John Bravo, wee were by Mr Skone set forward in our journey from Cales to San Lucar, partelie by boate and partelie by hired mules, where wee were charitablie entertained by the good English priests of St Georges Residens[135] there and thence conveyed by water up the River Boetis, & upon the foreteenth day of the

---

[133] Wadsworth claims to have met up with his companions at Sanlúcar, where he had been staying with his uncle the consul, and to have accompanied them 'to their Colledge in Sivill, whence taking my leave I left them, being not willing to tast any more of their discipline, and wishing them withall to take order to satisfie the merchants daughter, having alreadie done it for me. The Rector made answer for them to me that he would take that to his charge'.

[134] = debauched. Wadsworth was a 'Captain' on the strength of the commission he obtained in the army of Flanders c.1624.

[135] The Hospice of St George at Sanlúcar, originally founded as a refuge for English sailors in 1517, was acquired by Robert Persons in 1591 as a residence for English priests. See CRS 73 (1992), 1, 5–6.

same month of November wee arrived at our long desired home, the Colledge of St Greg[ory] in the street called Calle de las Armas at Sevill.

Ad majorem Dei Deiparaeque Virginis gloriam.

INDEX

III
HORACE WALPOLE AND
BRITISH RELATIONS WITH
SPAIN, 1738

Edited by Philip Woodfine

INTRODUCTION

The memoir, or memorial, printed here was written by Horatio
Walpole, the younger brother of Sir Robert Walpole, and uncle of his
more famous namesake, Horace Walpole of Strawberry Hill.* This
memorial presents the reflections of a man of considerable diplomatic
experience and ability, for the consideration of the British ministry at
a time of crisis in diplomatic relations with Spain, and was presented
to the inner cabinet in January 1738.[1] British shipping in the Caribbean
had suffered various depredations at the hands of Spanish colonial
guardacostas, their vessels equipped rather like small privateers, and
commissioned to intercept foreign traders and check their ships for
contraband. Illicit trade certainly went on extensively, and the London
merchants who agitated the issue so fiercely were disingenuous in
insisting that the depredations were all committed against innocent
traders going about their business with Jamaica and the British American colonies. However, theirs was a voice which the ministry could
not ignore, especially when their cause was taken up by the Opposition
and made into a test of the effectiveness of the Walpole administration:
the power of London opinion was magnified by the press and orches-
trated by opponents who saw at last the prospect of a 'Patriot' alliance
of Tories and dissident Whigs, sufficiently strong to topple Walpole
from power.[2]

Horatio Walpole's paper was produced at a critical point of the
ministry's response to these pressures, and at a time when it was not
simply the 'Robinocracy' which was under pressure to produce results,

* I am grateful to the late Lord Walpole for his kind permission to work in, and quote
from, the Walpole archives at Wolterton Hall, and to his heir, the present Lord Walpole
for arranging my visit there. The Wolterton (Walpole) MSS have since been acquired by
the British Library. The staff development fund of the University of Huddersfield
generously provided some of my travel expenses.
[1] The memoirs are preserved as duplicates, endorsed 'Wrote Janry 1738. HW.', in the
Coxe Papers (Horatio Walpole), BL Add 9131, the first amounting to 51 folios, ff. 199–
250, and the second to 20 folios, ff. 251–271. The originals are not in Horace Walpole's
surviving papers. For cabinet discussions, see cabinet minutes in BL Add 32993, ff. 57–
8 and the lists in BL Add 33007, ff. 122–4.
[2] See e.g. Linda Colley, *In Defiance of Oligarchy: The Tory Party 1714–60* (Cambridge,
1982); Jeremy Black, *British Foreign Policy in the Age of Walpole* (Edinburgh, 1985); Philip
Woodfine, 'The Anglo-Spanish War of 1739', in J.M. Black (ed), *The Origins of War in
Early Modern Europe* (Edinburgh, 1987); Michael Harris, *London Newspapers in the Age of
Walpole: a Study in the Origins of the Modern English Press* (1987); Robert Harris, *A Patriot Press:
National Politics and the London Press in the 1740s* (Oxford, 1993).

but also George II. The prestige of the monarch was already involved
in the affair: there had been numerous petitions to the king for relief,
and several royal attempts to obtain justice for complainants since the
late 1720s.[3] Now the king was at the centre of the diplomatic storm. A
major petition from the City merchants, fomented by the Patriot
opposition, was put forward in November 1737 and dominated the
political agenda, not least in the press. In early March 1738 there was
to be a major Parliamentary debate on the merchants' grievances, and
in December 1737, when Horace Walpole arrived in England from his
ambassadorial post in the Hague and began writing his memoir there
was circulating a printed list of 52 ships plundered or taken by the
Spaniards. This broadsheet alleged:[4]

> In every one of the above instances, whether the Ship was taken
> or plundered, the Master and Crew were used with the utmost
> barbarity.

While this was not strictly true, as four of the ships listed had escaped
their pursuers altogether, the document claimed that many other
seizures were not included. The impression given by the list is of a long
succession of boarding and plundering from 1728 to 1737: a chain of
unredressed abuses throughout the king's reign. George II was actively
involved in the making of foreign policy decisions in this period, and
it was no mere formula that attached the king's name to documents,
so if the king could not obtain a satisfactory response from the Spanish
ministry it reflected directly on his standing. In November 1737 the
king had issued a long Memorial, drawn up by Secretary of State the
Duke of Newcastle, to the Spanish court, laying out the demand for
speedy justice and British expectations of action.[5] In the months that
followed the ministers in Whitehall had to digest the offensive slowness
of Spanish formalities, a reply coming only in late February 1738, while
the press made the most of the delay and the powerlessness of crown
and ministry. Two Commons' Resolutions of 30 March (OS) 1738
raised the stakes, pressing the King for relief from depredations and
pledging him effectual support, a coded way of saying that there could

---

[3] Examples included the taking of the *Robert*, Story King master, in 1728, on which
petitions to the king were made in May and August 1731, the case still unresolved in
1738; BL Add 32774 ff. 118–20; 15 May 1731, SP 94/129, unfoliated. The cases of the
Anne galley, Samuel Bonham, in 1728 and the *Betty* galley, Richard Copithorne, in 1727
were still being raised by the Opposition press in 1739; *The Case of Samuel Bonham and the
other Owners of the Anne Galley* ... (London, 1737); *Craftsman* 24 Feb (OS) 1739.

[4] *List of British Merchant Ships, Taken or Plundered by the Spaniards*, SP 94/128, p.3.

[5] The Memorial was sent 4 Nov (OS) 1737 and presented by Benjamin Keene, the
ambassador in Madrid, on 10 Dec (NS) 1737; SP 98/129 unfoliated.

be no excuse for not having prompt naval action.[6] Behind the scenes, the administration reviewed the possible options open to them in this embarrassing diplomatic game, complicated from the monarchical point of view by the death of George's consort, Queen Caroline, in November 1737. Indeed Horace Walpole's contribution to the discussions came about because of his return to London from the Hague in order to attend the obsequies of the Queen, whom he seems genuinely to have mourned as a personal loss.[7]

The content of the memorial which Walpole wrote at this time is significant in that he outlines there the main substance of the thinking which was to guide the ministry in the prolonged and difficult nego-tiations over the following twenty months, leading ultimately to war. He appraises the treaty position between Britain and Spain; sifts the issue of the searching of British vessels on the high seas; assesses the historical patterns of diplomacy, and the current power relationships, between the two countries, and their likely effects. He also offers a judgement on the thorny question of whether George II ought to issue letters of reprisal to allow injured British merchants to make seizures of Spanish shipping in order to compensate themselves for their losses. If Horace Walpole had confined himself even to this last issue alone, the document would deserve to be better known, not least because this rather primitive device of international law was one of the most striking ways in which one can observe the continuing personal contribution of the monarch to international relations. In effect, the sovereign was giving a personal commission to the injured subject to take a private revenge on the subjects of a foreign king. Indeed, these were not even the particular subjects who had offended against British trade in the first place, but any vulnerable foreign nationals who could be seized. Such an unusual procedure was justified by presenting international affairs as a matter of interchange between proud and equal monarchs, whose personal dignity was involved in the fortunes of their peoples. When justice was long denied, and the monarch found himself unable to give satisfaction by the normal workings of diplomacy and the courtesies between crowns, then he could have recourse to extreme action, rooted in the traditions of personal monarchy.

---

[6] The Dutch received a reply to their Memorial in December 1737; Trevor to Harrington, 17 Dec (NS) 1737, SP 84/369, f. 102. La Quadra's reply to Keene came at the Pardo, 21 Feb (NS) 1738; SP 94/130, unfoliated. For the Commons' resolutions, see BL Add 32797, ff. 257–261. A good impression of the press reaction can be gauged from, e.g. *Craftsman* 5, 12, 19 Nov (OS) 1737; *London Magazine* 27 Mar (OS) 1738; *Common-Sense, or The Englishman's Journal* 18 Feb (OS) 1738.

[7] He finally obtained a yacht from Helvoet Sluys on 11 Dec (NS) 1737; SP 84/369 f. 60. His letters and scrawled notes at this time do suggest an unusual distress: see, e.g., SP 84/369 ff. 16, 18 & 44.

The really important question in 1738 was how such a proceeding would fit into the existing interchanges between the countries, and whether such a personal intervention would make normal diplomacy impossible. Horace Walpole's advice was to allow the king's own ships to make reprisals, and to grant that right also to private ships armed for war, if the merchants would accept this remedy:[8]

> They cannot be refused them; the Cases of doing oneself Justice are so flagrant, & have subsisted so long, that such a refusal would make us appear a most Contemptible Nation with all our Maritime Power.

However, he was sceptical of the value of this remedy, a point made even more forcibly in the second version of his memoir. As the Spaniards relied on other nations for their carrying trade, there were few Spanish ships of any value to be captured other than the treasure ships of the Galleons or Flota. Unlike many Opposition politicians, and some in the Ministry, Walpole from the beginning was dubious of the allure of this silver windfall.[9] Instead, he saw reprisal as a measure which would yield little, and might bring on open war, but which, for reasons of monarchical and national prestige, was unavoidable. At first sight, it would seem that the old-fashioned device of reprisals had no place in delicate foreign-policy negotiations, yet the ministry seems to have been persuaded by the cautious and thorough exposition of Walpole's memorial. They adopted his somewhat legalistic view that the issuing of reprisals was indeed justified. Since this was so, they had only limited room to manoeuvre. Clamour from those 'without doors' and fears for the prestige of the Crown were irresistible pressures. A few months later the king authorised reprisals, a move which resulted in no benefit to British traders, but damaged the already sensitive relations with Spain.[10] Probably it was inevitable that ministers in Britain and in Spain should have widely differing views of the issues at stake between them in the late 1730s, and Horace Walpole's memorial did nothing to alter this basic diplomatic conflict. However, he was

[8] BL Add 9131, f. 245. The Cabinet later ruled that prizes taken by naval vessels between the general order for reprisals and the declaration of war should be divided between the captors and the suffering merchants. In time of war, captors would receive their prizes, in a manner to be announced by the king. Cabinet minutes, 11 Apr (OS) 1740, BL Add 33004, f. 31.

[9] Philip Woodfine, 'Ideas of Naval Power and the Conflict with Spain, 1737–1742', in Jeremy Black & Philip Woodfine (eds), *The British Navy and the Use of Naval Power in the Eighteenth Century* (Leicester, 1988).

[10] The best introduction to the subject of prizes and reprisals at this time is still Richard Pares' masterly *Colonial Blockade and Neutral Rights 1739–1763* (Oxford, 1938). The declaration of reprisals came in early March 1738; see BL Add 32797 ff. 142 & 154; Keene to Newcastle 12 Apr (NS) 1738, SP 94/130 unfoliated.

influential because he presented the differences very precisely, for the benefit of the leading British ministers, and clarified the issues of principle regarding British navigation rights. Above all he starkly analysed the question as being on the one hand a matter of legal, treaty rights, and on the other a question of power rivalries. Walpole's own conclusion was that Britain must use all the leverage it could to bring Spain into new and more secure treaties, but his analysis made war more likely if the treaty-making attempt should fail.

The memorial deserves attention also for the light it throws on the processes of cabinet discussion in this period, and the position of Horace Walpole as a ministerial adviser. Even abroad, he was kept constantly supplied with copies of all the correspondence in and out of the Duke of Newcastle's office, which is no doubt why his surviving papers bear such a resemblance to the Newcastle Papers and the State Papers Foreign.[11] When in England, Horace was treated as one of the small group involved in shaping the details of diplomacy. A letter of the Duke of Newcastle in the spring of 1738, for instance, sent 'dear Horace' various papers to be laid before Cabinet, including instructions to Lord Waldegrave, the British ambassador in Paris which had been amended by Horace himself. Walpole was to read them, present them to his brother, and arrange the time of meeting. In the meantime, Newcastle asked for assistance over the vexed Georgia issue:[12]

I should be Obliged to you, if you would sketch out something for Oglethorpe; I will be trying something myself.

It seems clear that the talks of the inner circle of ministers were like an orchestral rehearsal from which the King's leading violin was absent. Ministers had to guess his aims and wishes, and plan their performance accordingly. The finer tactics of this process were beyond the scope of Horace Walpole's written comments, but his input was to provide a base for ministerial discussion and decision. His two papers were drawn up as a formal attempt to inform and persuade his influential colleagues. They came from a man whose chief experience was in diplomacy, and who had for several years been the British envoy to the United Provinces at the Hague, a leading centre of intelligence and diplomatic news. Indeed, the style of this memorial, like that of a number of Walpole's other political papers, bears the imprint of the 'written Gazetins' and the printed Gazettes, usually in French, and often originating in the Hague, which circulated among diplomats in this period.[13] Walpole's

[11] Newcastle to Walpole, 11 Sep (OS) 1739, BL Add 15946, ff. 34–5.

[12] Newcastle to H. Walpole, Claremont, 3 Apr (OS) 1738, BL Add 32797, f. 219.

[13] See e.g. BL Add 32801 ff. 137–40 for two manuscript gazetins of July 1739; printed gazettes were often filed among the State Papers Foreign now in the Public Record Office.

sphere was that of diplomacy and treaties, as even his critics acknowledged, though with some degree of irony. Leading opposition politician William Pulteney wrote in 1731 to Francis Colman, the resident in Florence:[14]

> In the present Treaty making Age, there is but one way for a foreign Minister to gett into favour, & become considerable, and that is by trying to make a Treaty as well as the best of them. This I understand you have done ... The great Horace himself I dare say could not have done better.

The existence, and the form, of the present memorial do suggest that Horace Walpole occupied a place in the decision-making process of government rather more significant than one would imagine from the neglect which he has suffered at the hands of historians in recent years. It is common enough for historians to underrate the active voice, and to stress the role of those who (like Newcastle) leave voluminous papers, at the expense of those who (like George II) leave few. Yet here is an underrated politician whose main influence seems to have come precisely through his use of written memoranda. He was by nature a memorialist, a man who organised his thoughts into formal, often chronological papers. Contemporaries, by contrast, exaggerated his role, assuming for the sake of polemic that the brother of the all-powerful first minister must himself be both a force behind the throne and an incompetent place-holder. Neither was true, but the ballads, pamphlets and newspapers of the period often enshrine a simple view of the nepotistic *duumviri*, 'his Honour and his Excellency' in corrupt and blundering charge of the nation.[15] What Horace Walpole's written intervention in 1738 shows is that his part in the process of discussion among the political inner circle was confined to his sphere of acknowledged expertise, especially in treaty matters, and that his views were complemented and checked by those of the influential Lord Chancellor, Lord Hardwicke.

Hardwicke's hand can be seen in the numerous additions to the first draft of Walpole's memoir, comments which were almost all incorporated in the reordered and amended second version of the paper.[16] The first memoir was written in the then common draft form, with the paper folded vertically and the text written on only one of the resulting halves, leaving the other free for amendments. The shorter second

---

[14] Pulteney to Colman, 25 Aug (NS), BL Add 18915, f. 8.

[15] E.g. *An Historical Ballad, humbly inscrib'd to the Duumviri* (London n.d., c.1730); *The Negotiators. Or, Don Diego brought to Reason* (London, 1738).

[16] The hand in the margins matches that of Hardwicke in his voluminous legal notebooks, and in some undoubted holograph documents. E.g. BL Add 35870, ff. 18–28, attested by his son; Add 32692, ff. 280–82, 348–89; Add 34506, f. 174.

paper was written in bold black ink, on double-spaced ruled lines, and perhaps intended for the eyes of George II, who might well, at 55, have needed such assistance. This is the version which is printed here, with the addition of some more substantial material from the first draft. It is however worth noting that both versions of the memorial seem to have been laid before cabinet council meetings, so presumably the ministers were privy to, and discussed, the issues on which Walpole and Hardwicke had differences. Hardwicke was an important link between the two main camps within the ministry, that centring on Sir Robert Walpole, and that beginning to form around the Secretary of State for the South, the Duke of Newcastle. A valued and trusted protégé of Walpole, Hardwicke was also a close friend of Newcastle, supporting him by giving constant reassurance and advice on a wide range of government papers. No-one seeing the volume of Hardwicke's surviving legal notebooks and case papers could easily believe, unless compelled to it by the evidence of the political manuscripts, on how great a range of judicial, parliamentary, and diplomatic issues the Lord Chancellor was required to pass a judgement, almost always at short notice, and often in full law term, in the press of the business of his office. When Newcastle needed assistance, he was not prone to consider the convenience or the workload of those who could give it.[17] One such chore for the Chancellor was looking over bulky packets of ancient Board of Trade reports, in September 1738, with a view to putting forward ideas for a new treaty of commerce with Spain.[18] Such materials were not always easy to come by, as is shown by a revealing comment of Hardwicke's on Walpole's draft. He referred to the ambassador sent to Spain in 1714, who finally negotiated a working convention on the Asiento and the whole issue of Anglo-Spanish trade:[19]

> Sr. Paul Methuen's instructions were so ample & descriptive, of ye severall indulgences formerly allowed to the English in ye sailing of their goods, & levying ye dutys, in ye ports of Old Spain; that the Inspection of them may perhaps be of use at this juncture; if they are not to be found in ye Secretary's Office, yet Sr. Paul I suppose can furnish them.

[17] E.g. Hardwicke's comments on the memorial of la Quadra, the Spanish Secretary of State, to Keene, 21 Feb 1738 (NS), BL Add 35884, ff. 1–4. His comments on an earlier paper by Horace Walpole can be found in BL Add 32692, f. 300. A few examples of his range can be seen in e.g. BL Add 35875 *passim*, and his methodical approach to an extensive workload can be sampled in BL Add 36051 and 36052 *passim*.

[18] Newcastle to Hardwicke, 25 Sep 1738, BL Add 35406, ff. 49–51.

[19] BL Add 9131, f. 212. Hardwicke was trusted to offer his judgement on the most important matters too, as in his comment on a draft of the king's ratification of the Convention with Spain in January 1739: John Couraud, Assistant Secretary, to Hardwicke, 20 Jan 1739, BL Add 35406, f. 70.

In the absence of an organised civil service always on hand to provide
such analyses, ministers earned their places. Even the indefatigable
Hardwicke was moved to complain in September 1739. He had been
called upon by Newcastle to sift the provisions of the Utrecht treaties
of peace and commerce, following a dispute in which Admiral Haddock
had searched a French ship. In a holograph letter, Hardwicke urged
the Duke to put this kind of work on a more settled basis:[20]

> I could wish that some intelligent and careful person were employed
> to peruse & compare all ye Treaties of this kind now in force with
> any foreign Powers: otherwise, if our present Disturbances should
> continue, the King's Admirals & Officers may run into many
> mistakes; and their Ignorance or Inadvertency may be imputed as
> Blunders by ye Administration, when it is impossible for any man
> to have those minute Particulars always in his head.

It was an established practice, then, to circulate documents among the
inner circle of ministers and advisers, and those who had the task of
drawing up and amending such documents were undoubtedly influential
in forming ideas on policy. The present memoir, drawn up by Horace
Walpole and revised by Lord Hardwicke, formed a significant stage in
the evolution of the ministerial policy towards Spain. By comparison
with the first draft of the memoir, the revised paper is not so exhaustively
concerned with treaties, and has more to say on the position of the
South Sea Company, a major obstacle to harmonious Anglo-Spanish
relations. The revised memorial has more to say also on the use of
warships, and is in general more sanguine about naval power. Where
the first draft is the work of a diplomat concerned with the process of
agreement, the final version is more concerned with practical solutions
on the seas, and with fears about the possible seizure of British effects
in Spain by way of retaliation.

No evidence seems to exist as to how the paper came to be written,
whether by the invitation of Sir Robert Walpole or Newcastle, or simply
by Horace Walpole's own determination. The downfall of Sir Robert
in 1742, and the prospect of a full-scale investigation and impeachment,
led the elderly statesman, who as a young man had sampled the
lodgings in the Tower, to see to the burning of large quantities of
papers. Even had they been extant, they might not have thrown much
light on such questions, according to insider Henry Etough:[21]

> Had Lord Orford lived no Instance, I believe, could have prevailed
> on him to attempt even a Short Narrative of ye most material
> Affairs in which he had been concerned. He was utterly averse to

---

[20] Hardwicke to Newcastle, Carshalton, 10 Sep (OS) 1739, BL Add 32692, ff. 280–2.
[21] Etough to Rev. Thomas Birch, 16 July 1746, BL Add 4306, fo. 74.

all voluntary Trouble & Business; what was necessary he dispatched with great Care & Vigour . . . His Memory was great & amazing[;] a few short hints were sufficient to supply [him] with Notice of all past Transactions. These I believe were ye whole [of] his own MS & therefore had they been preserved would have been insignificant. The Papers he had from others were of such a Nature, as made them ye proper Subjects of Destruction. Both he & his Brother during ye Ferment & Enquiry were too comprehensive in what they devoted to ye Flames.

Horace Walpole's own papers, still kept at Wolterton Hall, contain noticeably few letters from and to his brother. Sir Robert Walpole's letters to his protégé Benjamin Keene were burned, on the minister's orders, before Keene gave up his post and left Spain in 1739. Nonetheless, the sequence of events at least can be outlined with some confidence, and the likelihood is that the initiative came from Horace Walpole himself. He was never a man to resist intervening in the affairs of his fellow diplomats, and regularly made known to Keene his views on the conduct of the Spanish negotiations. When the Spanish court made representations about the British occupation of Georgia, Walpole ordered Keene to supply him direct with information about the Spanish view of the Treaty of 1670.[22] He was also in the habit of penning similar 'position paper' documents; abstracts, states of the question, projects of treaties etc., though none of those which survive are so finished or so clearly composed for others as this present memoir.[23] Furthermore, Walpole can be considered at this time as at the apogee of his powers. In 1736 he had turned down the chance to become Secretary of State for the Northern Department, though supported for the post by Queen Caroline and by Sir Robert Walpole. As yet he was unaware of his impending loss of the king's favour, a change which, in a manuscript autobiographical memoir, he dated from soon after the fateful death of the Queen.[24]

Before that event, Horace Walpole must have felt that he was in a special position in the ministry headed by his brother. He seems almost to have viewed himself as a Secretary of State manqué rather than as envoy to the United Provinces. From his post in the Hague, he disagreed at a distance with the interpretations which the Duke of Newcastle placed upon the treaties in question between Britain and Spain. Much later, when commenting on the draft declaration of war against Spain

---

[22] Walpole to Keene, The Hague, 3 Sep (NS) 1737, BL Add 32795, ff. 250–1. For other testy interventions see, e.g., same to same 31 Oct (NS) 1737, BL Add 32796, ff. 39–40; same to same, 7 Nov (NS) 1737, ibid. ff. 59–60.

[23] See the Wolterton (Walpole) MSS, Original Draughts and Political Tracts (2 vols).

[24] 'Mr. Walpole's Apology', Coxe Papers Vol LV, BL Add 9132.

in October 1739, Walpole was to complain that the ordering and emphasis of the grievances stated in it owed more to opposition peers with whom Newcastle was friendly than to the advice and conduct of the ministry itself. In November 1737 the major petition from the City merchants had founded their grievances expressly on their rights of navigation under treaty. It laid great stress on the right to unmolested navigation given in the 1667 Treaty, a stress which Newcastle reproduced in the royal memorial sent soon afterwards to Spain.[25] Unfortunately, unlike the 1670 Treaty, that of 1667 related only to European waters. Walpole congratulated the Secretary of State on the 'Strong, well reason'd and becoming Memorial relating to the Spanish Depredations, which you have sent by His Maty's Order, to Mr. Keene'. However, in language which in the conventions of the day was extremely pointed, he went on, for Newcastle's eyes alone, to suggest a central flaw in the Memorial:[26]

> I am apprehensive, that if the Spaniards have a Mind, instead of giving Satisfaction, to enter into a nice Discussion of your Memorial, They will observe perhaps, That the Treaty of 1667, and the Articles cited in it, have no manner of regard, to the Navigation, and Commerce to the American seas and ports.

This was, in the event, precisely the mind of the Spanish Court, much to Newcastle's discomfiture.[27] Walpole presented to the States General a Memorial modelled on that to Spain, but took it upon himself entirely to omit the 1667 Treaty from his representations to them.[28] The anti-Spanish tone and the force of the memorial to the Dutch provoked concern at Horace Walpole's hawkish aims, and led to rumours of a split between him and Newcastle.[29] Certainly he must have looked very closely into the evidence in support of his position and soon after his arrival in England he set down the results of his reading and reflection on the issue of the treaties and the general case for action against Spain.[30] From that stem the long papers which with their various revisions were laid before cabinet. One thing is clear, despite the

---

[25] H. Walpole to Hardwicke, 14 Oct (OS) 1739, BL Add 35586, ff. 202–5. Memorial SP94/129, unfoliated.

[26] H. Walpole to Newcastle, The Hague, 26 Nov (NS) 1737, SP 84/369, f. 1.

[27] See e.g. la Quadra to Keene, Aranjuez 26 May (NS) 1738; SP 94/130, unfoliated.

[28] H. Walpole to Newcastle, The Hague, 26 Nov (NS) 1737; SP 84/369 ff. 1–6.

[29] St. Gil to Geraldino 10, 24 & 31 Dec (NS) 1737; Geraldino to St. Gil 17 Dec (NS) 1737; SP 94/206 ff. 17, 45, 60–62, 27.

[30] He did not of course have available a large body of diplomatic analysis or commentary on which to rely. He used in particular: Jean Dumont, *Corps Universel Diplomatique du Droit des Gens* (Amsterdam, 8 vols 1726–31); Thomas Rymer, *Foedera Conventiones* (London, 17 vols, 1704–17); William Camden, *Annales Rerum Anglicarum et Hibernicarum Regnante Elizabetha* (1677).

criticisms of contemporaries. The quality of analysis and the understanding of the wider political and historical context found in these documents show that the ministry was far from considering only domestic clamours and political expediency.

CONSIDERATIONS RELATING TO THE NAVIGATION, AND COMMERCE OF GREAT BRITAIN IN AMERICA, WITH RESPECT TO THE TREATYS WITH SPAIN, AND THE DEPREDATIONS COMMITTED BY THE GUARDA COSTAS

January 23rd. 1737/8

The Disputes depending between Great Britain and Spain, either relate to the Depredations committed by the Spanish *Guarda Costas* upon the British Merchant Men, by taking and confiscating their Ships under Colour of their carrying on an Illicit Trade; Or to the New Settlement made in Georgia, by the Trustees, in Consequence of Letters Patents, granted by his Majesty for that purpose. Before I enter into a particular Discussion of what is reasonable and Just to be done with respect to these Two Points according to the present Circumstances and Treatys subsisting between the Two Nations, it may not be improper to take a View of the Principles, and Practices which formerly prevailed on Both Sides, in the Various Controversys that happened between the Two Nations in different Reigns on Account of the West Indies.

As soon as the Spaniards had discovered, and made Themselves Masters of Considerable Settlements in the West Indies, and had received a formal Gift or Investiture from the Pope of all the Discoverys that had been made or should be made in Those Parts; They pretended to have an undoubted Right to all that Country, exclusive of any other Nation that might find out and make other Establishments there; And to interrupt the Navigation, and Commerce of every Body else to any Place, whether possessed or not possessed by the Crown of Spain.[1]

It is unnecessary to dwell upon the absurdity of this Chimericall Right derived from the Pope, to which no other Sovereign, but more

---

[1] As soon as Columbus first returned from the Americas in March 1493 the (Spanish) Pope, Alexander VI, issued bulls confirming Spain's exclusive title to the new hemisphere, extending, according to the bull *Inter caetera*, from 100 leagues west of the Azores. Vagueness about the exact whereabouts of America led the Spanish to be generous to their chief colonial rivals, though, and in June 1494 the Treaty of Tordesillas between Spain and Portugal moved this imaginary north-south line to 370 leagues west of the Azores, which in the event gave Brazil to the Portuguese.

especially Those that would not Acknowledge his Supremacy in any Case whatsoever, would submitt, or suffer Themselves to be excluded from the same Right, and Privilege, as the Spaniards had Exercised, to Discover and make new Acquisitions in America, and enjoy the free Navigation in Those as well as in any other Seas for the Benefit of their Subjects.

But every Prince or State has a Right to exclude others from trading to his Dominions and Colonys, as a Preeminence inherent to his Sovereignty: unless he has granted that Liberty to any Power by Custom or some Solemn Act or Treaty of Friendship and good Correspondence between Them. So far, therefore, as the Spaniards pretend to forbid and to interrupt by violent means, the English from all Traffick with the Spanish possessions in America, Where They have never allowed any Navigation or Commerce, They certainly proceed in a regular and justifiable manner; And the only Question is, whether the English by Custom or Treaty with Spain have ever had a permission to sail, or Trade to the Spanish West Indies, or not?

A Fleet with Land Forces, sent by Oliver Cromwell having in 1655 made an unsuccessfull Attempt upon Hispaniola, to make amends for that Disappointment, took Jamaica.[2] The Protector immediately caused a Manifesto to be Published, conceived in Terms, suitable to his Character, to justify this unexpected Enterprise: where, among other Grievous Complaints of the violent and Barbarous Treatment which the English had met with from the Spaniards, it is alledged, that they were not suffered to trade in the West Indies, notwithstanding in the Treaty made between Henry the 8th. and the Emperor Charles Vth. in 1542:

> Pax et Liberum Commercium inter utrosqs. et utrorumqu. Populos peromnem alterutrius Ditionem, Portus et Territoria quaecunque sancitum est, sine ulla Occidentalis Indiae exceptione quamvis illam tunc Temporis Imperator ille obtineret.

This Argument in all likelyhood is taken from what is said to the same Effect by Cambden in the Life of Queen Elizabeth on occasion of an Expedition, made in 1569 [sic; 1568] by Hawkins to the West Indies, who with five Ships under his Command was surprised by the Spaniards in violation of a solemn agreement with the Vice King of Mexico, at the Port of St. John de Ullua a little Island in Vera Cruz and very ill used by them; of which Cambden giving an account, says:

---

[2] This was a sore point for ministers at this time, since opponents made much of Cromwell's vigour and success, compared with the tameness of the Walpole administration. See e.g. The Craftsman 3 June 1738, 13 Jan 1739; (Anon) The British Sailor's Discovery. Or the Spanish Pretensions Confuted (London, 1739), 53–71.

Hinc viri militares et Natio Nautica per Angliam fremuerunt, contra Hispanos bellum expoposcerunt, eos foedifragos esse clamitantes quandoquidem [foedere] inter Carolum 5tum Imperatorem et Henricum 8tum convenerit ut Liberum esset Commercium inter subditos utriusque Principis in omnibus et singulis Regnis, Dominiis Insulis, America quidem, quae tunc ad Carolum spectavit, ne excepta; **Sed Regina his aures occlusit, rebus Scoticis avocata.**

But notwithstanding this great Authority: if the said Treaty between Charles the 5th. and Henry the 8th. be closely considered and Examined, it will appear that the Spaniards never granted, or intended to grant the English a Liberty of Trading to their Ports, and Possessions in America. This Treaty as the Title as well as the Tenor of it import[s] was in the nature of an Offensive and Defensive Alliance against the French King; and although there are in the beginning of it strong Articles in generall Terms of a strict Union and Friendship by Sea, and Land between the two Kings, and all their Dominions, and Subjects; yet in the 7th. Art: where a mutual Defence is stipulated, and explained against Invasions, that might be made, upon their Respective Countrys, Those Countrys are particularly expressed, and specified in the said Article. And it is observable that no mention is made of the Spanish Possessions in the West Indies, and consequently they are not Comprehended in it; But the 13th. Article relating entirely to the Commerce to be carried on between the two Nations, is expressed in the following remarkable Terms:

Item pro communi bono hujus pacis &ca. et ut subditi utriusque Principum [praedictorum] mutuis Commerciis **consuetis** *se in dies magis Complectantur, Conventum est &ca. Quod circa intercursum Mercium, et mutuum* **Commercium quo invicem uti consueverant** *aut Tractatus intercursus de Data XI diei Aprilis 1520, sit et maneat in eo Statu et Vigore, in quo ex tractatu Cameracensi de Data 5ti. Augusti 1529 esse et manere debeat.*

It appears by this Article that no mention is made of America, either one way or other, But that the Commerce between the two Nations is to be settled according to the Treatyes of 1520 and 1529, the first of which is not to be found in the *Corps Diplomatique* of Treaties, but is in Rymer's *Foedera*, and referrs to a former Treaty that had no relation to America; as appears by the following Articles of the Treaty of 1529 between Henry the Eighth and Charles the Fifth:

Conventum est quod circa intercursum Mercium et mutuum Commercium **quo invicem uti consueverunt, tractatus intercursus** *de data diei undecimi Aprilis Anno 1520 sit et maneat [et] eodem Statu quo erat ante insumationem Belli, et perinde valeat ac si bellum non fuisset indictum ...*

Item Conventum est quod praesens Pax et Amicitia in Regno Angliae, et in partibus Flandriae, Brabantiae, Hollandiae, Zelandiae &c. intra **Mensem; in regno vero Hispaniarum inter tres menses vel citius si fieri potest a data praesentium** *per edicta publica et proclamationes in Portubus Maris et aliis Locis celebribus ubi talia fieri consuetum est publicabitur.*

So that no Agreement is made to Publish this Treaty in the Indies, which would have named as usual Six Months for that purpose.

And the last Treaty made at Cambray so far as it relates to Commerce is expressed in Words to the same Effect as the foregoing Article of the Treaty of 1542, referring to the Treaty of 1520, and to what was practised before the Warr antecedent to that Treaty. All which makes it plain that **Commercia Consueta et Commercia quo uti Consueverant** was to be the Rule and Foundation of the Treaty between the Two Nations: – And I believe it cannot be shewn that the English ever traded before that time to the Spanish West Indies, and there is no doubt but these words, *usual Trade* and *used to Trade* were industriously inserted in the Treaties after the Discovery and Settlements made there by the Spaniards to prevent our having any such pretension, which will appear still more evident by the subsequent Treaties between the Two Crowns.

And in Fact, in all the Expeditions afterwards made by Hawkins, Drake and others, during the Reign of Queen Elizabeth, These bold adventurers were never suffered to trade quietly at the Spanish Ports; and particularly Hawkins in those Places where he had any Traffick was obliged constantly to be upon his Guard, and was always refused admittance into others, where the Spaniards thought themselves strong enough to resist him. He endeavoured to persuade them, that his Commerce with them was for their Advantage; and that they might enter into it without danger; because the Princes, on both sides, were in Amity with one another, and the English had free traffick with Spain and Flanders: But he was constantly answered, that they were forbidden by the King of Spain to trade with any Foreign Nation, upon penalty of forfeiting their Goods, and indeed during the whole Reign of Queen Elizabeth, even while the two Nations were in peace, and had a mutual Commerce in Europe, They were little better than in a State of War in America without the least Shadow of a free or quiet Trade there. But at the latter end of the Reign of that Princess in 1600, when she agreed to treat of a Peace with the Spaniards at Boulogne, In the Instructions relating to Commerce the English Plenipotentiaries were directed to obtain:

Ut Angli in Indiis libere negotiarentur, quandoquidem in Tractatu 1541 (Cambden's Qun. Elizabeth ao. 1600. It should be 1542) in omnibus Caroli Quinti Dominis hoc concessum, saltem in iis Locis, quibus Hispani Sedes non fixerunt, et cum Principibus Indicis qui Hispanorum Imperio non subsunt.

By these Instructions, the English were to claim a general Trade in the West Indies, but might be contented with having it fixed to such Places, where the Spaniards had no Settlements, and where the Indians are not subject to the Dominion of Spain; But this Negociation having had no effect; After the Death of Queen Elizabeth, James the First concluded a Treaty with Philip the 3rd. of Spain in 1604, In which, with respect to Trade it is settled by the 9th. Article that there should be a free Commerce between the two Kings, and their Subjects in all their Dominions and Islands &ca. Both by Sea and Land *where Commerce was held before the breaking out of the Warr, and according to the usage, and observance of ancient Covenants.* And therefore their Subjects may reciprocally without Passport or Lycence, enter into any Parts, where a Commerce was carried on before the Warr. And in 1630, when the Peace was made between Charles the 1st. of England, and Philip the 4th. of Spain; By the 7th. Article the Commerce between the two Nations was settled upon the same foot, as it was agreed by the 9th. Article of the Treaty of 1604, that is to say, to be used in all their Dominions where Commerce *and Trade was carried on between the two Kingdoms before the Warr broke out between Queen Elizabeth and Philip the 2d. of Spain.*[3]

Cromwell indeed in his Manifesto Complains of these two Treatyes being made against the general inclination of the People, intimating, that there had been no Exception before relating to Commerce in any former Treaty, and of their not having pursued the Instructions, given to English Ministers in the Negociation of Peace just before the Death of Queen Elizabeth for insisting strongly upon their having a free Trade in the West Indies. (*Ut de Commercio libero in Occidentali India habendo instanter agerent*)

But in truth Cromwell's Allegations, and Inferences were extremely forced, (in order to justify his own Conduct towards Spain). For it is Plain, that the Terms of these Treatyes relating to Trade were taken from those of the Treatyes between Charles the fifth and Henry the Eighth, and the usage and observance of those Treatyes never extended to allow the English to Trade to the Spanish Possessions in America, and that Queen Elizabeth would have been satisfyed in obtaining a

---

[3] It was a constant argument of the opposition in Parliament and press that the Elizabethan days were the truly glorious ones, in which trade and national honour were fiercely upheld. Horace Walpole constantly asserted that the way to real security and commercial growth was through treaty, a position for which he was often lampooned. See e.g. [Rev. James Miller] *Are These Things So? The Previous Question, from an Englishman in his Grotto, to a Great Man at Court* (London, 1741), 8.

free Commerce to those Places, where the Spaniards had made no Settlements, and where the Indian Princes were not subject to the Dominion of Spain.

Thus stood the Treatyes and Practise relating to the Navigation and Commerce in the West Indies between the two Nations, untill after the Restoration of King Charles the 2d. when two famous Treatyes were concluded between him and the Crown of Spain; The one on the 12/23[*sic*] May 1667, and the other on the 8/18 July 1670.

That of 1667 containing the usual General Articles of Peace and Friendship between the two Crowns, their Subjects, and all their Dominions whatsoever: But with respect to Trade it is restrained to such Havens and Ports *where hitherto Trade and Commerce has been usually Exercised*; And it is very plain by the repetition of those Words in severall Articles, that the Regulations relating to the Commerce in this Treaty which are very beneficial to the English nation in their Trade to Spain, do not extend to the Spanish Dominions in America, which is strongly Confirmed by the Eighth Article of the same Treaty, where it is said – 'And for what may concern both the Indies, and any other Parts whatsoever, the Crown of Spain grants to the King of Great Britain and his Subjects all that is granted to the united States of the Low Countries, and their Subjects in their Treaty of Munster in 1648, in as full and ample manner, as if the same was particularly inserted'; The same Rules being to be observed whereunto the Subjects of the United States are obliged: One of which Rules is, *that the States shall not be permitted to Trade to the Dominions belonging to Spain in the Indies.*

But notwithstanding this amicable Treaty extending to all Dominions whatsoever on both Sides, a sort of Buccaneering Warr was continued by the Subjects of each other in the West Indies, which gave occasion for making the Treaty entitled, *A Treaty for the Composing of the Differences restraining of the Depredations, and establishing Peace in America between the Crowns of Great Britain and Spain*, concluded at Madrid 8/18th. day of July 1670.[4]

By the 7th. Article of this Treaty the Right of Sovereignty Dominion and Possession is confirmed to the English Nation of all Lands and Colonies in the West Indies then held and possessed by them.

By the 8th. Article, The respective Subjects of each Nation are forbid to sail, and Trade to the Colonies and Dominions of each other in the West Indies.[5]

[4] An improved version of this treaty survives in an undated draft among the Wolterton papers; 'Heads of Articles for Explaining the Treaty of 1670', Political Tracts MSS. It seems to be designed in the hope of a settlement with Spain, and tries to secure against the main sources of friction which had hitherto taken place.

[5] Walpole here accepts what was also the Spanish view, that steering a course to trade in a Spanish port was forbidden, and not only the being found trading in one. Since the

But by the 9th. Article, the said Navigation and Commerce may be exercised according to a Lycence or permission to be granted for that purpose.

By the 10th. Article, if the Ships of either Nation be forced by storms, by Pyrates or Enemies, or other Inconveniencies into the Harbours of the other in America, they should be favourably treated, and suffered to refresh themselves, and buy all things necessary for their Sustenance and reparation of their Ships, and conveniency of their Voyage and to depart when and where they please.

By the 11th. Art. in Case of Shipwreck they shall meet with all Friendly relief, and the Persons shipwrecked shall not be imprisoned.

By the 12th. Art. if there be 3 or 4 Ships forced into the Ports together as may give Grounds for Suspicion, They shall acquaint the Governour with the Cause of their coming and shall stay no longer than the Governour will permit, and shall be requisite for furnishing themselves with victuals, and for repairing their Ships; And they shall take care neither to Load or Unload any Merchandise.

By the 14th. Art. it is agreed that no private Injury shall any way weaken this Friendship and Convention, nor raise any hatred or differences between the two nations, but each shall answer for his own Deeds, nor shall any one be punished for what another has done, Either by Reprisals or other odious Proceedings, unless Justice shall be denyed or unreasonably delayed, In which Case it shall be lawfull to the King whose Subject has suffered the Injury to proceed according to the Law of Nations untill reparation shall be obtained to the injured Person.

By the 15th. Art. this Treaty is not to Diminish the Pre-eminence or Dominion of either Confederate in the American Seas &c.. But it is always *to be understood that the Liberty of Navigation ought in no manner to be disturbed where nothing is committed against the genuine Sense and Meaning of these Articles.*

Although by the express Terms of this Treaty, the Subjects of each Nation, are forbid to sail, and Trade to the Places, and Ports of the Other in the West Indies; Yet Considering the Facility which is allowed for their putting into each others Harbours if forced by Storms, or other Inconveniencies, and for staying until they have refreshed themselves, and refitted their Ships; And that, without giving notice to the Governour, unless they are three or four in number; And that notwithstanding the Right and Preeminence of either Side in those Seas, care is to be taken, that the *Liberty of Navigation may not be disturbed*

clamour over Spanish searches was so great, this was a crucial concession. For the similar Spanish interpretation see Keene to Newcastle, 7 May (NS) 1738, BL Add 32797, ff. 321–5.

in any manner whatsoever, It looks as if the Spaniards were determined to connive at the English trading to their Ports in the West Indies. And indeed Spain had at that time of day, and always during the Reign of King Charles the 2d. of Spain, such an occasion for the Friendship and Support of England with respect to their Foreign Dominions against the formidable Power and Encroachments of France, and at the same time were in such awe of our Maritime Power, on accompt of the communication of those Dominions and Spain, that it is no Wonder, That Crown did all they could to ingratiate themselves with the English nation, by favouring their Commerce as they constantly did, as long as that Prince lived.

This Treaty is confirmed by the Treaty of Commerce between Great Britain, and Spain concluded at Utrecht in 1713, Although the Eighth Article of the Treaty of Peace between those two Crowns, concluded the same Year seems in some measure to restrain the former Indulgence, granted by that of 1670 with respect to British Ships, putting into the Ports of Spain in America on some occasions by the following Clause:

> Whereas it is by common Consent Established as a Fundamental Rule *that the Exercise of Navigation* and Commerce to the Spanish West Indies should remain in the same State it was, in the reign of King Charles the 2d. of Spain, That therefore this Rule may hereafter be observed with inviolable faith, and in a manner never be broke, and thereby all Causes of *Distrust and Suspicion* concerning that matter may be prevented and removed, it is especially agreed, that no Lycence or Permission at all shall at any time be given either to the French, or to any Nation whatever in any name or *under any pretence directly or indirectly* to sail or traffick in, or introduce Negroes, Goods, Merchandize or any things whatsoever into the Dominions Subject to the Crown of Spain in America, Excepting what may be agreed by Treaty, or Treaties of Commerce above-said, and the Privileges granted by a Convention commonly called, El Assiento de Negros.

Although the words (under any pretence directly or indirectly to sail) seem very extensive, Yet upon due Consideration this Article seems to go no farther than to tye up the King of Spain's hands from granting a Lycence or Permission to any prince to traffick in his American Ports, and therefore destroys the 9th. Art. of the Treaty of 1670; But the liberty granted by the 10th. Art. for treating Ships favourably if forced into the Ports by Stress of Weather or Enemies &c. seems to remain still in full force.

2dly. Notwithstanding the Right and Preeminence of Dominion which either Sovereign may pretend to in the American Seas, care is to be taken, that the liberty of Navigation be in no manner disturbed, where nothing is committed against the Genuine Sense and Meaning of this Treaty; And upon this Foot the Rule of Navigation and Commerce, between the two Nations in America stands at present; Those Treatyes having always upon accomodating the Differences that have happened in the late King and his present Majts. Reign, been renewed and confirmed.

The Depredations therefore committed by the Spaniards in taking and confiscating the British Ships navigating the American Seas on accompt of a right of Dominion there, or any other Pretence whatsoever unless they are found sailing into or trading in the Spanish Places and Ports are unjustifyable, and Contrary to the express words of the Treatyes, subsisting between the two Nations.

The Reasons generally alledged for the Condemnation of the British Ships, taken in their Navigation in the West Indies are either on accompt of some pieces of Eight, or other Goods of the Growth of the Spanish West Indies being found on board or on Accompt of their being found cutting or loading of Logwood in some of the American Bays, or Creeks.

If those Bays or Creeks are avowedly acknowledged to be part of the Dominions of Spain, there is no doubt but the Capture and Condemnation of British Ships cutting Logwood there is justifyable; But the taking and Confiscating any British Ships not found sailing into or trading in the Spanish Ports, by reason of their having any Effects of the Growth of their Country on board, cannot be justified by any Article of the Treaty of 1670, nor with any Colour of Justice or Equity.

It is indeed said by the 15th. Art. of the Treaty of 1667, that if any Prohibited Goods shall be *Exported* from the Dominions of either of the said Kings by the respective Subjects of one, or the other, in such Case the Prohibited Goods shall only be Confiscated, and not the other Goods, Except the said Delinquent shall carry out of the Dominions of Great Britain, the proper Coin, Wooll, or Fuller's Earth, or *out of the Dominions of Spain any Gold or Silver wrought or unwrought*; In either of which Cases the Laws of the Respective Countries are to take place; and this Article hath sometimes been cited for seizing and Confiscating the English Ships in the West Indies where any Spanish Silver is found on board; But it is plain by the very terms of this Article, as hath been hinted before of other Articles of this Treaty relating to Commerce, that it does not relate to the respective Possessions in the West Indies because it Supposes by the Word (Exported) that a Trade may be carryed on with those Places, which is absolutely forbid by the Treaties, and all Commerce there whatsoever is prohibited and Illicit. And therefore this Article can, in no sense, justify the taking Ships in the Open Sea, and Confiscating them, by reason of Spanish Silver being found on board.

The Spaniards then must have recourse to the Presumption of British Ships having traded in their Ports by the Nature of the Loading found on board, But such a Presumption cannot justify their taking our Ships in their Navigation and Condemning them on that Accompt; Because the 15th. Art. of the Treaty of 1670 expressly says that the liberty of the Navigation is in no manner to be disturbed, where nothing is committed against the Genuine Sense and Meaning of those Articles.

Neither can it be fairly presumed from finding Spanish Silver or other Commodities of the growth of the Spanish West Indies on board of an English Ship, that the Ship hath been trading at the Spanish Ports there; Because it may happen, as it certainly often does, that the Captain of an English Ship from London or Bristol loaden with English Goods or from the Coast of Guinea loaden with Negroes, may sail directly to Jamaica and sell her Cargo there, and receive in Exchange for it besides some Goods of the growth of that Island, some Spanish Dollars or other Effects of the growth of the Spanish West Indies, without knowing or troubling himself as he is not obliged to do, how those Spanish Effects came to Jamaica; and shall it be presumed, if he is taken in returning to Great Britain by a Spanish *Guarda Costa*, that he has by reason of such Loading Traded at the Spanish Ports, and be Condemned on that Account?

It is well known that there is no money in any Places of the West Indies; whether they belong to the English, French or Spaniards, but what originally comes from the Spanish Mines there: And altho the Subjects of all those Nations are expressly forbid to Trade with one another; Yet it is as well known that the French and Spanish Governours will often suffer the Northern Colonies of Great Britain to bring them Lumber and Provisions without which they cannot well Subsist; And those Colonies must often receive in return, Spanish Dollars, and other Effects of the growth of Spain, and may with these Returns trade to the rest of the British Islands and Colonies from whence They may afterwards be carried to Great Britain in Ships, that never traded in the Spanish Ports of the West Indies. And therefore the Spaniards interrupting and taking British Ships in their Navigation in America and condemning Them if they find pieces of eight or other goods of the growth of Spain, upon a presumption of their having traded at the Spanish Ports, If it were not directly contrary to Treatys, as it certainly is, would still be a most unreasonable and unjust Proceeding. But the Truth of this Matter I am afraid is that the reasons of State of Political Interest which induced King Charles the 2d. of Spain to be so friendly to the English Nation and to grant Them by Treatys such favourable Terms of Trade and Navigation in Europe and in the West Indies are entirely ceased; And while the English, on one side, cannot be such usefull Allys as they were formerly to Spain, So the Spaniards, on the other, have not so much to fear from the Enmity of England as they formerly had. During the Reign of King Charles the 2d. of Spain, that Crown and France were Rivals for Power and in Constant Opposition to one another: the foreign Dominions of Spain in Italy and Flanders especially were envy'd and earnestly desired by France, and no other Power could be so usefull an Ally to the Spaniards for Checking the Ambitious Encroachments of the French in the Low Countrys as the English which naturally led the King of Spain to be favourable to this Nation in Matters of Commerce. And in Consequence of it the English gained great riches in their Trade, and Navigation in the West Indies.

Upon the death of King Charles the 2d. of Spain, a Prince of the House of Bourbon having got Possession of the Spanish Monarchy, Great Britain in conjunction with other Potentates, allarmed at the formidable Power of such an Union took up Arms to make him quitt it. But the Peace being afterwards made, by leaving the same Prince Master of that Kingdom and the Spanish West Indies; and separating, at the same Time, from the Crown of Spain all the Foreign Dominions which belonged to it before in Europe, caused such an alteration in affairs, as could not fail of creating and settling a perfect Amity, and close understanding between France and Spain; and for these reasons the Dependance which Spain had upon the friendship and Assistance of England against so powerful and Dangerous a Neighbour as France, must necessarily end, and with it the great Indulgence and warm inclinations, which the Spaniards had before shewn towards the English Nation particularly in matters of Commerce, must, notwithstanding the renewall of former Treatys, naturally cool: especially if they were convinced that They should not from the Circumstances and Situation of Things have so much reason for the future as they formerly had to apprehend the Ill Consequences of disobliging and provoking the English Nation, which, I am afraid, is the Present unhappy and unavoidable State of Things.

After the Spaniards had discovered and made Themselves Masters of the rich mines in the Indies and would not suffer any other Nation to trade Thither, the English having got no Settlements or Commerce in America, ran no great hazard in attempting to force a Trade with the Spaniards. And indeed a sort of buccaneering war was carried on by them in Those Parts for several years with much advantage in bringing home great Quantitys of Silver and other effects of the growth of the West Indies, to the great encrease of the Riches of the English Nation, which was at that time the sole property of the Spaniards who for Wealth and Power became the Envy of all other Countries. But considering the large Establishment of Islands and Colonys we have made since in America, Their various and useful Productions, for which we send in Return our own Manufactures: Considering the vast quantity of Shipping employed backwards and forwards between our respective Colonies; and them, and Great Britain: Considering on the other side, that the Spaniards have no Trade in the West Indies but what is carried on by their Galeons, Flota, and Register Ships,[6] that are fitted out, and armed as Men of War, and that the greatest Part of their Effects belong to other Nations, and particularly to the French, and consequently as Mo. Patiño used to say they are under a Natural Guaranty and Protection of all Europe:[7] That their *Guarda Costas* that committ the Depredations against our Merchants are small armed vessels that can easily escape from a Man of War and if they chance to be taken are of little or no value, I say considering These Things, and that as I said before according to the present situation of Europe the Friendship of Great Britain can be of no service to the Dominions of Spain; It can not escape the reflection of the Spaniards, that they have not so much reason as they formerly had to cultivate and manage a good understanding with us either on account of the Utility and advantage, They may expect, or of the dangerous Consequences they may apprehend according to the manner in which they shall treat the British Merchants in their Navigation and Commerce in America And that our taking revenge by Letters of Mart [*sic*; Marque] Reprisals or otherwise for the Depredations committed by their *Guarda Costas* will expose our Extensive Trade and the fortunes of our Merchants to greater Mischiefs and Inconveniences than we can possibly hope to do the Spaniards.[8] And that too without the Prospect of obtaining by that Means sufficient satisfaction and Reparation for such Losses. To these

[6] The *Galeones* and *Flota* were the two main trading fleets leaving Cadiz for the two Spanish New World Viceroyalties. The *Flota* sailed in the early summer, bound for Veracruz in New Spain. The *Galeones* sailed in late summer for Cartagena and Portobello, the chief ports and homes of the annual fairs in the Viceroyalty of Peru. Both fleets exchanged their cargoes for holds full of precious metals, and in the spring sailed back together from Cuba – a tempting prize, if they were in fact sailing together, or sailing at all, and if they were caught. In practice, by no means in every year were these fleets despatched. Register ships, *registros*, were single ships licensed to trade for specific purposes, and often carrying high-value luxury cargoes. An excellent modern treatment of Spanish trade is Geoffrey Walker, *Spanish Politics and Imperial Trade, 1700–1789* (London, 1979). See also Richard Pares, *War and Trade in the West Indies 1739–1763* (Oxford, 1936).

[7] Don José Patiño (1666–1736) was the man responsible for the revival of the Spanish navy from January 1717, when he was appointed *Intendente General de Marina*. A firm advocate of centralisation and rationalisation, he promoted economic recovery and became Philip V's most trusted adviser. In 1726 Patiño became Secretary of the Office of the Indies, as well as naval minister, and in 1732 he became Secretary of State and Chief Minister of the Crown, dying in office in 1736.

[8] This point was later forcibly made in H. Walpole's influential pamphlet *The Grand Question, Whether War, or no War, with Spain …* (London, 1739), 16–17.

Considerations may be added, that of the great and costly Pledge which the Spaniards have always in their Hands of Effects belonging to the South Sea Company on account of the Assiento Contract.[9] For altho it is stipulated by the 40th. Art. of that Convention that in case of a War between the Two Nations the Company shall be allowed a year and a half, from the time of the Declaration of the rupture, to withdraw their Effects from Spain, and the West Indies; yet we have found by Experience that that Article was never observed on the Occasion of any Troubles between the Two Crowns nor can there be any Rule laid down to enforce the Observation of it in time of War. It must be owned that the British Merchants frequently attempt to Trade on the Spanish Coasts in America, contrary to Treaty, and they become thereby lyable to the Penalty of Confiscation; But that can not be a reason why the Navigation of others in those Seas should be Interrupted, and their Effects and Ships condemned as Prizes on frivolous Pretences, when they can not be convicted of having traded with the Spaniards; For altho the Spaniards do not professedly own, That they take and Condemn one Ship, that is innocent, because another has exercised Illicit Commerce, Yet by their insinuating often to us, that we should take care to prevent our Ships from carrying on an Illicit Trade:– And by its being evident that severall Ships are taken by them that have not carried on any such Trade, It looks as if they retalliate the Crime of one, by the Punishment of another, tho' innocent, which is directly contrary to the 14th. Art. of the Treaty of 1670, which says, that every one shall answer for his own proper fault neither shall one man satisfy for the offence of another by Reprisals &c.. Besides by the Nature of Treatys it can not be understood, That any Prince is answerable for any of his Subjects exercising a Particular Commerce, forbidden by an Article of a General Treaty of Peace, Friendship and Correspondence, between the two Nations. As for Example; when the British and Spanish Subjects are prohibited in such a Treaty, from trading to the Ports and Places of each in America; If either of them will venture on such a Trade, They do it at their own Peril, They forfeit the Protection of their own Sovereign and of the Pavillon [flag] they bear; are lyable to

[9] The *Asiento de Negros* was the exclusive concession of supplying slaves to Spanish overseas territories, granted in 1713 to the English South Sea Company. The 42nd article of the 1713 Asiento Treaty gave the Company the unprecedented right to send an annual ship of 500 tons along with the yearly fleets from Spain, to trade direct with Spanish ports. These trade goods were held by the Spanish colonial authorities in locked warehouses until the annual fairs, and company agents and stocks were always vulnerable to Spanish interference. In addition, the complex accounting of the Asiento and annual ship meant that the Spanish government had always on hand money and goods of the Company, which could be withheld or confiscated. This vexatious connection was one of the chief immediate causes of war in 1739, and was finally dissolved by the commercial treaty of October 1750.

the Laws, made by the other in such Cases; But neither the Sovereign of such Offender, nor any of his Subjects, that are innocent, can be answerable, or punishable for the behaviour of the Guilty. However, it is to be feared, That the Spaniards provoked by the Illicit Trade, carried on by some of our Ships, without their being able to take them, and seeing how easy it is for them to take their Revenge upon others, among the vast quantity that constantly navigate those Seas, and how difficult it is for us to have redress by Reprisals or otherwise, and having no particular reason of State to manage our Friendship, may have been induced to commit those unjustifiable Depredations of late.

But how to obtain redress for what is past, and to prevent the like mischiefs for the future, either by fair or forcible means? is a great and indeed a very difficult Question.

As to fair means Experience shews, that it is almost in vain by the Nature of the Proceedings Both in the West Indies, & at the Court of Madrid, to look for any Reparation, for any unlawfull Capture, and Condemnation.

As soon as a Spanish *Guarda Costa* has taken an English Vessell, it is carried into the neighbouring Port, such as Porto Rico or Cuba; And as the Captor and the Governor there, who sitts in judgement, have both frequently a share in the Prize, She never fails to be condemned. An Appeal, indeed, lyes to the Superior Court in the Indies; But whatsoever way it is determined there, the Sufferer has no immediate Redress; If the Sentence is confirmed against the Prize, the Ship is Confiscated, and a Distribution is made of the Effects, if that has not been done before.[10] The Owner of the Vessell has an Appeal to the Court of Madrid; But the distance is so great, the Expences so grievous, and the Examples of having obtained Restitution, and Satisfaction so few, That he chuses rather to sitt down by his first Loss & have recourse to the Insurance Office, than give himself any farther trouble about it. If the Sentence is repealed, Yet the Ship and goods are not restored, nor Satisfaction given, because the Captor has likewise an Appeal to the Court of Madrid, and the Restitution and Satisfaction must be suspended and depend upon the determination of that appeal; And Therefore for the same Reasons the British Owner will not give himself any farther Pains after the Condemnation of his Ship in the first Instance; But they have in this Case too immediate recourse to the Insurers, and they after having paid the Assurance Money think it more adviseable to pay it quietly than to fling away more money to no purpose in the Prosecution of it; But in the mean time Both Merchants

---

[10] On 17 March (OS) 1738 a draft letter was sent for presentation by Keene in Madrid, making these points very forcibly and protesting against Spanish legal procedures; BL Add 32797, ff. 182–5.

and Insurers join in the loud Clamours of being injuriously treated and Interrupted in their Lawfull Commerce and Navigation, which is not only a cruel Check to Trade, but highly reflects Upon the Honour and Dignity of the Crown, in not being able to protect her Subjects.[11]

As to forcible means, to redress and prevent these violent Proceedings, That of Letters of Reprisal will, I am afraid, prove ineffectual and must end in an open rupture between the Two Crowns.

For as it has been hinted before, the Spaniards have no ships in the West Indies, besides the *Guarda Costas*, and their Galeons, Flota and Register Ships. The first are armed vessels, fitted out either by the King's Commission, or by the Governors, to prevent the Trade of other nations to the Spanish Ports, but carry on no manner of Trade, nor have they ever any Effects of Value on board, and therefore, if taken, will neither make Reparations to the Sufferer, nor defray the Charges of fitting out an armed ship for making Reprisals. And as by the Treatys & Law of Nations, no Letters for making Reprisals, can be granted untill the Prosecutions have been followed thro' the several Courts, & justice denied, or delayed there, and by the Sovereign; Such Reprisals must soon end in an open rupture, And therefore the consequences of that, with respect to our Trade and Possessions in America must be well considered before Letters of Reprisal be granted; But if the Government should give Directions, either to Men of War, or authorize private men to arm Ships; and make Reprisals upon the Spaniards wherever they meet Them; and in Consequence the Galeons, Flota, or Register Ships, & the Azogues[12] should be equally lyable to be taken for procuring Reparation, and Satisfaction to the English Merchants, what would be the Consequence of such a Measure, which may affect the Property of our own, as well as the Subjects of all other Nations and particularly the French, will without Doubt, be well weighed before it be taken and put into Execution.

If these Depredations should therefore be continued, without obtaining Satisfaction from the Court of Madrid in consequence of the Instances, that have been, or may be made there, no other remedy seems to occur, besides that of declaring open war against Spain or of giving at first proper Instructions to the King's Ships for securing our navigation in America against the *Guarda Costas*, which, perhaps may

---

[11] This whole paragraph was an interpolation by Lord Hardwicke in the first draft; BL Add 9131, f. 228.

[12] In years when the main fleets did not sail (not least because of markets being flooded by illicit traders) the silver smelters in the New World still needed mercury for their process. The *Azogues* was the naval squadron – usually two ships – which took the mercury. On returning, they of course carried back whatever royal bullion had accumulated, and it was the return voyage which attracted British cupidity.

be done upon as Justifiable a Pretence, as that upon which our Ships are taken by those Pyraticall Vessells.

By the Treaty of 1670, which I look upon to be the rule for restraining Depredations and establishing Peace in America between the Two Nations, as the Title imports; As it is expressly stipulated by the 8th. Article, That the Subjects of each confederate respectively shall abstain, & forbear to sail unto, or trade in the Ports possessed by the other Party in the West Indies; so it is expressly agreed by the 11th. Art. that the Liberty of Navigation ought in no manner to be disturbed, where nothing is committed against the genuine Sense and meaning of these Articles.

As therefore the Spaniards think it necessary to grant Commissions to Ships to prevent our sailing or trading in the Ports belonging to them on account of that Trade being but too frequently practised: have we not the same Right to authorize our men of war to preserve our Navigation in the West Indies, and prevent our Merchant men from being taken, when they are sailing in the open sea, & have committed nothing contrary to the Genuine sense, and meaning of the Treaty, which is too frequently practised by the Spaniards? And as they take the liberty to seize and carry into their Ports our Merchantmen, without their being found sailing into or trading in their Bays or Harbours and Bring them to Examination & Tryal; may not our men of war be instructed & authorized upon having notice; that any Spanish *Guarda Costa* had taken unlawfully a British Vessell, to take them, in like manner and bring them to our Ports in America, in order to be examined and tryed for having taken ships belonging to Great Britain in their Navigation, without any Pretence.

But whether this will be an adequate Satisfaction for the Injury done, or a means to prevent the like mischief for the future; and whether any Thing of this Nature will not draw on a sort of Pyratical war between the Two Nations in the Indies, seems doubtfull at least; And indeed I do not see any effectual way to be revenged on the Spaniards, if they continue their unjust Depredations, but coming to an open war with them. And there is no doubt but the English might in such a Case, undertake some Enterprize on the Spanish Settlements, as might be of infinite prejudice to them, provided we were sure of having a War with Spain only, and that we should not be engaged immediately with other Nations at the same time.

It is, indeed, true that the Court of Spain in answer to the late strong Representations made to them from hence, have declared that Satisfaction shall be given to the Just complaints of the Merchants; and according to the present State of affairs in Europe, there seems no reason, except the Dispute about Georgia, why they should encourage the Interruption of the British Navigation & Commerce in America;

The Queen of Spain, who has so great an influence, must be sensible of the obligations she has to his Majesty for the Establishment of her Son in Italy; and of what consequence the Maritime Power of England must be with respect to his future Peace, & Security there. It is therefore to be considered, whether this may not be a seasonable Juncture for Instructing the King's Minister at Madrid, to enter into a Negociation for Confirming & explaining the Treaty of 1670, on such a foot, that the Spaniards may be restrained from Interrupting our Navigation in America under the Penalty of such forfeitures and Immediate Reprisals, as may Discourage them from such Unjustifyable Attempts.

Points, to be Consider'd with Regard to the Depredations of Spain

[Some extracts from the longer draft document. Interpolations by Lord Hardwicke are identified by a bracket {thus}.]

1°. A State of the Nature of Our Treatys with Spain

2°. The Breach, & violation of Them by the Subjects of that Crown, without Redress, or Satisfaction, & what may have been the Reasons, or Motives for such Violations.

3°. What means are proper to be used for obtaining Satisfactionfor what is past, & prevention of the like Grievances for the Future.

[1°. is much the same as in the memoir already given.]

2°. As to the Spaniards having taken, condemn'd, & Confiscated the British Ships, & Effects in navigating the American Seas, & treated the Mariners in a most Barbarous manner in Violation of the Treatys between the Two Crowns, & that without Satisfaction, or Redress, It has been so Notorious, & Constant, a Practise, from the Treaty of Utrecht to this Time, that there is no need to enter into a particular Detail, or Proof of it; but to take notice of the Facts in General.

1°. Upon the Conclusion of any Disturbances between the Two Nations, & the Renewal of Peace, & Treaties, notwithstanding Orders, or *Cedulas* were issued on the Part of Spain, in the most Explicit Terms for the Restitution of Ships, taken contrary to Treaties, or for preventing the like Grievances for the future, no obedience was paid to Them by the Spanish Governors in the West Indies; The *Guarda Costas* continued their Depradations, and upon application made to Spain; Answers were frequently returned, that were dilatory, & evasive, & no Satisfaction made.

2°. In other particular Cases, that have been very flagrant, & Destitute, by the Confession of Spain, of all Foundation, or Pretence, for taking the Ships, either on Account of the Nature of the Loading, or for not steering a due Course in their Navigation, or for any other Pretence whatsoever, Cedulas, or Orders have been Issued, & repeated with the Strongest Injunction for Restitution of particular Ships, therein mention'd, & sometimes Penalty upon the Captors. And yet no Obedience was paid to them, & they still remain unexecuted, & without Effect.

3°. After these violences had ceased, & the Navigation in the American Seas, for some few Years had been uninterrupted; On a sudden in the Year 1737, many unjust Captures, & Confiscations have been lately committed by the Spaniards on the British Shipping in America. And upon the most earnest Remonstrances for Redress, & with a Renewal of the former Complaints of the Disobedience of the Orders, granted by Spain & insisting upon the Execution of Them, as well as an Immediate Restitution of the New Seizures, no Satisfactory Answer has been given by that Court:- Frivolous Excuses are alledged for the Non-Complyance on the part of the Governors wth. the K. of Spain's own Commands on Account of former Injurys; And fair promises are given with respect to the present, tending to delay, without any Prospect of Obtaining more Justice, than has been experienced before in several cases of the like Nature.

This being the Cruel Situation of our Navigation, & Trade, in the W. Indies, it may not be improper to Consider, upon what Colour, & Foundation the Spaniards committ these violences.

1°. It is sometimes Alledged, that by the 8th. Art. of the Treaty of 1670, the Subjects of each side respectively are to abstain & forbear to sail, & trade in any of the ports, & Havens whatsoever &c., possessed by the other Party in the W. Indies; and therefore if the Subjects of England sail out of the Course of the Navigation, from, & to their own Colonys, & from, & to Great Britain in America, with an Intention to approach the Spanish Coasts, They may be lawfully taken, & Confiscated. This is so unreasonable a Pretext:- that the Spaniards, by making Themselves the Judges of the Course of Navigation, will take the British Ships whenever They please, contrary to Treaty, & the Law of Nations...

4to. It is impossible for the British ships in returning Home, from Jamaica to Great Britain, to avoid approaching the Spanish Possessions in America, which they must necessarily do, whether they go thro' the Windward Passage, or otherwise; As more plainly appears by the Situation of Cuba-Hispaniola, & the Gulph of Florida: This being the Case, with respect to the Course of Navigation both ways, the pretence of taking our Ships on account of not observing the direct Course to, &

from our own Colonys, or to, & from England & those Colonys, is a most unjustifiable Pretence.

The 2d. Colour for these Captures, & Condemnations, is grounded upon the English Ships having on board the Produce, or the growth of the Spanish Plantations, as being an Evidence of their having traded in those Ports. This is as frivolous, and groundless a pretence as the other. 1st. Because there are many things which are the growth of the Spanish Plantations, that are likewise produced in those belonging to the English, such as Logwood, & other Dying Goods, as well as Cacao, & almost every thing besides Silver, &c...

Add to all these frivolous Pretences, that the Governor, & other Officers of the Places, such as Cuba, & Porto Rico, whither the Prizes, when taken, are carried, & before whom they are tryed, have frequently a share in the Privateers, fitted out to Cruize, & that the Mariners have little, or no pay but in Proportion to the Captures; which makes it no wonder that the British Traders are so easily taken, & confiscated, when the same Person is Judge, & Party, & so many are concern'd in Interest to have them condemn'd; or that they proceed in such an Unjustifiable Method, as is usually practised in Condemning the Ships, after having seized, & carried them into their Ports. The Captain, & all the Men are immediately confin'd as Prisoners; Their Documents & Papers are taken & kept from them; They are examin'd without being suffer'd to have an Interpreter of their own; and they are required to sign that Examination without having any Certain way to know the truth of the contents of it. In Consequence of this a Tryal is set on foot, and instead of the Master of the Ship being allowed to prepare for his Defence from the Evidence of His own Papers, & Documents, or of His Crew, or by providing such Agents, & Councill, as He may think most usefull to Him; His Documents, as was said before are kept from Him; Himself, & His Crew, remain Prisoners, & are not suffer'd to convene or Correspond with any Person whatsoever; And the Governr. appoints such Sollicitors, & Lawyers, under Colour of Defending them, as He shall think fitt. So that the whole Proceeding of Condemning & Confiscating the Ship is no more than a Sham Tryal, & renders it impossible for the Captain, tho' never so Innocent, to justify Himself in the first Instance, or to have any Foundation for an Appeal to a Superior Court, being stript of all the necessary means for that purpose...

If this difficult Situation, as 'tis to be apprehended, is but too well known by the Spaniards, they have little reason to manage their Treaties, with us, as expecting no great benefit from our Friendship, and no great Danger from our Enmity; The Influences, which principally govern Princes, & States in respect to one another, are ever since the Peace of Utrecht, with regard to us, & Spain, turned to our disadvantage, according to the present Political Situation of Affairs, & of the Powers in Europe, & according to the respective Interest, & Concerns of Both Nations in America; And, indeed, the Conduct of Spain, these three or four last Years, makes what has been said on this Head, but too evident. From 1734 to 1737 they made few or no Captures upon us in America; that is during their Joint War with France, & Sardinia against the Emperor; And also as soon as a separate Peace was concerted between the Emperor, & France unknown to Spain. This latter Crown, in hopes that we might be brought into Measures to disappoint it, shew'd all imaginable regard for our Trade in the W. Indies.

{What is here sayd with regard to ye little reason ye Spanyards may have to observe their treatys with us on account of our not being so usefull allys to them as formerly from ye alteration of ye Political State of Europe is to be understood with respect of Dominion, & Power wch. seize vain arbitrary & ambitious princes more than ye true Interest of their Subjects; wch. is ye case of ye present King or rather Queen of Spain to ye highest degree; for as to ye Subjects of Old Spain, they must be sensible that ye commerce of England is more beneficiall to them, than that of any other nation whatsoever, & they would gladly see a perpetual peace and friendship between ye two Nations according to their own Proverb Peace with England, altho' in war with all ye World besides.} ...

The next Question is whether the Case for granting Reprisals does exist in the present Complaints.

And there is no manner of doubt, from what has been said, Upon the 2d. General Head, but the Case does exist, Both on account of several Complaints made before, & after the Conclusion of the Treaty of Seville, for which Cedulas had been Issued, & a formal Declaration made, by the Court of Spain, for a General Restitution, without any Redress, or Satisfaction: And on Account of the particular Cedulas for Restitution of certain Ships, which, notwithstanding frequent Repetition of Them, have met with no Compliance.

As to the last Case of New Captures, & Condemnations in the Year 1737; As the Spanish Court has declared, that the Cases, & *Autos* shall be examin'd, & justice done, if the Treatys are violated; The Case of Reprisals, strictly taken, does not yet exist. But as the Minister in Spain, in His Answer, seems to excuse, instead of Condemning the Disobedience to the former Orders for Satisfaction, & to lay down some Notions relating to Captures, such as having the Produce of the Spanish W. Indies on board, & our Ships, in sailing not observing a due Course of Navigation, with a Design to approach the Spanish Coast, as what may be Justifiable reasons for taking them; There seems to be but little hopes Considering past Experience in Things of the like

Nature, of obtaining Satisfaction for the last violences. And this may be such an Unreasonable delay of Justice as to fall under the Rules of Reprisals, tho', if granted in this last case, may be the cause of such a Retalliation on the side of Spain, as to occasion Hostilities in the W. Indies, equal to War.

If Reprisals are necessary in any Case, will it be sufficient for the King to authorize His Subjects, that are Injured to make them only, or may He likewise employ His own Men of War for that purpose?

As to the first; may the Merchants take *any* Ships, such as Galeons, Register Ships &c? To be sure they may, untill the Merchant, to whom those Letters are granted, shall have obtained Satisfaction.

As to the King's ordering His own Ships to make Reprisals, under certain Regulations; There appears to be no reason to the Contrary; And this Expedient of Reprisals, by Letters granted to the Merchants, or by the Men of War, seems to be the most natural, & justifiable Method, according to the Treatys; But by what has been said before, considering the few Ships that the Spaniards have, that can be taken, the little value they are of if taken, except the Galeons, Flota or Register Ships are met with; and considering to whom the last belong; It is to be apprehended that the granting Letters of Reprisal may prove a very unadequate Remedy, or a very dangerous one, by engaging the Nations, that have the Chief Property in the Galeons, against us; But yet if the Merchants will accept Letters of Reprisal, They cannot be refused them; the Cases of doing oneself Justice are so flagrant, & have subsisted so long, that such a refusal would make us appear a most Contemptible Nation with all our Maritime Power.

But considering the insufficiency of granting Letters of Reprisal, & what may be the Consequence of Them, if they should have any Success, our Commerce, in the W. Indies, is so extensive that it must be supported & protected, at the same Time, with a strong Squadron in those Parts, & the Commander must have very serious, & explicit Orders, with respect to the Navigation, to be observed by Him, & the manner of protecting our Lawfull trade against the *Guarda Costas*; with the severest Injunctions, not to employ the King's Ships in the Convoy, & Protection of Those, that will carry on an Illicit Trade to the Spanish Ports; And as no body can foresee what may be the Consequence of any vigorous measures, altho' very Justifiable, I believe some Considerations must be employed at the same Time about having a Maritime Force to protect our Trade in the Mediterranean, & to Lisbon, and for putting some of our weak Colonys into a better Condition of Defence.

To conclude; this whole Affair is of so extensive a Nature with respect to the Contested Rights relating to the Navigation in the West Indies, the unjust Pretences for the taking, & condemning the British Ships, the Methods, to be employ'd for procuring Satisfaction for what is past, & preventing the like mischiefs for the future, That it seems impossible for the Parliament to come to any other Resolutions besides what relate to the Notoriety of the Facts, concerning the violence, & Injustice of the Depredations committed for such a long time by the Spaniards, upon the British Trade in the W. Indies, contrary to Treaty, with the Strongest Assurances to support His Maty. in taking such Measures, as Honour, & Justice shall make necessary in Case He cannot, by His Amicable Instances, procure Justice; And Security for that freedom of Navigation, & Commerce, as His Subjects are entitled to by the Law of Nations, & the Treatys subsisting between the Two Crowns.

Should Spain show a Disposition to give Immediate & certain Satisfaction on Account of former Depredations, as well as for Those, that have been lately committed, it will be proper to consider, what may be necessary to be done, as a sufficient Security, to prevent the like violences, & Interruption of our Commerce in the American Seas for the future; which cannot be done by any other Method, but by a Negociation between the Two Courts, to explain the Articles of the Treaty of 1670, in such a Manner as may obviate, & remove all the groundless pretences, as well as unjustifiable Proceedings for taking, & Condemning our Ships.

And to answer which End, the following Points will naturally come under Consideration.

1st. To have it explain'd that it shall not be permitted for the Ships of either side, to stop, & search those belonging to the other, in the Navigation on the high seas in America, under pretence of their having sailed out of Course without necessity, with an Intention to approach the Havens, Coasts, or Ports of the other.

2dly. It may be consider'd whether, in order to prevent Disputes about the Limits, & Course of Navigation, & the having an Intention from the Course of Steering, to sail to, or Trade in the forbidden Harbours, Coasts, & Ports of each other, It may not be adviseable to Limit a certain distance for the Navigation of the Ships of each Party, with regard to their respective Ports, & Colonys; unless forced to alter their Course by stress of weather, Ennemys, or Pyrates, or any other urgent necessity.

{This seems plausible, & agreable to ye sense of ye Treaty of 1670, but I'm afraid not practicable because it is scarce possible to describe ye course of navigation, wch. is lyable to many accidents by wind or weather, & ye same course must be pursued in sayling to trade lawfully to Jamaica, wch. leads to some of ye Spanish ports, & it will be hard to determine at a tryall whether ye ship taken had or had not followed ye prescribed Route, or was forced out of it, by stress of weather, or an ennemy.

In short it seems very difficult to settle this affair to mutual satisfaction; there is no manner of doubt I believe but Spain would readily give sufficient security, in pursuance of ye 8th. Art. of 1670, that their subjects shall never trade or sayl to ye English colonys in America provided ye Government in England would take care, that ye English should never trade or sayl to ye Spanish ports there; butt there is no Law in England to lay that restraint upon ye Subject; & ye trade to ye Spanish West Indys, altho' illicit by treaty between Sovereign, & Sovereign, is so very lucrative that ye Parliament will never pass such a Law, & ye English merchants will run ye hazard of carrying it on in spite of treaty.}

3dly. That in Case of the Stopping, & searching of any Ship on either side, without being found actually sailing & trading in the Harbours, & Ports of the other; the finding on board some part of the growth of the Country with which the Commerce is prohibited, shall not be a sufficient Evidence, for seizing & Condemning such Ship as a Prize.

4thly. It may likewise be necessary to make some Regulations with regard to the Method of proceeding in the Examination, Tryal, and Condemnation of the Prizes taken, & brought into the Ports; So that the Masters, & the Men may not be cruelly treated, & confined as Prisoners, nor their Papers & Documents, without which they cannot possibly make their Innocence appear, taken, & kept from Them; But that they may be at full Liberty to employ such Agents, Councill, Interpreters, & all other proper means, as shall be necessary for their Defence; And some Rule should likewise be laid down with respect to appeals to superior courts & the final decision &c..

INDEX

IV
THE PARLIAMENTARY
DIARIES OF SIR JOHN
TRELAWNY, 1868-73

Edited by T. A. Jenkins

CONTENTS

PREFACE

This edition continues that begun in Camden Fourth Series XL (1990) when the diaries for the years 1858–65 were published. I am again extremely grateful to Sir John Salusbury-Trelawny, Bt., for granting permission for me to edit his great-grandfather's diaries. My thanks are also due to the Deputy Keeper of Western Manuscripts, and other staff at the Bodleian Library, for their help in the preparation of them for publication.

The Universities of Exeter and East Anglia have kindly provided financial assistance to help meet the costs of my research.

EDITORIAL NOTE

The editorial conventions adopted here are the same as those for the earlier edition of Trelawny's diaries, which was published in the Camden series in 1990. Abbreviations have usually been retained, expansions being confined to less familiar abbreviations whose presence in their original form might disrupt the flow of the text. The original capitalisation has also been followed. Trelawny's practice was to write up the diary, often the day after the events he was describing, and then to correct it at leisure. This edition follows the corrected version of the text, but in a few cases where a deleted passage appeared to be of interest, I have also included these within + signs. Trelawny used a facing-page system, sometimes adding marginal comments on the left-hand page: where appropriate, these passages have been printed here within * signs.

The place of publication of all secondary works is London, unless otherwise stated.

The following abbreviations have been used throughout the footnotes:

B.F.S.P. British and Foreign State Papers.
C.J. Commons Journals.
G.D. H.C.G. Matthew (ed), *The Gladstone Diaries* (vols VII–VIII, Oxford, 1982).
G.H.D. Nancy E. Johnson (ed), *The Diary of Gathorne Hardy, Later Lord Cranbrook, 1866–1892* (Oxford, 1981).
H Hansard's Parliamentary Debates, third series.
K.J. Ethel Drus (ed), *A Journal of Events During the Gladstone Ministry 1868–1874 by John First Earl of Kimberley* (Camden Third Series, XC, 1958).
P.P. Parliamentary Papers.
T.D. T.A. Jenkins (ed), *The Parliamentary Diaries of Sir John Trelawny, 1858–1865* (Camden Fourth Series, XL, 1990).

INTRODUCTION

After an absence from the House of Commons of nearly three-and-a-half years, Sir John Salusbury Salusbury-Trelawny, the ninth baronet (1816–85), resumed his diary[1] following his election as one of the members for East Cornwall, in November 1868. In his third and final period as a Liberal M.P. – he had previously sat in the Commons from 1843–52 and 1857–65 – Trelawny was a witness to the dramatic events associated with W. E. Gladstone's first administration. His diary records the early legislative achievements of the government, notably the Irish Church and Land acts of 1869–70, and the Education act of 1870, but it also observes the subsequent difficulties encountered by Ministers, and traces the alarming disintegration of the Liberals' majority in the House of Commons. While the extra-parliamentary dimension to the Gladstone ministry's problems is well known, Trelawny provides a specifically parliamentary perspective on the situation. The diary is also of interest for the way its accounts of parliamentary debates take us beyond the official record in *Hansard*, evoking the climate of feeling on the backbenches, and throwing light on the personalities of the various speakers, as well as recording Trelawny's own reactions to the issues of the day.

Major political changes had taken place during Trelawny's absence from the Commons, and it is hardly surprising that he found the atmosphere of the House very different from what he had known before.[2] Lord Palmerston, the dominant parliamentary figure for most of the period covered by Trelawny's earlier diaries, had died in October 1865, and his politically cautious regime had been succeeded by that of Lord Russell's, which quickly provoked a split in the Liberal party over the question of parliamentary reform (an issue Palmerston had always endeavoured to keep in the background). However, the subsequent minority Conservative government, formed by Lord Derby, proceeded to 'dish the Whigs' by carrying the Reform act of 1867, which roughly doubled the size of the electorate in England and Wales through its provisions for household suffrage in the boroughs and a £12 household franchise for the counties. This measure went at least as far, and possibly further, than Trelawny, a man with a reputation as

---

[1] The three exercise books containing the diaries for 1868-73 are deposited in the Bodleian Library, MS Eng Hist d. 417-19.

[2] See below, 16 Feb., 17 Mar., 22 Apr. 1869.

a radical, had ever contemplated.[3] Furthermore, the issue of Church rates abolition, one with which Trelawny's career had been closely associated in the past, was also removed from the agenda as a result of a bipartisan settlement, in 1868.[4] With the Conservative and Liberal parties now under the leaderships of Disraeli and Gladstone respectively, a new era of fierce political rivalry was inaugurated from which Gladstone initially emerged as the victor, having successfully rallied the whole of the Liberal party around the question of Irish Church disestablishment. The general election of 1868 produced a decisive majority for the Liberals, and Gladstone, having assumed the premiership in December, embarked upon an ambitious course of legislation.

Circumstances had altered for Trelawny in another sense, in that he now represented a different constituency. In the past, Trelawny had sat for the small Devonshire borough of Tavistock, where the Duke of Bedford exercised considerable territorial influence,[5] but the county constituency of East Cornwall had a registered electorate in 1868 of over 8,000, in which small farmers, many of them nonconformists, were the predominant force.[6] Trelawny, who was himself a local landowner with an estate of some 8,000 acres near Liskeard,[7] had been chosen to contest the seat in place of the retiring Liberal member, the Hon. T. J. Agar Robartes, but initially it seemed likely that he would be sharing the representation with the sitting Conservative member, Nicholas Kendall, who had first been elected in 1852 on a protectionist and 'no-popery' platform. By the summer of 1868, however, Kendall's reputation as the 'farmer's friend' had been seriously damaged owing to the widespread belief in the constituency that he had been instrumental in increasing the burden of county rates. His vulnerability encouraged the Liberals to believe that they might, after all, carry both of the seats, and another Cornish landowner, Edward Brydges Willyams, was therefore put forward to run in harness with Trelawny.[8] Strenuous efforts were made by the Liberals to register their supporters as electors under the new £12 franchise qualification, substantially enlarging the size of the constituency in the process.[9] In his election speeches, Trelawny fully exploited the fact that when he had previously been in

[3] T.D., 3 May 1860.

[4] G.I.T. Machin, *Politics and the Churches in Great Britain, 1832–1868* (Oxford, 1977), 349–55.

[5] Although the presence of a radical-nonconformist element had created frequent problems for Trelawny: T.D., 4–15.

[6] For the background to this constituency, see E. Jaggard, 'Farmers, Nabobs and County Politics in Cornwall, 1832–68', *Southern History*, vii (1985), 145–61.

[7] John Bateman's *Great Landowners of Great Britain and Ireland*, (4th ed., 1883), gives the annual rental of the Trelawne estate as £6,000, including the income from woodland.

[8] *The Times*, 25 July 1868, 5.

[9] Ibid, 24 Sept. 1868, 10

parliament he had introduced a bill for the creation of locally elected
county boards to administer expenditure from the rates.[10] He thus
described himself as 'a strong financial reformer', and asserted that
'Tenant farmers and yeomen of counties were as fully able to supervise
the heavy expenditure of the county rates as were town councillors and
people resident in boroughs'.[11] At Looe, as the campaign was drawing
to a close, he raised a variety of issues that were of concern to a largely
agrarian audience:

> Sir John Trelawny addressed one of the most enthusiastic meetings
> that have been held in the Division. The horses were taken from
> his carriage outside the town, and the vehicle was drawn by the
> people, headed by a band of music and a torchlight procession
> ... [in his speech] He claimed to be almost the father of the
> County financial board question, and was in favour of these boards
> being formed altogether on the elective principle. He believed that
> the increase of game was injurious to agriculture, and he would
> do the best he could to mitigate the game laws and improve the
> relation between landlord and tenant. He was in favour of the
> rating of mines and woodlands. On the subject of the turnpikes
> he was against imposing any burden on the Consolidated Fund,
> preferring to leave the management to local bodies.[12]

Some aspects of Trelawny's past record, though, were still liable to
be held up against him, and he complained on one occasion that 'his
opponents were resorting to gross misrepresentation in order to prejudice the electors against him'. In an area where nonconformity was so
powerful, Trelawny's identification with the 'Sunday question', namely
the proposal to open museums and other public galleries on the
Sabbath, together with his support, as long ago as 1845, for the
Maynooth grant, still proved capable of creating some awkward
moments. As he observed, in a speech at Torpoint, 'It had been said
that he was either a Roman Catholic or an infidel, but he emphatically
denied the statement'.[13]

In the event, Kendall found his position to be hopeless and decided
to withdraw from the contest, leaving Trelawny and Willyams to be
elected unopposed. Thereafter, Trelawny's political position within the
constituency seems to have been secure enough, but he evidently found
the routine business of a county M.P. far more demanding than
anything he had previously experienced.[14] In addition, there was a good

---

[10] See *T.D.*, 20 Mar. 1861.
[11] Speech at Bodmin, *The Times*, 24 Aug. 1868, 7.
[12] Ibid, 14 Nov. 1868, 4.
[13] Ibid, 10 Nov. 1868, 5.
[14] See below, 19 Feb. and 10 May 1869; 14 Feb. 1871.

deal of work to be done with regard to matters directly concerning the economic interests of East Cornwall, such as mines and fisheries bills, proposals for rating reform, and the amendment (or abolition) of the game laws.

The outstanding national issue during the general election of 1868 was, of course, Gladstone's proposal to disestablish and disendow the Church of Ireland, a policy which Trelawny had consistently advocated through-out his political career. In a speech at Bodmin, in August, he duly reiter-ated his view that the Church of Ireland was 'an incubus on the Church of England', and that the latter institution would be better off without its sister Church.[15] While the first major legislative enactment by Gladstone's ministry therefore had Trelawny's wholehearted support, it would be a mistake to suppose that Trelawny was generally sympathetic in his attitude towards Irish grievances. In fact he regarded the government's subsequent attempt to settle the agrarian problem in Ireland, through the Land act of 1870, as a politically necessary but otherwise regrettable step, which would not satisfy the Irish people, but would set a dangerous precedent for future legislation affecting England.[16] Nor does Trelawny appear to have been any more enthusiastic about the third part of Gladstone's programme to 'pacify Ireland', the ill-fated University bill of 1873.[17] On the other hand, he was angered by what he considered to be the weakness of Gladstone's government when it came to taking measures to suppress agrarian disorder in Ireland.[18]

If we are to fully appreciate the nature of Trelawny's concerns regarding the 'Irish Question', it is necessary to look back beyond the period of his earlier diaries (Ireland did not figure as a prominent issue during the Palmerstonian era) to his first years in the House of Commons, when he made a number of revealing contributions to the frequent debates prompted by the agrarian crisis of the 1840s. Trelawny entered the Commons in 1843 describing himself as an 'ultra-radical', and indeed he had clearly been influenced by the ideas of Jeremy Bentham and of the political economists.[19] Such formative influences, however, served only to fill Trelawny with contempt for the Irish people, an attitude that was not at all uncommon amongst radicals of his generation.

The starting-point for an analysis of Trelawny's views is to be found in his belief that the solution to the problem of Britain's troubled relations with Ireland did not lie simply in the repeal of the Act of Union of 1800. In opposing Feargus O'Connor's motion for a select

---

[15] *The Times*, 24 Aug. 1868, 7.
[16] See below, 7 Mar., 4–5 Apr. 1870.
[17] See below, 3, 4, 11 Mar. 1873.
[18] See below, 24 Feb. 1870; 2 Mar. 1871.
[19] *T.D.*, 3–4, 15–19.

committee of inquiry into this demand, in December 1847, Trelawny argued that repeal of the Union would have disastrous consequences in Ireland: the protestants of Ulster would resist such a move, and the result would be a civil war ending in the creation of a Catholic military despotism. Such a regime, inspired by hatred towards protestantism, would thereafter pose a serious threat to Britain's own security.[20]

Granted that repeal of the Union was out of the question, Trelawny believed that it was essential to deal with the land problem in Ireland. The answer here, though, was not the legislative enforcement of a system of tenant right of the sort being advocated in the 1840s by Sharman Crawford. If Ulster was more prosperous than the rest of Ireland, this had nothing to do, according to Trelawny, with its distinct 'custom' of tenant right, but was 'owing to the superiority of the Saxon over the Celtic race'.[21] Indeed, he made no bones of his belief that the root cause of all the trouble in Ireland lay in the way 'the people indulged their progenitive tendencies without having means at hand for the support of a rapidly increasing population'.[22] The only possible solution, therefore, was the eviction of tenants farming holdings that were too small to be viable, and the consolidation of the land into much larger, economically realistic, holdings.[23] Trelawny felt that such a policy could be justified once the British government had extended the poor law system to Ireland, as it did in 1847, thus providing the Irish people with a basic guarantee against actual starvation.[24] Once these arrangements were in place, Trelawny believed that the British authorities were fully justified in resorting to the use of coercion, including the suspension of *habeas corpus*, in order to stamp out social disorder for which the Irish people no longer had any reasonable excuse.[25]

Slightly earlier, in June 1846, *The Times* published a letter from Trelawny addressed to the Whig Prime Minister, Lord John Russell, containing a typically glib utilitarian formula for the solution of the Irish Question. Trelawny argued for the extension of the poor law system to Ireland on the grounds that 'Every man has a right to live who offers to devote his hands to the creation of wealth, and the rich should be contented to contribute a percentage of their wealth as a security for the enjoyment of the remainder'. The provision of poor relief would reconcile cottiers to the loss of their small holdings, which they at present clung on to as their only means of subsistence. Once the small farms were consolidated, and law and order restored, this

---

[20] 7 Dec. 1847, *H* xcv. 774–6.
[21] 22 Mar. 1848, *H* xcvii. 867–8.
[22] 9 Feb. 1849, *H* cii. 517.
[23] 22 Mar. 1848, *H* xcvii. 867–8.
[24] 31 Mar. 1847, *H* xcii. 685–6.
[25] 7 Dec. 1847, *H* xcv. 774–6; 9 Feb. 1849, *H* cii. 517.

would inspire the confidence necessary for the outlay of capital on the land. Indeed, Trelawny looked to the consequent restoration of a resident landlord class in Ireland. As capital investment led to a rise in land values, so, according to Trelawny's vision, 'the generally improved material condition of a misgoverned and ill-advised society would afford leisure for the settlement of religious differences and for the consolidation of the union with the sister Country'.[26]

Trelawny's approach to the religious dimension of the Irish problem is of particular interest for the way it reflects prevalent Liberal assumptions about the socially progressive nature of the Protestant faith. In his maiden speech in the House of Commons, calling for the disestablishment of the Church of Ireland, Trelawny had argued that the presence of the Established Church in Ireland served to alienate the Irish people from protestantism. By removing this symbolic grievance, therefore, and allowing the free-play of religious opinions, right would inevitably defeat wrong, and the weaning of the Irish people from their Catholicism could be confidently anticipated.[27] This was a classic piece of Benthamite optimism, on Trelawny's part, but it is important precisely because it was by no means an eccentric point of view among British radicals in the 1840s.

Impatient as he was, in 1847, with 'the constant howl of the Irish members ... their continual drumming and boring for money ... [and] their unreasonable demands',[28] Trelawny's overall perception of Ireland and the Irish people had not appreciably altered by the 1870s. His increasing disenchantment with the policies of Gladstone's first ministry therefore provides a valuable insight into the way that one mid-Victorian radical was becoming disturbed by certain tendencies within 'Gladstonian Liberalism'.

Ironically, the policy that did most to damage the Gladstone government's standing with the Liberal party in the Country was one which received Trelawny's full support. *Dod's Parliamentary Companion* for 1869 notes that Trelawny was an advocate of nonsectarian education, and, while W.E. Forster's Education act of 1870 adopted a more cautious approach, creating School Boards only in the areas where they were needed, and otherwise leaving the existing denominational schools in place, Trelawny recognised this to be a substantial achievement in the circumstances, especially given the strength of the vested interests involved. Important sections of nonconformist opinion were outraged by Forster's act, however, and the subsequent agitation against it in the Country did great harm to the Liberal cause. The government's prestige

[26] *The Times*, 27 June 1846, 5.
[27] 2 Aug. 1843, *H* lxxi. 175–81.
[28] 7 Dec. 1847, *H* xcv. 774–6.

and popularity thereafter diminished alarmingly, with the problem being compounded by the ill-conceived Licensing bills of 1871 and 1872, which succeeded in offending both the drink interest and the largely-nonconformist temperance movement.[29]

What Trelawny's diary shows is that the government's difficulties in the Country as a whole were also mirrored in the decline of its authority in the House of Commons. Once the wave of Liberal popularity had obviously past its peak, members of the Conservative opposition were emboldened to adopt a more aggressive stance, exploiting the laxity of parliamentary procedure, as well as their majority in the House of Lords, in order to obstruct blatantly such measures as the Army Regulation and Ballot bills of 1871. The consequent political frustrations, and especially the effects of late-night sittings, contributed to the increasingly widespread state of demoralisation amongst backbench Liberals. While the problems of parliamentary management facing the government were clearly a symptom of its growing unpopularity in the Country, Trelawny also felt that there were serious faults with the personnel of the ministry which were making matters worse. The Liberal chief whip, G.G. Glyn, was a pleasant but rather ineffectual parliamentary manager, while certain key ministers, notably the Home Secretary, H. A. Bruce, were weak, and others, like Robert Lowe and the notorious A. S. Ayrton, were personally unpopular.[30] Above all, the Prime Minister himself contributed to his government's decline by his volubility, excitability, and occasional losses of temper.[31] If the heroic legislation of 1869–70 had brought out the best in Gladstone as a parliamentarian, subsequent events revealed the limitations of a man with such a passionate temperament. Trelawny would undoubtedly have concurred with the diagnosis made by one of Gladstone's Cabinet colleagues, Lord Kimberley, in 1873, that 'Our old programme is completely exhausted: and Gladstone is not the man to govern without "measures", nor is he at all suited to lead a party in difficulties. He must have a strong current of opinion in his favour'.[32]

It was also Trelawny's belief that the government was exacerbating its problems in controlling the House of Commons by the dogged pursuit of certain measures which lacked the necessary momentum provided by a strong public opinion in their favour. This analysis was naturally influenced by Trelawny's own political prejudices, but he felt that it could be applied especially to the question of the secret ballot for parliamentary and municipal elections, a subject on which he had

[29] D.A. Hamer, *The Politics of Electoral Pressure* (Brighton, 1977), 122–38, 165–99.
[30] See below, 19 June 1872 (Glyn); 9 Aug. 1870 (Bruce); 15 Mar. 1870 (Lowe); 13 May 1870 (Ayrton).
[31] See below, 24 Feb. 1871; 23 Feb. 1872.
[32] *K.J.*, 18 Mar. 1873.

recently changed his mind. A consistent advocate of secret ballot since his first election to parliament in 1843, Trelawny had informed his prospective constituents, in 1868, that he would be opposing any future bills.[33] The precise reasons for Trelawny's conversion are not clear, but he may well have been influenced by the arguments of the philosopher, John Stuart Mill, who was a personal friend. Certainly, Trelawny seems to have shared Mill's view that voting was a public duty rather than a private right, and that publicity was therefore essential in order to ensure that voters were not betraying the 'public interest'.[34] It is also possible, in Trelawny's case, that the magnitude of the franchise extension granted by the Conservatives in 1867 may have aroused fears as to the potential cupidity of the new electorate, which could only be kept in check by open voting. Whatever the truth may be, Trelawny was dismayed by the Gladstone ministry's determination to press on with its Ballot bills, in 1871 and 1872, in the face of protracted Conservative opposition which was delaying other important parliamentary business and, Trelawny feared, damaging the reputation of the British parliament.[35]

To a lesser extent, Trelawny looked upon the government's reluctant willingness to attempt the repeal of the Contagious Diseases acts of 1866 and 1869 in much the same light. For him, the inspection and detention of prostitutes infected with venereal disease, in certain towns with large army or navy bases, was an essential public health policy,[36] and he was appalled at the way the government, in 1872, was prepared to devote precious parliamentary time to the repeal of the acts for no other reason than fear of the agitation by an extra-parliamentary pressure group. In this case, however, the defenders of the acts, a powerful cross-party grouping which also included many eminent members of the medical profession, were strong enough to be able to resist the government's plan. Trelawny himself was actively involved in the defence of the Contagious Diseases acts, finding in this a worthy cause of a kind he had not had since the days of his Church rates abolition bill.[37]

It would be misleading, however, to create the impression that Trelawny was becoming entirely alienated from the Liberal party. On the question of women's rights, for instance, Trelawny may have been a supporter of the contagious diseases legislation, and he also held

[33] *The Times*, 23 Nov. 1868, 4.
[34] For Mill's position, see Bruce L. Kinzer, *The Ballot Question in Nineteenth-Century English Politics* (New York, 1982), 73–81.
[35] See below, 11 July 1871; 8 Apr. 1872.
[36] Indeed he had pressured the Palmerston government to pass the first Contagious Diseases act: *T.D.*, 5 and 31 May 1864.
[37] See below, 21 Mar. 1872.

strong views on what he considered to be the impropriety of the behaviour by some of the women involved in the repeal campaign,[38] but on the other hand he regularly voted for Jacob Bright's bills to protect married women's property and to extend the parliamentary franchise to women who were householders. He also voted, in 1872, for G.O. Trevelyan's bill to apply the principle of household suffrage to the counties as well as the boroughs. Furthermore, when he complained about the congestion of parliamentary business, Trelawny was at the same time expressing his frustration at the government's failure to deal with certain issues which greatly concerned him: he was anxious, for instance, to see a settlement of the vexed question of the game laws (he was a member of the select committee of inquiry which sat in 1872–3), and, during the largely barren session of 1873, it was Trelawny who tried to promote an amending bill to the Prison Ministers act of 1863, designed to secure for Roman Catholic prisoners ministration by clergymen of their own faith. Nevertheless, when we recall his earlier reputation as a Benthamite radical, it is undoubtedly true that Trelawny's views in general appear much more moderate, in the altered circumstances of the 1868–74 parliament, and it therefore seems reasonable to follow a recent study of this period in classifying him as a 'Whig-Liberal'.[39]

In his earlier diaries, Trelawny had occasionally expressed some concern about the ability of parliament to conduct the nation's business under its existing rules,[40] reflecting his strong sense of the importance of maintaining Britain's constitutional machinery. After 1868, the situation threatened to reach crisis proportions due to the strains imposed by the ambitious legislative programmes of the Gladstone ministry, together with the abuse of parliamentary procedures by many backbench M.P.s.[41] Trelawny's contribution to the discussions about what needed to be done took the form of an anonymous letter to *The Times*, in February 1870, in which he pointed to the amount of time that was wasted as a result of the adherence to antiquated procedures such as the hearing of petitions, the unnecessary repetition of forms, and the inefficient method of taking divisions. This letter seems to be of sufficient interest to merit inclusion as an appendix to the diaries. Trelawny's letter also made a number of practical suggestions for the more efficient use of space within the Palace of Westminster, and, while most of his ideas were not adopted, the proposal to exclude strangers from the lobby

[38] See below, 20 July 1871; 22 July 1872.

[39] J.P. Parry, *Democracy and Religion: Gladstone and the Liberal Party, 1867–1875* (Cambridge, 1986), 321, 338.

[40] *T.D.* 30 July 1860; 7 Feb. 1861.

[41] Agatha Ramm, 'The Parliamentary Context of Cabinet Government, 1868–1874', *English Historical Review*, xcix (1984), 739–69.

was implemented at the beginning of the 1870 session. Sadly, it is impossible to establish the extent to which this change was the result of Trelawny's promptings.[42] One other action by Trelawny, which is worth mentioning in the context of his determination to uphold the dignity and authority of parliament, was his decision to make notes of the debate on the Contagious Diseases acts, on 24 May 1870, after another member had moved that strangers be removed from the gallery. Trelawny supplied his notes to *The Times* newspaper, and they seem to have provided some of the material for the report that was subsequently included in *Hansard*.[43]

Trelawny's political career came to an end with the sudden dissolution of parliament in January 1874. His decision not to stand for re-election seems to have been entirely due to reasons of ill-health: as early as 1871 he had indicated to his constituents that he would not be able to face another electoral contest, and the available evidence suggests that he almost certainly could have secured re-election had he wished it.[44] A further sign of the high regard in which he was held by the Liberals was the fact that in 1873 the chief whip, Glyn, had, without solicitation, suggested Trelawny's name to Gladstone as a suitable one for a peerage at the end of the parliament.[45] No offer was made, in the event, and there is no way of knowing whether Trelawny would have welcomed a new title.

Almost nothing is known of Trelawny's political opinions during the period between his retirement and his death, in August 1885. Leonard Courtney, the 'Little Englander' radical who won a by-election at Liskeard in 1876, did note that Trelawny had refused to support him, although this must at least in part have been due to the fact that the Conservative candidate was Trelawny's son-in-law.[46] We might well imagine that he would have recoiled from the melodrama of the Midlothian campaigns – it is clear that Trelawny had never been an uncritical admirer of Gladstone, for all the latter's acknowledged qualities – and he would certainly have been alarmed by the 'socialistic' tendencies of the 1880s associated with Joseph Chamberlain. Had he lived longer, there is every reason to think that he would have opposed Gladstone's plan of Home Rule for Ireland, and thus joined in the drift of so many Liberal landed families towards Conservatism. Whether under paternal inspiration or otherwise, it is interesting to note that by *c.* 1890 Sir William Trelawny, the tenth baronet, was chairman of the South East Cornwall Liberal Unionist Association.[47]

[42] See below, 14 Feb. 1870.
[43] See below, 24–25 Apr., 5 July 1870.
[44] *The Times*, 4 Dec. 1871, 6; 21 May 1872, 6; 26 Feb. 1873, 8.
[45] Glyn to Gladstone, 17 Sept. [1873], B.L. Add MSS 44348, fo. 275.
[46] G.P. Gooch, *Life of Lord Courtney* (1920), 123.
[47] Ibid, 282–3.

EIGHTH PARLIAMENT OF QUEEN VICTORIA

Thursday, 10 December 1868:[48] I arrived just before 2 p.m. A large crowd followed some one – I think it was Disraeli – and cheered loudly. In Westminster Hall was ranged a line of some hundreds along whose front we passed to the corridor.

House pretty full. I noticed that the benches behind the opposition front bench were thinly occupied, & that the benches below the gangway were nearly full. The ex-ministers looked downcast. On the ministerial side there seemed to be a tendency to crowd above the gangway, though places were pretty equally filled.

A great many new faces. Old members much grayer since 1865 when I last saw them.

* The Yeoman-Usher of the * Black Rod (Admiral Clifford) summoned members to the Lords. I remained. After a brief absence of those who followed the Black Rod, the clerk pointed to Sir Geo. Grey, who, thereupon, with great composure, appropriateness and skill, proposed Mr J.E. Denison as Speaker. Sir Geo. spoke far better than usual. His manner was less hurried, his matter well chosen & tersely put. He mentioned that Denison had been for 40 years a member and had been 3 times speaker.[49] Walpole[50] was apparently a little nervous &, as usual, pompous. But his real kindness and geniality reconcile hearers to minor defects. Mr Denison briefly acknowledged the honour conferred upon him – & submitted himself to the will of the House. He was then escorted by his mover and seconder to the chair when we all stood up. The Speaker now delivered a carefully-prepared speech & made allusion to the number of new members and the fact of their being elected under Household Suffrage. The Lord advocate (Moncrieff) congratulated the Speaker, and spoke with brevity and point – moving the adjournment.

Disraeli was followed on leaving the House by a crowd of admirers who cheered lustily.

---

[48] In the light of the results of the recent general election, the Conservative Premier, Benjamin Disraeli, had decided to resign immediately rather than face the new parliament. By 10 Dec., therefore, W.E. Gladstone had already been commissioned to form a Liberal administration.

[49] Elected in 1857, 1859 and 1865.

[50] Seconding Grey.

Saturday, 12 December: [...] The Ministry appears to be nearly complete. There is an ominous absence of many supposed candidates for posts. Still there is a strong cast.[51]

Tuesday, 15 December: The law relating to vacation of seats by members made ministers of the Crown, taken in connexion with a recent act affecting claims to seats, has rendered expedient an adjournmt. and, accordingly, the House is adjourned till the 29th.[52] There was a brief debate on this technical matter.

Tuesday, 16 February, 1869: House met at one. Arriving about 1/4 before 2, I found the swearing of members in progress. Adm[iral] Sir A. Clifford, Bt., CB, who looked frail, soon summoned us to the Lords. On the return of members the Queen's speech was read and the address moved by the Hon. H. Cowper who acquitted himself excellently. Mundella seconded him in a manner less successful. M. succeeded J.A. Roebuck for Sheffield and some think the choice of a seconder was a hit at R.[53] If so, R. is, in a certain sense, avenged. My belief is that M. was selected as a compliment to the working classes whom he is supposed to represent. A Premier who could be capable of low spite would be unworthy of a much lower office.

A great many good measures were promised by various members of the government and there are hopes of the session being a memorable one. Disraeli was subdued & moderate – indeed, it seemed to me, prosy.

The absence of many well known countenances was painful. New men on all sides.

I pitied John Bright, who looked unhappy. Samson has lost his hair.

There was a great crowd in West[minster] Hall, forming a long line. Walking up I was leisurely looking at the statues on my left when I was

---

[51] A number of former Whig ministers, such as the Duke of Somerset, Viscount Halifax and Sir George Grey, had declined offers from Gladstone. The most notable new recruit was the radical, John Bright, who became President of the Board of Trade; J.P. Parry, *Democracy and Religion: Gladstone and the Liberal Party, 1867-1875* (Cambridge, 1986), 278-9.

[52] And again until 16 Feb. 1869. The first adjournment was necessary in order to allow the statutory period of time (21 days) for election petitions to be presented, before new writs could be issued for those constituencies where Liberal ministers were obliged to seek re-election. Lord Ossington, *Notes from my Journal when Speaker of the House of Commons* (privately printed, 1900), 235.

[53] Roebuck was notorious for his anti-trade union views. Mundella, a hosiery manufacturer in Nottingham, sought to promote closer relations between employers and employees, and took a specialist interest in matters affecting the working men. W.H.G. Armytage, *A.J. Mundella 1825-1897: The Liberal Background to the Labour Movement* (London, 1951).

vociferously cheered. The people thus amused themselves as members entered, and it made one feel a little ridiculous.

Thursday, 18 February: Several questions were put and notices given. Gladstone informed the House that the Queen was prepared to come to London for the purpose of receiving her faithful Commons at the Palace. He excused her non-attendance at the opening of Parliament on the grounds of severe headache from which she suffered. The course of members going to see her in the way proposed was not, he said, without precedent and he adduced instances.[54] Disraeli consented, guardedly – he seems to be dropping his aggressive manner. Probably he feels that a particular responsibility attaches to a leader of opposition who has been Premier.

Gladstone looks somewhat worse thro' care & labour. Evidently, the smallest and greatest matters beget anxiety in him. Sir D. Le Marchant[55] read the address at length, which it was obviously tedious to Gladstone to hear. Will he bear his work?

Friday, 19 February: [...] I found plenty to do in the shape of duties not coming before the Public. My new post is far more laborious than any former one.

Monday, 22 February: Goschen & Bruce[56] again distinguished themselves by quiet practical & well-informed expositions. It is settled that some business of importance – in particular, a measure relating to our criminal caste – shall commence in the Lords.[57] Goschen introduced an important bill to secure uniformity of assessment in London and another for a similar object throughout the country.[58] It was proposed by McEvoy to abolish the ecclesiastical Titles act.[59] The House seems to maintain its tranquil and sensible demeanour.

Gladstone reported that the Queen would not receive her commons owing to the ill health of Prince Leopold.

[54] The only precedent was in 1805, after the death of the Duke of Gloucester. Normally, when the monarch did not open parliament in person, the Address was presented to him or her by the Privy Councillors. Ossington, *Journal*, 239. The suggestion for a public reception at Buckingham Palace was made by the Home Secretary, who was concerned about the possible adverse effects of 'the Queen's total abstention from all popular demonstrations'; H.A. Bruce to Gladstone, 9 Feb. 1869, B.L. Add MSS 44086, fo. 32.

[55] Clerk of the House of Commons.

[56] President of the Poor Law Board, and Home Secretary, respectively.

[57] The Habitual Criminals bill, introduced on 26 Feb.; Royal Assent, 11 Aug.

[58] The Rateable Property (Metropolis) bill and the Rateable Property bill. The latter was subsequently withdrawn; for the former, see Avner Offer, *Property and Politics 1870–1914* (Cambridge, 1981), 176–7.

[59] McEvoy's bill was later withdrawn.

Friday, 26 February: Newdegate moved for inquiry on the subject of Roman Catholic endowments & was defeated. I voted agt. him.[60] It strikes me that ministers might have replied to his speech: at least, briefly. Still I am of opinion a special motion of this kind, affecting a particular religious community, would not be expedient.

When Newdegate was moving, the whole front bench of the opposition was empty [...]

Monday, 1 March: The fullest House I ever saw.[61] Coming late, I made three attempts to obtain a seat, going up as many sets of steep staircases. For some two hours I heard Gladstone's marvellous exposition and then left my place. I have read the remainder of his speech since. It seems to me that he revels in distinctions. The use of his intellect is evidently not merely a delight but a necessity of his nature. The speech (and of this he was conscious) was at times wanting in the interest which has characterized some of his more remarkable speeches. But then the sense of responsibility must have been great. Opposite opinions must be conciliated. Catholics must be persuaded that they gain their due; Protestants that they only give up what ought not fairly to be in their hands. The orator's exordium & peroration were both excellent.

Wednesday, 3 March: The House divided on the great Tramways motion,[62] which was debated for nearly 3 hours. Mr Grosvenor & Lord Geo. Hamilton distinguished themselves. Pease, too, spoke well.[63] Several members described their experience of trams in American cities. Conflicting evidence. * I supported the 2d. reading. * [...]

Thursday, 4 March: [...] Bruce moved for the promised Committee on purity of Election &c. and intimated, to the unspeakable delight of members below the gangway, his conversion to the Ballot, upon which he propounded excellent arguments. Hardy agreed to the proposal for a Committee, concluding his speech with a remark to the effect that

[60] 85:46 against the motion for a select committee to enquire into the working of legislation relating to Roman Catholic charities; *H* cxciv. 384-99.

[61] For the 1st reading of the Established Church (Ireland) bill, to disestablish and disendow the Church of Ireland; no division. Disestablishment was to take place on 1 Jan. 1871, and the Church's property vested in a new ecclesiastical commission for the next ten years. After financial provision had been made for incumbents and curates, and compensation given to other denominations for the loss of the Maynooth grant, regium donum etc., Gladstone reckoned on a surplus of £7.8 millions which was to be applied to 'unavoidable calamities and suffering' not covered by the poor law. Parry, *Democracy and Religion*, 280- 2.

[62] 209:78 for 2nd reading of the Metropolitan Street Tramways bill. Later withdrawn.

[63] Moving the rejection of the bill on the grounds that it would give monopolistic powers to a private company; *H* cxciv. 542-5.

he hoped it was not to be a mere cloak for persons who had already changed their minds. (Laughter.)

A writ for Bewdley was moved by Noel. Some liberals objected, preferring postponemt. for a year on grounds of corrupt practices. On a division the writ passed.[64] In this my name will not appear as I had left the House.

[...] It occurs to me that inquiries into corrupt practices shd. be completed within a reasonable date after each gen[era]l election. Delay tends to degrade Parliamt. and familiarize the Public with low questions. The false swearing of venal voters and protestation of candidates that they knew of no illegal expenditure – in the face of acknowledged outlays of many thousands – must by habit harden the conscience.

The House heard the awful news of the supposed cost of the Abyssinian expedition, said to be over £8,000,000.[65]

Friday, 5 March: After the usual battery of interrogatories, the House settled down to hear Lord Eustace Cecil's motion on adulteration of food[66]. He is not equal to Lord Robert Cecil (whom we have lost) now Lord Salisbury. Probably Lord Eustace is a well meaning member and may do good service. At present he does not astonish anyone. Bright & Pochin spoke usefully – each sceptical as to the extent of wilful tampering with food.

The work of the evening was Collier's (att[orne]y gen[era]l) bankruptcy Bill[67] which pleased all the speakers except Jessel, a lawyer – which is a good sign.

The Tories were in disgrace about the appoint[men]t of Col[onel] Wetherall to an Irish civil post just before their vacation of office. Wilson Patten seemed to make but a lame defence of the course taken.[68]

Monday, 8 March: Attending at 1/2 past 4, I found Gladstone on his legs replying to Hutt's question whether the African Squadron was

---

[64] 128:65. The election in Nov. 1868 had been declared void. The by-election on 11 Mar. 1869 was won by a Conservative, but also declared void, the seat being awarded to the Liberal candidate, the Hon. A.H.A. Anson.

[65] Robert Lowe moved a supplementary vote of £3.6 millions, making a total of £8.6 millions; H cxciv. 641–3. For the war, see Freda Harcourt, 'Disraeli's Imperialism 1866–1868: A Question of Timing', *Historical Journal*, xxiii (1980), 87–109.

[66] For a government investigation of malpractices, and the amendment of the penalties attached to these offences; H cxciv. 718–27, withdrawn.

[67] Royal assent 9 Aug.

[68] Sir Edward Wetherall, a soldier, had been appointed Under-secretary for Ireland. Wilson Patten was the Conservative Irish Chief Secretary at the time. Wetherall died in May 1869.

to be withdrawn. Not all immediately, but a good beginning is to be made with hopes of complete eventual withdrawal.[69]

There was a good deal of skilful sparring between the late & present governmts. on the subject of new creations of offices. Sclater-Booth, Cardwell & Hunt were the chief speakers. All spoke well – in the best style of House-of-Commons thrust & parry.

The charge least successfully met was that levelled at the appointmt. of Lord Lansdown[e] without salary,[70] wh. appointmt. was objected to on constitutional grounds. No man, as a rule, is fit for high office without training thro' lower grades. To give this training to men who can afford to serve without pay is to deprive poorer men of an opening.

It struck me that some of the liberals were not pleased [...]

Tuesday, 9 March: Locke King moved the 1st reading of a bill for assimilating the law of descent of real property to that of personal. Gladstone seemed rather favourable to some change, but no time now to undertake more measures[71]. Nothing else very noteworthy.

Wednesday, 10 March: A long debate on Lord R. Montagu's Bill for preventing cattle Plague.[72] On a division he was defeated. Majority 56. Numbers 197 to 253. * I voted agt. Lord R.M. *

[...] The measure of govt., being an elaborate code,[73] deserves consideration before a measure introduced by an irresponsible member. Any good parts of Lord R. M.'s bill may be adopted in the measure of Ministers. To restrict trade to dead meat is to suppress it in hot weather. Live stock are wanted by buyers of store cattle. The Cattle trade of Liverpool is almost extinguished. That of Hull greatly curtailed. The measure of Ministers seems to be as effective as that of Lord R.M. which is ambiguous & inconsistent. However, I keep a report of the debate for reference.

Sir J. Coleridge followed. He moved the 2d. Reading of the University Tests Bill[74] in a very good speech and not a long one. Mowbray replied and (his case being considered) acquitted himself well – looking and speaking like a member for Oxford University – proper & prejudiced. As our time was short, the debate was adjourned.

[69] The squadron was deployed off the West Coast of Africa to suppress the slave trade.

[70] As a Junior Lord of the Treasury in Gladstone's ministry.

[71] The Real Estate Intestacy bill was later withdrawn.

[72] 2nd reading of the Contagious Diseases (Animals) bill, requiring that imported cattle be slaughtered at the port of entry; later withdrawn.

[73] The Contagious Diseases (Animals) (No. 2) bill, increasing the powers of the Privy Council to regulate the importation and transportation of live cattle. *P.P.* 1868–9, i. 511.

[74] The Solicitor General, acting in an independent capacity, sought to abolish religious tests for all lay posts in the Universities; rejected by the House of Lords.

Thursday, 11 March: White of Brighton made a long and very dreary speech (preliminary to supply) on the subject of the duties of the Minister of War and F[ield] M[arshall] com[mandin]g in chief.[75] This is a matter which interests a certain class of Financial & Military reformers. The motion was withdrawn and Cardwell made his statement[76] which was commended from opposite quarters. The reduction (over a million) will not, I think, satisfy the taxpayer. The army still costs a heavy sum. The remarks of 'the Times' of this morning are in this sense.

The Minister deals in part with the subject I formerly handled – viz, the manner in which the Guards are officered. He abolishes 3 superfluous L[ieutenan]t Colonels [...]

Wednesday, 17 March: I voted with Governmt. agt. Mr Monk's Bill for relieving officers of the Revenue Departments from certain disabilities and restrictions as to their conduct at elections.[77] At present such officers cannot canvas or take active part. It was argued that their great influence might be abused – for example, their power to insist upon immediate payment of sums due to the State. Promotion, too, might be held back from deserving subordinates.

Restriction, it was added, is no new thing – as contractors cannot sit in Parliament.

Gladstone warned us of the danger of making a change, reminding us that whoever has 9 sovereigns in his pocket may be pretty sure that 1 of them will find its way into the Public exchequer.

Lowe & Ayrton had previously spoken in a somewhat similar strain.

Gladstone referred to a rumour – he did not say it was true – that his non-election for S. Lancashire[78] was, in part, due to the opposition of civil servants who regarded him as too strict in his supervision of matters of finance.

Some one said in debate that the civil servants were fortunate in their disability.

It is diverting to notice the flutter of notice papers when a new question occurs. The new members are so diligent – new brooms! The whole Ho[use] is white as in a snow-storm.

Lowe shd. be more guarded in his replies and remarks. Why attribute the desire of revenue officers to take part in elections to vanity? What made Lowe desire to be a member of a Govt? Let us assume, Public

---

[75] i.e. the division of responsibilities between the two posts. The commander-in-chief was the Duke of Cambridge, the Queen's cousin.

[76] The Secretary of State for war, on the army estimates. £14,230,400 was required for the year, a reduction of £1,196,650.

[77] 207:88 against the 2nd reading of the Revenue Officers bill.

[78] South West Lancashire, in 1868.

spirit. Why may not other revenue officers have Public spirit?

I forgot to mention Ayrton's account of office-mongering in America. It hardly exaggerated the actual facts here. What member does not know this?

Thursday, 18 March: (Irish Church) 1/2 past 4. House very full. Almost every place taken. Numerous peers in attendance.

D'Israeli looks calm & serious, – his hat off, – his right hand across his left wrist, – awaiting the signal to begin. On his right hand Hardy, – on his left Claud Hamilton & Stafford Northcote.

Collier, Cardwell, Childers, & Bruce reply to questions. Little interest till Bright's turn came. Silence at once.

Near 5. Hughes asks a question. Some one violated a point of order. Much laughter. Heaps of Petitions.

Dizzy leapt up at 5.10 (Great cheers.)[79] I heard him during an hour and 35 minutes. He seemed to me to labour much more than usual, like a man in a false position. He raised no enthusiasm and his followers looked uneasy. A few of his jests were diverting enough, but hardly suited the occasion. At times he was mystic, at others paradoxical. I think he has materially strengthened ministerial hands [...]

By the way, Dizzy plied his tumbler incessantly as cheers afforded opportunities. A friend was sent for more. Going out, I said to an official + White the doorkeeper + that D. was obliged to drink often, which I thought might have been for a sore throat; but my friend said that it was brandy & water. I have no doubt D'Israeli's throat was not quite in the best condition. He evidently had a cold.

Friday, 19 March: At 10m. before 5, Ball began the debate[80] in a good manner & rich brogue.

Gladstone & Cardwell calm, cheerful, & ready for battle. As Ball made some point, they interchanged remarks. Gladstone uneasy as his conduct on the Maynooth grant was dissected.[81]

Ball has the tones & some of the gifts of an orator. But, like a lawyer, he sometimes draws minor distinction. *+ ex. gra. The Prot[estan]t Epis[copal] Ch[urch] was not established by conquest, existing clergymen were only required to conform! +* Lowe, Cardwell & Gladstone

---

[79] Moving the rejection of the 2nd reading of the Established Church (Ireland) bill.

[80] On the 2nd reading of the Established Church (Ireland) bill, continued.

[81] Gladstone had resigned from Sir Robert Peel's ministry over this issue, in 1845, because it conflicted with the principles he had stated in his book, *The State in its Relations with the Church* (1838). Nevertheless, he had still voted for the Maynooth grant. Ball therefore contended that Gladstone had no religious objection to State endowment of the Roman Catholic Church; *H* cxciv. 1791–1814.

are very cheerful, & seem comfortable as to the line of reply they will adopt.

Bright looks full of conscious power – & is all attention, not undervaluing his foe, & not fussy.

'The great evil' – says Ball – 'is the amount of absenteeism that exists in Ireland'. Droll expression! He deprecates voluntary support of religions. He instances America & alludes to Hepworth Dixon's acc[oun]t of religion there.[82] (oh! oh!)

He disapproves of mendicancy. 'You will not find an Erasmus except in a church which is endowed like Erasmus's'.

The glory of England mainly due to the Union of Church & State. (Cheers & ohs.)

He alludes to Gladstone's former works hereon – 'words that will outlive the ephemeral breath'.

Gladstone stretches across Childers to Bright, doubtless suggesting an argument to be used in reply.

Ball has the great advantage of the power of varying his tones, & dropping his voice in skilful contrast, running, as expression seems to require, over his whole scale.

'When Lord Stafford came t'Ireland' – He fell into this abbreviation several times: – a mere minor flaw, but worth avoiding.

5.55 p.m. House warming up, orator well heard – Tories more & more happy & contented.

He says a burthen will be thrown on land, that of supporting religion. Yet D'Israeli seemed to say the bill was a gift to landlords.[83]

Ball's elaborate calculations about an alleged error in the Bill, in omitting the charge of poor-rate, rather disturb Gladstone, Cardwell & Lowe, whose heads are laid together. As to the value of life interests – 'the clergy by no means remarkable for brevity of existence'. (laugh.)

He comes to the condition in which the Queen will be left with a barren sceptre in her hand. (Sensation.)

Bright very attentive, Gladstone cannot quite remain still. Palmerston rarely moved or betrayed emotion. The hat helped this. Gladstone's pallid & passionate lineaments lie exposed to full observation of every change.

Peroration excellent. (Great cheers.)

Sullivan[84] followed, & was a worthy antagonist. I heard him while he dealt Disraeli some heavy blows, & then went home.

[82] William Hepworth Dixon, *New America* (1867), described the state of religion in a country where a purely voluntary system operated.

[83] Disraeli, on 18 Mar., had ridiculed the plan for the extinction of the Tithe rent charge, predicting that the result would be that Church property would go into the pockets of the landlords; *H* cxciv. 1662–94.

[84] Irish Attorney General.

Lord Crichton, Miall, Stafford Northcote and Bright spoke – the last great as ever. Miall did not succeed very well, if one believe 'the Times'.

Sullivan seems to have been quite equal to Dr Ball.

Monday, 22 March: At prayers the House was nearly full, members being desirous of securing places with cards.

4.30. Questions. These almost amount to speeches read [...] The first time I ever heard a question (Dixon's) delivered close to the clock, from the seats newly used by members only.[85] Goschen very lengthy in reply.

5.10. Roundell Palmer began. (Cheers) 'imperious & overwhelming necessity determines his course'.[86]

6.15. Lowe very animated & attentive.

Splendid speech, just over in 2 hours & 12 minutes.

Roundell Palmer's manner & appearance are far more clerical than lay or forensic. Earnest & conscientious it is difficult not to believe him.

Gladstone was during parts of the speech nervous & fidgetty, & he took many notes. Quotations from one or more of his speeches affected him a good deal. He cheered energetically at one point as much as to say 'I admit all that & can explain it'.

Grand as the effort of Palmer was & fascinating as it was to listen to him, his speech leaves on the mind a sense of want of breadth, and was more worthy of an equity draughtsman than a statesman. I predict that it will fall to the lot of Lowe to tear the fabric to pieces. Many inconsistencies will be apparent to the critics of tomorrow. The nice distinctions Palmer drew will turn out, I suspect, to be but illusions of a refined & scholastic intelligence.

Lowe's countenance in profile as he watched Palmer I shall hardly forget. From time to time he jotted down notes bringing his paper close to his eyes.

It seems Coleridge was selected for immediate reply to Palmer. This explains the dreadfully mournful expression of + Collier's + countenance.

[...] Palmer looks delicate. His voice required repeated supplies of water, Headlam was his bottle holder. I never saw an orator before proceed with his speech for some sentences with a tumbler in his hand. Several great speakers are I think becoming weak in the throat: – notably D'Israeli & Bright.

[85] Recent changes had made available for members the two first benches on each side under the gallery: Ossington, *Journal*, 236.

[86] He opposed the 2nd reading of the Established Church (Ireland) bill, on the grounds that while he favoured disestablishment, he was opposed to disendowment. His views had precluded an offer from Gladstone of the Lord Chancellorship: Roundell, Earl of Selborne, *Memorials: Personal and Political, 1865–1895* (1898), i. 112–13.

Tuesday,[87] **23 March**: [...] 4.45. Gladstone calmly awaits the fray, his arms crossed, & his eyes tranquilly fixed on the stained glass windows. He looks ash-pale & sharp-visaged. On his right Cardwell, on his left Childers – who occasionally appear to take instructions.

Bright's rather aggressive reply about statistical returns of farm stock,[88] among which horses are not included. Farmers supposed not to like to render themselves liable for assessed Taxes.

5.22. Debate resumed.[89] Walpole began. I did not stay to hear him. At about 1/4 before 11 on my return I found Hardy on his legs, who poured forth a complete torrent for two hours & more. The monotony of his stentorian tones is very tedious. But he satisfied his party, who cheer him vehemently. It is now nearly 1 a.m. Stretched on a cushion in a corridor before a good fire, I heard a wag laughingly ask a brother member 'will you pair till 5?' Surely Hardy might compress his matter.

Just before 1, he sat down amid tremendous applause.

Gladstone in great force. (Repeated cheers.)

10 min. to 2, and he still flows on without a check.

Gladstone twitted D'Israeli with his charge of last year of a conspiracy of Romanists & ritualists to undermine the Royal supremacy, and reminded him of Lord Mayo's[90] willingness to give salaries to the priests. This R. Palmer has given up. D'Israeli's power of face is miraculous; – not a muscle does he move.

25 min. past 2. After a fine speech the House divided.

Ayes 368
Noes 250

118   I voted with the ayes.

House adjourned until Thursday week. Very few cabs in Palace Yard. I, foreseeing this, got a good start, &, by running fast, found one vacant, – & so home.

Gladstone administered a well deserved rebuke to Stafford Northcote for words used during the Election contest.[91]

The House of Commons will not hold its members, who suffer in consequence much inconvenience.

Friday, 9 April:[92] [...] Fawcett, agt. advice, would press his motion

---

[87] Trelawny accidently wrote 'Thursday'.

[88] Question raised by Clare Sewell Read; *H* cxciv. 2001–2.

[89] 2nd reading of the Established Church (Ireland) bill.

[90] Irish Chief Secretary in the Conservative ministries of Derby and Disraeli.

[91] In fact, Gladstone alleged that the speech, describing the bill as 'sacrilege, spoliation, perfidy', had been made at a Conservative dinner on 3 Mar. (reference not found in *The Times*).

[92] The House resumed its sittings on 1 Apr., but Trelawny had been absent through illness.

that all civil & diplomatic appointments shd. be obtained by Public competition. This was considered rather too hasty. Lowe & Lord Stanley gave reasons for caution.

I was still unfit for a long night of work & so lost the division.[93] No doubt I shd. have voted with Ministers [...]

Monday, 12 April: From the commencement of the sitting till 10, I was in attendance & heard the budget discussed at much length.[94] Hunt, Northcote, Thomas Baring & many others made criticisms. Lowe & Gladstone interchanged remarks and agreed to a sort of compromise to take pro forma all the resolutions but the 6th,[95] wh. is postponed. A suggestion was also accepted that the bill for repealing the 1/- corn duty shd. fix a definite day when the duty shd. cease.

Lowe's talent shone out conspicuously in his exhaustive and argumentative reply to speakers who raised numerous points. The extra payment of £400,000 of assessed Taxes in 1870 would have been recovered in 1872, while the Income Tax reduction of 1d. would be felt at once.

The following is what I jotted down at the time in my note-book:–

Lowe wants his Budget resolutions as a foundation for a Bill. Hunt draws distinctions. Lowe very anxious to get the resolutions pro forma. He & Gladstone confer across Childers.

Gladstone rises to put the discussion in a more intelligible condition. (Hear. Hear.) He said a certain resolution in one contingency wd. not be necessary, upon a proposal that the duty on servants be adopted.[96] Ayrton usefully corrects him across several Ministers. Hazardous feat! but he was right, & looked proportionably happy.

Lowe fell back on his power, & was content to challenge battle.

D'Israeli calmly criticized Lowe's 'misconception', & would not admit that the arrangement of proceeding pro forma was to be taken as a matter of course. He was very skilful.

Gladstone succeeded him, arguing that Lowe was quite right.

Hunt offered a suggestion to facilitate the progress of business. (A laugh.)

Lowe showed the difficulty. House cried 'go on, go on!' As the case

---

[93] 281:30 against the amendment.

[94] Lowe had outlined his budget resolutions on 8 Apr., *H* cxcv. 363–400. He proposed that the income tax and land tax should be collected in a single instalment, in January. He also proposed a comprehensive scheme for the revision and simplification of other assessed taxes, converting them into licence duties. Income tax was to be reduced by 1d., and the duties on fire insurances abolished along with the 1s. corn duty (a remnant of the old corn laws). James Winter, *Robert Lowe* (Toronto, 1976), 255–7.

[95] Relating to servants, carriages etc., *H* cxcv. 595–6.

[96] Reference not clear from *Hansard*, but evidently relates to the 6th resolution.

stands Hunt threatens a wider disagreement and begins a lengthy dissertation.

Lowe & Gladstone confer from time to time. Lowe is fussy, & seems like a man who is easily teased.

Ayrton rather too officiously makes suggestions to Gladstone, who politely but impatiently receives them with bows delivered without turning his head. Ayrton returns to the charge. There is no shaking him off. It is a wonder that a man could bear this kind of rebuff twice. But Ayrton is – Ayrton.

Hunt proceeds acutely & practically. Too much taxation at one part of the year.

Crawford (the Gov[erno]r of the Bank) follows pertinently. If small sums belonging to Govt. lie in the Bank at one period, the Bank will hold more for the taxpayer.

Ayrton again besieges Gladstone who c[oul]d hardly bear the renewed attack. Ayrton now leaves his post. But soon he reappeared on the left of Gladstone instead of his right.

Wednesday, 14 April: A very interesting and instructive debate on the married womens' protection Bill.[97] The mover was Mr Russell Gurney. Some of the cases of hardship which he described were exceedingly harrowing. We had forcible speeches from Jessel & the Solicitor general[98] and a very fair speech from H. Lopes who was on the other side. As some one said in my hearing 'the Jews are strong to-day'. There was no division on the 2d. reading.

Then came T. Hughes's Sunday Trading Bill upon wh. I gave 2 votes of a character wh. 'the Times' calls obstructive.[99] But why did not the mover put on the notice paper the amendments intended? The Bill is a plan for the alteration of the criminal Law on a point of importance. Very likely disturbances will spring out of it. I spoke, briefly. Probably, I was a little thrown off my guard by my feelings and sympathy with an active party below the gangway.

Gurney is full, fluent and earnest. His manner gentle and agreeable. Voice easily heard. Matter pertinent and case not overlaid [...]

Thursday, 15 April: Newdegate moved an amendment on going into

---

[97] The Married Women's Property bill, which later ran out of time in the House of Lords.

[98] Sir John Coleridge.

[99] *The Times*, 15 Apr. 1869, 8. The votes were 169:81 against Rylands' motion that the chairman of committee report progress, and 110:57 against Brady's motion that the chairman leave the chair. Thomas Chambers had proposed a number of 'verbal amendments' which were not on the order paper. The bill was later withdrawn.

Committee on the Irish Church Bill[100] and was defeated. Numbers 355 to 229. Of course, I voted with Ministers.

The policy of the liberal party was one of abstention from debate. Our opponents made speech after speech, but failed to provoke an answer – except a short (and able) description, by Gladstone, of the state of parties with reference to the question under discussion. He shewed abundantly that, whereas his party were as one man, the Tories were distracted by conflicting counsels. Some are for levelling up;[101] some for no surrender. Disraeli was unusually brief, – labouring, evidently, under the difficulties he encounters. He knows as well as any man that the country has taken its decision and has no hopes of convincing his extreme men of any alternative plan.

The House was very boisterous and unruly while Sinclair Aytoun was speaking.[102] Two or three Conservatives spoke well, notably Holt and Raikes, M.P. for Chester [...]

Friday, 16 April: We had a division on Sheridan's clause requiring smoking accommodation in Metropolitan Railway carriages. I voted agt. the clause. * 175 to 167.[103] *

Afterwards I paired for the night with Mr Drax. There was a division on the 2d. clause of the Irish Church Bill.[104] Numbers 344 to 221. The clause was carried.

The debate was lively. The lawyers had much to say. Collier, Dr Ball, R. Palmer, the Attorney gen[era]l for Ireland[105] among them. Disraeli and Gladstone distinguished themselves greatly. Disraeli was, I gather, very full of fire.

The hinge of the arguments was the effect of the Bill on the Royal Supremacy. The points raised were very subtle.

Monday, 19 April: [...] the Irish Church question was resumed. The Committee divided on the proposed postponemt. from Jan[uar]y 1st 1871 to 1872. In this I appeared.[106]

Then I paired from 7 to 11 1/2 with Mr Percy Wyndham – &, after

---

[100] To delay it for six months.

[101] i.e. the concurrent endowment of all denominations.

[102] Seeking to move an instruction to the committee regarding the Maynooth grant, but ruled out of order by the Speaker; *H* cxcv. 847.

[103] For Sheridan's clause, during the 3rd reading debate on the Metropolitan District Railway bill; *C.J.* cxxiv. 137.

[104] Disraeli moved to omit the clause, which dissolved the legislative union of the English and Irish Churches, claiming that he was seeking to preserve the Royal supremacy; *H* cxcv. 993– 9.

[105] Edward Sullivan.

[106] 301:194 against Hardy's amendment to clause 12, seeking to delay the transfer of Church property to the ecclesiastical commissioners; *H* cxcv. 1109.

my return, found there had been a division on the disendowing clause: 214 to 103.[107] Soon after we had another division – 330 to 232. This point touched the question of deducting curates salaries from rectors' incomes.[108]

The evening was rather a warm & boisterous one at times. Disraeli was absent – being gouty.

It seems to me that the fight made by the Tories is not well-judged. It tends to familiarize the Public mind with the subject & procedure of disendowing Churches. The discussion will leave on record everything that future reformers will desire to know. The Tories should have taken 2 great divisions & then succumbed to a tyrant majority [...]

Wednesday, 21 April: We had a division on the 2d. reading of the Bill to allow marriage with a deceased wife's sister. Numbers 243 to 144. Majority 99.[109] I voted with the ayes.

I heard excellent speeches from Lord Bury, B. Hope & John Bright – the last in great force. Sir Geo. Grey spoke briefly, giving in his adhesion to the measure, wh. Sir J. Coleridge opposed.

Bright's speech lasted just 1/2 an hour. Rarely has he been more caustic, more earnest or impassioned. His contempt for B. Hope's 'ecclesiastical rubbish' was quite refreshing. To hear his denunciation of the tyranny and domination of priests from the Treasury Bench was a thing worth living for.

Thursday, 22 April: After questions put to Ministers, the Irish Church Bill[110] became the topic of the evening. A little before 7, I paired till 1/4 before 10 with Sir F. Heygate. A division was taken at 7.35 p.m: numbers 221 & 128.[111] In this my pair was effective.

Another division on a point affecting clause 15 (Curates Compensation) followed at 9.35. Numbers 220 & 107.[112]

In this case, my pair held good. Some members were less fortunate. One + military + man was wandering about to find a pair after the event. This course does not recommend itself.

At 1/4 before 10, I was in my place again and voted on Mr Charley's amendmt. of clause 17. Numbers 314 and 199.[113]

---

[107] For clause 12.

[108] Hardy's unsuccessful amendment to clause 14, to omit the provision that compensation to curates be deducted from the incomes payable to incumbents; *H* cxcv. 1137–8.

[109] For Thomas Chambers' bill; later withdrawn.

[110] Committee stage.

[111] Against Palmer's amendment to clause 14 regarding 'permanent curates'; *H* cxcv. 1378–85.

[112] Against Pim's proposal for lump sums rather than annuities; *H* cxcv. 1386–7.

[113] Against Charley's proposed annuities for organists, vergers etc.; *H* cxcv. 1411.

Afterwards, about midnight, I paired with Sclater-Booth and went home. There was a division on reporting progress. Numbers 289 to 176.[114]

Notes. It was new to me to hear such cries as 'sit down'. A member told me that some one, a few nights since, shouted 'turn him out'. Truly I feel as if I were reporting progress – and that the wrong way.

It was very evident that Disraeli & the generals on his staff did not desire some of the divisions taken. There was one man who lustily cried 'No' when the question was put. Disraeli looked back as much as to say 'how can you be so unwise as to divide?' But the member persisted. 'Who is he?' people ask. 'Tom Conolly'. Meanwhile, the Ho[use] is cleared. Cigars are sacrificed (as a neighbour mournfully told me he had twice sacrificed his, one being a very fine one) – & the benches were filled, when, at the last moment, Conolly held his tongue.

On clause 17, Mr Charley moved certain words – & threatened a division. Doubting at last, he descended to Disraeli's place & apparently consulted him – (Laughter and banter from the Liberals). Charley then decided upon abstaining; in vain, unruly people behind the chair exclaiming 'aye' forced a division. The Committee was very wild & unruly. It is something to say it was good humoured.

Monday, 26 April: Attending at 1/4 before 4, I heard some 2 1/2 hours of discussion of the Irish Church Bill in Committee. Still, not being inclined to remain late, I paired from 1/2 past 7 for all night with Mr John Tollemache – & retired.

Disraeli was very diverting in alluding to inconsistencies betwn. the opinions expressed by Bright, Gladstone & Lowe at various times. Even Gladstone could not help admitting so much. A division, covered by my pair, occurred soon after I left. Numbers 232 to 132.[115]

The points mostly under notice were the treatment dealt to the Irish Church in respect of Churches & certain Cathedrals. Govt. was reproached for the severity of its terms as contrasted with the 'gracious & generous' proffers made, – especially in one of Bright's speeches.[116] The truth is, I think, this – if Ministers are too favourable to the Irish Church, the measure will be no settlemt.

Wednesday, 28 April: [...] Denman moved his Law of Evidence Bill, which, in one of its clauses, embodies my Affirmations Bill of

---

[114] Against Colonel Gilpin's motion.

[115] For Gladstone's proposal to drop from clause 25 a provision enabling the commissioners to provide money for the upkeep of certain Churches and Cathedrals as national monuments; *H* cxcv. 1603–4.

[116] Disraeli was referring to a speech made in the previous parliament; *H* cxcv. 1591.

1861.[117] Denman in his speech mentioned this, which was but fair. He spoke for an hour & 10 min: and stated the argument very clearly & succinctly.

Staveley Hill followed, opposing the part of the Bill making parties in Divorce Courts compellable to give evidence. He however did not contest the point of the objection to testimony of infidels.

Collier[118] was very forcible. He referred to the authority of Lord Penzance[119] who says justice has been constantly defeated. Denman had stated that that learned Judge had approved of the Bill moved.

Serjeant Dowse was very diverting. He told capital stories of the Courts. Lopes supported the Bill. Such is progress! Why, in 1861, the Tories I believe thought me inspired by the Devil, whereas today, the Bill was read a 2d. time without a division.

I watched the debate all day; well-armed with Parliamentary returns * see in 'accounts & Papers 10' 1861. Law of Evidence p. 375 Vol 43 * to shew that we are demanding for Englishmen a state of Law, on the subject of the effect of opinions on the right to give testimony, which has been for many years in force in India & the West Indies. But I resisted the temptation to speak, and I am glad I resisted.

Friday, 30 April: [...] Youghal writ was [...] moved, to which T. Collins objected.

Debate & Division. We carried the writ, although some said they were ashamed of their vote, as corruption must have taken place.[120] It seemed to me, however, that we had no option. Numbers 102 to 70.

Denman thinks I had better not introduce a Bill to enable parties in criminal cases to give evidence till his Bill is passed.[121]

I was a member of a deputation to Goschen from Cornwall in the evening. The object of the deputation was to obtain justice for owners of clay mines in the provisions of the new bill relating to the assessmt. of property.

Tuesday, 4 May: There has been a notion that John Bright was indiscreet in announcing to the House a day or two back that he was prepared to deal with the Irish land problem.[122] The Ministers were

---

[117] Clause 4 of the Evidence Amendment bill permitted affirmations in lieu of oaths in criminal cases; 2nd reading agreed. Cf. *T.D.*, 11 and 13 Mar. 1861.

[118] Attorney General.

[119] An eminent judge in the court of Probate.

[120] It was 'notoriously venal'; K.T. Hoppen, *Elections, Politics and Society in Ireland, 1832–1885* (Oxford, 1984), 290. The Liberal victor in 1868 had been unseated, but another Liberal won the subsequent by-election.

[121] i.e. to allow married couples to give evidence against one another; no such bill was introduced.

[122] 30 Apr., *H* cxcv. 2009–17, favouring the creation of a peasant proprietory.

asked, who is the chief? Some pessimists begin to think he will not long remain in the Cabinet. To-day we had an Irish Church debate again at 2 p.m. Whalley & Newdegate had an unseemly altercation. Remarks were interchanged between the two quondam-allies & champions of ultra-Protestantism which must have delighted the Catholics present. On a division we had a majority of 128. Numbers 324 to 196.[123] I paired with L[ieutenan]t Col[onel] Jervis for the evening sitting which begins at 9.

[...] Fawcett's objection yesterday to the scheme of permitting the Irish Landlords to buy the tithe at so many years purchase – that it is a gift to them – excited & continues to excite some attention. 'The Times'[124] handles the scheme severely [...]

Wednesday, 5 May: At 2.15 I attended. House pretty full for Wed[nesda]y. Gladstone was energetically replying to D'Israeli on the Bill provoked by the seditious language of the Mayor of Cork.[125]

Dr Ball followed him, questioning the legal propriety of introducing a Bill of Pains & Penalties in a House which cannot take evidence on oath. Coleridge, Northcote & others spoke briefly.

Hope, on behalf of the independent Conservatives, made a stout defence of the conduct of the Govt. The Irish Att[orne]y Gen[era]l[126] looked very happy, the Tories above the gangway very nervous. Hardy saw the necessity of rising.

He evidently does not concur with Dr Ball & Northcote, seeing that the objection as to proceeding in this house was by him distinctly put aside.

The Irish Att[orne]y Gen[era]l briefly closed the debate, & the Bill was read a first time.[127]

Thursday, 6 May: Clontarf Township Bill. Amendment moved by Sir J. Esmonde.[128] Some Liberal Irish for amendment. Tories against. Division announced.

Coming in suddenly, I met Irish saying 'vote with the noes'. Not satisfied I sought more evidence. Soon I heard our whip reply to a Whig official's question which side was to be supported by our people, &

---

[123] For clause 39, regarding compensation for the loss of the Maynooth grant; *H* cxcvi. 107–32.

[124] *The Times*, 4 May 1869, 8.

[125] Daniel O'Sullivan had made a number of pro-fenian speeches. A bill of pains and penalties was introduced in order to disqualify him permanently from office.

[126] Edward Sullivan.

[127] The bill was dropped on 11 May when it was learned that the mayor had agreed to resign.

[128] *C.J.* cxxiv. 182.

learned that the Irish were to be favoured by supporting the noes.

The fact is the amend[men]t was for a £4 instead of an £8 rating for purposes of certain local elections. But I enquired further of a member (C.F.)[129] well acquainted with the correct practice in similar cases, and was told what was Dodson's[130] view, – and this, like many other liberals, I supported, – that is, I voted with the ayes.

The Liberals mostly gave a wrong vote to please the Irish. We won – 121 to 154. Majority 33 [...]

Friday, 7 May: 2 p.m. Clause 58 of the Irish Church Bill chiefly occupied the Committee. Tedious, indeed, these debates are becoming. The Liberals talk too much, sometimes playing the enemy's game.

[...] 5.30 p.m. Lord Claud Hamilton on his legs. His gesticulation is convulsive, & his energy runs away with him. I shd. think him amiable & conscientious. Now, Gladstone is replying.

6.5. Clauses passing with more speed. We have just passed 62. The opposition is tired. All seem to wish to get on. Ordinary speakers are frequently requested from both sides to 'speak out'. But what is meant is – 'hold your tongue'.

6.15. p.m. Much cheering on approaching the termination of our work: – but when, as 7 o'clock approached, Mr Dodson said 'that I report this bill with amendments to the House' the cries of 'hear hear' were loud & continued [...]

Monday, 10 May: A good deal of work at the House. More interest than formerly is shewn by the Public in Public Petitions. They give a member a good deal of labour. Besides this, the Liskeard Election[131] has occasioned me many interviews with influential people, candidates & officials or persons possessing local influence [...]

Wednesday, 12 May: [...] I made private suggestions to Cardwell[132] in the matter of the contagious Diseases Bill, & as to shoe-reform for the Army, warning him that the French were, I believed, in treaty hereon with an English firm for a better form of shoe.

[...] I proposed to the Speaker that we shd. use the lobby for our purposes, (including Divisions on great occasions). My suggestion was that the great Central Hall might serve the Public, & cards might be sent in by the Police. I added we might thus save building by relieving the House of pressure, the lobby being made comfortable. He seemed

---

[129] Presumably Charles Forster.
[130] Chairman of committees.
[131] A by-election in which Trelawny was interested as a local landowner.
[132] Secretary of State for war.

to think the idea worthy of being entertained, & he said he would speak to Layard & the Govt. about it[133] [...]

Thursday, 27 May: The House re-assembled after the Holydays.[134] Hunt criticized the Budget. Lowe replied to him. Crawford, Gov[erno]r of the Bank, was a little caustic in dealing with Lowe's defence of his plan of collecting the revenue by an alteration of the times of payment, and affirmed that Lowe's language with regard to the Bank of England had produced 'consternation in the city'.[135]

[...] The 'Times'[136] says of the Budget that 'it repeals nearly 40 acts of Parliament, and substitutes for a labyrinth of imposts, qualified by reservations, exceptions & abatements, a simple Tariff of duties in respect of the use of taxable articles which everyone can comprehend'.

Friday, 28 May: [...] Country gentlemen walk about & congratulate each other on Lowe's surrendering the tax on brood mares![137] We are not, then, sent up to Parliament for nothing.

Monday, 31 May: I, along with Capt[ain] Vivian, introduced Horsman.[138]

Full House early. Plenty of work occupied me – & I hardly knew which matter to discharge first.

Paired from 5.5. till 11.30 with Bromley Davenport.

Debate commenced on the Irish Church.[139] Mr Glyn[140] demurred to pairing (he meant for all night), thinking that a good show in the lobby was desirable. So I resolved to be present, if possible.

Denman laughingly related how the Law of Evidence Bill got through.[141] Hardy & Mowbray had a later motion on the orders of the day * The Oxford University Statutes Bill * ; so, when a member noticed that 40 members were not present, and Denman appealed to him not to press a count, the count was escaped, the Speaker not proceeding to count as would be the usual course. I think Hardy

---

[133] For the outcome, see below, 14 Feb. 1870.

[134] The House had adjourned for Whitsun on 13 May.

[135] Crawford feared that the concentration of tax collection would have an adverse effect on the money market: *H* cxcvi. 823; Lowe's view was that 'the money market must look after itself', Winter, *Robert Lowe*, 257.

[136] *The Times*, 28 May 1869, 8.

[137] Lowe had proposed to abolish the exemption of brood mares from taxation. He reluctantly yielded to pressure from, among others, Speaker Denison: Ossington, *Journal*, 243-4.

[138] Victor in the Liskeard by-election.

[139] 3rd reading stage; Holt moving a delaying amendment.

[140] Government chief whip.

[141] 3rd reading passed on 28 May; Royal assent, 9 Aug.

opposed the Affirmations Bill when I introduced it;[142] and it is a marvel the Evidence Bill advanced a stage when Mowbray was in the House. There must have been an ecclesiastical measure of engrossing interest to follow. Religious toleration, like Law reform, advances like a crab – sideways.

[...] I forgot to mention a Division on a Bill from the Lords for making a sort of disendowment of a city church. All Saints District (Bishopsgate St.). Mr Crawford recommended it, & stated in private to me and another member that Coleridge & Hope opposed it. Clearly it was an ecclesiastical opposition. A division took place. I supported Crawford, who won. It was said that Coleridge hedged his vote on the Irish Church by thus voting in the supposed interest of the English one. I noted that Gladstone got up & left the House at the moment of the imminent Division. Ayes 173 Noes 137.[143]

11.25 p.m. D'Israeli is now baiting John Bright on the subject of the Irish land question.[144] D'Israeli has been a little effective upon this personal topic. He is continuing in an unusually serious & prophetic strain, & wound up in an impressive peroration (much cheering). What an actor!

11.45. Gladstone has commenced. Full House. Gladstone is unusually forcible & calm. I never knew a speech of his more terse. He is speaking like a winning man.

12.25 a.m. June 1st. Gladstone takes great advantage of one of Newdegate's interruptions, & points out the want of unity of plans between the Tories who evidently – that is, those on the ex ministerial Bench – ill dissembled their annoyance. + at the indiscipline of their party. +

12.30. He galls Newdegate to the point of indiscreetly rising again. Of course the orator gets more & more advantage.

12.45. He is now about to deal seriously with the probable conduct of the Lords, & is uttering words of caution.

12.55. Grand peroration. Cheers & clapping of hands.

The Division took 25 minutes. As usual, a great crush at the door & difficulty in getting conveyance so late. It was who could run fastest. For the amendment 247, Agt. it 361. Maj[ori]ty 114.

Tuesday, 1 June: Still tired through last night's work, I merely attended in order to meet in the Library of the H. of Lords my colleagues who had an appointment there at 1/4 before 5 with Lord

---

[142] He did; *T.D.*, 13 Mar. 1861.

[143] For the 2nd reading; *C.J.* cxxiv. 214–15.

[144] See above 4 May; Trelawny is now reverting to the 3rd reading debate on the Established Church (Ireland) bill.

Portman on the Stannaries Bill.[145] Lord Falmouth was there & later, Ld. Vivian. After a conference we heard Ld. P. introduce the Bill, which was read a 2d. time – & so home [...]

Friday, 4 June: Attending before 6 p.m. I heard Hadfield denouncing the delay in preparing a complete digest of the Statutes.

Locke King spoke very earnestly in this matter. Some £80,000 have been spent, – & 36 years – without adequate result. Gladstone made a statement intended to reassure members of the success of the proceedings already taken.

Others spoke; & Hadfield would have a division.

It seems that this gets rid of Gregory's opportunity of dividing on his question relating to opening institutions on Sundays.[146] He might however still make his speech. The original motion was 'that I do now leave the chair'. The amendment was to leave out all the words after the word 'that' &c. Question: – 'that the words proposed to be left out stand part of the question'. This the House affirmed, so that other resolutions are ipso facto annulled. 217 to 64.[147]

It is said that the Division had this object – to avoid a disagreeable vote. I supported Ministers, on the statement made by Gladstone.

It was too late for me to hear all Gregory's speech, which, so far as I heard it, was excellent. The House was soon counted out. 99/100ths of members agreed with Gregory, but everyone was glad there was no division. Fear of bigots or blockheads – and both.

Monday, 7 June: [...] Mr Bruce promised me that he would write to the chief constable in the district in wh. Hitchin is situate for information as regards the ill treatment of some women by a policeman who entered a house without authority & treated the women with indignity on a suspicion that a child found in the neighbourhood might have been born in their house. A Mr C.E. Serjeant wrote to me hereon.[148]

[...] On entering the House to-night Mr Gladstone was received with a burst of cheers, which were intended as a note of warning to the Lords.

---

[145] Sir John St Aubyn's bill, amending the law relating to mining partnerships within the stanneries of Devon and Cornwall, had already been passed by the Commons; Royal Assent, 24 June. *P.P.* 1868–9, v. 207.

[146] Gregory advocated the Sunday opening of museums etc.

[147] Against Hadfield's amendment to the motion for entering into committee of supply, calling for the discontinuation of expenditure on the digest of the Statutes; *H* cxcvi. 1244–8.

[148] The matter was not raised in the Commons.

Thursday, 10 June: I have a notice on the paper with the object in view of saving time & space in matters of practice in the conduct of business of the House.[149] There has been an ominous hint or two of more building in order to extend our accommodation within the area of the Palace! [...]

Wednesday, 23 June:[150] [...] On Tuesday night there was an important motion of Rathbone's on the incidence of local taxation in the matter of poor-rate.[151] This question is looming larger every day, as personal property increases, & population moves from side to side.

Noon sitting at the usual hour. Delahunty had a notice on the Irish Banknote system.[152] His observations elicited from Lowe a remarkable speech shewing how well he understands the theory of Banks & currency and how free he is from certain 'superstitions' (as he correctly calls them) hereon. It is a great advantage to possess a Chancellor of the E[xchequer] so capable of dealing with politics &c. from their speculative side. Still even he may be tripped up in details by the merely-practical people. We shall see.

Thursday, 24 June: I am vexed at my inability to attend the Committee on the Contagious Diseases Bill (1866).[153] It is not right to leave my bed [...]

Tuesday, 29 June: [...] a long debate on clauses of the University Tests Bill. Cavendish Bentinck made himself as disagreeable as possible to Gladstone & Grant Duff by quoting the latter agst. his present chief. Certainly Duff used, some 3 or 4 years ago, – very strong language about the Premier's erratic tendencies.[154] Duff has been in the habit of presenting to his constituents a kind of exhaustive account of recent Political History. The House laughed a good deal at Bentinck's expression – 'my humble self', – & no wonder.

Later he attacked Gladstone in his presence in order to induce him to speak, & herein succeeded.

[149] Not moved; but see below, 14 Feb. 1870.

[150] Trelawny had been ill since 10 June, and his attendance continued to be intermittent.

[151] *H* cxcvii. 430–8, urging that the burden of local rates be relieved by State grants; withdrawn.

[152] 2nd reading of the Money Laws (Ireland) bill; withdrawn.

[153] On 8 June Trelawny had been appointed a member of the select committee to inquire into the working of the act. For the background, see Paul McHugh, *Prostitution and Victorian Social Reform* (1980), 35–48.

[154] Bentinck noted that in 1866 Grant Duff had criticised Gladstone for defending the principle of denominational education in the Universities (Gladstone changed his position in 1868); *H* cxcvii. 767–72.

Several others spoke, – Hope, Raikes, Round, Palmer, Mowbray, G. Hardy, besides more.

I noticed that Disraeli sat calm & unperturbed as if he thought (and as he well might) that, in view of known or coming changes, shadowy distinctions on clauses relating to University tests were almost beneath notice. At one moment he seemed to be nearly asleep. I feel sure, from observing his manner at different times, that he despises the politics of men of the Hardy, Mowbray & Walpole type [...]

Friday, 2 July: Division 121 to 219. Assessed Rates Bill on C. Villiers' motion which was carried. 'Rateable Hereditaments' adopted in lieu of 'dwelling houses'.[155]

University Tests Bill. Committee Progress. Roundell Palmer's new Test, being a declaration not to teach opinions 'opposed to the Xtian religion or the doctrine & discipline of the Church of England'.[156] Is he dreaming? Sincere we know he is.

Dr Lyon Playfair delivered a very remarkable speech; indeed, a model speech. Sartoris spoke excellently too.

Roundell Palmer got little or no support on either side, and withdrew his motion. The Tories – at least, one of them – derided it, as a device of 'Mrs Partington'.[157]

Fawcett next moved an addition to the Bill. Bouverie answered him.

It is curious to note Disraeli's evident indifference to such Bills as the University Tests Bill. He appears to be sound asleep, but only appears. Fawcett's object is to give Colleges power to alter statutes so as to abolish tests. Coleridge opposed on technical grounds, for he distinctly said that he approved of the end sought to be obtained.

Denman counselled that the mover should not go to a division now, though he concurred with the views expressed in the motion. Afraid of the Lords.

Division. Ayes 147. Noes 234.[158] I voted in both these divisions – 1st with Villiers: 2d. with Fawcett. At 9 o'clock the House was counted out.

The usual strangulation of infant measures has commenced. The process will be rapid, I imagine [...]

Tuesday, 6 July: The Cattle Plague Bill. I heard Read who speaks

---

[155] With regard to compounding; *H* cxcvii. 1088–9.

[156] *H* cxcvii. 1090–1.

[157] She was a fictional village gossip; B.P. Shillaber, *The Life and Sayings of Mrs Partington* (1854). In one of her stories, she attempted to keep out the Atlantic with her mop.

[158] Against Fawcett's amendment. The bill was subsequently passed by the Commons, but ran out of time in the Lords.

well – also, McCombie, a very excentric character.[159] Ld. Robert Montagu added remarks. Forster's conclusion was thus stated: 'Read's amendt. wd. lead to the compulsory slaughter of almost the whole of the imported cattle'.

Forster's able statement contained various reasons why the Govt. plan shd. not receive the addition of Read's words to clause 15.

A three years restriction wd. exclude cattle of any country in which a single case of cattle plague has occurred in that period. Yet, under Read's words there is no security that Galician cattle might not come from a Russian port.

Hunt thinks the 3 years' limit might be shortened – suggesting 18 months. Forster objected that the question of time has not much to do with the case. Countries are very dangerous in which no cattle plague has existed.

Restriction diminishes ministerial responsibility. Discretion should be left to ministers. Some foreigners have let cattle come thro' a country itself uninfected. The 3 years rule would in this case be no security.

Henley agrees with Read. Henley created a titter when he said that 300 years ago a disease was introduced from America which still continues in this country [...]

Wednesday, 7 July: Trades Union Bill. Arriving about 3.30, I was in time to hear a good part of the debate. Edmund Potter pleased the House, & Mundella distinguished himself.[160]

Bruce is favourable to some legislation, but has not had time since the Report of the Royal Commission appeared. He seems to me to be a judicious Home Secretary, but is not very fluent. Still his matter is solid & good.

Forster announced on behalf of Govt. that the 2d. reading wd. have their support. Funds of Unions shd. be protected & combination Laws repealed. This is the opinion of Ministers.

Henley regrets delay, & think Unions have been hardly & cruelly treated. A millstone is hung round their necks which colours everything they do. Curious form of speech, but no one laughed! 2d. reading[161] amid cheers.

Thursday, 8 July: Rather a hard day's work. Committee at 1 p.m.

[159] Read's amendment, in committee, to enforce the slaughter of cattle at the point of debarkation, unless the country of origin had been free of disease for three years; *H* cxcvii. 1272–5. Supported by McCombie. Amendment defeated, 220:116.

[160] Both were supporters of the bill.

[161] Agreed without a division; the bill was later withdrawn. Gladstone had privately intimated to Walter Morrison, on 5 July, that he would support the bill on the understanding that it would proceed no further that session; *G.D.*, vii. 91.

(Contagious Diseases.) Dr John Chapman, Editor of the 'Westminster' was in attendance, but too late to be examined.[162] We had much discussion on the Report, & amicably arranged it.[163]

Our work done, I went to the House, where much discussion ensued on Dillwyn's amend[men]t on report of supply. Dillwyn objected to Layard's proceedings in the Central Hall, – in particular, his committing the country to a contract without first obtaining the consent of Parliament. This he frankly admitted was an error. Also, it appeared the plan was a good one on the merits. Still the error remained: but, after the apology, it seemed to many in the House to savour of truculence to press the amendmt; & so it appeared on a division. For Govt. – 187. Against – 97.[164] I voted with Ministers [...]

Friday, 9 July: Forster's words in clause 63 respecting the supply of food & water to cattle travelling on railways satisfied me.[165] A considerable discretion given to the Privy Council is better than a precise system which wd. probably be ineffective. Anstruther's question. Do *we* ever think of going 30 hours without water? (Great Laughter.) Irish cattle came over in a state likely to end – & often ending – in Pleuropneumonia. One member observed 'Irish beasts are much more unruly than other beasts'. (Much laughter.)

[...] Forster said there was difficulty as regards compulsory slaughter and compensation [...] Cawley wants compensation from a general rate or the consolidated fund. He won't get it[166] [...]

Monday, 12 July: [...] Seeing the Whips, I told them that I must pair and leave town. They are most anxious to keep me till the Lords amendmts to the Irish Church Bill come down. I bargained to remain on terms of my being allowed to go on Saturday next.

Tuesday, 13 July: [...] At the ev[enin]g sitting Earl Grosvenor was defeated by 126 to 85 votes, in his endeavour to obtain for Cheshire

---

[162] He was a medical opponent of the Contagious Diseases act.

[163] The report recommended additions to the towns covered by the 1866 act, and suggested another select committee be appointed to consider further extensions. The government subsequently passed an act (Royal assent, 11 Aug), adding six more towns to the schedule; McHugh, *Prostitution*, 48–52.

[164] Layard, the chief commissioner of works and buildings, thus carried his modified resolution for a vote of £31,026 (originally £34,026) for building work in the Palace of Westminster, Dillwyn having persisted in his attempt to reduce the vote by a further £2,500 because of his opposition to decorating the walls of the Central Hall; *H* cxcvii. 1429–30.

[165] Forster's amendment to his Contagious Diseases (Animals) (No. 2) bill, agreed; *H* cxcvii. 1530–1.

[166] His amendment to clause 67 was withdrawn; *H* cxcvii. 1535–7.

exoneration from its debt to the State incurred for money advanced to pay for slaughtered cattle. This preposterous proposal was well dissected in the speeches of Lowe & Gladstone. I regret to say that thro' illness, which confined me to my bed, I was neither in the Division nor paired.

Thursday, 15 July: Writing in bed at 1.37 p.m., I speculate what Gladstone will propose to do in the matter of the Lords amendmts to the Irish Ch. Bill.[167] Can he accept them – I mean, in substance? Few will think that course possible – nay, the indecision of the Lords who trifled with their own amendments would be a pretty plausible reason for rejecting the Bill as it stands. Inter alia the principle of it is disturbed – it has lost its equilibrium, being in the main a scheme treating the property of the State as a fund on which one set of Christians have a claim superior to the claims of other sets. Again the commutation of annuities at 14 years is a form of re-endowment. Also, the putting off sine die the application of the residual fund is not satisfactory.

Then, there is the glebe house question. Enough, however, to shew that Gladstone cannot give way.

Will the Lords do so? Eventually, yes. But at once? Something will depend on Public Meetings – Something on Gladstone's position with the Queen. He must I think succeed or resign.

3.40 p.m. Up & ready for battle.

Gladstone is going to make a statement we hear. It is very difficult to forecast what it will be. If matters have been well-managed, there must have been skilful negotiation thro' neutrals of known sense & probity. Perhaps, all has been thus settled.[168] Complicated with the fate of the Bill is the power of the constituencies with that of an hereditary chamber. The excuse of the Lords for the 2d. reading of a Bill disestablishing and disendowing the Irish Church – itself a portentous step & by them so considered – was deference to the undoubted wishes of the constituencies. But the bill sent down has not received their sanction. It is as if the Lords had sacrified their virtue for nothing. Their indecision & vacillation – for they have surged hither & thither

---

[167] The overall effect of the 62 amendments passed by the Lords was to make a nonsense of the disendowing clauses of the bill, restoring to the Church of Ireland most of its property and money. It was to be left to parliament in future to decide how the surplus funds should be applied, and the preamble of the bill was rewritten so as to permit the concurrent endowment of other denominations. An element of concurrent endowment was also introduced with the amendment providing that glebe houses and lands be given to Roman Catholic and Presbyterian clergy out of the Church of Ireland's surplus funds. Disestablishment was to be postponed from 1 Jan. to 1 May 1871. See the *Annual Register*, 1869, 95–100.

[168] Not yet. Gladstone moved the rejection of the most important of the Lords' amendments; *H* cxcvii. 1891–2.

like a hustings mob – will expose them to much severe criticism. Compare Gladstone's firm & resolute course [...]

Friday, 16 July: I heard Serjeant Dowse's speech[169] wh. was very diverting. Sometimes, he made his foes laughable; sometimes, himself. A thoroughbred Irishman! who else would make foes by contrasting Northern with Southern Celts? Old Hadfield surpassed himself to-night. Quite earnest, at moments effective, he was most frequently ridiculous.

I divided on the Ulster glebes question – & voted with Ministers. Num. 344 to 240.[170]

[...] I also paired, thro' Mr Noel & Mr Glyn, with Sir Hervey Bruce, from Monday the 19th inclusive, for the session.

Tuesday, 20 July: The course of the Lords[171] evidently influenced the tone of feeling in the Commons, where Gladstone, entering, was loudly cheered [...]

Friday, 23 July: The reception of the Lords amendments was the occasion of many speeches. Gladstone endeavoured to render the position of their Lordships as comfortable as the case would admit of.[172] The Irish Church Bill awaits the Royal assent. I fear that future discussion on the relative rights of sects & churches will grow out of the reservation of the surplus.[173] Yearly motions hereon may be expected for some time to come – & such motions will constantly suggest the English Church.

Monday, 26 July: [...] It is pleasant to notice the progress of the Law of Evidence Bill & the Bankruptcy Bill. If to these the contagious Diseases (Cattle Bill) be added[174] – with another measure or two – the session will have been almost memorable – apart from the Irish Church act.

Gladstone has been ill – & no wonder.

Friday, 30 July: Govt. incurred some severe criticism on the vote for completing certain fortifications. It seems that we are still paying for

[169] On the Established Church (Ireland) bill.

[170] To disagree with the Lords' amendment.

[171] Who, the previous day, had voted to restore their amendment to the preamble of the Established Church (Ireland) bill; *H* cxcviii. 323.

[172] After negotiations between Lord Granville and Lord Cairns, the House of Lords had given way on most of its amendments; *G.D.*, vii. 104–5.

[173] It was left to parliament to decide in future how the surplus should be applied.

[174] All 3 bills received the Royal assent on 9 Aug.

Palmerston's fancy. Numbers on going into Committee 100 to 32. Cardwell, however, has reduced the scheme.[175]

On clause 1 Capt[ain] Beaumont was only defeated by 9 votes. Numbers 82 to 73[176] [...]

Saturday, 7 August: [...] Interesting speeches were made (on friday 6th) by Sir R. Palmer and R. Lowe – the former on the marriage laws and their anomalies, the latter on our coinage and the effect of our making no charge for coining sovereigns. Lowe has lately been astounding City Financiers & he appears to have been generally in the right.

Palmer wants an uniform & certain form of marriage, Lowe points to the advantages of an international currency. He evidently regards the habit of using gold for exchange as a wasteful & superstitious luxury.

I think that Free trade in Banking – a doctrine I have held since 1844[177] – is not far off.

Wednesday, 11 August: Queen's speech and Parliament prorogued [...]

---

[175] The Fortifications (Provision for Expenses) bill proposed spending an extra £1,500,000 on the coastal fortifications initiated by Palmerston in 1860.

[176] Beaumont's amendment sought a reduction to £1,285,000 by reducing the number of guns at the Spithead forts; *H* cxcviii. 1008–9. The government chief whip subsequently complained of the poor attendance by ministers in this and other divisions; Glyn to Gladstone, 31 July [1869], B.L. Add MSS 44347, fos 307–15.

[177] See Trelawny's pamphlet, *Sketch of existing restrictions on banking and doubts of the soundness of the principles on which they rest* (1847).

SESSION OF 1870

Tuesday, 8 February: The Queen's speech gives promise of numerous measures. I attended at the ev[enin]g sitting and heard the speeches of the mover and seconder of the address. These gentlemen were Capt[ain] Egerton and Sir C. Dilke. Each occupied about 20 minutes. The former was rather dull. The latter had a decided success. Apparently, Cardwell thought so; who turned round and shook hands with Dilke.

Disraeli had some trouble in discovering in the Queen's speech points of attack. On the whole Ministers came off with flying colours [...] The address was agreed to.

Thursday, 10 February: I heard the whole debate on O'Donovan (Rossa's) case.[178] There was a wonderful splitting of hairs by lawyers. Mr G. Moore spoke of the 'Honble. Member for Tipperary' (laughter) & made the matter more insulting by the remark that at least he had been elected without any corrupt practice.

The seconder, Mr Matthews, spoke well & ingeniously. For his conclusion, however, he sought to prove too much as he argued in effect that the House had parted with its authority unless a petition were presented. Suppose for example a child of 12 were elected. Would the election be good if no one petitioned? Gladstone, Coleridge, Roundell Palmer & Bouverie all, more or less ably, handled the subject.

The division occupied 19 minutes! 301 to 8.[179]

Friday, 11 February: Mr Berkeley Hill[180] had a long interview with me on the subject of the acts wh. deal with Contagious Diseases. We conversed for an hour & interchanged views. He recently wrote to the 'Times' an able letter on recent legislation dealing with those diseases[181] [...]

Monday, 14 February: I went to see Mr Edwd. Webster, of the

---

[178] Gladstone moved that O'Donovan Rossa, elected for Tipperary, was incapable of being returned to the House of Commons on the grounds that he was a convicted felon; *H* cxcix. 122–3.

[179] For Gladstone's motion.

[180] Surgeon at the London Lock hospital, and honorary secretary of the Extensionist association, campaigning for the extension of the Contagious Diseases acts.

[181] *The Times*, 5 Feb. 1870, 4.

exam[ine]rs office (H. of C.), in order to confer about our plans of saving the time of the House in conducting business. In a letter to 'the Times' by me, signed MP, which appeared on the 7th, inst. the subject was handled at some length.[182] As I entered the great central Hall, I found one part of my scheme in full force. Policemen are stationed there whose duty it is to keep strangers from entering the lobby just outside the door of the House. Last year I suggested such a plan to the Speaker & others.[183]

[. . .] Leatham re-opened the Ballot question[184] on which Tories are beginning to exhibit symptoms of altered opinions.

Tuesday, 15 February: A little before 5 p.m., in a very full House, Gladstone introduced the Irish Land Bill.[185] It was of course the cause of intense interest. As he unfolded his scheme, it struck me that the blot, if any, will lie in its complexity and in the number & variety of the courts of one kind or another into which landlords & tenants may be drawn. Even if the measure were devised by an angel, it is doubtful whether, in the existing state of opinion in Ireland, there is enough respect for laws to insure the measure fair play. Only a few days ago a barrister received an anonymous warning not to proceed in a certain cause for a client! However, time may cure this & fiat justitia ruat calum.

The Conservatives listened very tranquilly to the speech of the Minister. The liberals occasionally cheered him – but not with quite as much confidence as one has witnessed. The fact is, both sides feel that

[182] Ibid, 7 Feb. 1870, 10; printed as an appendix to this edition, below pp. 502–4. Edward Webster had made a number of suggestions for procedural reform in a pamphlet, *The Public and Private business of the House of Commons considered in relation to the economization of the time of the House and its members* (1868).

[183] See above, 12 May 1869. Speaker Denison described the effect of the changes made as follows: 'The lobby up to the door of the House was open to strangers, and continually crowded by them, so that members could not get to the vote office, or to the refreshment rooms, or to and from the House, without being pressed upon and thronged, not only by constituents, but by members of deputations and strangers, to their excessive inconvenience. I arranged with the Sergeant-at-arms that this first lobby should be kept free of strangers, for the use of members. Strangers to remain in the large central hall, sending in cards or messages to members.' Ossington, *Journal*, 1900), 253. What influence, if any, Trelawny's suggestions had on these changes, is unclear.

[184] 1st reading of the bill to introduce the secret ballot for elections. Leatham agreed to postpone the 2nd reading until after the report of a select committee on the subject.

[185] The Landlord and Tenant (Ireland) bill, limiting the landlords' power of arbitrary eviction and enforcing a system of compensation for departing or evicted tenants. Compensation was to be paid to departing tenants for improvements made to their holdings, and for eviction itself (though not in cases of failure to pay the rent). The distinctive 'Ulster custom' of tenant right was to be legally recognised. For the background to the bill, see E.D. Steele, *Irish Land and British Politics: Tenant Right and Nationality, 1865–70* (Cambridge, 1974).

a measure of some sort is indispensable, yet the vastness of the difficulty represses hasty conviction; still more, enthusiasm.

I listened to Gladstone for 2 1/4 hours, but lost his peroration.

It struck me that his tribute to Disraeli (in his absence) was graceful & modest. The extract from Bright's letter lent weight to the Bill. Coming from him in the midst of a dangerous illness, it had a kind of solemnity.

It seems to me that the principles involved in the interference proposed with property in Ireland, will inevitably bear fruit in England in spite of circumstances being very different.

Cardwell is engaged in re-organizing the War Department; Lowe is astonish[in]g the world by his financial measures. To-day we learn, for the 1st time, that we shall receive a weekly balance sheet.

Recurring to Gladstone's speech, I was struck by his mention of Sharman Crawford's early efforts to settle the tenant right question. It seems he began as early as 1833.[186] Again & again, it used to be my fate to hear him on that subject. Most people thought him a bore – with a fixed idea & that socialistic & spoilatory. Gladstone paid a well-deserved tribute to O'Connell's efforts in the same direction, noticing his pamphlet in wh. he pointed out the differences betwn. English & Irish land laws[187] – the landlords of Ireland having very arbitrary & coercive powers & processes.

Thursday, 17 February: Edwd. Forster ably introduced the govt. education Bill, wh. is certainly a remarkable sign of the times. The plan purports to provide, where not now existing, schools in every district. Education will be compulsory. There will be a conscience clause.[188] Forster's style was characterized by 'rugged eloquence' (as 'the Times' calls it); he was copious, clear, fluent & candid. The measure not only astonishes me, but the manner of its reception [. . .]

Friday, 18 February: [. . .] In the R[eform] Club I met L. * Leatham * a member of some force, who asked me what I thought of the education Bill. I answered that there appeared to me to be much

---

[186] William Sharman Crawford was in fact elected for Dundalk in 1834. On 22 Mar. 1848 Trelawny had successfully moved for the rejection of his Irish tenant right bill; *H* xcvii. 867–8.

[187] Not traced.

[188] In its original form, Forster's bill provided for the creation of School Boards in England and Wales in areas where the existing provision of school places was deemed insufficient. Boards were to have the option of making school attendance compulsory. They were also to be allowed to decide what sort of religious instruction should be provided, with a conscience clause allowing parents to withdraw their children from this instruction if they so desired. Voluntary schools were to be eligible for rate aid. *P.P.* 1870, i. 505.

that was good in it. He rejoined 'I think there is nothing in it but what is bad'. Are the radicals going to oppose it?

Whalley indulges sometimes in rather highflown language, disproportionate to his matter in hand.[189] The inevitable T. Collins of Boston – ever on the look out for such cases – was ready at once with his ironical & emphatic applause in manner & tones well-understood in the House. Collins has a very loud voice and his 'hear, hear', following with cruel fidelity and simulated admiration each particular claim of the speaker to Public approval, or his use of stilted language in very matter-of-fact business, would have been enough to disconcert any one but Whalley, who, I think, fancied he sat down amid general enthusiasm, whereas the very strangers were, many of them, convulsed. + in laughter +

Monday, 21 February: Numerous questions as usual. Afterwards the Bill for inspection of Mines was introduced in a long & interesting speech from Bruce. It is a pity he has not a less hesitating and prosy delivery. However, he is painstaking & seems to deal skilfully with the matters he has in charge. Lyon Playfair spoke well & received respectful & attentive consideration such as the House usually accords to the deserving. How refreshing it is to hear a man of science speak within these walls! [...]

Tuesday, 22 February: Gladstone's deprecation of Mr Monk's motion in favour of removing certain disabilities of Revenue Officers at times of elections[190] had some humour. But Gladstone's jocularity is prolix & overcharged with statement. However, the substance of the appeal to the mover to give ministers some rest was sound, tho' I wondered at its scriptural enforcemt. by allusion to the unjust judge – who yielded from weariness (as Monk seemed to think Gladstone wd. yield). Jenkinson observed that there was no less authority for the statement that there is no rest for the wicked (a laugh).

Monk withdrew amid titters.

We divided on the motion to exempt Chelsea bridge from toll against good faith. Numbers 162 to 21. * T. with maj[ori]ty.[191] *

The Metropolitan Board of Works shd. consider of the purchase of the existing charge on Chelsea Bridge toll. There must be a limit to Imperial expenditure for Metropolitan purposes.

[189] An amendment to the supply motion, hostile to turnpike trusts; *H* cxcix. 551–3, withdrawn.

[190] Motion for a select committee; *H* cxcix. 697–702.

[191] Against Peck's resolution to end the toll; *H* cxcix. 708–11.

Wednesday, 23 February: [...] Grave fears seem to grow of the unworkableness of the Land bill. Will arbitrators be found in a country wherein 'Law secures not life'? if found, will they survive decisions adverse to tenants? Will even legal tribunals meet the difficulty? Perhaps, our wondrous persuader – Mr Gladstone – may remove all fears.

The education bill will be, I predict, rudely handled. Whoever expounds the Bible, teaches his own tenets. This will raise dissension.[192] Let us hope Forster may answer the criticism.

Thursday, 24 February: Numerous questions as usual. These are often printed at length, then read as notices, & read again or spoken on delivery. Our rules result in chaos.

Members are mostly thinking of that gravest of subjects – the Irish question. There is, I suspect, a rising feeling that the Ministry is unequal to the task of dealing with disaffection. Osborne is returned for Waterford. Fortunate if he escape the district with his life. We want a plain spoken member. There is a dead level of timid mediocrity in the House as it is constituted.

Friday, 25 February: A very conversational evening. Rather like a friday's proceedings under the existing distribution of business. The topic wh. most interested me – & wh. came on quite unexpectedly as far as I was concerned – was the state of the Royal Forests – Goldney moving.[193] Stansfeld wanted data before taking any definitive steps. It struck me that a return moved for by me in 1847 and printed June 10th in that year might be brought with advantage to the recollection of the House. So I sought it in the Library and apprized Stansfeld of the existence of the data he required [...]

Monday, 28 February: Gladstone's reply to Ld. J. Manners who questioned G. on murders in Ireland was rather evasive – a plain question of the kind might be answered with[ou]t a torrent of words [...]

Tuesday, 1 March: We had a long discussion on a motion of Torrens's, M.P. for Cambridge, in favour of emigration at the expense of the State.[194] It struck me that he did not make out his case, altho' his speech had merits, was well delivered and not too long. Luckily for

---

[192] A reference to the provision that School Boards could decide for themselves what religious instruction should be provided.

[193] *H* cxcix. 815–18, arguing that the New Forest and the Forest of Dean were badly managed and unproductive.

[194] *H* cxcix. 1002–10, arguing that this would alleviate poverty.

me I was able to restrain a disposition I had to speak. + utter a few words in favour of Political economy which hardly had fair treatment in the debate. + Monsell, in his uncouth manner, rather effectively replied to Torrens who had the + fluent & rather flippant + * fluent & by no means timid support * of the young M.P. for Middl[se]x, Lord G. Hamilton.

I lost the vote, having failed to get a pair. Numbers 153 to 48[195] [...]

Wednesday, 2 March: [...] Plimsoll proposed to compel Railway directors to supply footwarmers. This was strongly opposed by Dillwyn and we divided. Numbers 108 to 76.[196] My name was among the noes.

Sir T. Erskine May[197] and I had some talk ab[ou]t various plans of preventing waste of time. There is little, I fear, to be done. May thinks that the system of questioning ministers in effect saves time by diminishing the number of motions. True the license is abused. But it is not easy to impose a restraint upon members. He does not think that more division clerks would shorten the time spent in taking divisions, as members are as slow in passing out betwn. the tellers as the division clerks are in taking names.

Friday, 4 March: The main topic this evening was the Malt tax. Col[onel] Bartellot was leader of the abolitionist party & very well he acquitted himself.[198] Read, too, performed his part in a good & business-like manner.

Lowe I did not hear; I perceive he has engaged to consider the proposed substitute for the tax[199] [...]

Monday, 7 March: The Irish Land Bill (2d. reading) was moved by Gladstone. Of the speeches wh. I heard the most remarkable was that of Capt[ain] White who seconded Bryan's amendment.[200] White's speech was admirably delivered. He has a good presence & voice, and many qualities of an orator. I venture to predict that he will take a high place some day.[201] He was, I think, mistaken in dwelling upon his freedom from bias as regards pressure from constituents or fear of

---

[195] Against the resolution. Speaker Denison noted that Gladstone's speech against Torrens had been decisive; Ossington, *Journal*, 252–3.

[196] Against 2nd reading of the Railway Travelling bill.

[197] Assistant Clerk of the House of Commons.

[198] Calling for the substitution of the tax with licences for brewers; *H* cxcix. 1253–60, withdrawn.

[199] In his budget, Lowe merely removed the tax on farmers who steeped their own barley; 11 Apr., *H* cc. 1607–45.

[200] To delay the 2nd reading for six months.

[201] He retired from parliament in 1875.

losing his seat. A man worthy of being a Senator is of courtesy assumed to be superior to such influences.

The debate was not very sparkling as it strikes a reader, and, retiring about 7, I can only judge of what afterwards happened from newspaper reports.

Grave doubts constantly recur to me of the probability of the Bill giving satisfaction. That may be imperially right which is economically wrong. All parties concur in the opinion that some legislation is wanted – & so it is perhaps legitimate to vote for the 2d. reading.

Tuesday, 8 March: Maguire's was an earnest and impressive speech on the Irish land Bill. Certainly, he abundantly shewed the evil working of the system of land-managemt. in Ireland. The evil, when probed, is mainly reducible into over-competition for land and want of confidence in the protection of law agt. outrages, which want of confidence prevents the development of manufacturing industry so that the population only live by getting land [...]

Wednesday, 9 March: The subject of this days proceedings was a Bill purporting to be a Bill for the abolition of Scotch Church Rates[202] – a most disingenuous description, inasmuch as there are no Scotch Church Rates and the use of that expression was an attempt to use English Public opinion, moved agt. English Church Rates & still subsisting after their abolition, for the purpose of relieving Scotch heritors of a tax to wh. they are liable for various ecclesiastical purposes such as Minister's manses, Churches & even, as I understood, clergymen's salaries. The English Church rates were subject to rejection by rate-payers in vestry and were chargeable on occupiers in respect of their holdings. The rates were in personam. The fact is, the Scotch charge on heritors is an endowment belonging to the Nation. If the Scotch Church were disestablished & disendowed – as may come to pass – the charge would be a valuable capital & ought not to be relinquished. Arguments agt. the Bill were adduced by the Lord advocate[203] in a clear & cogent speech. It seemed to me not justifiable after that statement to support the Bill, so I voted with the noes. We were 225 agt. 108. Most of the radicals were agt. us. Hardcastle was with me. * Note. I shd. not forget that the Ministry were prepared to grant special redress for persons who have cause of complaint capable of substantiation – and some such were admitted even by the Lord Advocate. * [...]

---

[202] 2nd reading of Duncan McLaren's bill.
[203] George Young.

Thursday, 10 March: Col[onel] Wilson Patten supported the Bill[204] in a speech lasting about an hour. He is a halting orator, with a painful delivery. His matter, however, was useful & his criticisms fair.

Horsman, at 5.55 p.m., commenced his speech. The house was hushed at once. His voice is weak, and soon wanted water. He has been speaking for 20 minutes (6.15). Not being aggressive, he is rather prosy.

He adverted to crime & outrage, detailing instances. This sounded like a side-blow at the ministry. Gladstone looks serious.

He has drawn a picture of what the Irish tenant would be under a system of security. Some of the House laughed incredulously, as the picture seemed overdrawn.[205]

He noticed, rather unpleasantly for Ministers, their inertness in resorting to measures of repression. His tone, apologetic for the Cabinet, was rather like disguised reproof. The government looked a little frightened and incredulous of the heartiness of his praise. He is now finishing. Time 55 minutes.

The speech was considered very good. The Conservatives quite concur in his opinion on the indispensable necessity of insuring the safety of property and life.

The two most noteworthy speeches delivered afterwards were those of Sir Roundell Palmer and Mr Hardy. These were spoken after I left. The former strongly advocated measures in repression of outrages – the latter criticized the Bill in some of its details – apparently, to very good purpose.

Friday, 11 March: After the usual battery of interrogations levelled at ministers, W. H. Gregory spoke for about 1 hour on the Land Bill. His remarks were valuable & dispassionate. There is not room for a description of a sort of substitution-plan which he tendered.[206] Next came Lord Elcho, who, I think, distinguished himself not a little. He cited passages from speeches delivered in 1866 and 1868 by Robt. Lowe, which passages, if uttered by him now, would be quite inconsistent with his responsibility for the bill. It seems that he strenuously stood up for political economy as an 'oasis' in 'politics' and declared he would not be a party to measures for Ireland, in regard to private property, which he would not apply to England.

It was now about 7 p.m., so I went home. Returning at 1/2 past 10, I found Disraeli on his legs. The house was very full.

---

[204] The Landlord and Tenant (Ireland) bill, 2nd reading debate continued.

[205] He favoured the application of the 'Ulster custom' throughout Ireland; *H* cc. 1643–58.

[206] In effect the '3 f's', of fair rent, fixity of tenure and free sale, and no separate recognition of the Ulster custom; *H* cxcix. 1745–60.

Disraeli's speech was that of a man who felt that he shared in a grave responsibility – & this perhaps accounts for his rather slow & hesitating delivery at times. The flagellation he administered to Horsman will remain in his memory. He had reproved successive ministers for inattention to the report of the Devon Commission[207] & for culpable inaction. Yet, said Disraeli, this 'superior person' had been for some years Secretary for Ireland &, to the astonishment of Lord Mayo, said that he found the office a 'sinecure'.[208]

Disraeli's criticisms will be of use when we find ourselves in committee. He thinks the measure too complex and he sketched another plan.[209]

Some of his remarks, as usual, convulsed the House.

Gladstone succeeded. The most important announcement he made was that in several particulars the arguments propounded had affected the conclusions embodied in the Bill, which might he thought be reconsidered. He warmly appealed to the adverse Irish party not to divide. This, however, they did & so, at 2 min. before 1 a.m. we went into the lobby and spent there 27 minutes. After passing the tellers, we entered – that is, those who cared, entered – the lobby where at least were elbow room & refreshments.[210] At 1/4 before 2 I got to bed [...]

Monday, 14 March: [...] Visct. Crichton moved a resolution wh. the Ministry consider one of censure – for removal of Capt[ai]n Coote from the Shrievalty of Monaghan.[211] Ld. Crichton's speech was by no means wanting in research, nor was it ill-delivered but quite the contrary.

I paired with Mr Broderick till 10 & went home. There was a division – 183 to 113.[212] So my pair told.

At 1/2 before 10, Mr Dixon's motion on the 2d. reading of the Education Bill[213] came on & was subsequently adjourned. As I expected,

---

[207] Which reported in 1845, favouring compensation for tenants' improvements; *P.P.* 1845, xix-xxii. for the detailed evidence it collected.

[208] 3 June 1858; *H* cl. 1450–7.

[209] He felt that the Ulster custom should not be recognised by law, and that where a man with no lease was evicted in spite of having paid his rent, he should be allowed to appeal to a tribunal in which the Judge would decide each case on its merits; *H* cxcix. 1806–28.

[210] Bryan's amendment against the 2nd reading was defeated, 442:11. The Speaker had made special arrangements to cope with the likely large number voting in one lobby; Ossington, *Journal*, 254.

[211] Crichton's motion condemned the dismissal of Coote for tampering with a jury; *H* cxcix. 1877–87.

[212] For the government.

[213] Against allowing local authorities discretionary power to determine the religious instruction provided in schools supported by State funds or rates; *H* cxcix. 1919–31.

the nonconformists have found out the weak places in it and the House
is white with petitions every night [...]

Tuesday, 15 March: [...] Lowe, as usual, was very curt & caustic
in replying to questions. He raised much laughter & probably made
some enemies. Gladstone himself could not help laughing. What a
contrast betwn. Lowe's replies & Cardwell's! Of course, the former are
a rich treat to the House, whereas the pompous propriety of the latter
is rather the reverse.

The dissenters are vehemently opposed to a part of the education
Bill. Very many petitions have been sent agt. the clause which gives,
in effect, to local Boards discretion in the matter of religious doctrines
to be taught in certain cases. An unfair course has been taken by Mr
Dixon – that of raising, on the 2d. reading, a question more fit for
treatment in Committee, the mover professing to be in favour of the
Bill. A great debate has been on foot for 2 days & will be continued
for several more as seems likely. The Conservatives seem to be more
favourable to the Ministerial plan than the radicals. Several good
speeches were made.

I was nominated a member of the Prison Ministers Committee of
19.[214]

Wednesday, 16 March: The 4 Cornish County members considered
2 bills, severally called the Metalliferous Mines Bill and the Mines
Inspection Bill, in order to weld the best provisions of each into one
Bill – that of the governt. viz the Mines Inspection Bill. Afterwards, I
attended the sitting to hear the Ballot discussed.[215] Osborne was diverting
the House with his experiences at Nottingham & Waterford. He did
not contribute much that was new in the shape of argument.

The Tories adopted a motion for the adjournment of the debate,
which course put me in a difficulty. I was apprehensive lest a vote on
either side shd. be misunderstood. For example: – in voting with
Leatham I thought my vote would be taken as given in support of the
Ballot wh. I oppose; while, in voting with the mover of the amendmt,[216]
there was danger of my appearing to shirk a direct form of opposition
to the Ballot. So I left the House, intending to vote agt. the measure

---

[214] A select committee, chaired by J.F. Maguire, to enquire into the working of the
Prison Ministers act of 1863: *C.J.* cxxv. 85, for the membership; *P.P.* 1870, viii. 715 for
the report.

[215] 2nd reading of Leatham's Ballot bill. He agreed to postpone it after Lord Hartington,
who had chaired a select committee on the subject (of which Leatham was a member),
indicated that the government intended to introduce a bill of its own. Bruce L. Kinzer,
The Ballot Question in Nineteenth Century English Politics (New York, 1982), 119–34.

[216] Newdegate, whose adjournment motion was defeated, 226:116.

on the 2d. reading. There was some slight excuse for adjournmt. because the report of the Hartington Committee was not yet in print. When, however, the Tories became manifestly factious by adopting a motion for the adjournt. of the House, I voted with the Noes.[217]

My new position + change of opinion + was very deliberately adopted some years ago and announced in the address to the electors of E. Cornwall in 1868.[218] If anyone ask me to what I attribute it, I think I shd. reply that I have little trust in any check for corruption and intimidation except Publicity. * See accounts of American elections. In 1 case 18,000 more voted than the whole number of a constituency. 'Vote early & vote often' is sometimes the maxim there. * The security of the Ballot requires integrity in some Public officers; &, as an elector I shd. prefer the light of day to their ministrations or ink made of chloride of cobalt.[219] + I cannot see what answer can be rendered to the argument that the suffrage is either a possession or a trust. If a possession, why shd. anyone interfere with its exercise? If a trust, how is it congenial to our constitutional notions to fulfil it under the cloak of secrecy? +

While Public opinion is as it is, I fear that few will attach to corruption in electoral matters the same kind of criminality wh. is usually placed on that vice. A fraud by a Trustee in money matters would send him to Coventry. A bribe at an election has only of late begun to be regarded as disgraceful in the same degree.

With regard to the efficacy of the Ballot in securing secrecy, I am not quite clear that such end would be attained. Lately, there have been searching enquiries on elections in Boroughs extending over a field of nearly 40 years, & it appears that any question may be asked & that no lapse of time closes a transaction.

Who, then, is safe? or, if safe, what elector will not be apprehensive of a disastrous cross examination? If an election be likely to be decided agt. a darling of a large body of household suffragists, the Ballot Box will in excited times be smashed – & the fidelity of officials will be accused and inquiry demanded. Can the inquiry be refused in the face of an allegation of tampering with the Ballot cards? If it cannot be refused, where is secrecy?

As a convert, I have no right to express confidence in my judgment. Still, it is my judgment.

Thursday, 17 March: Chichester Fortescue propounded the Min-

---

[217] Bartellot's motion, which would have killed the bill, defeated 220:110.
[218] *The Times*, 23 Nov. 1868, 4.
[219] Used to mark the hands of those who had voted.

isterial plan for preventing outrage & sedition in Ireland.[220] He made a most unfortunate blunder at the end of almost his first sentence which was all the more laughable inasmuch as he spoke with the air of a minister dealing with a great crisis. In fact he described the scheme 'for the maintenance of life and above all property in Ireland'. Pausing amid universal laughter, he rather neatly recovered his equilibrium and proceeded. The House listened tranquilly to a somewhat tedious statement and, towards the end of his speech when a rigorous part of the plan was sketched, shewed signs of satisfaction. Liberals, below the gangway, were rather passive. Ministers stop short of the suspension of the Habeas Corpus act, F. affirming that there is no precedent for such a measure in cases of agrarian outrage.

Later in the evening, govt. had a rather rough experience on a motion of Lord Henry Lennox in disapproval of the Admiralty-retirement-scheme. The division presents the following numbers – 169[221] to 136. From this I was absent, not expecting any vote of importance after the debate on Irish outrages.

Several liberals opposed Ministers in the debate, notably, Bouverie, Whitbread & Ld. Henley. These names struck me. Very likely, there were others [...]

Friday, 18 March: On the amendmt. to the 2d. reading of the Education Bill,[222] Vernon Harcourt spoke ably during 45 minutes. It is said the controversy is 'squared'.

Coming into the House at 10 p.m. I found a tedious gentleman on his legs, Col[onel] Beresford, who appears to be a politician of a very square toed type. Col[onel] Sibthorpe[223] revived – without his fun; in lieu of it, prolixity (which Sibthorpe had not).

When Beresford sat down, from 25 to 40 members were on their legs. Mr Richard succeeded in obtaining precedence. It was evident that there would be no chance of a division till late, if at all; so, after consulting the whip, I retired.

Government are going to shape their plan so as to meet the approval

---

[220] 1st reading of the Peace Preservation (Ireland) bill, aiming e.g. to suppress the use of firearms in proclaimed districts, increase police powers of search, give magistrates powers of summary punishment, and give the Crown powers to seize newspapers; *P.P.* 1870, iii. 655.

[221] Trelawny mistakenly gave the figure for the majority as 161. Lennox was against the retiring of flag officers except on grounds of age or health, because of the expense involved; *H* cc. 127–36.

[222] Debate continued from 14 Mar.

[223] Charles Sibthorp, M.P. for Lincoln 1826–32 and 1835–55; an ultra-protectionist.

of those liberals whose spokesman Dixon has been.[224] No doubt he had a case, but should he not have reserved it for statement in Committee?

The amendmt. was negatived.

In effect Fawcett was heard almost immediately after I went. Does he not address the House rather too often?

Vernon Harcourt has many advantages. He has a powerful voice, a strong organisation, and, being in the prime of life, makes his mark in good time. He has talents & cultivation – also, sarcasm. His practice as a lawyer has not corrupted his style of delivery – a thing sometimes noticeable. It struck me that a longer knowledge of his audience would preclude allusions to opinions held by a member 'in his secret heart'. He referred to Lowe, with whom the speaker said he had long been acquainted. This made matters worse. Again, was it wise to speak of the service of the liberal party to Gladstone as service of 'perfect freedom'? There was a shudder at the words among the Conservatives.

Mr W. S. Allen has given a notice of motion in favour of opening Museums &c. on 3 evenings a week from 7 to 10. I have taken steps to secure the re-publication of the report of my Committee on this subject appointed in 1860.[225]

Monday, 21 March: The Cornish County members have been & are still engaged in arranging clauses for the Mines Inspection Bill.

If Ministers deal successfully with all three Bills now before the Country – on Irish Land, Irish Crime & English Education – Ministers must be more than human. It will be said that the first outrages Political economy, the 2d. the Constitution, the 3rd. the conscience!

The 2d. reading of the Peace Preservation Bill was under discussion throughout the evening. Wilson Patten seems to have blundered in his line of criticism. Dr Ball stoutly supported the Bill. Horsman shewed signs of one of his fits of discontent – which are not rare. Henley picked holes [...]

Tuesday, 22 March: The Irish question was resumed. A division was taken betwn. 12 & 1 a.m.[226] Having a cold, I did not remain so late.

Lord J. Manners made a bitter speech agt. Ministers whose hands he yet wants to strengthen by the Bill under discussion! It is sad when so fine a nature as his lordship's is thus warped by party feeling. I have watched his career for 35 years since we were at Cambridge, and know

---

[224] Gladstone, in a conciliatory speech, had announced that the government was willing to reconsider, during the committee stage, the conscience clause of the Education bill; *H* cc. 292–303.

[225] *P.P.* 1860, xvi. 1.

[226] 425:13 for the 2nd reading of the Peace Preservation (Ireland) bill.

him to be an amiable, painstaking and well-meaning man. But the name of 'liberal' is a red rag which drives him mad, altho' in office he has quietly appropriated our policy – household suffrage, for example.

It is right to observe that my vote would have been for the 2d. reading of the Peace Preservation Bill.

Wednesday, 23 March: The Burials Bill was the theme of to-day's debate. The introducer was the member for Denbighshire, Mr Osborne Morgan.[227] His speech was very effective – in delivery, reminding me a little of Roundell Palmer.

The cases he cited of perverse intolerance shewn by Ministers of the establishment were overwhelming and their natural defenders quailed under the onslaught. I hope his speech will be published at length.

He won on a division by 233 to 122.

Afterwds. Bruce, at Sir Geo. Grey's[228] suggestion, moved that the Bill be committed to a select Committee. The victorious party disapproved of this course wh. nevertheless was adopted on a 2d. division. Numbers 226 to 135[229] * T. agt. * [...]

Friday, 25 March: [...] At a morning sitting, Bouverie's amendment on the words 'or seditious' was discussed and a division occurred. Numbers 333 to 56.[230] The mover is scandalized at the new mode of dealing with 'sedition', an offence which some say is indefinable. Madness requires unusual treatment, and the Irish are at this moment mad. The Bill is an outrage on liberty and yet without it there would be no liberty. Is it not true that men cultivate land or not according to the mandates of a secret and irresponsible Body? Facts justify Ministers, and the powers given are given in trust that they will not be abused.

[...] Again, Lord J. Manners railed at Ministers agt. reason, justice & palpable facts. This Gladstone shewed. How wise Disraeli is in abstaining from attacks tending to weaken the executive!

Osborne indulged his oratorical powers. It is not quite easy to reduce his remarks to a tenable & consistent whole. In some parts of his speech – especially, as to the abolition of the Lord Lieutenancy – it was my good fortune to agree with him.

---

[227] Acting on behalf of a joint committee of the Protestant Dissenting Deputies and the Liberation Society; the bill would have permitted dissenters' burial services in Anglican Churchyards; G.I.T. Machin, *Politics and the Churches in Great Britain, 1869–1921* (Oxford, 1987), 42.

[228] The Home Secretary and his Liberal predecessor.

[229] Trelawny mistakenly gave the figure for the majority as 236. The bill was later withdrawn.

[230] Against the amendment to clause 27 of the Peace Preservation (Ireland) bill, providing for the seizure of 'treasonable or seditious' matter; *H* cc. 617–23.

It was curious to hear Mr G. H. Moore – the persistent opponent of the Bill – argue, in favour of 1 year as agt. 2 years imprisonment, that the former would be more probably carried out. Why, this doctrine suggests coercion which would be effective. Irishman to the backbone!

Saturday, 26 March: After a good deal of talk the Peace Bill was read a 3rd. time and passed. This is a great step. Would this have been allowed had the 13 patriots[231] not suspected their own wisdom?

Very possibly they will owe their lives to the merciful severity of Parliament.

Tuesday, 29 March: [...] Lowe's free spoken mode of treating deputations is highly to his credit. Thus, on the malt tax, he seemed to please persons who attended.[232] To-day 'the Times' notices his answer to a deputation of Financial Reformers to whom he preached economic truths little understood or appreciated by the general Public. Lowe does not see why – especially since the last Reform Bill was enacted – new taxation shd. be laid on the rich only. He speaks of taxation resembling a table wh. must have legs enough to stand on. Someone, I think Gladstone, said we must beware of pulling out the linchpin. I recollect that some 25 years ago I warned Parliament that taxation is a house of cards. One card falls – the edifice follows. Lowe thinks the entire relinquishmt. of a tax is unfavourable to sudden demands such as circumstances may call for.

Wednesday, 30 March: Most of my time was employed in attending to the arrangement of clauses to be printed in Mr Bruce's Mines regulations Bill. The Northern members for mining districts met the Cornish County members in one of the rooms occupied by officials of the House. * Mr Gosset's[233] (I understood) * There we came to an understanding, which St Aubyn will make known in the proper quarter.

Afterwards, being present in committee of the House on the Attorneys & Solicitors remuneration Bill, I took the liberty of moving two additions; severally, to the 5th & 6th clauses. On a division upon the 1st. I suffered a defeat. Numbers 95 to 10.

My objects were to prevent the detention of a clients securities until a bill of costs has been paid and to compel prompt delivery of accounts of charges due.[234]

---

[231] Those who had voted against the 2nd reading, on 22 Mar.

[232] *The Times*, 9 Mar. 1870, 12.

[233] Serjeant-at-arms.

[234] *C.J.* cxxv. 117, for the amendment to clause 5 relating to clients' securities; the amendment to clause 6, setting a twelve month deadline for solicitors' claims, was negatived on 1 Apr.; *C.J.* cxxv. 121.

Thursday, 31 March: After a sitting of four hours as one of the Select Committee upon Prison Ministers, I attended the House, when at least one hour and a half was wasted in wrangling upon loss of time and the question who is to be blamed for it. Gladstone sketched his programme which is not very hopeful.[235] The work of Parliament has beaten us. Its magnitude even in peace is beyond our powers. What would it be in war? Double sittings are already to be held even before Easter. Many subjects are in [the] charge of select committees [...]

Friday, 1 April: [...] The Lords amendmts. to the Peace Preservation Bill were in part agreed to. To portions we could not assent as they trenched on the privileges of the H. of Com[mo]ns[236] [...]

Monday, 4 April: [...] Disraeli's speech[237] was calm & temperate; it was intended I think to frighten landowners in England. Had Mr Henley delivered it, it would have been quite in keeping with the supposed-speaker's position. But Mr Disraeli supported the 2d. reading and it is too late to battle for the principles of political economy. If the measure do any good, it will be in virtue of its largeness of conception. An Irish liberal MP spoke to me of it with contempt and declared that it would not be received with satisfaction by anyone in Ireland. This in substance.

Lowe professed to reply categorically to all Disraeli's points. Lowe's delivery is not happy – too jerky & disjointed. He has no elocution, & his want of art in putting the excellent matter of his speeches must be a subject of regret to his admirers. It is in the Times report that one discerns the real force of his speeches.

Roundell Palmer & Gladstone spoke at length. The former appeared to agree neither with ministers nor with the opposition.

I sadly fear that, in our endeavour to give satisfaction to the Irish, we shall only succeed in rendering their dislike to us more intense. Should this be so, we shall have weakened confidence in the security of property to no purpose. This sounds gloomy, but the thought will rise.

Tuesday, 5 April: We had a 2 o'clock p.m. morning sitting. A good

---

[235] He proposed morning sittings for Friday 1st, Tuesday 5th and Friday 8th Apr.; *H* cc. 992–6.

[236] Gladstone had stated his objection to part of clause 38, relating to awards by Grand Juries to the relatives of murder victims, on the grounds that this was taxation by the House of Lords; *H* cc. 1050.

[237] On the Landlord and Tenant (Ireland) bill, in committee.

deal of lively controversy ensued upon Clause 3. Fortescue's amendmt.[238] was carried on a division. Numbers 293 to 182 * T. in majority. *

A smart encounter took place betwn. Hardy & Gladstone. Hardy considered that Gladstone had used language likely to engender in the unemployed a disposition to attribute their sufferings to owners of property. This seems to represent the spirit of Hardy's charge. The vociferous cheers of the House decidedly endorsed it. But is not the Bill liable to the same criticism? Why is the property of landowners dealt with? It is not because competition is so great that tenants have no alternative but to get land or starve? But is the landlord capable of repressing overpopulation? Is the fault of over-competition his?

The naked fact stares us in the face – we have turned our backs upon Political economy. The science appears to have broken down.

Such is the delay in the progress of business that I have predicted that, after some weeks more of debating, the House will resort, as in the case of Ld. Stanley's India Bill, to the method of resolutions.[239] It seems to me that we have not laid a definite basis of principles.

P. Taylor moved for payment of members. He took 24 into the lobby.[240] The £500 a year he would give a member is a pretty compensation for men who pay thousands for a seat. * T. absent. *

Wednesday, 6 April: Sites for places of worship Bill[241] was our theme. A long debate. The Conservatives on the whole more tolerant, as I thought, than the Liberals. With proper safeguards, the wants of dissenters may be satisfied. But they are very aggressive & rather resent by anticipation a conciliatory demeanour. No division.

Some law Bills followed. I succeeded in getting the excision of a clause too favourable to solicitors in the matter of lieu for costs.[242]

As we left the House, B-e[243] said 'T. Do you know the diff[eren]ce betwn. an attorney & a sol[icito]r?' No, I replied. 'The Speaker says the diff[eren]ce is that betwn. an alligator & a crocodile'. I fancy this is not new.

+ The worst impression I have of the breed is gathered from my

[238] Moved in the Irish Chief Secretary's absence by Gladstone; *H* cc. 1284-5. A verbal alteration to clause 3 of the Landlord and Tenant (Ireland) bill, clarifying the tenant's right to compensation on quitting his holding.

[239] In Apr. 1858; *H* cxlix. appendix.

[240] The hostile majority numbered 211.

[241] 2nd reading of Osborne Morgan's bill to facilitate (with powers of compulsory purchase) acquisitions of land for places of worship. Morgan pointed out that in Wales there was often difficulty in obtaining land for dissenters' chapels, because of the hostility of landlords; *H* cc. 1382-90. The bill made no further progress.

[242] The Solicitor General agreed to the omission of the clause from the Attorneys and Solicitors Remuneration bill; *H* cc. 1423.

[243] E.P. Bouverie.

intercourse with them. An eminent sol[icito]r spoke to me of a course being taken for the purpose of 'influencing costs'. Another used these words 'our rascally profession'. +

Free trade & short accounts are better than acts of Parl[iamen]t in the matter of costs. But no unfair advantage in respect of general lieu on securities. This is what I enforced.

Wednesday, 27 April:[244] An interesting debate on the marriage law.[245] The House divided twice and the Bill went thro' committee. Gladstone pronounced in its favour, yet did not conciliate Roundell Palmer who, as I thought, dealt with the subject in the manner of a special pleader.

T. Chambers was forcible & energetic. His notice of Palmer's arguments was very effective. Palmer was perhaps discreet in discussing some printed paper with his neighbour during the handling he received.

With what grace could he charge the bill as retrospective after the cruelty inflicted by Lord Lyndhurst's act?[246] That act it was wh. dealt the mischief. Before it passed, a marriage with a deceased wife's sister was not void, only voidable. But dissenters owed no moral fealty to decisions of our ecclesiastical courts.

What right had Palmer, disclaiming a theological treatment of the question, to attribute to the mover a Levitical line of supporting it, when Palmer well knew that the mover only meets opponents, relying on Levitical grounds by shewing that, if the old testament is to be taken as authority, it would be rather in his favour than agt. him?

Gladstone dwelt on the ripeness of Public opinion in favour of the Bill and the unfairness of requiring dissenters to be bound by the teaching of our ecclesiastical law. This in substance.

Thursday, 28 April: 'The Times' of this morning has a grave article on waste of Parliamentary time & obstructive courses. But the most noteworthy point in the article is the caution read to the Premier who is a chief offender in regard to speechmaking and engrosses the conduct of the Land Bill. The fact is, I fear, it shews a certain want of completeness of details – making fools of supporters who defend provisions doomed to be surrendered. The misfortune his backers labour under is the necessity of opposing the scheme or taking it with all its faults. To throw over Political economy & find that the sacrifice is after all in vain were very provoking. It is as well to be hung for a sheep as a lamb [...]

---

[244] Trelawny had been paired from 7–12 Apr., and the Easter recess followed until the 25th. His attendance was intermittent until the end of the month, due to rheumatism.

[245] i.e. the Deceased Wife's Sister bill, moved by Thomas Chambers. Later rejected by the House of Lords.

[246] House of Lords Sessional Papers, 1835, i. 195.

Monday, 2 May: [...] I voted agt. Dr Ball's amendment on clause 3 of the Land Bill to substitute 21 for 31 years as the minimum term of a lease relieving landlords from compensation to tenants[247] [...]

Wednesday, 4 May: The Times of this date has a paragraph accounting for my not appearing in the Divisions on Monday when Newdegate's Conventual motion came on & mentioning that I shd. have voted agt. it.[248]

Religious bigotry is at the bottom of the business. Newdegate is quite honest & courageous, but lacks judgment. His course favours Catholicism – rallying high & low agt. a common foe. The truth ab[ou]t English Convents is known pretty well by all who have read the trial 'Saurin v Starr'.[249] The Home Sec[retar]y could easily frame a Bill curing practical evil in law or facts. It does not, however, appear to me, when one considers the inevitable notoriety of transactions of persons & communities in England, – however strong their aim may be to maintain secrecy & seclusion – that it is not worth while to make the subject of Conventual life a theme for examination by a Parl[iamentar]y Committee. Sitting upon the Prison Ministers Committee I have very good & special means of judging what the disturbing effect would be of cross-examining priests on matters affecting their status and the civil position of the community to wh. they minister.

We voted to-day on Jacob Bright's Bill for giving the Parliamentary franchise to women who happen to be qualified by property. The Bill had my support. Numbers 124 to 91.[250] Bruce spoke for Ministers – or, rather, against them – seeing that he avowed their indecision in the matter. But, surely, this question was one ripe for the dignity of Ministerial treatment.

Bright's speech was delivered before I reached the House. The debate interested me, tho' it was provoking to hear bad arguments propounded witht. adequate exposure. Beresford Hope made an original speech in a good manner & pleased both sides. After offering him my congratulations I ventured to observe that he did not mark the distinction betwn. married and unmarried women in that the latter, owning income, have the duty of filling up Income tax returns & consequent

[247] 290:209 against Ball.

[248] On 2 May Newdegate had secured the appointment of a select committee to inquire into the matter; *H* cci. 51–84.

[249] A sensational court case, in 1869, in which Mary Saurin successfully sued the mother superior (Mrs Star) of a convent in Hull, for libel and conspiracy. Walter Arnstein, *Protestant and Catholic in Mid-Victorian England: Mr. Newdegate and the Nuns* (University of Missouri Press, 1982), 108–22. The case fuelled Newdegate's demands for a parliamentary inquiry.

[250] For the 2nd reading of the bill to enfranchise women householders.

liability. The contention was that the concession to unmarried women of necessity involved a concession to married.

[...] It struck me as curious that, at one stage of the debate on Women's Suffrage, not a single Conservative sat on the benches above the gangway.

Thursday, 5 May: [...] The Whalley episode was the first business. He had written to the Times, mentioning the remarks made in his hearing in a late debate[251] – 'kick him' 'strangle him'. Also, he adverted to his ineffectual challenge of the decision of the Speaker. Osborne commented on Whalley's proceedings with some severity. The Speaker took occasion to remind Whalley that matters relating to order should, under a rule of the House, be disposed of at once. Also, the conduct of a member in complaining to a Public Journal was censured.

During the evening there were some personalities betwn. Lord Elcho and Mr Robertson, whose almost injuriously-devoted adherence to Ministers & their measures excites notice. R. sits just behind Gladstone & is one of his most vociferous 'claqueurs'. Being a tall & conspicuous person, he naturally attracts attention.

Friday, 6 May: Sundry questions disposed of, Allen moved for opening certain Public Institutions (galleries & such like) on the evenings of week days.[252] He used the materials liberally supplied him in the report & evidence of my select Committee of 1860. Walpole, Kinnaird, W. Gregory & Hope spoke.[253] Also, Robert Lowe who begged the mover not to divide, holding out hopes of a new & fire-proof building. I could not resist a temptation to support the proposal of Mr Allen. 'The Times' (of May 7th) is not quite accurate in its notice of the words wh. fell from me – that is, according to my notion of that wh. I intended to convey and wh. I believe I conveyed. * See Daily News & Telegraph. I bought a copy of the last. * (I particularly allude to the Sunday question.) Now while I said 'I did not disguise' that in 1860, I meant to try to gain the opening of Collections &c. on Sundays, I added that I was well aware of the feeling on that subject & had felt its effects;[254] but I do not recollect that I last night said anything which committed me to the principle of going further at present as regards the sunday question – that not being specially under consideration. * Note, later: It is, however, true that I alluded by names to Kew

---

[251] On Newdegate's motion on convents, 2 May; *The Times*, 4 May 1870, 7.
[252] His amendment only applied to the National Gallery and parts of the British Museum; *H* cci. 330–3. Withdrawn.
[253] Kinnaird seconding and Gregory supporting Allen; Walpole and Hope were sceptical. *H* cci. 330–50 for the debate.
[254] *T.D.*, 16 Feb. 1860.

gardens & Hampton Court and the advantage the Public enjoy in those places of resort being open on Sundays. Also, I threw out for consideration a question whether some of the ancient works in the British Museum – those, for instance, illustrative of Biblical History such as the remains of Ninevah &c. – might not be collected & set apart for exhibition on Sundays. When 'the Times' speaks of the expression of my readiness to 'extend the principle', this must be the explanation. I have sent to the West Briton as accurate an account as possible of my speech; almost my very words.[255] * Allen's object was to obtain the advantage on weekday evenings. It is almost worse than the evil to attempt to set the newspapers right. At least, I despair of getting an exact version of my speech recorded in the Morning & evening papers without great trouble and so much delay as to render correction almost useless. Besides, the correction of one paper, looks too like approval of others.

[...] As to the Land Bill,[256] it is noteworthy that one amendmt. was rejected by 191 to 132; the other by 167 to 103. That is to say, the Committee is thinning & ministers have hardly, perhaps, majorities quite as large. What will the Bill be like when it shall return from the Lords? Will it live thro' the Session? Will it kill the Premier? Will English & Scotch landlords become alarmed?

An Irish nobleman of my club (Earl of D)[257] – a whig – yesterday expressed his surprise that English landlords endured the Bill. The fact is, we are apprehensive of the consequences of not dealing with a subject on which several governments have allowed the Irish to expect that Parl[iamen]t would legislate. Economically, the measure is, I fear, wrong. Imperially, it is, I think, necessary. However, I shall severely scrutinize it when it shall be presented for a 3rd. reading.

Monday, 9 May: [...] Lord Hartington's Bill[258] does not please Balloteers of the Leatham school, nor the Tories. It is not clear to me that Nomination day meetings shd. be discontinued. Is it not a good thing that a candidate shd. meet both friends & foes face to face at some point during an election? Might not a notorious rogue & adventurer slip in by the skilful management of an election agent & a docile committee? A nomination meeting is a disagreeable ordeal, so is physick. As a

---

[255] Published on 12 May.

[256] In committee, on clause 5.

[257] Possibly the Earl of Dunraven.

[258] The Parliamentary Elections bill, based on the report of Hartington's select committee (*P.P.* 1870, vi. 131), provided for a secret ballot, the abolition of public nominations, and banned the use of public houses as committee rooms. It did not, however, apply to municipal elections, and numbered counterfoils on the ballot papers left open the possibility of a scrutiny. 1st reading given, but no further progress made.

candidate, I shd. desire to avoid it. As a citizen, I think it doubtful whether it may not be a valuable security. The Bill will leave expenses of elections untouched. Money will still have its natural influence.

Thursday, 12 May: [...] Hardcastle proposed to pair with me on Women's Disabilities which J[acob] Bright was resolved to bring on – even as late as just before 1 a.m. if he could get the chance – and so it turned out, when he was defeated, Bouverie moving to negative the Bill. Numbers 220 to 94[259] [...] Bouverie's argument was hardly fair, because it by no means follows from the allow[in]g women, qualified by property & rated, to vote, that married women, leaving home, shd. be enfranchised. If a woman be fit to vote in Municipalities, I think she is fit to vote for a representative. * My opinion that heads of houses, male or female, shd. be enfranchised. *

Friday, 13 May: There was a smart encounter to-night on Cowper-Temple's motion relating to Barry's dismissal (as it is called) from the post of architect for the new Houses of Parl[iamen]t.[260]

Hope adverted to Ayrton's manner of treating gentlemen on which Hope thought he discerned improvement – for which he considered there was still room – & herein for once there will be unanimity – even among persons who pretend to taste. + His use of the word 'assumptions'[261] will hardly be warranted by reference to any received authority on the Queen's English. However, it may be said that the exceptional qualities of Ayrton justify the coining of a new word. +

Osborne answered Hope and, in defence of Ayrton as a financier, described him as a 'noble savage'. I am not quite sure that the adjective is not redundant.

Ministers only won by 43.[262] Had any one of them but Ayrton been Commiss[ione]r of works, the motion wd. have been defeated by (perhaps) 200.

[...] A friend (w.c.)[263] talking lately with me of political people observed that Disraeli was rather contemptuous of J.S. Mill when he

---

[259] Against the motion to enter into committee on the bill to extend household suffrage to women.

[260] *H* cci. 670–82. Edward Barry, the son of Sir Charles Barry, had been appointed by Cowper-Temple in 1860, but had quarrelled with Ayrton, the current chief commissioner for works and buildings. There was some doubt as to whether Barry was, strictly speaking, an office holder. For the long and controversial history of the new parliament buildings, see Roland Quinault, 'Westminster and the Victorian Constitution', *Transactions of the Royal Historical Society*, sixth series, ii (1992), 79–104.

[261] 'The offer was met by a dry and hard assumption as to the rights of the Crown'; *H* cci. 701.

[262] 152:109.

[263] Perhaps George Wingrove Cooke, a leader writer for *The Times*.

was in the Commons, – exhibiting his feeling (for example) in walking out in the middle of a speech of his. It is said that Disraeli called the Philosopher a 'well-educated governess'.

Thursday, 19 May: [...] I am informed that the writer of an excellent letter which lately appeared in the Times[264] on Contagious Diseases was Dr Carpenter of the London University. He is a great authority.

Monday, 23 May: [...] The Land Bill has passed thro' Committee and will surely go to the Lords. This is not quite as I predicted. I expected that the lower House would have been moved to proceed by way of resolutions. It seems to me that if the measure become law, a great many tenants will leave Ireland, bought out by Landlords who will increase the size of farms. Perhaps, this is right [...]

Tuesday, 24 May: [...] In my place soon after 4 p.m.[265] Several members wished to know whether I really intended to call attention to the presence of strangers. My reply was that I was considering what it were proper to do in that regard & that I shd. not take such a step with[ou]t consulting many good & experienced advisers.
[...] I met Gilpin who had just left the Speaker. He, as I was informed, desired to see me. I said 'I am now on my way to him'. Also, Glyn[266] spoke to me; deprecating the supposed step. The Speaker gave me sound & judicious reasons why it were well to avoid it. He considered that the subject could easily be treated without grossness, & that it would be unfortunate if it shd. seem that the House could entertain a matter without opportunity given to the Public of knowing all its bearings. I can only report a sketch of his arguments. He reminded me that the Public already knew almost everything that could be said ab[ou]t contagious diseases. I gave a statement of my only doubt, viz, whether the full horrors of the evils we wished by legislation to mitigate could be described if it were known that speeches would be reported at length. However, I agreed with the Speaker & accepted his judgment as being indeed my own. Leaving him, I met Craufurd for Ayr who inquired of me how matters stood, Craufurd knowing that I had thought of excluding strangers. I told him of my decision & stated that in any case there were reasons agt. action on my part – 1stly

---

[264] Not found.
[265] Ready for the 1st reading of William Fowler's bill to repeal the Contagious Diseases acts of 1866 and 1869. There had been a mounting public agitation against the acts during the early months of 1870; Paul McHugh, *Prostitution and Victorian Social Reform* (1980), 56–9.
[266] Government chief whip.

because I reported the debate when John O'Connell cleared the House[267] & 2dly because in my address to E. Cornwall on becoming a candidate I stated, on the subject of the Ballot, that the best cure for evils was a full & exhaustive knowledge of their nature. That was in a rough way of statemt. the ground I took.

[...] There was a debate and division on the subject of the Welsh Church – the mover being Mr Williams. * T. with Ministers.[268] * I confine myself to the remark that Gladstone very emphatically described his entire want of sympathy with Williams – 'putting his foot down' upon the position which he & his government mean to hold.

Fowler followed. Hereupon Craufurd observed to the Speaker that there were strangers in the gallery. There was a kind of appeal to Craufurd to let the strangers remain undisturbed. Bouverie observed that there was no motion before the House. The Speaker seemed, by a sort of hesitation, to deprecate their removal. Also, I think, Gladstone & others appealed to Craufurd to abstain from pressing his right. Craufurd persisted, the House demurring. So the galleries were cleared & my notebook came forth.

I was writing speeches for ab[ou]t 4 hours, sitting behind Gladstone. People soon found out what I was doing. At 10.20 the Speaker went out to get food. So went I but failed as the buffet was occupied, and I feared the Speaker would be too quick for me. Dinnerless, I proceeded with my reporting. When the debate finished & after a division taken on adjournt. (Col[onel] Anson mov[in]g.)[269] I went upstairs & inquired for the Times Reporter. I said I had a report & that my notion was to collect the members of the Press & read my notes. He did not see his way to this & proposed to send a short-hand writer to meet me in the Central Hall. I agreed. The Reporter there met me. The light hardly let me read my notebook. We went into the Telegraph office, where a wax candle was supplied to us. I read. The Reporter copied. The labour was long & tedious. In the midst hunger asserted itself. I went to the buffet & ate 2 cold beef pies washed down with some brandy & soda water, while the reporter wrote at my dictation. I heard that Lyon Playfair's speech[270] had already been sent to the Times & to-day I am sorry that my report of his speech had not been sent as it is more full than that published – a far better speech. In fact, the speech was too good to be dealt with in so summary & clumsy a fashion [...]

---

[267] In June 1849; Frederick Knight Hunt, *The Fourth Estate: Contributions towards a history of newspapers and of the liberty of the press* (1850), ii. 286.

[268] 209:45 against Watkin Williams' resolution for disestablishment; *H* cci. 1274–91.

[269] 229:88 to adjourn the House. The Home Secretary, Bruce, announced that a Royal Commission would be appointed.

[270] Supporting the Contagious Diseases acts.

Wednesday, 25 May: Finding that the Times's report of Dr Lyon Playfair's speech was not as full & satisfactory as it deserved, I sought him &, finding him, brought to his notice a draft report wh. represented pretty well the bulk of his arguments. A few points required elucidation & additions. These he supplied. I then went to the gallery in order to procure the insertion of the amended speech in the Times. But it was too late. The interest of the Times people was, I suppose, not concerned in correcting the report already published. At any rate, I was unsuccessful. Meanwhile, my labour may not be thrown away, as Hansard may want a full report of the debate.[271]

[...] In the matter of reporting the debates, there is to me this comfort – that if I cannot say good things, I can help convey good things to the Public. It has been my luck to take this task in 1843,[272] in 1849 and 1870.

Thursday, 26 May: It is said that one lady could hardly be induced to leave the gallery when strangers were ordered to withdraw. Some wag observed she was 'the deceased (diseased?) wife's sister' [...]

Friday, 27 May: St Aubyn convened a little Parliament on the Mines Inspection Bill. Pendarves Vivian, Lord G. Cavendish & Wentworth Beaumont were of the number. We discussed some of the clauses of the Bill [...]

Sunday, 29 May: The progress of the land bill was more rapid than I expected.[273] My prediction that it would come to being dealt with by way of resolutions has been falsified. Still there is no saying what the Lords may do. It is extra-ordinary how little good one hears of the Bill from Irishmen of any party.

Looking back on the Debate on Fowler's motion, I think Henley has laid himself open to serious comment. Was not he in Parliament in 1864 when this legislation commenced? Did he ever fail in detecting a flaw in a Bill? Was he for the only time in his life during the progress of a measure – asleep? He is distinctly in fault if 2 committees have sat & reported, & if 3 acts have passed full of unconstitutional & even immoral provisions without his interference & denunciation. An enemy would say that he waited for a wind before he set his sails. To say this were unjust, but I feel sure the fact of the breeze suggested its use.

---

[271] *H* cci. 1307–47 reports the speeches 'so far as they can be ascertained'. This was at least partly based on Trelawny's notes: see below, 5 July 1870.

[272] In a part of his diary entry for 20 Mar. 1872 (not printed), Trelawny mentions that this was on 12 May 1843, *H* lxix. 313–14, during a tempestuous debate on the corn laws.

[273] It was now through the committee stage.

Ayrton, too, was a strenuous opponent of the Bill in 1864. How came
he to let the bill of 1866 become law?

Monday, 30 May: St Aubyn, Lord G. Cavendish, Mr W. Beaumont,
Pendarves Vivian & I in company with Mr T.S. Bolitho (from Cornwall)
met Mr Bruce in Mr J.G. Dodson's[274] room for the purpose of settling
certain clauses in the Mines Inspection Bill so as to prevent unnecessary
collision in the House.

[...] Henley recurred to the late notice taken by Craufurd of the
presence of strangers. Gladstone judiciously replied, reminding Henley
that he[275] was a member of a committee upon the subject after John
O'Connell's exclusion of the strangers in 1849. * The Committee was
appointed 15th June 1849. * That Committee unanimously reported in
favour of the retention of the power. Shielding Craufurd a little
Gladstone observed that there was a division of opinion out of doors
upon Craufurd's course.

[...] Henley did not seem to like the publication of the account I
gave to the Times, calling it 'garbled'. The fact is the report of his
speech was in substance provokingly accurate – & perhaps he gave
himself a license in absurdity in the belief that the Public would not
know the worst. His sneer at the bishops[276] may have displeased his
constituents.

Friday, 31 May: [...] I omitted to mention a kind of duel betwn.
Corry & Baxter.[277] Baxter greatly distinguished himself. He seems to
have turned the admiralty office inside out, laying bare no end of
nefarious transactions.

[...] I note that the Press is by no means unfavourable in its view
of Craufurd's course. The fact is the violence of certain women in the
treatment of the Contagious Disease question has reacted against
them &, perhaps, the cause they so vehemently espouse. Calm &
discerning people have been led to make inquiries which have resulted
in exposure of much exaggeration [...]

Thursday, 9 June: Holidays over.[278] Again the Mill [...] On the
exemption from the horse tax for horses occasionally employed on
team work on the roads for hire, Ministers were defeated by 4 votes

[274] Chairman of committees.
[275] i.e. Gladstone.
[276] Describing the 5 bishops who had signed a petition supporting the Contagious
Diseases acts as 'a smartish lot to go into an affair of this kind'; *H* cci. 1338.
[277] Parliamentary secretary to the admiralty.
[278] Parliament had ajourned for Whitsun on 31 May.

(49 to 45), even Mr Speaker supporting the exemption[279] [...]

Friday, 10 June: [...] It is an inconvenience in our orders & proceedings that no one can foresee on which of the many questions standing as amendments on going into supply a division will be taken – indeed, one can[no]t foresee which question will actually be taken. To remain from 4 p.m. till 2 a.m. on the chance of some particular motion coming on is a serious addition to Parliamentary engagements. It so happened that Mr Campbell brought on his resolution in favour of County representation for purposes of local govt. Had I known that this would be certainly taken & at a suitable time, I shd. have been glad to hear his speech as his measure was at one time in my charge (1863?).[280] It seemed to me that Bruce's answer, as printed, was of the official type and not satisfactory. The terms of Campbell's motion were general & moderate.[281] Any one favouring the principle of County Representative governmt. might fairly have voted for that motion – unless, indeed, he shd. have had reason to prefer, in the Public interest, the motion to wh. Campbell moved an amendmt. that motion being 'that I do now leave the chair' for the purpose of going into committee of supply. * Mem. An amendment to the motion 'that I do now leave the chair' is not a well-chosen way of introducing a project of legislation. Votes given according to this manner of proceeding must be deceptive. A warm friend of Financial Boards might well vote 'aye' to the above question, such vote being in effect adverse to the objects of the mover of the amendment. *

Monday, 13 June: I note that Bob Lowe's Inland Revenue Bill has the new clause about horses employed occasionally on team work for repair of roads. Who can say that Mr Speaker's intervention was thrown away? If my memory deceive me not, he interfered in a recent session to save breeders from a tax on brood mares.[282] I know his interest in this kind of stock.

The University Tests Bill passed thro' Committee & 4 divisions were taken. My pair for the night was Mr Walter Powell. Gladstone exposed himself to adverse criticism by avowing the dependence of governmt. on the terms of an understanding entered into with certain University

---

[279] With the House in committee, the Speaker himself spoke in favour of Gregory's motion against the horse licence; Ossington, *Journal*, 257.

[280] It was slightly earlier; *T.D.*, 20 Mar. 1861.

[281] ' ... the principle of representation ought to be applied to the government and financial administration of Counties'; *H* cci. 1853–61. Defeated, 61:39.

[282] See above, 28 May 1869.

Reformers. The Times rather severely notices this matter.[283]

J. Talbot moved the omission of words wh. seemed to him to allow of atheists obtaining educational offices. Ministers accepted his suggestion. Yet, there was a division. Of course, he succeeded[284] [...]

Tuesday, 14 June: Buxton delivered a good speech on a project he has for a concerted revision of the Bible, the Queen co-operating with the President of the United States. His account of the Bible was carefully prepared and heard by many with interest. His speech shd. be re-published. As to his plan, Gladstone raised a smile at it. Old Henley croaked – likewise, Newdegate. Indeed, these two members croak almost nightly as if no debate could be considered at an end on other terms.

After Buxton,[285] Col[onel] French introduced Irish matters; in particular, local taxation. Soon it was evident that the House was dwindling. Members gathered outside the glass doors. The Serjeant at Arms was among them, and evidently hoped for a count out. T. Collins was very active for this object, but left it to another – a young member – to take the necessary step. As any member returned to the House – some having reasons for keeping a House – the idle faction laughingly remonstrated, while in turn they were reproached for their desire to close business.

A member, Mr Montague Guest (as I since heard), now called attention to the state of the House. The bell rang – & the glass was turned. Members collected. Over 40 were pres[en]t and the debate was resumed.

Soon after another such attempt succeeded.

The anxiety to get a holiday was pretty generally shared. It was amusing to hear a member complain of the slowness of the sand in the minute glass, which he said must be wet. The Premier probably hoped for a quiet evening; yet, he stuck to his post and seemed to curiously, yet calmly, survey the faces of men peering in at the glass door with the object of discerning how soon it would be safe to send in a member who should arrest proceedings. The ringleader, Collins, went in & – as it were virtuously – took a seat on the liberal side so that no one could accuse him of anything & was shortly followed by his coadjutor. * (Later.) At the 2d. count, as I learn T. Collins nobly sacrificed himself by calling the Speaker's attention to the paucity of members present. *

---

[283] *The Times*, 14 June 1870, 9. The bill had now been adopted as a government measure. Gladstone admitted that he had made an agreement to exclude the Heads of Colleges from the bill's provisions; *H* cci. 1949–51. Cf. Gladstone to Benjamin Jowett, 13 June 1870, *G.D.*, vii. 306.

[284] 181:113. *H* cci. 1966–7, for the amendment.

[285] Motion withdrawn.

I attended twice, hoping that Gilpin would bring on his motion about business hours. He wants to carry a scheme of early closing.[286]

Wednesday, 15 June: Hardcastle in a creditable manner moved the 2d. reading of his Bill for the repeal of the Minority clauses of the last Reform Bill.[287] The debate was instructive. Several members contributed to it valuable materials. T. Collins acquitted himself very well, moving the previous question. The opinions of the school of J.S. Mill were ably propounded by W. Morrison,[288] who had much to offer in the shape of personal experience of American politics.

Gladstone was in favour of the measure of Hardcastle, but (in substance) stated the question was an open one amongst his govt. Disraeli was never favourable to these 'refined and fantastic' schemes, but, regard paid to the circumstances amidst which the plan was adopted – for its rejection he said would have been 'fatal to the Reform Bill' – was disposed to prefer the previous question. Fawcett, amidst much interruption, insisted on a hearing which, the strength of his lungs availing him, was not a difficult matter. Dodson & several others spoke briefly, Newdegate & Henley (of course) among the rest. On a division we had a tie. The Speaker gave his voice so that members might have an opportunity in the lobby of reconsidering their votes (a laugh) – whereupon we divided a 2d. time and were beaten. * Hardcastle on the Minority clauses. T. with him. Tie 181 to 181 on Previous question, on main question 175 to 183. Bill lost.[289]*

Thursday, 16 June: In a pretty full house Gladstone made a statement of certain extensive alterations which Ministers have agreed to make in the Education Bill.[290] This was not very pleasant to Vernon Harcourt if one might judge by his countenance. He had, I shd. observe, certain resolutions on the notice paper which he meant to offer as essential to

[286] His resolution that no opposed business should be brought on after midnight was raised on 21 June, but withdrawn; *H* ccii. 704–6.

[287] The 1867 Reform act provided that the cities of Birmingham, Manchester, Liverpool, Leeds and Glasgow, together with certain counties, should each return 3 members. In such constituencies, electors could only cast two votes.

[288] A supporter of proportional representation, who favoured the extension of the minority clauses; *H* ccii. 149–57.

[289] In fact there had been a mistake, and the bill should have been rejected on the first division; Ossington, *Journal*, 257–8.

[290] Voluntary schools were to be financially supported only by State grants, and not out of the rates; and Cowper-Temple's clause, proposing that religious instruction in Board Schools should exclude any 'catechism or religious formulary distinctive of any particular denomination', was adopted. *H* ccii. 266–85. For the background to these changes, see J.P. Parry, *Democracy and Religion: Gladstone and the Liberal Party, 1867–1875* (Cambridge, 1986), 303–4.

a measure of education. Disraeli & others followed Gladstone. It was clear that we had before us so new a plan that the House could not be asked to adopt it with[ou]t notice, so I went home [...]

Disraeli was caustic and amusing as usual, but certainly did not contribute much to chances of the Bill's success. * At one moment Disraeli, with a puzzled air, sought enlightenment by trying to find on the notice paper the language of one of the amendments on the education Bill, when T. Collins, with audacious officiousness, actually leapt up from his place below the gangway & put the words wh. D. wanted directly under his eyes. *

* Very adroit was D. in extorting a general cheer from Gladstone's follow[e]rs below the gangway by adverting to the creation of a new sacerdotal class in the schoolmasters to be constituted. Humourous, too, was his allusion to the amount of explanation of the Holy Scriptures we all require – the inference being that the poor would require more & thus each instructor would be a priest. * Gladstone was very wordy & consumed, as Disraeli observed, one hour and a half in making his new proposals without wasting a word upon them (a laugh). Cowper-Temple was evidently much pleased at his doctrine being accepted. He raised ironical laughter by his commendation of the Minister on his Statesmanlike course [...]

Friday, 17 June: [...] Ministers are praised for diminishing their patronage by a recent step in relation to vacant offices and for a change which has at last fixed the position of the F[iel]d M[arshall] Com[mandin]g in chief as subordinate to the Sec[retar]y of State for war.[291] This is a matter on which I took some action several years ago.[292] In vain, then – for household suffrage had not alarmed persons in high places.

Sunday, 19 June: There are now materials for forming opinions on the measure of Ministers for the education of the People. It occurs to me to ask myself whether we do not owe it to the future and to ourselves to secure education for children who, with[ou]t our intervention, wd. be uneducated. To this my reply is affirmative. Next I ask myself shd. the education given be secular? If possible, yes. But is purely-secular education possible? Again, what is one to say to those who think that the best secular education presents an inadequate, if not an evil, result

---

[291] Trelawny is referring to the changes made by two orders-in-council, the first, of 4 June, introducing competitive examinations for entrance to parts of the civil service, the second, signed by the Queen on 28 June, regulating the position of the commander-in-chief.

[292] *T.D.*, 22 and 24 Mar. 1865.

for money levied from the general taxpayers? Could a purely-secular school be entrusted to any but a secularist master? If not, what is to be said to R. Catholic candidates for such a post?

Dissenters are opposing 'denominationalism'. But this has for many years been in force at the expense of the Public, since grants from the Treasury have been given to Committees of denominational schools.[293] How is the case of principle altered by entrusting education to local Boards? It may even be said that a more immediate control is thus given to the Public. In short is it not necessary, if state education be adopted at all, to resort to compromise. Reduce it to a minimum if you will, but compromise there must be. Is the Ministerial Bill a fair one?

It may be said that tho' purely-secular education may be impossible, education shd. purport to be secular. The party who would maintain a close alliance betwn. religious and secular knowledge might reflect that reading and writing are working tools which may be rendered subservient to any purpose. The efforts of the Sunday School teacher would be greatly facilitated by preliminary training in an elementary secular school. Discipline in itself is a good step gained.

The difficulty of Ministers will be when their measure has passed. If dissenters definitively condemn it, there will be a new anti-rate agitation like that agt. Church rates.

Dissenters are thro' their activity and organization formidable. But the masses might be powerful enough to overbear dissenters; and, coming to find the advantages of elementary teaching, might exclaim in a peremptory tone 'away with your crotchets!' Most legislation invades private liberty. The question is, is legislation good?

Monday, 20 June: Mr Rich[ar]d of Merthyr Tydvil made an excellent speech in favour of an unskilfully-worded motion in amendmt. to the proposal for the Speaker leaving the chair that the House might go into committee on the education Bill.[294] Rich[ar]d is, I hear, a preacher & a dissenter of some note. His speech was a little like a sermon & perhaps used the name of the Deity too frequently.

Several Cornish members and others consulted me as to the vote to be given. My deliberate decision was agt. the amendmt. – or, rather, in favour of this proposition 'that the words proposed to be left out stand part of the question'. Now those words would be 'I do now leave the chair'. I do not see, how after allowing the principle of the education

---

[293] Since 1833.

[294] Opposing any increase in State grants to denominational schools, favouring a national system of elementary education with compulsory attendance, and urging that religious instruction should be left to the voluntary efforts of the religious denominations; *H* ccii. 495–510.

Bill to be affirmed on a 2d. reading, we shd. with fairness refuse to Ministers an occasion of moulding it in detail so as to bring it into harmony with the wants & wishes of the people [...]

Thursday, 23 June: [...] there were several divisions on Gun licenses. Peter Taylor objected to a measure for disarming the people – & divided.

The tax, fixed at 10/- was carried on a division by Ministers.[295] Originally, the sum was to have been £1.

Then there was a division on adjournt. wh. was defeated – and another one in which an amendmt. was carried agt. Ministers[296] & which extended the immunity given in the Bill to persons carrying guns on their own 'curtilage' to persons carrying them 'upon lands in the occupation of the owner of the gun'. Numbers 112 to 90.

Lowe noticed that the words would dispense with the tax in cases where persons were fortunate enough to occupy land and impose it on those who were not.

The Lords are engaged on the Irish land Bill. Will Govt. accept their amendments? Cabinet councils are rather frequent. Is it intended, as some hinted to me last night, that Ministers will take their victory & postpone the education Bill till another year?[297] This would not be the most foolish act they could perform.

Friday, 24 June: [...] At a morning (2 o'clock) sitting the Education Bill went into Committee; on the division the numbers were 421 to 60.[298] My vote was with Ministers.

[...] Gladstone, in his usual diffuse & copious style, indicated the points in which alterations were possible in the Bill. These are no longer considerable as governmt. have made up their minds not to be chargeable with a plastic liability to yield at every summons according as the Bill fails to please particular objectors.

A brother member and I took great pains to induce two of our hesitating friends to vote for the resolution to go into Committee, and we were successful.

Many members were at Her Majesty's breakfast at Windsor. The House of Lords might have spent its time there better than in mutilating the Irish land Bill. Had they thrown out the Bill on a 2d. reading, they might have had something to say for such a course, but to [amend] a

---

[295] 163:106.

[296] By Clare Sewell Read.

[297] No evidence for this. There were Cabinet meetings on 18 and 23 June, as well as 'smaller and larger conclaves respecting Land Bill'; *G.D.*, vii. 310–13.

[298] Against Richard's motion, continued from 20 June.

Bill which will only be useful at all if it at least purports to give a large measure of relief and which is sure to be carried is not a well considered course. There may be this result. The Irish may specially attach to the Lords the aversion now felt for English Rule.

Recurring to Somerset Beaumont's motion,[299] I think the Cornish clergy who want another bishop ought to be pleased at my vote. Also, those conservatives who disapprove of life-peerages. Yet, this is the only good thing in the law as it stands. The creation of suffragan bishops shews that bishops find their ecclesiastical labours very exhausting. How cruel we are!

Thursday, 30 June: A very long and interesting sitting.

The religious difficulty in the education Bill was handled with conscientious & painstaking care. Speeches were brief & pertinent – distinctions most refined.

In the early part of the even[in]g there was a division on an amendmt. proposed by Mr Samuelson of no great moment & not involving any question of principle. In this I took no part.[300]

Stafford Northcote's amendmt. we defeated.[301] His object was to reject the securities agt. teaching particular catechisms or formularies. This security was inserted at Cowper-Temple's suggestion.

Pakington's proposal that the Holy Scriptures 'shall form part of the daily reading & teaching in such school' also failed after debate & division.[302] In this division my name appears. * T. agt. Pakington. *

Jacob Bright's amendmt. was not more successful.[303] In this too I had an opportunity of voting. * T. agt. Jacob Bright. *

Both these last votes will probably lead to misunderstanding on the part of persons out of the House. Having attentively listened to arguments on both sides, I could not hesitate how I should decide.

Forster said that under the Bill there is nothing wh. prevents the reading of the Bible. It may too be expounded provided the clause protecting pupils agt. distinctive formularies is adhered to. But the enactment wh. Pakington insisted upon would have nullified the possible

---

[299] His Lords Spiritual bill, to remove bishops from the House of Lords, was defeated by 158:102 on 21 June. Trelawny had paired for the bill with C.H. Mills.

[300] Amendment to clause 10 that twenty householders (rather than a majority of ratepayers) could apply for a School Board to be set up; *H* ccii. 1225–6. Defeated, 249:63.

[301] 252:95; *H* ccii. 1236–44.

[302] 250:81; *H* ccii. 1265–7.

[303] 251:130 against the amendment to prohibit teaching 'in favour of or against the distinctive tenets of any religious denomination'; *H* ccii. 1270–1. Gladstone argued that the effect of this would be 'to introduce a new kind of State religion'; *H* ccii. 1280–2. 133 Liberals abstained from the division and only 91 non-government Liberals voted with Ministers, but '132 Conservatives ensured government victory'; Parry, *Democracy and Religion*, 306.

formation of purely secular schools where desired by rate-payers.

As to Jac. Bright's proposal, the speeches of R. Palmer & Gladstone were very cogent. The insertion of vague words restricting teachers from teaching anything favourable or unfavourable to the distinctive tenets of any religious denomination would be a trap to tender consciences & would not do credit to us as workmanlike constructors of acts of Parliament – inasmuch as an indictment could never be constructed upon shadowy differences in language & illustration. The distinctive formularies of sects – such as catechisms – are definite things & the use of such is precluded in terms under the clause (14). With this a majority were satisfied. The points raised were nice & it is not easy to describe them fully in this hasty way.

* If an instructor in a purely-secular school created by a school-board shd. attack with arguments in the presence of his scholars the tenet of any religious Body, he would come within the meaning of Bright's provision, as it would neither allow an instructor to advocate or oppose any such tenet. But how difficult to draw a line! a skilfully-contrived epithet would tend to sap a dogma. *

It was urged by more than one speaker that the measure is mainly devised on behalf of little children, for whom doctrinal teaching is in practice treated as unsuitable. In existing schools common sense treats as cobwebs difficulties which occupy much time in a legislative assembly. When one comes to the attempt to define in a Bill the course which common sense ought to take, the attempt at once proclaims itself impracticable.

Friday, 1 July: Dixon's amendmt. which would supply education free of expense was rejected.[304] The Division occurred before I came [...] The Bill provides for the case of very poor children who will be enabled to obtain education free of cost.[305] It does not seem well to imply that parents who can afford to pay school pence shd. be exempted from this charge at the Public expense.

There are no doubts many faults in the Bill which deals with complicated facts & existing undertakings betwn. the State & Local Bodies who have provided education in part by Voluntary subscriptions. It is no small matter after all to have before us a measure which proclaims the title of every child to be educated. If the measure pass, it will be the charta of the unconsulted Born – and time and experience will soon enable the governmt. to point out in what respects the law will require alteration.

---

[304] 257:32; *H* ccii. 1308–10.
[305] Provided for in clause 25 of the bill.

Monday, 4 July: Much talk about changes in the cabinet in consequence of Lord Clarendon's death.[306]

This day has been a busy and important one. There was news that
Forster & Ld. Halifax enter the cabinet.[307] Forster was warmly welcomed
in the H. of C. Both sides are pleased.

Ayrton, in some of his replies to questions on topics such as refreshmt.
rooms for Lords & Commons, seemed likely to alarm his leader.
Ayrton's frank reference, twice, to the 'peremptory' tone of those who
speak for their lordships on matters affect[in]g the accommodation to
be provided for them, might have sounded new to old-fashioned ears.
Be this as it may, Ayrton shd. study condensation in his answers & not
unnecessarily shew front.

There was a good deal of talk about the late 'counts out', Eykyn
leading.[308] Opinions on this point are at variance. It is considered by
some that the system is a barbarous relic. This is Hibbert's view. Other
people think it a valuable possession; to be, however, sparingly used.
Disraeli suggested that a 1/4 of an hour of law shd. be given at an
evening – 9 o'clock – sitting (as I believe he meant).

A 'massacre of innocents' took place. Many bills drop for this session.
More lives are threatened.

Bouverie usefully recalled the manner in wh. the new system on
fridays has grown up.[309]

The real mischief is the enormous increase of business wh. the H. of
C. has in charge & its appetite for every subject, great & small.

[...] Sir C. Dilke nearly carried agt. Ministers his amendmt. for
making ratepayers, instead of town-councils in towns & vestries in
parishes, the constituency for the creation of School Boards. (Numbers
150 to 145). * T. absent paired with a Tory. *

Lord F. Cavendish's proposal to adopt cumulative voting in the
constitution of Boards was adopted.[310] Gladstone professed to be guided
by reasons adduced in the debate. But does not the admission bear a
wider significancy? Is not the plan equally good for the constitution of
the House of Commons? A passing speculation.

[...] I omitted to notice some remarkable murmurs among the

---

[306] The Foreign Secretary had died on 27 June, and was succeeded by Lord Granville.

[307] Forster retained his post as Vice-President of the Council; Halifax became Lord
Privy Seal in place of Lord Kimberley, who succeeded Granville at the Colonial Office.

[308] Complaining that the rule that a quorum of 40 members was required for
proceedings to continue was making it difficult for private members motions; *H* ccii.
1365-6.

[309] Fridays had changed from being government nights to supply nights, which enabled
M.P.s to raise issues of their choice in the form of amendments to the main motion; see
William White, *The Inner Life of the House of Commons* (ed. Justin McCarthy, 1897), ii. 191-
3.

[310] Agreed without a division.

Conservatives when, in reply to a question, Bruce said that, owing to a feeling prevalent in England, the Census of 1871 would not exact an account of the religious opinions of the inhabitants of that part of the Empire. Such an account is obtained now in Ireland & will be forthcoming in respect of Scotland. There are many secularists in England. Perhaps, these are afraid of the law if they avow their belief or they may dread social persecution.

Tuesday, 5 July: [...] In the morning I drove to Mr Hansard's in the Temple to give him another chance of adding Henley's speech to the Contagious Diseases debate. The speech was transcribed from my notes, the report in the Times being only a condensation of these made by the + staff + authority of that paper. It remains to be seen whether Henley will correct the speech & let it be inserted in Hansard's debates.[311]

I called Forster's attention to an important book on America – 'the Americans at home' by Macrae[312] – that he might use the facts therein related in meeting objections to his education Bill – these facts bearing upon the religious difficulty which in American Common Schools gives little or no trouble.

I wrote for Mr J. White a form of questions to the Minister for war with the object of eliciting the fact of the D[uke] of Cambridge remaining in command after 5 years have elapsed, there being a rule on this point affecting staff officers.[313]

Wednesday, 6 July: I gave my vote with Mr Brown in favour of his Bill intended to repeal the 25 & 26 Vic. 114.[314] This is a very harsh and unconstitutional game Law.

On this motion I hazarded a few observations. Sir Geo. Grey & Bruce distinguished themselves as apt observers of old official traditions according to which time is gained by frivolous objections and unreal pleas. Twenty five years ago, I sat on Bright's committee.[315] The whole Game Law was turned inside out. Now, an experienced ex-Home Sec[retar]y[316] suggests further inquiry, deprecating an 'early' repeal of a law which he opposed on its introduction in 1862!

After I had left the House, Hughes's Sunday Trading Bill was taken.

---

[311] It was; *H* cci. 1338.
[312] David Macrae, *The Americans at Home* (Edinburgh, 1870).
[313] Raised on 11 July; *H* cciii. 30–1. Cardwell, the War Secretary, confirmed that the commander-in-chief was exempted from section 106 of the Royal warrant.
[314] 2nd reading of the Poaching Prevention act repeal bill, defeated 140:62.
[315] *P.P.* 1845, xii. 331; 1846, ix. 1.
[316] i.e. Grey.

Division.[317] It will either drop or be torn to pieces in Committee.

The Law of Charles 2d. is unworkable. Magistrates inflict nominal penalties. Hughes seeks to pass a Bill that may be carried out. But this is virtually and up to a certain extent new legislation inasmuch as the Law of Charles 2d. is in many respects a dead letter.

It is worthwhile to make a note that the act Mr Brown sought to repeal is Sir Baldwin Leighton's act. I believe it passed in the summer of 1862. The Country gentlemen attended in great strength and forced it thro' the House[318] [...] The Law gives great power to the Police, who are virtually made gamekeepers.

Thursday, 7 July: On my arrival, I found the House had resolved itself into a committee on the Education Bill. Clause 45 was under discussion. Sir M. Lopes's proposal to limit rates to 1d. was opposed by Ministers on the ground that the total to be p[ai]d by rates would thus only amount to £200,000 – too small a sum to ensure local activity & care. My pair for the night was Baillie Cochrane, who stated that he was for Lopes.[319]

Vernon Harcourt discoursed on his projected amendmt. which would purport to limit the rates to 1/6th of the costs. Ministers, yielding apparently to pressure, have indicated an intention of proposing in clause 82 a proviso that costs betwn. the product of a 3d. rate and a capitation grant of 7/6 shd. be made good by an extra Privy Council grant.

Mr Forster argued that a dependence upon rates alone would be the starvation of schools, while dependence on the Public exchequer would put an end to efficiency.

Northcote had given notice of a proposal to divide the liability thro' any deficiency betwn. payers of rates & the Public taxpayer. This was to be adopted in clause 82. But Harcourt would have it at once. However, he was defeated (176 to 21) [...]

Friday, 8 July: Division occurred in Committee on the question of compulsion as distinguished from permissive compulsion which Forster's Bill proposes.[320] My voice in each case was with Ministers. Matters are not in a state for which direct compulsion seems applicable. That educational measures may gravitate tow[ar]ds compulsion is not unlikely.

At the even[in]g (9 o'clock sitting) Mr W.H. Smith defeated Ministers

---

[317] 109:64 for the 2nd reading, but it proceeded no further.
[318] *T.D.*, 23 and 24 July 1862.
[319] The amendment was defeated, 273:88.
[320] Sir Thomas Bazley's amendment to clause 65, defeated 230:92; *H* ccii. 1716–17.

by a large majority on his amendmt. to going into Committee of Supply. That amendmt. proposed a certain dealing with the Crown Foreshore property n[ea]r West[minste]r Bridge which would appear to be a confiscation of such property to the extent of £150,000 for the benefit of Metropolitan ratepayers.[321] No doubt, there is an allegation on their behalf that the land recovered was worthless till their rates were expended on it.

I was not present on the occasion of this motion coming on.

A note of what I observed on the Education Debate: – Fawcett haranguing at 20 minutes to 6. How he rants! Poor Ministers! There is Forster looking with eye glass most wistfully at the clock, Gladstone next, arms crossed over his legs with a look of fatigued resignation, Bruce wishing Fawcett at the devil. ('Divide Divide'.).

Monday, 11 July: [...] Trevelyan endeavoured to explain his abandonmt. of his place in the govt.[322] It is not clear to me that, if abandonment was proper, it did not come too late.

[...] The thorny point during the night was the favour shewn by Ministers to the principle expressed by the new word 'denominationalism'.[323] This was the avowed ground of Trevelyan's resignation [...]

Tuesday, 12 July: I have paired (except on the Mines Bill[324] and the Contagious Diseases Bill) from (after) frid[a]y the 15th till the end of the session with Lord Henry Scott. This is booked by Mr Adam & Mr Glyn.

[...] There were 5 divis[io]ns on Lords amendmts. to the Land Bill. These turn much on nice details & can hardly be handled here. I voted in 3 divisions.

Govt. seemed to exercise their power moderately, only insisting upon disagreemt. with the Lords in cases in which agreemt. would most likely peril the Bill. Disraeli seemed to be equally discreet. The Bill will pass.

[...] Fortescue[325] had the task of defending the scale of compensations

---

[321] Smith moved that no public buildings should be erected on that part of the embankment which was reserved to the crown and which had been reclaimed from the river at the ratepayer's expense; *H* ccii. 1752–8. Amendment carried, 156:106, the government's defeat 'not averted by Gladstone's angry & unconciliatory speech'; *G.H.D.*, 9 July 1870.

[322] He had resigned as a Lord of the Admiralty because of his opposition to the Education bill.

[323] Hostile speeches by Candlish and Dixon; *H* cciii. 66–7.

[324] Which was eventually withdrawn.

[325] Irish Chief Secretary.

to Irish tenants. No wonder the Peers could not understand it. Why, it is an arithmetical Sphinx! Disraeli's face in listening to Fortescue seemed to me to express confused wonder and sense of fun. Both, however, subdued to the very faintest expression.

The time lost in dividing to-day was even more than usual. It must have been at least 1 1/2 hours. As many stood imprisoned behind the glass doors, at which we pass the tellers, there was much grumbling of imprisoned members – which at length culminated in a dismal universal groan in loudest tones. On this the doors were opened [...]

Wednesday, 13 July: I heard the debate on Lawson's Permissive Bill[326] and he did not convince me to vote with him. There was great weight in Kennaways's remark that a majority of 2/3rds of the ratepayers might be a minority of the Inhabitants.

In America we are told drinks may be got by entering a house and asking for the baby, whereon a customer is directed to a backroom affording every facility for getting the supply required. The applicant then leaves the House, depositing a sum at the bar with another reference to baby's health.

A member told me that a native American laughs at the difficulty of getting whiskey. He goes at once for it to the chemists as for physic.

The poor, says Wheelhouse, cannot afford cellars. Again – why not close the clubs?

Lawson is reminded that he proposes to ruin a great industry without compensation. The value of the property of licencees is estimated at £100,000,000 – and the annual business is worth it is added £20,000,000! However this be, it is a strong thing to rob the Innkeepers &c. upon the grounds shewn by the mover.

The Bill is most unfair. A yearly disturbance of the question is allowed to those who wd. suppress the traffic. But if a vote suppress it, it is 3 years before rate-payers can release themselves from the law.

Lawson's contention that the Bill did not close a single Public house was not in spirit accurate. By the Bill, a majority of 2/3rds would eventually cause the refusal of new licenses and the non-renewal of expiring licenses. How can Lawson say, with a grave face, that his measure would not close a single Public house? I refer to the Times that I may not attribute to him language which he did not use.

[...] Bruce[327] might have saved his supporters much embarrassmt. had he prepared a measure for the improvemt. of our Licensing system. He pleads for time but a Bill might have been prepared under his orders, printed & read a 1st time.

---

[326] 2nd reading of the Permissive Prohibitory bill, empowering ratepayers to close down public houses.
[327] Home Secretary.

We won by a rather small majority. Numbers 121 to 90.

The House now resolved itself into Committee on the Burials Bill. We had one division – & the time we had was purposely wasted.[328] This mode of warfare was not even decently veiled. The reflection wh. occurred to me was that the Church will be ruined by her friends. * As the hand approached 1/4 before 6, a gallant Colonel who had been evidently engaged in these tactics, professed, on sitting down, with a smile on his face, to give his friend below the remaining time. This was Col[onel] Bartellot. Others rivalled him in this [illegible] * [...]

Thursday, 14 July: [...] It seems that Fowler will insist on the adjourned debate on contagious diseases coming on next Wed[nesda]y. Also, Craufurd will probably call attention to the presence of strangers. He is to let me know his decision on this. He told me that my reporting wd. be a breach of privilege. I replied that I did not care & they might commit me for contempt. He then said that he would raise the point. I said I did not care a – & that I would make him pay for my supper. (Much laughter.)

[...] I suspect the explanation of his [Fowler's] course on the Contagious Diseases question is that there is a rigorous system in force at Cambridge relating to these cases & that the system is unpopular there. Does the member attack the new laws as a mode of assailing the local institution?

[...] The evening – nay, the night – was in a great measure consumed in discussions of Ballot &c. as applied to the Education Bill (which was, however, triumphantly carried thro' committee). The Times mentions 12 divisions – mostly, factious. The House adjourned at ab[ou]t 5 1/4 a.m. (after the gas was turned off) on this **Friday July 15th!!** What will the Public say? Where are the Statesmen? Where is caution, moderation, Policy? Is the character of Parliament nothing? * I paired till 10.30 p.m. Afterwards, voted (1) agt. Bartellot's proposal to report progress[329] & (2) that the word 'provided' stand part of certain words – these being 'That any Poll shall be taken by a Secret Ballot'. I understood that on our carrying the word 'provided' any plan of voting papers or some form of Ballot might still be an occasion of voting. However, the Times, I see, reads the decision as a decision on the Ballot itself. Numbers 234 to 155.[330] *

The Ballot question in the education Bill presented difficulties – especially, as the word 'secret' was not to be used. It was explained

---

[328] 143:54 against Goldney's superfluous amendment; *H* cciii. 192. The bill was later withdrawn.

[329] Bartellot defeated, 244:136.

[330] Against Hope's amendment; *H* cciii. 296. Cf. *The Times*, 15 July 1870, 8.

that this meant not that votes would not be in practice secret, but that secrecy was not made absolute. * One form of Ballot leaves scrutiny as a possible incident, another purposes to be final. * However, the want of certainty as to this was a subject of hostile feeling on the part of Ballotists, while the opposition deprecated the introduction of the Ballot into an education Bill. It was urged that a great change of this kind ought to be adopted if at all after proceedings taken for that special object & that the change ought not to be the effect of a side wind.

Frankly, I was unable to come to a satisfactory judgment on the balance of arguments presented to me. Accordingly, so far as goes my interpretation of the complicated forms in which issues were put, no vote of mine was given committing me for or agt. the Ballot [...]

White, doorkeeper, told me that the reporters had left the House before business terminated. Certainly, the struggle was heroic & Ministers deserve great praise.[331]

Friday, 15 July: [...] War, it is reported, has been declared betwn. France & Prussia. Madmen!

Wednesday, 20 July: [...] The adjourned debate on Contagious Diseases followed, when Craufurd called the Speaker's attention to the presence of strangers, so speeches were delivered in camera. Elphinstone rose to order, adverting to the fact that a member was taking notes. The Speaker ruled that this was not contrary to order. The debate was continued till the moment at which it was closed by the operation of a standing order.[332]

Wednesday, 27 July: Memorable as the day on which the English Prime Minister declared to Parliament and justified so far as might be his adhesion to the Ballot.[333] The gist of his arguments is this:– The Ballot used to be opposed by Palmerston & others on the ground that voting is the act of a Trustee for the benefit of all including the unrepresented; that household suffrage is virtually universal suffrage in boroughs already & the adoption of household suffrage in counties is only an affair of time; & that hence a man is only responsible to himself and the Public are not concerned to know how he votes. Disraeli

[331] It has been suggested that the government was seeking to placate the radicals after having dropped the Parliamentary Elections bill; Kinzer, *Ballot Question*, 141–4. In the event, the House of Lords struck out the ballot clause from the Education bill.

[332] i.e. at a quarter to six. The bill did not come on again. See *H* cciii. 574–607 for an account of the debate as far as it could be ascertained: the extent of Trelawny's contribution to this report is unknown.

[333] Gladstone declared his support for Leatham's Ballot bill, which was given its 2nd reading without a division; *H* cciii. 1028–34. No further progress made.

severely criticized Gladstone's mode of treating the subject. It strikes me, after reading his statement carefully, that so long at least as household suffrage is confined to Boroughs, his contention is, on his own shewing, faulty.

It is rather alarming to some to observe the agility with wh. he conforms his opinions to those which he had but lately opposed.[334] The case of the deceased wife's sister was a case in point.[335] The premier has a high character for conscientiousness and may incur no suspicions where a less conscientious man would hardly escape injurious comments [...]

Friday, 29 July: [...] I was this ev[enin]g in conversation with a liberal ex-cabinet minister.[336] Our chief topic was the Ballot a propos of Gladstone's conversion to it.

The doctrine of my friend was this; – a vote is neither a property nor a trust. The Nation requires of a man his unbiassed judgment on the qualities of the candidates named. The machinery which elicits this judgment shd. be adopted & the Ballot would answer the purpose. How ab[out] the pride of consistency and the consequent desire to be careful at first in forming opinions? How ab[ou]t the useful effect on others, when a man of sense, cultivation & integrity has steadily maintained a particular opinion?

A passing remark with reference to the Permissive Liquor Bill,[337] – why shd. 2 out of 3 persons prevent the 3rd. from buying a glass of beer? It is replied, because some people may get drunk. This answer is inadequate; yet, in effect, it is almost all that can be said. If the use of ardent spirits has in general effects such as to warrant coercive measures, such measures shd. be general & be the effect of imperial legislation. Besides, 2/3rds of a body of ratepayers are not even a majority of the inhabitants of a place [...]

Monday, 1 August: [...] Great Britain is arming herself.[338] Shall we drift into war again?

Thursday, 4 August: [...] The education Bill appears now to be safe.[339] This is satisfactory to me, as I very steadily supported Ministers

---

[334] Gladstone had changed his mind on the subject in 1868, when he had been anxious to secure John Bright's adhesion to his new government; Kinzer, *Ballot Question*, 146–7.

[335] See above, 27 Apr. 1870.

[336] Probably either C.P. Villiers or Thomas Milner Gibson.

[337] See above, 13 July 1870.

[338] On 2 Aug. parliament voted for a £2 million credit and 20,000 extra troops; *H* cciii. 1300.

[339] Royal assent, 9 Aug.

upon the measure. I doubt if in any instance my vote was registered agt. them, though the secret ballot, had issue been joined on it, might have given me trouble. However, it was hardly on all fours with Political Ballot [...]

Tuesday, 9 August: Mr Bruce took occasion to indicate the subjects on wh. he intends to propose bills next session.[340] He takes this course in order, I think, to cover his inaction in this session – of which the Press seems to be disposed to complain.

[...] It is noteworthy that Jacob Bright & Sir W. Lawson protest agt. entanglements in Continental affairs, while P. Taylor distinctly disavows such notions of isolation.[341]

Wednesday, 10 August: Some serious carping at Ministerial policy on the War. Osborne the chief aggressor. J. White another. Long explanation by Gladstone. Notable abstinence of Disraeli.

It occurs to me that if the new treaty adds anything to the treaty of 1839,[342] we are committed to new entanglements; if it detract from that treaty, we shall seem to meditate a breach of faith. Should we stand in a worse position if we had calmly and inoffensively announced the course which in certain events duty would call upon us to perform? This is the crude question of an uninformed spectator.

So ends the session.

---

[340] The Home Secretary's speech mentioned, inter alia, a Licensing bill, a Trade Union bill and a Mines Regulation bill; *H* cciii. 1734–5.

[341] All were prominent radicals.

[342] On 9 Aug. Britain had signed a treaty with Prussia reaffirming the neutrality of Belgium (as guaranteed by the treaty of 1839), and stating that if either Prussia or France violated this neutrality Britain would intervene with the other in order to defend Belgium. *B.F.S.P.*, lx. 13–17. A similar treaty with France was signed on 11 Aug.: *B.F.S.P.*, lx. 10–13.

SESSION OF 1871

Thursday, 9 February: The House met about 2 p.m. and, after attend[in]g in H. of Lords, resumed at 1/4 before 4, when numerous notices of motions were made by Ministers & others. The faces of the front bench of conservatives looked more & more bleak as each Ministerial promise to deal with an important subject was given. Evidently the Premier has well-disciplined his corps and insisted on prompt performance of their duties.[343]

Mr J.G. Hamilton moved the address in a fair speech of 25 minutes duration. Morley followed him, with some credit. Both read a good deal from notes. In fact, the two speeches were in considerable part read – &, I may say, skilfully read. Not an easy feat. The House was very quiet & tolerant – & each speaker earned some cheers.

Disraeli at once launched out into criticism.[344] His speech I reserved for perusal; as, also, Gladstone's.

When Morley adverted to some plan of conciliation betwn. Nations in order to settle quarrels with[ou]t war, the usually-impassible face of Disraeli fairly gave way & he allowed himself a rather hearty laugh. That is for him, tho' of course I don't mean aloud. But, certainly, after the experience one has had of mankind during 1/2 a century, the idea does seem a little utopian. Possibly the sight of the great dissenting leader preaching peace & goodwill, in a flaming Dep[u]ty Lieutenants uniform, brand new, tickled Disraeli's fancy.

Monday, 13 February: [...] I heard Gladstone's lengthy speech on the vote in favour of Princess Louise,[345] wh. passed nem. con. It would appear that, after his speech & the reasons he advanced, the opponents hesitated; but, perhaps, we shall hear more of them at a later stage [...]

Tuesday, 14 February: Several measures of importance were intro-

---

[343] Gladstone's Cabinet notes of 2 Nov. 1870 and 25 Jan. 1871 show the government's intentions for an ambitious legislative programme; *G.D.*, vii. 390, 438. The latter note listed five issues as of prime importance: abolition of University Tests; abolition of the Ecclesiastical Titles act; an Army Regulation bill; a Ballot bill, and a Trade Union bill.

[344] Arguing that government economies in the armed forces had rendered Britain impotent in Europe; *H* cciv. 70–96.

[345] A dowry of £30,000 and an annuity of £6,000, on her marriage to the Marquis of Lorne.

duced. Mr Bruce seeks to amend the Laws relating to combinations of workmen &c. and appeared to meet the approval of the representatives of labour and capital.[346]

Mr Lefevre introduced a bill on Inclosures – & Collier a bill for the repeal of the ecclesiastical Titles act.[347] * Note. See a letter to the West Briton at the time.[348] The Cornish gentlemen had an indignation meeting. * It rejoices me to live to see the day when an obnoxious statute which I for one strenuously opposed comes to be properly dealt with.

Much of my time was employed in County business which involved attendance at the Treasury and writing letters relating to Post office vacancies.

Thursday, 16 February: Cardwell introduced his great scheme for the better organization of the Army.[349] He had a decided success, but doubts arise whether the 'advanced' Liberals will like the expense to be incurred. His voice is weak and we had some difficulty in follow[in]g his statement, wh. however was fluent and nearly faultless as a composition. Indeed, it was a good Review article. Opinions upon the changes proposed would be premature.

Peter Taylor opposed the dowry of £30,000 for the Princess Louise. The House was somewhat impatient; in fact, hungry. Sir Robert Peel severely commented upon Gladstone's statements made in recommending the grant. Peel considered that Gladstone overstrained the facts of the case as regards arrangements made on the accession of W[illia]m the 4th.[350]

But the noteworthy thing was Peel's animadversion on the Queen's neglect to entertain foreigners and the burthen cast upon the Prince of Wales, whose allow[an]ce Peel would double. As to the marriage, he thought it impolitic & stigmatized it as a marriage of the Princess with a minister at the advice of Ministers![351]

---

[346] The Home Secretary's Trades Union bill, giving legal recognition to unions, received the Royal assent on 29 June, along with a Criminal Law amendment bill containing provisions regarding peaceful picketing which were originally in the Trades Union bill; *P.P.* 1871, vi. 267; i. 347.

[347] The Home undersecretary's Inclosure Law amendment bill was later withdrawn; the Attorney General's repeal bill received the Royal assent on 24 July.

[348] *West Briton*, 10 Jan. 1851, 4–5.

[349] The Army Regulation bill, re-organising the army (particularly the reserve forces) and abolishing the purchase of commissions; Thomas F. Gallagher, '"Cardwellian Mysteries": The Fate of the Army Regulation Bill, 1871', *Historical Journal*, xviii (1975), 327–48.

[350] Peel challenged Gladstone's claim that William IV had received more for the civil list than Queen Victoria; *H* cciv. 367–8.

[351] Lorne was the eldest son of the Duke of Argyll, the Secretary of State for India.

On a division we were 350 to 1 – the 1 being Fawcett. People laughingly asked how he found his way into the lobby? It is said Taylor led him back.

During his[352] speech, when he spoke of a ministerial statement as worthy of the days of the Stuarts, Fawcett alone – in a silent House – cheered loudly – wh. was too much even for Disraeli.

[...] The new dining-room was crammed. The waiting seemed to me to be bad. Probably, more members than usual dined. Sir Henry Storks was there, who had just taken his seat after having been under a shower of stones thrown at him by some people at Ripon.[353]

Friday, 17 February: [...] There is reason for the opinion that the Contagious Diseases acts will fall – slain by their proper protectors – the Governmt! It is said that the mot d'ordre is somewhat of this kind, 'the acts are dying fast – *give them a kick*!' Of what use, then, was the appoint[men]t of a Royal Commission?[354] Probably, it has gained time for Ministers.

The Commission sits regularly thrice a week.

Monday, 20 February: [...] in Committee on University Tests. Stevenson moved to sweep away from clause 3 the exception in favour of Divinity Degrees wh. the Bill proposes.[355] Playfair's speech alone went far to convince me that the amendmt. was right. We were beaten. Numbers 185 to 140.

Next Fawcett proposed that the taking of holy orders shall no longer be a condition of holding the headship or fellowships of a college. Govt. won by Tory aid. Numbers 182 to 160.[356] There was much cheering. Gladstone was very resolute, alleging that govt. has already 'pondered' its course & the consequences.

Playfair's account of a Scotch system of instruction in divinity which is available by & useful to students holding any kind of religious creed

---

[352] i.e. Taylor's.

[353] General Storks had been brought into parliament to assist the government in passing its army reforms. His earlier attempts to gain election to the Commons were hampered by the hostile campaigns against him by opponents of the Contagious Diseases acts; H.J. Hanham, *Elections and Party Management: Politics in the Time of Disraeli and Gladstone* (2nd ed., Brighton, 1978), 218–20.

[354] In Nov. 1870, of which Trelawny was a member; Paul McHugh, *Prostitution and Victorian Social Reform* (London, 1980), 60–4.

[355] Divinity students could still be required to subscribe to a religious formulary; *H* cciv. 500–1.

[356] The majority included 112 Conservatives, and only 31 British Liberal backbenchers; J.P. Parry, *Democracy and Religion: Gladstone and the Liberal Party, 1867–1875* (Cambridge, 1986), 308. Fawcett's amendment only applied to *clerical* fellowships.

was very instructive [...] The principles held by all shd. I imagine, if any, be taught at Universities.

Some of us had doubts about our votes. It might have seemed important to send up the Bill in the form it had last year, but, really, little good seems to come of the endeavours made from time to time to render measures agreeable to the Lords. A step in advance may do no harm.[357]

Tuesday, 21 February: Trevelyan moved his resolutions on the Army.[358] His speech was good – full and energetic. The House gave him a very good hearing. Osborne taunted him with delivering a speech which had been already spoken over & over again in the provinces.

Vivian & Cardwell defended the Duke of Cambridge's tenure of office.

It was impossible that I who had frequently called attention to the exemption of the officer Command[in]g in chief from the 5 years rule applicable to other officers could abstain from supporting Trevelyan.[359] I paired with Sir Wm. Russell and went home.

Wednesday, 22 February: It being Ash Wed[nesda]y, the House met at 2 p.m. Plimsoll, in a long & energetic speech, moved the 2d. reading of a Bill for the inspection of ships. Henley, in his quaint way, tore the plan to bits amid much laughter. Plimsoll made the great mistake of overstating his case. Govt. has a measure, which purports to deal with the evils P. complains of.[360] There is no doubt ships unfit for use are sent to sea [...]

Friday, 24 February: For 4 1/2 hours I attended a sitting of the Commissioners on Contagious Diseases. The work is very heavy and I find it difficult to do much in the H. of C., where, however, I was present for sometime.

Disraeli made a long speech on the neutralization of the Black sea.[361] He appears to have annoyed Gladstone exceedingly. The speech was,

---

[357] The bill finally passed; Royal assent 16 June.

[358] That military re-organisation must include an alteration in the tenure of the commander-in-chief (the Duke of Cambridge, the Queen's cousin); *H* cciv. 590–612.

[359] Whose resolutions were defeated, 201:83.

[360] Plimsoll withdrew his bill; however the government's Merchant Shipping bill, introduced on 13 Feb., was also subsequently dropped.

[361] In Oct. 1870 Russia had seized the opportunity afforded by the Franco-Prussian war to denounce the clauses of the Treaty of Paris (1856) which excluded her warships from the Black Sea. A conference of the European Powers in London, in Jan. 1871, effectively accepted Russia's action, agreeing to the abrogation of the Black sea clauses; *B.F.S.P.* lvi. 1193–1227.

in my judgment, a good one. Gladstone has been wanting, of late, in temper, discretion & straightforwardness. How could he make such a mistake as that of citing alleged opinions of Lord Clarendon & Lord Palmerston without full assurance that such opinions were really held by those ministers? Of course, my allusion is to the notion that they attached small importance to the neutralization of the Black sea.[362]

How could Gladstone suggest to Sir S. Robinson to alter the date of his letter?[363] Even if Gladstone could shew that the alteration would be formal, why give the enemy cause to blaspheme?

It seems to me that he lost his temper – & Disraeli, who is provokingly calm, actually shone by contrast. It is not clear to me that the Tories will not soon put govt. in a minority by proposing a vote in wh. the radicals will join. On Fawcett's motion govt. only won by Tory aid.[364] 'Non tali auxilis &c.'

By the way, Gladstone's reply to Disraeli on the subject of Odo Russell's threat to Bismarck that we might have to go to war with Russia with or with[ou]t allies is quite indefensible. No one, scarcely, will believe that Gladstone meant what he said.[365] We, liberals, are in a sad plight – under a cloud, at least.

Monday, 27 February: [...] Lord Hartington, abandoning the proposal of a secret committee, moved for a select committee to inquire into the state of Westmeath.[366] An energetic speech was made by Disraeli and, also, one of the same character by Hardy. Ministers shd. not have mentioned the word 'secret' if they had not made up their minds to abide by it. There are signs that Ministers are wanting in decision & self-confidence. Is it that they were the men for work which has been done?

I begin to think the advanced liberals meditate revolt. They have lost their chief watchwords.

[362] Gladstone defended his assertion, made in the debate on the Address, that the two dead Liberal statesmen had believed that the Black sea clauses could be no more than temporary; H cciv. 854–65.

[363] A separate issue. Robinson had resigned as controller of the navy and third sea lord after a dispute with the first lord, Childers. Gladstone asked Robinson to change the date of his minute to the day after his resignation, so that there would be no formal difficulty about publishing it. Their correspondence was printed in The Times, 16 Feb. 1871, 10.

[364] See above, 20 Feb.

[365] Russell was a special envoy to the German army at Versailles. Gladstone denied that he had thrown him over; H cciv. 854–65.

[366] The committee was to inquire into the agrarian conspiracy, known as ribbonism, in County Westmeath and adjoining areas; H cciv. 989–1000. Hartington, the Irish Chief Secretary, had originally proposed on 23 Feb. that the committee should take evidence in private. Both Hartington and the Lord Lieutenant, Spencer, had favoured immediate legislative action, but this was resisted by Gladstone; G.D. vii. 449–50.

Tuesday, 28 February: This was Sir Massey Lopes's great Field day. He brought on, in an excellent speech occupying ab[ou]t 2 hours, a resolution in favour of an enquiry into local taxation with the object of greatly extend[in]g the area of chargeability for purposes now provided for by rates on lands & houses.[367] Govt. thro' Goschen moved the previous question on the ground that the necessity for enquiry does not warrant delay & that the time for action is come. They have a bill ready in pursuance of a paragraph in the Queen's speech calling attention to the subject in hand. This alone seemed to me to be a good ground for supporting the previous question. When an executive govt. adopts the principle of a proposal, so far as it is safe & wise to apply it, & indicates in so formal a manner an intention to act, can it be expedient or just to weaken their power by putting them in a gratuitous minority? I think not. My vote was with the Noes – we won by 46. Numbers 195 to 241.

It is certainly my opinion that mineral dues, game & plantations shd. be rated for local purposes, but some serious speculative difficulties beset any proposal to deal with the funds, mortgages &c. Hereon, were there time, it would be easy to dilate – perhaps, with advantage.

It shd. not be forgotten, with regard to our course, that had Lopes won, the Ministerial measure would have been delayed pending the inquiry sought for.

How would Fundholders like to pay 3/- in the pound on money lent to the State? How about wasteful expenditure of money so levied? Who would lend money on the security of land with an ever impending menace of a deduction in the shape of local rates? Would not the borrower have to give more? [...]

Wednesday, 1 March: A dull ecclesiastical Wed[nesda]y. The Burials Bill our topic of debate. Division 211 to 149.[368] * T. with majority. *

The Bill seems to me to be fair and moderate. Dissenters will have to pay Burial Fees.

Thursday, 2 March: Lord Hartington's resolution for a Committee on Westmeath &c.[369] was adopted after sundry delays and the delivery of many speeches. It struck me that the speech of Wilson Patten, a speech of a fair-minded and much-respected member, contained almost all that one would require to hear before coming to a decision. It was time for action, not for committees. He affirmed that the Irish govt.

---

[367] Lopes wanted an inquiry into the incidence of local and imperial taxation so as to ensure an equal burden for different types of property; *H* cciv. 1037–61.

[368] For the 2nd reading of Osborne Morgan's annual bill.

[369] See above, 27 Feb.

had knowledge with regard to conspirators which wd. enable govt. to put them down at once. Wilson Patten has been Secretary for Ireland[370] & ought to know what are the resources of that official. The course of Ministers, in every respect, seemed to me to be weak and inapposite. If it was necessary to have a 'secret' committee, why withdraw the proposal of secrecy? Why ask the House to nominate a committee to do the work of the cabinet? *It* is a secret committee, & ought to be equal to the occasion. Gladstone is falling in the estimation of his party. Govt. is going down hill.

I did not care to be led into the lobby in favour of a course almost universally censured & took an unusual line with me – that of not voting – being perfectly indifferent whether the Committee sit or not.[371]

In my judgment the nest of murderers shd. be broken up with a hand in a steel glove. The Habeas Corpus act shd. be suspended at once. The most direct way to an object is the best way. I don't ask for precedents where the end is to secure the existence of society [...]

Friday, 3 March: [...] govt. were defeated on a question of the mode of selecting engineers for India[372] [...]

The defeat of Ministers was serious. Numbers 46 to 52. The mover went out. He was Sir F. Goldsmid. It is a good rule in making a motion to reflect upon the results of its possible success – a thing sadly lost sight of by enterprising candidates for leadership on some question of detail. Such a defeat would not befall a ministry which had the art of attaching its followers.

Monday, 6 March: [...] The outlay in redemption of purchase in the army is the cause of much disagreement. Some of The Tories would prefer to leave things as they are.[373] The same party are looking out for a chance of combining with the radicals who chafe at cost. Great is one's perplexity. The subject is charged with difficulties.

---

[370] In Disraeli's ministry, Sept.-Dec. 1868.

[371] The vote was 256:175 in favour of a committee. Disraeli and some 50–60 Conservative M.P.s walked out in order to save the government from a possible defeat; Disraeli to Northcote, 10 Mar. 1871, in W.F. Monypenny and G.E. Buckle, *Life of Benjamin Disraeli, Earl of Beaconsfield* (1929 ed.), ii. 478–9. Following the committee's report, on 31 Mar., the government introduced a Protection of Life and Property bill, suspending Habeas Corpus in Westmeath and surrounding areas; Royal assent 16 June. *P.P.* 1871, iv. 701.

[372] Amendment to the supply motion, that civil engineers need not have been educated at government colleges; *H* cciv. 1326-30.

[373] Colonel Loyd Lindsay's amendment to the 2nd reading of the Army Regulation bill, that in the light of recent additional defence expenditure it was unjustified to vote public money for the abolition of purchase; *H* cciv. 1397–1415. Lindsay put the cost of abolition at £12 millions, compared with the government's estimate of £8 millions.

Wednesday, 8 March: A rather dreary debate on Loch's Scotch Game Law amendmt. Bill. Strong arguments were urged agt. it as interfering with liberty of contract and likely to lead to great injustice – putting leases in jeopardy by forfeiture & leaving collusive arrangements open to landlords who might apparently let the game to 3rd. parties in trust for their lessors. The Lord advocate[374] opposed the Bill, promising to introduce another Bill the next day. But the course of Ministers was shabby. Disapproving of the Bill, they & their followers walked out in a large body. Division 154 to 85.[375] T. in majority.

Afterwards, came the everlasting deceased wife's sister who might I think marry and let us have done with her. The Speaker seemed to me very deaf when the cry 'the Noes have it' was raised. He quietly left the chair. So, a division was taken at once in committee. Numbers 84 to 149.[376] * T. with the ayes. *

Then the policy was adopted of talking agt. time. The eccentric T. Collins repeated platitudes, and re-told a jest which he told in my hearing much more forcibly a year or two back. And so our day was wasted.

Recurring to the Scotch Game Law Bill, I remember saying to several members that the measure was apparently devised for the purpose of teaching Scotchmen how to drive a bargain. (This produced some mirth.)

Tuesday, 14 March: We had a little discussion on Lambert's motion for a committee on Salaries.[377] A few sentences of mine appear in the reports published [. . .] It has for many a year been my opinion that the higher political offices are underpaid. The effect is to the disadvantage of the State, because no one has much chance of office unless he is possessed of good means of living during the necessary period of apprenticeship.

Wednesday, 15 March: Three members of the Contagious Diseases Commission – the chairman (Mr Massey), Mr Applegarth[378] & I – went to Aldershot in order to visit the Lock Hospital there & judge of the treatment of the poor women. On my return to town, it was too late for attending the House of Commons. No divisions.

[374] George Young.
[375] Against the 2nd reading. The government introduced its own Game Laws amendment bill on 9 Mar., but it was later dropped.
[376] Against Hunt's motion that the chairman leave the chair. The bill was rejected by the House of Lords.
[377] i.e. salaries from office of members of both Houses of Parliament; H cciv. 1985–90. Negatived.
[378] The trade union leader; an opponent of the acts.

The business of the Commission is very absorbing.

Thursday, 16 March: Attending early, I foresaw a terrible night of useless work & paired with Mr Fielden. We escaped 6 divisions on adjournment,[379] the House sitting till 3 1/4 a.m. [...]

Friday, 17 March: [...] At the commencement of the evening there was a squabble betwn. Cavendish Bentinck and Arthur Peel on a charge of irregular comment by him when Bentinck was speaking last night. Peel, it seems, used words reflecting upon Bentinck on account of his attributing to the Premier total want of principle. Peel adhered to his words & justified them. Bentinck apologized for his observation − if, which he did not recollect, he had made it − & altogether cut a sorry figure. I fear he is a victim of exaggerated self-esteem.

Lloyd Lindsay's amendmt. on the Army Organization Bill collapsed.[380] The Bill was read a 2d. time [...]

Saturday, 18 March: A long day's work on the R. Commission.

The celebrated Mrs Josephine Butler was examined. If she were as prudent as she is clever, fluent & beautiful, she would be even more dangerous than she is to the causes she opposes.[381] I have no doubt but that she is an earnest believer in the cause she has espoused [...]

Monday, 20 March: We had some discussion on the motion of Trevelyan for the abolition of Army colonels[382] − a body of officers not required by the service and being in fact a relic of a corrupt past. Cardwell's hesitating & feeble opposition plainly shewed his heart was with us, tho', perhaps, there may be lions in his path.

Pakington referred to the 'presumption' of liberal members below the gangway, and a few impromptu sentences fell from me amongst others in support of Trevelyan.

We divided and govt. with the aid of the Tory opposition beat us (111 to 204).

Afterwards Govt. yielded to Mundella's application that the Army question shd. be postponed to thursday, Mundella being desirous of an opportunity for his motion which stood to be brought on 'in committee'. But Leatham had a motion for reduction of the army & he, it is said, was annoyed at the loss of his chance. Govt. exposed itself to severe

---

[379] On the Army Regulation bill.

[380] See above, 6 Mar. On the Conservative side, it appears that 'few liked Lindsay's amendment & our party wd. have mustered badly'; *G.H.D.*, 17 Mar. 1871.

[381] Her tone had been aggressive and hysterical; McHugh, *Prostitution*, 64–5.

[382] Amendment to the supply motion, that no further appointments should be made unless they involved active command of a regiment; *H* ccv. 274–9.

comment from Disraeli. There are signs of hesitation in ministerial tactics and a certain loss of prestige [...]

Wednesday, 22 March: Rather an eventful sitting. Carnegie moved the 2d. reading of his Law of Hypothec abolition Bill. This Law is analagous to the English Law of distress (with a difference).[383] After several speeches delivered by members of more or less note the Lord advocate,[384] in the name of govt., approved of the Bill, but, giving reasons, raised a vehement opposition. In giving his reasons, he glanced at the English Law and used language decidedly calculated to alarm English lessors.[385]

[...] Curious that another Bill shd. be introduced to teach Scotchmen how to drive a bargain!

Carnegie thinks that Hypothec encourages small tenancies. Why, does he desire that none but large farmers shd. have farms? or that landlords shd. cultivate in propriâ personâ?

A tenant is in a different position from the butcher or baker. The tenant uses land & takes a crop many months before the rent day. The butcher may insist on prompt payment. How would tenants like it, if landlords, alarmed at legislation, shd. require a deposit before entrance on an estate?

Young (Lord advocate) was not well-advised in his line of remarks. His leader will not thank him for them.

Leaman made an energetic speech – by no means a bad one in point of logic. His delivery is good. E. Ellice spoke – rather caustically – moving an adjournmt. in order that Ministers might have time for considering the law of both countries to which law Young had referred.[386]

Thursday, 23 March: [...] Mundella moved a resolution as an amendmt. on going into supply. His object is to limit Ministers to our ordinary army expenditure. Yet, he approves of the abolition of purchase. I failed to concur with him on his motion. * T. agt. him. (294 to 91.) *

When the House had resolved itself into committee of supply, Leatham proposed to reduce the army by 20,000 men. This, also,

---

[383] The law of distress allowed for the seizure of chattels in order to recover a debt; the law of hypothec gave a prior claim to the landlord for his rent over the crops and stock of the tenant farmer.

[384] George Young.

[385] Asserting that the bill would set a precedent for the abolition of the law of distress; *H* ccv. 430–5.

[386] This was negatived, and the 2nd reading of the bill defeated, 186:105, with many English county members voting against it.

seemed to me objectionable. * T. agt. him (304 to 74) *

Mundella spoke well. Leatham was, as usual, fluent. Neither was very practical.[387]

[...] About 1/2 past 10 p.m. there was quite a scene. House full, 4 Burmese in magnificent apparel, many ladies behind the screen. Sir H. Hoare was delivering a dull speech[388] on the floor, below the gangway. On a sudden the great Hippy (Hippopotamus) Damer – who it is said had dined with some liberal host having a fine cellar – crossed the House between Hoare and the table. (Loud cries of 'order' and much mock indignation, with shouts of laughter long continuing.) Damer found himself planted between Gladstone & Forster. To Gladstone he was apparently communicating some information from notes which he had. (Loud cheers.) Damer seemed afraid to leave his post for fear of breaking the rules & so poor Gladstone, half-astounded, half-amused and studiously-gracious, had to keep up a conversation with Hippy for a considerable time. The roars of laughter at last quite extinguished Hoare & so we went to division. The story is that Hippy had just returned from Paris & thought it necessary to tell the Minister of his experiences there. What boys members are – especially towards 11 p.m.! As I was walking about the entrance lobby, Hippy who did not know me, came up & would give me the whole story – how he had dined with Dr. Russell & + how Hippy thought of telling Gladstone what he knew of affairs at Paris. It was most difficult to save him from the fresh ridicule he was exciting among several bystanders. He thought it necessary to describe himself as a 'd-d fool' & to 'apologize to every one'. In fact I might have hence begun to think him sober but for unmistakeable evidences to the contrary. 'The Times' I see refers to the proceeding & wickedly mentions that the member is described in Dod as of 'Conservative principles, free and uncontrolled'. After sitting for (say) 10 minutes between Gladstone & Forster, apparently puzzled how to escape without offending the rules again, the offender was adroitly spirited away by some one, * I think I heard it was Lord Otto Fitzgerald * who came from behind the speaker's chair + [...]

Monday, 27 March: [...] My time is almost engrossed by the Contagious Diseases Commission, which, at my suggestion, is sitting daily. It is very important to conclude it soon.

Tuesday, 28 March: [...] During an hour or thereabouts I was in the Lords where Lord Vivian moved for a committee on the subject of Lords Lieutenant and their position. The debate had much interest for

---

[387] And both were defeated.
[388] During the debate on Mundella's amendment.

me, because it grew out of a controversy regarding my brother's command of the Royal Cornwall Rangers Militia.[389] The subject has already been the occasion of a debate in the Lords.

Thursday, 30 March: Sir C. Dilke moved a resolution wh. was virtually a resolution expressive of want of confidence in Ministers. This motion referred to their conduct in the matter of the Black Sea Conference.[390] I paired with Sir James Elphinstone & went home. The motion was abortive – negatived ignominiously without division. Dilke wants experience. He is fluent & ready. Both dangerous advantages in a young member [...]

Monday, 3 April: We have a report of the select Committee appointed to consider of the best way of expediting our business. The Speaker and Sir T. Erskine May were the only witnesses.[391]

The Ballot Bill, Bruce's Licensing Bill & Goschen's Local Govt. & Local Taxation Bill were subjects of debate. Very long and very important speeches were made. It seems to me that Bruce's Bill is very complex.[392]

Ministers must have worked very hard during the recess. I have doubts whether their recent measures will have the success which the Irish Church Bill, the Land & Education Bills had. Pressure will be less strong. Interests more divided. It takes time for measures to ripen.

Tuesday, 4 April: [...] A speech of Shaw Lefevre's shewing the progress of enclosures in England interested me for some time as I once spoke on the subject about 1845.[393] The Enclosure Bill of that period has produced excellent results. Some 3 or 4 hundred thousand acres brought into cultivation out of waste.

Tuesday, 18 April:[394] Monk moved on the subject of superannuations

---

[389] Vivian, the Lord Lieutenant of Cornwall, was at loggerheads with the War office. He had differed from the diarist's brother, H.R. Trelawny, over the date for the militia's manoeuvres, and had sought his removal. *H* ccv. 734–7. Motion negatived.

[390] *H* ccv. 894–918; regretting the government's agreement to the London conference at which the Black sea clauses of the Treaty of Paris had been abrogated. Gathorne Hardy seems to have suspected that 'Disraeli secretly egged on the movement'; *G.H.D.*, 31 Mar. 1871.

[391] *P.P.* 1871, ix. 1.

[392] It also provoked a storm of protest from the drink interest, fearing that publican's licences would be withdrawn; Brian Harrison, *Drink and the Victorians* (1971), 263–8.

[393] 4 July 1845; *H* lxxxii. 25–6.

[394] The House had adjourned for Easter on 4 Apr., resuming on the 17th.

of civil servants and received from Bob Lowe the tender of a compromise
which the mover accepted.[395]

C. Reed wanted to exempt some 20,000 postmen from Sunday
labour in the country. Gladstone, considering that even for civil reasons
abstinence from labour on Sundays is a benefit, was willing to meet
Reed as far as was possible compatibly with Public advantage and
made him an offer tending tow[ar]ds the lightening of labour on
Sundays.[396] So there was no division.

Then came Lord H. Lennox who brought under notice the story of
the dismissal of Admiral Sir Spencer Robinson. It is far from clear to
me that ministers were in the right in this matter, which I fear grew
out of the loss of the Captain.[397] After reading the Bluebook containing
an account of her loss and its probable causes, I incline to the conclusion
that, had the views of Robinson & Reed (the controller) been attended
to, the Captain would never have been built.

Gladstone waxed warm at Bouverie's remarks: so reports 'the Times'.
Ministers would not let Lennox withdraw his motion & he was defeated
(104 to 153).[398] * T. at home, didn't vote. *

[...] It strikes me that Ministers are more frequently carped at in
this year than in last. The want of decision they have shewn in the
Westmeath business has an ugly appearance. Goschen's Bill is hardly
a project describable as one presenting a definitive settlement.[399] Bruce's
Licensing Bill will never pass as it stands. The game Bill will be deemed
to be an imperfect treatment of a serious difficulty. Whether Cardwell
will succeed is a question by no means solved. The budget may not
add to any good temper still remaining in the Public mind.

Wednesday, 19 April: [...] Peter Taylor moved his Game Law
abolition Bill – which to my mind is simple spoliation, as he does not
pay owners of game the compliment of a nominal protection of their
rights.

I was tempted to say that Taylor is the Nemesis of neglect. Since

---

[395] Lowe offered to allow the commutation of pensions for those whose posts had been
abolished; *H* ccv. 1256–8.

[396] *H* ccv. 1272–8, for Gladstone's offer of an inquiry into what could be done.

[397] Robinson, the former controller of the navy and third sea lord, had been opposed
to the mode of construction of the 'Captain', which had sunk in the Bay of Biscay in
Sept. 1870.

[398] Against the motion for a select committee of inquiry.

[399] The Local Taxation bill was an ambitious scheme, summarised by one historian as
follows: 'A single local rating authority and one single consolidated rate were to be
substituted for the many that existed before. New Parochial and County Boards were to
become the organs of local government, posing a threat to the existing structure of
landed hegemony in the Countryside.' Avner Offer, *Property and Politics, 1870–1914*
(Cambridge, 1981), 177–9.

1846 (I think it was) when I served on Bright's Committee,[400] the game question has been ripe for legislative interference. No measure is before us wh. is up to the mark.

Taylor is as unjust to some tenants as to owners. Where a tenant has a lease of a farm on wh. game is not reserved, a poacher might kill the game & so rob the tenant under his very eyes!

My vote was agt. his Bill.[401]

Several members voted with him as a mode of protesting agt. Ministerial dawdling & inefficiency. This reason for voting agt. conviction is I consider immoral. Sir Henry Hoare was a delinquent in this sense; as, also, Capt[ain] Carnegie. Hardcastle moved the amendmt., he hav[in]g a bill of his own which he took the opportunity to describe. His measure is simply preposterous. If he intend it for a jest, it may pass – as a jest. Why, it is a harsher game law![402]

McLagan followed. He, too, presented a game Bill, which is perhaps more near being solution, tho' I am not prepared to say it will be so. He saw that time was wanting for more than a division, so he spared us a speech. An adjournt. was very properly come to that we might learn more of Ministerial intentions on the several Bills laid before the House. This adjournt. had my support,[403] but this did not commit me in any way as to the measure of McLagan.

Thursday, 20 April: We had Bob Lowe's Budget. 'The Times' uses, in allusion to it, Disraeli's phrase when he spoke once of 'harum scarum budgets'.[404] Lowe's manner is not happy. His shortness of sight renders his difficulty in finding his figures great; &, apparently, he has not Fawcett's faculty of carrying any amount of prepared matter in his head. Lowe has much of the clumsiness which Goschen (another able man) exhibits. Yet, Lowe propounds many sound principles of taxation with boldness & even with unction. Indeed, I am not sure he does not relish the task of recommending that which is unpopular. The tax on matches struck the House with some astonishmt. Dixon could not bear

---

[400] *P.P.* 1845, xii. 331; 1846, ix. 1.

[401] 2nd reading defeated, 172:49.

[402] Hardcastle's plan would have made game the property of the occupier, so that poaching would be regarded as common theft; *H* ccv. 1364–6.

[403] 106:37 for Craufurd's adjournment motion. Gladstone's Cabinet note of 3 Mar. 1871 reads: 'Game Laws. 2R M'Lagan's bill. Not to object. Proposed reference of Bills including our own to a Committee'. *G.D.*, vii. 458. This was the course adopted, but no legislation resulted.

[404] *The Times*, 21 Apr. 1871, 9. In order to cover an anticipated deficit arising from the costs of army reform and extra military expenditure, Lowe added 1d. to the income tax, imposed a tax of 1/2d. on small boxes of matches and 1d. on larger ones, and doubled the succession duties to 2% in cases where the heir was the eldest son; *H* ccv. 1391–1419.

it – so he divided.[405] Unfortunately, it did not strike me that any important action would be taken at once, so I was not pres[en]t. [...] The budget will not, I think, be popular.

Monday, 24 April: Foul air in the Cont:Dis: Commission room was the climax to impending gout. A sharp attack sent me home to bed. – So I lost an opportunity of voting agst. White's resolution on amendment to going into Ways & means.[406] It is not clear to me that the items of the Budget are all sound, or expedient to be adopted, & it is quite open to me to oppose them in detail; but having accepted the responsibility for the plan of getting rid of the Purchase system & for the scheme of Army organization, I do not think fit to throw impediments in the way of passing the bill.

I have written to the Times and stated why I was absent from the Div[isio]n – specifying how I should have voted. Govt. only won by 27 votes. Nos 257 to 230.

Thursday, 27 April: The Budget has collapsed. 'Lucifer' Lowe and his coadjutors are routed horse and foot.[407] Disraeli skilfully pointed out all the disagreeable circumstances in the position of Government. Fawcett signalized the occasion by the valuable remark, coming from him as a democrat, that exemptions of the working classes from a share in increased expenditure held out to them a temptation to waste. This remark had the evident approval of the Conservative party. After some broad farce of Osborne's, & some very undignified personalities in answer from Auberon Herbert, the motion for Ways & Means was postponed till Monday.

I forgot to notice a rather ominous speech from Lord Geo. Cavendish, to the effect that, if the Govt. did not take care, there would be no liberal county members left.

Friday, 28 April: The Budget is giving occasion to very hostile notices. This evening Wm. Cowper-Temple moved in favour of reserving as an open space for purposes of health & recreation those parts of Epping Forest which have not been enclosed with the assent of the Crown or by legal authority. Government opposed the motion and were defeated by a majority of 101[408] [...]

[405] The 1st resolution, regarding the match duties, was passed, 201:44.

[406] Opposing additional taxation; *H* ccv. 1585–93.

[407] By the matchgirls' demonstration organised by Bryant and May. The government now dropped both the match duties and the increased succession duties, and instead put 2d. on the income tax. James Winter, *Robert Lowe* (Toronto, 1976), 274–8.

[408] 197:96 for the supply amendment; *H* ccv. 1852–8. Cf. *G.D.*, vii. 487: ' ... circumstances of much indignity'.

Monday, 1 May: Government appear to have strained every nerve. They defeated Mr W.H. Smith's motion[409] by 335 to 250. There was a great debate, and considerable injury was done to the Government by the inconsistencies into which they were shown to have fallen. Trelawny absent, ill.[410]

Wednesday, 3 May: Today was the field day of the discontented ladies,[411] Jacob Bright being their spokesman, who took occasion in one portion of his speech, to insult his three chief opponents Bouverie, Elcho & Newdegate apparently without the excuse of warm blood or provocation. Probably he wanted to intimate to the ladies in the Gallery that if it had been 30 years sooner & if he had not been a quaker, he would have fought 3 duels for them. Bouverie took an opportunity of insulting John Stuart Mill, whom he described as a sophist & plagiarist. The secret of this is that Mill some years ago sent Chadwick to oppose Bouverie at Kilmarnock.[412] Bouverie had his revenge then, which one would think was enough. Gladstone trimmed his sails,[413] which evolution was pointed out by Mr Henry James and Lord John Manners, the former of whom spoke ably. The Ladies were beaten by 220 to 151.[414] T. absent ill.

Thursday, 4 May: T.M. Torrens preferred 5d. to 6d. income tax ('I give thee 6, I will see thee damned first' as Osborne observed in his speech). He moved accordingly and was beaten by 46. Numbers 294 to 248. I was in bed under medical orders to remain quiet. Suddenly, at 8.30 p.m. I was summoned by Glyn[415] in extremis. Fortunately I had had a glass of champagne; possibly public principle was thus made less inert. So I was dressed & went down to the House, where I remained till near 2 a.m., cursing the prolixity of leading speakers, and really tired of hearing the Lancashire twang of our verbiose and diffusive leader. Glyn came up and spoke apologetically for having brought me down so early. I told him I wished Gladstone would only read a speech of Livy, & see that the whole of what he had to say might be got into fifteen lines [...]

---

[409] Against the increase in income tax; *H* ccv. 1937-43.

[410] Ill-health affected Trelawny's attendance for the remainder of this session.

[411] 2nd reading of the Women's Disabilities bill, extending the parliamentary franchise to female householders.

[412] In 1868; Edwin Chadwick was defeated.

[413] Saying that the government had no view on the matter, that personally he was against it, but even this was expressed ambiguously; *H* ccvi. 88-95.

[414] Trelawny mistakenly gave the minority as 157.

[415] Government chief whip.

Monday, 8 May: [...] Gladstone stated his intentions with regard to public business. Several bills to be wholly or partially withdrawn; Local rating Govt. bill for instance; and the licensing part of the Licensing Bills.[416] It seems to me the House is getting very unruly; and representative institutions are more than ever on their trial. Erskine May's proposal of reinstituting grand committees, each, I presume to take charge of a special subject, may hereafter be adopted.[417]

Tuesday, 9 May: I attended and heard the commencement of Mr Miall's speech in favour of Disestablishment of the English Church.[418] The portion which I heard was remarkably good, & showed signs of much elaboration. A full House and a very patient audience. A few Conservatives cried 'oh! oh!' when he expressed the absence of hostility to any church as a church, regarding all as entitled to respect on account of the mission on which they were engaged. The state of my health precluded my remaining for the division. Meeting my colleague Mr B. Willyams later, I paired with him.[419] * The reason for my line in regard to the Church Disestablishment was glanced at as I perceive by the Telegraph newspaper. The writer deprecated the danger of a powerful religious community, untrammelled by State control, & administering a capital, estimated at 80 millions of money. * On a division the resolution was negatived by 374 to 89.

Wednesday, 10 May: [...] Mr Muntz had a bill for exempting charitable buildings from local taxation. Stansfeld[420] talked against time to defeat it, moving an adjournment. This motion was rejected by 117 to 84. This course was considered to be not a very good example in a minister, and may be taken as a disastrous precedent. Since this was written, my colleague,[421] who was in the House, reports that as soon as Hibbert sat down Stansfeld rose & the House hearing him with impatience, said he should propose the adjournment of the Debate. The opposition laughed & cheered, & he said 'If you mean to divide upon that, I shall talk it out'. And he persisted, offering the strange sight of a member of the Government speaking from the Treasury Bench, amidst a storm of interruptions & cries of 'Divide', and regardless

---

[416] The whole measure was later dropped.

[417] Recommended by the recent select committee; *P.P.* 1871, ix. 1.

[418] The resolution was for disestablishment in England, Scotland and Wales; *H* ccvi. 474–97.

[419] i.e. against Miall.

[420] President of the Local Government Board.

[421] E.B. Willyams, the other member for East Cornwall; Trelawny was absent ill.

of the efforts of Glyn who came behind him & pulled him by the coat tail.[422]

Monday, 15 May: There was a great party fight on Muntz's motion relating to the Purchase question.[423] For Muntz 195. Against 260. T. absent, ill. Muntz's was an attempt to defeat Cardwell by a side wind, favoured by the Conservatives. Still, these repeated shocks are disintegrating the strength of Govt. seriously.

Thursday, 18 May: Disraeli, according to notice, discursively viewed the conduct of Lowe & the Govt. as respects the Budget. Apparently he made no unanswered point, or at least no point for which he had not himself created a precedent [...]

Tuesday, 23 May: Several (3) divisions on the Lords amendments to the University Test Bill. The House disagreed with the Lords on material points; but at Gladstone's instance consented to bid for the passing of the Bill by acquiescing in the amendment that religious worship suited to members of the Ch: of England should be provided in college chapels [...]

Thursday, 25 May: Col[onel] Anson moved an amendment on the Army Bill, – negatived. Govt. had a majority of only 19; 81 to 62. Sir George Jenkinson's amend[men]t was negatived by 58 to 38. Much recrimination between the Govt. & opposition. Sir Wm. Russell's amend[men]t. was negatived by 170 to 154; which division was taken as a triumph by the opposition.[424] The bill is postponed till after Whitsuntide. Afterwards the Metropolis Water bill was the occasion of a motion for adjournment. After vast waste of time the House adjourned at 20 min: to 3.[425] It seems to me that Cardwell's plan relating to purchase, will fail to pass.

---

[422] In fact, the government chief whip reported to Gladstone that the House had misunderstood Stansfeld's intention, which was '*to protest agst a division being taken without discussion*'; Glyn to Gladstone, 10 May 1871, B.L. Add MSS 44348, fo. 94.

[423] Amendment in committee to clause 2 of the Army Regulation bill, seeking to restrict compensation for the abolition of purchased commissions to the official, 'regulation' price; *H* ccvi. 811–16.

[424] Three time-wasting amendments to clause 3, relating to compensation for officers.

[425] The adjournment motion was defeated, 87:57, but the Home Secretary then agreed to it after Tom Collins moved to adjourn the House (which, if passed, would have killed the bill). The bill received the Royal assent on 21 Aug.

Friday, 26 May: Three absurd divisions on the Irish Protection to Life & Property Bill.[426] T. absent.

I believe Irish members really wish that the Bill pass, but it would not please some of their constituents to let the cat out of the bag.

Friday, 2 June: An interesting speech was elicited from Lowe by White's motion in favour of relieving the poorer consumers from taxation applied to liquidation of the debt. Lowe's speech will go far tow[ar]ds rehabilitating him after the temporary loss of prestige due to the late abortive budget.[427]

Gladstone is better, but has not yet returned to his Parl[iamentar]y work[428] [...]

Monday, 5 June: [...] there occurred the now usual faction-fight and 3 obstructive motions for adjournmts.[429] Gladstone suffers seriously in encounters with Disraeli, who surpasses his rival in calm & premeditation – also, in point. His allusion to Gladstone's change on the Ballot was a very palpable hit. How could it be seriously said that the Ballot measure was urgent in the face of the fact that the Minister only became a convert to it last year?[430] Such a statement approached the comic (laughter). It is difficult to believe that either the Army Bill or the Ballot Bill will pass this year.

Tuesday, 6 June: Armitstead (for Mr H. Herbert) asked a question ab[ou]t interference with mounted officers of Volunteers entering Hyde Park & his question referred to their 'gratuitous' services.[431] This was too much for me, so I rose to order, asking the Speaker if a question was in accordance with the rules when it contained something not true – the proof being a Parl[iamentar]y return then in my hands shew[in]g that the Volunteers cost in this year over £800,000. The Speaker, who seemed puzzled, did not consider that the question was out of order, but Sir Geo. Grey hoped it would be, when next put

---

[426] Committee stage of the bill to suspend Habeas Corpus in County Westmeath and surrounding areas; the minorities in the three divisions numbered 7, 8 and 11.

[427] White's motion urged that priority be given to reducing indirect taxes; *H* ccvi. 1436–43, withdrawn. Lowe's speech, reasserting the principle that the working classes must pay their share of taxes, was published in pamphlet form: R. Lowe, 'The National Debt Speech ... on the 2nd of June 1871', (1871).

[428] He was suffering from a fever, 28 May–4 June; *G.D.*, vii. 502–4.

[429] On the Army Regulation bill, in committee. Trelawny mistakenly wrote that there were 2 motions.

[430] See above, 27 July 1870. Disraeli pointed to the delay in passing the Irish Protection of Life and Property bill, while the government was pressing its Ballot bill which, he argued, was not urgent; *H* ccvi. 1587–92.

[431] *H* ccvi. 1601–2.

amended. The renewed notice omits, I perceive, the objectionable word. The fact is, I believe, the Speaker shd. have corrected the notice as at least irregular or inconvenient. Before I put my question I consulted the Jun[io]r clerk [...]

Thursday, 8 June: [...] Army regulation was the main topic.[432] Col[onel] Anson imprudently used a tone of menace as if the army were likely to be unfaithful. He had reason to regret this course & made an apology. If officers do not take care, over-regulation prices will be treated as being what in truth they are – illegal.[433] The discussion was rather in that direction. Cardwell, on a hint from Sir Geo. Grey, spoke somewhat ominously about the course the executive might think it a duty to take now that over-regulation prices were officially under notice. Rylands & V. Harcourt must have considerably disturbed the minds of the Colonels who have carried their game a little too far.

Friday, 9 June: [...] It is quite out of my power to do more to-day than attend on the Royal Commission. We are endeavouring to frame a report. Our disagreement is remarkable. Hardly two Commiss[ione]rs hold exactly the same opinions. My analysis, printed by order, is found to be useful.[434]

Tuesday, 13 June: The opposition is becoming more and more factious. The Government rather weakly defers to it. Roundell Palmer very seriously warned the party of Anson & Elcho[435] that their course was neither likely to benefit the Army, the Conservative party or the cause of the constitution.

[...] A certain self constituted-Revd. Beewright is improv[in]g each shining hour by obtaining summonses agt. the vendors of Lollypop on the Lord's day!

Friday, 16 June: [...] It daily strikes one more & more that govt. cannot keep their house in hand. Is there a want of a mastermind in the cabinet? Is Lowe too tall for Gladstone? Law reform surely need not wait so long.[436] Is it endurable that the Colonies shd. be able to

---

[432] In committee.

[433] The bill provided for compensation to officers on the basis of the unofficial price paid in practice for commissions, rather than the 'regulation price'.

[434] An analysis of the evidence given to the Royal Commission; *P.P.* 1871, xix. 33.

[435] Who were obstructing the Army Regulation bill.

[436] Lord Chancellor Hatherley's expected Judicature bill had not been introduced.

taunt us with some 300 unadjudicated causes in the Privy Council?[437]
Who is responsible?

Sunday, 18 June: + George Grote[438] died this morning at 20 min.
past 7. My wife was with him till 4 a.m. She was called back about 1/2
an hour before his death and was present with him till the last – at
that moment supporting his head with her arm. +

Monday, 19 June: [...] There was a close division (176 to 174) on
the question whether Armouries stores &c. for the militia shd. or shd.
not be defrayed hereafter by the State instead of out of the County
Rates.[439] The agriculturists will closely scrutinize our votes heron. It
was news to me that the proposal was to be made.

  Govt. proposed that the subject shd. stand over with[ou]t prejudice
till the final adjustmt. on local & Imperial taxation shd. be made.

Tuesday, 20 June: [...] W. Fowler withdrew his notice of motion
on the Contagious Diseases question, but why could he not have
apprised the House at an earlier moment? It was preposterous to have
thought of proposing to abolish the Acts before the Commission had
reported [...]

Wednesday, 21 June: To-day my foot swelled and I did not attempt
to go to the House. So I was not in the division on Mr Rylands Sale
of Liquors on sunday Bill.[440]

  John Locke made a courageous and useful speech.[441] He is a man of
excellent sense & ability.

Thursday, 22 June: [...] there was a smart preliminary skirmish
betwn. Disraeli & Gladstone. The occasion was Mr J. Lowther's
proposal that the Committee on the Ballot Bill be instructed to provide
for the disposal of certain vacant seats.[442] Gladstone, unfortunately, let
fall words which seemed to glance at the further treatment of the
electoral Laws. This gave Disraeli an opening & he inveighed agt. the
Minister's indiscretion. Gladstone resisted the interpretation put on his
words which however Hardy declared had produced a visible shudder

---

[437] Two new puisne judges were added to the judicial committee of the privy council;
G.D., vii. (17 June 1871 and note).

[438] The former radical M.P. and historian (1794–1871); a friend of the diarist.

[439] Lord G. Hamilton's proposed clause to the Army Regulation bill; *H* ccvii. 275–81.

[440] 2nd Reading passed, 147:119; defeated on 26 June.

[441] Opposing the bill to ban the opening of public houses; *H* ccvii. 380–3.

[442] *H* ccvii. 402–4; defeated 254:145. The vacancies arose from the disfranchisement of
Beverley, Bridgwater, Cashel and Sligo, for corrupt practices.

among the Liberal party. We divided. My vote was with Ministers [...]

Tuesday, 27 June: A great portion of the day's work consisted in baiting Ayrton.[443] An unseemly spectacle to Gods & Men. The news-papers make it useful in amusing some of the Public; but working members will groan over such waste of time at the end of June.

Wednesday, 28 June: A day nearly wasted on fruitless squabbling over the Parish Churches & the Burials Bills. Each Bill nibbles at the established Church & keeps alive a controversy betwn. its clergy and the nonconformists[444] [...]

Friday, 30 June: [...] Betwn. 9 & 10 p.m. I went down to the House again – at the express wish of some of my St Austell friends. Gilpin's motion on Slavery was the attraction[445] [...]

Tuesday, 4 July: A wasted day. The Conservatives were bent on presenting to the progress of the Ballot Bill every form of obstruction. We were in Committee, when Fielden moved that the Chairman leave the chair and proceeded to speak to the main question as if the stage were the 2d. reading. This most unfair & unparliamentary course was defended by others and 5 hours were consumed in talk. Newdegate had the honour of closing the discussion. Disraeli sat a long time nearly at the rear of the Speaker's chair, but probably he intended to emerge, as turned out to be the case, at some suitable moment. Gladstone read the House a lecture on the state to which members are bringing the conduct of business. The notice paper is daily crowded with amend-ments; particularly on the Ballot Bill. Members seem to throw control to the winds – in fact, the House is nearly resolved into its elements. It is a question whether Disraeli is a whit more happy in ruling his men than Gladstone in ruling us. Geo. Bentinck renounces allegiance to the Tory chief, whom Beresford Hope likes no better. Perhaps, he cannot forget his 'Batavian grace' to which Disraeli once alluded[446] [...]

[443] The chief commissioner of works and buildings, dealing with the civil service estimates in committee of supply.

[444] 2nd Reading of West's Parish Churches bill; withdrawn. It sought to prevent bishops in future from appropriating pews for the use of landowners and others at the expense of ordinary parishioners. Osborne Morgan's annual Burials bill was in committee, but never completed this stage.

[445] Amendment to the supply motion calling for action against the East African slave trade; *H* ccvii. 952–5. Withdrawn after the offer of a select committee of inquiry.

[446] Beresford Hope, of Dutch extraction, was a heavy, clumsy figure. Disraeli had once referred (in 1867) to the 'Batavian grace' of his invective, which took the sting out of it; Monypenny and Buckle, *Disraeli*, ii. 265.

Wednesday, 5 July: My vote was given agt. McLaren's Scotch Church Rates Abolition Bill.[447] The title is disingenuous. In fact, this Scotch Church rate is a charge upon heritors, who acquired their land subject to the Tax. The English Rate was a charge upon the person & was contingent upon the vote of a majority of a vestry.

[...] The course of Ministers is not very straight-forward on the subject. They were stout ab[ou]t the maintenance of the Welsh Church[448] & I thought equally stout ab[ou]t this Scotch Church rates – which are in essence tithe. Now, the Lord Advocate[449] talks encouragingly of dealing with the subject in some way acceptable to dissenters!

Mr Norwood made an useful motion on a measure for compelling tradesmen in partnership to state their names in full. The debate hereon was interesting & instructive. The Attorney gen[era]l,[450] with some levity, ridiculed the Bill, which the House appeared to like, so Arthur Peel got up & capitulated on terms – a committee to be next year. Thus we are governed! When Osborne Morgan said publicity was honesty, secrecy was fraud, vehement cheers greeted him on the opposition side.

Thursday, 6 July: Called to a meeting at the Treasury Downing St. I attended it along with a large number of the Liberal party.[451] Gladstone, Forster & several members made remarks. The object was a policy with which the opposition may be met – their tactics being decidedly factious. It sounded comical in the Premier to counsel abstention from speeches. The meeting cheered him lustily and there was much determination to aid him. He did a very wise thing in proposing to leave the conduct of the Ballot Bill to Ed. Forster.

At the sitting of the House – after preliminaries – Dodson took the chair and Newdegate moved that Dodson shd. leave it at once. There was a division.[452] It seemed to me that my place was not in the House. How could I seem to vote for a Ballot Bill? on the other hand, how could I support a merely dilatory motion? I walked out.

Floyer next moved a resolution by way of amendmt. on clause 2, which would put an end to open Nomination meetings at Elections.

---

[447] 121:76 for the 2nd Reading, but no further progress.
[448] See above, 24 May 1870.
[449] George Young.
[450] Sir Robert Collier.
[451] *The Times*, 7 July 1871, 5, 9.
[452] 154:63 against Newdegate.

On this my voice was heard for a short time – and in a sense unfavourable to Forster's Bill. I voted with Floyer.[453]

[...] Before my arrival at the House after dinner, there was some 'sensational' business. During Newdegate's speech – I think it was – all the Liberals but two left the House. On this, many Tories went over to take possession of the unoccupied benches below the gangway. There was, also, an attempt to count out the House, when back came a whole posse of Liberals & the attempt was defeated. The House is in a very unruly state. Gladstone's prestige is waning. He wants several of the happy qualifications in a leader, which Palmerston had.

Friday, 7 July: Nomination days were again the theme. A great deal of desultory talk was uttered & 2 divisions were taken on the subject. Forster frankly admitted that the words of the clause were insufficient as they stand.

It was not my wish to offer obstruction to Ministers and I was contented with one protest agt. the clause in my vote given on thursday – so I went home. Indeed, my health required this, for I am unable to bear so much work. Luckily, the Royal Commission concluded its sittings to-day.[454]

Monday, 10 July: [...] There were 2 divisions on the Ballot Bill; 1st on Mr Bourke's motion for postponemt. of the question of the mode of voting till a later stage, and 2dly, on Mr Walter's proposal to limit Ballot to Boroughs. Both movers were defeated.[455]

My name will not be in either list. It is my desire not to share in plans of obstruction, but to reserve myself for points to which I entertain a serious objection.

The discussion is very hollow. It is not at all likely that the Bill will pass in the Lords. It is in the highest degree artificial & open to important objections in almost every clause. The more one examines it the less one likes it [...]

Tuesday, 11 July: [...] The mode of conducting opposition to Ministers is very ominous of future evil. Constitutional government is rudely tried. The Conservatives below the gangway are incurring a heavy responsibility.

[453] His amendment, to continue nomination meetings, passed 296:183; *H* ccvii. 1259–64.

[454] *P.P.*, 1871, xix. 1, for the anodyne report recommending that the regulation of prostitutes be continued, but not the periodic medical examinations. There were seven minority reports; Trelawny signed the one by Pakington which defended the periodic examination of prostitutes; McHugh, *Prostitution*, 65–8.

[455] 210:134 and 240:142 respectively.

Ministers are by no means free from blame, as they are attempting to force upon Parliament measures which might as well wait and meantime grievances of a pressing and practical character remain unredressed.

Thursday, 13 July: A good deal of preliminary skirmishing occurred, Geo. Bentinck moving the adjournment.[456] Disraeli was very amusing. The House was in fits of laughter. * Speaking of the delay or neglect of practical measures of the most pressing kind – he attributed it to the resuscitation of an antiquated frivolity. The Minister, he said, had suddenly become a convert to an expiring faith & had passionately embraced a corpse. *

[...] Govt. were defeated afterwards on the new site for the Mint.[457]

Friday, 14 July: Another day wasted. There was a division on Cave's amendment to clause 3 the object of which was to secure the power of tracing voting papers by means of some distinguishing mark correspond[in]g with a counterfoil. Kennaway, in Cave's absence, moved this.

I supported Ministers[458] considering that the plan was only one of many plans conceived for the purpose of delaying the Bill. If we are about to have a system of secret voting, it shd., I think, be a system for which a government is responsible.

[...] Business is very unusually in arrear. The exigencies of party are supposed to require our almost exclusive devotion to the Ballot Bill. This is only kept on the books by way of warning the Lords that they had better allow the Army Bill to pass. If it be otherwise, the Ballot Bill would begin to loom large. Gout clings to me and my health is seriously impaired by the duties which my post exacts.

Monday, 17 July: [...] So, the Lords have rejected the Army Bill![459]

Thursday, 20 July: Four divisions on amendments to clause 3, which is the Ballot clause. Afterwards a good deal of crimination and recrimination accompanied with loss of temper in various members. Disraeli was called to order by Dodson.[460] * T. has left town *

The early part of the sitting will be memorable for an announcement

---

[456] To prevent the Parliamentary Elections bill coming on; negatived.

[457] 118:115 for Charley's amendment, in committee on the New Mint Building site bill, that the chairman leave the chair.

[458] Who defeated the amendment, 201:177.

[459] 155:130 against the 2nd Reading, that day.

[460] Chairman of committees.

of a Royal warrant abolishing purchase altogether.[461] This led to an interesting discussion. The measure is described by Lord Elcho as a coup d'état and by the 'Times' as a 'wrench' to the constitution.[462]

It will be necessary to study this subject. Primâ facie it is difficult to understand to what purpose the House of Lords was invited to consider the Army Bill if its decision was to be held to be of no account. On the other hand, it will be said that they have brought down the blow on themselves.

Bruce has received a deputation anent the question of Contagious Diseases.[463] Many ladies of various ages thought it decorous to take part. This strikes me as a sign of the times. Surely male representatives might have conveyed to the Minister the remonstrances of the other sex.

Monday, 24 July: The House is still in Committee on the Ballot Bill. Three divisions on or relating to clause 3 were taken. Being an absentee, I have written to the 'Times' to say that, had I been pres[en]t I shd. have voted agt. clause 3, which adopts the Ballot.

The idea of carrying the Bill in this session looks like a grim jest. Not a soul believes this possible. Persistence in the endeavour is deemed to be essential to cohesion betwn. Ministerialists above & below the gangway.

An Autumn session has been recommended & is a proposal actually entertained.[464]

Thursday, 27 July: [...] It is difficult even for a supporter of the government to defend their recent management of affairs. How different would have been the conduct of some of the Premiers whom it has been my lot to observe &, generally, follow! [...] A quarrel has been established with the House of Lords – a quarrel which might have been avoided. If Gladstone do not exhibit more care, his Ministry will soon totter to its fall.

Friday, 28 July: [...] Ministers have a rough time of it. They have so managed matters that very severe comments have been provoked in both Houses. It is easy to say that Ministers are not responsible for the effects of an obstructive policy in the opposition. Such policy were hardly possible + Public opinion would not bear it + were there nothing reprehensible in ministerial tactics.

---

[461] Announced in the House of Lords by Granville; *H* ccviii. 2–9.
[462] *The Times*, 21 July 1871, 9.
[463] *The Times*, 21 July 1871, 12.
[464] It was considered at a Cabinet meeting that day; *G.D.* viii. 12.

Monday, 31 July: There was opposition to the motion for an allowance to Prince Arthur. Two divisions were taken[465] [...] It is noteworthy that the Court is not in very good odour. People of opposite sections are discontented; there are friends of the monarchy who like to receive a quid pro quo[466] and radicals & republicans who disapprove of the institution.

Tuesday, 1 August: No less than eight divisions on the Ballot Bill. There was a two o'clock sitting till 7 p.m. and a 9 o'clock sitting till 25 min. to 3 a.m. Was such management of the House ever known? Who has strength equal to the careful discussion of a highly-complex subject for so many hours in 24?[467]

There is an evident waste of power. The spectacle presented to the Public is not a satisfactory one. If the two Houses cannot mend their relations,[468] it will begin to be a question whether life peerages will not be inevitable.

In the Commons, abuse of the privilege of moving adjournments – so that members speak on any subject without notice and virtually set aside business prescribed on the notice paper – will eventually require a change in forms of proceeding.[469] No sense of decency restrains members from the irregular course referred to.

Tuesday, 8 August: [...] Were I not disabled, it would be my desire to attend on thursday next the debate on Col[onel] Anson's vote.[470] This desire cannot be gratified. Whatever constituents may say or think, one owes a little, after all, to one's own health & mine has been seriously shaken in this year – chiefly, thro' labour on the Royal Commission. Some 50 sittings absorbed almost all my leisure & curtailed my few opportunities of systematically dealing with my physical condition.

---

[465] Dixon's amendment that the allowance be reduced to £10,000 per annum was defeated, 289:51; Gladstone's original motion for £15,000 was then carried, 276:11.

[466] A reference to the growing impatience with the Queen's seclusion from public life since the death of Prince Albert in 1861.

[467] The bill was later rejected by the House of Lords on the grounds that it had been sent up to them so late in the session.

[468] The previous day, the Lords had passed Richmond's censure motion condemning the government's action in using a Royal warrant to abolish the purchase of army commissions as an 'interposition of the Executive during the progress of a measure submitted to Parliament'; *H* ccviii. 455–63.

[469] On 8 Nov. 1871 the Cabinet considered far-reaching changes including restrictions on factious adjournments, the clôture, and Grand Committees; *G.D.* viii. 59. But see below, 26 Feb. 1872, for the result.

[470] His amendment to the 2nd Reading of the Military Manoeuvres bill, criticising the War Office administration; *H* ccviii. 1337–41. The 2nd Reading was eventually agreed without a division.

The Treasury whip with its three lashes has therefore – so far as I am concerned – smacked in vain.

Wednesday, 9 August: The loss of the Captain was Lord H. Lennox's theme to-day and a long debate ensued.[471] This must be read. It is a puzzle to me how the Admiral in command (Milne) has not been tried by Court Martial.

It seems to me that govt. is daily losing ground in the Public estimation. Goschen is an able man – but can it be said that he has adequate experience for the conduct of a great shipbuilding department? The cabinet shd. have called Milner Gibson to the Helm.[472]

Monday, 14 August: [. . .] votes in supply. Among contested points was the sum asked for to defray the expense arising out of the Contagious Diseases Acts. Governmt. manfully stood by these acts and, in my judgment, deserve very great praise.[473]

Friday, 18 August: Wrangling over spilt milk. Elcho and Cardwell. Elcho laid himself open to repartee – a kind of luxury in which Cardwell rarely indulges. As to Elcho, when does he not lay himself open? or, rather, is he not all over vulnerable? Cardwell knew that the Army Bill[474] and appropriation act were safe, otherwise I imagine he would not have punished his assailant so severely tho' the punishment was richly deserved.

Monday, 21 August: The Queen's speech and the Prorogation.

---

[471] Motion for a select committee; withdrawn. The 'Captain' was a newly-designed turret ship which had sunk in the Bay of Biscay, in Sept. 1870, with the loss of 500 men. Stanley Sadler, "In Deference to Public Opinion": The Loss of H.M.S. Captain', *Mariner's Mirror*, lix (1973), 57–68.

[472] The former Liberal minister had lost his seat in 1868, and never returned to the Commons.

[473] William Fowler's motion to reduce the army estimates by £3,793, defeated 65:44; *H* ccviii. 1616–20.

[474] Having abolished the purchase of army commissions by Royal warrant, the government was able to reintroduce its Army Regulation bill which had to be passed by the Lords if any compensation was to be given to officers. Royal assent, 17 Aug.

SESSION OF 1872

Tuesday, 6 February: The House met & there was no opposition; but, nevertheless, much discursive criticism. The Alabama question is the serious point of attack.[475] Ministers have, I think, much trouble in store for them.

A large batch of notices was presented to the House.

Strutt moved, Colman seconding the address. Disraeli's was a good speech – in a graver style than usual. He is rising as a statesman & is fast gaining upon his rival who has less self-command.

Wednesday, 7 February: [...] Government has offended the licensed victuallers & thus a Yorkshire seat has been lost.[476]

The language of the Anglo-American treaty has been so carelessly worded as to cause doubts at least of its obligations.[477] [ink faded] distinctly perceived the blot as long ago as last June. I confess I begin to be anxious for the credit of my leaders [...]

Thursday, 8 February: I was in attendance to-day. Milbank was discomfited in his attempt to get Sir C. Dilke into a new scrape by putting to him a question relating to his recent anti-monarchical utterances.[478] As might have been expected it was decided that the question would be irregular. J. White talked to some of the ruling

---

[475] By the treaty of Washington, 8 May 1871, the British and U.S. governments had agreed to submit a number of disputes between the two countries to independent arbitrators at Geneva. *B.F.S.P.* LXI 40–56. The most important of these disputes involved the American claim of compensation for the damage inflicted on Federal shipping by the 'Alabama', a warship supplied from Britain to the Confederates during the American civil war. It later became clear, however, that the Americans intended to revive their 'indirect claims' for damages, i.e. that they should also receive compensation for the undue prolongation of the civil war allegedly caused by Britain's action. The British government denied that the indirect claims were admissible under the treaty of Washington. Adrian Cook, *The "Alabama" Claims: American Politics and Anglo-American Relations, 1865–1872* (Cornell University Press, 1975).

[476] The Northern division of the West Riding of Yorkshire, where the Conservative candidate won by 54 votes. The abortive Licensing bill of the previous year had provoked great hostility towards the government on the part of the drink interest. *The Times*, 5 Feb. 1872, 8.

[477] i.e. whether the treaty covered the indirect claims.

[478] In a speech at Newcastle, Dilke had criticised the cost of the monarchy; *The Times*, 6 Nov. 1871, 6.

spirits & lay by so as to intercept Milbank before he could say above a word or two.

To-day we had motions on the Speaker's retirement.[479] Gladstone & Disraeli ably discharged a very difficult task. Bouverie's face indicated no very contented feelings.[480]

* In many ways he is qualified for the office. But he has not had sufficient modesty & may have somewhat officiously manifested a relish for the task of reminding Premiers or Premiers expectant of their shortcomings. He, it was, who took the round robin to Lord Russell[481] – & the on dit is that when, years after, Bouverie, on an occasion presenting itself at an interview or business with his lordship, expressed a hope that the memory of the fact had passed away, Lord R. observed, in his dry hoarse manner, 'you think so, do you?'

It was Bouverie who a few years ago spoke of leaders who could not lead & followers who would not follow. This, I think at least, must have involved Gladstone. There is no love lost betwn. the 2 men. Bouverie rates himself too highly. I think it was Roebuck who once described him as a 'political prig'. *

When the Speaker rose to speak, members removed their hats at once. Bouverie had a moment or two of indecision. I also at first abstained from this act, being in doubt if it was usual. But my indecision was only momentary. Bouverie persistently wore his hat, till Lord Ernest Bruce, who sat on my left just above the gangway made, apparently, a king of good natured suggestion to B. to follow the course of the rest & he then acted accordingly [...]

Friday, 9 February: A full house. An empty chair.

Brand sat on the first seat below the gangway on the liberal side. The Serjeant brought up the mace 'advancing with it in his arms – not upon his shoulder – & placed it underneath the table'. (See Times of the 10th.)

After Gladstone had announced the permission of the Queen to elect a new Speaker, the chief clerk (Sir Erskine May) pointed to Roundell Palmer who proposed Brand in a rather long speech. * Note. In the journals of the House it is mentioned that the chief clerk pointed to Gladstone, but not to Palmer. I thought I saw May point to Palmer, but perhaps I was mistaken. * It struck some of us as remarkable that, in a case of this kind, an orator like Palmer shd. have referred so frequently to the notes he held in his hand. However, the effect will be

---

[479] Speaker Denison had informed Gladstone that the strain of the previous session had been too much for him; 24 Nov. 1871, B.L. Add MSS 44261, fo. 322.

[480] He had been passed over for the vacant post, which was offered to H.B. Brand, a former Liberal chief whip.

[481] Reference unclear.

all the better in the print of his speech, as an exact order of ideas will conduce to its written effect (the ideas being well worthy of a studied arrangement).

Locke King seconded him, & I fancied might as well have avoided any reference to disorderly proceedings wh. sometimes occur. L. King's delivery was excellent. His speech was in the main a good one, – perhaps a little too long.

At this moment, mover & seconder got up & were on their way to Brand in order to drag or conduct him to the chair, when he rose to acknowledge the kindness of his reception. The proposer & seconder, shrink back abashed (amid laughter) to any places which chanced to be available, R. Palmer wedging himself in below the gangway to his own & righthand neighbour's inconvenience. Brand delivered a careful speech in excellent taste & with a good clear voice & afterwards proceeded to the chair, not (as I thought usual) dragged to it with violence agt. his will but actually *leading* the file betwn. the legs of Ministers & the table. If he gently resisted (as 'the Times' says) at any moment, the resistance did not appear to my eyes. * Brand again spoke briefly on the top of the steps. *

The ceremony concluded, Gladstone moving the adjournment. This gave him an opening for another florid & rather over coloured speech. I observed to Osborne that Brand must tremble. There is always a danger of Gladstone's saying too much; he is the victim of his facility of expression. At least he shd. be the sole victim.

[. . .] It shd. be mentioned that when the Speaker-elect took his post, the mace was placed on the table.

Tuesday, 13 February: I attended twice to-day. The main topic of debate was the subject of dealing by legislation with Contagious Diseases.[482] Bruce's sketch of the Bill he has prepared was partially unfolded before my arrival. His course is not satisfactory. There were delivered several speeches, & one fell from me. What will the House of Lords say to a measure for the repeal of the acts of 1866 & 1869? They are working well, as even Bruce admits; & he, confessedly, yields to clamor. But thus we are governed. It appears to be the duty of Ministers to find out what is the latest impulse of any powerful section & obey it. Right in the abstract is henceforward to be of no account.

His Bill was read a first time. Then Rylands moved W. Fowler's Bill for a repeal of the acts (66 & 69), on which I objected on a ground of

---

[482] The government had decided to repeal the acts of 1866 and 1869, and rely on other existing laws to deal with brothels; see Gladstone's Cabinet note, 15 July 1871, *G.D.* viii. 7–8.

order.[483] In this objection the Speaker concurred. So Fowler's proposal must wait.

A friend, D.,[484] told me of a recent remark by the late Chancellor (Bethell)[485] on the character of our very orthodox (present) Chancellor, Lord Hatherley – 'that the monotony of his existence is not redeemed by the practice of a single vice'. There actually ought to be a collection of the utterances of the excentric ex-chancellor.

Wednesday, 14 February: I voted to-day for the 2d. reading of the Burials Bill.[486] Miall spoke, giving the Tories distinctly to understand that he was not prepared to accept the Bill as anything like a settlement of the claims of Dissenters & that he regarded the measure as a mere branch of a general adjustment. This frankness was exactly what the Tories wanted & they cheered its expression vociferously.

Jacob Bright very straightforwardly commented to me on my severity tow[ar]ds him yesterday. I told him that he had called a measure which I thought most excellent an 'infamous' act. Also, I reminded him that his brother was as a member of the government responsible for the legislation complained of (the act of 1869 at least might have been specified) & that I had a right to defend Mr John from Mr Jacob Bright.

Many members expressed approval of my speech.

Thursday, 15 February: [...] The Collier question occupied the Lords[487] & looms in the Commons. Ministers had the luck to win by one vote & that the Chancellor's. How wd. it have been had there been no Alabama difficulty.

Monday, 19 February: Ministers only escaped by 27 voices a vote of censure on the appointment of Sir R. Collier![488] Cross spoke well, I

[483] Not recorded in *Hansard*; presumably the objection was that the bill's sponsor was not present.

[484] Unidentified.

[485] Richard Bethell, 1st Baron Westbury; Lord Chancellor 1861–5.

[486] Which passed, 179:108; but Osborne Morgan's annual bill, to permit Dissenters' burial services in Anglican churchyards, again failed to complete its passage through the Commons.

[487] Sir Robert Collier, formerly Attorney General, had been appointed a judge of common pleas solely in order to qualify him for an appointment to the judicial committee of the privy council. Lord Stanhope's resolution, regretting this procedure as a violation of the spirit of the rules governing appointments to the judicial committee (which required a judicial qualification), was defeated by 88:87; *H* ccix. 376–88.

[488] R.A. Cross moved the same resolution as Lord Stanhope's.

gather. Denman's attack was most damaging. Sir Roundell Palmer[489] was, as usual, very effective. It is clear that he, like many others, holds the opinion that the course taken in regard to Collier was a mistake tho' not a mistake worthy of a vote of censure. * T. paired for the night with G.W.P. Bentinck (W. Norfolk). *

Gladstone's government is on the wane. He wants judgment & moderation – in short, ballast. As to his subordinates, they are with few exceptions not first rate men. Hence the scandals which have lately shocked the country. The admiralty is, I fear, in complete chaos.[490]

Tuesday, 20 February: [...] a meeting took place in a room behind the chair to concert measures in opposition to the Ministerial Bill for the abolition of the Contagious Diseases acts. Pakington, Mitford, Playfair & Kinnaird were of the party. I thought it right to apprise Glyn[491] of my hostility to Ministers on this matter. He considered that my recent speech left no doubt about this & he wished all members were as plain spoken as I was. Of course, these are not his exact words [...]

Wednesday, 21 February: Nothing very noteworthy. My vote was given for the Bill enabling a man to marry his deceased wife's sister.[492] Parliament has, I think, rather grown tired of this subject which takes a deal of time.

Thursday, 22 February: [...] Bethell's compliment to the Attorney general's management of the Tichborne case amused me – 'the attorney gen[era]l has detected 2 imposters'. I suppose this was when the cross examination was on foot, as this was considered by some as unskilful.[493]

Friday, 23 February: I gave notice of a 'Call of the House'[494] on the day for which stands fixed the 2d. reading of the Contagious Diseases Bill. My object is to require the whole House to share the responsibility of the course taken.

[...] There was, also, a division on the Parks Bill.[495] This Bill has

---

[489] Moving an amendment that there was no cause for censure; *H* ccix. 677–95. This was carried, 268:241.

[490] See N.A.M. Rodger, 'The Dark Ages of the Admiralty, 1869–85, part 1', *Mariner's Mirror*, lxi (1975), 331–44.

[491] Government chief whip.

[492] 2nd reading of Thomas Chambers' annual bill carried, 186:138.

[493] The Attorney General, Sir John Coleridge, had been counsel for the defence in the celebrated case of Tichborne v. Lushington; *Annual Register*, 1872, part 2, 239–50.

[494] Requiring all members to attend unless they had been given leave of absence.

[495] The Royal Parks and Gardens bill, to regulate public meetings, in committee; Goldsmid's motion to report progress defeated, 140:24.

been the cause of much turmoil. 'Heroic talk' it has been called. Mere scolding, I shd. say. Hardy, Gladstone & Disraeli have called forth severe comments in the 'Times'.[496]

Members on the liberal benches very freely criticize Gladstone's vehemence & excitability. His majorities are dwindling.

Monday, 26 February: A very long time was expended in discussing Lowe's motions relating to the conduct of Public business. There were late at night 2 divisions,[497] which were taken in my absence.

The conduct of the late Speaker in selecting members to speak was referred to by G. Bentinck. It seems that a mode of arranging a list prepared in concert with the whips was the subject of an article in a newspaper.[498] The fact is there must have been enough in the impeachment to found comments.

The present Speaker, it was gathered, will not avail himself of the kind of aid objected to.

The question of excluding strangers at the will of one member was the occasion of a long and useful discussion. The difficulties of innovation were felt to be more serious than had at first appeared.

Ministers will get more elbow room on supply when it stands for Mondays under the new order adopted this evening.

Glyn[499] made a brief speech in his own defence on Bentinck's question. Glyn described his speech as his first, after a membership of 15 years duration. No wonder he did not select oratory to win withal. He has a strong impediment in his utterance, which causes a repetition of several words in every sentence. That which he was understood to deliver was well enough, only that it seemed in a great degree to own Bentinck's case.

If a whip selects members who shd. speak, what chance would an independent member have?

Wednesday, 28 February: [...] Men are curious about my call of the House. There is more interest in it than one might have expected. Glyn affected to be glad of my bringing up members.

---

[496] *The Times*, 24 Feb. 1872, 9. Hardy accused Gladstone of having incited the Hyde Park riot of 1866. His diary records that his speech 'caused such an explosion of passion & temper from Gladstone as even he has seldom exhibited. Constant storms followed. His abuse of me amused me a good deal more than hurt me. He could scarcely get it out for rage. What a leader of the House'; *G.H.D.*, 23 Feb. 1872.

[497] Lowe carried his resolution to facilitate the passing of the Estimates, by avoiding debates on the motion to enter into committee of supply on Mondays, 132:92; *H* ccix. 1058–61. Selwin-Ibbetson's call for a select committee was defeated, 152:120.

[498] Not specified in the debate.

[499] Government chief whip.

Thursday, 29 February: [...] My motion for a call of the House on the 21st March stood for this evening. But hearing a rumour that the Contagious Diseases Prevention &c. Bill would probably not come on then, I took the precaution of eliciting this in Public by a question to the Minister. Gladstone confirmed the rumour & promised to let me have notice of the new day to be fixed. Is there indecision again on this legislation?[500] [...]

Friday, 1 March: [...] a long debate commenced on Sir R. Palmer's motion in favour of creating a great school of Law.[501] This motion was an amendment to the motion for going into Committee of supply, so that the division list does not satisfactorily express the opinions of all who voted. Palmer's was an excellent statement which I listened to with pleasure. It is always a charm to hear a really competent and thoroughly informed advocate speak.

Being very lame – with difficulty ascending & descending the long staircases – & having still a cold, I could not return to the House for a late sitting & hence my name was not in the division list. How I shd. have voted, is uncertain. It seems to me that the Inns of Court, spurred by Palmer, may, ere next year, make regulations superseding his scheme as not necessary. There was much in its favour as the case stands. It seems that England hardly holds an advanced position among nations having schools for instruction in jurisprudence. Lawyers, it is said, study only enough for practice. Division 116 to 103.[502]

Monday, 4 March: My vote, on the Metrop[olitan] Street improvement Bill was in the sense of preferring the regular tribunal to be constituted by the Committee of selection to a tribunal of 10 members, five to be chosen by the said Committee & 5 by the House.[503]

Members seem to me to have no civil shame. If each in turn seek to introduce new courses in order to further projects of particular persons or bodies out of doors, chaos must reign. It seems to me we have too many new members who will not attend to the cautions offered by experienced men [...]

Tuesday, 5 March: Two attendances this evening tried me sorely.

---

[500] The subject does not appear to have been discussed in Cabinet since 3 Feb.; *G.D.* viii. 106.

[501] *H* ccix. 1221–38.

[502] Against the motion. Trelawny mistakenly gave the figure for the minority as 113.

[503] Hinde Palmer's motion for the irregular procedure, *H* ccix. 1318, defeated 170:122. Dodson, the chairman of committees, argued that such a committee would be partisan. The bill was a private one, empowering the Metropolitan Board of Works to borrow £2.5 millions to build a new street between Old Street, Shoreditch, and Oxford Street.

But Dixon's resolutions on education were almost an imperative call. After two divisions E. Forster's amendment was triumphantly carried.[504] The course taken by Dixon of the League[505] & the Dissenters calls to my mind some remarks in this journal in 1870, which remarks are, I think, borne out. The education system is regarded as a new Church Rate. The subject is a very large one. I heard Dr Playfair & Fawcett who distinguished themselves. It was ab[ou]t 1 a.m. when I got home.

Wednesday, 6 March: [. . .] My vote yesterday with Ed. Forster was dictated by the policy sketched in his amendment – that of giving the system already at work a longer trial. His critics on our side are much at loggerheads & have not been by any means consistent. Fawcett honestly admitted that he had made a mistake in 1870. Should we have made the progress we have made towards the education of the whole People had we, at the outset, nailed to the mast the motto of Mr Dixon's party?

Friday, 8 March: We went to Brighton. There was much controversy in the House on two recent appointments – that of Homersham Cox[506] & that of Mr Hervey to the Rectory of Ewelme.[507] Bouverie was very severe in his references to certain peculiarities of Gladstone's mind [. . .]

Monday, 11 March: Army estimates were the topic this evening. I was compelled to nurse a cold & could not return to the House late at night and so I lost 3 divisions. Holms & Muntz moved amendments. Also, there was a vote on Army agencies.[508]

---

[504] Dixon's 6 resolutions criticising the operation of the 1870 Education act, especially the failure in many areas to have School Boards set up, and the use of public money to support denominational schools; *H* ccix. 1395–1407. Defeated 355:94. Forster's amendment, urging that it was too soon to assess the working of the act; *H* ccix. 1418–38, carried by 323:98.

[505] The National Education League, based in Birmingham, which led the opposition to the 1870 act.

[506] Osborne Morgan's resolution that county court judges in Welsh-speaking areas should speak the Welsh language; *H* ccix. 1648–58. Withdrawn. Prompted by the appointment of the non-Welsh speaking Cox to the mid-Wales circuit.

[507] A long debate on the appointment of the Revd. William Harvey as rector of Ewelme, in Oxfordshire. By statute, the rector had to be a member of the Oxford University convocation, but Harvey was a Cambridge graduate: Gladstone had therefore arranged from him to be made a member of the Oxford convocation in order to qualify him. This episode raised similar doubts about Gladstone's methods to those raised in the recent Collier case; see above, 15 and 19 Feb.

[508] Holms' amendment to reduce the army by 20,000 was defeated, 234:63, and Muntz's proposed 10,000 reduction by 216:67; Lea's amendment to omit the item for agencies was lost, 87:43. The Estimates amounted to £5,238,000.

Undoubtedly, the estimates are high. But, really, it does not seem to me that Cardwell is managing our affairs badly. As the Country becomes richer, it presents to enemies more temptations. The cost of labour, too, has greatly increased. My vote would certainly have been given in favour of Governmt.

Tuesday, 12 March: [...] Sir D. Wedderburn moved a resolution with the object of expediting Scotch business. After some debate – Macfie being on his legs – the House was counted out. This I suppose was done in order to gain time[509] [...]

The fact is undeniable that business is very seriously retarded by want of will or want of power in some one.

Wednesday, 13 March: We had a division on a Bill for affording facilities for Public worship under authority of the bishop of a diocese.[510]

Henley uttered the common sense of the case, as I at least thought, so, seeing no reason why the Church shd. not have every means of enabling her 'to overtake population' I voted with the ayes.

The afternoon was not altogether unprofitably passed, as I had much talk with members about the game laws.

Thursday, 14 March: Three times the Committee on the Ballot Bill divided. Little progress was made. My voice was with Ministers on an amendment to clause 1.[511]

There was a good deal of time wasted & it is likely the tactics pursued last year will be repeated in this.

Torrens wanted to throw the costs of Elections on the Consolidated Fund, but took few votes.[512]

The Speaker had one or two opportunities of exhibiting his qualifications & he did his work well.

J. Locke & I had some conversation on the Game Laws. It occurred to me that he & I might jointly prepare a Bill. He is a great authority on this subject, having written on it an able treatise which I must get.[513]

---

[509] Wedderburn wanted a select committee. Gladstone's Cabinet memorandum of 9 Mar. notes obliquely, 'Wedderburn's motion: act for the best'; *G.D.* viii. 122.

[510] Salt's Public Worship Facilities bill, allowing bishops to licence clergy to perform certain services in e.g. school rooms. 122:93 for the 2nd reading, but later withdrawn.

[511] 265:108 against Gregory's amendment to prevent nominations being made without the candidates' consent; *H* cciv. 1956.

[512] Defeated, 362:54.

[513] *The Game Laws*, (5th ed., 1866). No bill was prepared, but Trelawny's concern about this subject reflected constituency pressure for action: see his speech at Liskeard, *The Times*, 9 Jan. 1872, 5. Trelawny's own position was that he was prepared to give tenants control over game on their holdings, but he was against abolishing all penalties for poaching. The audience at Liskeard seems to have favoured total abolition of the game laws.

Ministers are sinking daily. All sorts of subjects require immediate attention, & our leaders want grasp. The admiralty is in a horrid state of confusion.

It will be very difficult to defend our chiefs at banquets in the Country.

I served on a Committee in 1870 chosen to enquire into the expediency of appointing R. Catholic chaplains in some of the Queen's Prisons. Our recommendation was made,[514] but is not yet adopted in an act. This is weakness in Ministers as they are simply afraid of exciting the ire of fanatical protestants.

About 1/4 of a century ago (in 1845–6?)[515] I served on Bright's Game Laws Committee. The subject was then threshed out & yet Ministers are ab[ou]t to refer it to a new Committee!

The Alabama case is their great rock ahead. On that I think it quite possible that they may receive a vote of censure.

Tuesday, 19 March: There was an unusually full House, there being much curiosity ab[ou]t Dilke's motion on the Civil list.[516] When his turn came, Lord Bury rose to raise a point of Privilege – citing the oath taken by members and implying, as it would appear, that Dilke's republican opinions were inconsistent with that oath. The speaker ruled that he had no ground for interference – & Bury sat down, with a diminished reputation for good sense.

This incident gave Dilke a fair chance of a hearing as the House was not very favourable to Lord B's interposition.

In a long speech delivered most fluently but with a very disagreeable voice & in a most monotonous tone, Dilke unfolded his case. His self-possession was complete but his style wanting in experience. He evinced proofs of considerable industry, yet from want of methodical arrangement & neatness I think he failed to do his case full justice.

Members became very riotous & disorderly. Strangers were excluded; attempts were made several times to count the House & cockcrowing was heard – nay, even a hiss. * Some other farm bird may have waddled into the building. *

There was a division on a motion for adjournt. & on the main question Dilke had 2 votes.[517]

I only remained till 1/4 before 7, so failed to witness the disorderly

---

[514] *P.P.* 1870, viii. 715.

[515] *P.P.* 1845, xii. 331; 1846, ix. 1.

[516] Motion for returns; *H* ccx. 251–91.

[517] 276 voted against him. Dillwyn's earlier motion to adjourn the House (defeated 261:23), by forcing a division, had made it possible for strangers to return.

portion of the sitting. The 'Times' blames Gladstone for his excited manner in replying to the mover.[518]

Wednesday, 20 March: [...] Several people have seemed to think that the treatment experienced by Auberon Herbert[519] will give a certain strength to Republicanism which it otherwise might have wanted. Gladstone's attempt to stifle discussion was unwise. Palmerston would have pursued very different tactics: perhaps, he would have entered the lists with Dilke who might have been handled as skilfully as the Tiverton Butcher (Rowcliff).[520] As the matter now stands, there lurks a suspicion that there are facts not to be disclosed with credit to H. M.'s advisers [...]

Thursday, 21 March: I had a few words with Glyn[521] ab[ou]t the Contagious Diseases Prevention Bill. Was it coming on on the day for wh. it stands on the paper Viz, Ap[ril] 8th? He said it would not come on that day, & added that notice enough would be given me of its coming on so that I might make my motion for a call of the House. This information I communicated to Sir John Pakington, adding that I shd. take no further step till after Easter.

[...] Glyn asked whether I wd. serve on the Game Laws committee. Yes, I replied – but with some warnings to him that my division of E[ast] C[ornwall] expects action.

Col[onel] Anson had some talk with me on my intended course with respect to the Bill of Ministers on Contagious Diseases Prevention &c. He is keenly opposed to it. There is little doubt but we shall, numerically speaking, present a powerful phalanx united in resistance to the mischievous change projected.

Amidst sham conflicts and half-hearted men one finds at last a cause which is real.

Friday, 22 March: A very instructive day's work. Dodson's resolutions on the management of private business by a new tribunal were discussed. Many members who are listened to with deserved respect on account of their praiseworthy labours in conducting the comparatively unseen routine of private Bill legislation delivered their opinions. The immense demands on the time & health of the House caused by the existing system necessitate change – and that without delay.

---

[518] *The Times*, 20 Mar. 1872, 9. Cf. Speaker Brand to Gladstone, 20 Mar. 1872, expressing concern at the 'turbulent proceedings'; B.L. Add MSS 44194, fo. 143.

[519] The main target of the disorderly conduct during the previous day's debate.

[520] Who had customarily spoken against Palmerston at each election; Hon. E. Ashley, *Life of Viscount Palmerston, 1846–65* (1876), ii. 151–3.

[521] Government chief whip.

Heavy costs are often equal to a denial of justice – & it is considered that travelling by railway has been rendered very dear by the same cause. Dodson's first resolution was carried & now we await further proceedings. Probably, a bill will be brought in[522] [...]

Saturday, 23 March: Several persons interested in C[ontagious] D[iseases] legislation met at Mr Mitford's house. Among others Dr Skey & Dr Spencer Smith. Also, Mr Lane, Mr Berkeley Hill, & Nassau Senior.[523] We discussed various points. Over 2,000 doctors have signed a memorial in favour of the acts now in force.

Monday, 25 March: After preliminary exhibitions of egotism in members putting questions to ministers and several mistakes committed by persons whom no rebuffs will ever instruct, Lowe propounded his budget. It was on the whole very well received[524] [...]

Tuesday, 26 March: The O'Donoghue spoke ably agt. the Dublin Universities Bill which Fawcett conducts. There was a division during the evening upon it, wh. I missed.[525] During the early part of the debate I was present.

The O'Donoghue evidently comes forward as the organ of the priests who I gather wish to have an exclusively Catholic University. The abolition of Tests in the existing University seems to be unfavourable to this object.

Thursday, 4 April: The House resumed its labours.[526] V. Harcourt moved an amendment to the estimates of the Chancellor of the exchequer & was defeated by only ab[ou]t 2 to 1.[527] There was but a small attendance. It seems to me that the Tories must have left to Ministers the task of doing their own unpopular work. * T. absent (in the country). *

There was, later, a division on the Chancery Suitors Fund Bill. Governmt. propose to take charge of this fund, paying £2 per cent

[522] There was no bill. The chairman of committees' 1st resolution, that the private legislation system 'requires reform', was agreed; *H* ccx. 507.

[523] Senior was an eminent economist; the others were members of the medical profession. For the surgeon, F.C. Skey, see Paul McHugh, *Prostitution and Victorian Social Reform* (1980), 38–42.

[524] *H* ccx. 603–27. With a large surplus in hand, Lowe took 2d. off the income tax and gave extra relief to those on incomes under £300 per annum.

[525] 94:21 for the 2nd reading of the bill to abolish religious tests at Trinity College, Dublin.

[526] Having adjourned for Easter on 26 Mar.

[527] 78:35 against the motion to reduce national expenditure; *H* ccx. 735–47.

upon it & making a profit out of the same for the Public.[528] This Henley calls 'a grab' at other people's money. Bouverie does not quite approve of the proceedings, which is one of scores of cases illustrative of the tendency of all business to gravitate to a centre & that centre the House of Commons. Nothing, great or small, escapes the action of this law. Observe this in the daily questions put to Ministers.

Friday, 5 April: [...] Newspapers comment upon the thinness of the House when the Sanitary Bill of Stansfeld was moved.[529] Will Boards of guardians have virtue & self denial enough for the intelligent performance of the kind of duties devolved upon them by this legislation? *How do they pay medical men now?*

Monday, 8 April: [...] There were 3 divisions after I left – 1. on voting papers, 2. on a more open kind of Ballot (!) & [3] on providing machinery for the detection of personation by a scrutiny.[530] This has long been a difficulty I have as regards a Ballot Bill. A fearless voter, valuing his rights & anxious to be secure that his vote really told for the candidate of his choice, would desire to retain the power of proving the fact. If he have this power, there can be no absolute secrecy; and, if no absolute secrecy, no security for the oppressed.

Every debate exhibits the childishness of the measure. Really, the House shd. give a little of its time to serious matters such as the scourges which afflict us in the shape of preventible diseases. We are wasting another session & putting constitutional govt. in jeopardy [...]

Tuesday, 9 April: I conversed with Horsman & Pakington on possible courses in relation to the C[ontagious] D[iseases] question & Ministerial conduct – Stansfeld's[531] in particular. Quieta non movere seems the best course at this moment.

I voted with the majority agt. deviation from the ordinary course in the matter of hearing by counsel Metropolitan Ratepayers. * Metropolitan Improvements. T. followed Bonham Carter & Dodson's lead.[532] *

---

[528] 2nd reading passed, 89:37; Royal assent 6 Aug.

[529] The 2nd reading of the Public Health bill was passed without a division.

[530] Parliamentary Elections bill, in committee. Lowther's amendment allowing postal votes, *H* ccx. 914–16, defeated 81:36; Bentinck's to omit candidates' names from the ballot paper, *H* ccx. 926, defeated 143:99; Gregory's for numbered ballot papers, *H* ccx. 932–3, defeated 166:126.

[531] A government minister who had come out in favour of repeal in a speech at Halifax; *The Times*, 4 Apr. 1872, 12.

[532] The new chairman of committees and his predecessor opposed Hinde Palmer's motion that petitions by London ratepayers against the Metropolitan Streets improvement bill be heard by the select committee; *H* ccx. 955–6. Defeated 150:108.

[...] W. Fowler moved a resolution agt. entails & took a fair number with him.[533] Gregory, who is a solicitor, made, as I think, as good a defence of the law as the case admitted. Gladstone was undecided, and Fowler advised him to walk out. Rather sarcastic! * T. was paired generally with Northcote. How wd. he have voted?

Wednesday, 10 April: [...] Gladstone rather frequently takes some step or makes some speech which tends to shake confidence in him as a leader. His course on tuesday on the Metropolitan Bill was in the very teeth of the opinions of experts on Private Bill legislation & seemed to justify a remark I overheard that his vote was given qua member of Greenwich.[534] Then why lay himself open to Fowler's taunt? Surely, Gladstone might have said Fowler had failed to convince Her Majesty's government! Waning, waning, waning. This seems to me to describe its state. How will they escape an adverse verdict on the Megara?[535]

Thursday, 11 April: [...] I saw Osborne, who informed me he had failed in finding a remarkable precedent I had mentioned to him for his coming motion in the case of Lady Mayo[536] & begged me to help him, so I went to the Library of the Commons & soon found the whole story in the records of debates of 1845 when Hume compelled Peel to give Sir Henry Pottinger an annuity.[537] It was fortunate that I thought of this. I took into the House 2 vols of Hansard and handed them to Osborne who mastered them very soon &, returning, said 'you have made me'. The fact is he has now a whole mine of arguments in the many speeches made at the period alluded to – among the rest Palmerston's.[538]

After an interesting debate on a private Bill, the House resolved itself into Committee on the Ballot Bill and a division was taken on the question of the word 'secretly'. On this my vote was with the Tories.[539]

[533] But he was beaten, 103:81; *H* ccx. 992–1004.

[534] In the case of private bills introduced by representative bodies like the Metropolitan Board of works, those represented by that body had no right to petition against such bills. But Gladstone had questioned whether the MBW was really a representative body, as it was not elected by the ratepayers; *H* ccx. 964–5. There was strong opposition to the bill from London M.P.s, and it made no further progress.

[535] A ship used for transporting seamen to Australia, which had run aground in June 1871. A court martial in Nov. 1871 exonerated Captain Thrupp, and the general view was that the Admiralty was to blame for sending out an unseaworthy vessal; *Annual Register*, 1871, appendix, 243–6.

[536] Whose husband, the Viceroy of India, had been murdered in Feb.

[537] 3 June 1845; *H* lxxx. 1374–80.

[538] Osborne withdrew his motion on 18 Apr. after receiving assurances from Gladstone; *H* ccx. 1479–81.

[539] 202:126 against Bentinck's amendment to omit 'secretly' from clause 2; *H* ccx. 1091.

Altho' I care little for the Bill which is the source of much delay of business, the word gave me a good opportunity of recording a protest agt. the principle of the measure [...]

Craufurd divided the House on the formation of a Borough Funds Bill & there were none but tellers. One effect of very late sittings is, I think, that members really have not the calmness required for a wise exercise of their judgment.

Friday, 12 April: Gladstone described the existing state of affairs in the matter of the Alabama claims.[540] Rathbone's question elicited so much that Disraeli had little left to do, and I suspect missed an opportunity of uttering some of the speech he had prepared. His usually impassive or well-disciplined features never I think exhibited so much concentrated bitterness as at the moment when he sat down & just afterwards. This I particularly observed. Gladstone was very calm & I think rejoiced at the skilful movement by which his foe had been discomfited – for I conclude Rathbone had had a hint of the course which would be convenient.

It struck me that Lawson's motion on treaties of guarantee[541] was not one which it would be wise to indorse. Cast-iron rules are not applicable to politics. W. Cartwright seemed to me to speak with knowledge & force.

My name was not in any division this evening. The Ballot Bill came on. It is daily assuming a more & more ridiculous aspect. Pity it is that so good a man as W.E. Forster is used up to such little purpose [...]

Monday, 15 April: 10.30 a.m. A rather hard week before us, I fear.

So, in fact, it commenced. Our committee lasted over three hours – nearly 3 1/2 – and very keenly debated were the clauses of the Bill (Masters & servants).[542] Poor Political economy appears to be in very bad odour. It can, however, still get a hearing.

The business in the House was the Ballot Bill, on which, after 5 divisions, Ministers received a defeat, though only by a single vote. This defeat was on Harcourt's amendmt. to the penalty for breach of confidence in the voter not to divulge proceedings.[543] The tone of

---

[540] The government had prepared its counter-case to the 'indirect claims' made by the U.S. government; *H* ccx. 1144–9.

[541] That Britain should withdraw from all treaties binding her to military intervention; *H* ccx. 1151–7, defeated by 126:21.

[542] Committed to a select committee of which Trelawny was a member; *H* ccx. 214–21. The bill was to replace the Truck act of 1831, with the same object of ensuring money payments to labourers.

[543] Leatham, backed by Forster, had moved an amendment imposing penalties on those who revealed their vote; Harcourt moved an amendment to this replacing the word 'wilfully' with 'with corrupt intent', and this was carried, 167:166; *H* ccx. 1292–5.

several Ballotists is that they intended the Bill shd. confer safety to voters who might desire freedom thro' secrecy, not that a fearless voter shd. be punished for speaking of his vote & for whom he gave it. On this rock I expect the Bill will split. Forster doggedly stood to his guns and fought his ship as long as there remained anything on wh. he could hang a rag of bunting. But the motion to report progress looks like an admission that fortune has deserted him. What will Ministers do? or, if they persevere, how can it be expected that the House of Lords will pass the Bill? They will say, 'why, Gentlemen, you send us a discredited measure!'

Tuesday, 16 April: Lopes spoke well for one hour and thirty five minutes and obtained a great Victory – a majority of 100![544] Govt. must have managed matters carelessly. When I went down for a 2d. time, I considered that a division would not take place on the main question, as it was 11 o'clock and there were many candidates for the Speaker's eye. So I paired for ministers with Sir D. Salomons & went home. How could Gladstone content himself with the amendment of Acland?[545] Nothing could be more mistaken. Acland seemed to admit the gist of Lopes's case. Situated as I found myself, I felt that I could not accept Lopes's words explained by the light of his speech. He seeks that some £2,037,000 be taken off the shoulders of rate-payers & placed on those of the general tax-payers. But why £2,037,000 only? On his shewing twice that sum shd. be thus dealt with. How about centralisation? How ab[ou]t probate duties on real property? Will landowners relish their condition after such changes as may come of a full inquiry into the whole subject of the incidence of taxation? What tax has the full assent of taxpayers? How would the House of Commons have looked if Lowe had asked for 1 1/2 [d.] in the £1 in the shape of Income tax in order to meet charges now falling on the rates?

    * Palmerston would have treated the difficulty very lightly. Perhaps, he would have kept the debate alive till 1 a.m. and then have moved an adjournment on account of the strength of Lopes's case and interest felt in it. Gladstone has managed matters almost as badly as possible. *

---

[544] 259:159 for the resolution to relieve owners and occupiers of the burden of local taxation for charges such as the police and the administration of justice, which were beyond local control; *H* ccx. 1331–55. 37 Liberal M.P.s voted with Lopes; J.P. Parry, *Democracy and Religion: Gladstone and the Liberal Party, 1867–1875* (Cambridge, 1986), 351.

[545] Agreeing that relief to ratepayers was desirable, and that rates for new objects should be shared equitably between owners and occupiers, as in Scotland and Ireland; *H* ccx. 1355–69.

Thursday, 18 April: 'The Times' of this date has a serious warning to Gladstone.[546]

[...] the House soon went to its work on the Ballot Bill. Ministers experienced a crushing defeat.[547] The hero of the evening was Vernon Harcourt who made a telling and most amusing speech. His line is to enact a Ballot Bill which will give protection to the timid or persecuted but not to enforce secrecy upon people undesirous of it and this appeared to be the mature judgment of the Committee. Sir Geo. Grey & Bouverie made speeches in this sense. A very good one was made from the opposite point of view by Henry James, who seems to me to have some of the gifts of an orator. I consider that he evinced qualities which, with proper cultivation and more experience, are likely to carry him far.[548]

There were, I count, six divisions on the Ballot. My vote was given in favour of Harcourt's motion – which was in denunciation of three months imprisonment with hard labour for shewing a voting paper.

Osborne seemed to think Ministers would let the Bill drop, but Gladstone – who managed to keep his temper – preferred to continue the fight.

The Tories were half-frantic with delight and would hardly let the tellers announce the victory tho' it was their own.

There was afterwards a division on the Parks Bill upon which opposition has nearly died out. Early in the session the Bill gave considerable trouble. I believe there has been a compromise.[549]

Monday, 22 April: [...] I was for some 3 1/2 hours in the committee on Masters & servants &c. A very lively discussion was kept up on sections of the Bill. I did my best to obtain a hearing of the Cornish miners case.

Then, I went to the House, but took no part in divisions. It is not my wish to vote frequently in these – even could I remain most of the night. I don't like the Ballot & don't like to oppose it obstructively – and in my peculiar condition of opinions pairing for the night is almost impossible.

'The Daily News' threatens a dissolution in the case of Fawcett's

---

[546] *The Times*, 18 Apr. 1872, 11, criticising Gladstone's failure to recognise the discontent of ratepayers, and pointing to the ominously large number of Liberal absentees from the division on Lopes' resolution.

[547] In the debate continued from the 15th, Leatham's amendment was defeated 274:246. Trelawny was one of 37 Liberals in the majority, another 70 were absent unpaired; Bruce L. Kinzer, *The Ballot Question in Nineteenth Century English Politics* (New York, 1982), 210.

[548] He joined the government in Oct. 1873.

[549] 3rd reading of the Royal Parks and Gardens bill, passed 114:19; Royal assent 27 June.

beating ministers in a division on his Dublin University Bill.

[...] Mismanagement is more & more attributed to the government which seems to be 'all abroad'.

Tuesday, 23 April: I attended at 4 p.m. A Petition of interest from certain poor women at Windsor was presented by Roger Eykyn. At my instigation he moved that it be read by the clerk. Sir Erskine May accordingly read it – silence having been first obtained by cries of 'order order' from some of us. The petition was cheered by the great body of the House.[550]

[...] Government is in a weak state. After several damaging defeats, there is looming a motion by Fawcett on University matters in Ireland on which motion he will, it is said, have the support of the Conservatives.

Forster's speech on Candlish's motion[551] was to my mind conclusive. Compulsion is necessary. Between 3 and 4 hundred thousand children would not be educated without it. Parents have a right to name the kind of instruction children shd. have.

Wednesday, 24 April: Mitford has very usefully employed himself in collecting names of members willing to join a deputation to the Home Sec[retar]y to remonstrate agt. the projected repeal of the Sanitary acts of 66 & 69 which interest many of us [...]

Thursday, 25 April: [...] Fawcett moved the adjournment of the House and in a lively and caustic speech complained of the conduct of Ministers in regard to the subject of University Tests.[552] Playfair followed him in a similar spirit. Both speakers were very effective. Bouverie gave additional weight to the charges made. The Speaker twice endeavoured to keep Fawcett & his seconder within the rules of debate – & with some success. Gladstone very skilfully pleaded the great pressure of business and the smallness of the time at his disposal. Not a point was left out in his speech – I mean, every charge was dealt with. The Liberal part of the House was not as jubilant in its reception of the reply of the Minister as it would have been three years ago. In fact,

---

[550] Eykyn proceeded to introduce an Offences Against Women and Children bill, imposing punishment by whipping for certain offences; *H* ccx. 1798, no progress made.

[551] To repeal clause 25 of the 1870 Education act, which allowed School Boards to pay the fees of pauper children so that they could attend denominational schools; *H* ccx. 1714–18, defeated 316:115. The majority contained 188 Conservatives, 42 Irish Liberals, and only 67 non-official Liberals; Parry, *Democracy and Religion*, 337.

[552] He complained about the government's failure to unreservedly support his bill to abolish religious tests in Trinity College Dublin; *H* ccx. 1813–22. Bill withdrawn. Ministers had wanted to divide the bill, accepting the abolition of tests, but opposing the clauses relating to the government of Trinity College Dublin, and they had threatened to make the issue one of confidence; Parry, *Democracy and Religion*, 344–8.

the government is on its trial and on an issue of the govt's choice, and yet Gladstone does not, as usual, select an early day for a decision of the question 'is the House contented with the executive?' [...]

Friday, 26 April: Trevelyan moved an amendment to the usual order for supply in favour of Household suffrage in counties & I went into the lobby one of 70 who voted for his proposal. We were defeated by 2 to 1.[553]

Gladstone spoke agt. Trevelyan. Fawcett made an able speech on our side. Clare Read was on the other side. After his speech St Aubyn, conversing with me, commented on Disraeli's marked attention to Read, who, sitting on the 2d. bench below the gangway, received a sort of visit from his leader and I am inclined to think some compliments. It is a very rare thing to see Disraeli leave his place except to go out of the House. He sits watchful & impassive, yet sometimes slightly betrays the effort it costs him to repress emotion. To-day, when Fawcett commented upon D's clever 'tactics' in 'dishing' his opponents (with an illustration), he seemed to affect for a moment somnolence but he failed to disguise the reception of a 'palpable hit'.

Fawcett is well heard – but it is possible that the House may in the end resent so many fluent lectures. There is in his accent something provincial which is the more disagreeable thro' the loudness of his voice. Not seeing the expression of his audience[554] he loses an advantage possessed by other speakers.

Tuesday, 30 April: [...] I strongly pressed on the Game Laws Committee the duty of accepting the law & the facts as established, & proceeding to consider the bills introduced in 1871 & 1872 relating to England. This as a practical step. In the main my proposals received assent, but I hear they were deemed to be not in conformity with the order of reference. But is a committee of the House a court of Chancery – bound by rigid rules? I think not. Are we destined to waste 2 more years on an enquiry? It is intended to put the question on the shelf?

Wednesday, 1 May: The debate of this day was on Jacob Bright's bill for giving unmarried women the franchise. This motion had my support.[555] The principle on which my decision stands is this that heads of houses owning property & paying taxes ought to be represented. The case of married women is quite distinct. Many fallacies were

---

[553] 148:70.
[554] He was blind.
[555] 2nd reading of the Women's Disabilities Removal bill defeated, 222:143.

imported into the question. Several witty speeches were made – the wittiest that of Serjeant Dowse. Scourfield, too, spoke with humour & force – like a cultivated man as he is.[556]

In the evening I dined with the Speaker, who did the honours as host capitally. The party was a mixed one, I think intended to consist of independent members.

Friday, 3 May: [...] I was in attendance in the early part of the evening, having a considerable number of petitions for presentation. Hardly a day passes, but I have a batch – chiefly for Sir W. Lawson's Permissive Prohibitory Bill [...]

Monday, 6 May: Government experienced a crushing defeat on Gordon's motion relating to religious teaching in Scotland.[557] I paired for the night with Sir L. Palk. * T. with govt. *

It seems to me that ministers cannot continue much longer to hold office with advantage to the Country or with credit to themselves.

The state of the Alabama question may preclude immediate resignation.

The course taken by Dixon & the Birmingham League on the 25th clause of the education act 1870 appears to be bearing fruits – little, perhaps, contemplated by that party.[558] The best chance for state education lay in moderation and mutual allowances for inevitable differences of opinion [...]

Wednesday, 8 May: The first deed of this day was a refusal to adopt the usual motion that committees shd. not sit till two o'clock to-morrow, that being Ascension day. Bouverie led in this affair, but said he did not mean to divide. However, a division was challenged & Glyn met with defeat.[559] Bouverie's argument was that the loss of two hours to persons concerned in private Bills involved a loss of some £2,000. * T. not arrived in time. *

Next came the great Permissive Prohibitory Bill, Lawson as usual moving. A very powerful speech was delivered by Henley who spoke

---

[556] Both opposing the bill; *H* ccxi. 66–8, 34–7.

[557] Amendment to the Scottish Education bill, for retaining the existing system of religious instruction in publicly funded schools; *H* ccxi. 288–302, carried 216:209. For the government's mishandling of the debate and division, see *G.H.D.*, 7 May 1872.

[558] The Scottish Education bill (Royal assent, 6 Aug.) was a blow to the National Education League's campaign for non-denominational education; G.I.T. Machin, *Politics and the Churches in Great Britain, 1869–1921* (Oxford, 1987), 51.

[559] 52:47 against the government chief whip's motion. Glyn complained to Gladstone that 'It was a most unfair proceeding on the part of the Radicals', who had forced a division which Bouverie had not intended; 8 May [1872], B.L. Add MSS 44348 fo. 166.

of that great canvasser, the Quart Pot. Towards 1/2 past 5, some one moved the adjournment, which, thinking that many wanted to speak – for many had risen at the same moment during the debate & one told me he had come from America in order to be present – I supported.[560] 'The Times' will have it that this was an unworthy manoeuvre.[561] Now, so far as I was concerned this charge is most unjust. My vote was deliberately given on the principle of obtaining 'more light'. * T. for adjournt. The principle was not touched by the division. * [. . .]

Thursday, 9 May: I have hardly time for the task of recording votes.[562] Hodgkinson moved for limiting the expenses to be charged by returning officers. His motion seemed to me not a good one, because in fixing a limit, he almost gave a legislative sanction to a charge, when, in reality, there ought to be no charge at all. Mr Forster's answer to Hodgkinson tended to convince me that his amendmt. was inexpedient – & I opposed it.[563]

Mr Sclater-Booth proposed to leave out clause 1 wh. would abolish nomination meetings as now held & for these substitute private meetings. These Sir G. Grey & Bouverie denounced, while Osborne (with his usual raciness) supported the Ministerial proposal. My vote was agt. it.[564]

Mr Forster's plan for altering the hours of polling being propounded, there was much discussion & it was eventually defeated by Ministerial voters – Forster renouncing his own policy (350 to 48).[565] This vote was taken while I was not in attendance; as, also, was taken the vote on Sir R. Knightley's amendmt. to the effect that, in lieu of an illiterate voter being required to go before a magistrate (which he thought would in effect disfranchise many) the voter shd. make a declaration before the returning officer.[566]

Really this is too bad. The House adjourned only at two o'clock & the debate stands over till monday next. More & more it comes to be admitted that the framing of a Bill which shd. present a workable scheme of secret voting is a matter 'bristling' with difficulties. In a country where the will of one man acting thro' Prefets is equivalent to Law, Ballot may be carried out by arrangements adapted to exceptional

[560] Sir F. Heygate's motion was defeated, 369:15; the bill was later withdrawn.

[561] *The Times*, 9 May 1872, 9.

[562] The Parliamentary and Municipal Elections bill, in committee.

[563] 349:82 against the amendment; *H* ccxi. 511–12.

[564] 253:177 for retaining clause 1.

[565] *H* ccxi. 550, for Forster's plan of variable closing times according to the time of year.

[566] 183:168 against the amendment, *H* ccxi. 557–8, which was contrary to the principle of secret voting, and probably merely intended as a delaying tactic.

cases; but when these have to be foreseen & dealt with in clauses embodying penal sanctions – there is no end to difficulties which may be expected.

What will the House of Lords have to say to all this? [...]

Saturday, 11 May: On this day, by appointment, a deputation of 150 members of the House, of the most varying shades of Political opinion, went up to Mr Bruce in order to urge upon him the expediency of maintaining the Sanitary acts of 1866 and 1869.[567] Sir J. Pakington & I headed the deputation. Just before 1 p.m. doors were opened and we entered the Home Sec[retar]y's room. There were Bruce and Winterbotham.[568] We found a good number of chairs arranged in a segment of a circle. Pakington & I had chairs side by side, opposite to Bruce, & we were in the centre of the deputation. Pakington then opened proceedings in a plain & effective manner. When he concluded, he presented a document which had been confided to him – viz, a memorial signed by some 2,400 docters strongly opposed to the abolition of the acts. The list comprised many names of the highest authority in the Profession. J.S.T. followed Sir J. Pakington and, on sitting down, received marks of the approval of the deputation. Others spoke briefly, adding each a little to our statements. Mitford, Eykyn & some one or two more.

Bruce spoke at length and very frankly described the difficulties by which government is beset. He is evidently in agreement with us, but some of his colleagues think differently. His reference to my little contribution to the days proceedings was, I fear, more than my due. About 2 or somewhat sooner we all rose and, interchanging bows with the Minister, retired [...]

Monday, 13 May: [...] In a very full House – the galleries occupied by numerous persons of great distinction (including, as I learn, the King of the Belgians) – Gladstone described the state of affairs in relation to the Alabama dispute. He spoke for nearly 1/2 an hour & had no more anxious listener than Lord Granville.[569] The Premier was very careful in his language &, paying high compliments to the House on its forbearance hitherto, especially begged that it might be continued for a little longer. Disraeli followed – but had little to say in substance

[567] See *The Times*, 13 May 1872, 8.

[568] The under-secretary.

[569] The Foreign Secretary was listening to Gladstone's account of the fact that the supplemental article to the treaty of Washington, whereby the U.S. was to drop her 'indirect claims' for damages in return for a pledge that Britain would not make such claims in any analagous case in future, had been referred to the U.S. Senate for approval; *H* ccxi. 654–63.

beyond words expressive of acquiescence. Of course, interest ceased when Gladstone had spoken & Disraeli need not have uttered more than a single sentence. The galleries were soon nearly empty & I presumed the House of Peers was the attraction [...]

Monday, 27 May: At the close of the Whitsuntide recess,[570] the aspect of political affairs is for the moment brightened, the American Senate being favourably disposed to the supplemental (Alabama) treaty.

At the usual time when questions are put Disraeli wanted to know how we stand on this matter. Gladstone was cautious – & gave but little news. The truth is, I believe, ministers are in the throes of negociation [...]

Thursday, 30 May: The first business in progress at the time when I came was on an amendmt. by Dillwyn in opposition to a private Bill for the sale of All Saints Church, Cardiff. This was the occasion of a rather smart controversy. Old landmarks gave no certain indication of any member's vote. Dillwyn was successful.[571]

It seemed to me, after listening to arguments, that, unless one were hostile to the established Church, there was no adequate reason for refusing to indorse the plan contained in the Bill. My vote was, therefore, in its favour.

[...] The rumour is general that the Alabama Treaty is virtually dead.[572] If this rumour prove to be correct, Ministers will have a rather rough time during the remainder of the session. Legislation is very much in arrear. Many measures which have for long past been wanted have been put aside, for the sake of the Ballot Bill. Adderley's question as to the great measure for promoting & preserving the health of the People ominously reminded the House of its precious time wasted. He wanted for the Bill a morning sitting, but could not get it.[573]

Friday, 31 May: We sat 4 hours and 10 minutes in the Game Laws Committee Room. Our little Parliament consists of 19 members. Ward Hunt (otherwise mother Hunt) ably guides our deliberations. He is a very pleasant & genial gentleman.

[570] The House having adjourned for Whitsun on 13 May.

[571] Defeating the bill, which had originated in the House of Lords, by 172:153 on the 2nd reading.

[572] It now appeared that the U.S. government would not agree to the supplemental article; Granville to Gladstone, 29 May 1872, in Agatha Ramm (ed), *The Political Correspondence of Mr. Gladstone and Lord Granville, 1868–1876* (Royal Historical Society, Camden Third Series, LXXXI-II, 1952), ii. 328–9.

[573] The Public Health bill did finally receive the Royal assent on 10 Aug.

[...] Glyn[574] tells me that there is no chance of the Contagious Diseases Prevention &c. Bill coming on on the 10th, but I keep my motion for 'a call of the House' on the list for a little time longer. In my opinion the Bill will die a natural death [...]

Monday, 3 June: [...] Mr Howard, the Librarian, supervises the printing of Parl[iamentar]y papers. He desired to know if I wished that the whole return presented to the House by the War Office on my motion relating to Colonels shd. be printed.[575] I answered in the affirmative for certain reasons founded on past experience. * Mem. In regard to the Colonels my object was to shew how these valuable appointments to sinecure offices being rewards for distinguished services are disposed of. I moved hereon in Gen[eral] Peel's time, many years back & regret that I did not insist upon the order of the House being carried into effect. I hesitated on learning how much labour the return would cost. * [...]

Tuesday, 4 June: [...] lively proceedings on a deputation of miners & others interested in the masters & servants Bill to Mr Bruce — when many members gave expression to their opinions[576] [...]

St Aubyn, Pendarves Vivian & I conferred on the question of rating mines. We agreed to propose to Bolitho the holding of another county meeting that we may receive a fresh opinion of the county under altered circumstances — H. Lopes hav[in]g given notice of a Bill to rate minerals. Thus far our abstention has been due to a resolution adopted at a county meeting[577] [...]

Thursday, 6 June: [...] Sir Massey Lopes put to Gladstone a question whether govt. mean to take any step towards giving effect to the decision taken on Lopes's resolution.[578] The reply was rather misty. One might, perhaps, gather from it that Lopes has greatly widened the area of the subject to be dealt with in a new general measure on rating; and, if I mistake not, he or his party will rue the day when the resolution was carried.

Monday, 10 June: [...] Maguire requested that I would move the first reading of the Prison Ministers Bill. The object is to give Catholic prisoners the religious superintendence of priests of the prisoners'

[574] Government chief whip.

[575] *P.P.* 1859 (2), xvii. 7, 9.

[576] Not reported in *The Times*. Trelawny shortly afterwards resigned his interest in this subject to another Cornish member, Pendarves Vivian.

[577] See below, 12 June.

[578] On local taxation; see above, 16 Apr.

communion. On this question a committee sat and reported some time in this Parliament and of that committee I was a member.[579] It will rather seriously add to my work to watch the Bill. Maguire thought it better that I shd. move in the matter because he is a R. Catholic, & the Ministers have not, it seems, the courage of their opinions. Maguire went to urge the matter on Gladstone, but took little comfort [...]

Tuesday, 11 June: To-day the Game committee sat for the usual four hours. We had an excellent witness, Mr Irvine, a Scotch lawyer and country-gentleman [...]

Wednesday, 12 June: The Cornish members have received the endorsement of a county meeting for their course in regard to the rating of mines. Perhaps, the conservative member for Launceston[580] may have been a little hasty in endeavouring, as it would seem, to move in advance of his brother members, who, in concurrence with the wishes of the county as expressed at a county meeting, have forborne to act until action would take place under most favourable conditions. H. Lopes's Bill, for the rating of Lords' dues, maybe a good one; but before we support it, it were well to be sure that, taken in connexion with a recent decision in a court of law, it does not rate mine property twice over.[581]

[...] Ministers are in a sad scrape about the Washington treaty and some of them, as it struck me, look rather crestfallen.[582] Earl Grey severely criticized them in his late speech on the Ballot.[583] His reference to their weakness in regard to C[ontagious] D[iseases] legislation was very noteworthy.

Friday, 14 June: My first labour was a four hours attendance on the Game Laws Committee; our witness was a member of the House, Clare Sewell Read, a tenant farmer. He seems to me to be a gentlemanly & sensible man, of good information on agricultural subjects. [...] We patiently proceeded with our enquiry till close upon 4 p.m.

---

[579] See above, 15 Mar. 1870.

[580] Henry Lopes.

[581] The Mines Dues bill received its 2nd reading on 14 June, but was later withdrawn. See *The Times*, 12 June 1872, 9, for the meeting of the Cornwall mines assessment committee at Truro. It was noted that in the recent case of 'Guest v. the overseers of the Parish of East Deane', in the court of Queen's Bench, the ruling had been that the mine surface (buildings, machinery etc) were liable to rates. If mineral dues were also to be liable, therefore, the result would be double rating.

[582] The previous day, Gladstone had stated that there was no agreement on the supplemental article; *H* ccxi. 1589–90.

[583] Moving the rejection of the 2nd reading in the upper House, on 10 June; *H* ccxi. 1427–37.

when the bell rang, 'division' was loudly called &, on the Chairman saying that we had better adjourn, we all rushed as fast as our legs could carry us along the passage, down the main staircase, thro' the Central Hall, to the House & were in time to vote on Collins's amendmt.[584] How Mother Hunt brought his body down was a marvel till he told me that he had descended by the staircase near the Ladies' gallery.

There was some uncertainty how we shd. vote about Collins' proposal, as Ministers were not keen in its favour. They felt bound by words used at an earlier stage to let Collins have his way. My vote was agt. him. From one of the whips I ascertained that the question was not of much interest to the government [...]

Monday, 17 June: Capt[ain] Trench took his seat.[585] As he came up escorted by Capt[ain] Beaumont & Dodson, some of the Conservatives cheered. Liberals seemed to hope he would join their ranks. Not so. He went to the opposition side. Kinnaird, who greeted the new member, tried, I thought, to bring him our way. Some amusement was produced by the little scene, of which the Tories took the honours [...]

Tuesday, 18 June: A very tedious sitting for 4 hours in the Committee on the Game Laws.

In the midst the Bell sounded for a division on the Birmingham Sewage Bill, which division I tried to overtake. In vain – as time failed me. The truth is I discovered that I had taken another member's hat, which I was obliged to carry back.

[...] There is a growing impression that tenant farmers ask too much in regard to the Game Laws and that the real object sought is to get the game for the tenants for nothing, with a severe law of trespass agt. strangers encroaching!!

The Lords have made an example of the Ballot Bill.[586] Forster will hardly know his own child. What will the Commons do?

My health is a good deal shaken again by the work there is to do – under unfavourable conditions.

Wednesday, 19 June: [...] a measure introduced by Bass for

---

[584] On the Scottish Education bill, designed to protect the rights of denominational schools to public funding; *H* ccxi. 1744. Carried by 203:109.

[585] Following the Galway by-election. The Home Rule candidate, Captain Nolan, had won the election, but he was unseated on the grounds that the Roman Catholic clergy had intimidated voters, and the seat awarded to Trench instead. K.T. Hoppen, *Elections, Politics and Society in Ireland, 1832–1885*, (Oxford, 1984), 158.

[586] Passing a number of amendments during the committee stage; Kinzer, *Ballot Question*, 213–30.

abolish[in]g the power now held by county court judges to imprison persons who disobey orders of paym[en]t of debts under 40/-. It seemed to me that Henry Lopes made out a complete case agt. the bill, setting forth that it is only where the debtor has effects & won't pay that liability to imprisonment is incurred. My vote was on the side of Lopes.[587] Government as usual appeared unequal to the occasion. Jessel was put up just at the end, but, + being laughed at for his trivial contribution to the debate, he + did not save a division. Lopes won [...] Standing at the door I endeavoured to find out how ministers were going to vote. Glyn[588] said to some one 'you had much better not vote'!! (or equivalent words). Where are we drifting?

Thursday, 20 June: [...] Newgate raised a question of order – viz, as regards the disadvantage under which independent members are placed by the existing practice when morning sittings (2 p.m.) are resorted to. These are used for the government's purposes and the House is so worn out that at the 9 p.m. meeting a count is almost sure to take place. A division occurred on some question with this result – Ayes 3 Noes 13.[589] So the House at 1/2 past 1 stood adjourned.

Lowe, early in the evening, was rather hard on his wordy chief. In reply to a question of Newgate – a question of some length[590] – Lowe simply said 'No, Sir'. Both sides laughed – apparently concurring in the wisdom of only saying what an occasion requires. Gladstone would have very likely drawn several distinctions & wound up with an exhaustive (and exhausting) peroration.

Friday, 21 June: For four hours I presided over the Game Laws Committee in the absence of Mr Ward Hunt. It was no easy task to keep members within the subject intrusted to us. McCombie, frankly admitting his want of experience, comes armed with a long series of written questions & doggedly puts them in their order.

[...] Tenant-farmers examined turn out to hold very communistic ideas.

Monday, 24 June: [...] Disraeli made a speech at a great Conservative meeting at the Crystal Palace.[591] Scarcely any member of note

[587] Helping to defeat the 2nd reading of the Imprisonment for Debt abolition bill, by 136:34.

[588] Government chief whip.

[589] On Newgate's motion fixing a date for his Monastic and Conventual Institutions bill; *H* ccxi. 2030. He was defeated.

[590] On the parliamentary count-outs; *H* ccxi. 1992.

[591] His famous speech to the Conservative National Union; *The Times*, 25 June 1872, 7.

remained to represent his party on the first opposition bench except Pakington.

Tuesday, 25 June: I notice that the Liskeard Board of guardians have charged the County members with neglect in the matter of the question of rating mines. Can anything be more unjust? We have scrupulously followed the wishes of successive County meetings.[592] The idiots at Liskeard are not aware of the difficulty private members have in carrying bills and the importance of gaining, if possible, ministerial aid [...]

Wednesday, 26 June: Gregory moved the 2d. reading of a Bill for facilitating transfer of land.[593] T. Collins & Jessel thoroughly picked it to pieces. Hinde Palmer assisted this operation. It was really a treat to hear Jessel who, handling a subject thoroughly within his grasp, amply established his legal title to the office of solicitor general. I say this, because some think that he has something to learn before he will have, as a general debater, the ear of the House. The Bill was withdrawn.

Afterwards, the occasional sermons Bill of Cowper Temple was debated for some hours. Giving to the subject my best attention, I deemed it to be a measure which it was not safe to support. It is very doubtful, to say the least, whether an incumbent & a bishop shd. have power to let a layman & a stranger preach to a congregation of the established Church. While such an institution exists, I think the best security for the rights of the laity is the law affixing to definite & regular functionaries responsibility for their conduct. It is quite possible that some good might accrue from the proposed innovation; but, on the whole, it seems to me insufficient to justify risk.

Mr Richard was very bitter in his reference to the humiliation it must cause to the Ch. of England to be compelled to sue to Parliament for liberty of the kind sought. He has been a dissenting minister. A.B. Hope was no less bitter in his allusions to preachers not being within the pale of the church. Each representative of a school of thought was, I thought, wanting in the true breadth of charity. On a division the Bill was lost. My vote was given in Hope's lobby.[594] There was a good deal of cross voting & many doubted up to the moment of leaving the House [...]

Thursday, 27 June: So, the Alabama question relating to indirect

---

[592] See above, 12 June.
[593] The Real Estates Titles bill.
[594] Helping to defeat the 2nd reading, 177:116.

claims is settled by its withdrawal from the record.[595] Luck for Ministers! + whose fate turned on it. + Gladstone sketched the position of the Ballot Bill on its return from the Lords & declared how much of the alterations made he could accept[596] [...]

Friday, 28 June: [...] + Last night Herbert Spencer called here & we had a long & animated discussion on the Contagious Diseases acts.[597] +

I attended, as usual, at the sitting of the Committee on the Game Laws. Mr Smith proved to be an able witness – speaking as chief of the Agricultural chambers of Scotland.

After about 4 hours work, the bell called us to vote on the Lords amendments to the Ballot Bill. Hereon my vote was with the Tories and the Lords agt. compulsory secrecy; for the promised plan of scrutiny proposed by Forster; for the use of school houses for polling and for the Lords amendments as to the hours of polling i.e. till 5 in winter & 7 in summer[598] [...]

Monday, 1 July: Civil servants estimates were the first business. The usual discursive talk. Ayrton was almost civilized. He is by no means a bad Public servant.

[...] I framed a motion for a return wh. will set forth the injustice of the treatment Catholics meet with in the matter of payment of Prison Ministers.[599] Shame on Protestant dissenters! whose petitions agt. a most just Bill crowd our table.

Tuesday, 2 July: After 4 hours of tedious work in committee Room No. 17 (Game), the bell caused our sudden adjournment & we were in our places & ready for a division in committee on the coal mines Regulation Bill. Hours of talk followed & another division was taken against the judgment of almost every member present, as there appeared to be a general murmur of 'agreed agreed'. Bonham-Carter probably caught the voice of some one dissentient & felt bound to pronounce

---

[595] *H* ccxii. 293–8, for Gladstone's statement. The U.S. had accepted the Geneva arbitrators decision to rule out the indirect claims.

[596] Cf. Gladstone's Cabinet note, 26 June 1872; *G.D.* viii. 170.

[597] Spencer of course opposed State intervention in this area. He had been a friend of Trelawny's for some years: see Spencer's *An Autobiography* (1904), ii. 19, 40. In 1860, Trelawny had been a subscriber to Spencer's proposed 'Synthetic Philosophy'; ibid, appendix A.

[598] Respectively: *H* ccxii. 347, defeated 302:234; *H* ccxii. 369, carried 382:137; Lords' amendment against use of school rooms, *H* ccxii. 375, defeated 365:86; *H* ccxii. 378–9, defeated 227:190 although Forster was favourable.

[599] See below, 9 June 1873.

his fiat 'strangers must withdraw'.[600] It is unnecessary to describe here
the effect of each vote. Suffice it to say that my course on these Mines
Regulation Bills is to support Ministers – at least, till proof be adduced
of the needlessness of the intervention proposed.[601]

We sat till 7 p.m., then I went home, returning at 9. An attempt was
made to count out on Miall's rising.[602] This attempt failed. Miall spoke
ably for an hour and Leatham, who was aggressive in his tone, seconded
the mover.

T. Hughes followed. In the middle of his speech I left the House,
after 9 hours of attendance.

It seemed to me that support of Miall would have put me in a false
position. He does not disguise his hostility to the Church establishmt. &
that hostility was the key to his proposed commission of Inquiry. On
the other hand, it is not agreeable to oppose the ascertainment of facts.
Yet, even here there is ground for demurring to a costly investigation
into matters mostly discernible already in official documents [. . .]

Wednesday, 3 July: A bill was introduced by Sir C. Dilke & others
which purported to deal with lands belonging to corporations &c. &
which was deemed to savour of socialism. On a division – after a
debate – the Bill was rejected.[603] * T. agt. *

Being much the worse in health thro' the length & labour of this
session, I have been compelled to resort to arrangements for obtaining
some relief.

By the way, I must mention that the Bill for closing Public Houses
throughout the whole of Sunday[604] was – as the saying goes – 'talked
out'. But, in performing this function, that excellent, sensible and genial
member – John Locke – shd. not turn repeatedly to watch the hands
of the clock. Members detected this & laughingly marked their notice.
But Locke is a favourite & may usually have his way.

The Prison Ministers Bill will be watched by Maguire and I expect
to be summoned to town if a day can be obtained for the Bill.
Meanwhile, an appeal for a day from Irish members is on foot. The
session is too near its close to admit of our carrying thro' all its stages
a measure tending to religious equality.

Monday, 8 July: [. . .] During the evening Sir J. Pakington, Mitford &
I considered whether we shd. allow Gilpin to have the first reading of

---

[600] Presumably on Elliot's amendment, *H* ccxii. 508–9, which was defeated by 298:20.
[601] Royal assent, 10 Aug.
[602] Motion for a Royal Commission on Anglican property; *H* ccxii. 527–40, defeated 295:94.
[603] 184:17 against 2nd reading of the Commons Protection bill.
[604] Introduced by Hugh Birley.

Wm. Fowler's Bill for the repeal of the Con. Diseases acts.[605] Pakington thought that there was no reason why we shd. give Gilpin this advantage. We met in a room behind Mr Speaker's chair. Mitford thought differently from Pakington. I was content to follow him, so I apprised Gilpin that, unless he would undertake for himself & supporters not to speak beyond simple words of course in a mover, we shd. stop him under a rule of the House that a member cannot, if the objection be taken, move in the name of another member. Gilpin said he could not undertake for his friends that they should not speak.

[...] The great political event of this day was the decision of the Lords on the Ballot Bill.[606]

Tuesday, 9 July: [...] finding that proper steps were to be taken in the business to follow at 9 p.m. under Gilpin's conduct, I returned to Upper Norwood. It was understood that Wm. Fowler would not be at his post. Subsequently when at 9 p.m. the House resumed, it was counted & less than 40 were present. This is a heavy blow for the opponents of the acts of 1866 & 1869.

Maguire informed me of the fact that 29 members had asked of Gladstone a day for the Prison Ministers Bill.[607] I await orders. If a day can be obtained for me, I must be in my place. 'The Times' of this day has a petition from Plymo[uth] agt. the Bill & a petition from others for it.

Wednesday, 10 July: Remaining in the country, I only know thro' newspapers the proceedings of this day.

Walter Morrison moved the 2d. reading of the Proportional Representation Bill & shewed considerable grasp of the subject dealt with.

The thinness of attendance – for at one time only 12 were present – indicates the unripeness of the Public Mind for 'fanciful' experiments on the constitution. It is right to say that some very able theorists eagerly support the plan – e.g. Mr J.S. Mill and Mr Hare.

Dilke moved an amendment[608] which so far satisfied Morrison as to induce him to withdraw his motion in favour of Dilke's. There was a division (26 for Dilke, 154 agt.).

Thursday, 11 July: After questions St Aubyn headed some 25 County

[605] Fowler was absent owing to the death of his wife.

[606] They had ceased to press their amendments. Gladstone's Cabinet note of 6 July shows that the government had been prepared for an autumn session, and if necessary a dissolution, if the bill was rejected; *G.D.* viii. 174.

[607] Gladstone's Cabinet note of 6 July, ibid, states: 'Regret we cannot give time'.

[608] That any redistribution of seats must give equal power to all voters; *H* ccxii. 905–12.

members who formed a deputation to Mr Gladstone having for their object to apprize him of the feelings of agricultural electors on local taxation & representation of ratepayers. Mr Gladstone enquired whether other members desired to make any observations & some made a few. Then, he gave us his substantial acquiescence in the request which had been put; viz, that he shd. announce in some Public manner his intention to deal with the matters referred to. All this occurred in a room behind the Speaker's chair. We then retired.

Many questions were put this evening. It is pretty clear that the fate of many bills is sealed. Glyn told me there was no chance for the Prison Ministers Bill, & he evidently has no more notion of the progress of the govt. bill for the abolition of the acts of 1866 & 69.[609] Indeed, Pakington had private authority from Bruce for the statement that the bill is to be dropped.

[...] Bruce moved the 2d. reading of his Licensing Bill. Can it pass in this session? Hardly.[610]

St Aubyn told me the course taken by the deputation entirely arose out of a conversation he & I had on the subject [...]

Monday, 15 July: [...] The Call of the House, of which I had a notice on the paper, has been withdrawn, the reason for it having ceased. That reason was to make the whole House share the responsibility of any action taken in regard to the repeal of the acts of 1866 & 1869. The govt. was prepared to move against experience & light – some of them against their own convictions – & it seemed to me that in such a strait the House was to be considered as the govt. & each member equally responsible.

Thursday, 18 July: [...] The House was in Committee on the Public Health Bill wh. was under a close scrutiny. Members lost their tempers & much valuable time. Bonham Carter's decision was contested.[611] Unseemly disturbance. The sitting was carried into the small hours. Surely it is time for a better organization of our industry.

Monday, 22 July: Jacob Bright moved in (army) supply an amendment agt. the vote for expenses of carrying out the Contagious Diseases acts.[612] He spoke at some length – say, for 35 min & alluded to me &

[609] Gladstone's Cabinet note of 29 June shows that they had discussed dropping the abolition bill; *G.D.* viii. 171–2.

[610] 2nd Reading agreed. The bill had originated in the House of Lords. For the way it had been hurriedly put together, see *K.J.*, 20 Apr. 1872.

[611] Osborne questioning whether Hicks Beach's speech was relevant; *H* ccxii. 1379–83.

[612] *H* ccxii. 1522–32, to cut the army vote by £3,648. Defeated, 140:74.

my speech agt. him early in this session.[613] Our cue was to say nothing –
and to be contented with the money which is incurred & must be paid.
This liability is a very distinct matter from the policy of the acts.

Members were much disgusted at the presence of women in the
Ladies gallery where they sat complacently fanning themselves. * See
Livy Book 34 ch. 1 on the conduct of women. (Porcius Cato's speech.) *
[...]

Tuesday, 23 July: Elcho expected that I shd. have spoken at length
in answer to Jacob Bright. No, said I, not a word. Our policy was not
to speak. This evidently disconcerted Bright's party. To-day we took
the Licensing Bill and I voted once in mitigation of severity * T. would
allow a child under 14 to buy a glass of beer.[614] *

Wednesday, 24 July: On Capital punishment J. D. Lewis greatly
distinguished himself.[615] There were no two opinions on this. The
debate was by no means uninteresting or ill-sustained. Richard (for
Merthyr) made a good speech. Henley announced his conversion to
the opinion of the mover.

Thursday, 25 July: [...] Several members who discussed the penalty
for drunkenness last tuesday were evidently under the influence of
drink. One member who was again and again on his legs so far
betrayed his condition that the committee did not disguise its notice of
it. Yet, it was hardly a fit subject for laughter.

Thursday, 1 August: St Aubyn put to Gladstone a question which
elicited a reply likely to be of service during the Autumn to County
members as he has declared the intention of Ministers to endeavour to
deal with the whole subject of Local Taxation & the representation of
ratepayers. There appears to be but little hope of a speedy termination
of this session.

Saturday, 3 August: The Licensing Bill has been discussed &
considered by the House with exemplary patience[616] [...]

Saturday, 10 August: The Queen's speech. So ends the session.

---

[613] See above, 13–14 Feb.
[614] Osborne Morgan's amendment forbidding sales to children under 14; *H* ccxii. 1679,
defeated 129:60.
[615] Opposing Charles Gilpin's Capital Punishment abolition bill, which lost its 2nd
reading, 167:54.
[616] It received the Royal assent on 10 Aug.

SESSION OF 1873

Thursday, 6 February: We met about 2 p.m. & the formalities often herein described were as usual respected.

It seemed to me that Mr Lyttelton & Mr Stone[617] acquitted themselves creditably.

Disraeli & Gladstone received loud cheers on entering the House. Disraeli had most & it was noteworthy that both sides warmly expressed their sympathy with him.[618]

The Queen's speech was thought tame. Numerous notices were given – some 60 or 70 in all.

I gave a notice of my Prison Ministers Bill ab[ou]t which I am under an engagement to the late John Francis Maguire.

It occurred to me to ask Miall what he would think of the Bill & I was fortunate in obtaining his prompt acquiescence in it. He rightly considers that towards prisoners the State stands in loco parentis. I hope Osborne will assist me actively [...]

Friday, 7 February: We had more last words on the report of the address. Cochrane could not resist his disposition to talk. Afterwards came numerous first readings of Bills. Among others was the Prison Ministers Bill[619] for which are sponsors J.S.T., Osborne & Lord A. Russell. *+ I think the names of those who supported me judiciously chosen. +* When I had moved, the Premier looked back at me & made a kind of gracious greeting which seemed to say 'thank you'. And he might feel accordingly, for at this juncture the introduction of the Bill is not ill timed. Governmt. feared the performance of their duty & of course it shields them if any independent member undertake it. Osborne readily acceded to my request that he would join with me & the same may be said of Lord Arthur Russell. They are both brave men & risk something in battling for the weak and unprotected agt. the intolerant & bigoted. It seemed to me inexpedient to put on the back of the Bill the name of a Catholic. I tried to get the name of Pakington & then Walpole, but unsuccessfully. I hope, however, for their support in debate. Osborne has notes of my materials to be used in introducing the subject and it is my purpose to offer him more data

---

[617] Moving and seconding the Address.
[618] His wife had died in Dec. 1872.
[619] *P.P.* 1873, iv. 233.

such as the evidence given to the Committee in 1870 underlined by me. The Prison Ministers Bill involves a great principle & must be pressed upon the House daily without intermission.

[...] I named our next sitting (Monday the 10th) for my bill, well knowing the poor chance it wd. have in a scramble for a vacant Wednesday. My success will depend upon persistency 'in season & out of season', and the grievance being great gives one a right to plead urgency. Besides, Ministers may cure the evil by adopting the Bill and they ought to adopt it. Hence they cannot complain.

Monday, 10 February: I sent a message to the Clerk to postpone my Prison Ministers Bill to thursday fortnight.[620] The ev[enin]g was spent partly in wrangling over the dead bodies of Ayrton's late Park rules,[621] & partly in discussing & readopting, upon a division, the rule of last year under which Supply can be taken on a Monday, without being intercepted by preliminary motions.[622] This rule was said to work well, as Members were enabled to foresee what wd. be the topics likely to be handled that evening.

Thursday, 13 February: In a speech of prodigious length, Gladstone unfolded his Irish University scheme. So far, it is difficult to forecast whether the ultra montane priesthood in Ireland will accept it.[623] Fawcett too, will have something to say on it. The newspapers contain the Lord Chancellor's new scheme for the fusion of Law & Equity, and the constitution of an Appellate tribunal.[624]

Tuesday, 18 February: Vernon Harcourt moved an abstract resolution on the increase of our Public Expenditure.[625] Gladstone replied, tendering the offer of a Select Committee on Civil Service expenses. Harcourt, disclaiming the belief that the Committee would be of any use, accepted it, and condemned himself by allowing his main question

---

[620] Trelawny was again ill, and his attendance was intermittent until Easter. Gout, affecting his fingers, made writing-up the diary difficult.

[621] The new rules under the Royal Parks Regulation act were laid on the table.

[622] Lowe's resolution, *H* ccxiv. 244–5, carried 148:78; see above, 26 Feb. 1872.

[623] Gladstone's bill proposed to create a new Dublin University, embracing Trinity College and the Queen's Colleges of Belfast and Cork, with an undenominational governing body and a purely secular curriculum (theology, philosophy and modern history were thus excluded). Roman Catholic and Presbyterian colleges were to be allowed to affiliate, but would not receive any State endowment. The bill was condemned by the Roman Catholic bishops, who wanted a State-endowed University under their control; J.P. Parry, *Democracy and Religion: Gladstone and the Liberal Party, 1867–1875* (Cambridge, 1986), 353–68.

[624] i.e. the Supreme Court of Judicature bill; *P.P.* 1873, v. 443.

[625] That it was excessive; *H* ccxiv. 602–21.

to be negatived. Altogether the proceeding was abortive and useless. Expense goes on, in spite of the affectation of all sides to diminish it.

Thursday, 27 February: [...] The Irishmen seem to me very anxious about the Prison Ministers Bill. I endeavoured through Glyn[626] to get a day from the Govt., not as yet successfully.

Friday, 28 February: [...] In the House I saw Bruce & endeavoured to obtain a Govt. day for the Prison Ministers Bill. He agreed with me that such legislation was required, and spoke of the bigotry of its opponents. As to a day, Mr Gladstone, he said, arranged the course of public business; but Mr Bruce added he wd. mention it in the Cabinet on Saturday[627] [...]

Monday, 3 March: It appears to me that the debate on Mr Bourke's motion on the Irish University question was most damaging to Govt.[628] Fawcett and Ld. E. Fitzmaurice distinguished themselves on the Liberal side, speaking against the Bill.

Tuesday, 4 March: [...] The University Bill (Ireland) seems to me to be in a very weak & sickly condition.

Tuesday, 11 March: I was summoned by no less than 3 private whips during the day & night, – the last not far from the division. My attendance was out of the question. Government underwent a most damaging debate & on division were defeated by 3. Numbers for: 284, against: 287.[629] It seems to me that this defeat is mainly the effect of bad judgment and mismanagement. The measure was not one on which the existence of a Govt. ought to turn. Gladstone ought to have been more sure of his ground before committing his party so far. And now – the Deluge?

Thursday, 13 March: Gladstone in a full house, announced the resignation of the Govt. House adjourned till Monday.

Monday, 17 March: Gladstone announced the state of affairs in

---

[626] Government chief whip.

[627] No specific reference to this in Gladstone's Cabinet note of 1 Mar.; *G.D.* viii. 293–4.

[628] Condemning the government's failure to name the 28 members of the proposed new governing council; *H* ccxiv. 1194-1202.

[629] On the 2nd reading of the Irish University bill, Bourke's amendment (from 3 Mar.) having been negatived. 38 Irish Liberals either voted or paired against the bill, 10 British Liberals opposed it and 9 abstained; Parry, *Democracy and Religion*, 365.

regard to the Govt., which state of affairs seems to be transitional. The House is adjourned till Thursday. It may be gathered from the newspapers that D'Israeli has a government ready but is unwilling to accept of office during the existing Parl[iamen]t.[630] It wd. appear that Gladstone in resuming office will have to prepare the way for D'Israeli by completing business which presses, & advising H.M. to dissolve Parl[iamen]t.

Thursday, 20 March: [...] Gladstone & D'Israeli made explanations on the late interregnum. [...] I think D'Israeli had the best of it in the discussion.

Friday, 21 March: A motion of Hardy's was made on the subject of the new rules under the Geneva Arbitration.[631] It struck me that Ministers underwent a damaging discussion. The Att[orne]y Gen[era]l[632] evidently held opinions different from Forster & the Govt. Gladstone rather tamely acquiesced in the principle of the motion. Why was Forster put up to speak instead of Enfield? I fear it is not enough to be able 'to answer questions'. – Three divisions on matters relating to Supply, which seem to have arisen out of a grave scandal in the accounts. The Post Office authorities have been spending large sums without votes of Parl[iamen]t.[633] If I mistake not, there will be a serious party division on this matter, wh. is expounded at large in Times of today. The financial reformers, White, Fawcett, Sclater-Booth & others were very savage.

Wednesday, 26 March: It is thought that D'Israeli made a mistake in using the Burials Bill as an occasion of a trial of strength. The Division goes some way towards the reconstruction of the Liberal party. Numbers 280 to 217. – Majority 63.[634] T. in majority.

---

[630] For the proceedings leading to the reinstatement of Gladstone's ministry, see John Morley, *The Life of William Ewart Gladstone* (1903), ii. 340–7.

[631] Arguing that the 6th article of the treaty of Washington unduly enlarged the rights of belligerant powers against neutrals; *H* ccxiv. 1963–84, withdrawn.

[632] Sir John Coleridge.

[633] It had emerged that Frank Scudamore, assistant secretary of the Post Office, had applied nearly £1 million to the extension of the telegraphic service taken from Post Office receipts and Savings Banks deposits (which ought to have been paid into the consolidated fund and to the National Debt commissioners respectively). Scudamore had been improperly allowed direct communications with the Chancellor of the Exchequer, Lowe, by-passing the Postmaster-General, Monsell. James Winter, *Robert Lowe* (Toronto, 1976), 285–7.

[634] For the 2nd reading, Disraeli having moved the rejection of Osborne Morgan's annual bill. The High-Churchman, Gathorne Hardy, lamented that 'the desertion of Irish and Scotch on our side enhanced the majority. I begin to doubt those allies when Church questions are at issue'; *G.H.D.*, 27 Mar. 1873.

Friday, 28 March: Trelawny put some questions to Gladstone on the Prison Ministers Act (1863) Amendment Bill, of which J.S.T. has charge. His object was to establish Gladstone's responsibility for the defect in the Act referred to, which leaves to the discretion of local Prison authorities the decision of the question whether non-conformists in prisons should have as good a title as members of the Established Church to religious instruction and associated worship. Gladstone's answer was not satisfactory; though he will support the Bill of which J.S.T. has charge, he will neither take upon himself the task of curing the defect, nor give up a Govt. day for the discussion of that Bill.

There was an animated discussion this ev[enin]g on a point of order, arising out of proceedings in relation to Fawcett's University Test Bill. Most of the experts on the rules of the House, including the Speaker's two late rivals Bouverie & Dodson, made remarks. The Speaker was calm & decided, & his judgments appeared to give satisfaction. Here & there he might have been slightly wrong in verbiage. I had amusing instances illustrative of this as I sat just behind Bouverie, who kept up a running fire of half audible interjections; such as when the Speaker said 'read & discharged', – Bouverie said 'read for the purpose of being discharged'. Gladstone seemed fussy, & I thought unacquainted with a well known rule of the House;[635] & so others seemed to think. Cardwell was precise. On the whole, Fawcett had a success, in spite of the well-laid powder mine under him, for the Irish Catholics were attempting by a point of form to defeat a measure to which the priests are opposed.

I had some trouble in arranging a little affair in regard to the conduct of the opposition to Fowler's Bill upon the Contagious Diseases Acts. Mitford had written to me on this point. It was difficult for me to pronounce whether Sir J. Pakington or J.D. Lewis was the fitter leader against Fowler. So I contented myself with summing up the reasons in favour of either – the weightier being for Pakington. Mitford sent on my letter to Lewis. Finding Lewis & Pakington both in the Lobby, I sounded each, & after some trouble arranged to the satisfaction of both as I understood, that Pakington shd. move the amendment & Lewis second it. I deem this to have been a fortunate stroke of work as it was more difficult than I have time to describe.

Monday, 7 April: An unusual number of questions & notices kept the House in cruel suspense as to the budget. The Speaker was called

[635] Fawcett had sought to fix a date for the 2nd reading of his bill to abolish religious tests in Trinity College, Dublin, but an Irish member, Philip Callan, objected on the grounds that the bill had been altered since its 1st reading. Fawcett offered to withdraw the bill and introduce it again for a 1st reading, but Gladstone questioned whether this could be done when the 1st reading of the original bill had been unopposed; *H* ccxv. 307–8. The 1st reading was given.

upon once or twice to set a member right. This kind of duty our chief performs with great firmness & decision. He seems to me to be very watchful.

The budget will not I think have a very enthusiastic reception. Most people would have preferred payment of the indemnity out of the income in 73–4[636] [...]

Monday, 21 April:[637] [...] Some of the Irish stoutly opposed Fawcett's Bill on University tests, but had not the hardihood to divide.[638] Indeed there was a decided want of harmony among the Irish liberals who had been in favour of the abolition of tests in English Universities & some no doubt saw what a false position they would be in if they fought for the maintenance of tests in Ireland [...]

Tuesday, 22 April: Auberon Herbert, in a long speech delivered amidst signs of impatience & even discourtesy, moved for leave to bring in a bill having the object of providing that in the possible event of the suppression of certain fellowships compensation should be based on a principle to be laid down now so as to avoid future waste.[639] An unusual course was adopted on a division, viz that of rejecting the Bill on its first stage. For this course there was a plausible excuse in that the matter is under the charge of Royal Commiss[ione]rs & the mover's step therefore premature & rather inconsiderate.

Altho' this is true, it is fair to say that Herbert's speech had some excellent and suggestive remarks & it seemed to me that the House was prejudiced agt. him by his rather conceited manner which was not improved by his constant references to lengthy manuscripts. Had he condensed his speech & delivered the best of it without notes, it is possible that he would have fared better [...]

Thursday, 24 April: [...] I gave notice to omit clause 20 in Dillwyn's Salmon fisheries bill. This would inflict heavy penalties on the Fowey fishermen for using their fishery during most of the time wherein the

---

[636] Lowe proposed to pay the £3.2 millions indemnity to the United States, resulting from the Geneva arbitration on the 'Alabama' question, half from current revenue and half from government borrowing. (Gladstone himself had wanted to pay the whole amount from current revenue; *K.J.*, 5 Apr. 1873.) With the economy buoyant, Lowe was still able to reduce the income tax by 1d. to 3d. in the £, and to halve the duty on sugar; *H* ccxv. 654- 70.

[637] The House had resumed after adjourning for Easter on the 7th.

[638] 2nd reading agreed; Royal assent 26 May.

[639] *H* ccxv. 801–9, seeking to limit the compensation given for Oxbridge Fellowships that might be abolished; defeated 107:81.

fish are fit for the table. I may force a compromise & then withdraw my motion.[640]

Monday, 28 April: Lowe seemed to crush W.H. Smith's case on his motion agt. part of the budget.[641] Lowe was certainly very caustic & at the same time humorous & original. He fastened on the opposition their acceptance of the reduction on the Income tax – a benefit to the rich – &, their rejection of the reduction on the sugar duties – a benefit to the poor. As a party view of a course, the hitting was fair enough if a little ad captandum [...]

Wednesday, 30 April: Much business at the House. Women's Disabilities. I voted with Jacob Bright.[642] In a few sentences I warned women to use their power if they get it with moderation and adverted to their improper conduct in inciting persons to break the law – alluding to the Contagious Diseases acts. * See Mrs Lewis's evidence before the Royal commission on C.D. acts.[643] * [...] Also, I adverted to the indelicate conduct of women obtrusively exhibiting themselves in the gallery when the above acts were discussed.

Thursday, 1 May: I paired with Sir John Hay till 11 o'clock, & promised the Whips I would then return as I could not get another pair. The subject was the adjourned debate on W.H. Smith's motion relating to the Budget.[644] When I got back to the House at 11, I found numerous members smoking in the cloakroom. No sooner had I come in than I observed Mr Glyn,[645] who was taking a pinch of snuff at the table, & heard him say with considerable delight as he looked at me, that he had just 'spotted' 2 more members. I suspect he thought I was going to shirk him. Finding I had no chance of pairing, I went up & took a sofa in one of the upper corridors, where I could just hear the laughter & cheers awarded to the rival orators D'Israeli & Gladstone. I confess I did not care to have a nearer acquaintance with what they were saying, which appeared to consist, in the main, of criminatory & recriminatory banter. I had prophesied they would never divide, as the Tories would have put themselves in a most unpopular position. In fact Lowe's speech on Tuesday night convinced me that the motion would

---

[640] Trelawny was acting here in the interests of his constituents; but see below, 15 July.
[641] That before considering indirect taxes the government should make known its views regarding the maintenance and adjustment of direct taxes; *H* ccxv. 1030–41.
[642] His annual bill to extend household suffrage to women was defeated, 222:155.
[643] *P.P.* 1871, xix. 515.
[644] Continued from 28 Apr.
[645] Government chief whip.

collapse.[646] As we were coming away from the House, near 2 o'clock, member after member observed 'what a shame to keep us here uselessly'. To one, (Headlam) I replied 'yes, & to have to hear this Lancashire twang – spun out too'. It seemed to me the same thought must have struck him as he laughed in evident sympathy. I had some conversation with W.E. Forster on Cornish business, who charmed me by his prompt & painstaking manner of action, following me up in order to clear up a point about which there might still be uncertainty.

Friday, 2 May: [...] Mr Joseph Arch, labourer, was the witness summoned to give evidence on the Game Laws.[647] He astonished us all by expressing his readiness to substitute for these laws an effective law of trespass – even trespass without damage done. I think he is an able and straightforward man and probably one of the best of his class. We shall hear more of him, I predict.[648]

Pell pointed out to Arch that he had learned two pieces of information during his examination & these were important. I mention this because it illustrates the vagueness of ideas floating in the minds of the Public in respect of laws impugned.

Monday, 5 May: Stansfeld introduced three Bills on Local rating[649] in an able and well-considered speech. Unfortunately his voice was weaker than usual & not more than 3/5ths of the House present could have heard what he said. Sir M. Lopes immediately raised the note of criticism which seemed premature [...] It strikes me, after some study of the subject, that he has greatly modified his opinions about the area of taxation since he commenced his movement.

Gladstone looked very pale and ill. They say he cannot sleep.

Tuesday, 6 May: Sir C. Dilke spoke well in moving for a redistribution of seats so as to remove palpable anomalies in the representation. My vote was in favour of his motion, which had but 77 supporters[650]

Wednesday, 7 May: Lawson had his field day;[651] he experienced a

---

[646] Which it did; no division. Many Conservatives had apparently not wanted Smith's motion to be brought on at all; *G.H.D.*, 2 May 1873.

[647] i.e. to the select committee, continued from the previous session.

[648] Arch was President of the National Agricultural Labourers union. He became a Liberal M.P. in 1885.

[649] The Rating (Liability and Value), Valuation and Consolidated Rate bills. The first was rejected by the House of Lords, the others withdrawn.

[650] 268 opposed the motion to 'redress inequalities' in the distribution of electoral power; *H* ccxv. 1561–70.

[651] 2nd reading of the Permissive Prohibitory bill.

heavy defeat on the division. Numbers 321 to 81. The different forms of casuistry by which members strove to defend their votes or their abstention from voting were really most diverting. The House greatly resented the pressure exerted upon it from outside. In two letters direct requests were made to me to absent myself if I failed to make up my mind to support the motion. Osborne made a vigorous speech against it. Dr Dalrymple described his experience of the utter failure of the Maine Law.[652] Lawson appears to be mad. It is really *difficult* to regard him as sane. He is fluent, energetic and well able to sustain the attention of his audience (for he by no means wants wit); but there I must stop.

Osborne observed, in the corridor where we were writing letters, that Sir Wilfrid's question & Miall's[653] would break up the liberal party.

The Tories cheered Lord Chelsea who took the oaths & his seat for Bath. The licensed Victuallers shewed their power at the election for that city.[654]

Thursday, 8 May: [. . .] the Liberal party is beginning to be alarmed at the changes at elections which are rather in favour of the Conservatives. Bath, Londonderry & Gloucester have thus pronounced.

Friday, 9 May: I attended the Game Laws Committee. A wide range of topics occupied the evening sitting of the House. There is an impression that there is danger of the session being but a barren one. Law reform hangs fire and there appears to be a great want of energy in dealing with it [. . .]

Monday, 12 May: [. . .] Conservatives are dissatisfied with Ministerial measures relating to local taxation. That great mountain, the motion of Lopes hereon,[655] seems to have ended in the production of 3 mice in as many govt. proposals. Disappointment is natural when members vote for a vague resolution tending to raise false hopes.

Wednesday, 14 May: Cowper-Temple's occasional sermons Bill was the thesis of the day. J.D. Lewis made a clever speech agt. the Bill. Gladstone, too, spoke ably as usual.[656]

[652] Legislation passed in 1846 and 1851 forbidding the manufacture or sale of intoxicating liquor in the State of Maine; later adopted by several other American States.

[653] Church disestablishment.

[654] Within weeks Chelsea succeeded his father as Earl Cadogan, prompting another by-election at Bath in which the temperance question was again prominent; D.A. Hamer, *The Politics of Electoral Pressure* (Brighton, 1977), 184–6.

[655] See above, 16 Apr. 1872.

[656] Opposing the 2nd reading of the bill to allow non-anglican laymen to preach, which was defeated 199:53; *H* ccxv. 1973–9.

The movers did not care to divide, but some member of the opposition cried 'aye' & would have a division in spite of their convictions. This is a course rarely resorted to and not well looked upon. My vote was, as in last session, agt. the Bill [...]

Thursday, 15 May: Bouverie very savagely attacked Ministers on their making a proposal to appoint a committee on the Callan case (O'Keefe's) so as to deprive Bouverie of his initiative in the matter by pre-occupying the ground & gaining delay.[657] Lord Hartington seemed justly indignant when Bouverie compared the course taken as analagous to 'roping', a process resorted to on the Turf.[658] The process is to press a horse tow[ar]ds the ropes [...]

Friday, 16 May: Miall moved a resolution for the disendowment and disestablishment of the English & Scotch Churches.[659] His speech was well-prepared but his voice was weak. The House accorded to him a kindly hearing and, as the thought struck me, the Conservatives seemed to pay close attention to his arguments. No one, I think, – unless Miall himself be excepted – believed that the resolution was more than an abstraction having little or no immediate interest. Gladstone made a remarkable speech which seemed to delight the Conservatives. The admission he made that since the abolition of the Irish church there had been no increase of tolerance among religious communities was a melancholy one. He spoke tow[ar]ds the close of his speech of the value of Church property in England if the Irish method of abolition were adopted, which property he put at 90 million £. I could not help thinking that the pains he had given himself in making this estimate were rather calculated to alarm the Conservatives & reminded me of Blucher's observation on seeing London from St Paul's 'What magnificent loot!'

The numbers on a division were 356 to 61.[660]

[...] J[ohn] Bright was present, sitting just under Miall once bench above the front bench below the gangway. He is, some one told me, in good spirits. To my mind he appeared to be flushed, restless & fatigued. I observed that he put up his hand from time to time tow[ar]ds his temples with the air of one who is conscious of being weak. It was pleasant to notice his hearty appreciation of one of Miall's best points.

---

[657] 159:131 for Hartington's motion for a select committee to inquire into the dismissal of the Revd. Robert O'Keefe, manager of the Callan national schools, by the Irish education commissioners; *H* ccxv. 2023. See Parry, *Democracy and Religion*, 350–1, 370–1; only 99 backbench Liberals supported the government, and 17 voted against it.

[658] The Irish Chief Secretary was a devotee of horse racing.

[659] *H* ccxvi. 16–37.

[660] Against Miall's resolution.

But, sad as it is to be a bird of ill omen, I cannot think Bright will ever make any more of his great speeches. * (Note 1877) This prophesy I rejoice to say has been falsified by the event. * Indeed, I earnestly hope he may not be tempted that way. Gladstone looks very ill. All conscientious statesmen are living too fast. It is self-murder.

Wednesday, 21 May: Fowler moved the repeal of the Contagious Diseases acts (66 & 69). His speech dwelt chiefly on statistics, – not, in the same degree, on the moral & constitutional objections to the acts. Altogether his speech was temperate & not in the style of a former speech of his and of a speech once delivered by Mr Jacob Bright.[661]

Pakington opposed Fowler's proposal & very completely demolished his case. J.D. Lewis made a capital speech as Pakington's seconder. Mundella & others spoke, among these J.S.T. who was impelled by a sense of fair play to defend Pakington whose statements had been unfairly denied by Mundella. We remained masters of the field, having routed our foes horse & foot.[662] But they are more numerous than one likes to find them.

Thursday, 22 May: My pair [...] was Mowbray. There were two divisions on adding more names to the Committee on the case of the Callan Schools. Ministers were defeated. The names were those of Dr Lyon Playfair, & Cross.[663] These defeats of Govt. are very galling.

[...] The division list on the late question introduced afresh by W. Fowler contains several members of the Cabinet.[664] I hear that the ladies received a notice that the subject of discussion was one not suited for their ears. In truth I believe the gallery into which ladies are allowed to come was empty.

Friday, 6 June:[665] The Masters and servants Bill occupied much of this day. Some people think that the working classes are more severely treated by the law in cases of breach of agreement than masters.

---

[661] See above, 14 Feb. 1872.

[662] 2nd reading defeated, 251:128.

[663] Harcourt's amendments to add Playfair and Cross to the committee, carried 200:182 and 205:165; *H* ccxvi. 319–21, 330. One Cabinet minister described Harcourt's conduct as 'a piece of sheer mischief – he was supported by Dizzy & all the opposition, & by some 14 Scotch & ultra Protestants on our side. Hartington made a speech wh. really gave the thing up. Gladstone lost his temper & walked out after the first division ... The whole animus towards the Comm[issione]rs & the Catholics of Ireland was very bad.' Chichester Fortescue's diary, 22 May 1873, B.L. Add MSS 63682.

[664] Forster and Stansfeld supported Fowler, Cardwell, Fortescue, Goschen and Hartington opposed.

[665] The House adjourned for Whitsun on 27 May, resuming on 5 June.

Vernon Harcourt takes the grievance, if it be properly so described, in hand.[666] Indeed, what topic escapes his ken?

Monday, 9 June: [...] The return on Prison Chaplains which was granted last year at my instance has been printed & very curious it is.[667] They tell me that a good many copies have been sent to the Country. It appears to me, as I observed to Leveson Gower, that we have caught dissenters tripping, since they rely on the Voluntary principle & yet take little or no interest in the state of mind of prisoners who are also dissenters. The religious instruction of prisoners is a duty or is not a duty. If it be a duty, it is either the business of individuals or of the State. It appears to me that dissenters will not perform their part nor let the State perform it [...]

Tuesday, 10 June: Three subjects on this day threatened me with exhaustion. At 12 o'clock (noon) the committee on the Game Laws had its meeting for the purpose of considering draft reports. At 2 p.m. the rating Bill in which my county is deeply interested was under discussion till nearly seven p.m. and then loomed the Prison Ministers [Act] (1863) Amendment Bill of which I have charge. It was evident that this Bill could not be taken, so as to effect any good, at the evening (9 p.m.) sitting, because, altho' it stood first on the orders of the day, it could only be taken after motions wh. have prior claims on tuesdays.[668] Accordingly, my Bill was postponed & stands now for tuesday fortnight, but Glyn[669] thinks that I have no chance for this year. However that may be, the return moved for by me last year & lately printed, I mean the return on Prison chaplains, will gradually sink into the Public mind & very likely give the Bill a good chance next year.

On Stansfeld's rating Bill we had 2 divisions. If it pass as it is, several classes of hereditaments not now rateable will become rateable. Mines, woods & plantations will be of this number. St Aubyn has an amendment which would limit rating to Lords dues in the case of tin & copper mines. It is doubtful whether this amendmt. will be accepted & I expressed to St Aubyn & others that I must watch the debate before I shd. come to my decision. Had the Bill of St Aubyn for the same object been the matter in hand, I shd. have said 'half a loaf is better than no

---

[666] His motion for an amendment of the law affecting trades unions followed the conviction of members of the gas stokers union for intimidation; *H* ccxvi. 572–88. No division.

[667] *P.P.* 1873, liv. 749, a list of the salaried and unsalaried prison chaplains in the U.K., in 1872, recording their religious affiliations.

[668] Sir John Hay's motion for a select committee regarding the system of navy promotions and retirement; *H* ccxvi. 751–71.

[669] Government chief whip.

bread'. But the Ministerial measure seems to be more efficacious for the interest of the whole ratepaying classes than that of St Aubyn. At least the question is doubtful.

The Tories have disturbed the incidence of taxation at Lopes's instance & are evidently in alarm. The rating of sporting rights & country houses does not delight the possessors. So, I suspect the measure of Stansfeld will be 'talked out' & drop till after the general election.[670] The tenant farmers will be bamboozled again on the old cry of 'Burthens on land'.

[...] Stansfeld distinguished himself on the Rating Bill.

Numerous petitions were presented in favour of the Prison Ministers [Act] 1863 Amendmt. Bill. Gladstone was understood to promise that no new changes shd. be laid on rates pending the question of the incidence of local taxation. How am I to be reconciled to this when I call to mind that he promised the aid of govt. tow[ar]ds my Bill?

Wednesday, 11 June: Much work. My first business is to come to a judgment upon the various draft reports on the Game Laws. I hardly see how we can hope to concur in a satisfactory scheme.

There are many petitions in favour of the Prison Ministers Bill. Perhaps, Catholics waited till Protestant fanaticism had exhausted itself? or is it that the late return 'Prison Chaplains' No. 156 has altered the opinions of Non-conformists?

Gladstone explained that he did not make the supposed promise ment[ione]d herein yesterday, which would have been inconsistent with Bills on the table. Certainly, his language seemed otherwise.

Mundella urged upon the House further factory restrictions on labour of Women & young persons & was opposed by Fawcett. In fact, Mundella is described as having talked out his own Bill[671] and no doubt a long speech on a Wed[nesda]y leaves too little time for full discussion.

Thursday, 12 June: The Judicature Bill was read a 2d. time after a good deal of discursive criticism chiefly by lawyers. H. Lopes made a good speech. He is a rising man & will very likely have office when Disraeli forms a government.[672] His style is by no means ill-adapted to the House and he puts his points tersely.

The education Bill followed & E. Forster described his intended

---

[670] It was rejected by the House of Lords.

[671] The debate on the Factory acts amendment bill being adjourned under the quarter to six rule.

[672] He was made a judge in 1876.

alterations in it.[673] These gave no satisfaction to Dixon, the leader of the Education League. It is a great gain to hear that a million & a half of children will soon be at school. In 1846 it was I believe that I put a resolution on the paper that £2,000,000 ought to be annually expended on education.[674] How I wish some Forster had then been Minister! It was about the same time that I recommended the setting apart of 2 million a year tow[ar]ds the Public debt.[675] Alas! too soon [...]

Friday, 13 June: A second long morning nearly wasted. Sir Geo. Jenkinson, in his washy & self-complacent style, re-opened the principle of Stansfeld's Local Rating Bill instead of permitting the examination into its details in Committee. In my judgment he made a speech which his party will have occasion to regret, for he talked wildly of bringing into rateability classes of property to which thoughtful men of all parties refer with caution as possible subjects of taxation.[676] A great part of the sitting was occupied, when we were allowed to deal with the framework of clauses, with the case of timber & undergrowth. Difficulty after difficulty presented itself & no one seemed to be trustworthy as a guide tho' several had experience. The end was that, after six hours work (at 7 p.m.), we had little to shew beyond doubts.

My observation was this that there is a settled plan to defeat the bill by delay. Sir M. Lopes has led his party into a quagmire & they have found out the fact. Many thought that Lopes's party would rue the day when they encouraged the disturbance of the question of relative burthens as betwn. land & personalty – & so it proves [...]

Monday, 16 June: [...] By the way, there shd. have been notice here of the mistake made in the manner of introducing to the House the Zanzibar contract. The rules of the House were not followed & this was perhaps lucky for Ministers as it was intended to treat their conduct in a hostile spirit.[677] Bouverie pointed out the defect in form &

---

[673] 1st reading of the Elementary Education act (1870) amendment bill, transferring from School Boards to Poor Law guardians the decision whether to pay the school fees of pauper children attending denominational schools, introducing the secret ballot for School Board elections, and enforcing compulsory attendance for pauper children under the age of 13. The first provision was later dropped; Parry, *Democracy and Religion*, 378–80.

[674] He spoke in this sense on 23 Apr. 1847; *H* xci. 1284–5.

[675] 4 Apr. 1851; *H* cxv. 1075–6.

[676] His amendment called for the inclusion of income from personal as well as real property; *H* ccxvi. 912–16, withdrawn.

[677] The Treasury was alleged to have awarded the mail contract for the Zanzibar–Cape Colony route to the Union Steamship Company on unduly generous terms, and without following normal procedures; Winter, *Robert Lowe*, 288–91. In the House of Commons, Bouverie pointed out that when the contract was laid on the table, the government had omitted to provide the required Treasury minute justifying the contract.

suggested the reference of the proposal to a Select Committee. Ministers have not been fortunate of late in their dealings with finance. There looms the scrape of the Post Office,[678] which scrape will occasion some rather proud financiers a disagreeable quarter of an hour – at least.

Tuesday, 17 June: A hard day's work again! The Game Laws Committee met at 12 o'clock, when the further consideration of Ward Hunt's draft report occupied us. In the midst of our deliberations the House met – that is to say, at 2 p.m. – when the Rating Bill was taken in Committee. It was my duty to attend this as soon as possible, because Cornwall is greatly interested in the mode in which Mines are to be assessed. When I came downstairs, I heard that Sir John St Aubyn had in effect made good his case, as Govt. admitted; so appropriate words are to be prepared in the sense of the mover's amendment.[679]

The limitation of this to tin & copper mines leaves the case of lead mines, & some others in a rather anamalous position.[680] This was noticed by some speakers. At the same time, it would not have been discreet in well wishers to the scope & object of the Ministerial Bill to offer opposition to a mode of rating in which Govt. acquiesced [...]

Wednesday, 18 June: My vote was in favour of the payment of Election expenses out of rates.[681] This will be a subject of a grumble in my county.

Fawcett's arguments were very cogent. It appears that the total cost of legal expenses is estimated at £90,000 & the cost to each householder once in three years would be ab[ou]t 1 1/2d!! Now, the rateable property of England is about £107,000,000!!! The landed interest I believe are afraid of this new burthen.

Thursday, 19 June: [...] The Zanzibar contract[682] was moved by Lowe & after discussion Bouverie's amendmt. proposing its reference to a committee was accepted, so Govt. escapes censure for the present.

It strikes me there must be a certain languour or indiscipline in the Ministerial ranks. Gladstone can hardly be the man he was. It must be very galling to a prude to be so often discovered in questionable

It was therefore necessary for the government to delay moving for the confirmation of the contract; *H* ccxvi. 1000–01.

[678] See above, 21 Mar.

[679] See *H* ccxvi. 1065–8.

[680] Trelawny himself was part-owner of the dues on a lead mine on his Cornish estate; *T.D.*, 9.

[681] Fawcett's Parliamentary Elections (Expenses) bill lost its 2nd reading, 205:91.

[682] See above, 16 June.

positions & then to be rescued by the adroitness of a candid friend. I suspect that there is disunion in the cabinet on several matters.

Friday, 20 June: [...] Talking with Mr Vargas who is an official acting in Mr Glyn's[683] department, I asked Mr V. how long he had served in his post. He said since 1817. No pension, yet? Yes, but Mr Glyn had been so kind to Vargas in his illness attending his bedside & sending Champagne & turtle soup that he felt the desire to remain at his post. Mr Glyn, I make my bow to you.

I have heard much of Mr Vargas before this. His patient & good-humoured face, as he sits longs hours at the entrance to the Secretary of the treasury's door (next the Post office), has something genial in it which attracts conversation. Very useful, too, one finds him; his forecast of the proceedings of an evening saves one, if attended to, many an hour. I asked him if he had kept a diary. No, he replied, regretfully. Disraeli, it appears had asked him the same question. Vargas served in the time of Castlereagh.

Monday, 23 June: [...] I called the Speaker's attention to a statement in the Journals of the House for frid[a]y the 20th shewing that fraudulent petitions had been presented for the repeal of the contagious diseases acts.[684] The Speaker, after a few inquiries (inter alia what I proposed to do) said he would consider of the matter & kept my copy of the Journal. It seemed to me that the case was one of urgency & that he ought to have taken or suggested immediate action, as the wrong done was a double one – that is to say, a wrong to the House & a wrong to numerous young ladies whose names were appended to a petition not being theirs at all. In fact the proceeding is a peculiarly rascally one, adding cruelty to fraud.

It is noteworthy that W. Fowler and Henley stole a march on me, for, while I was out of the House, they again grumbled at the Contagious Diseases acts, finding an opportunity on a vote in Supply on Army estimates. But these gentlemen abstained from a division. In fact, the mighty are somewhat crest fallen.

Government are again in trouble. Cardwell proposed some increase of expense in the department of the Field Marshall Com[mandin]g in chief (Duke of Cambridge). It came out thro' Anderson that the Treasury disapproved of granting the sum required. This disapproval could not be denied, so the vote, at Gladstone's suggestion, awaits

---

[683] Government chief whip.
[684] *C.J.* cxxviii. 202–3.

inquiry. A new Secretary & an increase of pay to an existing one together formed the bone of contention.[685]

Tuesday, 24 June: Well, I had more talk with the Speaker, who inclined to the opinion that it would be well to deal leniently with the delinquent, W.H. Cornish of Stroud. The petition 14,619 purported to be signed by a number of pupils of some ladies at that town, whereas it was not signed by any of the pupils & the heading was inserted by him after the signatures had been appended to the petition. The Speaker proposed that I shd. consult Mr Dickinson M.P. for Stroud on the matter & asked me to send to him that gentleman a little later. This, after some conversation with him, I did. Dickinson shewed me 2 letters from W.H. Cornish who seems to be alarmed. After Dickinson had exhausted his reasons in favour of mercy for the sake of the women especially, the school mistresses, the misses – I relented & suggested that he shd. write to Cornish & obtain from him an apologetic letter, to be shewn to me. It is far from clear that some other member will not move in the matter.

I gave a notice for friday to call attention to the Prison Chaplains Return No. 156 & move 5 resolutions. * See notices June 25th 1873. *

A division was taken on the Canada Loan guarantee which had my vote on the ground that it is part & parcel of the settlement of the Alabama question[686] [...]

Thursday, 26 June: [...] The Commander in chief's office is in disgrace ab[ou]t the falsification of a return of chest measurement of recruits. Col[onel] Anson wrote of this to the 'Times'. Cardwell said 'it was a grave error'.[687]

Friday, 27 June: [...] I took the precaution to withdraw the Prison Ministers Bill in order to obviate a complaint that I had 2 motions on the notices relating to the same subject. Lucky I took this precaution as the Speaker had some talk with me on the point, but I at once told him that the Prison Ministers Bill was withdrawn. This removed any objection to my proceeding by resolutions to-night (after first calling attention to the return). But it was not to be. The Irish apparently

---

[685] Anderson moved to reduce item 8 in the army estimates by £900, i.e. the £600 for a new assistant secretary and the £300 for the increased salary of a military secretary to the commander-in-chief. Cardwell agreed to omit the £300 portion; *H* ccxvi. 1287–97.

[686] 2nd reading carried 117:15; Royal assent 21 July. See *K.J.*, 24, note 3.

[687] In answer to a question from Pakington, *H* ccxvi. 1413-15, referring to the letter in *The Times*, 24 June 1873, 12, showing that the number of under-sized recruits had been concealed.

deserted their posts, the O'Conor Don being, so far as I could perceive, almost the only Irish member present. McLaren moved on Scotch Church Rates & the House was counted out.

As Glyn said, the Catholics have played their game so badly there is no hope of the success of a move in their favour at present. Meanwhile, my return will sink into the Public mind[688] & better luck may attend future efforts.

Monday, 30 June: At Sir John St Aubyn's request I attended at the office of Sir James Lindsay to confer on the projected employment of the Royal Cornwall Rangers at the Dartmoor manoeuvres.[689] I described to Sir James the state of the case as impartially as I could, for altho' the withdrawal of (say) 180 agriculturalists from the corn harvest is inconvenient, it ought not to be looked at solely from that point of view. I carefully expressed that I could not take the responsibility of recommending a decision. It was settled that Sir James shd. communicate with L[ieutenant] Col[onel] H.R. Trelawny[690] of the Rangers & request that he should consult the Chamber of agriculture.

[...] Vernon Harcourt made a long speech which it was observed he failed in delivering a few nights back.[691] In this case he used profuse notes. If he is prolix & tedious when he speaks without notes, how will it be if he continue to use them? As the case stands, he speaks too often & his slow delivery makes matters worse. He seems, too, to have a plum in his mouth. Let it not, however, be forgotten that there is always good stuff in his speeches & that his sentences are well put together & in excellent language.

A friend mentioned to me that Ministers were in + another mess + trouble again, they hav[in]g decided on recasting the scheme of the Judicature Bill in respect of Scotch & Irish appeals[692] [...]

Tuesday, 1 July: [...] On the whole the Committee (of 21 members)[693] has been very well attended and members have been good natured to each other and have kept their tempers. I think the committee will be a memorable one the matter in hand being most important.

---

[688] It was noticed in *The Times*, 11 July 1873, 4.

[689] Since the passing of the Army Regulation act of 1871, control of the militia had been transferred to the Crown.

[690] The diarist's brother.

[691] Criticising aspects of the Judicature bill, on the motion to go into committee; *H* ccxvi. 1569–79.

[692] The Lord Chancellor's bill had been amended in the Commons so that the proposed new court of appeal, rather than the House of Lords, would deal with cases from Scotland and Ireland, as well as from England and Wales; *H* ccxvi. 1561–6, for Gladstone's statement.

[693] On the game laws.

[...] After the close of our proceedings in the Committee Room, we found that the Shah[694] was in the Lords & was about to make a visit to the Commons. There was in the lobby a double row of members of the House besides strangers, & many ladies & after some delay the Shah & his attendants were met by Mr Speaker to whom the Shah was, as it were, passed over by Admiral Sir A. Clifford.[695] Then, the Speaker – who, by the way, did not look as if he was much at ease – conducted the Shah into our chamber where, apparently, a little scene was provided for him. Gladstone spoke. There was a farce of an adjournmt. moved by Mr R.N. Fowler upon a complaint made of proceedings in the absence of a member & a division taken.[696] Members laughed more loudly than usual; 'divide divide' & so forth were freely called & the puzzle was unriddled by the Shah's English attendant Sir H. Rawlinson.

At the 9 o'clock sitting, Sir H. Selwin-Ibbetson rose, when almost immediately there was a count. Thus, Peter Taylor's motion for opening museums on Sundays fell through. Independent members have a growing difficulty in obtaining a hearing. The powers of members are exhausted at morning sittings and this gives people excuses for non attendance when dangerous subjects are mooted. Now, the great Sunday question is one of these.

Wednesday, 2 July: This day was mainly spent in debating New-degate's Bill on Monastic institutions[697] of which he has great suspicions. Mr Matthews and Serjeant Sherlock severely censured the mover and I think with reason. It certainly appeared that Newdegate had spoken in ignorance of the law & thrown out unworthy insinuations against Catholics leading monastic lives. It was stated that when Newdegate sat as a member of a committee on this subject he put 1,222 questions and elicited nothing to the advantage of his cause. Matthews spoke well – in the style of a well-trained lawyer. Newdegate took a good number into the lobby * 96 out of 227 * but met with defeat. The general election is approaching and members fear a certain faction. Otherwise many more wd. have opposed Newdegate than the number found in the winning side. I chanced to hear an official say words like these 'this Parliament cares about nothing'. *He* ought to know if any one. My vote was against N. [...]

Thursday, 3 July: Col[onel] North re-opened the case of the dishonest

[694] Of Persia, on a State visit.
[695] Black Rod.
[696] 218:142 against the adjournment during the 2nd reading debate on the Turnpike acts continuance bill.
[697] 2nd reading of the Monastic and Conventual Institutions bill.

petitions from Stroud.[698] W.H. Cornish was let off be me on my seeing his apologetic letter written to Mr Dickinson M.P. So I did not speak on this occasion. But I notice that Mr C. Forster, chairman of the Committee on Public Petitions, referred to a letter of apology wh. I presume was the letter just alluded to. The House was content to take no further notice of the subject.

There soon followed an amusing combat of wits betwn. Disraeli & Gladstone on the Judicature Bill. Disraeli was very plausible and Gladstone was far more genial & facetious than usual [...]

Friday, 4 July: The Judicature Bill filled up the morning sitting. The proposal of Hardy to refer ecclesiastical appeals to the new appellate court was greedily accepted. The object I suspect is to connect the church more closely than ever with the State.[699] Decisions in which Bishops have a share are not the decisions of experts in the law. Hence want of Uniformity + which of course tends to the weakening of the authority. +

In the evening (after the 9 p.m. meeting of the House) Plunket carried agt. government an amendment in favour of a higher payment of Irish civil servants.[700] I suspect considerable embarrassment will grow out of this vote. The case is another instance of a small body exercising an undue influence in Public councils. The battle is like a battle betwn. a small force of trained Europeans & a horde of undisciplined orientals. Besides, a general election impends.

I paired for the night with Mr J. Fielden. We settled this tow[ar]ds the close of the Judicature debate. So, the arrangement covered the case of the civil servants.

Ministers get weaker day by day.

Tuesday, 8 July: We divided in the Game Laws Committee on the report as amended. On the whole, it appears to me that it does not present a settlemt. of the question.[701] Therefore I said 'no' & had as a following Winterbotham & C. Sewell Read. * Serjeant Sherlock & McLagan told me they would have supported me. No doubt McCombie

[698] See above, 23–24 June.

[699] In fact, the amendment seems to have been a High Church maneouvre designed to protect ritualist clergy from persecution by the bishops, but the bill was altered again by the House of Lords; G.I.T. Machin, *Politics and the Churches in Great Britain, 1869–1921* (Oxford, 1987), 59–60.

[700] 130:117; *H* ccxvi. 1805–10.

[701] It advocated the ending of protection for rabbits, the assimilation of English and Scottish law, and the creation of an arbitration procedure for landlords and tenants; *P.P.* 1873, xiii. 1.

would have done so had he been well enough. * In a very short time many people will, as I venture to predict, concur with us [...]

Wednesday, 9 July: [...] A.B. Hope 'talked out' the Burials Bill.

This 'talking out' process was never resorted to in a more unblushing manner as the talker who spoke for 3/4 of an hour deliberately referred to his object & kept coolly looking at the clock thro' his eye glass to see how many minutes remained to him. It must be admitted that the Burials Bill had no chance in this session & might as well have followed the fate of the government's innocents − a family of six.[702]

[...] The late division on Mr Richard's motion − on wh. Ministers were defeated[703] − excites some sensation. Absentees are censured. But how is it possible to flesh & blood to attend so often in a day? [...]

Thursday, 10 July: Really work is too heavy even for members who pair. My pair to-night was Lord Geo. Manners.

There was a knotty point of privilege at the outset. Gladstone was unfolding notices on it when Disraeli rose to order. G. moved 'that this House do now adjourn' & so forced the situation. Then, he proceeded − shewing that the House of Lords has no case in contending if it shd. contend that the alteration of the Judicature Bill in respect to Scotch & Irish appeals is an interference with the rights of the upper House. Cairn's doctrine goes this length.[704] Bouverie's remarks were very pertinent, but he thought the Ministerial plan of sending up the Bill so worded as to leave to the Lords a discretion to adopt or reject the proposed change (as we adopt or reject Bills sent down to us so worded or printed as to avoid any encroachmt. of our privileges) was not the best possible.

Afterwards the House went into committee on the Judicature Bill. Late at night there was a grand fight of adjournments on the Turnpikes Continuance Bill & this fight lasted till 4 o'clock! It appears that the Bill contained a provision relating to Highway Boards which provision involved a question beyond the understood purview or scope of the Bill. No less than 6 divisions were taken which were, I think, evidence of heat & passion − frequently observable towards the end of a session. Work done in such haste can hardly be good work. The Speaker who was perhaps in bed at 5.30 after midnight must return to the chair for a morning sitting today at 2 p.m. (that is on the 11th fri[day]), & will be again due at 9 p.m. for night work.

---

[702] See Gladstone's Cabinet note, 5 July 1873; *G.D.* viii. 351 and note 9.

[703] On 8 July, Richard's motion for a general and permanent system of international arbitration was carried by 98:88; *H* ccxvii. 52−73. Trelawny was absent, as were 13 members of the government; *The Times*, 10 July 1873, 11.

[704] In the House of Lords on 8 July; *H* ccxvii. 10−24.

Friday, 11 July: [...] It may be observed in the slang of the day that the O'Keefe squabble has been squared. Bouverie has achieved a victory over Ministers.[705] How Gladstone must love his 'right Honble. friend'! [...]

Sunday, 13 July: Note that I have written to Goschen[706] recommending Trotman's anchors which I think this diary will shew I recommended at least 13 years back.[707] Goschen has my hint that a motion hereon could not be opposed conscientiously by any one hav[in]g practical knowledge of seafaring matters.

I have lately been asked to put a question in the House hereon. My reply in part was that I prefer to let the Minister first have a private suggestion of the change recommended.

Monday, 14 July: I Represented to the Sec[retar]y of the admiralty, Shaw Lefevre, the behaviour of the Kite, Gunboat, at the late review of the fleet at Spithead in honour of the Shah. The Kite, in saluting, fired in the direction of Allan Young's steamboat, Lynx, in which were several ladies & gentlemen & more than one of the party were dangerously injured.[708] The defence was that the yacht was in forbidden waters. True, said I, but the Gunboat might have elevated her gun. Nothing could be said in reply to this. The truth is the Admiralty in a very unfeeling way, had been casting blame on persons to whom an expression of sympathy & 'regret' was due – & this I extracted & conveyed to one, the gentlemen most deserving of it [...]

Tuesday, 15 July: The Salmon Fisheries Bill was carried thro' committee at near four o'clock in the morning of this day. This, it seems to me, is hardly fair. It was my wish, if possible, to see that some amendmt. shd. be introduced more favourable to the Fowey Fishery which has now a close time unsuited to the habits of Salmon in Fowey waters. Dillwyn pointed out to me that the Bill bettered the case of the Fowey fishermen by adding a month to the open time. It would therefore have been imprudent to throw out Dillwyn's Bill.[709] Had I remained till 4 a.m. on the chance of its coming on, my pair with Mr Gore Langton precluded my taking part.

---

[705] His motion for a select committee was withdrawn following assurances from Gladstone that the position of O'Keefe, the dismissed manager of an Irish National school (see above, 15 May), would be reviewed; *H* ccxvii. 210–13.

[706] First Lord of the Admiralty.

[707] *T.D.*, 9 May 1861.

[708] Trelawny's interest in this matter may well have stemmed from the fact that he was also a keen yachtsman.

[709] Which received the Royal assent on 5 Aug.

[...] I obtained thro' Col[onel] Taylor[710] a session pair with Mr Bruen, Carlow Co., and high time!

Friday, 18 July: The close of the Session was spoken of as likely to be within 3 weeks. But temper or party feeling may put it off further.

Ministers grow daily weaker. Not only are they unfortunate in their measures but in their administration. Lowe's evidence before the Committee on the Zanzibar contract[711] has a disagreeable aspect. He seems to be not only maladroit but petulant.

The Scudamore scandal[712] will be another source of trouble. If the checks on expenditure are insufficient, why are they insufficient? If sufficient whence arose the misappropriation of money? Disraeli will have something to say on these matters. Perhaps, he may again speak of Ministers playing 'ducks & drakes' with our Public resources.

Whether any blame will attach to the government in the affair of the Gold coast,[713] time will shew.

Wednesday, 23 July: Trevelyan's motion on Household suffrage in counties was 'talked out'. This is noteworthy that Gladstone's letter in favour of the measure, being referred to by Forster,[714] became as it were 'part of the record' and members treated it as a message of Public import & even one indicating ministerial policy. The radicals seemed to chuckle amazingly & to joyfully accept the taunt that the measure is to be a new liberal 'platform' (as the term is) for the next election.

Thursday, 24 July: I count ten divisions on this one evening!![715] Dillwyn & Hardy had a little sparring. Hardy had expressed that though defeated in the H. Of C., he would look to another quarter to remedy the injustice which had been done. Dillwyn in Hardy's absence complained of the threat thus held out. Later in the evening, Hardy returned to his place & to the subject. Gladstone raised a point of order, alleging that Hardy was repeating his speech. But the chairman ruled that Hardy had not exceeded the license extended to members who had to set themselves right. Fag ends of subjects have been

---

[710] Former Conservative chief whip, and still involved in managing the party's Irish affairs.

[711] See below, 24 July.

[712] i.e. the misappropriation of Post Office funds; see below, 29 July.

[713] After a long delay, troops were sent out in Nov. to confront the king of Ashanti; *KJ.*, xviii-ix.

[714] Gladstone had asked Forster to state that, while the government had no view on the question, it was one which he considered to be 'just and politic in itself, and which cannot long be avoided'; *H* ccxvii. 841–2.

[715] On the Endowed Schools act (1869) amendment bill; Royal assent 5 Aug.

disposed of, but it is not easy to admire the manner of the workmen. The above description is mere condensation. But surely Gladstone's leadership is imprudent & fussy. Moreover, he was in error & was corrected by Bonham Carter.

The report of the Committee on the Zanzibar contract[716] is very condemnatory of Lowe & others. Will any resignations follow? The Times, newspaper, has an ominous article on the subject (date July 25th).

Friday, 25 July: Nothing noteworthy – except that there were more asperities of non conformist Christians towards Edward Forster. His speech was a noble refutation of charges of inconsistency hurled upon him by Candlish & Richard[717] [...]

Monday, 28 July: [...] Ayrton made a curious speech in which he seemed to rebuke the government for their conduct in placing a sum on the estimates in regard to land adjoining the new Houses without consulting his department &, also, for the step of seeking a grant of money for a part of a Public object without laying before the House the whole scheme & its cost.[718]

Tuesday, 29 July: On Cross's motion of censure in relation to recent proceedings in the Post Office an amendment in a milder, altho' still condemnatory sense, was moved by Sir Jno Lubbock & this he carried.[719] But governmt. have lost character in the transaction. There seems good reason for saying that some of the ministers want confidence in their colleagues. Ayrton's language shews that this is so. Osborne's censure was most damaging. Almost every sentence he uttered was a cutting reproof. There must, I think, be some change during the recess.[720]

---

[716] *P.P.* 1873, ix. 243, recommending that the contract be re-negotiated.

[717] During the 3rd reading debate on the Education Act (1870) amendment bill; Royal assent, 5 Aug.

[718] *H* ccxvii. 1123–4 and 1127–8, for Ayrton's comments, in committee of supply, regarding the project for the further embankment of the Thames, on which he had not been consulted by the Treasury, and the £8,500 vote for building work in the Palace of Westminster.

[719] The resolution by the Conservative, Cross, disapproved of the irregularities in the Post Office (see above, 21 Mar.) and the inadequacy of Treasury control; *H* ccxvii. 1189–1202. The Liberal, Lubbock's, amendment regretted what had happened and called on the government to ensure that there was no recurrence; *H* ccxvii. 1205–10. Cross's resolution was defeated, 161:111, and Lubbock's amendment agreed.

[720] A major ministerial 'reshuffle' took place during the summer and autumn: e.g. Lowe was moved to the Home Office, replacing Bruce who went to the House of Lords as Lord President of the Council; Ayrton became Judge-Advocate-General; Monsell was retired, along with Childers and Ripon; John Bright re-entered the Cabinet as Chancellor of the Duchy of Lancaster, and the backbench critics, Harcourt, James and Playfair, were all given office.

Wednesday, 30 July: [. . .] There was a damaging debate on Ayrton's relations with the rest of the government. 'We have muzzled *him*!' said a leading Minister to me some years back. But Ayrton has broken the muzzle!

Thursday, 31 July: [. . .] A long discussion on the late dissensions in which Lowe was severely handled[721] [. . .] It would take pages to describe the humiliations Ministers have undergone during this week. Members of the government have been attacking each other while Ward Hunt, Sclater-Booth, Bouverie & White have blown the coals. Ayrton, Lowe & Gladstone have, each & all, been in the wrong & richly deserved a direct vote of censure. No manners, no temper, no conduct.

Friday, 1 August: More folly of Gladstone. Why charge an opponent of the grant to the D[uke] of Edinburgh with indecency?[722] A severe rebuke was dealt to the Minister by Muntz. Gladstone & Disraeli opposed the grant of £50,000 a year to the Prince Consort in 1840.[723] One is tired of chronicling our leader's faux pas. Will he hold his office next session?

Tuesday, 5 August: The Prorogation.[724]

---

[721] During the debate on the Appropriation bill; *H* ccxvii. 1358–85.
[722] Gladstone had attacked Dilke's conduct in opposing the £10,000 annuity for the Queen's son; *H* ccxvii. 1441–3.
[723] When the Conservative opposition succeeded in reducing Prince Albert's annuity to £30,000.
[724] Trelawny's last entry: parliament was dissolved in Jan. 1874, and he did not seek re-election.

APPENDIX
TRELAWNY'S LETTER TO 'THE TIMES',
7 FEB. 1870

Economy of Parliamentary Time.

Sir,

A Parliamentary session of unusual interest is on the eve of commencement. The old faults will recur – waste of time at first, lassitude later, impetuosity at last.

There should be economy in three points – time, space and nervous energy. In time, because each fortnight saved may mean another such act as the Bankruptcy Act, or that which has so much disgusted habitual criminals. In space, because 120,000£ may be rescued from the hands of builders who may disfigure, without rendering more convenient, the existing chamber or its precincts. In nervous energy, because the work done in the House overtaxes and even exhausts the powers of members most competent by long experience and matured judgment to give the nation the best counsel.

Time is lost in dreary repetitions of forms, disorderly motions, debates on Metropolitan smoking cars and such like matters, irregular questions without notice, the defective system of taking divisions, resumption by members in general of business intrusted to the discretion of carefully selected committees, and, worst of all, uncertainty upon any given day as to which out of 40 or 50 subjects on the notice paper will in fact be taken in hand.

'A bad workman quarrels with his tools'. The house is a pretty good one if a better disposition were made of the space available.

Divisions might be taken in five minutes instead of 20, and that to the great comfort of all concerned. Any adjutant of a regiment would suggest a better plan than that in which members are languidly content to acquiesce. The Ayes, for example, might file right and left, – the Noes into the lobby outside the doorkeeper's chairs. Two or three couples of Division clerks might take members' names, and two or three passages, instead of one, might diminish the indecorous haste of senators clubbed in gangways who have keen eyes at 3 a.m. to the only cab vacant in Palace-yard.

With regard to space – why build at all? The great central hall is the best place for the public. Two policemen might secure the privacy of the lobby, which might easily be made a convenient withdrawing room or even library, containing books most likely to be wanted. Seats and tables might be provided, and competitive buffets, at which good tea and coffee might be obtained without the necessity of resorting to a distant room. As the case stands members are beset, earwigged, obstructed, almost mobbed, by obtrusive idlers, who won't take a civil assurance of an imperative engagement, and too often seek unfair opportunities of pre-occupying the judgment of representatives supposed to be unbiased.

A member in the midst of a debate wants to ascertain a fact. Stumbling over the knees of an indignant row of neighbours, and putting his seat in jeopardy, he is obliged to walk a good part of a sabbath day's journey to the library, whereas in the old House the library was close at hand.

Of seats there is an inadequacy, obliging members to come down several hours before business begins in order to secure a chance of hearing anything. This is a defect, no doubt, in the construction of the House, but it would be mitigated if a comfortable room were provided such as already suggested, for reading and refreshments. It is far from clear that some of the library and committee-rooms should not be converted into dining- rooms. The first half hour of business – sometimes it is an hour – is almost wasted. Many members endeavour to invite attention to petitions which no one listens to, and which we all know will pass the ordeal of a Select Committee and be printed if at all out of the common way, and mentioned in any case. All petitions might be handed to a petition clerk, and the Speaker might propose once for all that the list presented lie on the table. In this manner a good deal of time would be saved, especially in cases where the whole House represents the effect of a snowstorm, as it did when the Education Clauses of the Factory Bill [in 1843] were the cause of general insanity.

The great desideratum is a better organization of Industry. Unfortunately, there is a superstitious reverence for forms, – quite necessary in days when members were afraid of the Court and the Tower, and when there was no Press as a guarantee for the trustworthiness of proceedings – but obsolete in the present days.

There is no doubt a feeling among members that measures should be taken to secure some of the objects herein suggested. There are not wanting those who have endeavoured to show in detail how time might be saved in the conduct of the business of Parliament. Mr. Edward Webster (of the Examiners' office, House of Commons) has written an excellent pamphlet on the subject which every member should study. It is impossible to give more than its net result, which is as follows:- By the removal of subjects from the daily attention of the House, 7 1/4 sitting days' saved; by the reduction of the number of stages of Bills, 11

1/2 sitting days' saved; by modification of rule as to irregular discussions, 3 3/4 sitting days' saved; total sitting days' saved, 22 1/2. Equal to one month and 2 1/2 days' sitting of the House.

To which would have to be added:- saving by prevention of 'counts out', saving by limitation of abstract resolutions.

A result so important deserves attention. Allow me to submit it in good time to my brother sufferers.

M.P.

INDEX

Details of the constituencies represented and offices held by individuals are confined to the period covered by the diary, Dec. 1868 to Aug. 1873. Further information may be found in *Dod's Parliamentary Companion*.